KT-466-216

# Hands On Pascal

A Self-Study Guide to Pascal

Alistair Stewart

**Digital Skills**
Milton
Barr
Girvan
Ayrshire
KA26 9TY

First printed January 1999
Reprinted August 1999
Reprinted August 2000
Reprinted August 2001
Reprinted January 2002
Reprinted September 2002

ISBN:1-874107-05-X

# TABLE OF CONTENTS

## Introduction



## Chapter 1 Background

## Chapter 2 Starting Pascal

# Chapter 3 Control Structures

# Chapter 4 Routines and Units

# Chapter 5 Data Structures

# Chapter 6 File Handling

# Chapter 7 A Software System

# Chapter 8 Tables

# Chapter 9 Dynamic Linear Types

# Chapter 10 Advanced Data Structures



# Chapter 11 Classes and Objects

# INTRODUCTION

## Learn by Doing

The only way to become a programming expert is to practice. No one ever learned any skill by simply reading. Hence, this is not a text book where you can sit back in a passive way slowly reading through each chapter; rather it is designed as a teaching package in which you will do most of the work. The tasks embedded in the text are included to test your understanding of what has gone before and as a method of discovering for yourself some of the subtler aspects and techniques of the language. It is therefore important that you tackle each task since they are designed to test your knowledge and develop your skill. In addition, many of the short programs developed in the early chapters of the book are used to construct a final project in the last section of the text.

## Who this Publication is For

This book is designed for the following groups

- People new to programming who want to develop a high degree of skill in Pascal.

- People wanting to learn basic Pascal before moving on to Windows programming using Borland's Delphi.

- Anyone requiring a practical introduction to object-oriented design and programming.

No previous knowledge of programming or software design is required since what follows assumes you are new to these topics. However, you should be familar with the basics of a computer operating system such as MSDOS or Microsoft Windows.

This text is designed for independent self-study by students in the first and second years of a degree or HNC/D Computing course, professional programmers who wish to develop skills in the most popular object-oriented language, as well as any individual curious to discover the fascinating world of Pascal.

## The Contents

Chapter 1 covers some background material including number systems and a simple program definition language.
Chapters 2 to 9 cover the conventional aspects of Pascal.
Chapter 10 covers Borland's graphics routines.

## How To Get the Most out of this Package

Experience has shown that students derive most benefit from this material by approaching its study in an organised way. The following strategy is highly recommended:

1. Read a chapter or section through without taking notes or worrying too much about topics that are not immediately clear to you. This will give you an overview of the purpose of that chapter or section.

2. Re-read the chapter. This time take things slowly; make notes and summaries of the material you are reading (even if you understand

the material, making notes helps to retain the facts in your long-term memory); re-read any parts you are unclear about.

3. Embedded in the material are a series of tasks. Do each task as you reach it. These are designed to test your knowledge and understanding of what has gone before. Do not be tempted to skip over them, promise to come back to them later, or to make only a half-hearted attempt at tackling them before looking up the answer (there are solutions at the end of each chapter). Once you have attempted a task, look at the solution given. Often there will be important points emphasised in the solution which will aid your understanding.

4. As you progress through the book go back and re-read earlier chapters since you will often get something new from them as your knowledge increases.

## Language Syntax Diagrams

The text contains many syntax diagrams which give a visual representation of the format of various statements allowed in Pascal. These diagrams make no attempt to be complete but merely act as a guide to the format most likely to be used when constructing a Pascal statement. The accompanying text and examples should highlight any more complex options available.

Below is a typical diagram:

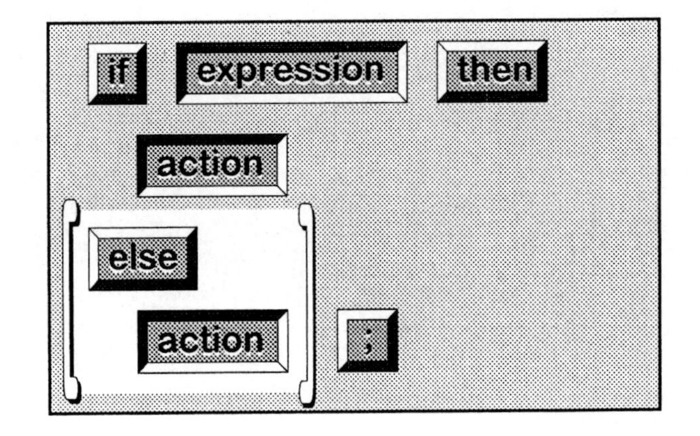


Each tile in the diagram holds a **token** of the statement.

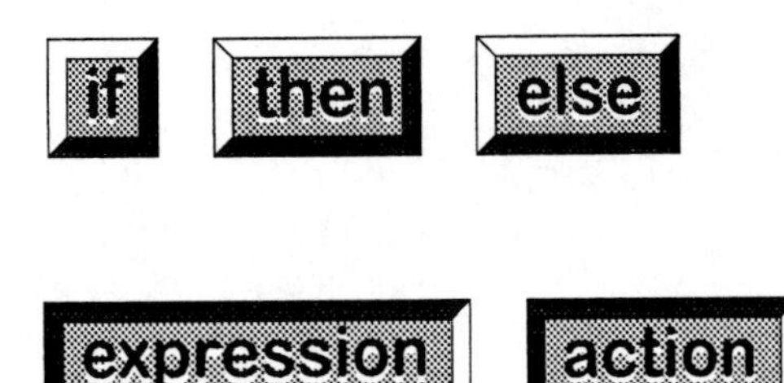


Raised tiles represent fixed terms in the statement which must be entered exactly as shown.

Sunken tiles represent tokens whose exact value is decided by you the programmer but again these values must conform to some stated rule.

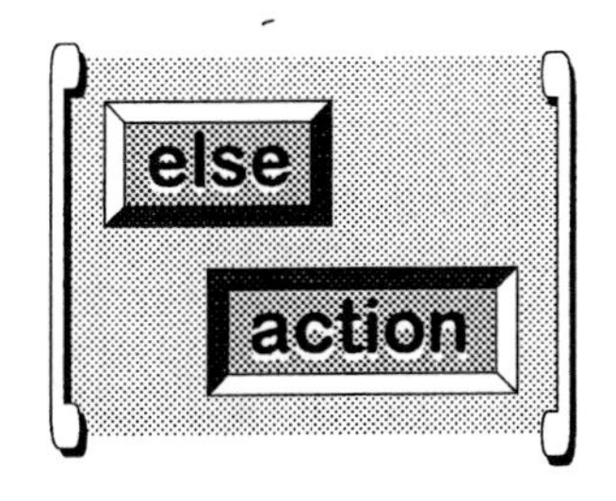


Items enclosed in parentheses may be omitted if not required.

action

statement

OR

begin

statement ;

end

Some tiles will be given a diagram of their own in order to explain their meaning in more detail. For example, the token, **action**, given above is defined in more detail by the diagram shown overleaf.

This shows that action has two possible interpretations: either a single statement, or a series of statements enclosed in the terms `begin` and `end`.

Where one or more tokens in a diagram may be repeated indefinitely, this is shown using the curved, arrowed line. For example, we can see from the previous diagram that the sequence **statement ;** may be repeated within the `begin end` terms.

Pascal makes use of three types of brackets: ( ), { }, and [ ]. Rather than use this informal term, the correct names for each is used throughout this text. These names are shown in the table below.

| Symbol | Name |
|---|---|
| ( ) | Parentheses |
| { } | Braces |
| [ ] | Brackets |

# Versions of Borland Pascal

Over the years Borland's Pascal has developed and grown and although it is now several years since the last update (version 7.0), there are still likely to be many people using earlier versions.

What follows should help you make the small modification necessary from the listings given within this text.

## Running Under DOS

If you are running a DOS version of Pascal, then you need to make the following changes:

Any references to the unit WinCrt should be changed to Crt.
The Unit WinDOS should be changed to DOS
Remove any calls to the routine DoneWinCrt.

## Using Version 6.0

Version 7.0 introduced three main features that are used with this text:

the keywords

```
break
continue
```

Open arrays as parameters to routines.
Allowing function calls without reference to the value returned.
For example, version 7.0 would allow the statement

```
ReadKey;
```

while earlier versions must assign the returning value

```
ch := ReadKey;
```

If you are not using version 7.0 these features must be omitted.

# CHAPTER 1
# Background

**This chapter covers the following topics:**

Binary Numbers

Boolean Expressions

Character Codes

Control Structures

Converting between Number Bases

Designing Algorithms

Floating Point Numbers

Hexadecimal Numbers

Octal Numbers

Stepwise Refinement

The Compilation Process

The Development Life Cycle

# DESIGNING ALGORITHMS

## Following Instructions

We're all used to following instructions: anything from fire evacuation procedures to how to assemble a flat-pack kitchen unit. Such a sequence of instructions is designed to allow us to perform some specific task. Sometimes the instructions we are carrying out are so familiar to us that we are not even aware of them; for example, driving a car requires us to perform various actions such as changing gear, pressing the brake or accelerator pedals, or turning the wheel. Other tasks, which are new to us, require a more deliberate adherence to the instructions given; for example, when we prepare a pre-packed meal from the freezer we are supplied with instructions such as:

```
Remove meal from carton
Remove lid
Preheat oven to 200°C
Place on baking tray in top half of oven
Leave for 35 minutes
```

A sequence of instructions designed to perform some specific task is known as an **algorithm**.

Every computer operates by following instructions. Such a set of instructions is known as a **computer program**.

The American spelling of program is used to differentiate a computer program from other uses of the word such as a TV programme.

Just as we may perform a great diversity of tasks by following a different set of instructions, so the computer can be made to carry out any task for which a program exists.

Computer programs are normally copied (or **loaded**) from a magnetic disk into the computer's memory and then executed (or **run**). Execution of a program involves the computer performing each instruction in the program one after the other. This it does at impressively high rates, possibly exceeding 200 million instructions per second (200mips).

Depending on the program being run, the computer may act as a word processor, a database, a spreadsheet, a game, a musical instrument or one of many other possibilities.

Of course, as a programmer, you are required to design and write computer programs rather than use them.

Computer programs are written in a very formal style using a limited number of commands known to the computer. Like us, computers use many different languages; in this publication we use a relatively new programming language called Pascal.

## Program Structures

Although programming is certainly complicated, there are only a few basic concepts and statements which you need to master before you are ready to start producing software. Luckily, the concepts are already familiar to you in everyday situations; all that is needed is to formalise their use to better suit a programming environment.

## Sequence

The set of instructions from the frozen meal was given as:

```
Remove meal from carton
Remove lid
Preheat oven to 200°C
Place on baking tray in top half of oven
Leave for 35 minutes
```

This is an example of a **sequence** of instructions. In other words, instructions which are to be carried out one after another, beginning at the first and continuing, without omitting any, until the final one is completed.

> **Activity 1.1**
>
> Write down the set of instructions required to wash clothes in an automatic washing machine.

## Binary Selection

Often one or more instructions in an algorithm should only be carried out when certain circumstances arise. For example, if we were producing a set of instructions to record a programme on the video we might write:

```
Put a new tape in the machine if there isn't enough space on the
current tape.
```

Such a statement contains two components:

a condition : *there isn't enough space on the current tape*

and

an instruction : *put a new tape in the machine*

A condition which is either *true* or *false* is sometimes referred to as a **Boolean expression**

The instruction is only to be carried out if the condition is *true* and hence this is sometimes known as a **conditional instruction**. Although we could rewrite the above instruction in many different ways, when we produce a set of commands in a formal manner, as we are required to do here, then the following format is always used:

```
IF condition THEN
    conditional instructions (executed when condition is true)
ENDIF
```

Using this layout, the instruction to insert a new video tape would be written as:

```
IF there isn't enough space on the current tape THEN
    Put a new tape in the machine
ENDIF
```

Sometimes, there will be several instructions to be carried out when the condition specified is met. For example,

```
IF light bulb is not working THEN
    Switch off power
    Remove old bulb
    Insert new bulb
    Switch on
ENDIF
```

Of course, the conditional statement will almost certainly appear embedded in a longer sequence of instructions. For example, the instructions for sitting an exam may be given as:

```
Write your name and class on the front sheet
When told to do so, turn over and read the exam paper
IF you have any questions THEN
    Raise your hand
    When the invigilator approaches you, ask any questions
ENDIF
Answer all questions in Section A of the paper
Answer only three questions from Section B
When you have finished, give your answer paper to the invigilator
Leave the room quietly
```

This longer sequence of instructions highlights the usefulness of the term **ENDIF** in separating the final conditional instruction, `When the invigilator approaches you, ask any questions`, from subsequent unconditional instructions such as `Answer all questions in Section A of the paper`

> **Activity 1.2**
>
> Write a sequence of instructions to make a cup of tea. Start with the instruction `Fill kettle`, end with `Drink tea` and allow for options to add milk and sugar.

The **IF** structure is also used in an extended form to offer a choice between two alternative actions. For example, our earlier cooking instructions could give alternatives for using a conventional cooker or a microwave:

```
IF using a microwave THEN
    Place meal in microwave
    Set to HIGH
    Leave for 12 minutes
ELSE
    Preheat oven to 200°C
    Place on baking tray in top half of oven
    Leave for 35 minutes
ENDIF
```

If the condition is *true* then the statements following the term **THEN** are executed otherwise those following **ELSE** are carried out. The general form of this extended IF statement is:

```
IF condition THEN
    statements to be carried out when condition is true
ELSE
    statements to be carried out when condition is false
ENDIF
```

> **Activity 1.3**
>
> Write a set of instructions to write and post a letter. Start with `Write letter`, end with `Place letter in Post Box` and allow for the choice of sending by first or second class post.

Instructions that choose between two alternative actions is called **binary selection**.

## Multi-way Selection

Sometimes choosing from two alternatives is not enough. If our frozen food example gave separate instructions for gas and electric cookers as well as microwaves, we could use two **IF** statements to describe this:

```
IF using a microwave THEN
    Place meal in microwave
    Set to HIGH
    Leave for 12 minutes
ELSE
    IF using an electric oven THEN
        Preheat oven to 200°C
        Place on baking tray in top half of oven
        Leave for 35 minutes
    ELSE
        Preheat oven at gas mark 7
        Place on baking tray in bottom half of oven
        Leave for 40 minutes
    ENDIF
ENDIF
```

Where one IF statement occurs inside another IF statement this is termed **nested IFs.**

**Activity 1.4**

In the following nested IF statements, what instruction is to be carried out when it's 10.00am?

```
IF it's between 4.00pm and 6.00pm THEN
  park the car in a metered space
ELSE
  IF it's after 6.00pm THEN
      park the car beside the house
  ELSE
      park the car in the car park
  ENDIF
ENDIF
```

Although this approach is quite acceptable, it is rather difficult to follow. A better method would be to have labelled alternatives:

```
IF
    using microwave:
        Place meal in microwave
        Set to HIGH
        Leave for 12 minutes
    using an electric oven :
        Preheat oven to 200°C
        Place on baking tray in top half of oven
        Leave for 35 minutes
    using a gas oven:
        Preheat oven at gas mark 7
        Place on baking tray in bottom half of oven
        Leave for 40 minutes
ENDIF
```

Each option is explicitly named and only the one which is *true* will be carried out, the others will be ignored. Of course, we are not limited to merely three options; there can be as many as the situation requires.

**Activity 1.5**

Write a set of instructions to pay for items bought in a large store in which you have an account. Allow options to pay by cash, credit card, cheque or through your account. Start with *Find out total cost*, end with *Take purchases*. You should include statements such as *Hand over credit card*, *Sign authorisation slip*, *Give account number*, *Take change*, and *Show cheque card*.

When producing a program for a computer, all possibilities have to be taken into account. If we apply that approach to our instructions for cooking the meal, we have to allow for any other possible methods of preparing the meal. Since we cannot know exactly what other methods might be used (possibly portable gas stove, grilling etc.) we need an option which groups all the other possibilities together and supplies a set of instructions to deal with them. This is done using an ELSE clause:

```
IF
    using microwave:
        Place meal in microwave
        Set to HIGH
        Cook for 12 minutes
    using an electric oven :
        Preheat oven to 200°C
        Place on baking tray in top half of oven
        Cook for 35 minutes
    using a gas oven:
        Preheat oven at gas mark 7
        Place on baking tray in bottom half of oven
        Cook for 40 minutes
    ELSE:
        Heat meal until edible
ENDIF
```

The additional **ELSE:** option will be chosen only if none of the other options are applicable. This gives us the final form of:

```
IF
    condition 1 :
        statements to be carried out when condition 1 is met
    condition 2 :
        statements to be carried out when condition 2 is met
         .
         .
    condition x:
        statements to be carried out when condition x is met
    ELSE :
        statements to be carried out when none of the previous
        conditions are met
ENDIF
```

**Activity 1.6**

Rewrite the set of instructions given in Activity 1.4 using the IF format described above.

Choosing between several alternatives is known as **multi-way selection**.

**Complex Conditions**

Often the condition given in an **IF** statement may be a complex one. For example, if a college only admits a student to a course when he has the academic qualifications and good references, then this can be described in our more formal style as:

```
IF student has sufficient qualifications AND has good references
THEN
    Admit student to course
ELSE
    Reject student
ENDIF
```

Note the use of the word **AND** in the above example. **AND** (called a **Boolean operator**) is one of the terms used to link simple conditions in order to produce a more complex one. The conditions on either side of the **AND** are called the **operands**. Both operands must be *true* for the overall condition to be *true*. We can generalise this to describe the **AND** operator as being used in the form:

```
condition 1   AND   condition 2
```

The result of the **AND** operator is determined using the following rules:

1. Determine the truth of condition 1
2. Determine the truth of condition 2
3. IF both conditions are *true* THEN
        the result is *true*
    ELSE
        the result is *false*
    ENDIF

The results of the **AND** operator are summarised in TABLE-1.1.

**TABLE-1.1**

The AND Operator

| condition 1 | condition 2 | condition 1 AND condition 2 |
|---|---|---|
| FALSE | FALSE | FALSE |
| FALSE | TRUE | FALSE |
| TRUE | FALSE | FALSE |
| TRUE | TRUE | TRUE |

Simple conditions may also be linked by the Boolean operator **OR** as in the instruction:

```
IF it's raining OR it's cold THEN
    Put on coat
ENDIF
```

Like **AND**, the **OR** operator works on two operands:

```
condition 1   OR   condition 2
```

When **OR** is used, only one of the conditions involved needs to be **true** for the overall result to be **true**. Hence the results are determined by the following rules:

1. Determine the truth of condition 1
2. Determine the truth of condition 2
3. IF any of the conditions are **true** THEN
        the result is **true**
    ELSE
        the result is **false**
    ENDIF

The results of the **OR** operator are summarised in TABLE-1.2.

**TABLE-1.2**

The OR Operator

| condition 1 | condition 2 | condition 1 OR condition 2 |
|---|---|---|
| FALSE | FALSE | FALSE |
| FALSE | TRUE | TRUE |
| TRUE | FALSE | TRUE |
| TRUE | TRUE | TRUE |

The final Boolean operator which can be used as part of a condition is **NOT**. This operator is used to negate the meaning of a condition. Hence ***NOT*** *over 21* has the opposite meaning from *over 21*; that is to say that if *over 21* is **true** then ***NOT*** *over 21* is **false**. Unlike **AND** and **OR**, **NOT** is used with a single operand:

```
NOT condition
```

The results of the **NOT** operator are summarised in TABLE-1.3.

**TABLE-1.3** The NOT Operator

| condition | NOT condition |
|---|---|
| FALSE | TRUE |
| TRUE | FALSE |

Complex conditions are not limited to a single occurrence of a Boolean operator, hence it is valid to have the statement:

```
IF it's raining OR it's cold OR it's windy THEN
    Put on coat
ENDIF
```

In this situation, the final result is produced by first determining the truthfulness of each simple condition. If we assume it's a dry, warm but windy day then the original expression can be reduced to:

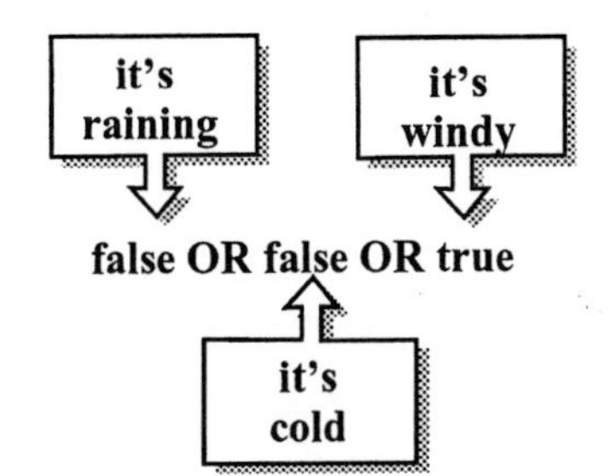


Next, the result from each Boolean operation is substituted. The left-most operator is dealt with first giving:

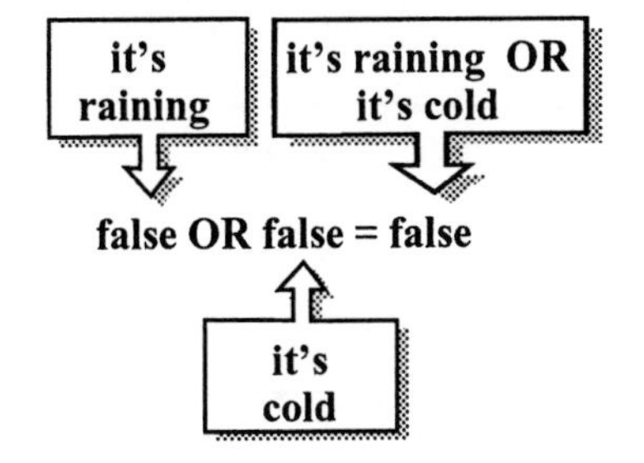


Replacing this result in the original expression gives:

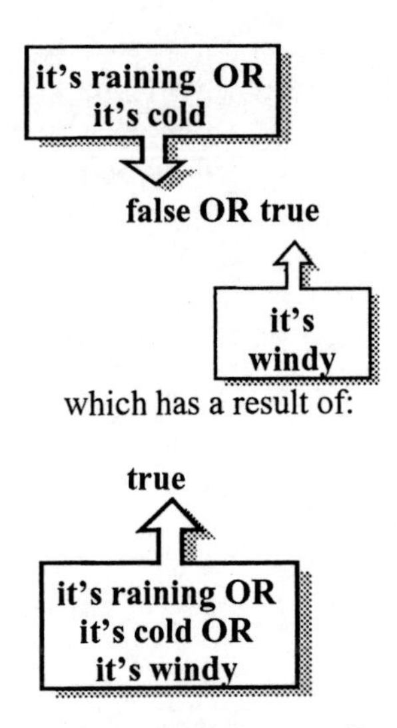


which has a result of:



And, since the overall result is **true,** *Put on coat* is performed.

Finally, **AND**, **OR** and **NOT** operators may be used in any combination. For example, we might define people due to retire to be those which met the condition:

```
IF you are male AND aged over 65 OR
    you are female AND aged over 60
THEN
    You may retire
ENDIF
```

When various operators are used, **NOT** operations are performed first, followed by **AND** and finally **OR** operations. Where there is more than one identical operator these are calculated from left to right. In the above example, for a 53 year old female we get:

**false AND false OR true AND false**

Since there are no **NOT** operations, the **AND**s are determined first. Being more than one such operator, the left-most is handled first giving:

**false OR true AND false**

The second **AND** results in

**false OR false**

which gives as a final result:

**false**

Boolean operator priority is summarised in TABLE-1.4.

**TABLE-1.4**

Boolean Operator Priority

| Operator | Priority |
|---|---|
| NOT | Highest |
| AND | |
| OR | Lowest |

Sometimes the priority of operators works against what we are trying to express. For example, if an insurance company wants to add an excess to the premium of people under 25 living in Glasgow, Manchester or London then we might be tempted to write:

```
IF living in Glasgow OR living in Manchester OR
    living in London AND under 25
THEN
    Add excess to premium
ENDIF
```

We would not expect a 26 year old living in Glasgow to pay the excess. But, if we look at the calculation for such a case, we get:

**true OR false OR false AND false**

The **AND** is calculated to give:

**true OR false OR false**

Next the left-most **OR** is reduced to give

**true OR false**

which finally reduces to **true**.

To achieve the correct results, we need the **OR** operations to be performed first and this can be done by giving the **OR** operators a higher priority than the **AND**. Luckily, operator priority can be modified by the use of parentheses. Items in parentheses are always performed first. Rewriting the condition as

```
IF (living in Glasgow OR living in Manchester OR
    living in London) AND under 25
THEN
    Add excess to premium
ENDIF
```

we now evaluate this as:

**(true OR false OR false) AND false**
= **(true OR false) AND false**
= **true AND false**
= **false**

> **Activity 1.7**
>
> Write the expression for the conditions required in order for a laser printer to produce output. It will be necessary for the printer to be on-line and the toner should not be empty. There must also be paper in the main tray or in the auxiliary tray.

## Iteration

There are certain circumstances in which it is necessary to perform the same sequence of instructions several times. For example, if a student sits three tests (each having a possible score of 100) and is given a pass only if his average mark for the tests is 50% or above, then we might describe the logic required in making such a decision as:

```
Set the total to zero
Read mark from test paper
Add mark to total
Read mark from test paper
Add mark to total
Read mark from test paper
Add mark to total
Calculate average as total divided by 3
IF average is not less than 50% THEN
    Student has passed
ELSE
    Student has failed
ENDIF
```

You can see from the above that two instructions,

```
Read mark from test paper
Add mark to total
```

are carried out three times; once for each test taken by the student. Not only does it seem rather time-consuming to have to write the same pair of instructions three times, but it would be worse if the student had sat 10 tests!

What is required is a structure which allows us to specify that a section of the instructions are to be repeated a fixed number of times. This is done using the **FOR..ENDFOR** structure:

```
FOR .. ENDFOR
```

Now the above can be rewritten as:

```
Set the total to zero
FOR 3 times DO
    Read mark from test paper
    Add mark to total
ENDFOR
Calculate average as total divided by 3
IF average is not less than 50% THEN
    Student has passed
ELSE
    Student has failed
ENDIF
```

The instructions between the terms **FOR** and **ENDFOR** are now carried out three times. Should the students have to sit 10 tests then all we need to do is rewrite the **FOR** statement as:

```
FOR 10 times DO
    Read mark from test paper
    Add mark to total
ENDFOR
```

The general form of this statement is:

```
FOR number of times required DO
    instructions to be repeated
ENDFOR
```

This structure is often referred to as a **loop structure** and the instructions to be repeated are known as the **loop body**.

**Activity 1.8**

Write a set of instructions to list the names of those students who achieve a score of less than 50% in an exam. There are exactly 20 students in the class. Your solution should contain the statements:

```
Read mark and name
Add name to list of fails
IF mark is less than 50% THEN
```

REPEAT .. UNTIL

There are other circumstances in which, although we want to repeat instructions, the number of times we wish to do this cannot be specified. For example, if we were describing the action of playing a simple slot machine we might write:

```
Put coin in machine
Pull handle
IF you win THEN
    Collect winnings
ENDIF
Repeat the previous statements above until you want to stop
```

Although this describes exactly what is required, the final statement is too clumsy and informal. The instructions can be rewritten as:

```
REPEAT
    Put coin in machine
    Pull handle
    IF you win THEN
        Collect winnings
    ENDIF
UNTIL you want to stop
```

This is a better format since the start and end of the loop body are identified using the terms **REPEAT** and **UNTIL** respectively. The **UNTIL** statement also specifies the condition under which iteration is to stop; this is known as the **terminating condition**.

The general form of this structure is:

```
REPEAT
    loop body
UNTIL terminating condition
```

The terminating condition may use the Boolean operators **AND**, **OR** and **NOT** as well as parentheses, where necessary.

**Activity 1.9**

Write instructions to look through the articles in a magazine until one written by *Liz Herron* is found. Your solution should contain the instructions:

```
Find start of article
Read the author's name
```

WHILE .. ENDWHILE

A final method of iteration, differing only subtly from the **REPEAT.. UNTIL** loop, is the **WHILE .. ENDWHILE** structure which has an **entry condition** at the start of the loop.

For example, when weighing out a half kilogram of individually wrapped sweets, most shopkeepers will empty out roughly the correct amount on to the scales and then add or remove individual sweets until the weight is correct. Using the WHILE structure to describe this action we get:

```
Empty approximately the correct weight of sweets on to the scale
WHILE the weight is incorrect DO
    IF the weight is over THEN
        Remove one sweet from scales
    ELSE
        Add one sweet to scales
    ENDIF
ENDWHILE
Place sweets in paper bag
```

The instruction between the **WHILE** and **ENDWHILE** will be carried out as long as the weight is incorrect. Once the weight is correct (that is, when the condition *weight is incorrect* is **false**) looping terminates and the statement following **ENDWHILE** is performed (*Place sweets in paper bag*).

In what way does this differ from the **REPEAT** statement? There are two differences:

1. The condition is given at the beginning of the loop.
2. Looping stops when the condition is **false**.

The main consequence of this is that it is possible to bypass the loop body of a **WHILE** structure entirely without ever carrying out any of the instructions it contains. If the shopkeeper gets lucky and empties the correct amount on to the scales at the beginning then the condition, *the weight is incorrect*, will be **false** and hence control jumps directly to *Place sweets in paper bag*. In contrast, since the condition is at the end of the loop, the loop body of a **REPEAT** structure must be carried out at least once.

If we try to replace the **WHILE** loop directly with a **REPEAT** loop we get:

```
Empty approximately the correct weight of sweets on to the scale
REPEAT
    IF the weight is over THEN
        Remove one sweet from scales
    ELSE
        Add one sweet to scales
    ENDIF
UNTIL the weight is correct
Place sweets in paper bag
```

Note that the condition has been reversed from that in the original description.

But this doesn't work properly since, if the correct amount is placed on the scales at the beginning, we nevertheless go inside the **REPEAT** loop, find *the weight is over* to be **false** (since the weight is correct), jump to **ELSE** and *Add one sweet to the scales;* but now the condition, *the weight is correct*, in the **UNTIL** statement is no longer **true** and hence we go back round the loop structure to the **IF** statement where the condition, *the weight is over*, is now **true** and hence we remove a sweet. At this point, by first adding then removing a sweet, we have returned to the correct weight so that the condition in the **UNTIL** statement (*the weight is correct*) is at last **true** and the loop is exited and the sweets placed in the bag.

Although the **REPEAT** loop has produced the correct result in the end, it generated some unnecessary actions.

**Activity 1.10**

A game involves throwing two dice. If the two values thrown are not the same, then the dice showing the lower value must be rolled again as often as is necessary until both dice show the same value. Write a set of instructions to perform this game. Your solution should contain the statements

```
        Roll both dice
and     Choose dice with lower value
```

**Infinite Loops**

A potential problem with REPEAT and WHILE loops is, since they do not specify exactly how many times the loop body is to be executed, it is possible to set up a loop structure which will never terminate. For example, we might attempt to describe the logic of weighing sweets as:

```
Empty approximately the correct weight of sweets on to the scale
WHILE the weight is incorrect DO
    Remove sweet from scales
ENDWHILE
Place sweets in paper bag
```

The above logic is fine - as long as we don't put too few sweets on the scale at the beginning! Should that happen removing a sweet will only take us further from the goal of getting the correct weight of sweets. With no chance of the condition, *the weight is incorrect,* being **false**, iteration will continue forever (although it won't be possible to keep removing sweets). This is known as an **infinite loop** and should be avoided. You can guard against such loops by mentally checking that some activity within the loop body will eventually result in the loop being exited.

# Data

Imagine we need to write down instructions for a trainee insurance salesman who sells car insurance policies by phone. The caller will supply details of the car, his age and the city in which he lives, the salesman will calculate the premium due adding any excess where necessary, and tell the caller the cost. If the caller accepts the offer, the salesman will take additional personal details from the caller and fill out an application form which he then places in a *New Policies* tray on his desk. Our formal description of the operation might be:

```
Get details of car model, engine size, caller's age and city
Calculate premium as half the engine size in cc
IF (city is Glasgow OR Manchester OR London) AND
    age is under 25
THEN
    Calculate excess due as £50 for each year under 25
    Add excess to premium
ENDIF
Tell caller the amount of the premium
Ask if he wishes to accept the policy
IF policy accepted THEN
    Get caller's name, street, post code, phone number and car
    registration number
    Transfer details to policy form
    Get policy number from the top right hand of policy form
    Tell the policy number to caller
    Place form in New Policies tray
ENDIF
```

This example and the previous test marks example introduce the need to process facts and figures (known as **data**). In a computing environment most algorithms involve the processing of data. An item of data has two basic characteristics :

a name
and a value.

The name of a data item is a description of the type of information it represents. Hence *caller's name*, *caller's age* and *car registration number* are names of data items; *"Fred Bloggs"*, *27*, and *"M1 CKY"* are examples of the actual values which might be given to these data items.

Note that textual values are enclosed in double quotes while numeric values are not.

In programming, a data item is often referred to as a **variable**. This term arises from the fact that, although the name assigned to a data item cannot change, its value may vary.

**Activity 1.11**

List the names of five other data items in the insurance example above and give a possible value for each.

There are four basic operations which can be performed on data:

**Input**

The first involves obtaining a value for a data item. For example, the insurance salesman's instructions include *Get car model. Car model* is the name of a data item and the command requires the salesman to obtain a value which he may associate with that name from the caller. In a computer environment, the request to get a value for a data item requires the user of the computer to enter a value at the keyboard. We describe this as a value being **input** to a data item.

**Calculation**

The second operation involves calculating the value of a data item. For example, *Calculate premium as half the engine size in cc* produces a value for the data item *premium* by calculation. This calculation involves the value of another data item (*engine size*). If *engine size* had been given as 2000cc then *premium* would be £1000.00. Notice also that it is possible to modify the value of a data item; for instance, later in the algorithm we have the instruction *Add excess to premium*, which, for a 21 year-old living in London would result in an excess of £200.00 being added to *premium*; changing the value of that data item from £1000.00 to £1200.00. This is referred to as a **calculation operation**.

**Comparison**

The value of a data item may be compared against some other value. The insurance example compares the value given to *city* to see if it is equal to "Glasgow", "Manchester" or "London".

**Output**

The final operation is to disclose the value currently held in a data item. For example, the instruction, *Tell caller the amount of the premium*, is a request to state the value associated with the data item, *premium*. In a computer environment, the equivalent operation would normally involve displaying information on a screen or printing it on paper. This is called **output** of data.

**Activity 1.12**

Identify other input, calculation and output statements in the insurance premium example above.

When describing a calculation, it is common to use arithmetic operator symbols rather than English. Hence, instead of writing the word *subtract* we use the minus sign ( - ). A summary of the operators available are given in TABLE-1.5.

**TABLE-1.5**

Mathematical Operators

| English | Symbol |
|---|---|
| Multiply | * |
| Divide | / |
| Add | + |
| Subtract | - |

Like Boolean operators, mathematical operators are dealt with on a priority basis. Multiply and divide have the higher (and equal) priority; add and subtract, the lower.

As well as replacing the arithmetic operator words with symbols, the term `calculate` is often replaced by the shorter but more cryptic symbol, **:=**

Using this abbreviated form, the instruction:

```
Calculate premium as half the engine size in cc
```

becomes

Read the symbol := as "is assigned the value".

```
premium := engine size in cc / 2
```

# Levels of Detail

Although we might write the instructions for setting a video to record a program as

```
Put new tape in video
Set timer details
```

this lacks enough detail for anyone unfamiliar with the operation of the machine. We could replace the first statement with

```
Press the eject button
IF there is a tape in the machine THEN
    Remove it
ENDIF
Place the new tape in the machine
```

and the second statement could be substituted by:

```
Switch to timer mode
Enter start time
Enter finish time
Select channel
```

This approach of starting with a less detailed sequence of instructions and then, where necessary, replacing each of these with more detailed instructions can be used to good effect when tackling long and complex problems. By using this technique, we are defining the original problem as an equivalent sequence of simpler tasks before going on to create a set of instructions for each of these simpler problems. This divide-and-conquer strategy is known as **stepwise refinement**.

The following is a fully worked example of this technique:

**Problem:**
*Produce a wage slip for an hourly paid worker. The worker gets paid £5.60 per hour when working between 0900 and 1700 Monday to Friday. If he works on Saturdays or after 1700 during the working week, he is paid £8.40 per hour. Sunday working pays a rate of £11.20 per hour. He has to pay 9% of his gross wage to superannuation, 10% of the gross wage to National Insurance. Of the remainder, the first £80.00 is tax free and the remainder is taxed at 25%.*

**Outline Solution**

```
1.  Get details of hours worked
2.  Calculate gross wage
3.  Calculate deductions
4.  Calculate net wage
5.  Write details on to wage slip
```

This is termed a **LEVEL 1 solution**.

As a guideline, we should aim for a LEVEL 1 solution with, at most, 20 statements - preferably significantly less.

Notice that each instruction has been numbered. This is merely to help with identification during the stepwise refinement process.

Before going any further, we must assure ourselves that this is a correct and full (though not detailed) description of all the steps required to tackle the original problem. If we are not happy with the solution then changes must be made before we go any further.

Next, we examine each statement in turn and determine if it should be described in more detail. Where this is necessary, rewrite the statement to be dealt with and, below it, give the more detailed version. For example, *Get details of hours worked* would be expanded thus:

```
1.  Get details of hours worked
    1.1 Get hours at basic rate
    1.2 Get hours at time-and-a-half
    1.3 Get hours at double time
```

The numbering of the new statement reflects that they are the detailed instructions pertaining to statement 1. Also note that the numbering system does not represent a decimal fraction, so if there were to be many more statements, they would be numbered 1.4, 1.5, 1.6, 1.7, 1.8, 1.9, 1.10, 1.11, etc.

It is important that these sets of more detailed instructions describe how to perform only the original task being examined - they must achieve no more and no less. Sometimes the detailed instructions will contain control structures such as IFs, WHILEs or FORs. Where this is the case, the whole structure must be included in the detailed instructions. That is to say, it is not possible to have, say, a FOR statement to start in the breakdown of statement 1 and the corresponding ENDFOR statement to appear in the breakdown of statement 2.

Having satisfied ourselves that the breakdown is correct, we proceed to the next statement from the original solution:

```
2.  Calculate gross wage
    2.1 Calculate gross wage as hours at basic rate * £5.60 +
        hours at time-and-a-half * £8.40 +
        hours at double time * £11.20
```

This time we haven't expanded into more statements but simply added detail to the original instruction.

The other statements expand as follows:

```
3.  Calculate deductions
    3.1 Calculate superannuation as 9% of gross wage
    3.2 Calculate national insurance as 10% of gross wage
    3.3 Calculate taxable pay as gross wage -
        (superannuation + national insurance + £80.00)
    3.4 IF taxable pay is greater than zero THEN
    3.5     Calculate tax due as 25% of taxable pay
    3.6 ELSE
    3.7     Set tax due to zero
    3.8 ENDIF
```

The **IF** statement allows for the possibility that the gross wage is not sufficient to incur tax.

Note that we have introduced a new data item, *taxable pay*, which although useful in arriving at *net wage* is not itself one of the data items required by the system. Such data items are called **temporary** or **local variables**.

```
4.  Calculate net wage
    4.1 Calculate net wage as gross wage -
        (superannuation + national insurance + tax due)

5.  Write details on to wage slip
    5.1 Write gross wage on payslip
    5.2 Write superannuation on wage slip
    5.3 Write national insurance on wage slip
    5.4 Write tax due on wage slip
    5.5 Write net wage on wage slip
```

Finally, we can describe the solution to the original problem in terms of the more detailed sequence of instructions:

```
1.1 Get hours at basic rate
1.2 Get hours at time-and-a-half
1.3 Get hours at double time
2.1 Calculate gross wage as hours at basic rate * £5.60
    + hours at time-and-a-half * £8.40
    + hours at double time * £11.20
3.1 Calculate superannuation as 9% of gross wage
3.2 Calculate national insurance as 10% of gross wage
3.3 Calculate taxable pay as gross wage -
    (superannuation + national insurance + £80.00)
3.4 IF taxable pay is greater than zero THEN
3.5     Calculate tax due as 25% of taxable pay
3.6 ELSE
3.7     Set tax due to zero
3.8 ENDIF
4.1 Calculate net wage as gross wage -
    (superannuation + national insurance + tax due)
```

```
5.1 Write gross wage on payslip
5.2 Write superannuation on wage slip
5.3 Write national insurance on wage slip
5.4 Write tax due on wage slip
5.5 Write net wage on wage slip
```

This is a LEVEL 2 solution. Note that a level 2 solution is produced by bringing together, in the correct order, the individual solutions of the LEVEL 1 instructions.

### A Few Points to Note About Stepwise Refinement

For some more complex problems it may be necessary to repeat this process to more levels before sufficient details are achieved. That is, statements in LEVEL 2 may need to be given more detail in a LEVEL 3 breakdown.

Not all statements need to be broken down to a lower level. For example, a LEVEL 1 solution might contain the statement `FOR 10 times DO` which may be left unaltered in a LEVEL 2 solution.

**Activity 1.13**

An orders clerk for a mail order company takes orders over the telephone. Customers begin by stating the number of different items they wish to purchase. For each item the clerk requests the catalogue number, which if given incorrectly, will require to be restated (it is possible that an invalid number will be given several times before the customer finally gives a recognised value). The clerk also asks the quantity required before checking if the item is in stock. If the item is out of stock or there is insufficient quantity, the clerk will offer an alternative if one is available. The clerk adds available items to an order list. Once the call is complete, the order list is sent to the dispatches department.

A possible LEVEL 1 solution to this task is:

```
1.  Get number of items
2.  FOR each item DO
3.      Get order details
4.      Process item
5.  ENDFOR
6.  Send order to dispatches department
```

Write a LEVEL 2 solution which should include statements such as:

```
IF item in stock AND sufficient quantity THEN
WHILE catalogue number is invalid DO
Check for alternative
IF alternative acceptable THEN
```

# Summary

- Computers can perform many tasks by executing different programs.
- An **algorithm** is a sequence of instructions which solves a specific problem.
- A **program** is a sequence of computer instructions which usually manipulates data and produces results.

- **Three control structures** are used in programs :
  Sequence;
  Selection;
  Iteration.

- A **sequence** is a list of instructions which are performed one after the other.

- **Selection** is performed using the IF statement.

- **There are three forms of IF statement:**

```
IF condition THEN
    instructions
ENDIF
```

```
IF condition THEN
    instructions
ELSE
    instructions
ENDIF
```

```
IF
    condition 1:
        instructions
    condition 2:
        instructions
        .
        .
    condition x :
        instructions
    ELSE:
        instructions
ENDIF
```

- **Iteration** is performed using one of three instructions:

```
FOR number of iterations required DO
    instructions
ENDFOR
```

```
REPEAT
    instructions
UNTIL condition
```

```
WHILE condition DO
    instructions
ENDWHILE
```

- **An infinite loop** may result from an incorrectly formed iteration.

- A **condition** is an expression which is either *true* or *false*.

- A **Boolean expression** is an alternative term for a condition.

- **Simple conditions can be linked** using **AND** or **OR** to produce a complex condition.

- **The meaning of a condition can be reversed** by adding the word **NOT**.

- **Data items** (or variables) hold the information used by the algorithm.

- **Data item values** may be:

  Input
  Calculated
  Compared
  or Output

- **Calculations** can be performed using the operators

  | | |
  |---|---|
  | Multiplication | * |
  | Division | / |
  | Addition | + |
  | Subtraction | - |

- **The symbol :=** is used to assign a value to a data item. Read this symbol as *is assigned the value.*

- In programming, a data item is referred to as a **variable**.

- The divide-and-conquer strategy of **stepwise refinement** can be used when creating an algorithm.

- **LEVEL 1 solution gives an overview** of the sub-tasks involved in carrying out the required operation.

- **LEVEL 2 gives a more detailed solution** by taking each sub-task from LEVEL 1 and, where necessary, giving a more detailed list of instructions required to perform that sub-task.

- **Further levels of detail** may be necessary when using stepwise refinement for complex problems.

- **Further refinement may not be required** for every statement.

- The order of priority of operators are:

| Operator | Meaning | Priority |
|---|---|---|
| * | Multiply | 1 |
| / | Divide | 1 |
| + | Add | 2 |
| - | Subtract | 2 |
| NOT | | 3 |
| AND | | 4 |
| OR | | 5 |
| := | Is assigned the value | 6 |

Items of equal priority are evaluated from left to right.

- The order of priority may be over-ridden using parentheses.

# THE DEVELOPMENT LIFE CYCLE

Designing algorithms is only one stage in producing any significant piece of software. The stages involved depend on the approach used. However, generally the following stages can be identified:

## Statement of Requirements

This is a document, produced by those requiring the software, which specifies what the system is required to do.

## Requirements Analysis

Since the statement of requirements is often brief, as well as containing contradictions, ambiguities and omissions, there is a need to examine the requirements in more detail, clearing up any outstanding problems. This activity is known as **requirements analysis**. The **System Specification** is the document produced as a result of the requirements analysis and is basically an organised, correct and full definition of the system to be developed.

## System Design

This involves defining the structure and architecture of the system. Each component is described in terms of what task it has to perform. The **System Design Document** is the by-product of System Design stage and contains descriptions of each component of the system.

## Detailed Design

Whereas Systems Design involves producing a description of what each component of the system must do, Detailed Design describes how each component functions; that is, it is in this stage of the development that the many algorithms of a system are specified. The processing to be performed may be described in Structured English or in a more computer program-like, **program design language** (PDL) - sometimes referred to as **pseudocode**.

## Implementation

Each component of the design must now be written in a form which can be understood by the computer. In other words, the program design language must be translated into a programming language. As the components are coded they must be tested for errors. This is called **unit testing**.

Tested units are then added to the system and the partially finished system is tested to ensure that the components integrate correctly into the system. This is called **integration testing.** The code produced during implementation will be listed for future reference. In addition, the programs are also retained in a form readable by the machine (probably held as files on a magnetic disk). The output produced by the programs during testing will be retained as evidence of the software's performance and correctness.

By this stage a complete working system has been produced. This system is then given to the customer who will perform his own set of tests on the software before accepting it. This is called **acceptance testing**.

## Iterating the Development Cycle

At each stage it may be necessary to back-track to an earlier one. For example, in creating a System Specification, it may be necessary to return to the customer who requested the software and revise the Statement of Requirements, or problems found at the testing stage may require us to rethink the System Design.

This continual requirement to return to earlier stages in the life cycle makes the whole design process an iterative one, but excessive revision of earlier work and late detection of errors carried forward from earlier stages can add significantly to the time and costs involved in producing the software.

## Validation and Verification

An obvious requirement which must be kept in mind while developing a system is that it meets the customer's requirements. The actions applied by the developer to ensure this is the case are known as verification and validation.

Verification ensures that the product of a given phase of the life cycle satisfies the document on which that phase is based. For example, the System Design Document (the product of System Design activity) is checked to see that it satisfies the description given in the System Specification. To summarise, verification involves ensuring that the output of a given stage correctly reflects the input to that stage.

Validation, on the other hand, is the process of checking that a document or piece of software accurately reflects the requirements of the customer.

## Maintenance

After delivery to the customer further work is often required on the system. In fact, as much as 80% of the total time spent working on a system can take place during the maintenance phase.

Maintenance may be required because of errors which have remained undetected until the software was in operation. Such corrections are considered to be part of the original contract for the system.

Another reason for maintenance is caused by changes to the environment in which the software operates. For example, software which calculates monthly salary payments will require to be changed if a local income tax system is to be introduced.

Finally, a system may require maintenance because the customer wishes extra features to be added. For example, a store's stock control system may require an additional feature to give statistical details of sales.

The last two causes of maintenance are not considered to be part of the original contract and hence the customer will be charged for any changes made.

The maintenance period is from the date of delivery to the time when the software is replaced. This may be many years.

# NUMBER SYSTEMS

## Introduction

The counting system we use today is the decimal or, more correctly, the denary system. It uses ten different symbols (0,1,2,3,4,5,6,7,8,9) to represent any value. The number of digits used in a number system is known as the **base** or **radix** of the system. Hence denary is a base 10 system.

In our number system, the position of a digit affects the value. Hence, 19 and 91, although containing the same digits, represent two different values.

In primary school we are often taught the theory of numbers by the use of column headings:

*Thousands* *Hundreds* *Tens* *Units*

To represent a value, we merely write the required numeric symbol in each of the appropriate columns. For example, to write down the number seven hundred and thirteen we place a 7 in the Hundreds column, a 1 in the Tens column and a 3 in the Units column:

| *Hundreds* | *Tens* | *Units* |
|---|---|---|
| 7 | 1 | 3 |

A more mathematical heading for these columns would be

$10^2$ is simply short-hand for 10*10.

The result of raising any number to the power zero is 1.

| $10^2$ | $10^1$ | $10^0$ |
|---|---|---|
| 7 | 1 | 3 |

Note that the column value is based on the number radix being used. Hence, for any number system (say, to the base R) the value of the columns can be written as:

$$\ldots \; R^4 \; R^3 \; R^2 \; R^1 \; R^0$$

## The Binary System

The modern computer stores all the information it holds, be it instructions, numbers or text, as a sequence of number codes. But the number system used by the computer has a base of two rather than ten. This is the **binary system** where every value is represented by only two digits: 0 and 1. Columns in this system have the values:

$$\ldots \; 2^7 \; 2^6 \; 2^5 \; 2^4 \; 2^3 \; 2^2 \; 2^1 \; 2^0$$

which, replacing the powers of two headings, gives the column values:

128 64 32 16 8 4 2 1

The binary digits, 0 and 1, are referred to as **bits** (short for **b**inary dig**its**). Values are most often stored in 8 bit groups.

This collection of 8 bits is called a **byte**.

## Converting from Decimal to Binary

From this information we can begin to see how we might represent a decimal number, say 23, in binary. Since 23 can be constructed from the values 16 + 4 + 2 + 1, we simply need to place a 1 in each of those columns, filling all other columns with zeros. Using the standard 8 bit grouping the decimal value 23 is represented as:

| *128* | *64* | *32* | *16* | *8* | *4* | *2* | *1* |
|---|---|---|---|---|---|---|---|
| 0 | 0 | 0 | 1 | 0 | 1 | 1 | 1 |

Generalising this approach, we can construct a simple algorithm to convert any decimal number to its binary equivalent:

```
Get positive decimal number
REPEAT
    Divide by 2, writing down answer and whole number remainder
UNTIL the answer is zero
Write down the remainders in a line, last one first, from left to
right
```

The operation is shown in FIG-1.1.

**FIG-1.1**

Converting Decimal to Binary

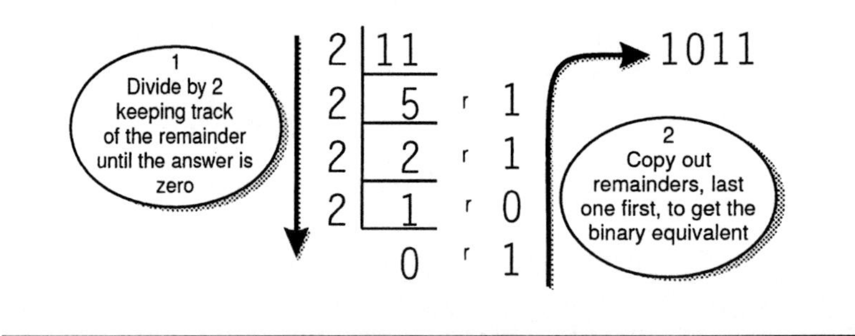


> **Activity 1.14**
>
> Convert the following numbers to 8 bit binary:
>
> 19
> 72
> 63

## Binary to Decimal

To convert from binary to decimal, take the value of each column containing a one and add these values to arrive at the decimal equivalent. An example is shown in FIG-1.2.

**FIG-1.2**

Binary to Decimal Conversion

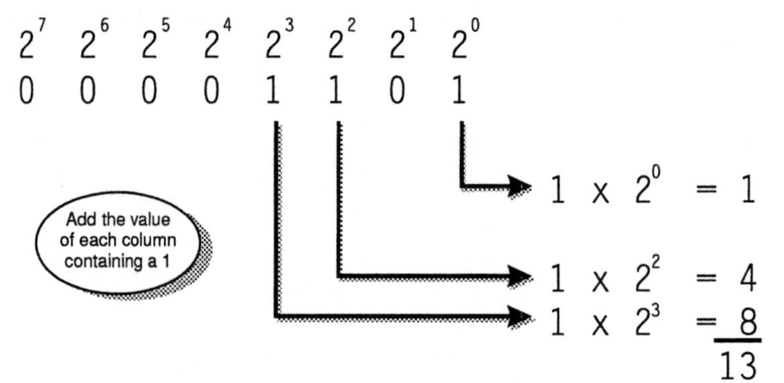

**Activity 1.15**

Convert the following binary values to decimal.

```
00101001
11111111
10101010
```

## Converting Fractions

So far we have only looked at converting whole numbers (integers) but we also need to be able to represent decimal fractions in binary.

Decimal fractions have column values of

**Decimal point** → . $10^{-1}$ $10^{-2}$ $10^{-3}$ etc.

which can be written as the fractions

. $\frac{1}{10}$ $\frac{1}{100}$ $\frac{1}{1000}$

Binary fractions, on the other hand, have column values of

**Binary point** → . $2^{-1}$ $2^{-2}$ $2^{-3}$ etc.

or

. $\frac{1}{2}$ $\frac{1}{4}$ $\frac{1}{8}$ etc.

To convert from a decimal fraction to the binary equivalent, the following algorithm can be employed:

```
Get decimal fraction
Set worked value to the decimal fraction
Write '.'
REPEAT
    Multiply worked value by 2
    Write down integer part of the result
    Remove the integer part from the worked value
UNTIL worked value is zero OR required degree of accuracy obtained
```

The first iteration of this operation is shown in FIG-1.3.

**FIG-1.3**

Decimal Fraction to Binary

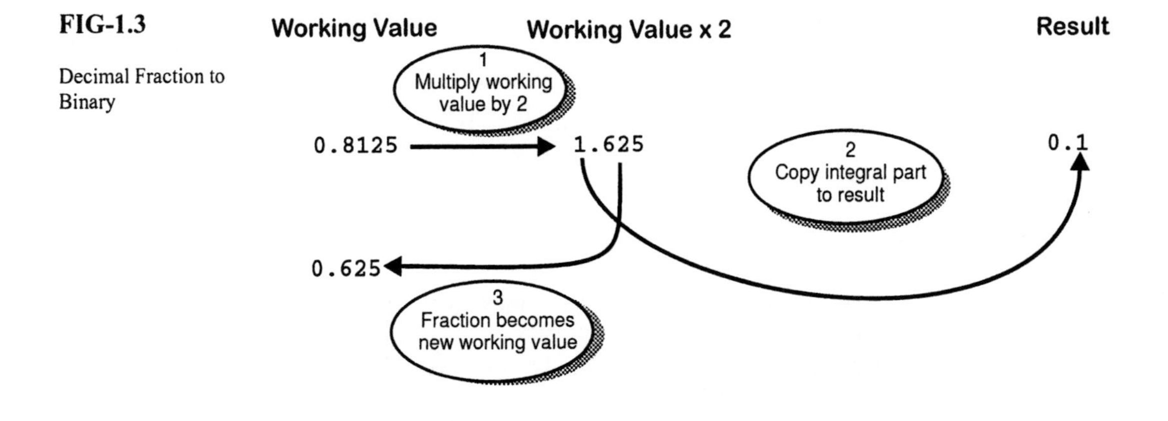

A full example of the conversion is shown below:

Value to be converted : 0.8125

| *Working value* | | *Working value x 2* | *Result* |
|---|---|---|---|
| | | | 0. |
| 0.8125 | x 2 | 1.625 | 0.1 |
| 0.625 | x 2 | 1.25 | 0.11 |
| 0.25 | x 2 | 0.5 | 0.110 |
| 0.5 | x 2 | 1.0 | 0.1101 |
| 0 | | | |

**Activity 1.16**

Convert the following decimal fractions to binary (stop after 6 binary places):

```
0.75
0.3125
0.38
```

Binary fractions to decimal present no problem since, like integers, it is simply a matter of adding the values of any column containing a 1.

To convert decimal numbers which contain a whole number and fraction part, such as 3.1415, simply split the number into its two parts, integer and fraction, and convert each separately.

**Activity 1.17**

1. Convert the binary value 0.01011 to decimal.

2. Convert the decimal value 12.625 to binary.

# Hexadecimal

The **hexadecimal** system is another number system which is widely used in computing. It has a base of 16 which implies there are 16 different digits. However, since our own decimal system has only 10 digits, we are left with the problem of representing values between 10 and 15 (decimal) by a single digit. This is achieved by using the first 6 letters of the alphabet. Thus decimal 10 is represented by A, 11 by B and so on.

Column values in hexadecimal are:

... $16^3$ $16^2$ $16^1$ $16^0$

or

4096 256 16 1

Conversion from decimal to hexadecimal uses the same technique as that for binary, except this time we divide by 16 and any remainders greater than 9 are converted to the equivalent letter code. FIG-1.4 shows an example of decimal to hexadecimal conversion.

**FIG-1.4**

Decimal to Hexadecimal Conversion

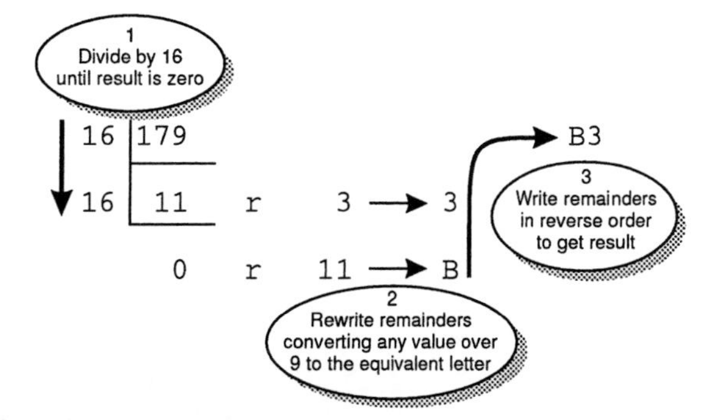


Hexadecimal to decimal uses the same method as with binary to decimal; only the column values are different (see FIG-1.5).

**FIG-1.5**

Hexadecimal to Decimal Conversion

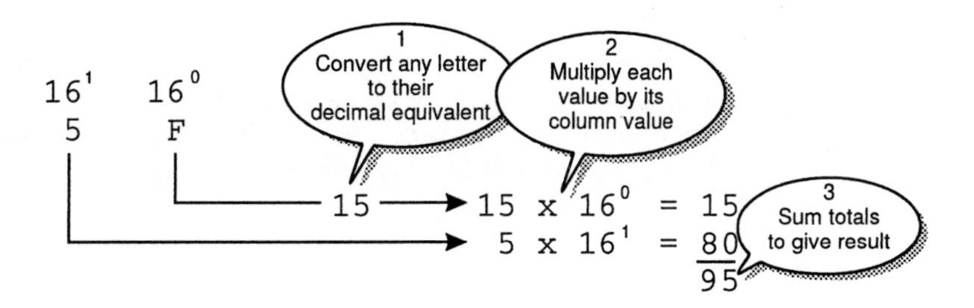


The most likely conversions when using hexadecimal are to and from binary. Four binary digits can range between 0000 and 1111 in value. Since this represents the values 0 to 15 we can use a single hexadecimal digit, 0 to F, to represent these four bits. Thus the contents of a single byte can be shown as two hexadecimal digits. The conversion technique is shown in FIG-1.6.

Conversion from hexadecimal to binary simply involves reversing this process as shown in FIG-1.7.

**FIG-1.6**

Binary to Hexadecimal Conversion

10011101

1001 1101

9 13

9 D

1 Split the value into 4 bit groups

2 Convert each group to decimal

3 Convert each decimal value to hexadecimal

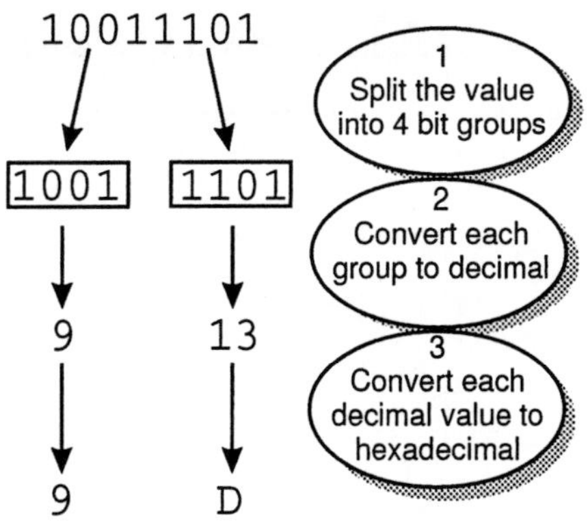

**FIG-1.7**

Hexadecimal to Binary Conversion

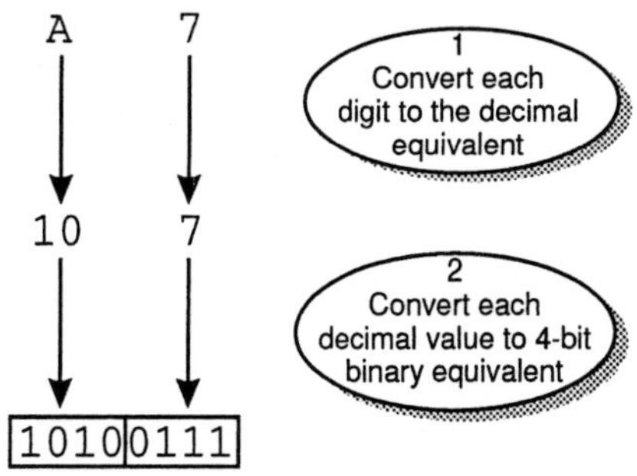

A 7

10 7

1010 0111

1 Convert each digit to the decimal equivalent

2 Convert each decimal value to 4-bit binary equivalent

**Activity 1.18**

1. Convert the following binary values to hexadecimal:

```
01000111
11111111
11001011
```

2. Convert the following hexadecimal values to binary:

```
73
A2
FE
```

# Octal

A final number system, which is useful in machines that use a 6 bit configuration rather than the more widespread 8 bit organisation, is **octal**. Octal is a base 8 numbering system using the digits 0 to 7.

Column values are

... $8^2$ $8^1$ $8^0$

that is

... 64 8 1

Decimal to octal is achieved by continually dividing by 8 until a result of zero is arrived at and then copying out the remainders (last one being the most-significant).

Octal to decimal is performed by multiplying each digit in the octal value by its column value and summing these values.

Binary to octal requires the binary value to be split into groupings of 3 bits. Grouping starts from the right-hand side; where the number of bits is not exactly divisible by 3, the left-most group may have only 1 or 2 bits. Each group is converted to its decimal equivalent; these digits give the final result.

Octal to binary requires each octal digit to be converted to exactly 3 binary digits.

It will not be necessary to convert octal to or from hexadecimal.

**Activity 1.19**

1. Convert the following binary values to octal:

```
101001
10011100
11111111
```

2. Convert the following octal values to decimal:

```
75
121
333
```

### Identify a Number's Base

Where a piece of text may refer to several number systems it is usual to include a subscript giving the number base being represented. Hence the decimal value 77 would be written as

$77_{10}$

while the hexadecimal value 57 would be shown as

$57_{16}$

# Negative Numbers

In an 8 bit byte we can store any binary value between 00000000 and 11111111 which, in decimal, is 0 to 255. But how are negative numbers, such as -17, stored?

Imagine we are sitting in a car whose current journey odometer is set to 0000. If we drive forward one mile then we will have a reading of 0001. If, on the other hand, we were to drive in reverse for one mile the reading would be 9999. Now, if we consider moving forward in the car as equivalent to moving up through the positive numbers while reversing is a movement through the negative range (as illustrated in FIG-1.8), then we can think of the reading on the odometer as representations of both positive and negative numbers (e.g. 0001 = +1; 9999 = -1). Some of the values are shown in TABLE-1.6.

**FIG-1.8**

Representing Positive and Negative Values on the Odometer

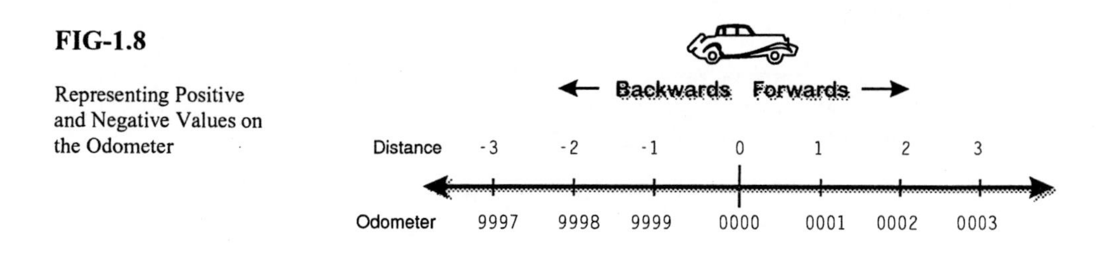


**TABLE-1.6**

Representation of Positive and Negative Values

| Integer value | Reading |
|---|---|
| -3 | 9997 |
| -2 | 9998 |
| -1 | 9999 |
| 0 | 0000 |
| 1 | 0001 |
| 2 | 0002 |
| 3 | 0003 |

Of course, using this approach has a cost since the range of positive numbers we can represent has now been reduced since readings such as 9996 no longer represent the value +9996 but rather -4. And what of the reading 5001? Does it represent the value +5001 or -4999? At some point on our readings we have to decide on a split between those which represent positive values and those which are negative. If we make the split half way (giving 5000 positive values - if zero is included; and 5000 negative values) we get the reading split as shown in TABLE-1.7.

**TABLE-1.7**

Negative and Positive Ranges

| Reading | Integer value |
|---|---|
| 0000 | 0 |
| 4999 | 4999 |
| 5000 | -5000 |
| 9999 | -1 |

This representation of negative values works rather well when performing arithmetic operations. For example, the subtraction

47 -12

which can be rewritten as:

47 + (-12)

This is represented in our new system as

0047 + (9988)

which, when added, gives:

0035

Remember, the odometer only has 4 digits, so the fifth digit (1) of the above addition is not stored in the result.

## 2's Complement

This same approach is used in binary where this method of representation is known as **2's complement**. With an 8 bit storage unit, values between -128 and +127 can be stored (as shown in TABLE-1.8)

**TABLE-1.8**

Negative and Positive Ranges

| Byte | Integer value |
|---|---|
| 00000000 | 0 |
| 01111111 | 127 |
| 10000000 | -128 |
| 11111111 | -1 |

### Decimal to 2's Complement

We already have a technique for converting a positive whole number to its binary equivalent and this can be extended to find the 2's complement value for negative numbers. The algorithm required is:

```
Get negative value
Ignoring the sign, convert to binary using all bits
Starting at right hand digit
REPEAT
    Copy current digit into result
    Move to the next digit to the left
UNTIL digit copied is a 1
FOR each remaining digit DO
    Copy the opposite digit into the result
ENDFOR
```

*Opposite digit* means 1's are changed to zeros and vice versa.

For example, to find the 2's complement form of the value -68, we first find the binary representation of +68:

```
01000100
```

This example assumes the value is being stored in a single byte (8 bits).

Next copy every digit (from the right) unchanged up to and including the first 1:

```
     100
```

Finally, copy the remaining digits but changing 1's to 0's and vice versa:

```
10111100
```

Where a number is stored over 16 bits ( 2 bytes ) this allows a larger range of values: -32,768 to 32,767 to be held, but the same 2's complement strategy is employed Hence, the value -68 would be stored in 16 bits as

```
11111111 10111100
```

> **Activity 1.20**
>
> Convert the following values to 2's complement form in both 8 and 16 bit format:
>
> ```
>   -3
>  -42
> -127
> ```

**2's Complement to Decimal**

Before converting a 2's complement value to decimal we must first decide if we are dealing with a negative value or a positive one. Looking back at TABLE-1.8 we can see that the left-most digit of all negative values is a 1 while it is 0 for positive values. Hence, where the left-most digit is a zero, conversion is achieved by following the same technique as that described earlier for positive binary values: add the values of each column containing a 1.

This means that, for negative values, we first convert the value to the equivalent positive value. Therefore, faced with the value

```
11001110
```

we begin by copying all the digits from the right up to and including the first 1

```
      10
```

and then changing each of the remaining digits:

```
00110010
```

This results in the positive form of the original number which can then be converted in the usual way. Obviously, a minus sign must be placed in front of the result:

```
        128 64  32  16   8   4   2   1
         0   0   1   1   0   0   1   0

=   -(32 + 16 + 2)

=   -50
```

To summarise, whole numbers are stored in a computer's memory as a binary pattern. The representation used may not allow for negative numbers (the storage format is said to be **unsigned** or **absolute**). Alternatively, by using 2's complement (or **signed** format), both positive and negative values may be stored. If a value is stored in a single byte, using unsigned format any value between 0 and 255 can be represented while 2's complement will allow values in the range -128 to +127.

When presented with a binary value it is necessary to know which of the above storage formats is being used before converting the value to decimal. For example, 11111111 represents the value 255 in unsigned format and -1 in 2's complement form.

# Floating Point Values

Real numbers (those with fractional parts) are stored in a different format. The format used within the computer is similar to that employed when writing numbers in scientific notation. Numbers such as 12.8 are said to be written in **fixed point format** but the same number can also be written as 1.28E1. This is **scientific** or **floating point** notation. Although it may look somewhat unfriendly, if you're unfamiliar with this form, it is simply a formula for the original number. Hence,

$$
\begin{aligned}
& 1.28 \times 10^1 \\
= \ & 1.28 \times 10 \\
= \ & 12.8
\end{aligned}
$$

The value 365.249 would be written as 3.65249E2 which is:

$$
\begin{aligned}
& 3.65249 \times 10^2 \\
= \ & 3.65249 \times 100 \\
= \ & 365.249
\end{aligned}
$$

The first part of the floating point number (e.g. 3.65249) is termed the **mantissa**; the second part following the letter E is the **exponent**. The exponent represents the power of ten by which the mantissa must be multiplied to give the value being represented. The mantissa is always shown as a value greater than or equal to one and less than ten. This is called the **normalised mantissa**.

For small numbers, such as 0.00013 the exponent will be negative:

```
   0.00013
=  1.3E-4
```

For negative values, the mantissa is negative:

```
   -6712.8
=  -6.7128E3
```

Again conversion from fixed to floating point notation can be explained using a simple algorithm:

```
Get the fixed point value
The mantissa is the original number with the decimal point
 moved between the first and second non-zero digit
Add an 'E'
IF the original value was less than 1 THEN
    Place a minus sign in front of the exponent
ENDIF
The exponent is the number of places the decimal point
 had to be moved to change the original number into the
 normalised mantissa
```

**Activity 1.21**

Convert the following values to floating point notation:

```
123.98
  6.9
 -0.00000001
```

When using floating point notation within the computer, the following approach is employed:

```
Get decimal value
Convert it to binary
Create the mantissa by moving binary point to left of the most
 significant 1
The exponent is the number of places the point was moved
 (written in binary)
IF the binary point was moved to the right THEN
    The exponent is negative
ENDIF
```

For example,

```
46.375
```

converts to

```
101110.011
```

giving a mantissa of

```
.101110011
```

and an exponent of

```
110
```

This format is changed slightly in most software to optimise the storage requirements and the efficiency of the algorithms used for manipulating floating point values.

There are two main changes. When storing real numbers in binary form, the exponent is usually held as a positive value. This is achieved by adding some value to the correct exponent, which may well be negative. For example, if the exponent occupies 8 bits of the space allocated to a real value this allows for a range of values from -128 to 127 when 2's complement form is being used. However, if we add 128 to the exponent once it has been calculated and hold the value in unsigned format, a range of 0 to 255 can be accommodated. This is called a **biased exponent**. The mantissa is also modified slightly by omitting the most significant digit when it is stored. Since the first digit of the mantissa must be a 1, there is little point in storing it, hence freeing 1 more bit to hold the remaining digits of the mantissa which results in slightly increased accuracy.

The storage format used is shown in FIG-1.9. The number of bits allocated to each component will depend on the implementation.

**FIG-1.9**

Floating Point Storage

| Biased Exponent | Mantissa |
|---|---|

**Activity 1.22**

Assuming floating point numbers are stored in 24 bits, the mantissa occupying 16 bits and the exponent 8 bits, show how the value 0.09375 would be stored. Assume an exponent with a bias value of 128.

# Character Coding

As well as numbers, computers need to store characters. Since everything in the machine is stored in binary this means that we need some coding system to represent these characters. This is much the same approach as employed in morse code where dots and dashes are used to represent letters.

ASCII stands for American Standard Code for Information Interchange

Although several coding methods are employed, originally the most universal one was the **ASCII** coding system. This uses a single byte (of which only seven bits are used) to store a letter in upper or lower case, or a punctuation character. This allows 128 different characters. For example the code for 'A' is:

```
01000001
```

This is also the binary equivalent of the decimal value 65 and in order to correctly interpret a binary pattern stored in the machine, the computer needs to be aware of the type of value the pattern represents (a number or a character).

The IBM extended character set is an extension of the ASCII coding which makes use of the $8^{th}$ bit to allow an extra 128 characters. Some of these codes are used for special European characters, others allow for simple graphics characters.

A new coding system using 16 bits is currently being finalised. This allows for every character used throughout the world and is referred to as **unicode**.

The full IBM extended character set is shown in APPENDIX A.

# Summary

- Computers store all data in **binary**.
- **Binary is a base 2 number system.**
- **Binary uses the digits 0 and 1.**
- **A binary digit** is often referred to as a **bit**.
- **Bits are most often organised into 8 bits**. An 8 bit group is known as a **byte**.
- **Decimal to binary** conversion of integer values is achieved by continually dividing by 2 until a result of zero is achieved. The remainders (last one being the most-significant digit) form the result.
- **Decimal to binary** conversion of fractions is achieved by continually multiplying the remaining fraction by 2 until a result of zero or the required accuracy is achieved. The integral part of each result forms the binary value.

- **Real decimal values greater than 1** are changed to binary by converting the integer and fractional parts separately.
- **Before converting from binary to decimal** it is necessary to know which format is being used: **unsigned** or **2's complement** format.
- **For positive values,** binary to decimal conversion is achieved by summing the value of each column containing a 1.
- **For negative values,** binary to decimal conversion is achieved by first converting to the positive equivalent.
- **Hexadecimal is a base 16 number system** using the digits 0 to 9, A to F.
- **A single byte can be represented by** two hexadecimal digits.
- **Decimal to hexadecimal** conversion is achieved by continually dividing by 16 until a result of zero is achieved. Any remainder over 9 is converted to the equivalent hexadecimal letter (10 = A, 11 = B etc.). The remainders (last one being the most-significant digit) represent the result.
- **Hexadecimal to decimal** conversion is achieved by summing the value of each column containing a non-zero digit.
- **Binary to hexadecimal** conversion is achieved by grouping the binary value into 4 bit groups; converting each group to the decimal equivalent; converting each decimal value to the hexadecimal equivalent.
- **Hexadecimal to binary** conversion is achieved by converting each hexadecimal digit to the decimal equivalent; converting each decimal value to the equivalent 4 bit binary value.
- **Octal is a base 8 number system** using the digits 0 to 7.
- **Decimal to octal** conversion is achieved by continually dividing by 8 until a result of zero is achieved. The remainders (last one being the most-significant digit) represent the result.
- **Octal to decimal** conversion is achieved by summing the value of each column containing a non-zero digit.
- **Binary to octal** conversion is achieved by grouping the binary value into 3 bit groups; converting each group to the decimal equivalent.
- **Octal to binary** conversion is achieved by converting each octal digit to the equivalent 3 bit binary value.
- **The base of a value** can be shown as a subscript following the number.
- **Signed binary values** are held in 2's complement form.
- **Floating point values** are constructed from a mantissa and exponent.
- **Normalising a decimal mantissa** involves moving the decimal point until its value is not less than 1 and less than 10.
- **Normalising a binary mantissa** involves moving the binary point until the most significant 1 is to its immediate right.

- **The exponent represents** the number of places the mantissa's point must be moved to restore the original number. The exponent is negative if the point needs to be moved to the left.

- In the computer, **floating point values are often held with a biased exponent and the first 1 missing from the mantissa.**

- **The IBM extended character set** is used by most computers. This allows for 256 different characters and is an extension of ASCII.

# THE COMPILATION PROCESS

Since computers are only capable of recognising and executing commands given in their own native processor instruction set (known as **machine code**) and since computer programs are normally written in other languages, the computer is required to perform some translation process to convert the original program code (known as the **source code**) into the equivalent sequence of machine code instructions (the **object code**) which can then be executed by the computer.

This operation is known as **compilation** and is performed by a piece of software called a **compiler**. Each compiler is designed to translate one specific source language, in this case Pascal.

Any practical compiler is more complex than this simplified model. For example, it is often the case that the source code which makes up the complete program is not held within a single file but is constructed from several files. In this situation, the compiler must first bring together the contents of each source file involved before beginning the main compilation process. This task is carried out by part of the compiler known as the **preprocessor**.

The term **function** is used here to mean pieces of program code which perform some specific operation. Hence a function may exist to calculate the cosine of an angle.

Most programs are unlikely to contain the source code for all the functions they require. More likely, a program will make use of existing functions which are available only in object code form. For example, a program may require to calculate the square root of some value, move the cursor to a new position on the screen, or open a disk file. A collection of such precompiled functions is held in a disk file known as a **library**. Although libraries are provided as part of the compiler package, the programmer is free to create a library of his own more specialised routines.

**FIG-1.10**

The Compilation Process

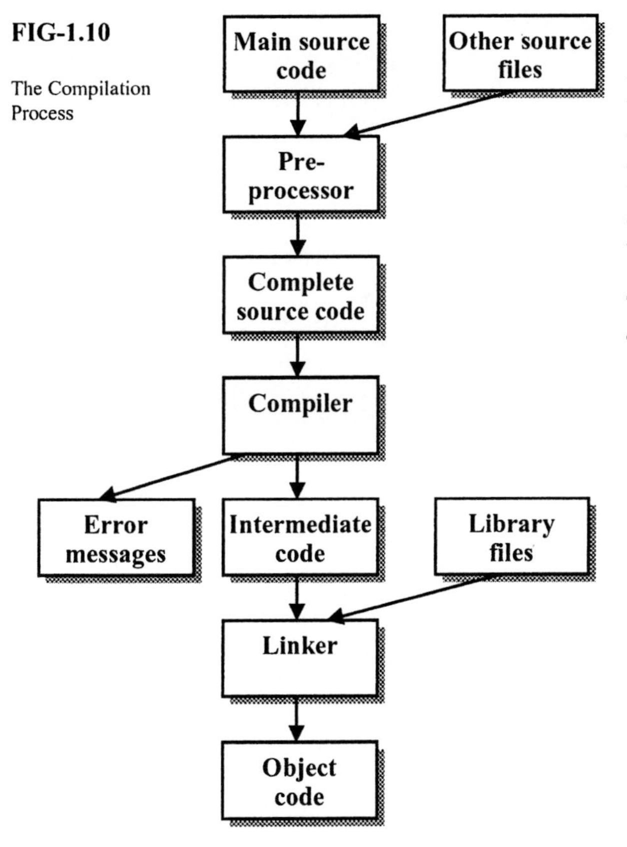


When the first stage of compilation takes place the source code is converted to object code, but where there is a call to a precompiled function held in other files the compiler merely makes a note of which additional functions it requires to insert in the final version of the program. These are embedded in the final source code by part of the compiler known as a **linker**.

This, more complete model of the compilation process is shown in FIG-1.10.

# SELF-ASSESSMENT REVIEW

1. Name the three basic control structures.

2. A, B and C are Boolean expressions. A and B are **true** while C is **false**. What is the result of the compound expression:

   A **AND NOT**(B **OR** C) ?

3. Define the term **infinite loop**.

4. Using stepwise refinement, write the set of instructions necessary to place a music cassette in a personal stereo and to begin playing at tape counter position 312 on side B of the tape. Start by removing any tape which may already be in the machine; end with pressing the play button.

5. Convert the following values to binary

   $103_{10}$
   $8E_{16}$
   $17_{8}$

6. Convert the following unsigned binary values to decimal, hexadecimal and octal:

   ```
   01000111
   10001010
   11001100
   ```

7. Convert the following signed values to decimal:

   ```
   01110001
   10001101
   11101001
   ```

8. Convert the following value to binary floating point using an 8 bit exponent and 16 bit mantissa.

   ```
   121.0783
   ```

# SOLUTIONS

## Activity 1.1

A possible solution is:

```
Open door of washing machine
Place clothes in washing machine
Put washing powder in powder tray
Close door
Choose required setting
When washing cycle complete, remove clothes
from machine
```

Of course, you will almost certainly have produced a solution which differs from the one above. But, as long as your logic is correct, (for example, it would be wrong to put the clothes in the machine before opening the door) then any solution is acceptable.
Remember to take a separate line for each instruction.

## Activity 1.2

```
Fill kettle
Switch on kettle
Put tea in teapot
When water boils, pour into teapot
Wait for tea to infuse
Pour tea into cup
IF milk is required THEN
     Add milk
ENDIF
IF sugar is required THEN
    Add sugar
    Stir tea
ENDIF
Drink tea
```

Other solutions are possible but make sure the milk and sugar are dealt with by two separate IF statement, and that the ENDIF terms are included.

## Activity 1.3

```
Write letter
Fold letter
Place letter in envelope
Seal envelope
Write address on envelope
IF sending first class THEN
    Stick first class stamp on envelope
ELSE
    Stick second class stamp on envelope
ENDIF
Take letter to post box
Post letter
```

Ensure you use an IF .. THEN .. ELSE structure when selecting the stamp.

## Activity 1.4

The statement carried out is:

```
park the car in the car park
```

## Activity 1.5

```
Find out total cost
IF
    paying by cash:
        Give cashier sufficient money
        IF any change is due THEN
            Collect change
        ENDIF
    paying by cheque:
        Write out cheque
        Give cheque to cashier
        Show cheque card
    paying by credit card:
        Hand over credit card
        Sign authorisation slip
        Take back credit card
        Take credit transaction slip
     paying through account:
        Give account number
ENDIF
Take till receipt
Take purchases
```

## Activity 1.6

```
IF
    it's between 4.00pm and 6.00pm:
        park the car in a metered space
    it's after 6.00pm:
        park the car beside the house
     ELSE:
        park the car in the car park
ENDIF
```

## Activity 1.7

```
printer on-line AND toner not empty AND (paper
in main tray OR paper in auxiliary tray)
```

## Activity 1.8

```
FOR 20 times DO
    Read mark and name
     IF mark is less than 50% THEN
        Add name to list of fails
    ENDIF
ENDFOR
```

## Activity 1.9

```
REPEAT
    Find start of next article
    Read author's name
UNTIL author's name is "Liz Herron"
```

## Activity 1.10

```
Roll both dice
WHILE both dice are not equal DO
    Choose dice with lower value
    Throw dice
ENDWHILE
```

## Activity 1.11

Possible data items are:

```
car model
engine size
city
premium
street
post code
phone number
policy number
```

## Activity 1.12

Input statements:

```
Get caller's name, street, post code, phone number
and car registration number.

Get policy number from top right hand of policy form
```

Calculation statements:

```
Calculate excess due as £50 for each year under 25

Add excess to premium
```

Output statements:

```
Give the policy number to caller
```

## Activity 1.13

Only two statements need to be expanded to give more detail:

```
3. Get order details
4. Process item
```

Possible expansions are:

```
3. Get order details
    3.1 Get catalogue number
    3.2  WHILE catalogue number is invalid DO
    3.3      Tell customer number is invalid
    3.4      Get catalogue number again
    3.5  ENDWHILE
    3.6 Get quantity required

4.  Process order
    4.1 IF item in stock AND sufficient quantity THEN
    4.2      Add details to order list
    4.3 ELSE
    4.4      Check for alternative
    4.5      IF there is an alternative THEN
     4.6             Tell customer details of
                  alternative
    4.7          IF alternative acceptable THEN
    4.8              Add alternative's details
                     to order list
    4.9           ENDIF
    4.10     ELSE
    4.11         Tell customer item not available
    4.12     ENDIF
    4.13 ENDIF
```

This gives a final LEVEL 2 algorithm of:

```
1.      Get number of items
2.      FOR each item DO
3.1         Get catalogue number
3.2         WHILE catalogue number is invalid DO
3.3             Tell customer number is invalid
3.4             Get catalogue number again
3.5          ENDWHILE
3.6         Get quantity required
4.1          IF item in stock AND sufficient quantity
             THEN
4.2              Add details to order list
4.3         ELSE
4.4              Check for alternative
4.5             IF there is an alternative THEN
4.6                 Tell customer details of
                    alternative
4.7                 IF alternative acceptable THEN
4.8                     Add alternative's details
                        to order list
4.9                  ENDIF
4.10             ELSE
4.11                Tell customer item not available
4.12            ENDIF
4.13        ENDIF
5       ENDFOR
6.      Send order to dispatches department
```

## Activity 1.14

```
0010011
01001000
00111111
```

## Activity 1.15

```
41

255

170
```

## Activity 1.16

```
0.11
0.0101
0.011000
```

## Activity 1.17

```
1.
0.34375

2.
1100.101
```

## Activity 1.18

```
1.
    47
    FF
    CB

2.
    01110011
    10100010
    11111110
```

## Activity 1.19

```
1.
    51
    234
    377

2.
    61
    81
    219
```

## Activity 1.20

| 8 bits | 16 bits |
|---|---|
| 11111101 | 1111111111111101 |
| 11010110 | 1111111111010110 |
| 10000001 | 1111111110000001 |

## Activity 1.21

```
1.2398E2

6.9E0

-1.0E-8
```

## Activity 1.22

```
011111001 1000000000000000
```

Remember the most-significant 1 in the mantissa is omitted.

Chapter 2

# Starting Pascal

## This chapter covers the following topics:

- Arithmetic Operators
- Assignment Operator
- Basic Program Structure
- Clearing the Screen
- Declaring Variables
- Identifiers
- Reading from the Keyboard
- Outputting to the Screen
- Pascal Reserved Words
- Program Constants
- Sample Programs
- Using Pascal under Microsoft Windows and DOS
- Variable Types

# A BRIEF HISTORY OF PASCAL

The Pascal language was defined by Niklaus Wirth in 1971 and was based on earlier languages such as Algol. By the mid-seventies it was widely used as a teaching language on mini and mainframe computers.

Its strengths are the good structuring and modular approach it encourages (and enforces) on program implementation. It is also a relatively simple language to learn.

An international standard for the language was eventually set out in 1983. However, around about this time Borland created the first version of Turbo Pascal for the newly emerging personal computer market.

It is probably fair to say that this product revolutionised how programs were created and compiled. Instead of using separate editor, compiler and linker to produce the executable program, all of this was achieved in a single Integrated Development Environment. In addition to this, Turbo Pascal extended the original language to allow for graphical output and easier text handling.

Turbo Pascal, and later the more up-market Borland Pascal, became a standard teaching language throughout the United Kingdom. In the USA, where Turbo Pascal was produced, the language was not as all-pervasive.

Now, both the USA and UK have moved on - primarily to C and C++. However, Pascal is still widely used as a first language in teaching programming skills.

Borland's Pascal has gone through many revisions over the years. It now stands at version 7.0. This, however, is the last version of the DOS based language to be produced. It is now several years since version 7.0 was released and Pascal development efforts at Borland are directed to Borland Delphi which has, itself, reached a version 7.0 release.

# PASCAL : PROGRAM STRUCTURE

## An Overview

Before describing the basic elements of Pascal, we'll begin with a quick look at some code to give you the general structure of a simple Pascal program. The program in LISTING-2.1 displays the message *Hello world* on the screen.

**LISTING-2.1**

A Simple Pascal Program

```
program first(input,output);
uses WinCrt;
begin
  writeln('Hello world');
end.
```

**An Explanation of the Code**

In fact, Borland's compiler allows this first line to be shortened or omitted.

| | |
|---|---|
| `program` | This is a keyword in Pascal and is used to mark the start of the program. |
| `first` | This is the name of the program. As the programmer, you are at liberty to choose any name, but it must conform to certain rules: it must begin with a letter and continue with letters, numbers or the underscore character; no spaces are allowed. |
| `(input,output);` | The terms `input` and `output` refer to the names given by the language to the keyboard and screen respectively. In modern versions of Pascal the inclusion of these terms has no significance. However, some Pascal compilers require them to be present. |
| `uses WinCrt;` | This tells the compiler to include various items from a library file called *WinCrt*.<br>If you're working in DOS mode this line may be omitted. |
| `begin` | Marks the beginning of a block of code. In this case, the code for the main program. |
| `writeln` | The term `writeln` is used to produce screen output. After the output is produced, the cursor will move to the start of the next line. |
| `(` | Is used to enclose the values to be displayed. |
| `'Hello world'` | Is the argument of `writeln` and is the text string to be displayed. Note that strings are enclosed in single quotes. When the program is executed, the phrase *Hello world*, is displayed. |
| `)` | This marks the end of the values to be displayed. |
| `end.` | Block terminator symbol.<br>In this case, the end of the main program. Note that the term is followed by a full stop. |

In programming the term **string** is used to denote a sequence of characters.

The next program, (see LISTING-2.2) which inputs and sums two values, introduces program variables, comments, data input and calculations.

**LISTING-2.2**

Input, Variables and Assignment

```
program ex2;
uses WinCrt;
var
  no1, no2, answer : integer;
begin
  (* Program adds two numbers *)
  { Read in two values }
  write('Enter 2 values ');
  readln(no1 , no2);
  { Add values entered }
  answer := no1 + no2;
  { Display result }
  writeln('The sum of ', no1, ' and ', no2, ' is ', answer);
end.
```

### An Explanation of the Code

The general term for names created by the programmer is **identifier**. Hence, the program name and the names of the variables are classified as identifiers.

In subsequent programs comments will be highlighted for ease of reading.

`program ex2;`
The shortened version of the first line is used here.

`var`
This keyword must precede the declaration of program variables.

`no1,no2,answer:integer;`
This defines the three variables, *no1, no2* and *answer* as integers.

`(* Program adds two numbers *)`
This is a comment. Comments are enclosed between (* and *) and can span several lines of the program.

`{ Read in two values }`
An alternative to `(* .. *)` is to use `{ .. }`.

`write`
This is similar to `writeln`, which we met in the previous program. However, `write` does not move the cursor to the next line after displaying the requested values.

`readln`
The `readln` command accepts input from the keyboard.

`( )`
The parentheses enclose the variables to which the values entered are to be copied.

`no1 , no2`
Specifies where in memory the values input are to be stored. Hence the first value entered from the keyboard is stored in the variable *no1*; the second in *no2*. The program uses a comma to separate each item to be input.

`answer := no1 + no2;`
This instruction adds the values held in *no1* and *no2* and places the result in *answer*.

`writeln('The sum of ', no1, ' and ', no2, ' is ', answer);`
Outputs a combination of strings and variable

values to the screen. Each item to be displayed is separated from the next by a comma.
The instruction is a command to display the string *The sum of*; followed by the value held in the variable *no1*; the string, *and*; the contents of *no2*; the string, *is* and finally, the contents of *answer*.
Since `writeln` is used, the cursor moves to the start of the next line once the output has been produced.

If working in DOS, the line `uses WinCrt;` must be omitted from both programs.

If you are working in a Windows environment, the output will be displayed in a separate window which should be closed before returning to the Edit Window.

**Activity 2.1**

Type in and run both of the above programs.

In the second program, enter the values 4 and 2. The values should be entered separated by a space.

If you are working in DOS, press **Alt F5** to see the output produced.

Next, press any key to return to the edit window.

All Pascal programs consist of a set of instructions which are themselves constructed from keywords, variable names, fixed values and operators.

A **keyword** is a term known to the Pascal compiler - for instance, `if`, `write` and `readln` are examples of keywords.

**Variable names** identify storage areas reserved for data held by the program (e.g. *no1, no2* and *answer*).

**Fixed values** are specifically stated values. These values may be either numeric, such as *12, -9* and *8.7*, or non-numeric such as *'Hello world'*. Fixed values such as these are known as **constants**.

**Operators** are used to manipulate values. The commonest operators are the arithmetic operators such as + and - .

# Summary

A simple Pascal program has the following structure (see FIG-2.1).

**FIG-2.1**

Structure of a simple Pascal program

program identifier ;
variable declarations ;
begin
executable statements
end .

# CREATING OUTPUT

## write

Almost all computer programs create some sort of results. Generally, we want these results to be displayed on the screen. To do this we can use the `write` statement. For example, the statement

```
write(12);
```

will result in the number 12 being displayed on the screen.

**Activity 2.2**

Type in and run the following program:

```
program out1;
uses WinCrt;
begin
    write(12);
end.
```

If we want to display text (known as a string), it must be enclosed in single quotes:

```
write('This text will be output on the screen');
```

The string will be displayed on the screen without the quotes.

**Activity 2.3**

Change the `write` statement in the program above to read:

```
write('dozen');
```

Re-run your program and examine the output produced.

For those of you working in a DOS environment, you'll see from the results of Activity 2.3 that the *12* displayed in the first run and the text *dozen* from the second run of the program have been displayed side-by side:

```
12dozen_
```

Under Microsoft Windows, each program will open its own output window, hence the displays produced by different programs will not be combined in this way.

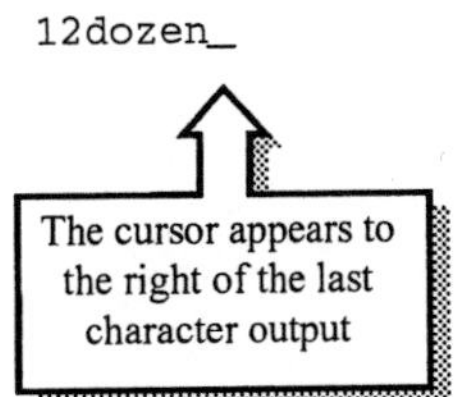
The cursor appears to the right of the last character output

Notice that the cursor (the flashing underline on the output screen) is placed to the immediate right of the *n* in *dozen*. You'll also see that the two values output, *12* and *dozen*, are displayed without any gap between them.

This brings us to the main characteristics of the `write` statement:

- Output starts at the current cursor position.
- The cursor ends up to the immediate right of the last character output by the `write` statement.

Hence, we can see that by running the program in Activity 2.2 the output would be

```
12_
```

and the modified version of the program in Activity 2.3 would start its output from this cursor position (on the right of the *12*) when outputting the word *dozen*.

## writeln

Often, we won't want all our output to be displayed on a single line. For example, we might want the data *12* and *dozen* to be output using the layout

```
12
dozen
```

To achieve this we need to replace the term `write` in our program with `writeln`. This new command (pronounced *write line*) differs from the earlier `write` statement in one respect only:

*It moves the cursor to the start of a new line after the output has been produced.*

Therefore, if a program contained the lines

```
writeln(12);
writeln('dozen');
```

it would produce the output

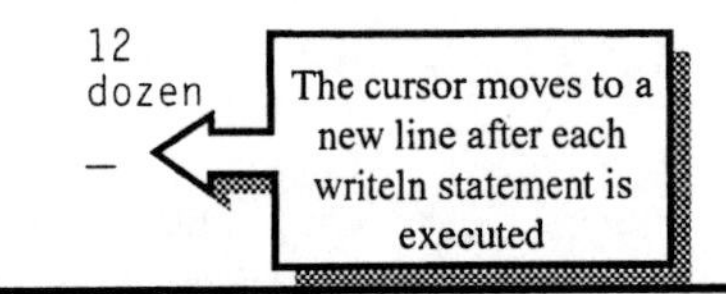
12
dozen
_
The cursor moves to a new line after each writeln statement is executed

**Activity 2.4**

Enter and run the following program:

```
program out2;
uses WinCrt;
begin
    writeln(12);
    writeln('dozen');
end.
```

Look at the output screen (using **Alt F5**, if in DOS mode).

After Activity 2.4, the output screen (in DOS) should look like:

```
12dozen12
dozen
```

Why did the second *12* end up on the same line as the previous output? Remember, the `writeln` command only moves to a new line **after** its data has been output to the screen and, like the `write` statement, output starts at the current cursor position. Now, since the previous program ended with the output screen showing

```
12dozen_
```

the next value to be displayed (*12* from `program out2`) will be placed at the position of the cursor - after the *n* of *dozen*:

```
12dozen12
```

Only after this will the cursor move to a new line:

```
12dozen12
_
```

which is where the final output (produced by the line `writeln('dozen');`) will begin, giving:

```
12dozen12
dozen
```

and finally, the cursor again moves to a new line:

```
12dozen12
dozen
_
```

# Other Display Options

## Clearing the Screen

You'll have noticed (in DOS) that the output screen isn't cleared between programs. This means that the results produced by the first program are still visible when we look at the results of the second.

It is possible to clear the screen at any point in your program using the command

```
ClrScr
```

This is a rather cryptic version of the phrase *clear screen*. The command has two effects:

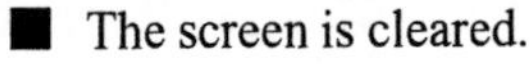

- The screen is cleared.
- The cursor is moved to the top left corner of the screen.

However, to make use of this command we need to add the statement

```
uses WinCrt;
```

If working under DOS, use
`uses Crt;`

as the second line of our program. Without this additional instruction, the compiler won't recognise the term `ClrScr`. We'll see the reason for this in a later chapter - for the moment just accept that the `uses` statement is necessary.

The next Activity shows the effect of using the new instruction.

**Activity 2.5**

Enter and run the following program:

The changes to the previous program are highlighted

```
program out3;
uses WinCrt;
begin
    ClrScr;
    writeln(12);
    writeln('dozen');
end.
```

Examine the output screen.

This time, you'll see the output (*12* and *dozen*) is at the top left of a blank screen, rather than appearing on a screen containing values from previous programs.

## Displaying Several Values

We've already seen that the two commands, `write` and `writeln` can be used to output values to the screen. But both commands are also capable of determining the style in which data is displayed.

If we want to display several values in a single statement, we can do this by simply adding the other values within the parentheses of the output statement. For example, we could output the numbers *1, 2* and *3* by writing:

```
writeln(1, 2, 3);
```

Notice that each value to be displayed is separated from the next by a comma. Without this, the compiler would normally raise an error.

Using this method, we can display as many values as we want in a single `write` or `writeln` statement. The values don't have to be of the same type. So, for example, we might write

```
writeln(1, 'A', 2, 'B', 3);
```

to output a combination of numbers and strings.

**Activity 2.6**

Enter and run the following program:

```
program out4;
uses WinCrt;
begin
    ClrScr;
    writeln(1, 2, 3);
    writeln(1, 'A', 2, 'B', 3);
end.
```

Examine the output produced.

It would appear from the first line output by Activity 2.6 that we've printed the number *123* rather than three distinct values. In the second line, although the characters all appear together, at least the letters separate the numbers from each other.

We can see from these examples that the values output in a single statement are displayed in consecutive locations on the screen.

So how can we display values such as 1, 2, 3 at a distance from one another? The second `writeln` in our previous program gives us a clue to how it can be done. Rather than use letters to separate the three numbers, we can tell the program to print spaces. Unlike written text, where we think of the spaces between words as simply blank bits of paper, to a computer a space is just another character; to be treated in the same way as say an 'A' or an 'M'. So to get the machine to display our three numbers separately we write

```
writeln(1, ' ', 2, ' ', 3);
```

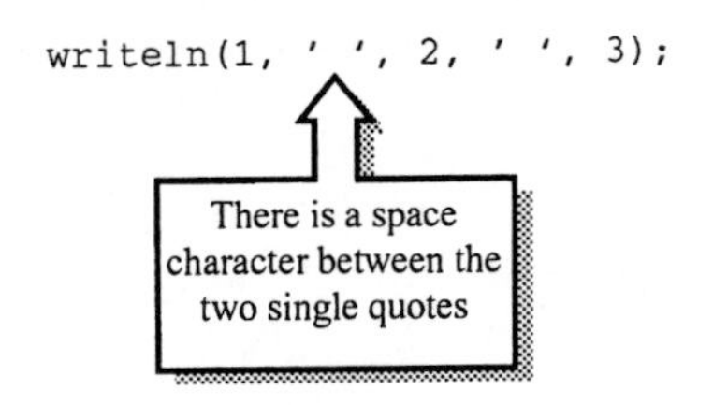
There is a space character between the two single quotes

Since it is often important to emphasis space characters in a program, from now on we'll use a triangle (∇)to represent any important space characters in a piece of code or the display produced.

It's also often useful to use a space to start or end longer strings. For example, the display from the command

```
writeln('I am', 21, 'years old');
```

will be output as:

```
I am21years old
```

But by adding spaces to the strings in the instruction,

It's important that the spaces are within the quotes of the string otherwise they will not be part of the final output.

```
writeln('I am∇', 21, '∇years old');
```

the output will be a much more readable

```
I am 21 years old
```

**Activity 2.7**

Using a `writeln` statement similar to that given above, write a program to output the text:

*I am 5 feet 7 inches tall*

Use a combination of strings and numbers to create the output.

## Defining Field Sizes

Another way to control the layout of what appears on the screen is to use a **field size.** A field size tells an item of data how many positions on the screen it should occupy when being displayed. For example, if we use the instruction

```
writeln(12:4);
```

we're telling the machine to display the number *12* using four screen positions. Now since the value *12* only requires two of those positions, the other two are space filled:

```
∇∇12
```

You can see from this example, that a field size is defined using a colon followed by the number of positions on the screen the data is to occupy. When the field size is larger than the required number of positions, the displayed value is right-justified within the field.

Using this technique, we can display our three values: 1,2, and 3 with a statement such as

```
writeln(1:2, 2:2, 3:2);
```

which would produce the output

```
∇1∇2∇3
```

We can also use field sizes when displaying strings. For example, the statement

```
writeln('Hello world':15);
```

produces the output

```
∇∇∇∇Hello world
```

This feature can also be used to create a gap of a specific size between values. For example, if we wanted to print the numbers *1* and *2* with 15 spaces between them, then we could use the statement

```
writeln(1, '∇':15, 2);
```

which, by forcing one space character to be displayed in a field 15 places in length, effectively displays 15 spaces. This is much easier than trying to place all 15 spaces inside a set of quotes within the `writeln` statement.

What if the field size given is too small? For instance, if we use the statement

```
writeln('Hello':2);
```

will we only get the first two characters ('*He*') displayed? The answer to that is, no. When the field size given is too small for the value to be displayed, the field size is ignored and the machine uses the minimum positions necessary to produce the complete output. So the statement above would still produce the output *Hello*.

**Activity 2.8**

Write a set of programs to produce the following outputs:

1. The letter 'X' at the top left of the screen.

2. The letter 'X' at the start of the fourth line of the screen.

3. The letter 'X' in column 40 of the seventh line of the screen.

**Continued on next page**

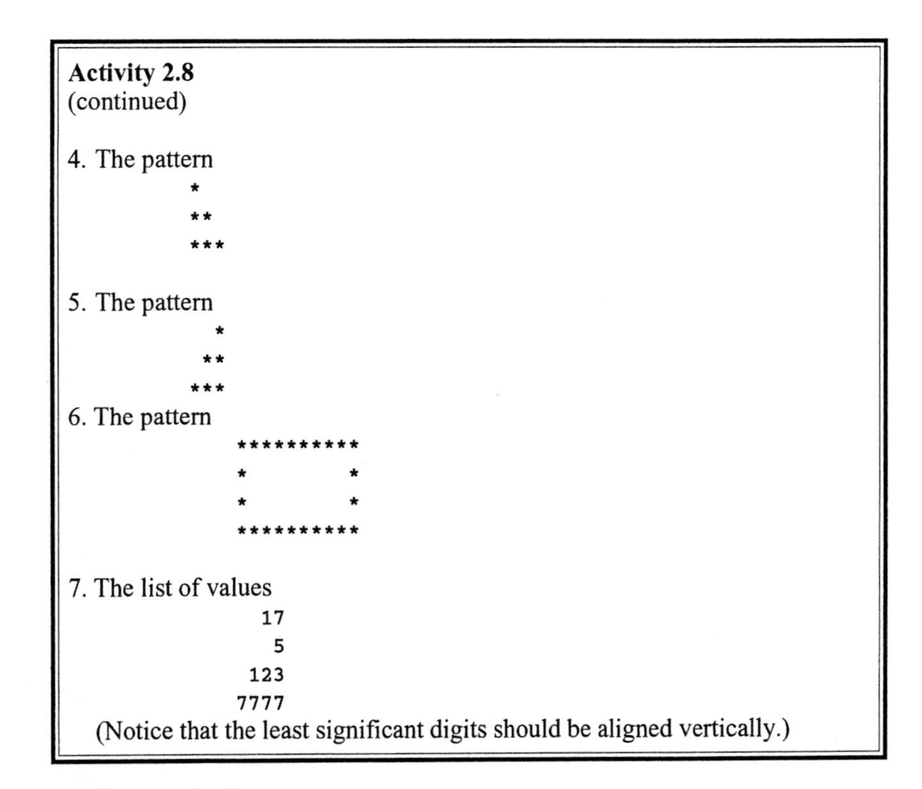

**Activity 2.8**
(continued)

4. The pattern

```
*
**
***
```

5. The pattern

```
  *
 **
***
```

6. The pattern

```
**********
*        *
*        *
**********
```

7. The list of values

```
  17
   5
 123
7777
```

(Notice that the least significant digits should be aligned vertically.)

## Displaying Real Numbers

So far the numbers we displayed have been integers, but there's nothing to stop us printing real numbers as well. For example,

```
writeln(358.67);
```

However, the resulting display might not be what you expected. The output produced will be

```
3.586700E+02
```

This is scientific notation. And, unless you're familiar with that format, it can be pretty unreadable.

If you want to get the more usual fixed point format on the screen, then you need to include a field size. However, this time the field size comes in two parts:

```
writeln(358.67:7:2);
```

The first part, as before, tells the machine the number of character positions to be occupied by the display on the screen; the second part tells us the number of decimal places required. So the above `writeln` statement tells us that the value 358.67 is to be displayed over 7 character positions on the screen, two of which are after the decimal place. This gives us the display:

Notice that there is only one leading space since the decimal point itself occupies one of the 7 display positions.

```
∇358.67
```

If we choose to give less decimal places in the field size than the number is specified to, the displayed value will automatically be rounded. Hence,

```
writeln(358.67:7:1);
```

gives

```
∇∇358.7
```

It's even possible to specify no decimal places, in which case, the decimal point does not appear as part of the display. Hence

```
writeln(358.67:7:0);
```

displays

```
∇∇∇∇359
```

There's one more trick we can play when displaying real values: by specifying a field size of zero, we can get a fixed-point display which occupies the minimum number of spaces:

This works because the program ignores the field size (since, at zero, it is too small) but makes use of the information given about the number of decimal places to create a fixed point display.

```
writeln(358.67:0:1);
```

displays as

```
358.7
```

### Displaying Blank Lines

One last possibility with the `writeln` statement is to use it without specifying any values to be displayed:

```
writeln;
```

This simply moves the cursor to the start of the next line on the screen. If the cursor is already at the start of a new line, this will result in a blank line in your output.

## Statement Format

The format of the `write/writeln` statement is shown in FIG-2.2 below.

**FIG-2.2**

The Output Statement

Items in braces, { }, are alternatives.

Items within brackets, [ ], are optional and may be omitted.

The arrowed line indicates items that may be repeated.

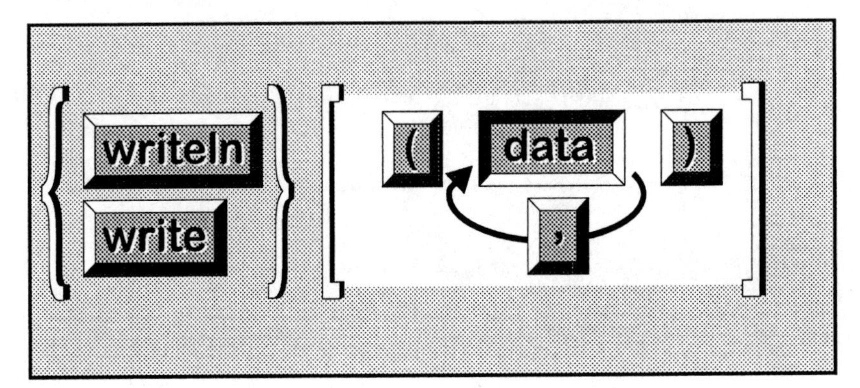


Where **data** can be:

These data types will be dealt with in detail later in this chapter.

a number,
a character,
a string,
a Boolean value (i.e. *true* or *false*)
a variable name
or an expression

In addition, **data** may contain a field size specification.

## Summary

- **Output** is achieved using the `write` or `writeln` statements.
- **The `write` statement** leaves the cursor to the immediate right of the last character output.
- **The `writeln` statement** moves the cursor to the start of a new line after the last character is output.
- **When displaying individual characters or strings**, these data items must be enclosed in quotes.
- **Scientific notation** is the default format for displaying real values.
- **Displaying several values** can be done in a single `write/writeln` statement. Each value must be separated from the next by a comma.
- **A field size** may be used when displaying a value. This determines the number of character positions on the screen that the value will occupy.
- **Field size format** for most values is

```
: field_size
```

- **Where a field size is too small**, it will be ignored.
- **When defining a field size for real values** include the number of decimal places using the format

```
: field_size : no_of_decimal_places
```

- **Use `writeln` without any values** to move the cursor to the start of the next line.
- **To clear the screen** and move the cursor to the top left of the display use the command

```
ClrScr;
```

- The `ClrScr` command can only be used if the statement

  **`uses WinCrt;`** (or **`uses Crt;`** in DOS)

  is included at the start of the program.

# VARIABLES AND CONSTANTS

## Variables

### What is a Variable?

Almost everyone has had to fill in a form similar to the one shown in FIG-2.3. Each entry in the form has a boxed area in which we are required to enter information. Beside each box is a label (or name) giving us an indication of what information we are meant to place in that box. Each box differs in size and format depending on the type of information it is designed to hold. Hence the *address* box is long because it requires several lines of information whereas the *sex* box has sufficient space for only a single character ('M' or 'F') and the *date of birth* box contains two forward slash characters ( / ) to separate the day, month and year values.

**FIG-2.3**

A Typical Form Layout

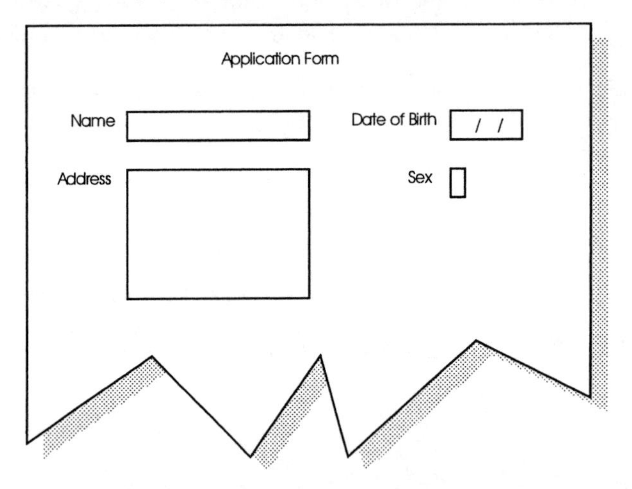


If a computer program requires to store similar information, then it too needs areas in which to hold that information (more commonly called **data**). However, in a program, data is stored in **variables** and, like the boxes on the form, variables need to be given names. LISTING-2.2 (on page 43) defined three variables: *no1*, *no2* and *answer*.

### Variable Types

Just as the boxes in the form are designed with the type of value they are going to hold in mind (such as a date, single character, amount of money etc.), so the type of value a program variable is to hold must also be specified.

Pascal recognises several types of values. Two value types are **integer** (whole numbers - positive or negative) and **real** (numbers containing fractional parts). The term `integer` is used when defining integer variables; in LISTING-2.2 the three variables were defined as integers with the statement:

```
no1, no2, answer : integer;
```

Real values are defined using the term `real`. For example:

```
angle, discount : real;
```

Of course, not everything we need to store is a number. For example, a name or address needs to hold letters or a combination of letters and numbers. Occasionally, we need only store a single character (e.g. an 'F' or 'M' to signify *Female* or *Male).*

Pascal has two basic variable types to store this sort of detail: `char` (short for *character*) variables which can store a single character, and `string` variables which can hold up to 255 characters.

A final basic type, called `boolean`, allows the values **true** and **false** to be stored. We might use such a variable to hold the result to questions such as *Are you over 21?* Unlike a form, in which we might literally write the word true or false, `boolean` variables are simply switched between two possible values. One of these represents *true*, the other *false*. We'll see more about `boolean` variables later.

## Naming Variables

The name given to a variable in a Pascal program must conform to the following rules:

Although there is no limit to the length of variable names, Borland Pascal recognises only the first 32 characters of a variable name.

- The first character must be a letter or an underscore ( _ ).
- Subsequent characters can be a letter, underscore or numeric.
- Capital and lower case **ARE NOT** significant (*NO* and *no* are the same).
- A variable name must **NOT** be a reserved word.

A **reserved word** is a word recognised by Pascal to have some specific meaning. A list of reserved words is given in TABLE-2.1.

**TABLE-2.1**

Pascal Reserved Words

| Pascal Reserved Words | | | | |
|---|---|---|---|---|
| and | end | label | repeat | while |
| array | exports | library | set | with |
| asm | file | mod | shl | xor |
| begin | for | nil | shr | |
| case | function | not | string | |
| const | goto | object | then | |
| constructor | if | of | to | |
| destructor | implementation | or | type | |
| div | in | packed | unit | |
| do | inherited | procedure | until | |
| downto | inline | program | uses | |
| else | interface | record | var | |

**Activity 2.9**

Indicate which of the following are invalid variable names:

```
no1
first_ans
3no
no_1
_result
file
final total
```

## Memory Allocation

Computer memory is often organised in bytes with each byte being allocated a unique identifying value known as the **memory address**. This setup is shown in FIG-2.4.

**FIG -2.4**

Memory Organisation

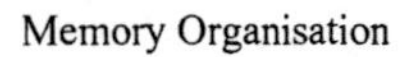

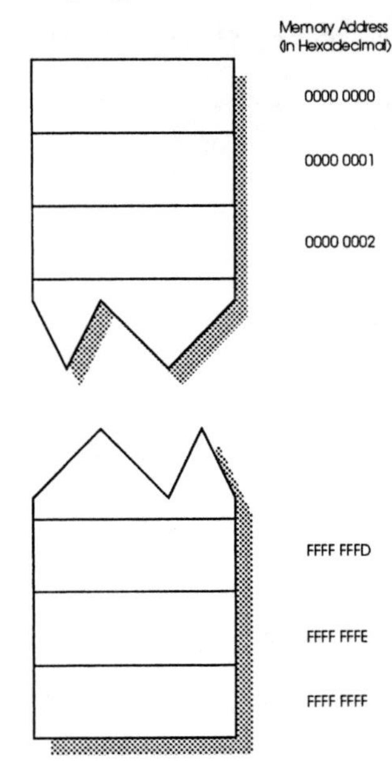


A ***byte*** is enough memory to store a single character (e.g. the letter 'A' will occupy one byte of computer memory when stored) and consists of 8 bits.

Every variable defined in a program is allocated its own space in the computer's memory. The amount of space, that is the number of bytes, allocated depends on the variable's type. This memory space will be used to store, in binary, any value placed in the variable by the program.

A single byte is not sufficient to store a reasonable range of numeric values and hence variables are normally allocated more than one byte.

We have already used type `integer` variables. Most compilers for small computer systems allocate two bytes to an `integer` variable which, using 2's complement notation, allows values in the range -32,768 to 32,767 to be stored. However, there are several other types capable of holding integer values which require a different number of bytes, or store data in an unsigned format. For example, `word` variables also occupy two bytes but store only positive values in the range 0 to 65,535, whereas a `longint` variable occupies four bytes and can store values over the range -2,147,483,648 to 2,147,483,647. Smaller integer values can be held in `shortint` variables which occupy a single byte and hold the range -128 to 127.

Single characters (e.g. 'A','?','$' etc.) are stored in `char` variables which are allocated a single byte in memory. Where more characters are required, a `string` variable can be used. This can store up to 255 characters.

TABLE-2.2 lists all the variable types available in Borland Pascal along with the range of values which may be stored and the number of bytes allocated.

To summarise, every variable defined in a program has four characteristics associated with it:

- A name e.g. no1
- A type e.g. integer
- A value e.g. -17
- An address in memory e.g. FFFF FFFD

Where the variable is allocated several bytes, the address associated with the variable is that of the first location allocated.

**Activity 2.10**

A Pascal program uses two *integer* and three *real* variables. State the total number of bytes allocated to these variables.

**TABLE-2.2**

Pascal variable types

| Variable type | Range of values | Number of bytes |
|---|---|---|
| **Integer Types** | | |
| `shortint` | -128 to 127 | 1 |
| `byte` | 0 to 255 | 1 |
| `integer` | -32,768 to 32,767 | 2 |
| `word` | 0 to 65,535 | 2 |
| `longint` | -2,147,483,648 to 2,147,483,647 | 4 |
| **Real Types** | | |
| `real` | $2.9 \times 10^{-39}$ to $1.7 \times 10^{+39}$ | 6 |
| `single` | $1.5 \times 10^{-45}$ to $3.4 \times 10^{+38}$ | 4 |
| `double` | $5.0 \times 10^{-324}$ to $1.7 \times 10^{+308}$ | 8 |
| `extended` | $3.4 \times 10^{-4932}$ to $1.1 \times 10^{+4932}$ | 10 |
| `comp` | $2^{-63}+1$ to $2^{+63}-1$ | 8 |
| **Character Types** | | |
| `char` | a single character | 1 |
| `string` | up to 255 characters | 256 |
| **Boolean Type** | | |
| `boolean` | true or false | 1 |

# Constants

As well as variables, most programs make use of **constants**, that is, fixed numeric or non-numeric values. We've already met examples of such constants in the `write/writeln` examples given earlier. For example, a program might use the value 3.1415 when calculating the area of a circle, or the message "*Enter name*" as a prompt for the user to key in a value. 3.1415 is a **numeric constant**; "*Enter name*" is a **string constant**.

## Numeric Constants

There are two main classes of numeric constants: *integer* and *real.*

### Integer Constants

An integer constant in Pascal is any non-negative whole number, hence 0, 7 and 124 are all examples of integer constants. Although integer values are, by default, assumed to be given in decimal (base 10), it is also possible to specify integer constants in hexadecimal (base 16) . Hexadecimal values are preceded by a dollar symbol (e.g. $F7).

Constant values in the range 0 to 32,767 are stored in two bytes (i.e. in `integer` format) while greater values are held in `longint` (four bytes) format.

> **Activity 2.11**
>
> What range of values would be stored in :
>
> a) `shortint` format?
>
> b) `byte` format?
>
> Give the range for each in decimal, hexadecimal.

**Real Constants**

Real values may be given in fixed or floating point notation. For example, we may use 3.1415 or 0.31415E+1 to represent the approximate value of $\pi$.

Real values of less than 1 must be shown with a zero before the decimal point (e.g. 0.5 not .5).

## Non-Numeric Constants

Non-numeric constants fall into three types: character, string and boolean.

**Character Constants**

A character constant is any single character and is normally shown enclosed in single quotes:

```
'a'
'*'
'9'
```

Character constants are stored in `char` format.

In the USA, the hash character is referred to as the *pound* symbol.

In addition, any character can be specified using the hash character (#) followed by the ASCII value of the required character in either octal or hexadecimal. Hence the letter 'A' may be specified as #65.

**String Constants**

A string is a collection of zero or more characters enclosed in single quotes. For example:

```
'This is a string.'
```

An empty string (i.e. a string with zero characters) is depicted as two adjacent single quote characters

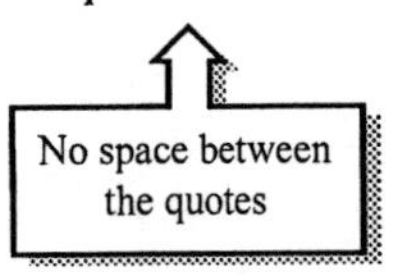


A string may contain a single quote character. However, this could cause a problem: if we were to write the string

The apostrophe and single quote are the same keyboard character.

'It's Friday'

the Pascal compiler would assume the apostrophe in the word *It's* marked the end of the string. To tell the machine that we actually want an apostrophe within a string we need to insert two! Hence, we get

```
'It''s Friday'
```

which the machine correctly interprets as *It's Friday*.

### Boolean Constants

Boolean constants are the terms *true* and *false*. Note that these terms are not enclosed in quotes (if they were, they'd just be other examples of string constants).

# Defining Variables

Every variable used in a Pascal program must be explicitly defined before the start of the executable code. A variable definition begins with the reserved word `var` followed by the list of variables being defined. The list consists of variable names and their type. For example, the code

```
var
    total       : integer;
    square      : real;
    sex         : char;
    address     : string;
    ok          : boolean;
```

defines five variables, one of each of the main types.

As well as using meaningful names, it is advisable to add a comment explaining the purpose of a variable:

```
total : integer;    {*** Number of phone calls ***}
```

Where several variables of the same type are required, they can be defined in a single statement using commas to separate each item.

```
x1,y1,x2,y2 : integer; {*** Co-ordinates of rectangle ***}
```

This can be split over several lines to allow comments to be added to each variable:

```
   x1,            {*** x ordinate of top left corner ***}
   y1,            {*** y ordinate of top left corner ***}
   x2,            {*** x ordinate of bottom right corner ***}
   y2:integer;    {*** y ordinate of bottom right corner ***}
```

The general format for declaring variables is shown in FIG-2.5.

**FIG-2.5**

Defining Variables

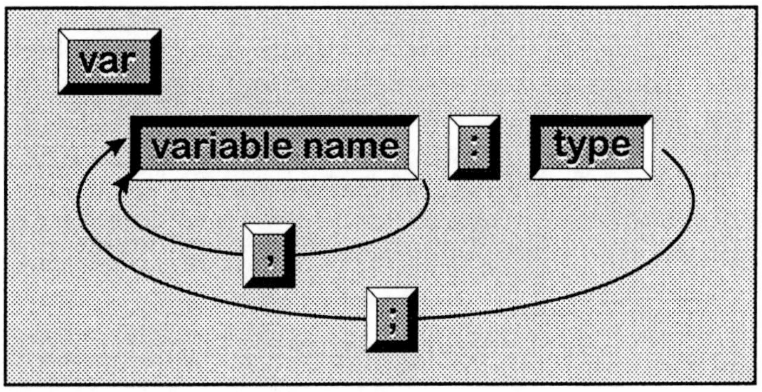

# Summary

## Variables

- Variables hold the values used within a program.
- A variable has:

| | |
|---|---|
| a name | Used to identify it from other variables. |
| a type | That defines the type of value that may be held. |
| a value | This is the value held within the variable. This value may be changed as the program runs. |
| an area of memory | This is the area allocated to the variable. The variable's value is held in this memory area. |

- A variable's name is constructed from letters, numbers or the underscore character. It must not start with a number. There can be no spaces within the name. It should not be a keyword of the Pascal language.
- The following variable types are available:

```
shortint
byte
integer
word
longint
real
single
double
extended
comp
char
string
boolean
```

- The initial value of a variable is undefined.
- The number of bytes allocated to a variable depends of the variable's type.
- Variables are defined in the `var` statement.

## Constants

- A constant is a fixed value.
- Constants can be integer, real, character, string or Boolean.
- Integer constants can be defined in either decimal (the assumed number base) or hexadecimal (precede the number with a dollar ($) sign.
- Real constants can be specified in fixed point format (e.g. 3.1415) or scientific notation (e.g. 2.1756E02).
- Character constants can be defined within single quotes (e.g. 'A') or by specifying the ASCII code for the character and preceding it with the hash sign (e.g. #65).
- String constants can be from zero to 255 characters in length.

- When including an apostrophe within a string, use two apostrophes. For example *It's* is specified as *'It''s'*.
- Boolean constants are the terms *true* or *false*.
- Boolean constants are not enclosed in quotes.

# THE ASSIGNMENT OPERATOR

## Introduction

As a program begins execution, space will have been allocated for all the variables declared in its `var` statement. However, the contents of these variables will be undefined. That is, they will have some unpredictable initial value created from the random pattern of 1's and 0's already in the memory locations allocated.

One method of storing a known value within a variable is to use the assignment operator (`:=`). For example, assuming a program contains the declaration

```
var
    count : integer;
```

we might begin the executable part of the program by setting this variable to zero using the statement:

```
count := 0;
```

If we read the assignment operator as meaning *is given the value*, then the above Pascal statement can be read as:

count *is given the value zero*

The assignment statement takes the form defined in FIG-2.6.

**FIG-2.6**

The Assignment Operator (:=)

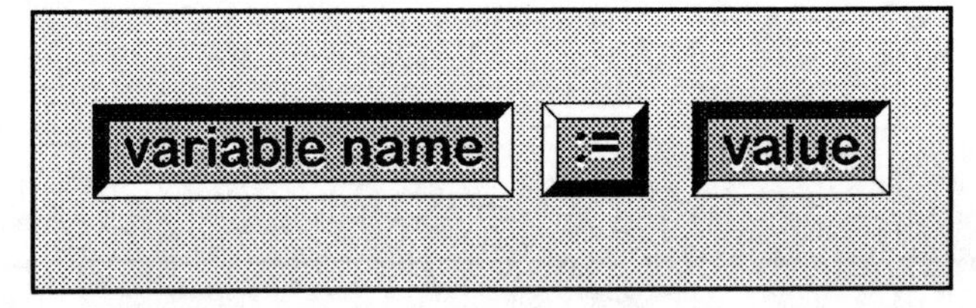


Execution of an assignment statement results in *value* being copied to the memory allocated to *variable name*. Any previous value held by *variable name* is lost.

*value* must be one of the following:

a constant
another variable
or an expression

## Assignment Options

The value to be assigned to a variable must, in general, be of the same type as the variable. Hence. an integer value should be assigned to an integer variable.

There's only one exception to that rule: an integer value may be placed in a real variable.

### Constant

Where *value* is a constant, that fixed value is assigned to the variable. See LISTING-2.3 for examples.

**LISTING-2.3**

Assigning a Constant to a Variable

```
program constassign;
var
   no1,no2       : integer;
   rno1,rno2     : real;
   letter        : char;
   name          : string;
   over21        : boolean;
begin
   no1      := 6;
   no2      := -10;
   rno1     := -4.891;
   rno2     := 12;          {*** Integer assigned to a real ***}
   letter   := 'D';
   name     := 'Elizabeth Heron';
   over21   := true;
```

## Variable

Alternatively, the value held in one variable can be copied into another. The contents of the right-hand variable are unaffected. See LISTING-2.4 for examples.

**LISTING-2.4**

Assigning the Value of a Variable to some other Variable

```
program varassign;
var
   no1,no2       : integer;
   rno1,rno2     : real;
   letter,ch     : char;
   name          : string;
   over21        : boolean;
begin
   {*** Constant assignments ***}
   no1      := 6;
   rno1     := -4.891;
   letter   := 'D';
   name     := 'Elizabeth Heron';
   {*** variable assignments ***}
   no2      := no1;
   rno2     := no1;         {Integer assigned to a real ***}
   ch       := letter;
```

## Expressions

An expression is usually, but not always, an arithmetic expression containing constants, variables and arithmetic operators. The basic arithmetic operators are those already described in Chapter 1:

| | |
|---|---|
| Addition | + |
| Subtraction | - |
| Multiplication | * |
| Division | / |

### Addition, Subtraction and Multiplication

There are no surprises in how these operators function. We may write assignment statements such as

```
no1  := no2 + 7;
rno2 := 8.9 - rno1;
no2  := no1 * 4;
```

or have longer expressions using several operators:

```
rno2 := no1 + no2 - rno1 * 3.1;
```

In all cases, the machine reduces the expression on the right-hand side to a single value and then assigns that value to the variable on the left of the assignment operator.

**Division**

The division operator ( / ) needs a little more thought when being used. Although it used in the same style as the other operators (e.g. 6/2 ), it always gives a real result. This means that a statement such as

```
no1 := 8 / 2;
```

where the variable to be assigned a value is an integer, will raise an error during compilation. To avoid this problem we must use a real variable on the left hand side of the assignment operator:

```
rno1 := 8 / 2;
```

A problem will also arise if you try to divide by zero. For example, attempting to execute the statement

```
rno1 := 8 / 0;
```

will cause the program to terminate.

There are two unfamilar operators: `div` and `mod`. These provide integer division and remainder operations and can only be used with integer values.

**The Integer Division Operator ( `div` )**

Unlike the normal division operator, `div` returns only integer results. That is, any fraction in the result is ignored. For example:

```
 7 div 2   gives the result  3
23 div 3   gives the result  7
 8 div 9   gives the result  0
-9 div 4   gives the result -2
```

**The Remainder Operator ( `mod` )**

The remainder operator, `mod`, is used to determine the integer remainder after division. For example,

```
9 mod 5
```

gives the result 4 since 5 divides into 9 once with a remainder of 4.

Where both values have the same sign, the result has that sign. Hence,

```
-8 mod -5
```

gives the result -3

Where the two values have different signs, the result has the same sign as the first value.

Examples:

```
     -8 mod 5              8 mod -5
=    -3                =   3
```

The remainder operator can also be used to perform the modulus operation. Remainder and modulus, give the same result when the signs of both values are equal. However, when dealing with values of different signs as in

-7 modulus 3

the mathematical operator gives a result of 2,

while in Pascal

```
-7 mod 3
```

gives a result of -1.

We can ensure that the `mod` operator is equivalent to modulus by using the following algorithm:

```
Calculate the remainder when value1 is divided by value2
Add value2 to the result
Calculate the remainder when the modified result is divided by
value2
```

This translates into Pascal as

```
result  := value1 mod value2;  {Variables defined as integers}
modifiedresult := result + value2;
answer  := modifiedresult mod value2;
```

and can be reduced to a single, though more cryptic, statement:

```
result = ((value1 mod value2)+ value2) mod value2;
```

Using the division or remainder operator where the second operand is zero will result in an error.

**Activity 2.12**

Determine the values of the following expressions:

```
   8 div  4          8 mod  4
   9 div  4          9 mod  4
   9 div  4.0        9 mod  4.0
   7 div  0          7 mod  0
   0 div  7          0 mod  7
   2 div  8          2 mod  8
 -11 div  3        -12 mod  3
 -15 div -6        -15 mod -6
   9 div -2          9 mod -2
```

It's important always to leave a space either side of **div** and **mod**, otherwise they will not be recognised by the compiler.

As with Structured English, an arithmetic expression can contain an unlimited number of operators in any order. Normal operator precedence applies with the `div` and `mod` operators given the same priority as multiplication and division. Operator precedence is overridden by the use of parentheses - expressions in parentheses being evaluated first. For example, in the expression

```
(no1 + 6) / 10
```

the addition operation will be performed before that of division.

Where there is more than one set of parentheses in an expression, such as

```
(no1 + 6) / (no2 + 10)
```

then the contents of the left-most parentheses are evaluated first.

Where parentheses are nested, as in

```
((no1 + 6) * (12 - no3) + 1) / (no2 + 10)
```

the contents of the inner most parentheses are evaluated first. For the expression above, the terms are evaluated in the order:

1. `(no1 + 6)`
2. `(12 - no3)`
3. `((no1 + 6) * (12 - no3) + 1)`
4. `(no2 + 10)`
5. `((no1 + 6) * (12 - no3) + 1) / (no2 + 10)`

The arithmetic operators and their precedences are given in TABLE-2.3.

**TABLE-2.3**

Arithmetic Operators

| Operator | Description | Priority |
|---|---|---|
| () | parentheses | 3 |
| * | multiplication | 2 |
| / | division | 2 |
| div | integer division | 2 |
| mod | remainder | 2 |
| + | addition | 1 |
| - | subtraction | 1 |

LISTING-2.5 gives several examples of expressions used with the assignment operator.

**LISTING-2.5**

Assigning the Result of an Expression to a Variable

```
program expassign;
var
   no1,no2,no3 : integer;
   rno1,rno2,rno3,result,ans : real;

begin
   no1      := 3;
   no2      := 4;
   rno1     := 1.56;
   rno2     := 7.8;
   no3      := no1 + no2;
   rno3     := rno1 - rno2;
   no1      := 23 * no2;
   rno2     := rno3 / 12;
   result   := (rno1 + rno2) / rno3;
   ans      := ((no1 + 2) * 3 - 1) / (no3 - 2);
```

**Activity 2.13**

Determine the value of the expression `7 * 3 div 10 + 5 mod (3 + 2)`.

### Converting Expressions

The code

```
program assign4;
var
    no1 : integer;
    answer : real;
begin
    no1 := 34;
    answer  :=  no1 * 12.3;
```

contains two data types in the final line: reals (*answer* and 12.3 ), and an integer (*no1*). In order to evaluate any part of an expression, Pascal requires the values associated with an operator (such as +, - , * etc.) to be of the same type. Where this is not the case, Pascal converts one of the values involved to the same type as the other value. In the example above, this means that the integer value (*no1*) is converted to a real value before the multiplication operation is performed

```
    34.0 * 12.3
=   418.2
```

which is then assigned to *answer.*

## Assigning Values to Character and String Variables

A character variable can only be assigned a single character. This must be in single quotes. For example,

```
ch := 'D';
```

we can assign any character we wish. Hence all of the following are valid assignments to a character variable.

```
ch := '5';      {The character 5}
ch := '+';      {A plus sign}
ch := '∇';      {A space}
ch := '''';     {An apostrophe}
```

However, it is not possible to give it an empty value

```
ch  :=  '';     {No space between the quotes}
```

since character variables must always contain one character - no less and no more.

Character codes are given in Appendix A.

It's also possible to assign a character constant to a variable by preceding the character's ASCII code number by a hash sign. Hence, to assign 'A' to *ch* we can write:

```
ch := #65;  {65 is the code for a capital 'A'}
```

String variables are assigned values in much the same way as character variables. This time, however, the value can be zero or more characters (to a maximum of 255). All of the following are valid string assignments:

```
txt := '';                  {Empty - no space between quotes}
txt := 'A';                 {A single character}
txt := '14 High Street';    {Multi-character string}
```

You can also use the plus (+) operator to join two or more strings together:

```
txt1 := 'to';
txt2 := 'get';
txt3 := txt1+txt2+'her';     {txt3 contains 'together'}
```

# Common Assignments

Of course, we're free to assign any valid value we want to a variable, but some assignments are so common, yet a little strange at first sight, that it's worth mentioning them at this point.

Programs often contain counter and sum variables. A counter variable is one which is used to count how often an event has occurred. For example, we might want to count how often the number 7 has been entered at the keyboard, or how many attempts someone has taken to arrive at the solution to a problem.

To do this we need to declare an integer variable such as:

```
var
    count : integer;
```

Because the starting value of any variable is undefined, one of the first things we need to do within the program, is to make sure *count* starts at zero:

```
count := 0;
```

Later in the program we'll need to add 1 to *count*. To do this we use the instruction

```
count := count + 1;
```

If you come from a mathematical background, it might seem strange to see the variable on both the left and right sides of the assignment operator. But the statement above simply translates to

*The new value of* nbr *is its current value plus 1.*

Another unusual statement is

```
nbr := - nbr;
```

which negates the contents of *value*. For example, if the variable *nbr* contains the value -12, then the statement

```
nbr := - nbr;
```

will result in *nbr* containing the value 12.

**Activity 2.14**

A similar requirement arises when we need to total a list of values. We need to declare a variable in which to hold our total (this may be integer or real, depending on the type of values to be summed). The variable has to be initialised to zero and subsequently have values added to its contents.

Which of the following statements will add the contents of *value* to *total*?

a) `total := value;`
b) `value := total;`
c) `total := total + value;`

# Converting a Value to a Different Type

## From Integer

Although we shouldn't need to do it often, it is possible to convert a constant or variable of one type to another. For example, the expression

```
char(65)
```

converts the integer value 65 to the corresponding character value (65 converts to the character 'A' - see Appendix A for the full character set codes).

An integer can also be converted to a Boolean using an expression such as:

```
boolean(12)
```

The above expression will convert to the value *true*; so will all other non-zero values. Only the expression

```
boolean(0)
```

will give the result *false*.

## From Other Integer Types

A variable declared as an integer type (`integer`, `word`, `shortint`, etc.) can have its value assigned to another variable from the same class of types. Hence, with the declarations

```
var
    a : longint;
    b : integer;
```

we can use the code

```
b := a;
```

to copy the contents of the `longint` variable *a* to the `integer` variable *b*.

However, it is your responsibility to ensure that the value being copied is not too large to fit into the space allocated to *b*.

**Activity 2.15**

Type in and execute the following program, observing the results displayed:

```
program ConvertingBetweenTypes;
uses WinCrt;
var
   a : integer;
   b : word;
   c : shortint;
   d : byte;
   e : longint;
```

**Continued on next page**

**Activity 2.15** (continued)

```
begin
  e := 1155;
  a := e;
  b := e;
  c := e;
  d := e;
  writeln(a);
  writeln(b);
  writeln(c);
  writeln(d);
end.
```

As you can see the value 1155 is successfully copied from *e* to *a* and *b*, but *c* and *d* produce apparently random values.

**Activity 2.16**

Convert the number 1155 to binary.

The values in *c* and *d* can be explained if we look in more detail at what's going on. This is shown in FIG-2.7 below.

**FIG-2.7**

Converting between Integer Types

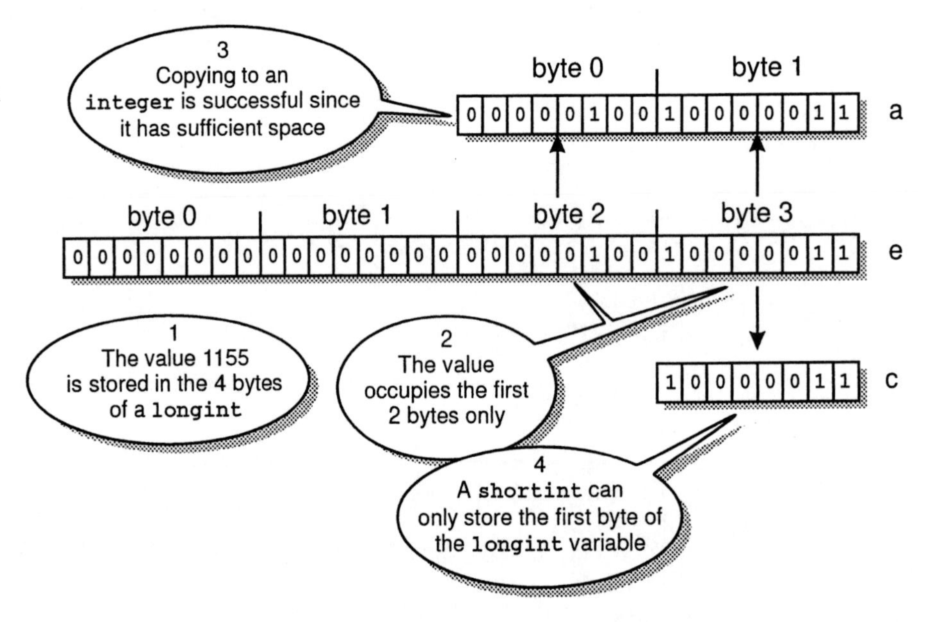


**Activity 2.17**

Covert the value 10000011 to decimal, assuming:

a) The value is held as an unsigned binary value.
b) The value is held in 2's complement form.

## From Real

Real values cannot be converted to `char` or `boolean` types, but they can be assigned to integer variables by eliminating any fractional part of the value.

This can be done in one of two ways: the fraction can be removed or the fraction can be taken into account and the value rounded to the nearest integer.

For truncation, we use the term `Trunc`. For example, assuming the declarations

```
var
    a : real;
    b : integer;
```

and the assignment

```
a := 12.6;
```

the statement

```
b := Trunc(a);
```

will assign the value 12 to *b*.

Rounding is achieved by the term `Round` as in

```
b := Round(a);
```

This will assign the value 13 to *b*.

**Activity 2.18**

What values will be assigned to the integer from the following assignments?

a) `a := Trunc(13.9);`
b) `a := Round(-7.8);`
c) `a := Round(67.2);`

## From Character

A character value can also be converted to either an integer or Boolean using expressions such as

```
integer('B')        and      boolean('C')
```

which would convert to 66 and *true* respectively.

Only the *null* character ( #0 ) converts to the Boolean value *false*. All other characters convert to *true*.

A character value can be copied directly into a string variable. Hence, assuming the variable declaration

```
var
    s  : string;
    ch : char;
```

the statement

```
s := ch;
```

is allowed. However, the reverse is not possible, so the instruction

```
ch := s;
```

is invalid.

### From Boolean

The symbols for the characters #0 and #1 are given in Appendix A

There are only four options open to us when converting a Boolean and these are

`char(true)` (gives #1) and `char(false)` (gives #0)

and

`integer(true)` (gives 1) and `integer(false)` (gives 0)

**Activity 2.19**

What are the final values of the variables *a,b* and *c* in the following code?

```
var
    a:integer;
    b:char;
    c:boolean;
begin
    a := 8;
    c := boolean(a);
    b := char(integer(c) + 64);
end.
```

## Structured English Equivalents

Table-2.4 shows some statements as they might appear in Structured English and their equivalent in Pascal.

**TABLE-2.4**

Assignment Equivalents

| Structured English | Pascal |
|---|---|
| Set total to zero | total := 0; |
| Subtract 1 from count | count := count + 1; |
| Add mark to sum | sum := sum + mark; |
| Calculate dividend as 10% of total | dividend := total * 0.1; |
| Calculate remaining ounces as remainder of (oz1 + oz2) divided by 16 | remoz := (oz1+oz2) mod 16; |
| Clear address | address :=''; |
| Set result to 'Fail' | result := 'Fail'; |
| Set ch to 'A' | ch := #65; |

# Variables and Output

We saw previously how `write` and `writeln` can be used to display values on the screen. We can also use these statements to display the value held in a variable.

By specifying the name of a variable within a `write(ln)` the contents of that variable are displayed. Hence, the code

```
var
    no:integer;
begin
    no := 12;
    writeln(no);
```

will display the value 12 (the contents of *no).*

Note that the variable name must not be included in quotes, since the program would interpret this as a request to display a string (the contents of the quotes).

Like other data items, variables can be specified with a field size. For example,

```
writeln(no:5);
```

displays the value of *no* over five screen positions.

The field size for a real variable must be given in two parts, specifying the total screen positions and the number of decimal places.

Typically, an output statement involving variables will also include explanatory strings. For example:

```
writeln('Circle radius is ',radius:0:2,'Area of circle is ',area:0:2);
```

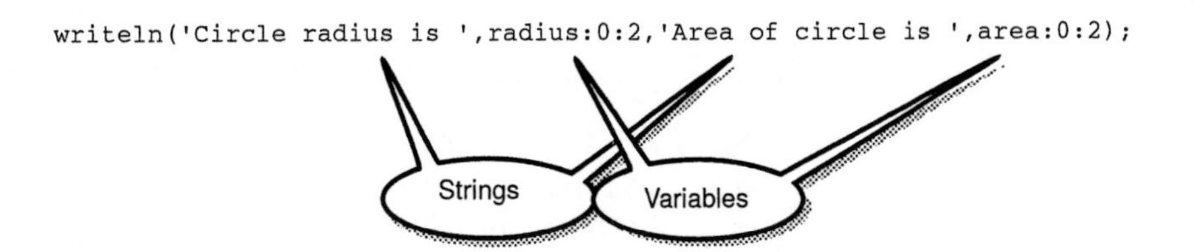


It's also possible to use a field size as a variable. Hence, if a program contains the following relevant code

```
var
    na, b   : integer;
    r       : real;

a := 6;
b := 2;
r := 678.958;
```

we can use the statement

```
writeln(r:a:b);
```

to display the value of *r* over 6 screen positions to 2 decimal places.

# Summary

- **The assignment operator** is used to give a value to a variable.

  Any previous value held by the variable is overwritten by the new value.

- The simplest assignment has the form `variable := value`

- Generally, `value` must be of the same type as `variable`. However an integer value can be assigned to a real variable.

- **The value assigned** may be one of the following:

  - a constant
  - the value contained in some other variable
  - the result of an expression

- **Arithmetic expressions** can use the operators:

  | Operator | Meaning |
  |---|---|
  | * | Multiplication |
  | / | Division |
  | `div` | Integer division |
  | `mod` | Remainder |
  | + | Addition |
  | - | Subtraction |

- **The division operator** ( / ) returns a real result. Hence the variable being assigned a value must be real.

- **The integer division operator** ( `div` ) can only be used with two integer values.

- **The remainder operator** ( `mod` ) can only be used with two integer values.

- When using the `div` and `mod` operators, make sure to leave a space on either side of the operator.

- **Where the second operand is zero**, an error will occur when using the division or remainder operators (e.g. 8/0).

- **When evaluating expressions**, multiplication, division and remainder operations (*, / , `div` , `mod`) are performed before addition and subtraction (+, -).

  This rule is modified by the use of parentheses: expressions in parentheses being performed first.

- It is the programmer's responsibility to ensure that **the variable type being used is adequate to store the value to be placed in it.**

# KEYBOARD INPUT

It is rather difficult to think of any worthwhile program which is not going to require some input from the keyboard (or some other device). The programs we have looked at up to now have used the assignment operator (:=) to store a value in a variable, but this means we must decide what values are to be used when we are writing the program. It's a bit like selling a television where the viewer doesn't get to choose the channel he wants to watch.

To allow the user to decide the value to be placed in a variable we need to delay placing a value in the variable until the program is running. Then we can ask the user to type in the value required. For example, if we were to write a program that calculated the area of a circle, we could ask the user to enter the figure to be used for the radius of the circle. In Pascal, user input is accepted using the `readln` statement.

## readln

The `readln` (pronounced *read-line*) command allows a variable to be assigned a value entered from the keyboard.

Instead of assigning the value 3 to the variable *month* in a statement such as

```
month := 3;
```

`readln` can be used to allow a value for *month* to be entered at run time from the keyboard:

```
readln(month);
```

The term `readln` is followed by parentheses enclosing the name of the variable in which the value is to be placed. We can interpret the above Pascal statement as:

*Get a value from the keyboard and insert it in the variable* month.

When the computer executes this statement, it will wait patiently for a value to be entered at the keyboard. Once the *ENTER* key is pressed, the value keyed in is assigned to the variable specified. It is possible to enter more than one value at a time using `readln` by simply separating each variable name by a comma:

```
readln(day, month, year);
```

This time, when the program is run, three values may be entered. All three values should be keyed in (separated by spaces) before pressing *ENTER*. The first value entered will be placed in *day*, the second in *month* and the third in *year*.

The general format for the `readln` statement is given in FIG-2.8.

**FIG-2.8**

The `readln` Statement

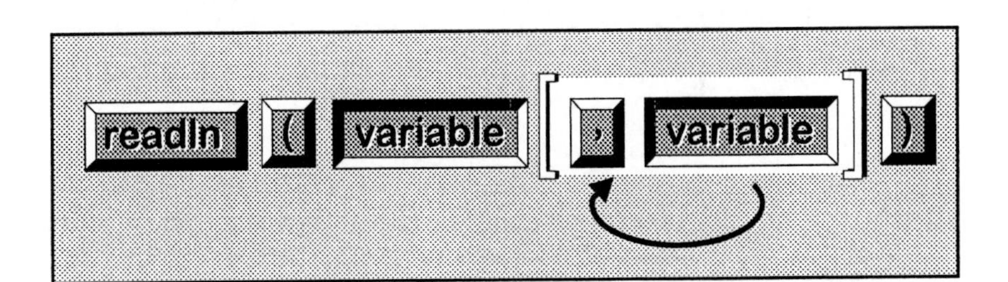

In general, it is best to have a separate `readln` statement for each value that is to be input unless the values are closely related in some way, as is the case with *day, month* and *year*.

At this stage in our knowledge, it will be up to the user of the program to ensure that the values entered are valid for the variables specified. For example, we will have to assume that when asked for a value for *month*, that an integer between 1 and 12 will be entered. Later we will look at ways which allow the program to check whether the values entered by the user are acceptable.

## User Prompts

We have already seen that `readln` can be used to accept values from the keyboard. However, when a `readln` command is executed by the machine it simply sits and waits for a value to be entered. If the user of the program did not write the code, he is likely to be blissfully unaware of the fact that the program has stopped and is awaiting data entry. Good programming practice requires that the user be issued with a meaningful screen prompt. Hence rather than write

```
readln(year);
```

a better approach would be:

```
write('Please enter year : ');
readln(year);
```

Prompts should be as helpful as possible. For example, if a measurement is required from the keyboard, specify the units of measurement:

```
write('Enter your height in metres : ');
readln(height);
```

It may also be appropriate to give a range of acceptable input values:

```
write('Enter a number between 1 and 12 : ');
readln(no);
```

**Activity 2.20**

Enter the following program:

```
program keyboardinput;
uses WinCrt;
var
    number : integer;
begin
    ClrScr;
    write('Enter a value : ');
    readln(number);
    writeln('Your number was ', number);
end.
```

Run the program several times, entering the following values:

16
-9
12.7
six

How does the program react to each of the values entered?

When working out the details of a program we will often identify the need for new variables. For example, here we need variables to store the total ounces in weight 1, the total ounces in weight 2 and the sum of these totals

You can see from the last Activity that entering a value of the wrong type causes the program to terminate. We'll discover in a later chapter how to prevent this.

## Structured English Equivalents

TABLE-2.5 gives some Structured English input/output statements and their Pascal equivalents.

**TABLE-2.5**

Assignment Equivalents

| Structured English | Pascal |
|---|---|
| `Get age` | `write('Enter age : ');`<br>`readln(age);` |
| `Display weight` | `writeln('Weight is ', weight:0:2);` |
| `Get date` | `write('Enter date(dd mm yyyy) : ');`<br>`readln(day, month, year);` |
| `Display date` | `writeln(day, '/', month, '/', year);` |
| `Get name and sex` | `write('Enter name : ');`<br>`readln(name);`<br>`write('Enter sex (M or F) : ');`<br>`readln(sex);` |

## Summary

- `readln` allows values to be entered from the keyboard.
- `readln` allows the user to assign values to variables as the program is running.
- **The value entered** must be of a type appropriate for the variable in which it is to be stored.
- **Several variables can be specified** in a single `readln` statement. This should only be done when the values are closely related.
- **If an inappropriate value is entered** from the keyboard the program will crash.
- **Precede a `readln` statement by a `write` statement** giving the user details of what is to be entered.

# NAMED CONSTANTS

A named constant allows us to associate an identifying name with a constant. So rather than write statements such as

```
tax_deduction := gross_wage * 0.25;
```

with its obscure reference to a tax rate of 25%, it is possible to define a variable constant for this value using

```
const
    tax_rate = 0.25;
```

and then use this name, *tax_rate,* to create a more readable version of the original statement:

```
tax_deduction := gross_wage * tax_rate;
```

The value assigned to a named constant cannot be changed at a later point in a program.

A named constant can be assigned any constant value. For example:

```
const
    tax_rate = 0.25;
    delete_code = 'D';
    lower_age = 18;
```

**Activity 2.21**

Write a program to calculate the area of a circle. You should read the value of a variable, *radius*, from the keyboard and define a constant, *pi*, equal to 3.1415. A second variable, *area,* should be assigned a value equal to *pi*radius*radius*. The value of *area* should be displayed with an appropriate message.

# PUTTING IT ALL TOGETHER

We have now covered enough Pascal to start creating simple programs.

However, the logic of even the simplest program should be thought out before we attempt to create the final code. After all, learning the grammar of the various Pascal statements is a relatively easy task; what makes programming a skill is the learning how to create solutions to problems.

The following example explains the informal stages involved in creating a simple program.

**Step 1**: Get a clear definition of the problem being tackled.
*A program is required that will allow two weights to be entered from the keyboard and the sum of the two weights displayed. The weights are to be given in pounds and ounces.*

**Step 2:** Identify the data items required by the program.

*Weight 1*
*Weight2*
*Sum of the weights*

**Step 3**: Write down the main steps involved in solving the problem.

1. *Read in a value for the first weight*
2. *Read in a value for the second weight*
3. *Add the two weights*
4. *Display the sum of the two weights*

**Step 4**: Where necessary, add more detail to any of the steps involved.

*3. Add the two weights*
*3.1 Convert the first weight to ounces*
*3.2 Convert the second weight to ounces*
*3.3 Add the two weights together*
*3.4 Calculate the pounds part of the sum as [total ounces/16]*
*3.5 Calculate the ounces part of the sum as total ounces modulus 16.*

and replace the original outline step by its more detailed equivalent

*1. Read in a value for the first weight*
*2. Read in a value for the second weight*
*3.1 Convert the first weight to ounces*
*3.2 Convert the second weight to ounces*
*3.3 Add the two weights together*
*3.4 Calculate the pounds part of the sum as [total ounces/16]*
*3.5 Calculate the ounces part of the sum as total ounces modulus 16.*
*4. Display the sum of the two weights*

**Step 5**: Convert data identified in Step 2 and the logic given in Step 3 and 4 into a program.

```
program addWeights;
uses WinCrt;
var
    weight1lbs, weight1oz, {*** First weight ***}
    weight2lbs, weight2oz, {*** Second Weight ***}
    sumlbs,sumoz,          {*** Holds sum of weights ***}
```

```
    totaloz1, totaloz2      {*** Total ounces in each weight ***}
        :integer;
begin
    ClrScr;
    {*** read in a value for the first weight ***}
    write('Enter first weight : ');
    readln(weight1lbs,weight1oz);
    {*** read in a value for the second weight ***}
    write('Enter second weight : ');
    readln(weight2lbs,weight2oz);
    {*** add the weights together ***}
    totaloz1 := weight1lbs*16 + weight1oz;
    totaloz2 := weight2lbs*16 + weight2oz;
    grandtotaloz := totaloz1 + totaloz2;
    sumlbs := grandtotaloz div 16;
    sumoz := grandtotaloz mod 16;
    {*** display the sum of the two weights ***}
    writeln(weight1lbs,' lbs ',weight1oz,' oz  + ',
    ↳weight2lbs,' lbs ',weight2oz,' oz = ',
    ↳sumlbs,' lbs ',sumoz,' oz');
end.
```

**Step 6:** Test the program. We need to make sure that the program gives the results expected of it. Later we'll look at formal ways of doing this, but for now we'll satisfy ourselves with simply thinking of some values to type in for the two weights and working out what the answer should be. For example, we might use the values 8lbs 10 oz for the first weight and 3lbs 8oz for the second. This should give us a result of 12lbs 2oz.

The next section of this chapter takes a closer look at each of these steps.

# CASE STUDY

Most chapters in this book contain small case studies. These are an attempt to show how the statements covered in that chapter are used within a larger program. In addition, it is a chance to discuss some of the other aspects which go to make up a good approach to programming.

## The Problem

The program to be installed in a new cash register allows the total due by the customer to be entered along with the amount offered in payment. The register then specifies the notes and coinage to be given in the change. For example, if £1.00 is offered for a purchase of £0.76 then the result would be COINAGE: 1x20p 2x2p.

## Clarification

As a software designer, you will almost certainly be presented with problems which are not completely defined. That is, you will probably be able to find parts of the description which are ambiguous, unclear or do not describe what is to be done under unusual conditions.

With the cash register software, the problem lies in the rule to be used in determining which coinage is to be returned: we could give all of the change in 1p coins! Where software is being written for a customer you MUST get a ruling on such matters from the customer rather than make your own assumptions. In this case, we wish to give the highest value coinage possible in change. Also the largest note offered in change will be £5.

## The Approach

Before getting involved with a detailed solution to any complex problem, it's worth taking some time to think, only in a very broad sense, the strategy to be used in tackling the problem.

Sometimes it is useful to take a few specific examples, work them through and see if their solutions suggest any general algorithm which might be applied to the problem.

**Change Examples**

| Money Given | Cost | Change | Coinage £5 | £1 | 50p | 20p | 10p | 5p | 2p | 1p |
|---|---|---|---|---|---|---|---|---|---|---|
| 10.00 | 3.75 | 6.25 | 1 | 1 | 0 | 1 | 0 | 1 | 0 | 0 |
| 20.00 | 8.51 | 11.49 | 2 | 0 | 0 | 2 | 0 | 1 | 2 | 0 |

The strategy employed in solving these examples is to examine first the change figure, and then each column in turn, looking to see how often that column's value will divide into the change. We then remove the corresponding amount from the change and try the next column until no change remains.

# The Algorithm

Our examples have given us an approach, and from that we developed a general strategy for solving the problem. The next stage is to change the informal explanation in the strategy above into the more formal style of Structured English:

```
1.  Get amount offered
2.  Get cost
3.  Calculate change as amount offered - cost
4.  Calculate £5 notes as number of times £5 goes into change
5.  Subtract the value of the £5 notes from the change
6.  Calculate £1 notes as the number of times £1 goes into change
7.  Subtract the value of the £1 notes from the change
8.  Calculate 50p coins as the number of times 50p goes into change
9.  Subtract the value of the 50p coins from the change
10. Calculate 20p coins as the number of times 20p goes into change
11. Subtract the value of the 20p coins from the change
12. Calculate 10p coins as the number of times 10p goes into change
13. Subtract the value of the 10p coins from the change
14. Calculate 5p coins as the number of times 5p goes into change
15. Subtract the value of the 5p coins from the change
16. Calculate 2p coins as the number of times 2p goes into change
17. Subtract the value of the 2p coins from the change
18. Calculate 1p coins as the number of times 1p goes into change
19. Display coinage
```

Next we need to check that the algorithm has no major flaws. This may be done by working our way though the algorithm using one of the examples we had calculated out earlier, to ensure it gives us the same results. This **dry run** should be done in a formal way so as to avoid mistakes when working through the algorithm. This can be achieved by creating a table to record each step and the latest value of all the variables involved. See TABLE-2.6.

**TABLE-2.6**

Dry Run

| Statement | Variables | | | | | | | | | | |
|---|---|---|---|---|---|---|---|---|---|---|---|
| | paid | cost | change | £5 | £1 | 50p | 20p | 10p | 5p | 2p | 1p |
| 1 | 20.00 | | | | | | | | | | |
| 2 | | 8.51 | | | | | | | | | |
| 3 | | | 11.49 | | | | | | | | |
| 4 | | | | 2 | | | | | | | |
| 5 | | | 1.49 | | | | | | | | |
| 6 | | | | | 1 | | | | | | |
| 7 | | | 0.49 | | | | | | | | |
| 8 | | | | | | 0 | | | | | |
| 9 | | | 0.49 | | | | | | | | |
| 10 | | | | | | | 2 | | | | |
| 11 | | | 0.09 | | | | | | | | |
| 12 | | | | | | | | 0 | | | |
| 13 | | | 0.09 | | | | | | | | |
| 14 | | | | | | | | | 1 | | |
| 15 | | | 0.04 | | | | | | | | |
| 16 | | | | | | | | | | 2 | |
| 17 | | | 0.00 | | | | | | | | |
| 18 | | | | | | | | | | | 0 |
| 19 | Displays 2,1,0,2,0,1,2,0 | | | | | | | | | | |

# The Program

The program is created by converting each statement in the Structured English algorithm to the equivalent Pascal statement. Depending on how much detail is given in the algorithm, one statement in Structured English may translate to one or more Pascal statements. Where there are many occurrences of a single statement in the Structured English translating to several Pascal statements, it is possible that the original Structured English needs to be broken down into more detail before attempting the translation.

When writing a program (rather than just short exercises) you should include documentary details in the program comments. These should list such things as the program title, author, date written, version number (which is updated each time a change is made), the equipment on which the program is to be run, the compiler used to create the executable version, etc. See LISTING-2.6 for the full code.

**LISTING-2.6**

Change Calculator (version 1)

```
program ChangeDispenser;
{***************************************************}
{* PROGRAM     : Change Calculator                *}
{* AUTHOR      : Patricia Stamp                   *}
{* DATE        : 20/7/1997                        *}
{* VERSION     : 0.1                              *}
{* DESCRIPTION : Calculates the change and coinage *}
{*               to be given for a given purchase  *}
{* HARDWARE    : PC Compatible.                   *}
{* SOURCE      : Borland Pascal v7.0              *}
{***************************************************}

uses WinCrt;

var
   cash,              {*** Amount paid by customer        ***}
   cost,              {*** Total cost of items purchased ***}
   change:real;       {*** Total change to be given       ***}
   pnds5,             {*** No. of £5 notes in change      ***}
   pnds1,             {*** No. of £1 coins in change      ***}
   pence50,           {*** No. of 50p coins in change     ***}
   pence20,           {*** No. of 20p coins in change     ***}
   pence10,           {*** No. of 10p coins in change     ***}
   pence5,            {*** No. of 5p coins in change      ***}
   pence2,            {*** No. of 2p coins in change      ***}
   pence1:integer;    {*** No. of 1p coins in change      ***}

begin
   {*** Enter cash and cost ***}
   ClrScr;
   write('Enter the amount paid : ');
   readln(cash);
   write('Enter the cost : ');
   readln(cost);
   {*** Calculate the change *** }
   change := cash - cost;
   {*** Calculate coinage ***}
   pnds5   := Trunc(change/5);
   change  := change - pnds5*5;
   pnds1   := Trunc(change);
   change  := change - pnds1;
   pence50 := Trunc(change/0.50);
   change  := change - pence50*0.50;
   pence20 := Trunc(change/0.20);
   change  := change - pence20*0.20;
   pence10 := Trunc(change/0.10);
   change  := change - pence10*0.10;
   pence5  := Trunc(change/0.05);
```

**Continued on next page**

The term `Trunc` is used to convert a real value to an integer. Any fractional part is ignored.

```
    change := change -pence5*0.05;
    pence2 := Trunc(change/0.02);
    change := change -pence2*0.02;
    pence1 := Trunc(change/0.01);
    change := change -pence1*0.01;
    {*** Display Total change and coins ***}
    ClrScr;
    writeln('Change Coinage');
    writeln('        £5 £1 50p 20p 10p 5p 2p 1p');
    writeln((cash-cost):5:2,'   ',pnds5,'  ',pnds1,'  ',pence50,
    '   ',pence20,'  ',pence10,'  ',pence5,'  ',pence2,'  ',
    pence1);
end.
```

# Testing

Every program must be tested. Testing attempts to highlight errors in a program. To test a piece of code, we need to devise a set of values to be used for any variables whose value needs to be input. This is called the **test data**. Next, we need to predict the effects such test data will have on the program's output. Where the output is text or numeric values, we need to determine what these values will be.

In this program we could use as test data the values we looked at earlier while deciding on the approach to be used:

Cash = 10.00; Cost = 6.25

When creating test data, our minimum aim is to ensure that the test data created will result in every line of code in the program being executed at least once. In this program we have a simple sequential structure, so our one set of test data will be sufficient to meet this requirement. However, in this case we'll go beyond the minimum requirements and use the second set of values :

Cash = 20.00; Cost = 8.51

**TABLE-2.7**

Test Data

| TEST DATA | | |
|---|---|---|
| **Test Run** | **Test Data** | **Expected Results** |
| 1 | cash = 10.00<br>cost = 3.75 | pnds5 = 1<br>pnds1 = 1<br>pence50 = 0<br>pence20 = 1<br>pence10 = 0<br>pence5 = 1<br>pence2 = 0<br>pence1 = 0 |
| 2 | cash = 20.00<br>cost = 8.51 | pnds5 = 2<br>pnds1 = 1<br>pence50 = 0<br>pence20 = 2<br>pence10 = 0<br>pence5 = 1<br>pence2 = 2<br>pence1 = 0 |

In order to know if the program is behaving correctly, we have to predict in advance what results to expect from our test data. Therefore, the expected outputs for the test data must also be determined.

All this information is usually laid out in tabular form (TABLE-2.7).

> **Activity 2.22**
>
> Type in the program above and run it using the test data given.

# The Flaw

The results of the above exercise show the importance of testing. Even when the algorithm seems to be correct, problems can occur in the computer program. One possible problem is that the translation from Structured English to Pascal has introduced an error. This time, however, the problem is a subtle one involving fractions and the binary system.

In the decimal system, we are quite familiar with values which cannot be expressed exactly. For example, one third can only be approximated as 0.33333 (taken to 5 decimal places). This is not a problem when dealing with money, since pence, which are expressed as a decimal fraction of a pound can all be represented exactly. Hence the change from our first set of test data can be represented exactly as the real number 6.25. Unfortunately, as with one third in decimal, binary cannot represent some fractions exactly. As the program extracts coinage values from the change figure, we arrive at a point where only 5p remains. This is expressed in decimal as 0.05 but again the binary representation is not exact. Were we to take the binary value held by the computer and convert it back to decimal we would have a value of 0.049998. If we attempt to divide this inaccurate figure by 0.05 to determine how many 5p pieces are in the change, we get a result of 0 rather than the 1 we are expecting. In fact, this highlights a major problem when computers are dealing with money : their inability to accurately represent fractions of a point in floating point notation, where such errors could be of critical importance.

# A Second Attempt

One way to overcome this is to deal only with integers when handling money values. This can easily be achieved by converting all amounts of money into pence by multiplying by 100. This approach gives rise to the second version of the program given below (LISTING-2.7).

**LISTING-2.7**

Change (version 2)

```
program ChangeDispenser;
{***************************************************}
{* PROGRAM     : Change Calculator                 *}
{* AUTHOR      : Patricia Stamp                    *}
{* DATE        : 20/7/1997                         *}
{* VERSION     : 0.2                               *}
{* DESCRIPTION : Calculates the change and coinage *}
{*               to be given for a given purchase  *}
{* HARDWARE    : PC Compatible.                    *}
{* SOURCE      : Borland Pascal v7.0               *}
{***************************************************}
```

**Continued on next page**

**LISTING-2.7**
(continued)

Change (version 2)

```
uses WinCrt;
var
   cash,             {*** Amount paid by customer ***}
   cost:real;        {*** Total cost of items purchased ***}
   change,           {*** Total change to be given ***}
   pnds5,            {*** No. of £5 notes in change ***}
   pnds1,            {*** No. of £1 coins in change ***}
   pence50,          {*** No. of 50p coins in change ***}
   pence20,          {*** No. of 20p coins in change ***}
   pence10,          {*** No. of 10p coins in change ***}
   pence5,           {*** No. of 5p coins in change ***}
   pence2,           {*** No. of 2p coins in change ***}
   pence1:integer;   {*** No. of 1p coins in change ***}
begin
   {*** Enter cash and cost ***}
   ClrScr;
   write('Enter the amount paid : ');
   readln(cash);
   write('Enter the cost : ');
   readln(cost);
   {*** Calculate the change in pence *** }
   change := round((cash - cost) * 100);
   {*** Calculate coinage ***}
   pnds5   := change div 500;
   change  := change - pnds5 * 500;
   pnds1   := change div 100;
   change  := change - pnds1 * 100;
   pence50 := change div 50;
   change  := change - pence50 * 50;
   pence20 := change div 20;
   change  := change - pence20 * 20;
   pence10 := change div 10;
   change  := change - pence10 * 10;
   pence5  := change div 5;
   change  := change - pence5 * 5;
   pence2  := change div 2;
   change  := change - pence2 * 2;
   pence1  := change;
   {*** Display results ***}
   ClrScr;
   writeln('Change Coinage');
   writeln('         £5 £1 50p 20p 10p 5p 2p 1p');
   writeln((cash-cost):5:2,'     ',pnds5,'   ',pnds1,'   ',pence50,
       '   ',pence20,'   ',pence10,'   ',pence5,'   ',pence2,
       '  ',pence1);
end.
```

Note that, in converting the change to pence, the term `round` is used. This automatically rounds any fraction to the nearest integer. Hence, if the change (6.25) is stored inaccurately (say as 6.24998) then multiplication by 100 will result in 624.998 pence and `round` will change this to 625 which is then copied to *change* Other changes include multiplying by 100 the value of each coin, since we are now working in pence and updating the version number.

When any change is made to a program, all testing must be redone. This is necessary since the program modifications may have introduced new errors and hence it cannot be assumed that tests which had previously given correct results will continue to do so.

**Activity 2.23**

Enter and test this new version of the program.

**Activity 2.24**

1. Read in a decimal integer and display it. Include appropriate text.

2. Read in an integer value between 30 and 254. Display the value in decimal and the equivalent character.

3. Read in 4 values representing two weights given in pounds and ounces. Print the sum of the weights in pounds and ounces. There are 16 ounces to 1 pound.
   OUTLINE LOGIC:
```
Get pounds and ounces of first weight (lbs1,oz1)
Get pounds and ounces of second weight (lbs2,oz2)
Calculate totaloz as oz1 + oz2
Calculate carry as integer part of totaloz/16
Calculate ouncessum as remainder of totaloz/16
Calculate poundssum as lbs1 + lbs2 + carry
Display poundssum and ouncessum
```

4. Read in a character. Print the character and also the preceding and succeeding characters in the ASCII set.
   (e.g. if B is input, output would be A B C)

5. Read in two integer values (using variables *no1* and *no2*). Without using any other variables, swap the contents of *no1* and *no2*. For example, if *no1* = 5 and *no2* = 1 at the beginning of the program, at completion the contents of *no1* and *no2* should be 1 and 5 respectively.

6. Read in an alphabetic character in lower case and display the upper case version of the letter.
   HINT: Look at the ASCII codes for letters in APPENDIX A.

7. Input a value in centimetres and convert it to yards, feet and inches.

   There are 2.4cm to an inch; 12 inches in 1 foot and 3 feet in 1 yard.

8. Zeller's Congruence is used to discover which day of the week a given date fell on.

   The formula is:

   d = ([2.6M-0.2] + D + Y +[Y/4] + [C/4]-2C) modulus 7

   Where

   | | |
   |---|---|
   | d | is the day of the week (0 = Sunday, 1 = Monday...) |
   | D | is the day of the month |
   | M | is the month number (March = 1. December = 10 January and February are month 11 and 12 of the previous year) |
   | C | is the 2 most significant digits of the year. |
   | Y | is the 2 least significant digits of the year. |
   | [*x*] | is the largest integer not greater than *x*. |

   Thus for 28/2/1961

   D = 28<br>
   M = 12<br>
   C = 19<br>
   Y = 60

**Continued on next page**

**Activity 2.24** (continued)

Write a program to accept a date as 3 integers and print out the day of the week on which it fell represented by a value between 0 and 6.
OUTLINE LOGIC:

```
Get  day month and year
Calculate M as (month+9)modulus 12 + 1
Calculate CY as year - integer part of (M/11)
Calculate C as the integer part of (CY/100)
Calculate Y as the remainder of (CY/100)
Calculate temp as integer part of (2.6*M-0.2)
Calculate d as (temp + day + Y + integer part of (Y/4) +
           integer part of (C/4)-2*C)modulus 7
Display d
```

# SOLUTIONS

### Activity2.1 to Activity 2.6

No solutions required

### Activity 2.7

```
program Act7;
uses WinCrt;
begin
    writeln('I am ',5,' feet ',7,' inches tall');
end.
```

### Activity 2.8

```
1.
program Act8_1;
uses WinCrt;
begin
    ClrScr;
    writeln('X');
end.
```

```
2.
program Act8_2;
uses WinCrt;
begin
    ClrScr;
    writeln;
    writeln;
    writeln;
    writeln('X');
end.
```

```
3.
program Act8_3;
uses WinCrt;
begin
    ClrScr;
    writeln;
    writeln;
    writeln;
    writeln;
    writeln;
    writeln;
    writeln('X':40);
end.
```

```
4.
program Act8_4;
uses WinCrt;
begin
    ClrScr;
    writeln('*');
    writeln('**');
    writeln('***');
end.
```

```
5.
program Act8_5;
uses WinCrt;
begin
    ClrScr;
    writeln('*':3);
    writeln('**':3);
    writeln('***':3);
end.
```

```
6.
program Act8_6;
uses WinCrt;
begin
    ClrScr;
    writeln('**********');
    writeln('*        *');
    writeln('*        *');
    writeln('**********');
end.
```

```
7.
program Act8_7;
uses WinCrt;
begin
    ClrScr;
    writeln(17:4);
    writeln(5:4);
    writeln(123:4);
    writeln(7777:4);
end.
```

### Activity 2.9

| | | |
|---|---|---|
| 3no | - | cannot begin with a numeric digit. |
| file | - | a reserved word |
| final note | - | no spaces are allowed. |

### Activity 2.10

22 bytes

2 integers at 2 bytes each = 4 bytes
3 reals at 6 bytes each = 18 bytes

### Activity 2.11

| | |
|---|---|
| shortint | decimal : -128 to 127;<br>hexadecimal : 00 to FF |
| byte | decimal : 0 to 255;<br>hexadecimal : 00 to FF |

### Activity 2.12

| | |
|---|---|
| 2 | 0 |
| 2 | 1 |
| invalid | invalid |
| invalid | invalid |
| 0 | 0 |
| 0 | 2 |
| -3 | 0 |
| 2 | 3 |
| -4 | 1 |

### Activity 2.13

```
7 * 3 div 10 + 5 mod (3 + 2)
7 * 3 div 10 + 5 mod 5
21 div 10 + 5 mod 5
2 + 5 mod 5
2 + 0
2
```

### Activity 2.14

c)

### Activity 2.15

The program produces the values 1155, 1155, -125, 131

### Activity 2.16

1155 decimal is 10000011 in binary.

## Activity 2.17

a) 131
b) -125

This is exactly the values displayed by the program in Activity 2.14

## Activity 2.18

a) 13
b) -8
c) 67

## Activity 2.19

a = 8
b = 'A' {65 is the code for 'A'}
c = true {Any non-zero value converts to true}

## Activity 2.20

The first two values are accepted and displayed; the final two values cause runtime errors because they do not match the variable's data type.

## Activity 2.21

```
program Act17;
uses WinCrt;
const
    pi = 3.1415;
var
    radius, area : real;
begin
    {*** Clear the screen ***}
    ClrScr;
    {*** Get the user to enter the radius ***}
    write('Enter radius of circle in cms : ');
    readln(radius);
    {*** Calculate the area ***}
    area := pi * radius * radius;
    {*** Display the result ***}
    writeln('The area of a circle with radius ',
    ↳radius:0:2,' is ',area:0:2);
end.
```

## Activity 2.22

No solution required.

## Activity 2.23

No solution required.

## Activity 2.24

1.
```
program Act20_01;
uses WinCrt;
var
     nbr : integer;
begin
    {*** Clear screen ***}
    ClrScr;
    {*** Get value ***}
    write('Please enter a value : ');
    readln(nbr);
    {*** Display value entered ***}
    writeln('The number entered was ',nbr);
end.
```

2.
```
program Act20_02;
uses WinCrt;
var
    nbr : integer;
    ch  : char;
begin
    {*** Clear screen ***}
    ClrScr;
    {*** Get value ***}
    write('Please enter a value : ');
    readln(nbr);
    {*** Copy to char variable for display ***}
    ch := char(nbr);
    {*** Display required output ***}
    writeln('Decimal   Char');
    writeln(nbr:4,'          ',ch);
end.
```

3.
```
program Act20_03;
uses WinCrt;
var
    lbs1, oz1 : integer; {First weight}
    lbs2, oz2 : integer; {Second weight}
    poundssum, ouncessum : integer;{Total weight}
    totaloz   : integer; {Total of ounces part
                         {of both weights}
    carry : integer;{Carry from ounces to pounds}
begin
    {*** Clear screen ***}
    ClrScr;
    {*** Get weights ***}
    write('Please enter first weight  : ');
    readln(lbs1, oz1);
    write('Please enter second weight : ');
    readln(lbs2, oz2);
    {*** Add weights ***}
    totaloz := oz1 + oz2;
    carry := totaloz div 16;
    ouncessum := totaloz mod 16;
    poundssum := lbs1 + lbs2 + carry;
    {*** Display total weight ***}
    writeln('Total weight is ',poundssum,
    ↳' lbs ',ouncessum,' ozs');
end.
```

4.
```
program Act20_04;
uses WinCrt;
var
    letter, previous, next : char;
begin
    {*** Clear screen ***}
    ClrScr;
    {*** Get value ***}
    write('Please enter a character : ');
    readln(letter);
    {*** Determine previous and next characters
***}
    previous := char(integer(letter) - 1);
    next := char(integer(letter) + 1);
    {*** Display characters ***}
    write(previous,' ',letter,' ',next);
end.
```

5.
```
program Act20_05;
uses WinCrt;
var
    no1, no2 : integer;
begin
    {*** Clear screen ***}
    ClrScr;
    {*** Get values ***}
    write('Please enter first number : ');
    readln(no1);
    write('Please enter second number : ');
    readln(no2);
    {*** Swap contents ***}
    no1 := no1 + no2;
    no2 := no1 - no2;
    no1 := no1 - no2;
    {*** Display contents ***}
    writeln('First variable now = ',no1);
    writeln('Second variable now = ',no2);
end.
```

6.
```
program Act20_06;
uses WinCrt;
var
    lowercaseletter, uppercaseletter : char;
begin
    {*** Clear screen ***}
    ClrScr;
```

```
    {*** Get lower case letter ***}
    write('Please enter lower case letter : ');
    readln(lowercaseletter);
    {*** Determine upper case letter ***}
    uppercaseletter := char(integer(lowercaseletter) - 32);
    {*** Display contents ***}
    writeln('Lower case = ',lowercaseletter);
    writeln('Upper case = ',uppercaseletter);
end.
```

7.

```
program Act20_07;
uses WinCrt;
var
    centimetres   : integer;              {Metric length}
    yards, feet, inches : integer;        {Imperial length}
    total_inches, total_feet : integer; {temporary variables}
begin
    {*** Clear screen ***}
    ClrScr;
    {*** Get weights ***}
    write('Please enter length (cms): ');
    readln(centimetres);
    {*** Convert to imperial ***}
    total_inches := round((centimetres / 2.4));
    inches := total_inches mod 12;
    total_feet := total_inches div 12;
    feet := total_feet mod 3;
    yards := total_feet div 3;
    {*** Display result ***}
    writeln(centimetres,' cm = ',yards,' yards ',feet,' feet ',inches,' inches');
end.
```

8.

```
program Act20_08;
uses WinCrt;
var
    day, month, year : integer; {Date to be converted to day of week}
    M, CY, C, Y      : integer; {Modified date values}
    temp             : integer; {temporary variable}
    d                : integer; {Day of week on which date falls}
                                {0 = Sunday, 1 = Monday etc..}
begin
    {*** Clear screen ***}
    ClrScr;
    {*** Get date ***}
    write('Enter date in form dd mm yyyy : ');
    readln(day, month, year);
    {*** Determine modified version of date ***}
    M    := (month + 9) mod 12 + 1;
    CY   := year - M div 11;
    C    := CY div 100;
    Y    := CY mod 100;
    temp := Trunc(2.6 * M - 0.2);
    d    := ((temp + day + Y + Y div 4 + C div 4 - 2 * C) mod 7 + 7) mod 7;
    {*** Display results ***}
    writeln(day,'/',month,'/',year,' is a ',d);
end.
```

Chapter 3

# Control Structures

**This chapter covers the following topics:**

Binary Selection

Boolean Operators

Compound Statements

Debugging

Iteration

Jump Statements

Multiway Selection

Nested Loops

Operator Precedence

Relational Operators

White Box Testing

# SELECTION

## Binary Selection

Binary selection allows us to choose between two alternative actions within a program. In Structured English, the simplest form of binary selection is implemented using the form:

See Chapter 1 for a fuller explanation of Structured English.

```
IF condition THEN
    statement
        .
    statement
ENDIF
```

Pascal also uses an `if` statement to implement binary selection. The simplest form of this statement is

```
if condition then
    action
```

where

`condition`
is any expression that can be reduced to a *true* or *false* value.

`action`
is any executable Pascal statement. If `condition` evaluates to *true*, then the action will be executed, otherwise it will be bypassed.

### Condition

REMEMBER

A Boolean expression is one which produces the result *true* or *false*.

The condition is usually a Boolean one in which the relationship between two quantities is compared. For example, the expression `no < 0` will be *true* if the contents of the variable *no* is less than zero (i.e. negative). Boolean expressions have the general form:

*value1* relational operator *value2*

where

*value1* and *value2*
may be constants, variables or expressions.

*relational operator*
is one of the operators given in TABLE-3.1.

**TABLE-3.1**

Relational Operators

| **Relational Operators** | |
|---|---|
| **Symbol** | **Meaning** |
| > | Greater than |
| >= | Greater than or equal to |
| < | Less than |
| <= | Less than or equal to |
| = | Equal to |
| <> | Not equal to |

As with the assignment statement, the values involved must be of compatible types (or be cast to compatible types).

**Activity 3.1**

Assuming the following definitions

```
var
    no1, no2, no3:integer;
    let1, let2    :char;
    s1            :string;
```

which of the following are NOT valid Boolean expressions.

1. `no1 < no2`
2. `let1 = let2`
3. `let2 => no3`
4. `no1 * 2 = no3 / 4`
5. `let1 <> 65`
6. `s1 = good`

TABLE-3.2 shows some Structured English IF statements and the equivalent Pascal code.

**TABLE-3.2**

Simple Pascal if Statements

| Structured English | Pascal Code |
|---|---|
| IF *no* is negative THEN<br>    Make *no* positive<br>ENDIF | `if no < 0 then`<br>`    no := -no;` |
| IF *day* is zero THEN<br>    Display "Sunday"<br>ENDIF | `if day = 0 then`<br>`    writeln('Sunday');` |
| IF *value* is even THEN<br>    Subtract 1 from *value*<br>ENDIF | `if value mod 2 = 0 then`<br>`    value := value - 1;` |

**Activity 3.2**

What output is produced by the following code?

```
program test1;
uses WinCrt;
var
    no1, no2, ans1, ans2 : integer;
begin
    no1:=6;
    no2:=2;
    ans1 := no1 - no2;
    ans2 := no1 + no2;
    if ans1 = ans2 then
        writeln('TRUE 1');
    if ans1 = ans2 / ans1 then
        writeln('TRUE 2');
    if ans2 < ans1 * 4 then
        writeln('TRUE 3');
end.
```

### Compound Relations - AND and OR Operators

Simple conditions, such as those used in the examples above can be combined using the AND and OR operators to form compound relational tests.Where the AND construct is used to link expressions, then all conditions must be *true* for the overall result to be *true*. For example, if we want to test if the variable *salary* is greater than 20,000 and *maritalstatus* is "*single*" then the required expression is:

```
(salary > 20000)and(maritalstatus = 'single')
```

Notice that each simple expression must be enclosed in parentheses. This is because the AND operator has a higher priority than the relational operators > and =. This priority is changed by the parentheses.

The full expression is evaluated in the following steps:

1. Evaluate `(salary > 20000)` (we'll assume this is *true)*
2. Evaluate `(maritalstatus = 'single')` (we'll assume this is *false*)
3. Evaluate the AND (*true* AND *false* gives *false*)

When OR is used, at least one of the conditions must be *true* for the result to be *true*. It is also possible to construct complex expressions involving several AND and OR operators. Where this is done it may be necessary to insert additional parentheses to adjust the priority of the operators or simply to clarify the meaning of the condition. TABLE-3.3 gives several examples of Structured English statements and the Pascal equivalent.

**TABLE-3.3**

Compound Expressions

| Structured English | Pascal Code |
|---|---|
| IF *no1* = 6 AND *no2* < 0 THEN | `if(no1=6)and(no2<0) then` |
| IF *sex* = 'M' OR *sex* = 'F' THEN | `if(sex='M')or(sex='F') then` |
| IF letter not uppercase THEN | `if(letter<'A')or(letter>'Z') then` |
| IF *temp* in the range 15 to 20 THEN | `if(temp>=15)and(temp<=20) then` |
| IF female AND older than 59 OR male AND older than 64 THEN | `if((sex='F')and(age>59))or ((sex='M')and(age>64)) then` |

Nested parentheses are allowed in expressions. Where used, the inner-most brackets are evaluated first. Parentheses of equal depth are evaluated left to right.

Assume the following declarations:
`weight,code,mark,key masterkey,quantity: integer; option,command:char;`

**Activity 3.3**

Write the Pascal equivalent for the following expressions:
(Assume any variables are already defined)

1. `IF weight > 16 THEN`
2. `IF code is not 17850 THEN`
3. `IF mark between 75 and 85 THEN`
4. `IF option = 'C' AND key = masterkey THEN`
5. `IF(command = 'D' OR command = 'A') AND quantity > 100 THEN`

### The NOT Operator

As well as using AND and OR to link simple expressions, we may negate the meaning of an expression by use of the NOT operator.

The general structure is:

```
if  not(condition) then
```

The parentheses are required because the NOT operator has a higher priority than AND, OR and relational operators and assignment statements. Table-3.4 gives several examples of Structured English statements and their Pascal equivalent; with and without using the `not` operator.

**TABLE-3.4**

Expressions using the NOT Operator

| Structured English | Expression (using NOT) | Expression (without NOT) |
|---|---|---|
| IF *no* not equal to 10 THEN | `if not(no=10) then` | `if no<>10 then` |
| IF *no1* not equal 10 AND<br>↳*no2* not equal 6<br>THEN | `if not(no1=10)AND`<br>↳`not(no2 =6)`<br>`then` | `if (no1<>10)AND`<br>↳`(no2 <> 6)`<br>`then` |
| IF *weight* not greater than 16<br>THEN | `if not(weight>16)`<br>`then` | `if weight<=16`<br>`then` |

## Compound Statements

Where there are several statements to be performed when the condition is *true*, then they must be enclosed within the terms `begin` and `end`. The general form is shown below:

```
if condition then
begin
    statement;
    statement;
        .
    statement
end
```

For example, the Structured English statement

```
IF ozs >= 16 THEN
    Add 1 to lbs
    Subtract 16 from ozs
ENDIF
```

is coded as:

```
if ozs >= 16 then
begin
    lbs:=lbs + 1;
    ozs := ozs - 16;
end
```

The positioning of the reserved words `begin` and `end`, and the use of indentation should be consistent throughout your program. Although the positioning of the text is of no concern to the compiler, we humans, who have to correct programs, sometimes weeks after they have been written, will find them much easier to decipher if a clear, neat style is used.

The rule is simple: indent any code within an `if` statement (or any of the other control structures we have yet to cover).

## if else

Like Structured English, Pascal allows the `if` statement to be extended to include an `else` option that will be executed only if the condition specified is *false.*

Structured English uses the format:

```
IF condition THEN
    statement
        .
    statement
ELSE
    statement
        .
    statement
ENDIF
```

Pascal uses:

```
if condition then
    statement
else
    statement
```

So the Structured English lines

*nbr* is assumed to be a numeric variable.

```
IF nbr is negative then
    display "Negative value"
ELSE
    display "Positive value"
ENDIF
```

would be coded as

```
if nbr < 0 then
    writeln('Negative value')
else
    writeln('Positive value');
```

Note that there is no semicolon in the statement preceding `else`.

Where there is more than one statement in any section of the `if` statement, those statements must be enclosed between the terms `begin` and `end`:

```
if condition then
begin
    statement;
        .
    statement;
end
else
begin
    statement;
        .
    statement;
end
```

For example, the Structured English statement

```
IF nbr is negative THEN
    Display "Negative value"
    Add nbr to negsum
ELSE
    Display "Positive value"
    Add nbr to possum
ENDIF
```

translates in Pascal to

```
if nbr < 0 then
begin
    writeln('Negative value');
    negsum := negsum + nbr;
end
else
begin
    writeln('Positive value');
    possum := possum + nbr;
end
```

The general form of the `if` statement is shown in FIG-3.1.

**FIG-3.1**

The if Statement

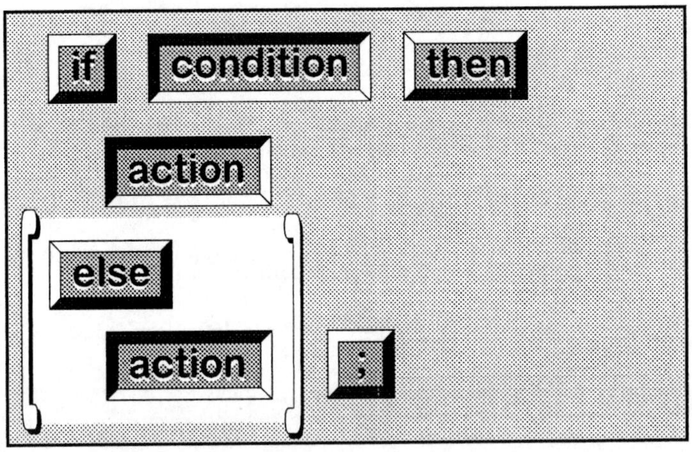

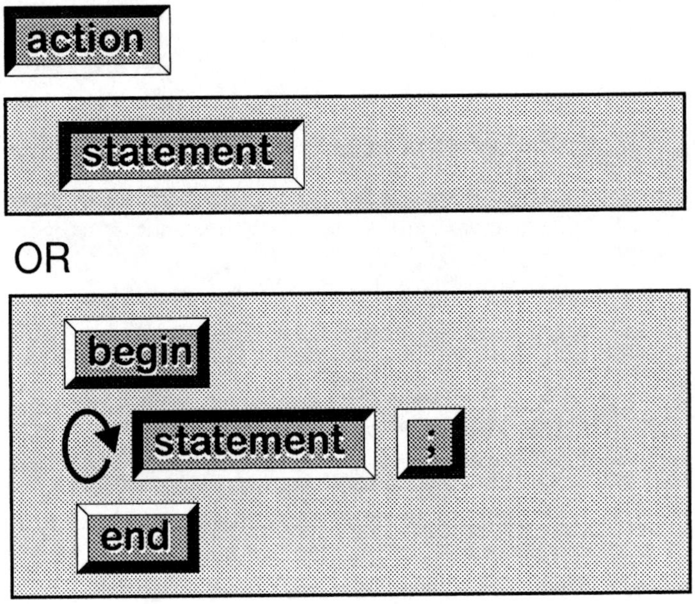

## Nested `if` Statements

When dealing with more complex problems, it is sometimes necessary to place one `if` statement inside another. This is termed **nested `if`** statements. For example, we might divide males into those of working age and those of retirement age with the logic

```
IF sex = 'M' THEN
    IF age >= 65 THEN
        Display "Retired male"
    ELSE
        Display "Working male"
    ENDIF
ENDIF
```

which in Pascal is coded as

```
if sex = 'M' then
    if age >= 65 then
        writeln('Retired male')
    else
        writeln('Working male');
```

Unfortunately, there is potential ambiguity in this structure since the `else` option could belong to the first `if` structure (`if sex = 'M' then`) rather than the second, as suggested by the indentation used. This uncertainty is avoided by applying the rule that an `else` is always assigned to the most recent `if` structure which does not already have a matching `else`.

Where the `else` statement is required to match with the first `if` rather than the second as in the logic

```
IF sex = 'M' THEN
    IF age >= 65 THEN
        Display "Retired male"
    ENDIF
ELSE
    Display "Female"
ENDIF
```

then this can be achieved by separating the second `if` statement from the `else` using `begin .. end`:

`begin` and `end` enclose the second `if` statement thus forcing the `else` to match with the earlier `if`

```
if sex = 'M' then
begin
    if age >= 65
        writeln('Retired male');
end
else
    writeln('Female');
```

**Activity 3.4**

Modify and extend the above `if` statement to print one of the four following messages:

*Retired male*
*Male working*
*Retired female* (Females retiral age =60)
*Female working*

## The `else if` Option

Although a simple `if..else` structure is ideal for choosing between two alternative actions, the nested `if` statements necessary to implement a wider range of choices can produce code which is less than easy to follow. For example, if a program requires to read in a transaction code and display one of the following messages

| **Code** | **Message** |
|---|---|
| 1 | CASH |
| 2 | CREDIT |
| 3 | RETURNED |
| other | INVALID CODE |

then this requires the logic

```
IF code = 1 THEN
    Display "CASH"
ELSE
    IF code = 2 THEN
        Display "CREDIT"
    ELSE
        IF code = 3 THEN
            Display "RETURNED"
        ELSE
            Display "INVALID CODE"
        ENDIF
    ENDIF
ENDIF
```

which, if programmed using the conventional layout, produces

```
if code = 1 then
    writeln('CASH')
else
    if code = 2 then
        writeln('CREDIT')
    else
        if code = 3 then
            writeln('RETURN')
        else
            writeln('INVALID CODE');
```

Without affecting the logic of the code, the above layout can be improved by placing each `else` and subsequent `if` expression on the same line:

```
if code = 1 then
    writeln('CASH')
else if code = 2 then
    writeln('CREDIT')
else if code = 3 then
    writeln('RETURN')
else
    writeln('INVALID CODE');
```

The effect of executing such code is to test each expression in turn until one is found to be *true*. The instruction associated with that `if` statement is then executed. If no expression is *true* then the final `else` option is executed.

Where more than one statement is required after any of the options then, as usual, `begin..end` must be employed giving the general form for this structure:

```
if condition then
begin
    statement;
        .
    statement;
end
else if condition then
begin
    statement;
        .
    statement;
end
        .
        .
else
begin
    statement;
        .
    statement;
end
```

**Activity 3.5**

Write Pascal programs to perform the following tasks:

1. Read in two numbers and display the word EQUAL if the values are the same, otherwise display NOT EQUAL.

```
OUTLINE LOGIC:
    Read in both numbers
    IF first number is equal to the second THEN
        Display "EQUAL"
    ELSE
        Display "NOT EQUAL"
    ENDIF
```

2. Read in two real numbers (*rno1, rno2*). If the second value is not zero calculate and display the value of *rno1/rno2*.

```
OUTLINE LOGIC:
    Read in values for rno1 and rno2
    IF rno2 isn't zero THEN
        Calculate result as rno1/rno2
        Display result
    ENDIF
```

3. Read in a letter and print VOWEL or CONSONANT as appropriate.

```
OUTLINE LOGIC:
    Read in value for letter
    IF letter is 'A', 'E', 'I', 'O' or 'U' THEN
        Display "VOWEL"
    ELSE
        Display "CONSONANT"
    ENDIF
```

**Continued on next page**

**Activity 3.5** (continued)

4. Read in two numbers and display the smaller of the two. If both values are equal then display "EQUAL".

```
OUTLINE LOGIC:
     Read no1 and no2
     IF no1 < no2 THEN
          Display value of no1
     ELSE
          IF no2 < no1 THEN
               Display value of no2
          ELSE
               Display "EQUAL"
          ENDIF
     ENDIF
```

5. Modify Zeller's congruence program from the previous chapter to display the day of the week in text form.

```
OUTLINE LOGIC:
     Read date
     Determine day of week code (stored in d) for date
     IF
          d = 0:
               Display "Sunday"
          d = 1:
               Display "Monday"
          d = 2:
               Display "Tuesday"
          d = 3:
               Display "Wednesday"
          d = 4:
               Display "Thursday"
          d = 5:
               Display "Friday"
          d = 6:
               Display "Saturday"
     ENDIF
```

6. Gauss developed a formula for calculating the date on which Easter Sunday falls. The formula is:

k = [year/100]
a = year modulus 19
b = year modulus 4
c = year modulus 7
q = [k/4]
p = [(13+8k)/25]
m = (15p+k+q)modulus 30
d = (19a+m)modulus 30
n = (4+k-q)modulus 7
e = (2b+4c+6d+n)modulus 7

| | |
|---|---|
| if d+e <=9 | day = 22+d+e and month = 3 |
| if d = 29 and e = 6 | day = 19 month = 4 |
| if d = 28 and e = 6 and a >10 | day = 18 month = 4 |
| all other cases | day = d+e-9 month = 4 |

**Continued on next page**

**Activity 3.5** (continued)

6. (continued)

[x] = largest integer not greater than x.

Write a program to read in a year and output the date on which Easter Sunday falls in that year.

```
OUTLINE LOGIC:
        Read year
        Calculate k as integer part of year / 100
        Calculate a as year modulus 19
        Calculate b as year modulus 4
        Calculate c as year modulus 7
        Calculate q as integer part of k / 4
        Calculate p as integer part of (13 + 8k) / 25
        Calculate m as (15p + k + q) modulus 30
        Calculate d as (19a + m) modulus 30
        Calculate n as (4 + k - q) modulus 7
        Calculate e as (2b + 4c + 6d + n) modulus 7
        IF d + e <= 9 THEN
            Calculate day as 22 + d + e
            Set month to 3
        ELSE
            IF d = 29 AND e = 6 THEN
                Set day to 19
                Set month to 4
            ELSE
                IF d = 28 AND e = 6 AND a > 10 THEN
                    Set day to 18
                    Set month to 4
                ELSE
                    Calculate day as d + e - 9
                    Set month to 4
                ENDIF
            ENDIF
        ENDIF
        Display day and month
```

# Multi-way Selection

Multi-way selection means choosing one option from many. Although we have already dealt with this situation using nested `if` statements and the `else if` structure, there is an alternative approach which often results in clearer code. This is the `case` statement. Earlier we looked at a program to read in a transaction code and display one of the following messages:

| **Code** | **Message** |
|---|---|
| 1 | CASH |
| 2 | CREDIT |
| 3 | RETURNED |
| other | INVALID CODE |

This could be coded in Structured English as:

```
IF
    code = 1:   Display "CASH"
    code = 2:   Display "CREDIT"
    code = 3:   Display "RETURNED"
    ELSE
                Display "INVALID CODE"
ENDIF
```

Pascal's `case` statement has a similar effect :

```
case code of
    1:      writeln('CASH');
    2:      writeln('CREDIT');
    3:      writeln('RETURNED');
    else    writeln('INVALID CODE');
end;
```

During execution, *code* is evaluated and control jumps to the label (1:, 2:, 3:) whose value matches that of *code.* Where *code* does not match any of the `case` values, then control jumps to the `else` option. When the selected option's code has been executed, control skips to the end of the `case` statement. The process is shown in FIG-3.2 below.

**FIG-3.2**

Executing a `case` Statement

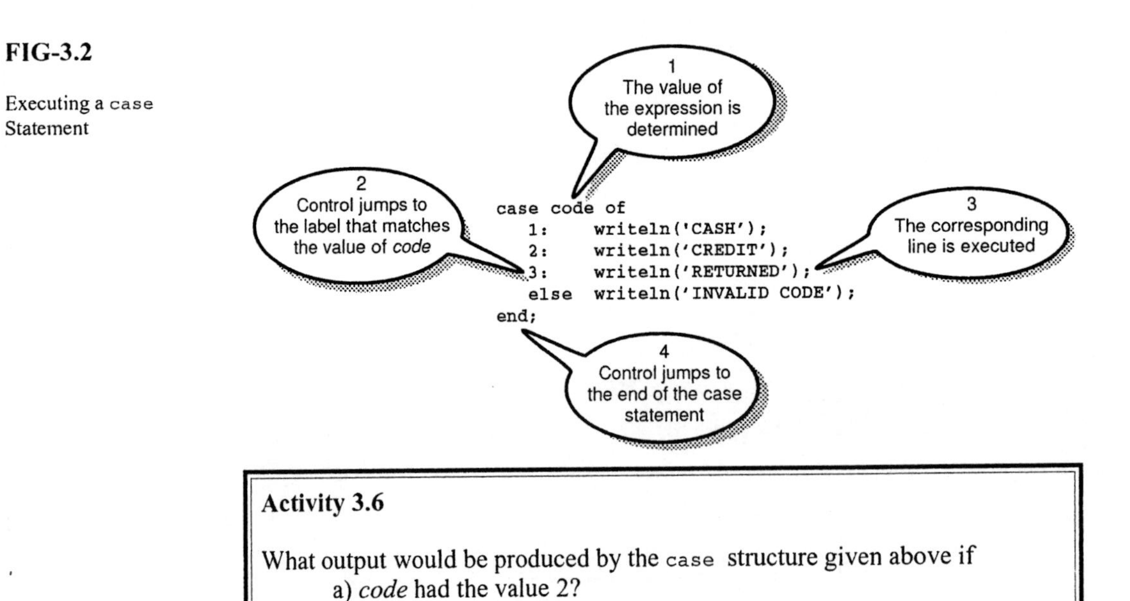


**Activity 3.6**

What output would be produced by the `case` structure given above if

a) *code* had the value 2?

b) *code* had the value 5?

**Activity 3.7**

Using a `case` statement, write a Pascal program that reads in an integer value (in the range 0 to 6) and displays the corresponding day of the week.

```
Outline Logic
  Read in a value for day
  IF
      day = 0 : Display 'Sunday'
      day = 1 : Display 'Monday'
      day = 2 : Display 'Tuesday'
      day = 3 : Display 'Wednesday'
      day = 4 : Display 'Thursday'
      day = 5 : Display 'Friday'
```

**Continued on next page**

**Activity 3.7** (continued)

```
    day = 6 : Display 'Saturday'
ELSE
    Display 'Invalid value for day'
ENDIF
```

## Multiple Statements

When several instructions are to be associated with a label in a `case` statement, those instructions must be enclosed within the terms `begin .. end`. This is shown in the example below in which the user must enter more detail when *code* is equal to 3.

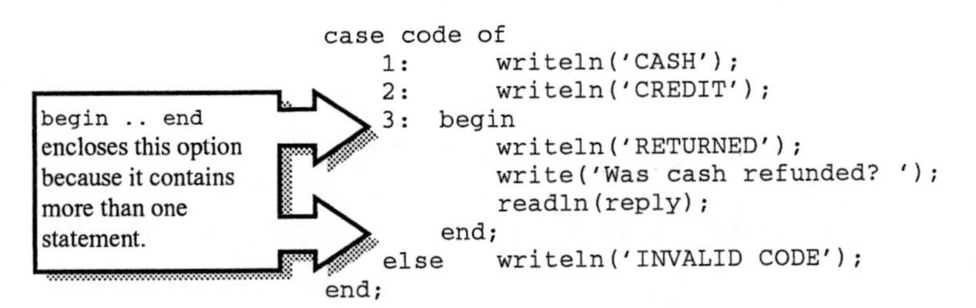

begin .. end
encloses this option
because it contains
more than one
statement.


```
case code of
    1:      writeln('CASH');
    2:      writeln('CREDIT');
    3:  begin
            writeln('RETURNED');
            write('Was cash refunded? ');
            readln(reply);
        end;
    else    writeln('INVALID CODE');
end;
```

**Activity 3.8**

Modify the program you created in Activity 3.7 so that when *day* is 6, the user is asked if he was working that day. If the response is YES, then display 'So sorry', otherwise display 'Hope you had a nice day'. The response should be read into a string variable called *reply*.

## Character Labels

The values specified within a `case` statement can also be character constants. The following program (LISTING-3.1) reads in two numbers and an operator ('+', '-', '*', or '/') and displays the corresponding result.

**LISTING-3.1**

Character Labels in the `case` statement

```
program Calculator;
uses WinCrt;
var
  no1, no2  : integer;
  operation : char;
begin
  ClrScr;
  {*** Read in details ***}
  write('Enter first value : ');
  readln(no1);
  write('Enter second value : ');
  readln(no2);
  write('Enter operation required (+-* or /) : ');
  readln(operation);
  {*** Calculate result ***}
  case operation of
      '+' :    writeln(no1, '+', no2, '=', no1 + no2);
      '-' :    writeln(no1, '-', no2, '=', no1 - no2);
      '*' :    writeln(no1, '*', no2, '=', no1 * no2);
      '/' :    writeln(no1, '/', no2, '=', no1 / no2:0:2);
      else     writeln('Invalid operator');
  end;
end.
```

It is also possible to have two or more values relating to the same section of code. For example, the code above expects the asterisk ('*') to be entered when using the multiply option but non-programmers are much more likely to enter an 'x'. Therefore, an improvement to the program would be to allow for both options. To do this we simply list all the values that are to take us to that option, separating each value by a comma:

```
'*','x' :  writeln(no1, '*', no2, '=' ,no1 * no2);
```

**Activity 3.9**

Type in the calculator program in LISTING-3.1.

Test it with the values 8, 0 and '/'.

Why does this cause a problem?

It's also possible to have any one of a continuous group of values execute the same `case` option using a label of the form: *lower_value..upper_value*. For example, if a `case` statement required all values between -70 and zero to display the word *Freezing*, then that section of the statement would be coded as:

```
-70..0 : writeln('Freezing');
```

Where continuous and disjoint values are required together we can have a label such as:

```
1..10,37,99 :
```

The general format of the `case` statement is shown in FIG-3.3

**FIG-3.3**

The `case` Statement

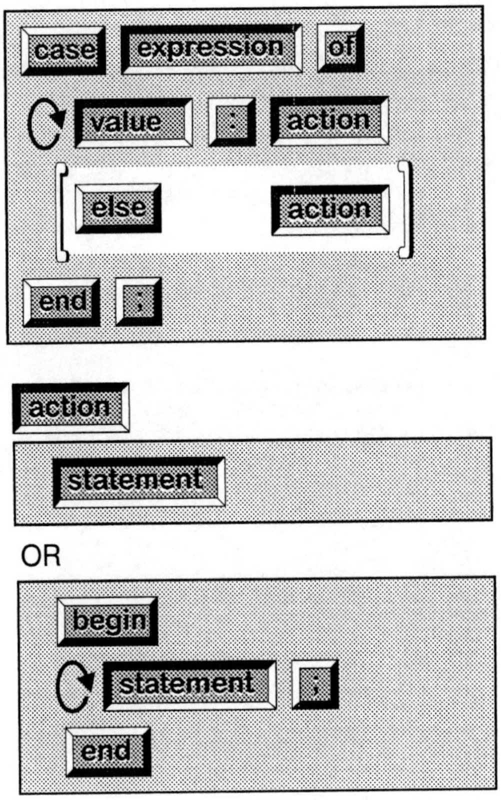

case expression of
value : action
else action
end ;

action
statement
OR
begin
statement ;
end

**Activity 3.10**

Using a `case` statement, write Pascal coding which converts an amount in pounds sterling to a given currency. The target currency is given by a single character:'$' for US dollars (1.66 to the pound), 'G' for German Mark (2.78 to the pound) and 'F' for French Franc (8.93 to the pound). Both upper and lower case letters should be acceptable. You need not validate the input. Display the amount in pounds and the target currency.

# Summary

- **Selection control structures** are used to choose between two or more alternatives.

- **Binary selection** is achieved using the `if` statement.

- **The `if` statement has two possible forms**:

```
if condition then
    action
```

and

```
if condition then
    action
else
    action
```

- **If the *action* to be performed** is more than a single Pascal statement, those statements must be enclosed within the terms `begin..end`.

```
if condition then
    statement;           {one statement - no begin ..end}


if condition then
begin
    statement;
    statement;
    statement
end                      {multiple statements - begin..end}
```

- **The condition being tested** must be a Boolean expression.

- **Boolean expressions** produce a result of either *true* or *false*.

- **Boolean expressions** have the form:

```
value     relational operator     value
```

- **Relational operators** are:

```
=       Equal to
<>      Not equal to
<       Less than
<=      Less than or equal to
>       Greater than
>=      Greater than or equal to
```

- **The condition can be a complex** one created by linking two or more simple conditions with the terms AND or OR.

- In complex conditions, **each simple expression must be enclosed within its own parentheses.**

```
(no1 < 4) and (no2 > 6)
```

- **A logic value can be reversed using not.** (e.g. `not(age > 18)` )

- **Multi-way selection** can be achieved using either nested `if` statements or the `case` statement.

- **Nested `if` structures** can be used where a choice between more than two options has to be made.

- **When `if` statements are nested,** `else` statements match with the last `if` section which is not already linked to an `else` statement. This may be overridden using parentheses.

- **The `case` statement** has the following format:

```
case expression of
    label1 :    action;
    label2 :    action;
            .
            .
    labelx :    action;
    else        action
end
```

- **If the action contains more than one Pascal statement**, those statements must be enclosed within the terms `begin..end`.

- **The `case` statement will begin execution at the label matching the value of the `case` statement's expression.**

- **Where none of the options in the `case` statement are appropriate, the `else` option is executed.**

  Where there is no `else` statement, the whole `case` structure is bypassed.

- **Label values within a `case` statement can be `integer` or `char` but not real or string.**

- **A contiguous range of value may be given in a label.**

```
12..25 :

'A'..'M' :
```

- **The range of values can also be disjoint.**

```
3,1,7 :

'A','E','I':
```

- **Contiguous and disjoint values can be used in a single label:**

```
1..10,83,99:

'A'..'M','Z':
```

# ITERATION

Iteration is the ability to execute some section of a program several times. Pascal has three distinct structures for achieving this. These structures are similar to those of Structured English (covered in Chapter 1) and translation between the two languages is easy.

## The `while` Structure

The `while` structure is probably the easiest to understand. This is an **entry-controlled loop**. That is, the condition to be tested is at the start of the loop. If the condition is *true* the action within the `while` statement (known more generally as the **loop body**) is executed; if not, then the loop body is bypassed. The action is repeated until the condition is no longer true.

The general form of a `while` loop in Structured English is:

```
WHILE condition DO
    action
ENDWHILE
```

The equivalent Pascal structure is:

```
while condition do
    action ;
```

Like the `if` statement, where the action to be performed is more than one statement, then these statements must be bracketed by the terms `begin..end`.

The structure of the statement is shown in FIG-3.4.

**FIG-3.4**

The while Statement

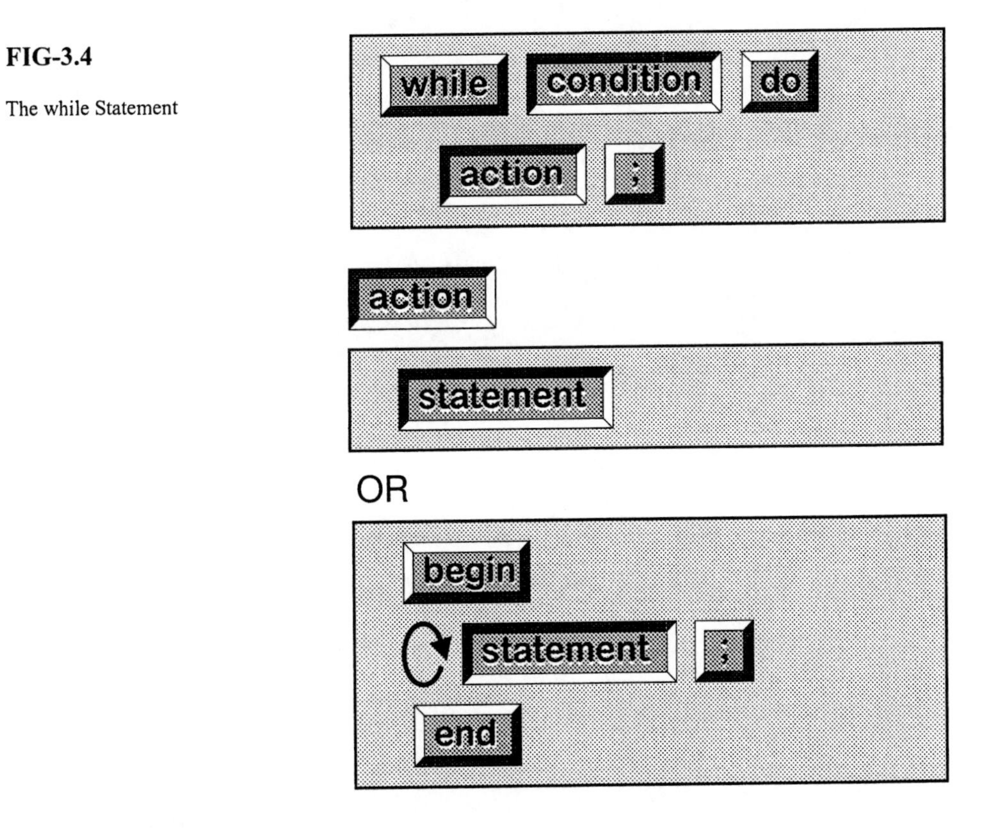

The operation of the statement is shown graphically in FIG-3.5.

**FIG-3.5**

Executing a `while` Structure

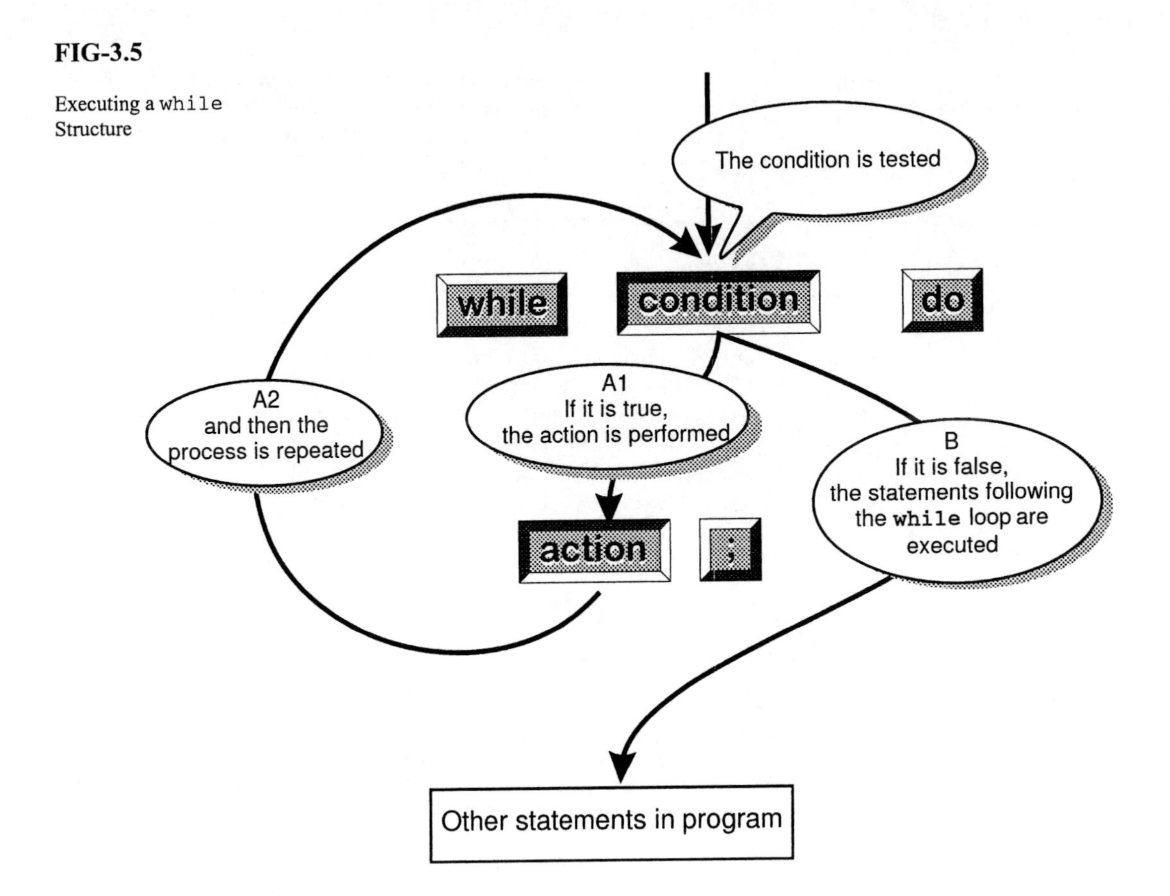


For example, we might define the logic determining the number of times one positive integer divides into another as

```
Get values for dividend and divisor
Set count to zero
WHILE dividend >= 0 DO
    Add 1 to count
    Subtract divisor from dividend
ENDWHILE
Subtract 1 from count
```

which can be coded in Pascal as:

```
readln(dividend, divisor);
count := 0;
while dividend >= 0 do
begin
    count := count + 1;
    dividend := dividend - divisor
end;
count := count - 1;
```

TABLE-3.5 gives several examples of Structured English *while* statements and the equivalent Pascal code.

**TABLE-3.5**

while Structures

| Structured English | Pascal |
|---|---|
| Get month<br>WHILE month outside range 1 - 12 DO<br>    Display "Invalid month"<br>    Get month<br>ENDWHILE | readln(month);<br>while (month<1)or(month>12) do<br>begin<br>    writeln('Invalid month');<br>    readln(month)<br>end; |
| Get value<br>WHILE value not zero DO<br>    Add value to total<br>    Get value<br>ENDWHILE | readln(value);<br>while value <> 0 do<br>begin<br>    total := total + value;<br>    readln(value)<br>end; |

**Activity 3.11**

Write the Pascal equivalent of the following Structured English:

```
Get previousvalue
Get currentvalue
WHILE previousvalue not equal to currentvalue DO
    Set previousvalue equal to currentvalue
    Get currentvalue
ENDWHILE
```

## A Common use for the `while` Structure

The `while` loop is often used to validate user input. It can be applied to force the user to re-enter data as often as necessary until it meets the requirements of the system. Generally, such `while` loops use the following logic:

```
Read data
WHILE data is invalid DO
    Display error message
    Get user to re-enter data
ENDWHILE
```

The example below uses this technique to ensure that the month requested from the user is in the range 1 to 12. The logic required is

```
Prompt for month
Get value for month
WHILE month is outside the range 1 to 12 DO
    Display error message
    Prompt for month
    Get value for month
ENDWHILE
```

and this could be coded as:

```
write('Enter month : ');
readln(month);
while (month < 1) or (month > 12) do
begin
    writeln('Month must be in range 1 to 12');
    write('Enter month : ');
    readln(month)
end;
```

# The `repeat..until` Structure

The `repeat..until` statement is an **exit-controlled** loop. The loop body is executed and then an exit condition is tested. If the condition is *true*, the loop is exited, otherwise the loop body is executed again. Iteration continues until the exit condition is *true*.

Pascal's `repeat .. until` statement is an exact match for Structured English's **REPEAT .. UNTIL** statement. Hence, in Structured English the general format is

```
REPEAT
    action
UNTIL condition
```

and the equivalent Pascal is:

```
repeat
    action
until condition;
```

The statements

```
REPEAT
    Get value
    Add value to total
UNTIL value is zero
```

are coded as:

```
repeat
    write('Enter value : ');
    readln(value);
    total := total + value;
until value = 0;
```

FIG-3.6 shows the structure of the statement.

**FIG-3.6**

The `repeat` Statement

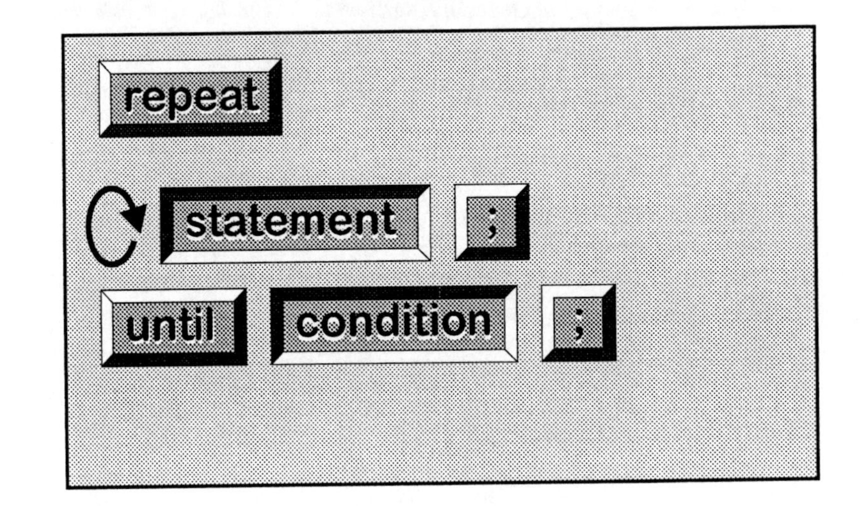


The operation of the statement is shown graphically in FIG-3.7.

**FIG-3.7**

Executing a `repeat..until` Structure

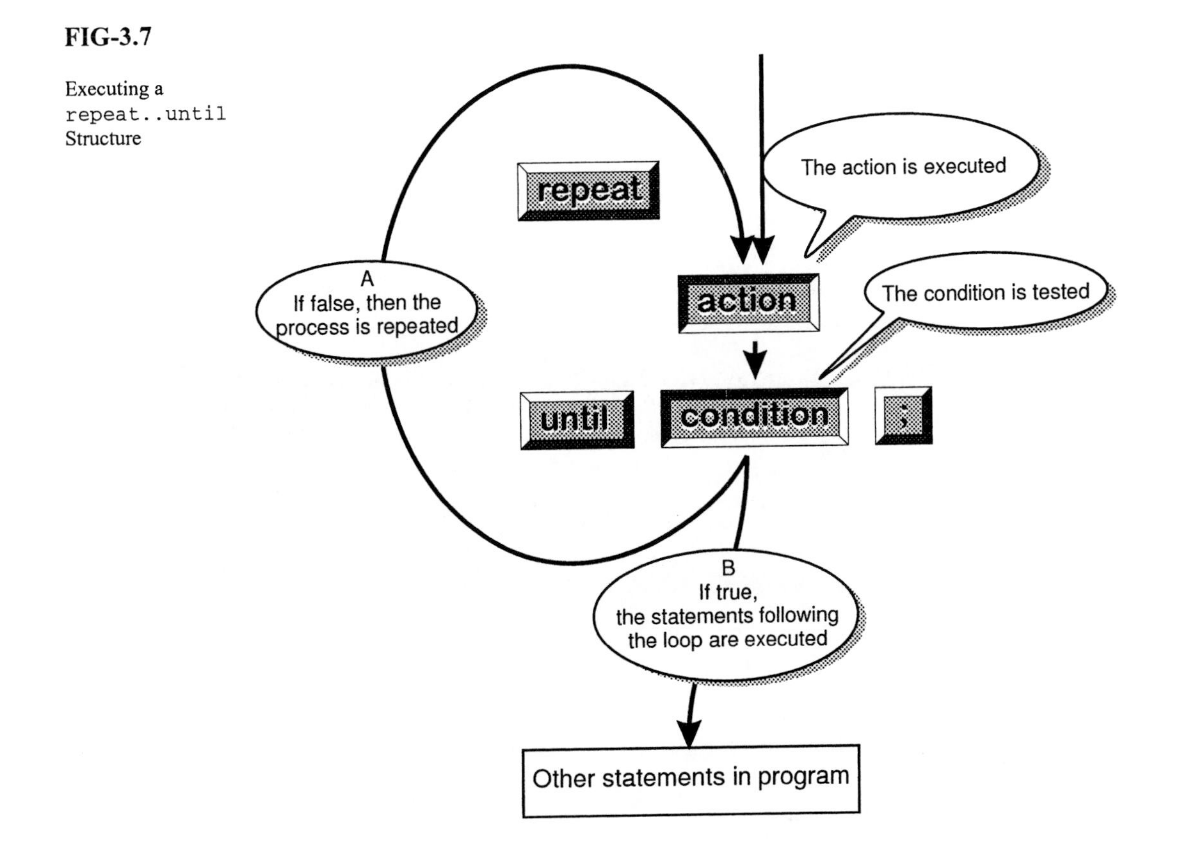


TABLE-3.6 gives some examples of Structured English **REPEAT .. UNTIL** loops and the equivalent Pascal `repeat..until` structures.

**TABLE-3.6**

`repeat..until` Structures

| Structured English | Pascal |
|---|---|
| Set target to 401<br>REPEAT<br>    Get score<br><br>    Subtract score from target<br>UNTIL target <= 0 | target := 401;<br>repeat<br>    write('Enter score :');<br>    readln(score);<br>    target := target - score;<br>until target <= 0; |
| Set total to zero<br>Set count to zero<br>REPEAT<br>    Get number<br><br>    Add number to total<br>    Add 1 to count<br>UNTIL count = 10 OR number = 0 | total := 0;<br>count := 0;<br>repeat<br>    write('Enter number :');<br>    readln(number);<br>    total := total + number;<br>    count := count + 1;<br>until (count = 10)or(number = 0); |

# The `for` Structure

In Structured English, the `for` structure can perform a sequence of tasks a fixed number of times using logic such as

```
FOR each student DO
    Get student's mark
    Add mark to total
ENDFOR
```

which, should there be 10 students, would carry out the statements *Get student's mark* and *Add mark to total* 10 times.

When we want to perform this type of loop in Pascal, we usually need to define a **loop counter variable** which the `for` loop increments each time the loop body is executed. For example, the 10 students would have their marks totalled by the code:

```
var
    count, mark, total : integer;
begin
    total := 0;
    for count := 1 to 10 do
    begin
        write('Enter mark : ');
        readln(mark);
        total := total + mark;
    end;
```

The method of execution of the statement is shown if FIG-3.8.

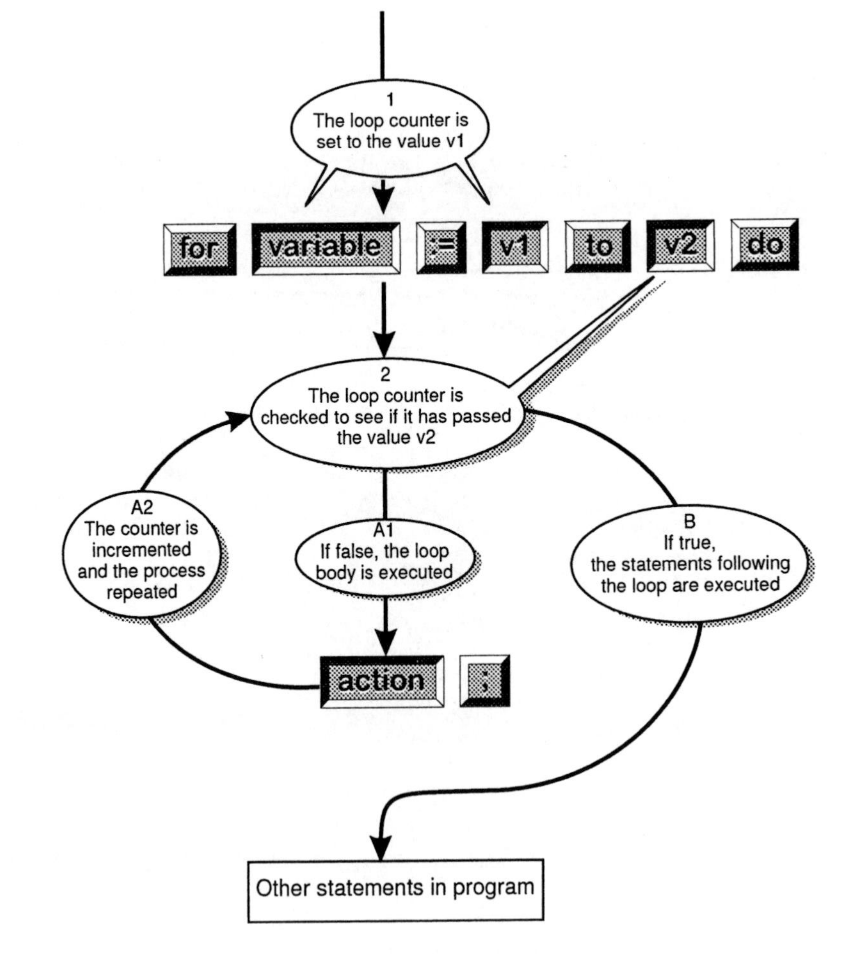


**FIG-3.8**

Executing a `for` Loop.

The same logic can be implemented in a `while` loop as:

```
count := 1;               {Set counter to start value (v1)}
while count <= 10 do      {Check if upper limit (v2) passed}
begin
    write('Enter mark : ');     {Execute loop body}
    readln(mark);
    total := total + mark;
    count := count + 1;         {Add 1 to counter}
end;
```

**Activity 3.12**

What output will be produced from the code below:

```
for nbr := 0 to 5 do
    writeln(nbr);
```

Like the `while` loop, when the loop body is constructed from more than one statement, those statements must be enclosed within the terms `begin..end`.

## A Second Form of the `for` Statement

As an alternative to adding one to the loop counter on each iteration, it is also possible to subtract 1. This is done by replacing the keyword `to` with `downto`. Hence, we could display the descending values of variable *count* as it began at 10 and reduced through each iteration to 1 by the statements:

```
for count := 10 downto 1 do
    writeln(count);
```

This is equivalent to the following logic:

```
count := 10;              {Set counter to start value (v1)}
while count >= 1 do       {Check if upper limit (v2) passed}
begin
    write(count);         {Execute loop body}
    count := count - 1;   {Subtract 1 to counter}
end;
```

## Non-Numeric `for` Loops

The `for` loop isn't restricted to using integer variables as loop counters, it is also possible to construct a `for` loop using a character variable. For example, we could display the letters of the alphabet using the code:

This code assumes *ch* has been declared as a `char` variable

```
for ch := 'A' to 'Z' do
    writeln(ch);
```

However, `for` loops cannot use *real* or *string* variables as loop counters.

## Other Variations

The start and finish values of a `for` loop can be variables or expressions. So, for example, a loop containing the lines:

```
write('Enter range of values to be displayed(lowest highest) :');
readln(lo,hi);
for c := lo to hi do
    writeln(c);
```

will display all the values between *lo* and *hi*.

**Activity 3.13**

If *lo* and *hi* in the above code were entered as the values -2 and 3, how often would the loop body be executed?

When the start and finish values of the `for` loop are given as variables, it is possible to have a situation where both values are the same (e.g. *lo* = 6 and *hi* = 6). In this case, the loop body is executed exactly once.

A second possibility is that the finish value is lower than the start value (e.g. *lo* = 12 and *hi* = 3). This time the loop body will not be executed at all and control will jump to the first statement following the `for` loop.

When an expression is used for the start and/or finish values such as in the code

```
for c:= 1 to hi * 3 + 2 do
```

the machine determines the start and finish values of the `for` loop by calculating the value of the expression(s) involved before execution of the loop begins. It will not recalculate these values on each iteration of the loop. Sometimes it would be useful if we could get the loop counter to increment by more than one on each iteration. For example, if we wanted to display the 3 times table from 1x3 to 12x3 this would be easy if we could get the loop counter to increment through the sequence 3, 6, 9, 12, etc. adding 3 each time. Unfortunately Pascal does not allow loop counters to be incremented in this way. However, we can get round the problem using the following logic:

```
FOR c := 1 to 12 DO
    Set nbr to 3 * c
    Display nbr
ENDFOR
```

**Activity 3.14**

Using the above logic, write a Pascal program to output the 3 times table.

When a `for` loop is complete, you should not assume that its loop counter has any specific value. For example, if a program contains the code

```
for c := 1 to 12 do
    writeln(c);
```

it would be wrong to assume that *c* will contain the value 13 after the loop is complete. Strictly speaking, the value of a loop counter is undefined when the loop has been completed.

Another situation to avoid is changing the loop counter in any way within the loop body. For example, the code

```
for c:= 1 to 12 do
    c := c - 1;
```

will lead to a lot of trouble!

## Structured English Equivalents

TABLE 3.7 gives some Structured English FOR loop examples and their equivalent Pascal code.

**TABLE-3.7**

`for` Structures

| Structured English | Pascal |
|---|---|
| Set total to zero<br>FOR each value between 1 and 10 DO<br>    Add value to total<br>ENDFOR | total := 0;<br>for c := 1 to 10 do<br>    total := table + c; |
| Set total to zero<br>Get no of students<br><br>FOR each student DO<br><br>    Get student's mark<br><br>    Display student's mark<br>    Add student's mark to total<br>ENDFOR<br>Calculate average as<br>    total/no of students | total := 0;<br>write('How many students:');<br>readln(noofstudents);<br>for c:= 1 to noofstudents do<br>begin<br>    write('Enter mark : ');<br>    readln(mark);<br>    writeln(mark);<br>    total := total + mark;<br>end;<br>average := total/noofstudents; |

## The Structure of the `for` Statement

The structure of the `for` statement is shown in FIG-3.9.

**FIG-3.9**

The `for` Statement

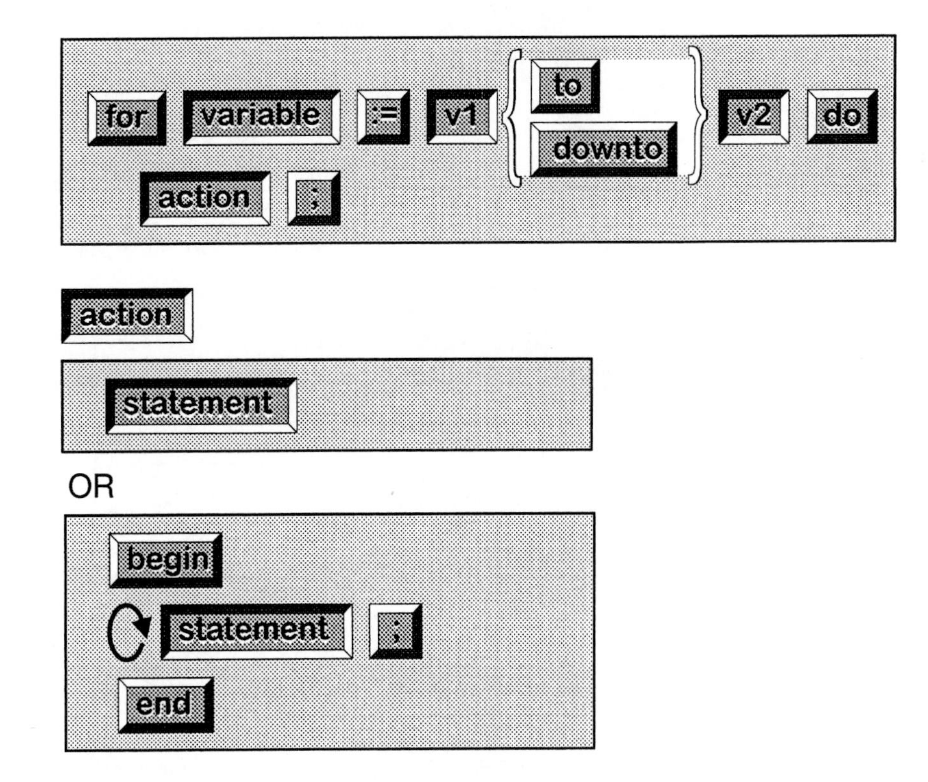

# Jump Statements

Statements which transfer the flow of control to some other part of a program are classified as **jump** statements. There are three such statements available in Borland Pascal: `break`, `continue`, and `goto`. Of these, `break` and `continue` were introduced in version 7.0, so if you're using an earlier version, these won't be available to you.

## The `break` Statement

The `break` statement can be used in any of the loop structures to allow early termination of the loop. For example, where we require to read in a maximum of 10 numbers, but with the possibility of terminating sooner if a zero is entered, we can use the code:

```
for c := 1 to 10 do
begin
    write('Enter value ',c,': ');
    readln(nbr);
    if nbr = 0 then
         break;     {*** for loop terminated by this statement}
    total :=  total + nbr;
end;
writeln(;Total was ',total,' after ',c,' numbers');
```

Included in the code is the conditional statement

```
if nbr = 0 then
     break;
```

which, when its expression `nbr = 0` is *true*, will cause control to jump to the `writeln` statement following the `for` loop body, hence terminating the execution of the loop (see FIG-3.10).

**FIG-3.10**

Executing the `break` Statement

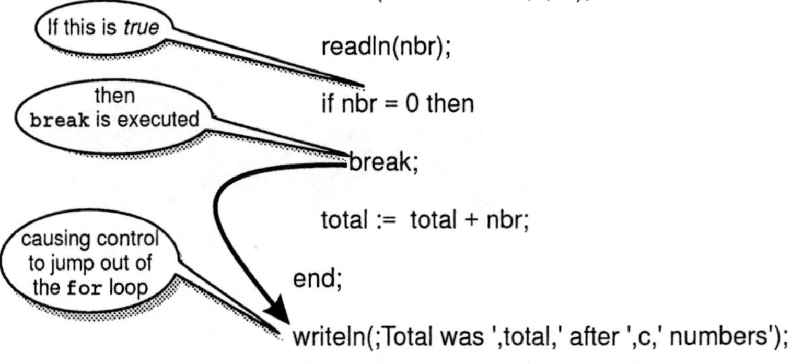


In general, the use of `break` in the manner described above is not considered good technique and should be avoided by rewriting the code.

## The continue Statement

The term `continue` is another statement which can be included in any loop structure. When executed, the `continue` statement causes the remaining statements in the current iteration of the loop to be skipped and transfers control back to the start of the loop. If `continue` is used within a `for` loop, the loop counter will be incremented (or decremented if it's a `downto` loop) before control returns to the start of the loop. If the loop is a `repeat` loop, the exit condition will be tested before returning to the start of the loop.

The following code accepts 10 numbers, summing those which are positive.

```
total := 0;
for c := 1 to 10 do
begin
    write('Enter number : ');
    readln(nbr);
    if nbr <= 0 then
        continue;
    total := total + nbr;
end;
writeln('Total of positive values entered is ',total);
```

Where `no <= 0` is *true* the remainder of the loop body, `total := total + no`, will be bypassed but the loop counter, *c*, will be incremented before control returns to the beginning of the loop. Hence, the `for` structure will terminate after 10 iterations irrespective of how often the `continue` statement is executed (see FIG-3.11).

**FIG-3.11**

The `continue` Statement

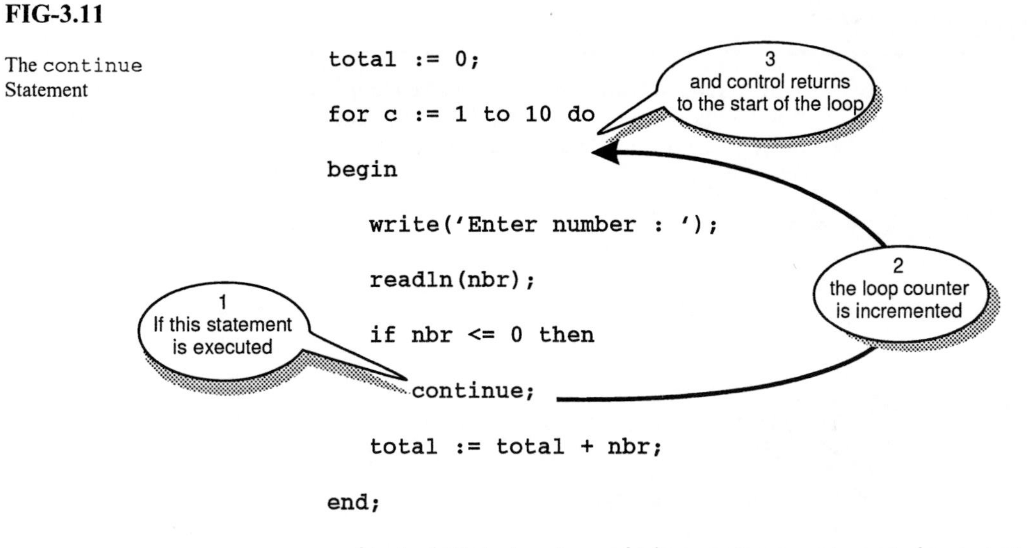
total := 0;
for c := 1 to 10 do
begin
write('Enter number : ');
readln(nbr);
if nbr <= 0 then
continue;
total := total + nbr;
end;
writeln('Total of positive values entered is ',total);
1
If this statement
is executed
2
the loop counter
is incremented
3
and control returns
to the start of the loop

> **Activity 3.15**
>
> Write a section of Pascal code using a `repeat..until` loop that makes use of the `continue` statement to accept and sum exactly 10 positive integers.
> The new total should be displayed each time a number is added.

Like `break`, `continue` should be avoided since it makes a program difficult to follow and debug.

### The goto Statement

The goto statement transfers control to a specified line of code. The destination line is identified by preceding it by a label. A label is any valid name followed by a colon.

```
total := 0;
for c := 1 to 10 do
begin
    readln(nbr);
    if (nbr = 0) and (c = 1) then {goto finish if first}
        goto finish;              {number is zero}
    total := total + nbr;
end
average := total / c;
writeln('Average is ',average:0:2);
finish:                          {label for goto statement}
writeln('Program terminated');
```

It is also possible to jump to a label given earlier in the program code but since this creates a looping situation it would be more appropriate to use one of the iterative statements (while, repeat..until or for).

Unlike break and continue, which can only be used inside control structures, the goto statement can be used anywhere in a program. Nevertheless, most guides to good programming technique would suggest its use should be avoided.

## Nested Loops

A common requirement is to produce nested loops, that is situations where one loop control structure appears within another. For example, if we want to read in and average six exam marks, each of which needs to be in the range 0 to 100, we could describe this logic as:

```
1. Set total to zero
2. FOR each exam DO
3.     Get valid mark
4.     Add mark to total
5. ENDFOR
6. Calculate average as total/6
7. Display average
```

This appears to have only a single loop structure beginning at statement 2 and ending at statement 5. However, if we add detail to statement 3, this gives us

```
3. Get valid mark
   3.1 Read mark
   3.2 WHILE mark is invalid DO
   3.3     Display"Mark must be between zero and 100"
   3.4     Read mark
   3.5 ENDWHILE
```

which, if placed in the original solution, results in

```
1.  Set total to zero
2.  FOR each exam DO
3.1     Read mark
3.2     WHILE mark is invalid DO
3.3         Display"Mark must be between zero and 100"
3.4         Read mark
3.5     ENDWHILE
4.      Add mark to total
5.  ENDFOR
```

```
6.  Calculate average as total/6
7.  Display average
```

giving a nested loops structure, where a WHILE loop appears inside a FOR loop.

> **Activity 3.16**
>
> Write the Pascal code for the Structured English above.

## Nested FOR Loops

Perhaps the most troublesome situation for someone just getting started in programming is where `for` loops are nested. The following example demonstrates the characteristics of such a structure. Consider the first two digits of a car's odometer. They begin set to 00. As the car moves, the least-significant digit (*units*) increments while the most significant digit (*tens*) remains unchanged (see FIG-3.12). But when the *units* value reaches 9, the *tens* value increments and the *units* is reset to zero (see FIG-3.13).

**FIG-3.12** Incrementing the Inner Loop Counter

**FIG-3.13** Incrementing the Outer Loop Counter

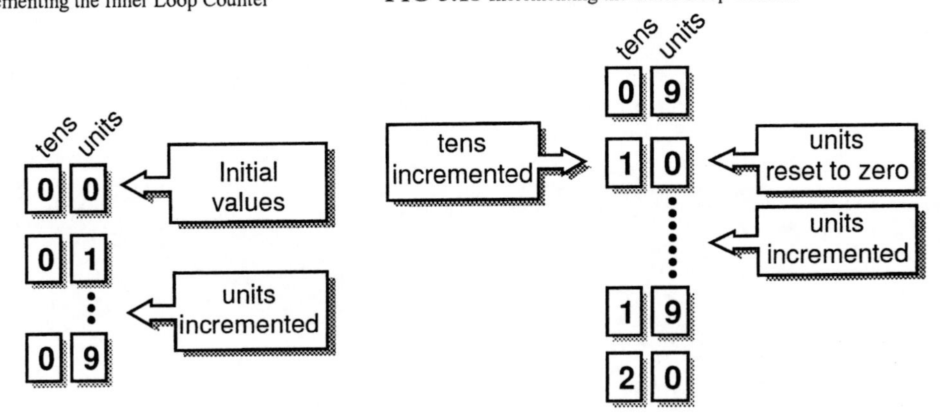


This process continues, with the *tens* value being incremented once for every ten increments of the units.

This situation is matched exactly by the code below:

```
units, tens : integer;

for tens := 0 to 9 do
    for units := 0 to 9 do
        writeln(tens:3, units:3);
```

The *tens* loop is known as the **outer loop**, while the *units* loop is known as the **inner loop**.

A few points to note about nested `for` loops:

1. The inner loop increments fastest.
2. Only when the inner loop is complete does the outer loop variable increment.
3. The inner loop variable is reset to its starting value each time the outer loop counter is incremented.

A common mistake, when implementing nested loops, is to use the same loop counter variable name in both `for` structures:

```
for count := 1 .....
{
        .
        .
    for count := 1 ......
```

This makes it impossible to maintain two independent counts for both the inner and outer loops - leading to disastrous results.

**Activity 3.17**

What would be the output of the following code?

```
for nol := -2 downto 1 do
    for no2 := 0 to 6 do
        writeln(nol:3, no2:3);
```

## Translating from Structured English

The nested iterative structures seen in the Structured English of Chapter 1 can be produced by simple translation. Where 10 students each sit six exams with a maximum possible mark of 100 for each exam, we can calculate each student's average mark using the following logic:

```
FOR each student DO
    Set total to zero
    FOR each exam DO
        Get mark
        WHILE mark is invalid DO
            Display "Mark must be in the range 0 to 100"
            Get mark
        ENDWHILE
        Add mark to total
    ENDFOR
    Calculate average as total / 6 (rounded)
    Display student number and average
ENDFOR
```

The corresponding code is:

```
var
    student, exam, mark, total, average : integer;

for student := 1 to 10 do
begin
    total := 0;
    for exam := 1 to 6 do
    begin
        write('Enter mark for exam ',exam' : ');
        readln(mark);
        while (mark < 0) or (mark > 100) do
        begin
            writeln('Mark must be in the range 0 to 100');
            readln(mark);
        end
        total := total + mark;
    end;
    average := round(total / 6);
    writeln('The average for student ',student,' was ',average);
end;
```

## `continue` and `break` in Nested Structures

Where `continue` or `break` is used in an inner control structure, as in the code below,

```
for j := 1 to 3 do
begin
    total := 0;
    for c := 1 to 10 do
    begin
        write('Enter number : ');
        readln(no);
        if no <= 0 then
            continue;
        total := total + no;
    end;
    writeln('Total of positive values entered is ',total);
end;
```

when the jump statement is executed, only the control structure in which the jump is placed is affected. For example, in the code above, if the 14th number entered was negative (at which point $j = 2$ and $c = 4$) $c$ would be incremented and control would return to the start of the inner loop. The loop counter would then be $j = 2$ and $c = 5$.

**Activity 3.18**

What results would be produced from the code

```
total := 0;
for m := 1 to 3 do
    for n := 1 to 5 do
    begin
        write('Enter number : ');
        readln(no);
        if no = 0 then
            break;
        total := total + no;
    end
writeln(total);
```

if the values entered are 6,0,3,1,0,0,7,8,0,5,0?

**Activity 3. 19**

1. Write a program that will output the numbers 1 to 7 three times. The first set of values should be output using a `for` loop; the second using a `repeat..until`; and the third using `while`.

2. Write a program that inputs numbers (positive or negative) one at a time. Each number is to be added to a total and the process continued until the total exceeds 100. Finally, display the total.

```
OUTLINE LOGIC:
    Set total to zero
    REPEAT
        Get a number
        Add number to total
    UNTIL total > 100
    Display total
```

**Continued on next page**

**Activity 3.19** (continued)

3. Write a program to display all numbers between 1 and 20 which are not divisible by 4 or 5.
   HINT: a number (*x*) is exactly divisible by some other number (*y*) when *x* divided by *y* gives no remainder.

```
OUTLINE LOGIC:
    FOR no := 1 TO 20 DO
        IF no is not divisible by 4 or 5 THEN
            Display no
        ENDIF
    ENDFOR
```

4. Write a program to read in two values (*column* and *line*) and place the character 'x' at the specified column and row on the screen. Check that *column* is between 1 and 80, the *line* between 1 and 24.

```
OUTLINE LOGIC:
    Get column
    WHILE column outside range 1 to 80 DO
        Display error message
        Get column
    ENDWHILE
    Get line
    WHILE line outside the range 1 to 24 DO
        Display error message
        Get line
    ENDWHILE
    Clear screen (move cursor to top left of screen)
    FOR line-1 times DO
        Move down one line
    ENDFOR
    Set width of display to column
    Display 'x'
```

5. One method of testing if a value is divisible by 37 is to split the value into groups of 3 digits which are then added. If the resulting sum is divisible by 37 then so is the original.
   e.g. 143412 = 143 + 412 = 555.
   Program this test and print an appropriate message.

```
OUTLINE LOGIC:
    Set sum to zero
    Get number
    WHILE number is not zero DO
        Extract the three least significant digits of number
        Add this extracted value to sum
        Remove the three least significant digits from number
    ENDWHILE
    IF sum is exactly divisible by 37 THEN
        Display "Value divisible by 37"
    ELSE
        Display "Value not divisible by 37"
    ENDIF
```

**Continued on next page**

**Activity 3.19** (continued)

6. The number of ways that *r* objects can be chosen from *n* objects is given by the formula

$$^{n}C_{r} = n!/((n-r)!*r!)$$

Write a program to read *r* and *n* (validate that $r < n$) and print the result.
NOTE: *r!* is pronounced *r* factorial and is *r * (r-1) * (r-2) *...... *1*

```
OUTLINE LOGIC:
    Get value for n
    Get value for r
    WHILE r>= n DO
        Display error message
        Get value for n
        Get value for r
    ENDWHILE
    Set factorialn to 1
    FOR I := 2 TO n DO
        Multiply factorialn by I
    ENDFOR
    Set factorialr to 1
    FOR I := 2 TO r DO
        Multiply factorialr by I
    ENDFOR
    Set factorialn_r to 1
    FOR I := 2 TO n-r DO
        Multiply factorialn_r by I
    ENDFOR
    Calculate nCr as factorialn /(factorialn_r*factorialr
    Display nCr
```

7. In ice skating, a number of judges (*N*) award marks. The highest and lowest of these are ignored and the others averaged to give a result. Write a program to input *N*, followed by *N* marks, and display the average score. Scores range from 0.0 to 6.0 in increments of 0.1.

```
OUTLINE LOGIC:
    Get first score
    Set highest_score to score
    Set lowest_score to score
    Set total to score
    Get value for N
    FOR N-1 times DO
        Get score
        Add score to total
        IF score is greater than highest_score THEN
            Set highest_score to score
        ELSE
            IF score is less than lowest_score THEN
                Set lowest_score to score
            ENDIF
        ENDIF
    ENDFOR
    Subtract highest_score and lowest_score from total
    Calculate average as total/(N-2)
    Display average
```

**Continued on next page**

**Activity 3.19** (continued)

8. If $X_i$ is an approximation of the cube root of $N$ then a closer approximation is:

$$X_{i+1} = (N/X_i^2 + 2X_i)/3$$

Write a program to calculate the cube root to 5 decimal places.

```
OUTLINE LOGIC:
    Get a value for N
    Set newx to N/3
    REPEAT
        Set oldx to newx
        Calculate newx as (N/(oldx*oldx)+2*oldx)/3
    UNTIL N-newx*newx*newx < 0.000005 AND
            newx*newx*newx - N < 0.000005
    Display newx
```

9. Making use of the date program written earlier, write a program which allows any date to be entered and the calendar for the month involved displayed in the form

| Sun | Mon | Tue | Wed | Thu | Fri | Sat |
|---|---|---|---|---|---|---|
| | | | | 1 | 2 | 3 |
| 4 | 5 | 6 | 7 | 8 | 9 | 10 |
| 11 | 12 | 13 | 14 | 15 | 16 | 17 |
| 18 | 19 | 20 | 21 | 22 | 23 | 24 |
| 25 | 26 | 27 | 28 | 29 | 30 | |

```
OUTLINE LOGIC:
    Get date
    Calculate day of week on which first day of month fell
    Display table heading
    Position cursor in correct column
    Display 1
    Display other day numbers on row 1
    Display numbers in subsequent rows
```

# Summary

■ **Iteration Structures**

**while**

```
        while condition do
            action
```

**repeat..until**

```
        repeat
            statement(s)
        until condition;
```

**for**

```
        for counter := start to finish do
            action
    or
        for counter := start downto finish do
            action
```

```
action
    statement;
  or
    begin
      statement;
          .
      statement;
    end
```

- **In the `while` structure,** *condition* is evaluated before each iteration of the loop body.
- The `while` loop body may be iterated a minimum of zero times.
- **The `while` loop terminates** when *condition* is *false.*
- **In the `repeat..until` structure,** *condition* is evaluated after each iteration of the loop body.
- **The `repeat..until` body** may be iterated a minimum of once.
- **The `repeat..until` loop terminates** when *condition* is *true.*
- **In the `for` structure,** the loop counter can be any ordinal type.
- **The `for` loop body** may be iterated a minimum of zero times.
- **The `for` loop's counter** is incremented (when using `to`) or decremented (when using `downto`) at the end of each iteration.
- **The `for` loop terminates** when the *finish* value is reached or exceeded.
- **Using `break` in an iterative structure** transfers control to the first statement following the loop.
- **Using `continue` in an iterative structure** transfers control to the end of the action defined in the loop body. However, the loop itself is not exited.
- **Using `continue` in an iterative structure** transfers control to the end of the action defined in the loop body. However, the loop itself is not exited.
- **Where loops are nested,** `break` and `continue` affect only the loop body in which they are used. That is, if they are defined in the inner loop control will be transferred to the end of that inner loop's body (`continue`); or to the first statement following the inner loop (`break`).
- **`goto` transfers control** to the specified label at some other point in the program.
- **`goto` can transfer control either to an earlier or later point** in the program code.
- **Use of `break`, `continue` or `goto` (especially `goto`) should be avoided** where possible since they can result in hard-to-follow code and violate guidelines of structured programming.

# TESTING CONTROL STRUCTURES

In an ideal world we would check our programs by entering every possible value and combination of values as test data. However, this is not practical even for simple programs since the time and effort required is prohibitive. Instead, a compromise is required.

One strategy used to test a piece of code is to create test data based on the structure of that code, the aim being to pick relevant test values each of which checks different parts of the code. This technique is called **white box** or **glass box** testing - so called, because we need to look at the internal structure of the program in order to create appropriate test values.

A minimum requirement of white box testing is that every statement in the code is executed by the test data. However, as we will see, this is a relatively poor strategy which can be improved on.

## Testing Sequences

To test a sequence of statements such as

```
write('Enter a number : ');
readln(no1, no2);
result := no1 * no2;
writeln(no1,' * ',no2,' = ',result);
```

we need only one set of test values (in this example that could be 12 and 2). This will result in all statements being executed.

## Testing Selection

### Simple `if` Statements

The simplest selection statement is an `if` statement without an `else` option. For example:

```
var
    nbr : integer;
begin
    write('Enter number : ');
    readln(nbr);
    if nbr < 0 then
        writeln('This is a negative value');
```

Although we can ensure that all parts of this statement are executed by using any value for *nbr* which results in the expression `nbr < 0` evaluating to *true*, it is also important to test the structure where the expression evaluates to *false*. Why is this?

Consider the code:

```
var
    no1, no2, ans : real;
begin
    write('Enter two numbers : ');
    readln(no1, no2);
    if no2 <> 0 then
        ans := no1 / no2;
    writeln(no1:0:2,' / ',no2:0:2,' = ',ans:0:2);
```

The code is meant to perform a division operation only if the divisor is not zero.

If we test this code by entering the values 6 and 2, the result will be 3 and all the statements will have been executed.

However, if we use the values 6 and 0, since the statement `ans := no1 / no2;` will not be executed, *ans* will not be assigned a value and the resulting output will be unpredictable.

Obviously, we want to detect such problems while testing the code. It is therefore important that even simple `if` statements are tested with two sets of data: one which evaluates the expression as *true*; the other giving a *false* result.

## `if .. else` Structures

Where an `else` is used, the need to test for both *true* and *false* situations is more obvious since this is the only way to execute all the instructions in the control structure. Hence, we might test the code

```
if nbr < 0 then
    writeln('Negative')
else
    writeln('Positive or zero');
```

with the values *nbr* = -8 and *nbr* = 3.

## Other Boolean Expressions

In Pascal, Boolean expressions turn up in other commands such as:

```
days_in_month = 28 + integer(year mod 4 = 0);
```

Statements such as these need to be treated like `if` statements and hence should be tested with values which give both *true* and *false* results for the expression involved.

## Nested `if` Statements

Since the path taken through an `if` statement is dependent on the truth of the statement's expression, where two `if` statements are nested, there are three possible paths. For example, in the code

```
if sex = M then
    if age >= 65 then
        writeln('Retired')
    else
        writeln('Working')
else
    writeln('Female');
```

we can identify the possible truth combinations for the expressions (`sex = 'M'`) and (`age >= 65`) (see TABLE-3.8).

**TABLE-3.8**

Possible combinations for Two Boolean Expressions

| Expression | |
|---|---|
| (sex = 'M') | (age >= 65) |
| TRUE | TRUE |
| TRUE | FALSE |
| FALSE | TRUE |
| FALSE | FALSE |

The last two combinations (*false,true* and *false,false*) execute the same section of code

```
else
    writeln('Female');
```

and hence we need only three combinations of data values to test the above code.

**Activity 3.20**

In the code

```
if sex = 'M' then
    if age >= 65 then
        writeln('Male retired')
    else
        writeln('Male working')
else
    if age >= 60 then
        writeln('Female retired')
    else
        writeln('Female working');
```

1. List all the conditions being tested.
2. How many *true/false* combinations are possible for the expressions involved?
3. How many combinations of test data are required to test all possible paths through the code?

## Complex Boolean Expressions

Where a Boolean expression is complex (i.e. contains linking AND or OR operators), as in

```
if (sex = 'M') and (age >= 65) then
    writeln('Male retired');
```

it is important to create test data which gives all possible combinations of *true* and *false* from the individual component of the Boolean expression. Hence, for the expression `(sex = 'M') and (age >= 65)`, test values resulting in each of the four possibilities shown in TABLE-3.8 are required.

Why is it important to perform all possible combinations?

Consider the situation where we had mistakenly written the above code as

```
if (sex = 'M') or (age >= 65) then
    writeln('Male retired');
```

using `or` rather than `and` to link the expressions.

The test data *sex = 'M', age = 66* (*true,true*) and *sex = 'F', age = 23* (*false,false*) would test both *true* and *false* options of the `if` statement without showing up any problems. However, by including the other combinations, for example, with the test data *sex = 'M', age = 45* (*true,false*) and *sex = 'F', age = 70* (*false,true*), the error in the code will be detected.

### `case` Statements

Since a `case` statement is equivalent to a series of mutually exclusive `if` statements, testing requires values corresponding to each of the labelled options as well as the `else` option. For example, given the code

```
case day of
    0:  writeln('Sunday');
    1:  writeln('Monday');
    2:  writeln('Tuesday');
    3:  writeln('Wednesday');
    4:  writeln('Thursday');
    5:  writeln('Friday');
    6:  writeln('Saturday');
    else
        writeln('Invalid value for day');
end;
```

then the test values required for *day* will be 0,1,2,3,4,5,6 and some invalid value, say, -1.

Where a `case` statement contains no `else` option we must still test the structure with a value that does not match any of the labels given.

Where two or more `case` options execute the same code, each `case` value should be tested separately. Hence, the section of code

```
a,e,i,o,u: writeln('Vowel');
```

would require that the values *a,e,i,o,u* are all used as part of the test data.

If a range of continouous values are used in a label, as in

```
1..5 : writeln('Cold');
```

it is sufficient to test that option using the lowest and highest value stated. Here that would be 1 and 5.

# Testing Iteration

### Infinite Loops

Iteration instructs the machine to carry out a sequence of instructions repeatedly. In order to stop this looping, the program must contain a loop-terminating condition. For example, in the code

```
readln(nbr);
while nbr > 10 do
    nbr := nbr - 1;
```

iteration of the single statement, `nbr := nbr - 1`, terminates when *nbr* is less than or equal to 10. No matter what value we enter, iteration will eventually halt. On the other hand, the code

```
readln(nbr);
while nbr <> 10 do
    nbr := nbr - 1;
```

may never exit if we give *nbr* a starting value of less than 10.

This situation is known as an **infinite loop**. If you are unlucky, you may have to reboot your computer to get out of this situation once your program has begun executing.

Infinite looping can occur in any of the three loop structures in Pascal.

We can minimise the chances of an infinite loop by checking that some of the code within the loop body has an affect on the loop's exit-condition in such a way that looping will eventually terminate.

## Testing `for` Loops

Where a `for` loop is coded for a fixed number of iterations, such as in the code

```
total := 0;
for c := 1 to 5 do
begin
    write('Enter number : ');
    readln(nbr);
    total := total + nbr
end;
writeln('Average is ', total / 5 :0:2);
writeln('Last number entered was ',nbr);
```

we have no influence over the number of times the loop will be executed and hence, only the five values required to be input need be supplied as test data.

However, it is important that we check that such loops do actually execute the expected number of times since either the upper or lower limit could have been coded incorrectly. For example,

```
for c := 0 to 5 do      {starts at zero instead of 1}
```

will result in the loop iterating six, rather than five times.

Loops which iterate either one too few, or one too many times are so common that these errors are often tested for explicitly.

If the `for` loop uses a variable to express the finish value, as in

```
total := 0;
write('How many values are to be entered : ');
readln(m);
for c := 1 to m do
begin
    write('Enter number : ');
    readln(nbr);
    total := total + no
end;
writeln('Average is ', total / m :0:2);
writeln('Last number entered was ',no);
```

we can influence the number of times the `for` loop is executed. In this situation, test data should be produced to execute the loop structure, zero, one and multiple times. For the example above, that would mean values of 0,1 and, perhaps, 4 for the variable *m*.

Not only do such checks ensure that the loop does not execute too many or too few times, but they also highlight certain errors which only appear when a loop is executed a specific number of times. For example, the code above will result in a run-time error when $m = 0$ and hence the loop iterates zero times. This is because the expression (*total / m*) will give a division-by-zero fault.

**Activity 3.21**

1. Identify the error(s) in the following code:

```
var
    total, m, c, nbr : integer;
begin
    readln(m);
    for c := 1 to m do
    begin
        total := 0;
        write('Enter number : ');
        readln(nbr);
        total := total + nbr
    end;
    if m > 0 then
    begin
        writeln('Average is ',(total / m):0:2);
        writeln('Last number entered was ',no);
    end
end.
```

2. In which case(s) will the above error be detected?
    a) During zero iterations test
    b) During one iteration test
    c) During multiple iterations test

### Testing `while` and `repeat..until` Loops

The `while` loop contains an entry-condition at the beginning of the loop body and, as such, is fundamentally the same structure as a `for` loop. The two structures should therefore be tested in the same fashion with test data to perform zero, one and multiple iterations.
On the other hand, the `repeat..until` loop has the exit-condition placed at the end of the loop structure. This means that it is not possible to test for zero iterations but one and multiple iterations should still be tested.

# Testing Complete Programs

Most programs will consist of a combination of control structures. To test the whole program, each control structure must be identified and test data constructed.
The following design describes a program which is intended to read in 10 values in the range 1 to 100 and count how many of the values entered are divisible by exactly 3 or 4. The logic required is shown below:

```
Set total to zero
FOR 10 times DO
    Read valid number
    IF number is divisible by 3 or 4 THEN
        Add 1 to total
    ENDIF
ENDFOR
IF any values were divisible by 3 or 4 THEN
    Display total
ELSE
     Display No values are divisible by 3 or 4"
ENDIF
```

The Pascal implementation of this logic is shown in LISTING-3.2.

**LISTING-3.2**

White Box Testing of a Program

```
program WhiteBoxTesting;
uses WinCrt;

var
  total  : integer;
  number : integer;
  count  : integer;

begin
  total := 0;
  for count := 1 to 10 do
  begin
      {***Read valid number ***}
      write('Enter number : ');
      readln(number);
      {*** While value entered is invalid re-enter it ***}
      while(number < 0) or (number > 100) do
      begin
          writeln('Invalid entry. Re-enter : ');
          readln(number);
      end;
      {*** If number divisible by 3 or 4 add 1 to total ***}
      if(number mod 3 = 0) or (number mod 4 = 0)then
          total := total + 1;
  end;
  {*** Display the total numbers divisible by 3 or 4 ***}
  if total > 0 then
      writeln('Number of values divisible by 3 or 4 :',total)
  else
      writeln('No values are divisible by 3 or 4')
end.
```

## Identifying the Test Requirements

**Activity 3.22**

Identify all selection and iteration control structures in LISTING-3.2.

We have two iterative and two selection structures in LISTING-3.2 to be tested.

Of these, the `for` structure is fixed to 10 iterations hence zero and one iteration tests are not possible.

The `while` structure contains multiple conditions and therefore, as well as being tested for zero, one, and multiple iterations, should also be tested for all possible combinations of *true* and *false* within the Boolean expression itself. Note that the combination *true, true* is not possible since *number* cannot be both less than zero and greater than 100 at the same time.

There are also two selection structures, both `if`'s.

The first of these also has a complex Boolean expression and this can be tested for all four possibilities.

The second `if` statement is a simple one and needs only *true* and *false* tests.

These test requirements are summarised in TABLE-3.9.

**TABLE-3.9**

White Box Test Requirements

| Structure to be tested | Purpose of test |
|---|---|
| `for count := 1 to 10 do` | Test multiple iterations |
| `while(number<0)or(number>100)` | Zero iterations<br>One iteration<br>Multiple iterations<br>true, false<br>false, true<br>false, false |
| `if(number mod 3=0)or(number mod 4=0)` | false, false<br>false, true<br>true, false<br>true, true |
| `if total > 0` | true<br>false |

## Choosing the Test Data

One data value may test several parts of the code. For example, if we assign the value 21 to *number* then the `while` loop

```
while (number < 0) or (number > 100)do
begin
     writeln('Invalid entry. Re-enter : ');
     readln(number);
end.
```

will be iterated zero times. Not only does this value perform the zero iterations test, but, since the Boolean expressions

```
        number < 0
and     number > 100
```

are both *false* when *number* is 21, this also tests the *false, false* combination for the expression `(number < 0) or (number > 100)`.

Once the `while` loop has been passed, the `if` statement

```
if(number mod 3 = 0) or (number mod 4 = 0) then
     total := total + 1;
```

will be executed. With *number* equal to 21, the first condition, `number mod 3 = 0` is *true* while, the second is *false*. Hence another of our test requirements is performed.

Since all of this code is within the `for` loop which is to be executed 10 times, other values must be chosen for *number* during subsequent iterations.

**Activity 3.23**

Write down a value for *number* which:

a) gives a *true/false* result for `while(number<0)or(number>100)`
b) gives a *false/false* result for `if(number mod 3=0)or(number mod 4=0)`

We need to continue this process of choosing values until all the required tests will be performed by the data. Each test value, the tests they are designed to perform and the expected results should then be listed in test documentation (see TABLE-3.10).

**TABLE-3.10**

White Box Test Data

| Run | Test Data | Reason for Test | Expected Result | Actual Result |
|---|---|---|---|---|
| 1 | number = | | | |
| | 21 | while iterated zero times | | |
| | | while false,false | | |
| | | if number mod 3... true,false | total = 1 | |
| | -6, 5 | while iterated once | -6 rejected with error | |
| | | while true,false | message | |
| | | if number mod 3... false,false | total unchanged | |
| | 101,-3,8 | while iterated more than once | 101 and -3 rejected | |
| | | while false,true | | |
| | | if number mod 3... false,true | total= 2 | |
| | 12 | if number mod 3... true,true | total= 3 | |
| | 100 | | total= 4 | |
| | 0 | | total unchanged | |
| | 1 | | total unchanged | |
| | 13 | | total unchanged | |
| | 31 | | total unchanged | |
| | 17 | | total unchanged | |
| | | for loop iterated 10 times | | |
| | | if total > 0 true | Displays | |
| | | | Number of values divisible | |
| | | | by 3 or 4 : 4 | |
| 2 | number = | | | |
| | 1 | | | |
| | 2 | | | |
| | 5 | | | |
| | 7 | | | |
| | 10 | | | |
| | 11 | | | |
| | 13 | | | |
| | 14 | | | |
| | 17 | | | |
| | 19 | if total > 0 false | Displays | |
| | | | No values are divisible | |
| | | | by 3 or 4 | |

There are a few points to note from TABLE-3.10 :

The RUN column refers to the program execution run number. This program will have to be run twice to test both options of the final `if` statement:

```
if total > 0 then
   writeln('Number of values divisible by 3 or 4 : ',total)
else
   writeln('No values are divisible by 3 or 4');
```

The TEST DATA column gives the values to be used when running the program. In this case, only one variable, *number*, needs to be supplied with a value. Where several variables are to be given values, the name of the variable to which a test value is to be assigned must be clearly stated in this column. Where a single variable is given more than one value on a single line (e.g. 101,-3,8), all but the last of these represent values which will be rejected by the input validation code.

The REASON FOR TEST column states the control structure and condition being tested by that specific test value.Where test data exercises a program condition already tested by an earlier piece of data, it need not be restated as a reason for test.

The EXPECTED RESULTS column states the expected reaction of the program to the data. This may specify the value to be taken by other variables or the output to be produced.

The ACTUAL RESULTS column is completed as the program is run. Hopefully, we may simply add an *as expected* message in this column with a reference to any printout produced during the test. But if the program should produce unexpected results, then this column should contain those results and reference made to other documentation detailing the error and the changes made to the program in attempting to correct that error.

If errors are detected during any test run, then all earlier test runs should be redone after corrections have been made. After all, the corrections may have introduced new errors. Where corrections have introduced new control structures or Boolean expressions, additional test data will have to be added.

> **Activity 3.24**
>
> Type in the program in LISTING-3.2 and run it using the test data given in TABLE-3.10.

# Debugging

Testing attempts to highlight errors in a program. When errors are discovered, their causes must be determined by examining the code and then changing the faults detected. This is known as **debugging**.

Borland supply several debugging aids to help track down errors in your code. Of these, the simplest and most useful are:

- Single step execution
- Watch facilities
- Breakpoints

## Single Step Execution

The debugging features may be activated by different keys in your version of Pascal. Check your manual for details.

Single stepping allows us to execute a program one line at a time. The program code appears on the screen and the next line to be executed is highlighted. A line of the program is executed each time the F8 key is pressed.

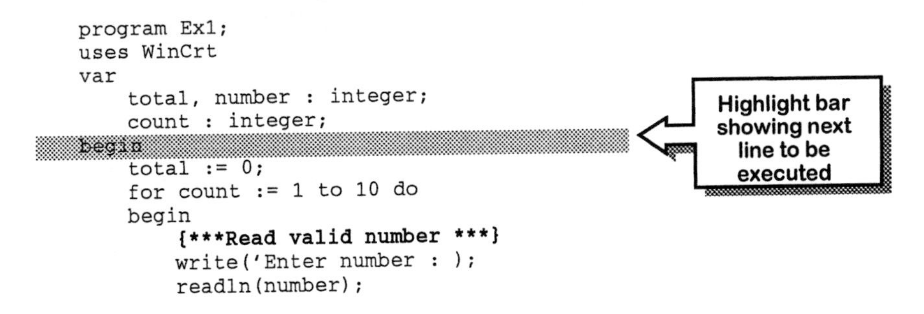

```
program Ex1;
uses WinCrt
var
    total, number : integer;
    count : integer;
begin
    total := 0;
    for count := 1 to 10 do
    begin
        {***Read valid number ***}
        write('Enter number : );
        readln(number);
```



This allows us to see which lines of code are being executed and hence allows us to detect when an unexpected route is taken through the program. For example, we may detect an `if` statement being treated as *true* when we were expecting it to be *false*.

Once the cause of an error has been detected we can halt execution of the program without running it to completion by choosing the PROGRAM RESET or TERMINATE PROGRAM option.

## The Watch Facility

A **watch** allows us to observe the value of any number of variables as the program executes. Hence we may see the value of *total* as our program counts the number of values divisible by 3 or 4.

The watch feature is switched on using the WATCH option in the DEBUG menu. This may be achieved using *Ctrl F7* or *Ctrl F5* depending on which version of Pascal you are using. The debugger prompts you for the name of the variable whose value is to be displayed.

Once chosen, the variable's value will be displayed as you single step your way through the program. Any changes in the variables value will be indicated instantly in the Watch window.

Any number of variables may be displayed.

## Breakpoints

Single stepping through a large program or one containing loop structures can sometimes be awkward and tedious. It may be that the part of the code we wish to step through is several hundreds of lines into the program. To avoid this time-consuming approach, we may set a breakpoint at any line in our program. Having set a breakpoint, we start execution of our program in the normal way. However, when the machine attempts to execute the line containing the breakpoint, we are returned to single-step mode at that point in the code.

To set a breakpoint, move the cursor to the line at which the break is required and press *Ctrl F8* or chose the SET BREAKPOINT option in the DEBUG menu.

Breakpoints may be made conditional. That is, they will only operate if a specified condition is **true** at the time the line containing the breakpoint is executed, otherwise the program continues normal execution.

When no longer required, breakpoints must be removed. This is done by returning the cursor to the line containing the breakpoint and again choosing the TOGGLE BREAKPOINT option in the DEBUG menu.

**Activity 3.25**

By placing a watch on *total*, and single-stepping through your program, find and correct the error in the program given in LISTING-3.2.

Does the correction require changes to the test data? If so, suggest additional test values; if no additional data is required, state why.

## Testing in this Book

As you can see, testing even a small piece of code is quite lengthy - and there are more testing techniques to cover yet! This means that, because of a lack of space, test data is generally missing or inadequate throughout this book.

# CASE STUDY

## The Problem

A program is required to allow the computer to be used as a simple calculator. The user should be able to enter simple expressions such as 10.1 * 10 and see the result displayed in the form *10.1*10=101.0* .

## Clarification

The program need only solve expressions with a single arithmetic operator. Any of the following may be used:

| | |
|---|---|
| + | Addition |
| - | Subtraction |
| * | Multiplication |
| / | Division |

Any other character entered as the operator should result in an error message being displayed.

Attempting division by zero should also result in an error message being displayed.

The program should continue to accept expressions until specifically terminated.

## The Algorithm

We begin with an overview of the solution:

```
1   Get expression
2   WHILE not terminating expression DO
3       Attempt to process expression
4       IF valid expression THEN
5           Display result
6       ENDIF
7       Get expression
8   ENDWHILE
```

These can then be expanded to give sufficient detail to produce the program code:

```
1   Get expression
    1.1 Clear screen
    1.2 Display prompt
    1.3 Get expression (value1 operator value2)

3   Attempt to process expression
    3.1 IF
    3.2     operator is +:
    3.3         Calculate result as value1 + value2
    3.4     operator is -:
    3.5         Calculate result as value1 - value2
    3.6     operator is *:
    3.7         Calculate result as value1 * value2
    3.8     operator is /:
    3.9         IF value2 isn't zero THEN
    3.10            Calculate result as value1 / value2
    3.11        ELSE
    3.12            Display "Divide by zero error"
    3.13        ENDIF
```

```
    3.14    ELSE
    3.15        Display "Invalid operator"
    3.16 ENDIF

7   Get expression
    7.1 Display prompt
    7.2 Get expression (value1 operator value2)
```

This gives us a final version of the logic from which to produce code:

```
1.1 Clear screen
1.2 Display prompt
1.3 Get expression (value1 operator value2)
2   WHILE not terminating expression DO
3.1     IF
3.2         operator is +:
3.3             Calculate result as value1 + value2
3.4         operator is -:
3.5             Calculate result as value1 - value2
3.6         operator is *:
3.7             Calculate result as value1 * value2
3.8         operator is /:
3.9             IF value2 isn't zero THEN
3.10                Calculate result as value1 / value2
3.11            ELSE
3.12                Display "Divide by zero error"
3.13            ENDIF
3.14        ELSE
3.15            Display "Invalid operator"
3.16    ENDIF
4       IF valid expression THEN
5           Display result
6       ENDIF
7.1     Display prompt
7.2     Get expression (value1 operator value2)
8   ENDWHILE
```

# The Program

**LISTING 3.3**

The Calculator Program

```
program Calculator;

{*********************************************************}
{* PROGRAM           : Calculator                        *}
{* AUTHOR            : Patricia Stamp                    *}
{* DATE              : 7/7/1998                          *}
{* VERSION           : 0.1                               *}
{* DESCRIPTION       : Calculates the result of single   *}
{*                     operator expressions              *}
{* HARDWARE          : PC Compatible                     *}
{* SOURCE            : Borland Pascal V7.0               *}
{*********************************************************}

uses WinCrt;

var
   value1, value2  : real;          {Values used in expression}
   op              : char;          {Expression operator}
   result          : real;          {Result of expression}
   valid           : boolean;       {Indicates validity of expression}
                                        {false - invalid}
                                        {true  - valid}
```

**Continued on next page**

**LISTING 3.3**
(continued)

The Calculator Program

The terminating value (-999) must be agreed and documented.

The expression has to be read in three parts. It would be easier for the user if we could avoid this.

Note that the program code differs from the design in that 'x' is accepted as an alternative to '*'. This is only acceptable if agreed with the customer and fully documented.

```
begin
   {*** Display options ***}
   ClrScr;
   writeln('OPERATIONS AVAILABLE');
   writeln('   +   Addition');
   writeln('   -   Subtraction');
   writeln('   *   Multiplication');
   writeln('   /   Division');
   writeln('Set first value to -999 to terminate the program');
   {*** Get expression ***}
   write('Enter first value : ');
   readln(value1);
   write('enter operator : ');
   readln(op);
   write('Enter second value : ');
   readln(value2);
   {*** While not terminating value, process expression ***}
   while value1 <> -999 do
   begin
        {*** Assume operation valid ***}
        valid := true;
        case op of
             '+':     {Add}
                  result := value1 + value2;
             '-':     {Subtract}
                  result := value1 - value2;
             '*','x': {Multiply}
                  result := value1 * value2;
             '/':     {Divide}
                  {*** If second value 0, division not allowed ***}
                  {*** and operation is invalid ***}
                  if value2 = 0 then
                  begin
                       writeln('Division by zero not allowed');
                       valid := false;
                  end
                  {*** otherwise perform division ***}
                  else
                       result := value1 / value2;
             else     {Invalid operator}
                  {*** Error message ***}
                  writeln('Invalid operator');
                  valid := false;
        end;
        {*** If valid expression, display result ***}
        if valid then
             writeln(value1:0:2,op:2,value2:0:2,'=',result:0:2);
        {*** Enter next expression ***}
        write('Enter first value : ');
        readln(value1);
        write('enter operator : ');
        readln(op);
        write('Enter second value : ');
        readln(value2);
   end
```

# Testing

By examining the program code we can identify several control structures:

Iteration:

```
while value1 <> -999 do
```

The `case` options:

```
'+':
'-':
'*':
'x':
'/':
else
```

If statements:

```
if value2 = 0 then

if valid then
```

To test the program we'll need to:

Execute the `while` loop zero, one and multiple times
Execute each `case` option and the `default` option in the `switch` statement
Execute each `if` statement for both *true* and *false* situations.

The test data is shown in TABLE-3.11.

**TABLE 3.11**

Test Data

| Run | Test Data | Reason for Test | Expected Result | Actual Result |
|---|---|---|---|---|
| 1 | value1 = -9999<br>op = '+'<br>value2 = 0 | while iterated zero times | Program terminates | |
| 2 | value1 = 6<br>op = '+'<br>value2 = 3<br>value1 = -9999<br>op = '*'<br>value2 = 0 | while iterated one time<br>case '+':<br>if valid , true | 6+3 = 9<br>Program terminates | |
| 3 | value1 = 7<br>op = '-'<br>value2 = 12<br>value1 = 9<br>op = '/'<br>value2 = 2<br>value1 = 7<br>op = '/'<br>value2 = 0<br>value1 = 8<br>op = '*'<br>value2 = 2<br>value1 = 3<br>op = 'x'<br>value2 = -6<br>value1 = 8<br>op = '?'<br>value2 = 1<br>value1 = -9999 | while iterated more than once<br>case '-':<br>case '/':<br>if value2 <> 0, false<br>if value2 <> 0, true<br>if valid , false<br>case '*':<br>case 'x':<br>case else<br>if valid , false | 7-12 = -5<br>9/2 = 4.5<br>Displays<br>Division by zero not allowed<br>8*2 = 16<br>3*-6 = -18<br>Displays<br>Invalid operator | |

**Activity 3.26**

Enter and run the program in LISTING 3.3 using the above test data.

# Problems

When using values containing fractions the results may be slightly out because of the inaccuracy that is unavoidable when storing real numbers in binary.

We have to enter expressions on three separate lines. For example:

```
12
+
3
```

It would be better if we could enter a more natural form such as:

```
12 + 3
```

Also the method of terminating the program is somewhat clumsy.

These problems cannot be easily avoided at this stage.

# SOLUTIONS

## Activity 3.1

```
3. let2 => no3
```

The conditional operator should be written as >=
a `char` variable cannot be compared with an `integer`

```
5. let1 <> 65
```

A `char` variable cannot be compared with an `integer`

```
6. s1 = good
```

The string constant, *good*, must be enclosed within single quotes

## Activity 3.2

True 3

## Activity 3.3

```
1. if weight > 16 then
2. if code <> 17850 then
3. if (mark >= 75) and (mark <= 85) then
4. if (option = 'C') and (key = masterkey then
5. if ((command = 'D') or (command = 'A')) and
     ↳(quantity >100) then
```

## Activity 3.4

```
if sex = 'M' then
    if age >= 65 then
        writeln('Retired male')
    else
        writeln('Male working')
else
    if age >= 60 then
        writeln('Retired female')
    else
        writeln('Female working');
```

## Activity 3.5

1.

```
program Act05_01;
uses WinCrt;

var
    no1, no2 : integer;
begin
    ClrScr;
    write('Enter two numbers : ');
    readln(no1, no2);
    if no1 = no2 then
        writeln('EQUAL')
    else
        writeln('NOT EQUAL');
end.
```

2.

```
program Act05_02;
uses WinCrt;

var
    rno1, rno2, ans : real;
begin
    ClrScr;
    write('Enter two numbers : ');
    readln(rno1, rno2);
    if rno2 <> 0 then
    begin
        ans := rno1 / rno2;
        writeln(rno1:0:2,'/',rno2:0:2,'=',ans:0:2);
    end
end.
```

3.

```
program Act05_03;
uses WinCrt;

var
    letter : char;
begin
    ClrScr;
    write('Enter uppercase character : ');
    readln(letter);
    if (letter='A')or(letter = 'E')or
    ↳(letter = 'I')or(letter = 'O')or(letter = 'U')
then
        writeln('VOWEL')
    else
        writeln('CONSONANT')
end.
```

4.

```
program Act05_04;
uses WinCrt;

var
    no1, no2 : integer;
begin
    ClrScr;
    write('Enter two numbers : ');
    readln(no1, no2);
    if no1 < no2 then
        writeln(no1)
    else
        if no2 < no1 then
            writeln(no2)
        else
            writeln('EQUAL')
end.
```

5.

```
program Act05_05;
uses WinCrt;

var
    {Date to be convert to day of week}
    day, month, year : integer;
    {Modified date values}
    M,CY,C,Y         : integer;
    {temporary variable}
    temp             : integer;
    {Day of week on which date falls}
    {0 = Sunday, 1 = Monday etc.}
    d                : integer;
begin
    {*** Clear screen ***}
    ClrScr;
    {*** Get date ***}
    write('Enter date in the form dd mm yyyy : ');
    readln(day, month, year);
    {*** Determine modified version of date ***}
    M  := (month + 9) mod 12 + 1;
    CY := year - M div 11;
    C  := CY div 100;
    Y  := CY mod 100;
    temp := Trunc(2.6 * M - 0.2);
    d := ((temp + day + Y + Y div 4 + C div 4 -
       ↳2 * C) mod 7 + 7) mod 7;
    {*** Display result ***}
    write(day, '/', month, '/', year, ' is a ');
    if d = 0 then
        writeln('Sunday')
    else if d = 1 then
        writeln('Monday')
    else if d = 2 then
        writeln('Tuesday')
    else if d = 3 then
        writeln('Wednesday')
    else if d = 4 then
        writeln('Thursday')
    else if d = 5 then
        writeln('Friday')
    else if d = 6 then
        writeln('Saturday');
end.
```

**Continued on next page**

## Activity 3.5 (continued)

6.

```
program Act05_06;
uses WinCrt;

var
    day, month, year              : integer;
                {Date on which Easter falls}
    k, a, b, c, q, p, m, d, n, e : integer;
                {Temporary variables}
begin
    {*** Get year ***}
    ClrScr;
    write('Enter year (4 digits): ');
    readln(year);
    {*** Calculate formula ***}
    k := year div 100;
    a := year mod 19;
    b := year mod 4;
    c := year mod 7;
    q := k div 4;
    p := (13 + 8 * k) div 25;
    m := (15 * p + k + q) mod 30;
    d := (19 * a + m) mod 30;
    n := (4 + k - q) mod 7;
    e := (2 * b + 4 * c + 6 * d + n) mod 7;
    if d + e <= 9 then
    begin
        day   := 22 + d + e;
        month := 3;
    end
    else if (d = 29) and (e = 6)then
    begin
        day   := 19;
        month := 4;
    end
    else if(d = 28) and (e = 6) and (a > 10) then
    begin
        day   := 18;
        month := 4;
    end
    else
    begin
        day   := d + e - 9;
        month := 4;
    end;
    {*** Display result ***}
    writeln('Easter Sunday falls on ', day, '/',
month, '/', year);
end.
```

## Activity 3.6

CREDIT
INVALID CODE

## Activity 3.7

```
program Act07_01;
uses WinCrt;

var
    day  : integer; {Day of week}
begin
    {*** Get day ***}
    ClrScr;
    write('Enter day as value between 0 and 6 : ');
    readln(day);
    {*** Display day of week ***}
    case day of
        0 : writeln('Sunday');
        1 : writeln('Monday');
        2 : writeln('Tuesday');
        3 : writeln('Wednesday');
        4 : writeln('Thursday');
        5 : writeln('Friday');
        6 : writeln('Saturday');
        else
            writeln('Invalid value for day')
end.
```

## Activity 3.8

```
program Act08_01;
uses WinCrt;
var
    day   : integer;    {Day of week}
    reply : string; {user's response to question}
begin
    {*** Get day ***}
    ClrScr;
    write('Enter day as a number between 0 and 6 : '
    ↳);
    readln(day);
    {*** Display day of week ***}
    case day of
        0 : writeln('Sunday');
        1 : writeln('Monday');
        2 : writeln('Tuesday');
        3 : writeln('Wednesday');
        4 : writeln('Thursday');
        5 : writeln('Friday');
        6 : begin
                {*** Ask if working ***}
                writeln('Saturday');
                write('Were you working? ');
                readln(reply);
                {*** Display response ***}
                if reply = 'YES' then
                    writeln('So sorry')
                else
                    writeln('Hope you had a nice day')
            end
        else
            writeln('Invalid value for day');
    end
```

## Activity 3.9

Division by zero results in a run-time error which terminates the program.

## Activity 3.10

```
program Act10_01;
uses WinCrt;
var
    pounds : real; {Money to be converted}
    amount : real; {Equivalent in target currency}
    target : char; {Target currency code}
begin
    {*** Get amount ***}
    ClrScr;
    write('Enter amount to be converted : ');
    readln(pounds);
    {*** Get target currency ***}
    writeln('What currency?');
    writeln(' $ - US dollar');
    writeln(' G - German mark');
    writeln(' F - French franc');
    readln(target);
    {*** Display day of week ***}
    case target of
        '$': writeln('£',pounds:0:2,' converts to $'
                    , (pounds*1.66):0:2);
        'G': writeln('£',pounds:0:2,' converts to D'
                    , (pounds*2.99):0:2);
        'F': writeln('£',pounds:0:2,' converts to F'
                    , (pounds*8.93):0:2);
        else
            writeln('Invalid target code');
    end
end.
```

## Activity 3.11

```
write('Enter previous value : ');
readln(previousvalue);
write('Enter current value : ');
readln(currentvalue);
while previousvalue <> currentvalue do
begin
    previousvalue := currentvalue;
    write('Enter current value : ');
    readln(currentvalue)
end;
```

## Activity 3.12

Output will be

0
1
2
3
4
5

## Activity 3.13

The loop counter would be given the values -2, -1 , 0, 1, 2, 3 on the various iterations of the loop. Hence, the loop would iterate 6 times.

## Activity 3.14

```
program Act14_01;
uses WinCrt;
var
    c   : integer;  {Loop counter}
    nbr : integer;  {value to display}
begin
    {*** Clear screen ***}
    ClrScr;
    {*** Display 3 times table ***}
    for c := 1 to 12 do
    begin
        nbr := c * 3;
        writeln(c:2,' * 3 = ',nbr:2);
    end
end.
```

## Activity 3.15

```
    count := 0;
    repeat
        write('Enter number : ');
        readln(nbr);
        if nbr <= 0 then
            continue;
        count := count + 1;
        sum := sum + nbr;
        writeln('Total now : ',sum);
    until count = 10;
```

## Activity 3.16

```
    total := 0;
    for exam := 1 to 5 do
    begin
        write('Enter mark : ');
        readln(mark);
        while (mark < 0) or (mark > 100) do
        begin
            writeln('Mark must be between 0 and 100');
            write('Re-enter mark : ');
            readln(mark);
        end;
        total := total + mark;
    end;
    average := round(total / 6);
    writeln('Average was ',average);
```

## Activity 3.17

There will be no output. The outer `for` loop has a starting value of -2 and a finishing value of 1. Since this is a `downto` loop, the counter starts at a value already beyond the finishing value, so the loop is bypassed.

## Activity 3.18

The output will be 10.

When a zero is encountered the inner loop will be terminated. Each time this happens, the outer loop's counter will be incremented. So, after three zeros, the `for` loops will be complete. By the time this happens, only 3 non-zero values will have been read and added to *total* : 6, 3 and 1, giving a total of 10.

## Activity 3.19

1.

```
program Act19_01;
uses WinCrt;

var
    c : integer;     {loop counter}
begin
    ClrScr;
    {*** Output using for ***}
    for c:= 1 to 7 do
        writeln(c);

    {*** Output using repeat until ***}
    c := 1;
    repeat;
        writeln(c);
        c := c + 1;
    until c > 7;

    {*** Output using while ***}
    c := 1;
    while c <= 7 do
    begin
        writeln(c);
        c := c + 1;
    end;
end.
```

2.

```
program Act19_02;
uses WinCrt;
var
    nbr   : integer;    {number input}
    total : integer;    {Total of values entered}

begin
    {*** Set total to zero ***}
    total := 0;
    ClrScr;
    repeat
        write('enter value : ');
        readln(nbr);
        total := total + nbr;
    until total >= 100;
    writeln('Total is ', total);
end.
```

3.

```
program Act19_03;
uses WinCrt;

var
    c : integer; {Loop counter}
begin
    ClrScr;
    writeln('The following numbers between 1'
        +' and 20 are not divisible by 4 or 5');
    for c := 1 to 20 do
        if (c mod 4 <> 0)and(c mod 5 <> 0)then
            writeln(c);
end.
```

4.

```
program Act19_04;
uses WinCrt;

var
    column, line : integer;
            {The screen position at which}
            {the character is to be displayed}
    c           : integer;  {Loop counter}
```

**Continued on next page**

## Activity 3.19 (continued)

4. (continued)

```
begin
    {*** Get valid position ***}
    ClrScr;
    write('Enter column : ');
    readln(column);
    while(column < 1) or (column > 80) do
    begin
        writeln('Invalid column. Must be '
          +'between 1 and 80. Please re-enter.');
        readln(column);
    end;
    write('Enter line : ');
    readln(line);
    while(line < 1) or (line > 80) do
    begin
        writeln('Invalid line. Must be '
          +'between 1 and 24. Please re-enter.');
        readln(line);
    end;
    {*** Output X on empty screen ***}
    ClrScr;
    for c := 1 to line-1 do
        writeln;
    writeln('x':column);
end.
```

5.

```
program Act19_05;
uses WinCrt;

var
    sum, nbr : longint;
begin
    {*** Set sum to zero ***}
    sum := 0;
    {*** Get number ***}
    ClrScr;
    write('Enter number : ');
    readln(nbr);
    {*** WHILE number not zero DO ***}
    while nbr <> 0 do
    begin
        {*** Extract last 3 digits & add to sum ***}
        sum := sum + nbr mod 1000;
        {*** Remove digits from original number ***}
        nbr := nbr div 1000;
    end;
    {*** Display appropriate message ***}
    if sum mod 37 = 0 then
        writeln('Value is divisible by 37')
    else
        writeln('Value is not divisible by 37');
end.
```

6.

```
program Act19_06;
uses WinCrt;

var
    n           : integer;{The total population}
    r           : integer;{Number of objects chosen}
    noofways    : longint;{Ways r chosen from n}
    c           : integer;{Loop counter}
    factorialn,
    factorialr,
    factorialnr : double; {Factorial results}
begin
    factorialn := 1;
    factorialr := 1;
    factorialnr := 1;
    ClrScr;
    write('Enter number of objects : ');
    readln(n);
    write('Enter number of objects to be chosen :');
    readln(r);
    while r > n do
    begin
        writeln('Number of objects chosen cannot '
          +'be greater than the total population');
        write('Enter number of objects : ');
        readln(n);
        write('Enter number of objects to be chosen :');
        readln(r);
    end;
    for c := 2 to n do
        factorialn := factorialn * c;
    for c := 2 to r do
        factorialr := factorialr * c;
    for c := 2 to n - r do
        factorialnr := factorialnr * c;
    noofways := Trunc(factorialn /
(factorialr * factorialnr));
    writeln(r, ' objects can be chosen from ', n, '
objects in ', noofways, ' ways');
end.
```

7.

```
program Act19_07;
uses WinCrt;

var
    score   : real; {Judge's score}
    highest : real; {Highest score awarded}
    lowest  : real; {Lowest score awarded}
    total   : real; {Total score awarded by panel}
    average : real; {The average score awarded}
    judges  : integer;  {No. of judges}
    count   : integer;  {for loop counter}
begin
    {*** Determine the number of judges ***}
    ClrScr;
    write('Enter the number of judges : ');
    readln(judges);
    {*** Get the score of the first judge ***}
    write('Enter score : ');
    readln(score);
    {*** Assume both highest & lowest score ***}
    highest := score;
    lowest  := score;
    {*** Set total to this first value ***}
    total := score;
    {*** Read in the remainder of the scores ***}
    for count := 2 to judges do
    begin
        {*** Get a score ***}
        write('Enter next score :');
        readln(score);
        {*** Add it to total ***}
        total := total + score;
        {*** If its an extreme score, store it ***}
        if score < lowest then
            lowest := score
        else
            if score > highest then
                highest := score;
    end;
    {*** Calculate average ***}
    average := (total - highest - lowest) /
                                (judges - 2);
    {*** Display overall score ***}
    writeln('Overall score : ',average:0:2);
end.
```

8.

```
program Act19_08;
uses WinCrt;

var
    N, oldx, newx : double;
begin
    {*** Get a value for N ***}
    ClrScr;
    write('Enter value : ');
    readln(N);
    {*** Set newx to N/3 ***}
    newx := N / 3;
    repeat
        {*** Set oldx to newx ***}
        oldx := newx;
        {*** Recalculate newx ***}
        newx := (N / (oldx * oldx) + 2 * oldx) / 3;
    until(N - newx * newx * newx < 0.000005)and
          (newx * newx * newx - N < 0.000005);
    {*** Display result ***}
    writeln('The cube root of ',N:0:2,
                              ' is ',newx:0:2);
end.
```

9.

```
program Act19_09;
uses WinCrt;

var
    day, month, year : integer;
          {Date to be convert to day of week}
    M, CY, C, Y   : integer; {Modified date values}
    temp          : integer; {Temporary variable}
    d             : integer;
               {Day of week on which date falls}
               {0 = Sunday, 1 = Monday etc.}
    daysinmonth   : integer; {Days in month}
    k             : integer; {Loop counter}
```

**Continued on next page**

## Activity 3.19 (continued)

9. (continued)

```
begin
    {*** Clear screen ***}
    ClrScr;
    {*** Get date ***}
    write('Please enter month and year in the
    ↳form xx xxxx : ');
    readln(month, year);
    day := 1;
    {*** Determine modified version of date ***}
    M    := (month + 9) mod 12 + 1;
    CY   := year - M div 11;
    C    := CY div 100;
    Y    := CY mod 100;
    temp := Trunc(2.6 * M - 0.2);
    d    := ((temp + day + Y + Y div 4 + C div 4 -
         ↳2 * C) mod 7 + 7) mod 7;
    {*** Determine the number of days in month ***}
    if (month = 1)or(month = 3) or (month = 5)
    ↳or (month = 7) or (month = 8) or (month = 10)
    ↳or (month = 12) then
        daysinmonth := 31
    else if (month = 2) then
        daysinmonth := 28 + integer(year mod 4 = 0)
        {*** Accurate between 1901 and 2099}
    else
        daysinmonth := 30;
    {*** Display calendar ***}
    ClrScr;
    writeln('   Sun  Mon  Tue  Wed  Thu  Fri  Sat');
    {** Display day one at correct position **}
    write(day:5+5*d);
    day := day + 1;
    {** Display remainder of first line **}
    for k := 1 to 6 - d do
    begin
        write(day:5);
        day := day + 1;
    end;
    writeln;
    {** Display other lines **}
    k := 1;
    while day <= daysinmonth do
    begin
        write(day:5);
        if k mod 7 = 0 then
            writeln;
        k := k + 1;
        day := day + 1;
    end;
end.
```

## Activity 3.20

1. The conditions being tested are:

```
sex = 'M'
age >= 65
age >= 60
```

2. The possible combinations are

```
sex='M' age>=65 age>=60
false   false   false
false   false   true
false   true    false
false   true    true
true    false   false
true    false   true
true    true    false
true    true    true
```

giving a total of 8

3. Not all combinations are relevant since `age >= 65` is only tested when `sex = 'M'` is *true* and `age>=60` tested only when `sex ='M'` is *false*. So a complete test requires the combinations:

```
sex='M' age>=65 age>=60
false     X     false
false     X     true
true    false     X
true    true      X
```

Conditions marked with an X can be either *true* or *false*.

## Activity 3.21

1. *total* is zeroed within the `for` loop.
2. c). *total* will be reset to zero before each input.

## Activity 3.22

```
for count := 1 to 10 do
while(number < 0)or(number > 100)do
if(number mod = 0)or(number mod 4 = 0) then
if total > 0 then
```

## Activity 3.23

a) Any value less than zero. e.g. -5
b) Any positive value under 101 which is not divisible by 3 or 4. e.g. 7

## Activity 3.24

No solution. This is a practical exercise.

## Activity 3.25

To ensure that zero is not considered to be a value which is divisible by 3 or 4 we need to change the first `if` statement to

```
if((number%3==0||number%4==0)&&number != 0)
```

Test data changes are required. With three expressions there are nine possible combinations. Some of these cannot occur. For example, *false/false/false* would mean that *number* gives a remainder when divided by 3 or 4 and is zero which is a contradiction.

| Possible combinations | Possible value |
|---|---|
| false/false/true | 1 |
| false/true/true | 4 |
| true/false/true | 3 |
| true/true/false | 0 |
| true/true/true | 12 |

## Activity 3.26

No solution. This is a practical exercise.

Chapter 4

# Routines and Units

## This chapter covers the following topics:

Calling Functions and Procedures

Creating Pascal Units

Function and Procedure Definition

How calls to a Routine Operate

Lifetime, Scope and Visibility

Modular Programming

Parameters

Routine Pre-conditions

Returning Values from Functions and Procedures

Standard Routines

Structure Diagrams

Test Drivers

# STANDARD ROUTINES

## What are Routines?

In programming, a routine is a piece of code designed to perform some specific task. That code is separated from the other program instructions and given an identifying name. There are many such routines available within Borland Pascal and we've already used some of these such as `clrscr`, which is a routine designed to clear the contents of the screen or window, and move the cursor to the top left of that area.

In Pascal, there are two types of routines:

functions
and
procedures

In the following sections we'll look at some of the routines that are available as part of the Borland Pascal language and how to create and use our own routines.

We'll begin by looking at some of the functions that are available within Pascal.

## Functions

### Functions in Mathematics

Anyone with a basic knowledge of mathematics will have come across functions. For example, a typical statement in trigonometry might be:

$$x = \cos(75)$$

This equation uses the function *cos* which calculates the cosine of an angle. The angle, in this case $75^{o}$, is known as the **argument** or **parameter** of the function. Mathematical functions act on the argument to produce a **result**. In the example above, the function *cos* produces the cosine of $75^{o}$ which happens to be 0.25882.

We may interpret the equation

$$x = \cos(75)$$

as short-hand for

*x is equal to the cosine of* $75^{o}$.

### Functions in Pascal

In Pascal, a function is a named section of code which performs some specific action and, normally, returns a single result.

For example, Pascal contains a function called `cos` for calculating the cosine of an angle (given in radians rather than degrees). The program in LISTING-4.1 reads in an angle in radians and displays the cosine of that angle.

**LISTING-4.1**

Using a Function

```
program UsingFunctions;
uses WinCrt;

var
  angle, answer : real;
begin
  {*** Get angle ***}
  ClrScr;
  write('Enter angle in radians : ');
  readln(angle);
  {*** Call function and assign value returned to answer ***}
  answer := Cos(angle);
  {*** Display results ***}
  writeln('Angle of ',angle:0:2,' radians has cosine of ',
          answer:0:2);
end.
```

Borland name their routines using a capitalised form which is also used within this text. However, since Pascal is not case-sensitive, the compiler will accept any form of a routine's name.

The line

```
answer := Cos(angle);
```

calls and executes the code held within the function `Cos`, supplying it with the value, called *angle,* as the argument to the function. The result returned by the function is assigned to the variable *answer.*

## Declaring Functions

Routines available within the Pascal language have their routine headings declared with Pascal Units (we'll be hearing more about these later). The declaration specifies the routine's type (function or procedure); its name (e.g. Cos); the type of value(s) it takes as arguments and the type of value returned by the routine if it is a function. For example, the declaration of the `Cos` function would be :

**FIG-4.1**

Function heading for *Cos*

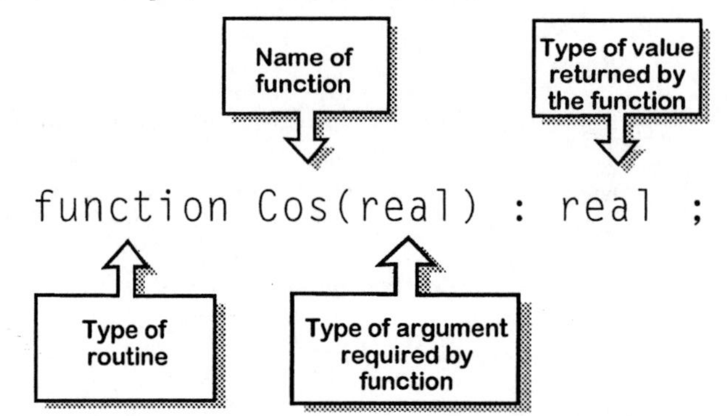


To use a routine defined within a Pascal Unit, the appropriate unit must be included in the `uses` clause of your program. For example, to make use of the `ClrScr` routine we need to include the statement

```
uses WinCrt;
```

in our program.

If you're working in a DOS environment, then `ClrScr` requires the statement

```
uses Crt;
```

Without this, the compiler would report an error when it encountered the term `ClrScr` within the program.

Many of the routines are in a Unit called *System*. Luckily, this Unit is automatically included in every program without the requirement of the `uses` statement.

## Calling Functions

The argument of a function, as well as being given as a constant, can also be specified as a variable or an expression. In the case of the function `Cos`, this allows expressions such as

```
Cos(no);
```

and

```
Cos(no * 3 - 0.6);
```

Where the argument is not a constant, Pascal will evaluate the variable or expression involved and use the resulting value as the argument passed to the function.

The value returned by a function can be assigned to a variable of the appropriate type allowing statements such as

These statements assume the variables *y* and *ans* have been declared.

```
y := Cos(x);
```

and

```
ans := Cos(0.5);
```

A function call may be placed anywhere in a program that it would be appropriate to place a constant of the type returned by that function. Therefore, it is quite acceptable to write

```
writeln(Cos(1.6):0:6);
```

since a `real` constant at that point (e.g. `writeln(-0.029:0:6)`) would be valid.

This means statements such as

```
if Cos(angle) < 0.4 then ...
```

and

```
result := 1.6 * Cos(angle);
```

are also legal instructions.

Pascal demands that the actual arguments used when calling a routine are of an acceptable type. Normally, this means that the arguments should be exactly the same type as those given in the routine's definition. However, a routine which has been defined to take a real value will accept an integer argument. In this, the rules match those used when assigning a value to a variable. Hence, we may write a statement such as

```
writeln(Cos(1):0:6);
```

and the integer argument will automatically be converted to a `real` before being used as the argument in the call to `Cos`.

Similarly, variables that are assigned the result of a function must also be of an acceptable type. This means that the statement

```
y := Cos(x);
```

is valid if *y* is a real variable, but invalid if *y* is an integer.

## Arguments and Return Values

Not all functions take a single argument, like `Cos`. Some have several parameters. One of these is `Copy` whose heading is:

```
function Copy(s: string; start : integer; nbr: integer) : string;
```

In order to explain the purpose of a function such as `Copy`, it is often useful to give names to the function arguments in the heading (as above) and then use these names in the function's description:

> *The purpose of the function* `Copy` *is to return part of the string* s. *The part returned starts with the* start$^{th}$ *character and is* nbr *characters long.*

A few functions are written in such a way as to allow parameters of various types and to return values of a corresponding type. For example, the `Abs` function, which returns the absolute value of the argument, can take any type of numeric value (real, integer, etc) and returns a value of the same type.

These functions' parameters are described in more general terms:

```
Abs(x:numeric type) : same as x
```

This means that an expression such as

```
Abs(-9)
```

will return an integer value, while

```
Abs(-6.57)
```

returns a real.

While some functions can accept any value of the type specified, others take a restricted range of values. For example, the `Sqrt` function returns the square root of its argument, but that argument cannot be a negative number (since the machine cannot calculate the square root of negative values).

This is a restriction on the possible range of values which may be passed as an argument to the routine and is described in the **pre-condition** of the function. Where the function can accept any value of the type specified (as with `Cos`), the pre-condition is simply written as **none.**

The following sections describe some of the routines available in Borland's Pascal compiler. Each entry gives the heading of the function and the Unit in which the routine itself is located. This is followed by the pre-condition placed on the arguments of the function, a description of the purpose of the function, and an example of it in use.

## Mathematical Functions

The following are some of the mathematical functions available. For a full list consult your Borland Pascal Library manual.

| | | |
|---|---|---|
| **Prototype** : | `function Abs(x: numeric type): as x` | |
| **Unit** : | System | |
| **Pre-condition**: | None | |
| **Description** : | Returns the absolute value of *x*. | |
| **Example** : | `writeln(Abs(-6));` | `{ Displays 6 }` |
| | `difference := Abs(x-y);` | `{ Absolute difference}`<br>`{ between x and y}` |

**Prototype** : `function Cos(x : real): real`
**Unit** : System
**Pre-condition**: None

**Description** : Returns the cosine of angle *x* (given in radians). Returns a value in the range -1 to 1.

**Example** :
```
writeln(Cos(0.73):0:6);
```

**Prototype** : `function Exp(x : real): real`
**Unit** : System
**Pre-condition**: None

**Description** : Returns $e^x$.

**Example** :
```
writeln(Exp(-0.68):0:6);
```

**Prototype** : `function Int(x : real): real`
**Unit** : System
**Pre-condition**: None

**Description** : Returns the integral part of *x*.

**Example** :
```
var
    result : real;
begin
    result := Int(12.9); {result set to 12}
    writeln('The integer part is ', result:0:0);
```

**Prototype** : `function Ln(x : real): real`
**Unit** : System
**Pre-condition**: None

**Description** : Returns the natural log of *x*.

**Example** :
```
ans := Ln(12.9);
writeln('natural log is ',ans:0:4);
```

Notice how the `if` statement is constructed here: when a function returns a Boolean value (as in the case of *Odd*), rather than write `if Odd(nbr)=true then` it is possible to use the value returned by the function in place of a Boolean expression.

`if Odd(nbr) = false then` could be written as `if not Odd(nbr) then`

**Prototype** : `function Odd(x : integer): boolean`
**Unit** : System
**Pre-condition**: None

**Description** : Returns *true* if *x* is an odd number; *false* if it is an even value.

**Example** :
```
if Odd(nbr) then
    writeln(nbr,' is an odd number')
else
    writeln(nbr,' is an even number');
```

| | | |
|---|---|---|
| **Prototype** | : | `function Pi: real` |
| **Unit** | : | System |
| **Pre-condition** | : | None |
| **Description** | : | Returns the value of $\pi$ as 3.14159265358979 |
| **Example** | : | `area := Pi*radius*radius;` |

We've already used `Round` and `Trunc` in Chapter 2 to convert real values to integer ones.

As you can see now, these conversions are done by function calls.

| | | |
|---|---|---|
| **Prototype** | : | `function Round(x : real): longint` |
| **Unit** | : | System |
| **Pre-condition** | : | *x* rounds to a value in the *longint* range |
| **Description** | : | *x* is rounded to the nearest integer |
| **Example** | : | `y := Round(12.9);      {y set to 13}`<br>`writeln('Nearest whole number is ',y);` |

| | | |
|---|---|---|
| **Prototype** | : | `function Sin(x : real): real` |
| **Unit** | : | System |
| **Pre-condition** | : | None |
| **Description** | : | Returns the sine of angle *x* (given in radians). |
| **Example** | : | `writeln(Sin(0.11):0:6);` |

| | | |
|---|---|---|
| **Prototype** | : | `function Sqrt(x : real): real` |
| **Unit** | : | System |
| **Pre-condition** | : | *x* >= 0 |
| **Description** | : | Returns the square root of *x*. |
| **Example** | : | `hypotenuse := Sqrt(side1*side1 + side2*side2);`<br>`writeln('Length of is ',hypotenuse:0:2);` |

| | | |
|---|---|---|
| **Prototype** | : | `function Trunc(x : real): longint` |
| **Unit** | : | System |
| **Pre-condition** | : | *x* truncates to an integer value. |
| **Description** | : | Returns the integral part of *x*. |
| **Example** | : | `ans := Trunc(12.9);    {ans set to 12}` |

The functions `Int` and `Trunc` may seem to be identical, but, whereas `Int` returns a *real* value, `Trunc` returns a *longint*. Hence, if the variable *ans* is declared as a *longint*, the statement

```
ans :=  Trunc(12.9);
```

would be valid, while

```
ans := Int(12.9);
```

would be invalid, since it attempts to place a *real* value in a *longint* variable.

## Using Maths Functions

The following program illustrates the use of mathematical functions. LISTING-4.2 lists the sine, cosine and tangent of all angles between $0^o$ and $90^o$ in steps of $5^o$.

**Program Logic:**

```
Display headings
FOR angle := 0 TO 90 DO
    Convert angle to radians
    Display the sine, cosine and tangent of the angle
ENDFOR
```

**Program Code:**

**LISTING-4.2**

Angle Table

```
program UsingFunctions2;
uses WinCrt;
var
  radians : real;        {angle in radians}
  c       : integer;     {Loop counter}
begin
  {*** Display column headings ***}
  ClrScr;
  writeln('Angle (degrees)  Sine      Cosine     Tangent');
  {*** FOR every 5 degrees DO ***}
  for c := 0 to 18 do
  begin
      {*** Convert to radians ***}
      radians := (c*5) * 3.1415/180;
      {*** Display sine, cosine and tangent of angle ***}
      writeln((c*5):7,' ':4,Sin(radians):10:2,Cos(radians):10:2,
                           Sin(radians)/Cos(radians):10:2);
  end
end.
```

> **Activity 4.1**
>
> Write the code necessary to display the square root of all integer values between 1 and 20 inclusive.

## Ordering Functions

Ordinal types are explained more fully in the next chapter. For the moment, we may think of ordinal types as anything other than real or string types.

The following functions operate on various ordinal types and the position of values within such sets.

**Prototype** : `function Chr(x:integer): char`
**Unit** : System
**Pre-condition**: *x* must be 0 to 255

**Description** : Returns the character that is at position *x* in the character set (see Appendix A for the character set). The first character is at position zero in the set.

**Example** :
```
for c := 65 to 90 do
    writeln(Chr(c));    {Shows 'A' to 'Z'}
```

**Prototype** : `function Ord(x: any ordinal type): integer`
**Unit** : System
**Pre-condition**: None

**Description** : Returns the position of *x* in its ordinal set. If *x* is the first position in the set, the value zero is returned.

**Example** :
```
writeln('A is character ',Ord('A'),
        ' in its character set');
                                    {Returns 65}
```

**Prototype** : `function Pred(x: any ordinal type): as x`
**Unit** : System
**Pre-condition**: None

**Description** : Returns the previous value in the ordinal set that *x* belongs to.

**Example** : `writeln(Pred('B'));     {Outputs 'A'}`

**Prototype** : `function Succ(x: any ordinal type): as x`
**Unit** : System
**Pre-condition**: *h:m:s:hs* should be a valid time.

**Description** : Returns the value that follows *x* in its ordinal set.

**Example** : `writeln(Succ('A'));     {Outputs 'B'}`

# Procedures

Whereas functions are usually designed to return a single result, procedures may return any number of values. Some, like `ClrScr`, return no values, while others, like `GetDate`, returns multiple values. Values being passed to a routine and the results being returned are stated together within the parameter list. Those that are returning values are preceeded by the term `var`.

## Declaring Procedures

Like functions, standard procedures are declared within Pascal Units. The heading for the procedure `Insert`, which inserts a new string at a specified position within an existing string, is shown in FIG-4.2.

**FIG-4.2**

The Construct of a Procedure

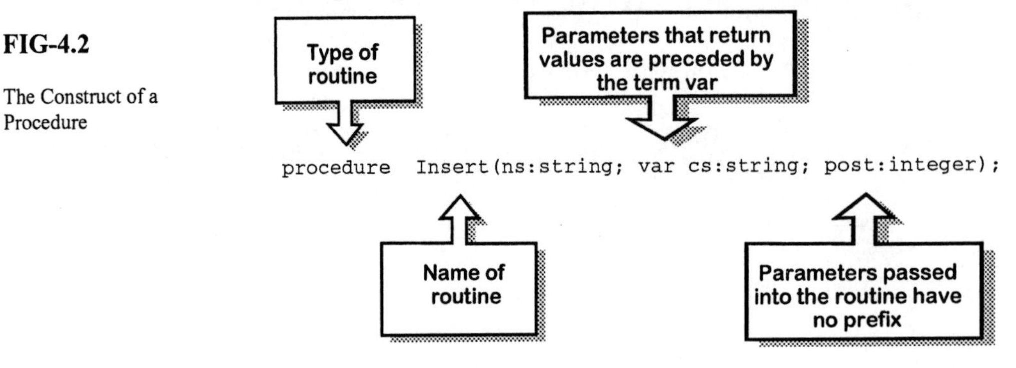

## Calling Procedures

Procedure calls always appear as stand-alone statements within a program - unlike functions, which are normally part of some other statement.

We've already seen this when using `ClrScr` in a program. It is always called with the line:

```
ClrScr;
```

The following code snippet uses the procedure `Insert` to change the contents of the string *s1* from *"sting"* to *"starting"*:

The procedure call is a request to insert 'art' starting at position 3 within s1.

```
s1 := 'sting';
Insert('art',s1,3);
```

Parameters being passed to a procedure can be constants, variables or expressions of the appropriate type, but parameters that are to hold the values returning from a procedure must be variables. This means that in the case of the procedure `Insert`, the first and third parameters may be constant, variable or expression terms, while the second must be a variable.

**Activity 4.2**

Assuming the following lines of code:

```
var
    s1,s2 : string;
    p     : integer;
begin
    s1 := 'tip';
    s2 := 'toe';
    p  := 3;
```

state which of the following are valid calls to `Insert`:

a) `Insert('r',s1,2);`
b) `Insert('n',s2,3);`
c) `Insert(s2,s1,p);`
d) `Insert(s2,'big',p);`
e) `Insert('w',s2,4 - 1);`

## Date-Handling Procedures

There are a few procedures designed to handle date and time related operations. These routines are defined in the Unit WinDOS (or Unit DOS, if you are not working in the Windows environment). The main ones are listed below:

| | | |
|---|---|---|
| **Prototype** | : | `procedure SetTime(h,m,s,hs:word)` |
| **Unit** | : | WinDOS (DOS) |
| **Pre-condition**: | | *h:m:s:hs* should be a valid time. |
| **Description** | : | Sets the systems time to h:m:s:hs. *hs* is hundredth of a second. *h* should be in the range 0 to 23. |
| **Example** | : | `SetTime(11,34,0,0);     {sets time to 11.34am}` |

| | | |
|---|---|---|
| **Prototype** | : | `procedure SetDate(y,m,d:word)` |
| **Unit** | : | WinDOS (DOS) |
| **Pre-condition**: | | *d,m,y* should form a valid date. Use a 4-digit year |
| **Description** | : | Sets the system date to *d/m/y*. |
| **Example** | : | `SetDate(1998,6,30);` |

| | | |
|---|---|---|
| **Prototype** | : | `procedure GetDate(var year,month,day,dow:word)` |
| **Unit** | : | WinDOS (DOS) |
| **Pre-condition**: | | None |
| **Description** | : | Returns the *day*, *month* and *year* as held within the operating system. It also returns, in *dow*, the day of the week in integer form (Sunday = 0, Monday = 1, etc.) |
| **Example** | : | `GetDate(y,m,d,dw);` <br> `writeln('Date is ',d,'/',m'/',y);` |

| | | |
|---|---|---|
| **Prototype** | : | `procedure GetTime(var h,m,s,hs:word)` |
| **Unit** | : | WinDOS (DOS) |
| **Pre-condition**: | | None |
| **Description** | : | Returns the current time in hours (*h*), minutes (*m*), seconds (*s*) and hundredth of a second (*hs*). <br> *h* will lie in the range 0 to 23. |
| **Example** | : | `GetTime(h,m,s,hs);` <br> `writeln('Time is ',h,':',m':',s);` |

## Increment and Decrement Procedures

Normally, we've incremented variables using statements such as

```
count := count + 1;
```

However, a more efficient way do this is to use the routine `Inc`, which adds to a specified variable. A second routine, `Dec`, decrements a variable. These routines are unusual in that they can be used with a second, optional parameter:

| | | |
|---|---|---|
| **Prototype** | : | `procedure Dec(var x:ordinal type [v:longint])` |
| **Unit** | : | System |
| **Pre-condition**: | | None |
| **Description** | : | If the second parameter is omitted, *x* is decremented by 1. When the second argument is included, *x* is decremented by *v*. |
| **Example** | : | `nbr := 12;` <br> `Dec(nbr);          {Sets nbr to 11}` <br> `Dec(nbr,5);        {Sets nbr to 6};` |

**Prototype** : `procedure Inc(var x:ordinal type [v:longint])`
**Unit** : System
**Pre-condition**: None

**Description** : If the second parameter is omitted, *x* is incremented by 1. When the second argument is included, *x* is incremented by *v*.

**Example** :
```
nbr := 12;
Inc(nbr,5);            {sets nbr to 17}
Inc(nbr);              {sets nbr to 18}
```

# Other Standard Routines

## Generating Random Numbers

Computers are often used to play games and many games need to generate random numbers to introduce an element of chance into the action. For example, if we want the computer to simulate throwing dice, then we need to get the program to generate random numbers between 1 and 6.

This is done using two routines:

**Prototype** : `function Random(x:integer): integer`
**Unit** : System
**Pre-condition**: None

**Description** : Returns a random number between zero and *x*-1 which is generated by the computer.

This function is normally used only after a call to the function `randomize()` which seeds the algorithm used by `random()` to generate values.

**Example** :
```
diethrow := Random(6) + 1;
```

**Prototype** : `procedure Randomize`
**Unit** : System
**Pre-condition**: None

**Description** : Initialises the random number generator. This command should be used before calling the `random` function, otherwise the program using `random` will generate the same sequence of values each time the program is executed.

**Example** :
```
Randomize;         {Initialise random number}
                   {generator before using Random}
diethrow := Random(6) + 1;
```

The next program generates a number between 1 and 200 using `random`, and allows the user up to seven guesses to determine the value of the number generated. The logic required is:

```
Generate number
Issue prompt
FOR up to 7 guesses DO
    Get guess
    IF guess is correct THEN
        Display winning message
        terminate FOR loop
    ELSE
        IF guess is too low THEN
            Display "TOO LOW"
        ELSE
            Display "TOO HIGH"
        ENDIF
    ENDIF
ENDFOR
IF the number wasn't guessed THEN
    Display failure message and value of number
ENDIF
```

This is coded as shown in LISTING-4.3.

**LISTING-4.3**

Guessing Random Number

```
program guess01;
uses WinCrt;

var
  number      : integer;     {Number generated by computer}
  guess       : integer;     {Number guessed by user}
  guessesmade : integer;     {Guesses made so far}

begin
  {*** Generate number ***}
  Randomize;
  number := Random(200)+1;
  {*** Issue prompt ***}
  ClrScr;
  writeln('Guess number between 1 and 200');
  {*** For up to seven times do ***}
  for guessesmade := 1 to 7 do
  begin
      {*** Get guess ***}
      write('Enter your guess : ');
      readln(guess);
      {*** If guess correct, issue message and quit ***}
      if guess = number then
      begin
          writeln('Correct after ',guessesmade,' guesses.');
          break;
      end;
      {*** If wrong guess, issue TOO HIGH or TOO LOW message ***}
      if guess < number then
          writeln('Too low')
      else
          writeln('Too high');
  end;
  {*** If all guesses wrong, give message and number ***}
  if guess <> number then
      writeln('You failed to guess. Number was ',number);
end.
```

**Activity 4.3**

Write a program to generate and display six random values between 1 and 49.

## String-Handling Routines

Strings are such an important part of many programs that there are several functions and procedures available to handle them. These routines allow us to perform various operations such as add text to an existing string, delete parts of a string, and search a string for a specific substring. The routines are desicribed below:

**Prototype** : `function Concat(s1,s2[,s3.....]):string`
**Unit** : System
**Pre-condition**: None

**Description** : Joins the strings of the argument to create a single string

**Example** :
```
result := Concat('al','to','get','her');
                {result set to 'altogether'}
```

This function performs the same operation as the + operater applied to strings. Hence, the line

```
result := Concat(s1,s2,s3,s4);
```

is equivalent to

```
result := s1 + s2 + s3 + s4;
```

**Prototype** : `function Copy(s:string;st,cnt:integer):string`
**Unit** : System
**Pre-condition**: None

**Description** : Returns that part of *s* that starts at position *st* and contains *cnt* charcaters.If *st* is not a valid position in *s*, an empty string is returned. If *cnt* is greater than the number of characters between *st* and the end of *s*, then the characters from *st* to the end of the string are returned.

**Example** :
```
result := Copy('altogether',5,3);  {'get'}
result := Copy('altogether',12,2);{''}
result := Copy('altogether',8,6);   {'her'}
```

**Prototype** : `procedure Delete(var s:string;st,cnt:integer)`
**Unit** : System
**Pre-condition**: None

**Description** : Deletes characters from *s*. *cnt* characters are deleted starting from position *st*. If *st* is not a valid position in *s*, *s* is returned unchanged. If *cnt* is greater than the number of characters between *st* and the end of *s*, then only the characters from *st* to the end of the string are deleted.

**Example** :
```
s1 := 'altogether';
Delete(s1,1,2);     {s1 set to 'together'}
```

**Prototype** : 
```
procedure Insert
        (add:string; var s:string; p:integer)
```
**Unit** : System
**Pre-condition**: None

**Description** : Inserts the string *add* into *s* starting at position *p*.

**Example** :
```
word := 'beg';
Insert('lon',word,3); {word set to 'belong'}
```

**Prototype** :
```
function Length(s:string):integer
```
**Unit** : System
**Pre-condition**: None

**Description** : Returns the number of characters in *s*.

**Example** :
```
s1 := 'Hello there';
writeln(Length(s1));        {outputs 11}
```

**Prototype** :
```
function Pos(sub,s:string):integer
```
**Unit** : System
**Pre-condition**: None

**Description** : This routine determines if a substring, *sub*, exists within a second string, *s*. The function returns the start position of the first occurrence of *sub* within *s*. If sub does not exist with s, then zero is returned.

**Example** :
```
writeln(Pos('get','altogether'));{outputs  5}
```

**Activity 4.4**

Write programs to perform the following tasks.

1. Read a string from the keyboard and display the number of characters it contains.
2. Read in a sentence as a string and display the number words in the string. You may assume that there is exactly one space between each word, that there are no punctuation characters in the sentence and that there are no spaces at the start or end of the string.
3. Read in a string and capitalise every word in the string.
4. Read in two strings, deleting every occurrence of the second string within the first.
5. Read in two strings and display how often the first occurs in the second.
6. Read in three strings and replace every occurrence of the second string in the first by the third.

# Console Input/Output

Reading from the keyboard and displaying information on the screen are two such important tasks that there are many functions and procedures dealing with these activities.

## Outputting to the Screen

The routines which affect screen output are listed below. They allow various operations such as clearing the screen, moving the cursor, and finding out the current position of the cursor.

**Prototype** : `procedure ClrScr`
**Unit** : WinCrt (Crt)
**Pre-condition**: None

**Description** : Fills the output window with space characters and moves the cursor to the top left of that window.

**Example** : `ClrScr;`

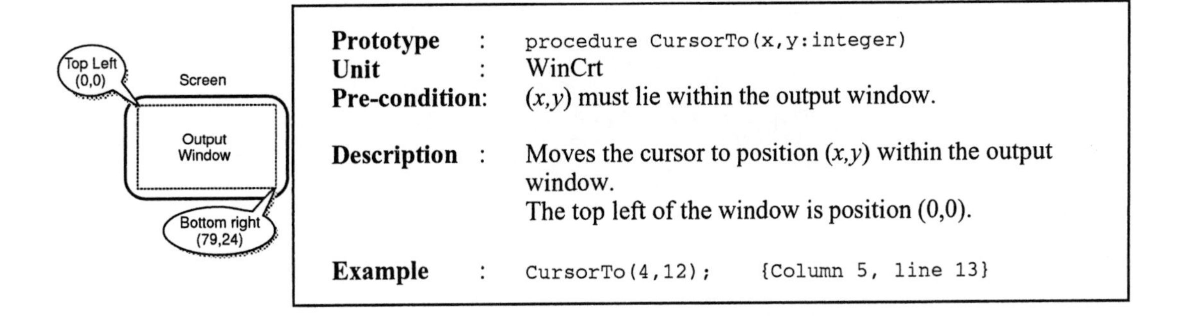


**Prototype** : `procedure CursorTo(x,y:integer)`
**Unit** : WinCrt
**Pre-condition**: (*x,y*) must lie within the output window.

**Description** : Moves the cursor to position (*x,y*) within the output window.
The top left of the window is position (0,0).

**Example** :
```
CursorTo(4,12);     {Column 5, line 13}
```

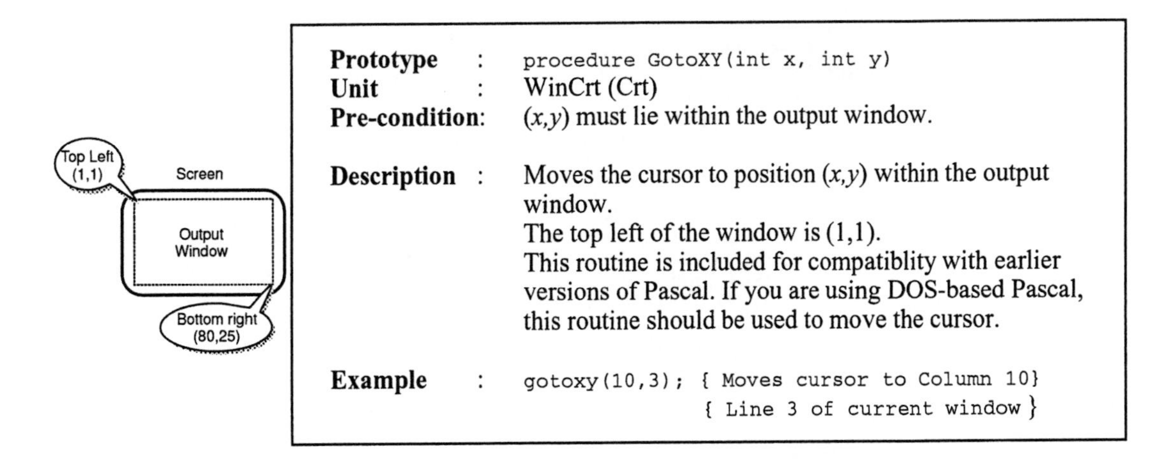


**Prototype** : `procedure GotoXY(int x, int y)`
**Unit** : WinCrt (Crt)
**Pre-condition**: (*x,y*) must lie within the output window.

**Description** : Moves the cursor to position (*x,y*) within the output window.
The top left of the window is (1,1).
This routine is included for compatiblity with earlier versions of Pascal. If you are using DOS-based Pascal, this routine should be used to move the cursor.

**Example** :
```
gotoxy(10,3); { Moves cursor to Column 10}
                { Line 3 of current window }
```

| | | |
|---|---|---|
| **Prototype** | : | `function WhereX` |
| **Unit** | : | WinCrt (Crt) |
| **Pre-condition**: | | None |
| **Description** | : | Returns the column in which the cursor is placed. Since the left-most column is taken as column 1, the possible result lies in the range 1 to 80. |
| **Example** | : | `ClrScr;`<br>`writeln(WhereX);   {Outputs 1}` |

| | | |
|---|---|---|
| **Prototype** | : | `function WhereY` |
| **Unit** | : | WinCrt (Crt) |
| **Pre-condition**: | | None |
| **Description** | : | Returns the line in which the cursor is placed. Since the top row is taken as line 1, the possible result lies in the range 1 to 25. |
| **Example** | : | `CursorTo(0,10);`<br>`writeln(WhereX);   {Outputs 11}` |

The program in Listing-4.4 places the character 'X' at a point specified by the user. The logic used is:

```
Clear the screen
Get the position required
WHILE position is invalid DO
    Issue error message
    Get the position required
ENDWHILE
Move cursor to the required position
write an 'X' to the screen
```

**LISTING-4.4**

Placing the Cursor

```
program ScreenOutput;
uses WinCrt;

var
  col, row : integer; {Cursor position}

begin
  {*** Get the position required ***}
  ClrScr;
  write('Enter the cursor position required (col line): ');
  readln(col,row);
  {*** WHILE position is invalid DO ***}
  while (col < 1) or (col > 80) or (row < 1) or (row > 25) do
  begin
      {*** Issue error message ***}
      writeln('Invalid position (col:1 to 80, line:1 to 25)');
      {*** Get the position required ***}
      write('Enter the cursor position required (col line): ');
      readln(col,row);
  end;
  {*** Write 'X' at required position ***}
  GotoXY(col,row);
  write('X');
end.
```

| | | |
|---|---|---|
| **Prototype** | : | `procedure ClrEol` |
| **Unit** | : | WinCrt (Crt) |
| **Pre-condition**: | | None |
| **Description** | : | Clears the screen from the current cursor position to the end of the current line in the text window. The cursor does not move. |
| **Example** | : | `GotoXY(65,12);`<br>`ClrEol;     {clears cols 65 -80 of line 12}` |

| | | |
|---|---|---|
| **Prototype** | : | `procedure DoneWinCrt` |
| **Unit** | : | WinCrt |
| **Pre-condition**: | | None |
| **Description** | : | This closes the output window.<br>By using this at the end of a program, the user will not have to close the inactive window that remains when a window is closed. |
| **Example** | : | `writeln('Press return to finish');`<br>`readln;`<br>`DoneWinCrt;` |

Although there are other routines available to modify screen output in both Windows and DOS mode, these are omitted from this text. Use Pascal's help features to discover what other routines are available.

## Reading From the Keyboard

When a key is pressed on the computer keyboard its code is transferred to an area of the computer's memory known as the **keyboard buffer** (see FIG-4.3).

**FIG-4.3**

The Keyboard Buffer

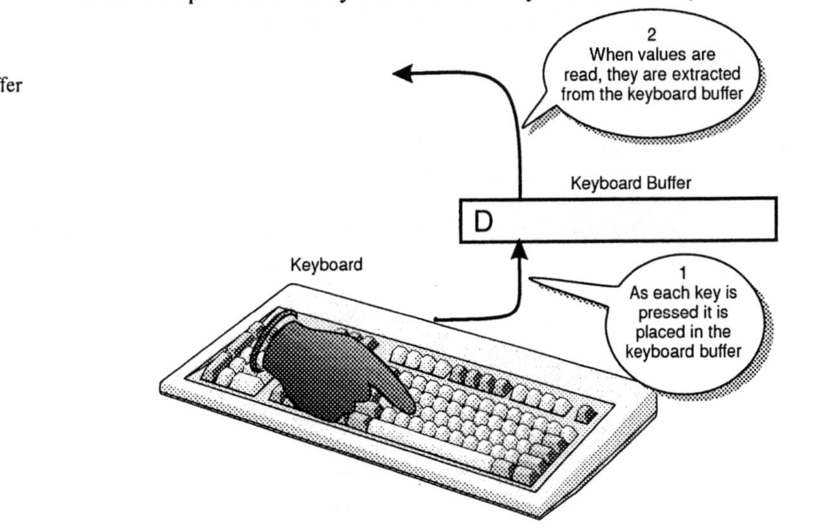


It is the contents of this buffer that is extracted by a `readln` statement. If the keyboard buffer is empty, `readln` halts the program until data appears in the keyboard buffer and the return key is pressed. The extracted data is then placed in the variable(s) specified within the `readln` statement. If there is insufficient data in the buffer, `readln` waits until more data is placed in the buffer; if there is too much data in the buffer, the surplus data is flushed from the buffer. The scenario below illustrates these points.

A program contains the statement

```
readln(a,b);
```

which is designed to read values for the two integers *a* and *b*. When executing the program, the user enters the data

```
12
```

This is placed in the keyboard buffer and then extracted to be placed in the variable *a*. However, a value is still required for *b*, so the program continues to wait until more data is entered. If the user now enters

```
5 79 23
```

this data is placed in the keyboard buffer and the value 5 is extracted and placed in the second variable *b*. The remaining data, 79 23, is then removed from the buffer and discarded.

In fact, an alternative to the `readln` statement is `read`. This has a similar affect to `readln`, but does not flush surplus data from the buffer. Hence, if a program contains the statement

```
read(a,b)
```

and the data entered is

```
12 5 79 23
```

then 12 and 5 are extracted and assigned to variables *a* and *b*, while 79 and 23 remain in the keyboard buffer to be read by subsequent input statements.

To gain more control over keyboard input we can use the function `ReadKey`. This reads a single byte from the keyboard buffer.

| | |
|---|---|
| **Prototype** : | `function ReadKey: char` |
| **Unit** : | WinCrt (Crt) |
| **Pre-condition:** | None |
| **Description** : | Reads a single character from the keyboard buffer. The character read is not displayed on the screen. |
| **Example** : | `writeln('Press any key to continue');`<br>`ch := ReadKey;` |

If you have a second look at the example given above for `ReadKey`, you'll see that it's purpose is to halt the program until a key is pressed, but since we are unlikely to make use of the character entered, we are at liberty to call the function without assigning the value it returns. Hence we may replace the line

```
ch := ReadKey;
```

with

```
ReadKey;
```

This is only true in Borland Pascal version 7.0. Earlier versions must make reference to the value returned.

In fact, any function can be called in this way - making no reference to the value it returns.

The `ReadKey` function can be used to create greater control over what keys are accepted from the user. For example, let's say we want the user to type in their age. Of course, we can use `readln`, but that gives the user too much freedom to enter invalid data. It would be better if we could restrict input to a maximum of two numeric digits.

The program in Listing-4.5 shows how `ReadKey` can be used in such a situation. The program uses the following logic:

```
Issue prompt
Set count to zero
Set input string to empty
Read character from keyboard
WHILE character not ENTER DO
    IF character is numeric AND count < 2 THEN
        Display character
        Add the character to the input string
        Add 1 to count
    ENDIF
    Read character from keyboard
ENDWHILE
Move cursor to next line
```

**LISTING-4.5**

Filtering Keyboard Input

```
program ControlledInput;
uses WinCrt;

var
   count   : integer;     {Count of characters entered}
   datain  : string[80];  {Contains the characters entered}
   ch      : char;        {Current character read from buffer}
begin
   {*** Issue prompt ***}
   Clrscr;
   write('Enter age : ');
   {*** Set count to zero ***}
   count := 0;
   {*** Set input string to empty ***}
   datain := '';
   {*** Read character from keyboard ***}
   ch := readkey;
   {*** WHILE character not ENTER DO ***}
   while ch <> #13 do
   begin
        {***IF character is numeric AND count < 3 THEN ***}
        if (ch >= '0') and (ch <= '9') and (count < 3) then
        begin
             {*** Display character ***}
             write(ch);
             {*** Add the character to the input string ***}
             datain := datain + ch;
             {*** Add 1 to count ***}
             inc(count);
        end;
        {*** Read character from keyboard ***}
        ch := readkey;
   end;
   {*** Move cursor to next line ***}
   writeln;
   {*** Terminate program ***}
   readkey;
   DoneWinCrt;
end.
```

**Activity 4.5**

Enter and run the program in Listing-4.5.

Modify the program so that it will accept a maximum of 10 uppercase letters.

What happens when you use backspace to delete the last character entered?

As you can see, a problem with the program above is that the backspace key can't be used to erase any characters entered by mistake.

To erase a character from the screen, we need to move the cursor one place to the left, erase the offending character by printing a space, and then move the cursor back one more time. This can all be done using the single statement:

```
write(#8,' ',#8);
```

This statement should only be executed when the backspace character has been pressed and there's something on the screen to delete. In addition, the count of how many characters are currently being displayed will have to be decremented.

The next Activity makes use of this information to allow you to create a more powerful version of the input program.

**Activity 4.6**

Re-program Listing-4.5 to allow for backspacing.

```
OUTLINE LOGIC:
  Issue prompt
  Set count to zero
  Set input string to empty
  Read character from keyboard
  WHILE character not ENTER DO
      IF
          character is numeric AND count < 2 :
              Display character
              Add the character to the input string
              Add 1 to count
          character is backspace and count > 0 :
              Remove last character from screen
              Remove last character from input string
              Subtract 1 from count
      ENDIF
      Read character from keyboard
  ENDWHILE
  Move cursor to next line
```

## Interactive Programming

So far, whenever a program requests input, the computer sits and waits for that input. However, there are situations when that would be undesirable. For example, when playing an interactive game on the computer, although it will react to input, such as the movement of a joystick, or hitting some key, the game does not wait for these input - it simply reacts to them if they occur. This is just one example of interactive programming, where the machine responds instantly to external events.

We can get our programs to react in the same way by interrogating the keyboard buffer.

The only reason that a program stops when executing a `ReadKey` operation is because there are no characters in the keyboard buffer, otherwise a byte would be extracted from the buffer and the program would continue without delay.

It is possible to place data in the keyboard buffer while a program is busy on some other tasks. For example, if you request the contents of a disk to be displayed on the screen, it is possible to hit a sequence of keys while the machine is busy listing the disk's directory. Each key pressed will be placed in the buffer, ready to be extracted when subsequent input statements are executed.

The function that determines if there is at least one character in the keyboard buffer is `KeyPressed`:

| | |
|---|---|
| **Prototype** : | `function KeyPressed:boolean` |
| **Unit** : | WinCrt (Crt) |
| **Pre-condition**: | None |
| **Description** : | Returns *true* if there is data in the keyboard buffer, otherwise *false* is returned. |
| **Example** : | `if KeyPressed then`<br>`    ch := ReadKey; {reads from buffer only if }`<br>`                   {occuppied}` |

The program in Listing-4.6 makes use of `KeyPressed` to modify the continual movement of symbol on the screen. The program employs the following logic:

```
Empty the screen
Set direction to UP
Place an 'O' in the centre of the screen
Read a key to start
WHILE key is not Enter DO
    IF at edge of screen THEN
        reverse direction
    move 'O' in current direction
    delay for 0.2 seconds
    ENDIF
    IF keyboard buffer not empty THEN
        read a key
        IF
            key = 'U' : Set direction to UP
            key = 'D' : Set direction to DOWN
            key = 'L' : Set direction to LEFT
            key = 'R' : Set direction to RIGHT
        ENDIF
    ENDIF
ENDWHILE
Close program
```

**LISTING-4.6**

Interactive Programming

```
program UsingKeyPressed;
uses WinCrt,WinDos;
const
  UP    = 1;        {Movement directions}
  DOWN  = 4;
  LEFT  = 2;
  RIGHT = 3;
```

**Continued on next page**

**LISTING-4.6**
(continued)

Interactive Programming

```
var
   direction       : integer;  {Holds current movement direction}
   ch              : char;          {Character read from keyboard}
   h,m,s,hs,oldhs  : word;          {Time variables}

begin
   {*** Empty the screen ***}
   ClrScr;
   {*** Set direction to UP ***}
   direction := UP;
   {*** Place an 'O' in the centre of the screen ***}
   GotoXY(40,12);
   write('O');
   {*** Read a key to start ***}
   ch := ReadKey;
   {*** WHILE key is not Enter DO ***}
   while ch <> #13 do
   begin
       {*** IF at edge of screen THEN ***}
       if ( WhereX = 2) or (whereX = 80) or (WhereY = 1) or
                                                 (WhereY = 25) then
           {*** reverse direction ***}
           direction := 5 - direction;
       {*** Move 'O' in current direction ***}
       {** Delete existing 'O' **}
       GotoXY(WhereX-1,WhereY);
       write(' ');
       {** Place in new position **}
       GotoXY(WhereX-1,WhereY);
       case direction of
           UP    : GotoXY(whereX,WhereY - 1);
           DOWN  : GotoXY(whereX,WhereY + 1);
           LEFT  : GotoXY(whereX - 1,WhereY);
           RIGHT : GotoXY(whereX + 1,WhereY);
       end;
       write('O');
       {** Wait for 0.2 seconds **}
       GetTime(h,m,s,oldhs);
       repeat
           GetTime(h,m,s,hs);
       until Abs(hs - oldhs) >= 20;
       {*** IF keyboard buffer not empty THEN ***}
        if KeyPressed then
        begin
           {*** read a key ***}
           ch := ReadKey;
           {*** Change direction ***}
           case upcase(ch) of
               'U' :{ UP }
                   direction := UP;
               'D' :{ DOWN }
                   direction := DOWN;
               'L' :{ LEFT }
                   direction := LEFT;
               'R' :{ RIGHT }
                   direction := RIGHT;
           end;
        end;
   end;
   {*** Close program ***}
   DoneWinCrt;
end.
```

The program uses a few approaches that are worth comment:

The directions, UP, DOWN, LEFT and RIGHT are set up as constants in such a way that the sum of opposite directions adds up to 5. This allows us to reverse direction using the line

```
direction := 5 - direction;
```

Also the left edge is tested for using the condition `WhereX = 2`. You might think we should be testing `WhereX = 1` but if the 'O' is placed in column 1, the cursor will then move to the right and be in column 2, hence the test for the cursor being in column 2.

The program includes a call to the function `UpCase`. This routine returns the uppercase version of its argument as described below:

| | | |
|---|---|---|
| **Prototype** | : | `function UpCase(ch:char):char` |
| **Unit** | : | System |
| **Pre-condition**: | | None |
| **Description** | : | If *ch* is a lowercase letter, the returned value is the uppercase version of the same letter. If *ch* is not a lowercase letter, the value returned is the same as ch. |
| **Example** | : | `writeln(UpCase('a'));  {Outputs 'A'}` |
| | | `writeln(UpCase(6));    {Outputs 6}` |

The program needs to delay for a short time between each movement of the symbol, otherwise the display would change too fast for us to see what was happening.

In Listing-4.6 we've done this with the code

```
GetTime(h,m,s,oldhs);
repeat
    GetTime(h,m,s,hs);
until Abs(hs - oldhs) >= 20;
```

which gets the current time and repeats that operation until at least 0.2 seconds have passed.

If you're working in the DOS environment, you can use the simpler *Delay* procedure described below.

| | | |
|---|---|---|
| **Prototype** | : | `procedure Delay(ms:word)` |
| **Unit** | : | DOS |
| **Pre-condition**: | | None |
| **Description** | : | The program stops execution for approxiametly *ms* milliseconds. |
| **Example** | : | `Delay(300);` |

# Summary

| ROUTINE HEADING | UNIT | DESCRIPTION |
|---|---|---|
| **MATHS** | | |
| function Abs(x: numeric type): as x | System | Returns the absolute value of x |
| function Cos(x : real): real | System | Returns the cosine of x radians |
| function Exp(x : real): real | System | Returns $e^x$ |
| function Int(x : real): real | System | Returns the integer part of x |
| function Ln(x : real): real | System | Returns the natural log of x |
| function Odd(x : integer): boolean | System | Returns true if x is odd; otherwise false |
| function Pi: real | System | Returns the value of $\pi$ |
| function Round(x : real): longint | System | Returns x rounded to the nearest integer |
| function Sin(x : real): real | System | Returns the sine of x radians |
| function Sqrt(x : real): real | System | Returns the square root of x |
| function Trunc(x : real): longint | System | Returns the integer part of x |
| **ORDERING** | | |
| function Chr(x:integer): char | System | Returns the character whose code is x |
| function Ord(x: any ordinal type): integer | System | Returns the value whose ordinal value is x |
| function Pred(x: any ordinal type): as x | System | Returns the value 1 less than x |
| function Succ(x: any ordinal type): as x | System | Returns the value 1 more than x |
| **DATE/TIME** | | |
| procedure SetTime(h,m,s,hs:word) | WinDOS | Sets the time |
| procedure SetDate(y,m,d:word) | WinDOS | Sets the date |
| procedure GetDate(var year,month,day,dow:word) | WinDOS | Returns the date |
| procedure GetTime(var h,m,s,hs:word) | WinDOS | Returns the time |
| **INCREMENT & DECREMENT** | | |
| procedure Dec(var x:ordinal type [v:longint]) | System | Decreases x by 1 or v |
| procedure Inc(var x:ordinal type [v:longint]) | System | Increases x by 1 or v |
| **STRING** | | |
| function Concat(s1,s2[,s3.....]):string | System | Joins the strinds s1, s2, etc |
| function Copy(s:string;st,cnt:integer):string | System | Copies cnt characters from sc, starting at st |
| procedure Delete(var s:string;st,cnt:integer) | System | Deletes cnt characters from sc, starting at st |
| procedure Insert(add:string; var s:string; p:integer) | System | Inserts add into sc, starting at p |
| function Length(s:string):integer | System | Returns the number of charcaters in sc |
| function Pos(sub,s:string):integer | System | Returns the start position of sub in sc |
| function UpCase(ch:char):char | System | Returns the upper-case form of ch |
| **SCREEN** | | |
| procedure ClrScr | WinCrt | Clears the screen; moves cursor to top left |
| procedure CursorTo(x,y:integer) | WinCrt | Moves cursor to (x,y). Top left is (0,0) |
| procedure GotoXY(int x, int y) | WinCrt | Moves cursor to (x,y). Top left is (1,1) |
| function WhereX | WinCrt | Returns the cursor's column (starts at 1) |
| function WhereY | WinCrt | Returns the cursor's line (starts at 1) |
| procedure ClrEol | WinCrt | Clears to end of current line |
| procedure DoneWinCrt | WinCrt | Close the appiaction window |
| function ReadKey: char | WinCrt | Reads a byte from the keyboard buffer |
| function KeyPressed:boolean | WinCrt | Returns true if keyboard buffer not empty |
| **MISCELLANEOUS** | | |
| function Random(x:integer): integer | System | Returns a random value between 0 and x-1 |
| procedure Randomize | System | Initialises the random seed |
| procedure Delay(ms:word) | DOS | Halts computer for ms milliseconds (DOS only) |

# USER-DEFINED ROUTINES

## Introduction

As well as using the standard routines supplied with Pascal, we can also create routines of our own.

By creating a routine for each of the main tasks to be performed by a program, we construct a set of building blocks which can then be linked to produce the complete software system.

This modular approach has many benefits. It allows each routine to be created and tested in isolation before being linked to others to form the final program. This tends to lead to shorter development time and more robust software.

We'll start by seeing how to create procedures.

## The General Format of a Procedure

The general layout of a procedure definition as shown in FIG-4.4.

**FIG-4.4**

The Format of a Procedure

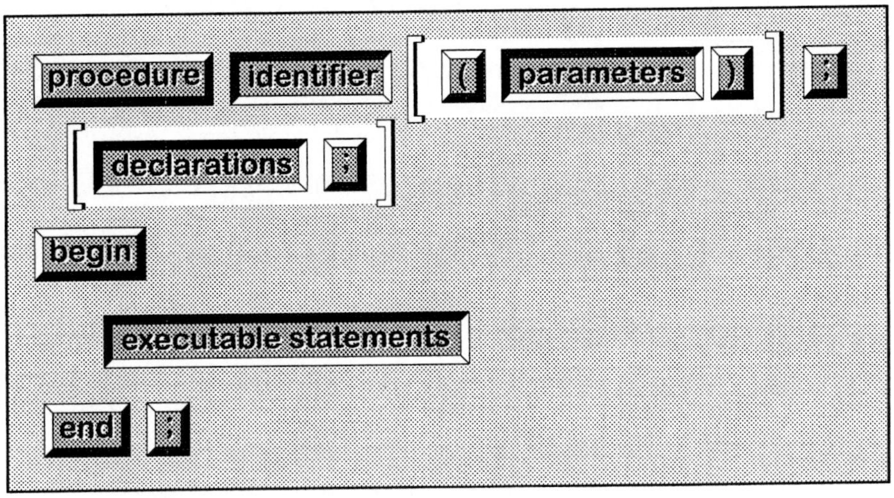

procedure identifier [ ( parameters ) ] ;
[ declarations ; ]
begin
executable statements
end ;

**KEY to FIG-4.4**

**identifier** Specifies the name of the procedure. It will be this name that is used when the routine is to be executed.

**parameters** The parameters specify the values that are to be passed in or out of the routine. Each parameter must be given a name and its type specified. Parameters which are to hold results returned from the routine must be preceded by the term `var`.

**Examples**

| | |
|---|---|
| `(a , b, c : integer)` | *a, b* and *c* are integer values being passed into the routine. |
| `(a:integer ; b:real)` | *a* and *b* are passed into the routine. Notice that the different parameter types must be separated by a semicolon. |

| | |
|---|---|
| `(a:char ; var b:real)` | *a* is passed into the routine;<br>*b* is returned by the routine. |
| `(var a, b : real)` | *a* and *b* are both returned. |
| `(var a:char ; var b:real)` | *a* and *b* are both returned.<br>However, since they are of differeing types, both must be preceded by `var`. |

**declarations** Routines can contain constant and variable declarations separate from those in the main program. Such items can then only be used within that routine. Often these are required as loop counters or to hold intermediate results when performing some calculation.

**executable statements** Any standard Pascal statement can be included within the routine.

The following example of a user-defined procedure displays a line of asterisks.

```
procedure Line;
begin
    writeln('*****************************');
end;
```

# Placing Routines in Your Program

The code for a Pascal routine must appear in your program before any call to that routine. This allows the compiler to check the validity of the call, ensuring the routine's name and parameters are correct.

Hence, the layout for a program using procedure *Line* would be as shown in LISTING-4.7

**LISTING-4.7**

Placing a Routine in Your Program

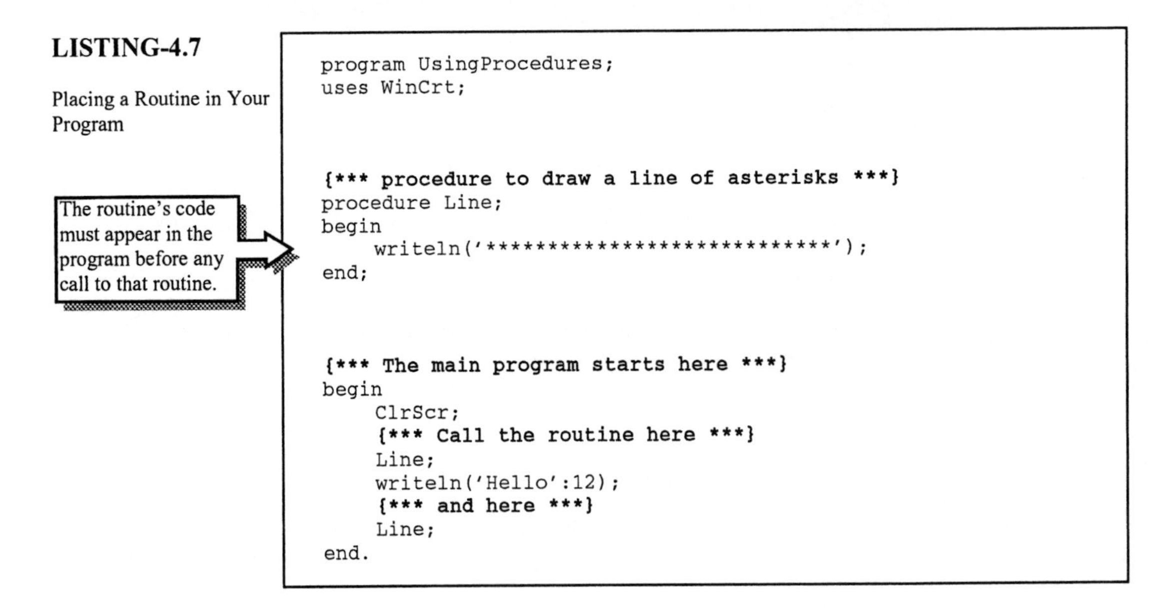
The routine's code must appear in the program before any call to that routine.

```
program UsingProcedures;
uses WinCrt;

{*** procedure to draw a line of asterisks ***}
procedure Line;
begin
    writeln('*****************************');
end;

{*** The main program starts here ***}
begin
    ClrScr;
    {*** Call the routine here ***}
    Line;
    writeln('Hello':12);
    {*** and here ***}
    Line;
end.
```

Notice from the program listing above that, with the routine's code inserted in the program, the routine can be called in exactly the same way we call those standard procedures available within the Pascal language.

**Activity 4.7**

Enter and run the program in LISTING-4.7.

# How the Program Executes

Every program instruction is stored in the computer's memory. Although these instructions are in machine code, they are equivalent to the original Pascal statements. Hence, we may consider, for the purpose of this explanation, that the program is held as a sequence of Pascal instructions.

We can identify two main sections of code in LISTING-4.7 : the code for the main program and that for *Line*. When we compile the program, the two sections of code will be stored separately in memory (see FIG-4.5).

**FIG-4.5**

Code Held in Memory

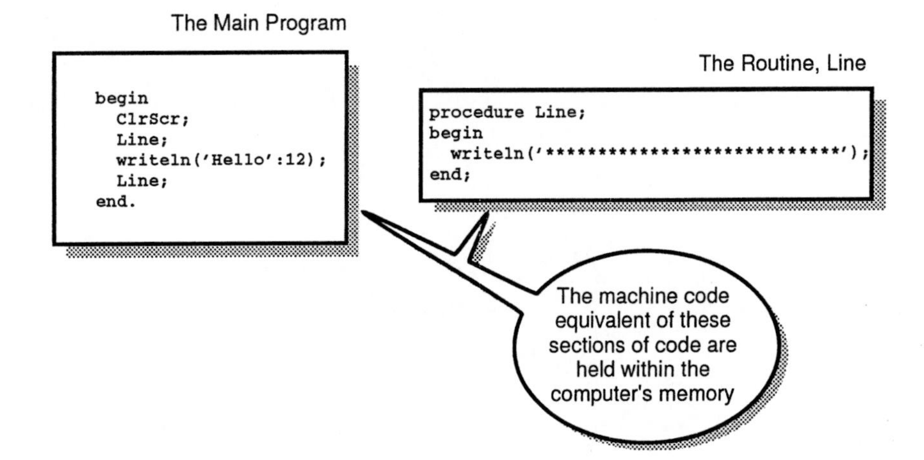


As always, execution begins in the main program. However, the first statement is a call to *Line,* the code of which is then executed. When this is complete, control returns to the statement in the main program following the original procedure call and execution of the main program continues. The stages involved in the execution of LISTING-4.7 are shown in FIG-4.6.

**FIG-4.6**

Executing a Routine

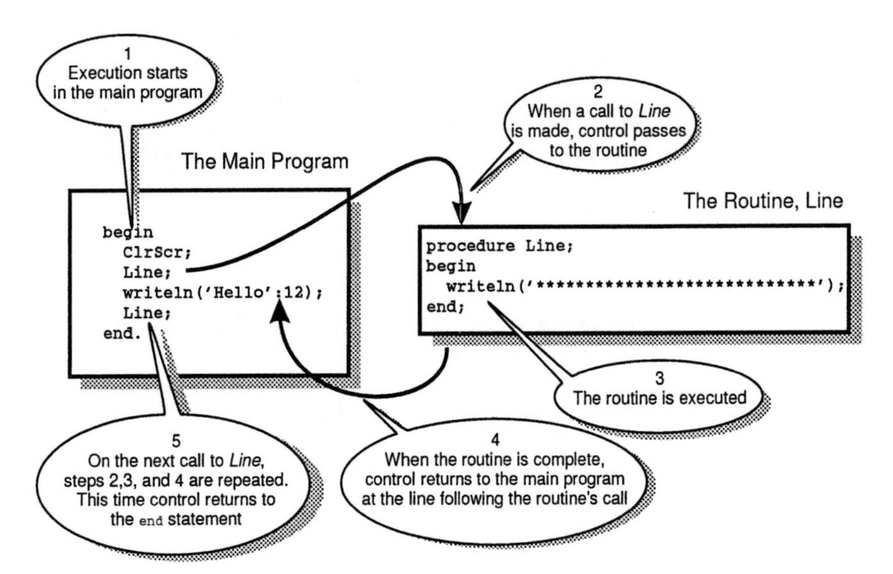

**Activity 4.8**

Type in LISTING-4.7 and use the single step trace facilities of the debugger to watch the execution of the program.

**Activity 4.9**

Write and test a procedure, *Box*, which draws a 10 by 10 square of asterisks.

# Passing Parameters

## A Single Parameter

User-defined routine names are shown in italics.

The *Line* procedure is not very useful as it stands since the length of the line is predetermined. A better routine would allow us to pass the required length as a parameter. Assuming a parameter, *width*, the new version of *Line* has the logic

```
FOR width TIMES DO
    Display a single asterisk (keeping cursor on the same line)
ENDFOR
Move cursor to start of next line
```

which is coded as

```
procedure Line(width : integer);
var
    count : integer;
begin
    {*** Output a single asterisk the required number ***}
    {*** of times ***}
    for count := 1 to width do
        write('*');
    {*** Move cursor to a new line ***}
    writeln;
end;
```

The new version of *Line* uses a `for` loop to display a single '*' *width* times. This requires the routine to declare a variable ( *count* ) to be used as the loop counter. Since *count* is declared inside *Line* it is known as a **local variable** and is allocated space in the computer's memory only while *Line* is executing. This is also true for *width*, which, although a parameter of the routine, is also created as a local variable in *Line.*

When our new version of *Line* is called, a value must be supplied in the parentheses. For example, the main program might contain the code:

```
Line(15);
```

This argument supplied is also known as the **actual parameter** of the routine. When the routine is called, the value of the actual parameter is copied into the formal parameter variable before execution of the routine begins. In the example above, this means that the value 15 is copied to *width* (see FIG-4.7).

The actual parameter may be a variable or expression as well as a constant. For example:

```
Line(nbr);          {*** Variable parameter ***}
Line(nbr * 2);      {*** Expression parameter ***}
```

**FIG-4.7** Passing Parameter Values to a Routine

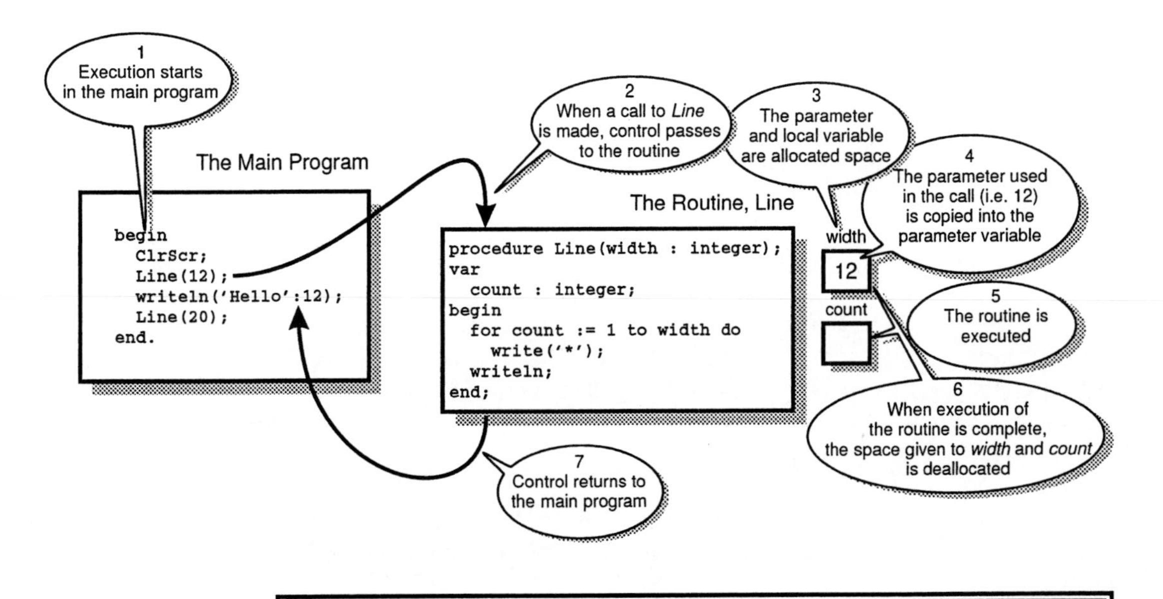


> **Activity 4.10**
>
> 1. Modify your *Box* routine to allow the size of the square to be defined as a parameter.
>
> 2. Write a procedure, *DisplayDayOfWeek*, that takes a number between 0 and 6 and displays the corresponding day of the week (0 = Sunday).

## Multiple Parameters

The procedure *Line* would be even more flexible if we could specify which character is to be used to create the line. This is achieved by making the character to be used in constructing the line another parameter of the routine:

```
procedure Line(width : integer; shape : char);
var
    count : integer;
begin
    for count := 1 to width do
        write(shape);
    writeln;
end;
```

A typical call to the new routine might be:

```
Line(30,'=');
```

> **Activity 4.11**
>
> What local variables will be created when a call to this new version of *Line* is called?
>
> What values will be copied to these variables before the routine begins execution?

**Activity 4.12**

1. Write a new version of *Box* to allow the border character to be specified.

2. Write a routine, *VertLine,* which will draw a vertical line of characters. Both the height of the line and the character from which it is constructed should be parameters to the routine.

When calling a routine, it is your responsibility as the programmer to ensure that the actual parameters (30 and '=' in the call to *Line* above) are given in the correct order - integer followed by character. Failure to do so will cause a compilation error.

# Returning Values from a Procedure

## Returning a Single Value

Most procedures produce results. For example, we might want to write a routine that determines the smaller of two numbers. Such a routine would need to have passed to it two values (the numbers being compared) and produce a result (a copy of the smaller of the two values input). Parameters that are designed to contain values being returned from a procedure must be preceded by the term var. Hence, our *Smaller* procedure would have the heading:

```
procedure Smaller(no1, no2 : integer; var ans : integer);
```

In the coding of the routine we need to assign a value to the parameter that is to contain the result. Therefore, the full coding for *Smaller* would be:

```
procedure Smaller(no1, no2 : integer; var ans : integer);
begin
    if no1 < no2 then
        ans := no1
    else
        ans := no2;
end;
```

The program in LISTING-4.8 shows this procedure being used. The program employs the following logic:

```
Read in two numbers
Find out the smaller of the two values
Display the results
```

**LISTING-4.8**

Returning a Value from a Procedure

```
program ReturningValues;
uses WinCrt;

{************************************}
{*       Procedure definition       *}
{************************************}
procedure Smaller(no1, no2 : integer; var ans : integer);
begin
  if no1 < no2 then
      ans := no1
  else
      ans := no2;
end;
{************************************}
{*        main program              *}
{************************************}
```

**Continued on next page**

**LISTING-4.8**
(continued)

Returning a Value from a Procedure

```
var
  n1, n2, result : integer;
  ch             : char;

begin
  {*** Read in the two values ***}
  ClrScr;
  write('Enter two numbers : ');
  readln(n1, n2);
  {*** Determine the smaller value ***}
  Smaller(n1,n2,result);
  {*** Display result ***}
  writeln('The two numbers were ', n1, ' and ', n2);
  writeln('The smaller value is ', result);
  {*** Close window when key pressed ***}
  ch := ReadKey;
  DoneWinCrt;
end.
```

Calling DoneWinCrt closes the Window.

## How it Executes

The call to *Smaller* within the program works in much the same way as with previous procedure calls:

This description of how var parameters are handled is sufficient to explain the end results of the action. However, the real truth about var parameters is out there - see pointers in the next chapter.

When the call is encountered within the main program, control passes to the routine. Parameters and local variables have their space allocated and the actual parameter values are copied across. In this case, that means that the contents of *n1* are copied to *no1*, *n2* is copied to *no2* and *result* is copied to *ans*. This last transfer, *result* to *ans*, may seem unnecessary since *result* is meant to be given a value rather than be sent one; also, because *result* was not assigned a value within the main program, its contents will be unknown. (We'll see in a later example why, nevertheless, it is necessary to perform this transfer.) As the procedure is executed, *ans* is assigned a value (overwriting any value transferred from *result*). Now, as the routine ends, but before its variables are deallocated, the contents of *ans* are copied into *result*, thereby passing the required value back to the main program.

The process involved is shown in FIG-4.8.

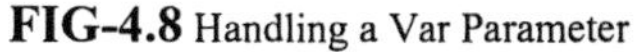

**FIG-4.8** Handling a Var Parameter

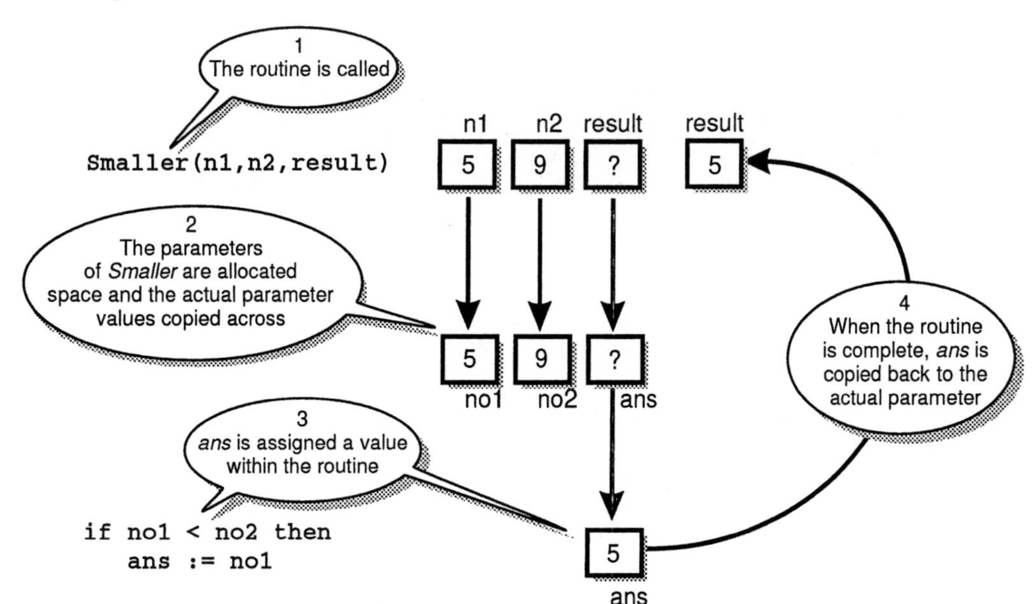

**Activity 4.13**

Create procedures with single `var` parameters that perform the following tasks:

1. Takes a date and returns the day of the week as a number between 0 and 6 (0 = Sunday). Call the routine *DateToDayOfWeek.*

2. Takes two input parameters, *x* and *y* and returns the result of *x* raised to the power *y* (i.e. $x^y$). Call the routine *Power. x* is raised to the power *y* using the formula: `exp(y * ln(x))`

## Returning Several Values

Some procedures require to return more than one value. For example, if an imperial weight is stored over two variables: one containing the pounds value, the other the ounces, and a routine is required which takes two such weights, and returns their sum, then the procedure will have to return two values.

The heading for such a procedure would be

The heading is split over two lines due to lack of space

```
procedure AddWeights(lb1, oz1, lb2, oz2 : integer;
                     var anslb, ansoz : integer);
```

and is coded as:

```
procedure AddWeights(lb1, oz1, lb2, oz2 : integer;
                     var anslb, ansoz : integer);
var
    totaloz : integer;
begin
    totaloz := (lb1 + lb2) * 16 + oz1 + oz2;
    anslb := totaloz div 16;
    ansoz := totaloz mod 16;
end;
```

LISTING-4.9 shows the routine in use.

**LISTING-4.9**

Using a Procedure with more than One Return Parameter

```
program ReturningValues;
uses WinCrt;

{*************************************}
{*       Procedure definition        *}
{*************************************}

procedure AddWeights(lb1, oz1, lb2, oz2 : integer;
                     var anslb, ansoz : integer);
var
  totaloz : integer;
begin
  totaloz := (lb1 + lb2) * 16 + oz1 + oz2;
  anslb := totaloz div 16;
  ansoz := totaloz mod 16;
end;
{************************************}
{*        main program              *}
{************************************}

var
  w1lbs, w1oz, w2lbs, w2oz, totlbs, totoz : integer;
  ch             : char;
```

**Continued on next page**

**LISTING-4.9**
(continued)

Using a Procedure with more than One Return Parameter

```
begin
   {*** Read in the two weights ***}
   ClrScr;
   write('Enter first weight (lbs oz) : ');
   readln(w1lbs, w1oz);
   write('Enter second weight (lbs oz) : ');
   readln(w2lbs, w2oz);
   {*** Add the weights ***}
   AddWeights(w1lbs, w1oz, w2lbs, w2oz, totlbs, totoz);
   {*** Display result ***}
   writeln('Adding ', w1lbs, ' lbs ', w1oz,' oz and ',w2lbs,
   ↳' lbs ',w2oz,' oz gives ', totlbs,' lbs ',totoz,' oz');
   {*** Close window when key pressed ***}
   ch := ReadKey;
   DoneWinCrt;
end.
```

**Activity 4.14**

Write and test a procedure called *AddLSD*, that adds together two amounts of money given in pounds, shillings and pence (There were 12 pence in 1 shilling and 20 shillings in a pound).

# Updating Parameters

There are occasions when we not only want to pass a value into a procedure, but also have that value changed and returned by the procedure. In fact, we've already met procedures in Pascal that do this: `Inc` and `Dec`.

Luckily, we don't have to do anything different to create such a routine. If you have another look at the description of how a `var` parameter is handled, you'll see that it already does everything we need since `var` parameter values are copied to the formal parameter variables.

The routine below, called *Twice*, doubles the value of its parameter:

```
procedure Twice(var v: integer);
begin
    v := v * 2;
end;
```

We could then call this routine as in the code snippet below:

```
var
    nbr : integer;
begin
    nbr := 10;
    Twice(nbr);
    writeln(nbr);
```

The `writeln` statement would display the value 20 on the screen.

**Activity 4.15**

Write and test a routine, *RemoveSpaces,* that removes all spaces from a string parameter.

Of course, it is possible to update the contents of more than one `var` parameter if required.

Next we'll look at how to create functions.

# The General Format of a Function

The general layout of a function definition is shown in FIG-4.9.

**FIG-4.9** The Format of a Function

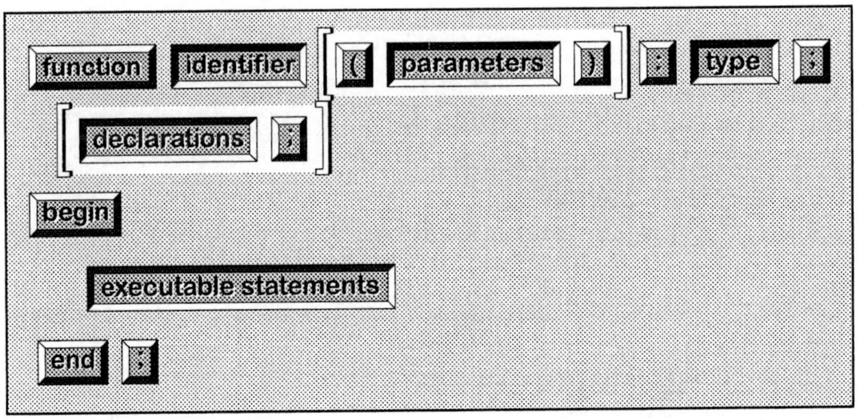

```
function identifier [ ( parameters ) ] : type ;
   [ declarations ; ]
begin
   executable statements
end ;
```

As you can see, the structure is similar to that of a procedure, the only differences being that the routine starts with the keyword `function` and that the parameter list is followed by a colon and a type.

**type** specifies the type of value returned by the function.

You may recall that the difference between a function and a procedure is that a function must return exactly one value whereas a procedure may return any number of values.

For example, if we wanted to create a function to return the tangent of an angle, it would have the heading

```
function Tan(angle : real) : real;
```

# Coding a Function

The coding of a function differs in one respect from a procedure in that somewhere within the function the value to be returned must be specified. This is done by assigning a value to the function name. You can see how this is done in the code for *Tan* below:

```
function Tan(angle : real) : real;
begin
   Tan := Sin(angle) / Cos(angle);
end;
```

It may seem strange to assign a value to the function name, but this is exactly what we need to do. Within the function, the name of that function is treated as if it were a variable of the same type as the value returned by the function. In this case, it means that we treat the term *Tan* as if it were a *real* variable. However, there is one restriction - the function name should only appear on the left-hand side of an assignment statement. Hence, the following statements would be inappropriate within *Tan*:

```
Tan := Tan + 1;      {Tan appears on RHS of assignment statement}
```

# Calling a Function

We've already seen how to call standard functions in the first half of this chapter, and calling your own is no different. So, for example, we might call *Tan* with statements such as:

```
x := Tan(y);
if Tan(angle) < 2 then
writeln(Tan(1.2));
```

**Activity 4.16**

Write and test functions to perform the following tasks:

1. Take a date and return the day of the week as a number between 0 and 6 (0 = Sunday). Call the routine *DateToDayOfWeek.*

2. Take two input parameters, *x* and *y* and return the result of *x* raised to the power *y* (i.e. $x^y$). Call the routine *Power. x* is raised to the power *y* using the formula:
   ```
   exp(y * ln(x))
   ```

3. Take an integer value and return double that value. Call the routine *Twice.*

# Choosing between Functions and Procedures

When we come to write a routine that returns anything other than a single value, we need to create a procedure. But where exactly one value is returned, we have a choice: procedure or function.

You've already seen some routines, such as *Power* and *Twice*, written in both styles. Often we will choose between the two styles based on how easy it is to call such routines. For example, if we wanted to use *Power* within our program, calling the procedure version would create a statement such as

```
Power(a,b,c);
```

with *c* being assigned the value $a^b$. On the other hand, calling the function would be coded as:

```
c := Power(a,b);
```

It is more obvious in the second version what variable is being assigned a value. But functions are even more convenient if they are to be used within an expression such as

```
if Power(a,b) > 1000 then
```

As a procedure we would have to code this as

```
Power(a,b,c);
if c > 1000 then
```

which is certainly more effort.

However, when a routine updates a parameter, as in *Twice*, a procedure may be preferable since this allows us to write

```
Twice(nbr);
```

rather than

```
nbr := Twice(nbr);
```

# Coping with Pre-conditions

The parameters to some routines have to be restricted in range. So, for example, although the parameter to the square root function is defined as a real value, not every real value may be used. For the square root function to operate correctly, the value passed must not be less than zero. These restrictions are described in the routine's pre-condition. Hence, assuming `sqrt` has the heading

```
function Sqrt(x:real):real;
```

its pre-condition would be stated as

```
x >= 0
```

If a call is made to the routine which does not satisfy the pre-condition, such as

```
writeln(Sqrt(-9));
```

the program will produce a runtime error and terminate.

Not all routines deal so severely with failure to meet a pre-condition. Some, like `GotoXY`, simply do nothing if the parameters are invalid.

Our own routines will often require pre-conditions. An example of this is *DayOfWeek* defined in Activity 4.13. The code given in the solution assumes that the value passed will be valid, but it would be better to check that the parameter is valid within the routine itself.

As a general rule, a routine should start by checking that its pre-conditions have been met. Where the pre-condition is not met, the routine should then either terminate the whole program or simply terminate itself, returning to the statement following its call. Which of these options is chosen depends on the importance of the routine. For example, it is unlikely that a program will produce the correct results if a calculation involving `sqrt` fails, hence the routine terminates the program. On the other hand, failure to move the cursor through a call to `GotoXY`, will spoil the layout of the screen but the results are unlikely to be affected, hence the routine simply returns control to the calling program.

### halt

To terminate the whole program we use the term `halt`. Hence, `sqrt` may start with the code:

```
if x < 0 then
    halt;
```

### exit

If we want to handle the error by simply returning from the routine, then we use the term `exit`. So `GotoXY` might contain the code:

```
if (x < 1) or (x > 80) or (y < 1) or (y > 25) then
    exit;
```

*DisplayDayOfWeek* was created in Activity 4.10.

**Activity 4.17**

Rewrite *DisplayDayOfWeek* so that it terminates the program if the value passed is outside the range 0 to 6.

## Summary

- **Procedures and Functions** can be defined in Pascal.
- **Procedures** return zero or more values.
- **Functions** return a single value.
- **The code for a user-defined routine** must appear within the program before any call to that routine.
- **Local variables** can be defined within a routine.
- **Parameters and local variables have space allocated** when a routine is called. These are destroyed when the routine is exited.
- **The term `var` is used in a procedure heading** to identify values being returned.
- **The return type of a function** is defined in the function heading following the parameter list.
- **The function name** is treated as a form of variable within the routine and is assigned the value to be returned by the routine.
- **The function name** can only appear on the left-side of an assignment statement inside the routine.
- **Generally, code a routine as a function** when it returns only a single value. However, if one of the parameters is updated, choose a procedure.

**Activity 4.18**

Write and test routines to perform the following tasks.

1. Return the second largest of four numbers.
   Create as a function called *SecLargest.*

```
OUTLINE LOGIC:
    IF n1> n2 THEN
        largest := n1
        second := n2
    ELSE
        largest := n2
        second := n1
    ENDIF
    IF n3 > largest THEN
        second := largest
        largest := n3
    ELSE
        IF n3 > second
            second := n3
        ENDIF
    ENDIF
    IF n4 > largest THEN
        second := largest
        largest := n4
    ELSE
        IF n4 > second
            second := n4
        ENDIF
    ENDIF
    return second
```

2. Identify a character parameter as a vowel, consonant or non-alphabetic character. (Return 1, 2 or 3 respectively).
   Create as a function called *ClassifyChar.*

```
OUTLINE LOGIC:
    IF ch is alphabetic THEN
        IF ch is a vowel THEN
            return 1
        ELSE
            return 2
        ENDIF
    ELSE
        return 3
    ENDIF
```

3. Return the value *true* if a specified year is a leap year, otherwise return *false.*

   Create as a function called *IsLeapYear.*

   This routine should terminate the program if the year passed to it is less than 1600.

**Continued on next page**

**Activity 4.18** (continued)

3. (continued)

```
OUTLINE LOGIC:
    IF (year exactly divisible by 4 but not 100)
        OR(year exactly divisible by 400) THEN
        return 1
    ELSE
        return zero
    ENDIF
```

4. Accept a month of the year and return the number of days in that month.
   Create as a function called *DaysinMonth.*
   February returns 28. The routine terminates the program if the month is not in range 1 to 12.

5. Read a date entered in the form day/month/year.
   Create as a procedure called *GetDate.*
   If the date as a whole is invalid, it is to be re-entered. Accept all entries from the same area of the screen. The date should be returned in three integer variables.

```
OUTLINE LOGIC:
    Record position of cursor
    REPEAT
        Set valid to FALSE
        Move cursor to recorded position
        Clear any previous entry
        Read date as string
        Separate string into day month and year
        IF unsuccessful THEN
            continue
        ENDIF
        IF month outside the range 1 to 12 THEN
            continue
        ENDIF
        IF year before 1600 THEN
            continue
        ENDIF
        Calculate days in month
        IF day outside range 1 to days in month THEN
            continue
        ENDIF
        Set valid to TRUE
    UNTIL valid
```

6. Accept a date (as three parameters) and return the number of days since 1/1/4713BC. Create as a function called *DateToJulian.*
   The formula for this is
   Y = year+(month-2.85)/12
   days = [ [ [ [367.0* Y]-[Y]-0.75*[Y]+day]-0.75*2.0]+1721115.0]
   where
   [x] is the largest integer smaller than or equal to *x*.

**Continued on next page**

**Activity 4.18** (continued)

7. Accepts the number of days since 1/1/4713BC and returns the corresponding date.

   Create as a procedure called *JulianToDate.*

   The formula for this is:

```
temp1 = (days - 1721119.0)+2.0
year = [(temp1 - 0.2)/365.25]
temp2 = temp1 - [365.25*year]
M = [(temp2-0.5)/30.6]
day = temp2 - 30.6 * M + 0.5
IF M > 9 THEN
     month = M - 9
     year = year+1
ELSE
     month = M+3
ENDIF
```

8. Read in an integer value and return another integer whose digits are the reverse of the accepted value (e.g. 145 will return 541).

   Create as a function called *Reverse.*

# LIFETIME, SCOPE, AND VISIBILITY

## Lifetime

With the introduction of user-defined routines, we now have a choice of where to define variables: they can be declared within a routine or within the main program. Variables defined within a procedure or function are known as local variables and exist only while the routine to which they belong is being executed. The **lifetime** of a variable is defined by the section of code during which it exists. In the code below, the variable *count* has the lifetime indicated:

```
procedure Line(width : integer);
var
    count : integer;
begin
    for count := 1 to width do      The lifetime of count
        write('*');
    writeln;
end;
```

## Scope

The **scope** of a variable is the part of the program in which a variable can normally be accessed. Any attempt to reference a variable outside its scope will cause the compiler to signal an error. For example in the code given below, the attempt to display the value of *count* is invalid.

```
program Scope1;
uses WinCrt;

procedure Line(width : integer);
var
    count : integer;
begin
    for count := 1 to width do
        write('*');
    writeln;
end;

begin
    Line(12);
    writeln(count);     {ERROR count does not exist here}
end.
```

If we declare a variable in the main program, after any user-defined routines, then that variable is available only within the main program.

## Global variables

But it is also possible to define a variable before the user-defined routines, as in the following code:

Different routines may also contain local variables whose names match. Since they have different scope, this is not a problem.

```
program Scope2;
uses WinCrt;

var
    big : integer;

procedure Line(width : integer);
var
    count : integer;
begin
    for count := 1 to width do
        write('*');
```

```
    writeln;
end;

begin
    Line(12);
end.
```

This is known as a **global variable**. Its lifetime and scope extend over the whole program. Hence, it can be accessed in any of the code which follows its declaration. For example:

```
program Scope3;
uses WinCrt;

var
    big : integer;

procedure Line(width : integer);
var
    count : integer;
begin
    big := 20;                      {big accessed here}
    for count := 1 to width do
        write('*');
    writeln;
end;

begin
    Line(12);
    writeln(big);                   {and here}
end.
```

Use of global variables is frowned upon and considered to be very bad programming since they often are responsible for errors within a program's logic.

## Visibility

An interesting situation occurs if the global variable has the same name as some other, local, variable. For instance, if we rename our global variable *count* and then try to access *count* within our procedure

```
program Scope3;
uses WinCrt;

var
    count : integer;

procedure Line(width : integer);
var
    count : integer;
begin
    count := 20;                    {which count is accessed?}
    for count := 1 to width do
        write('*');
    writeln;
end;

begin
    Line(12);
    writeln(count);             {global variable accessed here}
end.
```

it is not obvious which *count* variable will be accessed.

Although we are not normally allowed to define two variable with the same name, this rule does not apply if one is global and the other local.

When the code within *Line* is being executed, we now have two variables called *count* that are in scope. The compiler overcomes any problem in deciding which of the variables is being accessed by applying a simple rule:

*When more than one variable of the same name are in scope, any references are assumed to be to the local one.*

This means that while *Line* is being executed, although the global variable, *count*, is in scope, it is not visible to that code. The term **visibility**, therefore, is used to indicate the areas of code in which a variable can be accessed.

Of course, if we were to change the name of the global variable to anything other than *count* (or change the local variable in *Line*), then the problem of accessing the global variable would be solved.

## Typed Constants

A typed constant, despite its name, is a rather special type of variable. To understand its features and where it would be useful, consider the following problem:

A routine is required that takes an integer value. If that value is a 7, then 1 is added to a *count*. *count* is then displayed.

The logic for the routine would be

```
IF parameter's value is 7 THEN
    Add 1 to count
ENDIF
Display count
```

This seems a simple enough requirement, but how is it to be coded? We could try:

```
procedure NoOfSevens( v : integer);
var
    count : integer;
begin
    if v = 7 then
        count := count + 1;
    writeln(count);
end;
```

This would be called from a main program such as:

```
var
    c : integer;
    nbr : integer;
begin
    for c := 1 to 20 do
    begin
        write('Enter number : ');
        readln(nbr);
        NoOfSevens(nbr);
    end;
end.
```

But this won't work, since local variables are destroyed when the routine is exited, so *count* won't retain its value from one call to the next. In any case, we didn't even set *count* to zero.

We could try defining a global variable:

```
var
    count : integer;
procedure NoOfSevens( v : integer);
begin
```

```
    if v = 7 then
        count := count + 1;
    writeln(count);
end;
```

As long as we remembered to set *count* to zero in the main program, this would work. Since *count* isn't local it will remain in existence between calls to *NoOfSevens* and retain any value it is assigned there. However, it does use a global variable and these are to be avoided.

A third method is to create a **typed constant** within *NoOfSevens:*

```
procedure NoOfSevens( v : integer);
const
    count : integer = 0;
begin
    if v = 7 then
        count := count + 1;
    writeln(count);
end;
```

This is different from normal constant declaration where no type would be given (i.e. `const count = 0;`). Typed constants have several interesting characteristics. Firstly, they are allocated space as the program begins execution; in this respect they are similar to global variables. Also, at this time, they are assigned the value specified (e.g. *count* is set to zero). However, like local variables, they can only be accessed within the routine in which they are defined - in this case within *NoOfSevens*. Lastly, and most strangely, they aren't constants (despite the name) and may be assigned new values.

Now we have all the requirements of our program. Note that count will not be reset to zero each time the routine is entered, since a named constant is assigned the value specified in its definition only once, when its space is allocated.

# Summary

- **The lifetime of a variable is the section of code for which space is allocated to that variable.**

- **The scope of a variable is the section of code in which that variable could normally be accessed.**

- **The visibility of a variable is the area of code in which a variable can actually be accessed.**

- **Scope and visibility may differ** if a local variable has the same name as a global variable.

- **Named constants have a lifetime** that spans the whole program but scope for only the routine in which they are defined.

- **The value of a named constant** can be changed by a program.

- **Named constants retain their value** between calls to the routine in which they are defined.

# CASE STUDY

## The Problem

A program is required to perform a variety of tasks involving dates. The operations required are:

1. To calculate the number of days between two dates.
2. To calculate the resulting date when adding a number of days to a specified date.
3. To calculate the resulting date when subtracting a number of days from a specified date.
4. To determine the day of the week on which a specified date falls.

## Clarification

The program should display the options available in the form of a menu. Invalid entries should be flagged with appropriate error messages.

## The Algorithm

A basic description of logic required is given by:

```
1. REPEAT
2.     Display Menu
3.     Get option
4.     Process option
5. UNTIL QUIT option chosen
```

Rather than continue to stepwise refine the algorithm, an alternative approach is to identify statements in the description which may be converted to routines in the final program and treat these as separate problems to be tackled independently. In the above logic, steps 2,3 and 4 seem likely candidates.

The details of each routine is given in what is known as a Mini-Specification (or Mini-Spec). For example, the Mini-Spec for a menu function would be:

| | | |
|---|---|---|
| **NAME** | : | DisplayMenu |
| **PARAMETERS** | | |
| **IN** | : | None |
| **OUT** | : | None |
| **IN/OUT** | : | None |
| **PRECONDITION** | : | None |
| **DESCRIPTION** | : | User options are displayed on screen |
| **OUTLINE LOGIC** | : | |

```
Display "1  -  Days between dates"
Display "2  -  Add days to date"
Display "3  -  Subtract days from date"
Display "4  -  Day of week"
Display "5  -  QUIT"
Display "Enter option (1 to 5)"
```

As you can see, a Mini-Spec bears some resemblance to the description of a standard routine. However, there are some differences: rather than supplying a routine heading, separate lines are used to define the routine's name, parameters and return type.

IN parameters are equivalent to those passed on a *read only* basis in a function. For example, a routine which calculated an employee's wage based on the number of hours worked would require the hours worked to be passed as an IN parameter.

An OUT parameter indicates a value returned by the routine. For example, in the wage calculating routine the employee's wage would be an OUT parameter.

When coding routines with OUT parameters we may use a function if only one value is returned, otherwise a procedure with `var` parameters will be needed.

IN/OUT parameters are those where the actual parameter's value is updated by the routine. We met examples of this earlier in routines such as *Twice* and *ToUpper*.

The PRE-CODITION details any restrictions on the values of parameters passed into the routine.

The OUTLINE LOGIC gives details, in a Structured English, of the steps required to program the routine.

The routine required to get the user's option has the Mini-Spec:

**NAME** : GetOption
**PARAMETERS**
  **IN** : None
  **OUT** : option : INTEGER
  **IN/OUT** : None
**PRE-CONDITION** : None

**DESCRIPTION** : *option* set to value entered at keyboard. *option* should be in range 1 to 5. Values outside this range should result in an error message with the user being allowed to re-enter a value for *option*.

**OUTLINE LOGIC** :

```
Display "Enter option"
Get option
WHILE option outside range 1 to 5 DO
    Display "Invalid option. Must be in
            the range 1 to 5"
    Display "Please re-enter option "
    Get option
ENDWHILE
```

```
NAME            : ProcessOption
PARAMETERS
    IN          : option : INTEGER
    OUT         : None
    IN/OUT      : None
PRE-CONDITION   : 1 <= option <= 5

DESCRIPTION     : option specified is executed.

OUTLINE LOGIC   :
                  IF
                      option = 1:
                          Get first date
                          Get second date
                          Change first date to Julian days
                          Change second date to Julian days
                          Display the absolute difference
                          between the first and second
                          Julian days
                      option = 2 :
                          Get date
                          Get days
                          Convert date to Julian days
                          Add days to Julian days
                          Convert Julian days to date
                          Display new date
                      option = 3 :
                          Get date
                          Get days
                          Convert date to Julian days
                          Subtract days to Julian days
                          Convert Julian days to date
                          Display new date
                      option = 4 :
                          Get date
                          Convert to day of week
                          Display day of week
                      option = 5 :
                          Display terminating message
                  ENDIF
```

The outline logic for *ProcessOption* highlights some complex tasks:

```
Get first date
Get second date
Convert first date to Julian days
Convert second date to Julian days
Convert Julian days to date
Convert to day of week code
Display day of week text
```

Some of these tasks, such as `Get first date` and `Get second date` are basically the same task with different parameters. Recognising this, we can reduce our list of tasks to:

```
Get date
Convert date to Julian days
Convert Julian days to date
Convert date to day of week code
Display name of day corresponding to day of week code
```

Now each of these can be defined as functions in their own right:

| | | |
|---|---|---|
| **NAME** | : | GetDate |
| **PARAMETERS** | | |
| **IN** | : | None |
| **OUT** | : | day, month, year : INTEGER |
| **IN/OUT** | : | None |
| **PRE-CONDITION** | : | None |
| **DESCRIPTION** | : | Valid values for *day*, *month* and *year* accepted from keyboard. |
| **OUTLINE LOGIC** | : | |

```
REPEAT
    Set invalid to FALSE
    Clear area of screen used
    Read day, month, year
    IF month outside the range 1 to 12
    THEN
        Set invalid to TRUE
    ENDIF
    IF year before 1600 THEN
        Set invalid to TRUE
    ENDIF
    Calculate days in month
    IF month is February AND
     year is a leap year THEN
        Add 1 to days in month
    ENDIF
    IF day outside range 1 to
     days in month THEN
        Set invalid to TRUE
    ENDIF
UNTIL NOT invalid
```

| | | |
|---|---|---|
| **NAME** | : | DateToJulian |
| **PARAMETERS** | | |
| **IN** | : | day, month, year : INTEGER |
| **OUT** | : | noofdays : INTEGER |
| **IN/OUT** | : | None |
| **PRE-CONDITION** | : | *day*, *month* and *year* form a valid date |
| **DESCRIPTION** | : | Sets *noofdays* to the number of days since 1/1/4713BC to *day/month/year* inclusive. |
| **OUTLINE LOGIC** | : | |

```
Y = year+(month-2.85)/12
noofdays = [ [ [367.0* Y]-[Y]-0.75*[Y]
+day]-0.75*2.0]+1721115.0
```

| | | |
|---|---|---|
| **NAME** | : | JulianToDate |
| **PARAMETERS** | | |
| **IN** | : | noofdays : INTEGER |
| **OUT** | : | day, month, year : INTEGER |
| **IN/OUT** | : | None |
| **PRE-CONDITION** | : | *noofdays* >= 0 |
| **DESCRIPTION** | : | Returns the date (*day/month/year*) which is *noofdays* since 1/1/4713BC |
| **OUTLINE LOGIC** | : | |

```
temp1 := (noofdays - 1721119.0)+2.0
temp2 := temp1 - [365.25*temp1]
M := [(temp2-0.5)/30.6]
day := temp2 - 30.6 * M + 0.5
year := [(temp1 - 0.2)/365.25]
IF M > 9 THEN
    month := M - 9
    year := year+1
ELSE
    month := M+3
ENDIF
```

| | | |
|---|---|---|
| **NAME** | : | DateToDayofWeek |
| **PARAMETERS** | | |
| **IN** | : | day, month, year : INTEGER |
| **OUT** | : | dow : INTEGER |
| **IN/OUT** | : | None |
| **PRE-CONDITION** | : | *day, month* and *year* form a valid date |
| **DESCRIPTION** | : | Returns the code for the day of the week on which the date *day/month/year* fell. (0 - "Sunday" .. 6 - "Saturday"). |
| **OUTLINE LOGIC** | : | |

```
M    := (month+9) modulo 12+1
CY   := year-[M/11]
C    := [CY/100]
Y    := CY modulo 100
temp:= 2.6*M-0.2
dow := (temp+day+Y+[Y/4]+[C/4]-2*C)
        modulo 7
```

| | | |
|---|---|---|
| **NAME** | : | DayOfWeek |
| **PARAMETERS** | | |
| **IN** | : | dow : INTEGER |
| **OUT** | : | None |
| **IN/OUT** | : | None |
| **PRE-CONDITION** | : | 0 <= *dow* <= 6 |
| **DESCRIPTION** | : | Displays name of day corresponding to *dow*. (e.g. displays "Sunday" if *dow* = 0; "Saturday" if *dow* = 6) |
| **OUTLINE LOGIC** | : | |

```
IF
    dow = 0:
        Display "Sunday"
    dow = 1:
        Display "Monday"
    dow = 2:
        Display "Tuesday"
    dow = 3:
        Display "Wednesday"
    dow = 4:
        Display "Thursday"
    dow = 5:
        Display "Friday"
    dow = 6:
        Display "Saturday"
ENDIF
```

The detailed logic of *GetDate* introduces the possibility for yet more routines: one to determine if a year is a leap year and another to return the number of days in a specified month. This generates two additional Mini-Specs:

| | | |
|---|---|---|
| **NAME** | : | IsLeapYear |
| **PARAMETERS** | | |
| **IN** | : | year : INTEGER |
| **OUT** | : | result : BOOLEAN |
| **IN/OUT** | : | None |
| **PRE-CONDITION** | : | 1600 < *year* |
| **DESCRIPTION** | : | Returns *true* if *year* is a leap year, otherwise returns *false*. |
| **OUTLINE LOGIC** | : | |

```
IF (year divisible by 4 but not 100)
OR(year divisible by 400) THEN
    return 1
ELSE
    return zero
ENDIF
```

|  |  |  |
|---|---|---|
| **NAME** | : | DaysInMonth |
| **PARAMETERS** |  |  |
| **IN** | : | month : INTEGER |
| **OUT** | : | days : INTEGER |
| **IN/OUT** | : | None |
| **PRE-CONDITION** | : | 1 <= *month* <= 12 |
| **DESCRIPTION** | : | Returns the number of days in the *month* specified. No account is taken of leap years. |
| **OUTLINE LOGIC** | : |  |

```
IF month is 4,6,9 or 11 THEN
    return 30
ELSE
    IF month = 2 THEN
        return 28
    ELSE
        return 31
    ENDIF
ENDIF
```

The main program should also be described in a mini-specification:

|  |  |  |
|---|---|---|
| **NAME** | : | DateHandlingSystem |
| **PARAMETERS** |  |  |
| **IN** | : | None |
| **OUT** | : | None |
| **IN/OUT** | : | None |
| **PRE-CONDITION** | : | None |
| **DESCRIPTION** | : | Offers a selection of date processing operations.<br>Option 1 - the number of days between two dates.<br>Option 2 - Add a number of days to a given date.<br>Option 3 - Subtract days from a given date.<br>Option 4 - Display the day of the week on which a date fell.<br>Option 5 - Quit the program |
| **OUTLINE LOGIC** | : |  |

```
REPEAT
    Display menu
    Get option
    Perform option chosen
UNTIL quit option chosen
```

## Structure Diagrams

With so many routines used in the program, we are in danger of losing sight of the overall structure of the program. One graphical method of representing this overview is with a **Structure Diagram**.

**FIG-4.10**

Representing a Routine in a Structure Diagram

ProcessOption

A Structure Diagram shows the relationship between the routines of the system. That is, it shows calling/called relationship between routines and the values that are passed between these routines.

Each routine is represented by a labelled rectangle (see FIG-4.10).

Where one routine is called by another, this is shown by linking the corresponding rectangles (see FIG-4.11).

In the diagram, the **called routine** is placed beneath the **calling routine**.

Where data passes between the routines, this is shown using the symbol ○↗ and the name of the data items being transferred. The direction of the arrow indicates the direction in which the information is passed (see FIG-4.12).

If an item of data is updated by a routine (i.e. it's an IN/OUT parameter) it is shown as passing both into and out of the called routine (see FIG-4.13).

**FIG-4.11**

Calling and Called Routines

**FIG-4.12**

Returning Values from the Called Routine

**FIG-4.13**

Representing an IN/OUT Parameter

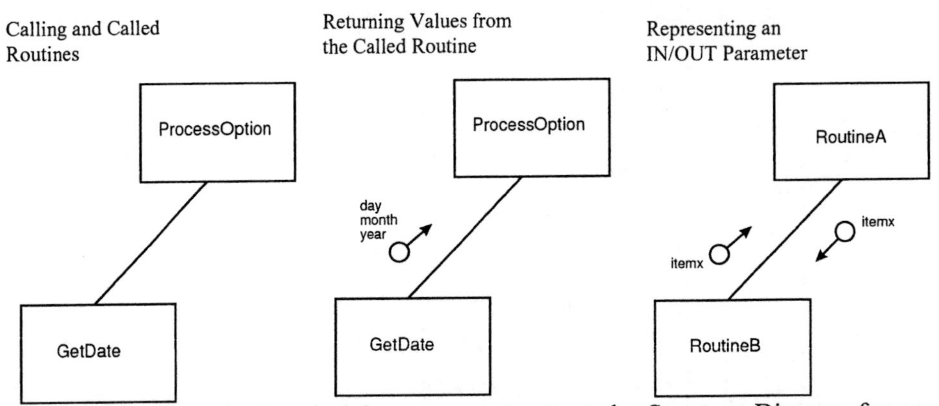


Using these basic principles, we can construct the Structure Diagram for our program (FIG-4.14).

**FIG-4.14**

The Case Study's Structure Diagram

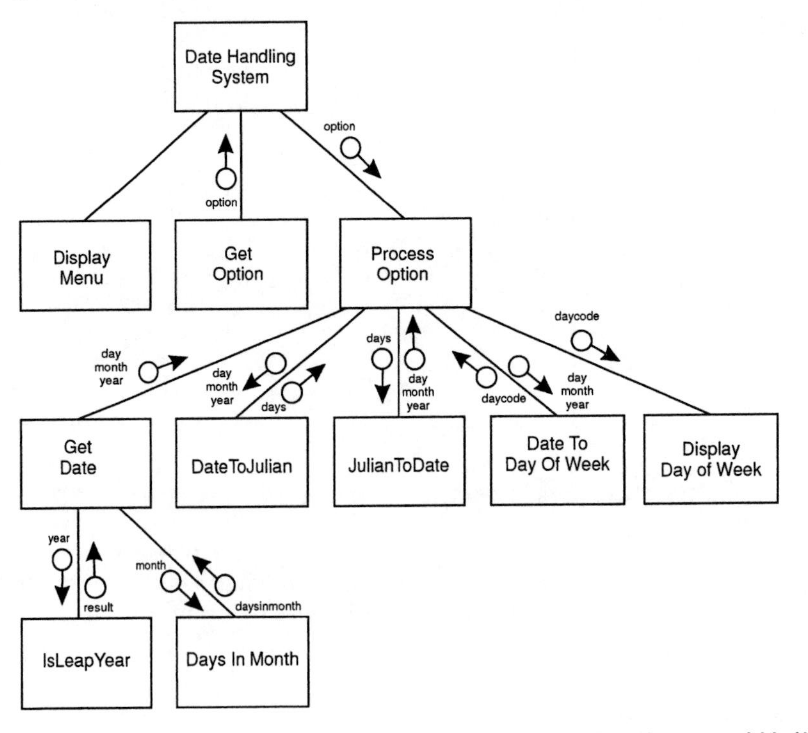

There are several details that do not show up on the Structure Diagram:

- The order in which routines are called
- How often a routine is called
- The actual parameters used in the routine call

# Testing the Routines

We've already seen in the previous chapter that test data can be created by examining the actual code of a program. This is called white box testing. By separating a program into several routines we can apply this technique to each routine. As long as routines are kept small and uncomplicated then the amount of white box test data required for each should be held at a level which can be easily handled.

## Black Box Testing

One problem with white box testing is that it only tests those control structures actually present in the code. If we've mistakenly omitted code from a program then tests which should be carried out will not be generated by this approach.

Another way to test code is to create test data based on the actions that the program or routine is supposed to perform. For example, if we know a routine called *IsLeapYear* is meant to return *true* when the year given as an argument is a leap year and *false* when it is not, then we might use the values 1992 and 1995 to check that we get the expected results under both circumstances.

We have created test data without reference to the code of the routine. In fact, the test data could be generated as soon as a complete description of the purpose of the routine is given, long before any code is ever written. This approach is known as **black box testing**.

The aim of black box testing is to identify the general group of responses that may occur in a routine, and from this to define the set of input values which should lead to each response. In the case of *IsLeapYear*, the responses are *true* or *false* and the input sets are:

1. Leap years
2. Non-Leap years

These input sets are known as **equivalence classes** since members of a given set or class should elicit the same response from the program.

Occasionally, we may want to divide an equivalence class into sub-classes simply because we feel this might result in more rigorous testing. Hence, we might decide to identify the equivalence classes for *IsLeapYear* as:

1. Leap years
   a) Century years (i.e. 1600, 2000, 2400 etc.)
   b) Non-century years (i.e. 1904, 1952, 1996 etc.)
2. Non-Leap years
   a) Century years (i.e. 1900, 2100,2200 etc.)
   b) Non-century years (i.e. 1901, 1973, 2001 etc.)

Again, we would use a single value from each class to test the routine.

Some routines have no obviously differing classes of response. For example, the routine *Twice* which doubles the parameter passed to it always gives back a number. So can we identify different reponse classes? Well, we might divide the results into negative, zero and positive classes.

The classes chosen will sometimes be obvious, other times we may need a bit of imagination and sometimes there will only be one class of responses.

When a routine has a pre-condition, it is important to specify that as one of the response classes and to identify the set of values which trigger that response.

> **Activity 4.19**
>
> Identify the various responses for *DaysInMonth* which returns the number of days in a specified month. The routine accepts an integer value in the range 1 to 12 and takes no account of leap years.

**Boundary Values**

Some equivalence classes are linear in nature. For example, one sub-class of rejected values in *DaysInMonth* is that containing integer values of 13 or more.

Experience has shown that with such classes the values on the boundary between one equivalence class and the next, when used as test data, often highlight problems in a piece of software. Hence, these **boundary values** should be used, along with some other value from each class, as test data.

**Creating Black Box Test Data**

To summarise: creating black box test data involves six steps:

- Identify the differing responses of the routine to be tested.
- Identify the equivalence classes for parameters or input data.
- Sub-divide the main equivalence classes where thought to be useful.
- Choose a value from each class as test data.
- Where the values of a class are linear, add all boundary values to the test data.
- Identify the expected response for each test value.

**Testing *DaysInMonth***

Responses: Pre-condition not met<br>
28<br>
30<br>
31

Equivalence classes:
1. Invalid month
    a) Less than 1
    b) Greater than 12
2. 2
    (February)
3. 4,6,9,11
    (April, June, September, November)
4. 1,3,5,7,8,10,12
    (January, March, May, July, August, October, December)

The actual test data is shown in TABLE-4.1.

**TABLE-4.1**

Black Box Test Data

| Class | Test Data | Expected Result |
|---|---|---|
| 1 a) | -7 | Not executed |
| 1 a) Boundary | 0 | Not executed |
| 1 b) | 20 | Not executed |
| 1 b) Boundary | 13 | Not executed |
| 2 | 2 | 28 |
| 3 | 6 | 30 |
| 4 | 5 | 31 |

Black box testing is not an alternative to white box testing. Rather, they complement each other and increase the likelihood of discovering errors in our code. For example, once we code *DaysInMonth* we'll end up with the following control structures:

```
if (month < 1) or (month > 12) then
if (month = 4) or (month = 6) or (month = 9) or (month = 11) then
if month = 2 then
```

These will determine the white box test data required.

As we create white box test values, we can incorporate, where possible, the values already chosen for the black box technique. The white box test data is shown in TABLE-4.2 with values extracted from the black box test data marked with an asterisk.

**TABLE-4.2**

White Box Test Data for *DaysInMonth*

| Run | Test Value | Reason for Test | Expected Result | Actual Result |
|---|---|---|---|---|
| 1 | month = -7* | if(month<1)or t,f | return 0 | |
| 2 | month = 13* | if(month<1)or f,t | return 0 | |
| 3 | month = 4 | if(month<1)or f,f<br>if(month=4)or t,f,f,f | return 30 | |
| 4 | month = 6* | if(month=4)or f,t,f,f | return 30 | |
| 5 | month = 9 | if(month=4)or f,f,t,f | return 30 | |
| 6 | month = 11 | if(month=4)or f,f,f,t | return 30 | |
| 7 | month = 2* | if(month=4)or f,f,f,f<br>if(month=2) t | return 28 | |
| 8 | month = 5* | if(month=2) f | return 31 | |

In addition to this, the test data table has to be extended to include any test values not yet incorporated from the black box test values. In the case of *DaysInMonth*, this would require two more test runs using the values 0 and 20. These would appear on the final test data table as the test data values for runs 9 and 10.

## A Test Driver

Like the components in a piece of equipment, the routines that go to make up the whole program should be tested separately. This is achieved by isolating the routine to be tested from the rest of the program and writing a small main program to call up the routine and display any results it produces.

This program is known as a **test driver**. Each routine should have its own test driver.

The results produced by a test driver should be compared with the expected results and, where there are differences, this should be documented and corrections made to the routine being tested.

Normally, testing begins at the lowest level of routine. LISTING-4.10 shows the program required to test *DaysinMonth*.

**LISTING-4.10**

Using a test Driver

```
program DaysInMonthDriver;
uses WinCrt;

{*** Calculate the days in a given month ***}
function DaysInMonth(m : integer): integer;
begin
  {*** If its April, June, September or November, return 30 ***}
  if (m = 4)or(m = 6)or(m = 9)or(m = 11)then
       DaysInMonth := 30
  {*** If its February, return 28 ***}
  else if(m = 2) then
       DaysInMonth := 28
  {*** Otherwise return 31 ***}
  else
       DaysInMonth := 31;
end;


{ *** Driver for DaysinMonth ***}
var
  month : integer;
  ch    : char;
begin
  repeat
       ClrScr;
       {*** Read test value ***}
       write('Enter month (1 to 12 or -99) : ');
       readln(month);
       {*** Call routine to be tested and display result ***}
       writeln('Days in month ',month,' = ',DaysinMonth(month));
       ch := ReadKey;
  until month = -99;
end.
```

Similar drivers would be created for routines such as *GetDate* and *DayOfWeek*. However, some routines depend on the results output by other routines. So, for example, it would be difficult to create a driver for *DateToDayOfWeek* without using the *GetDate* routine to supply a date. As a consequence some drivers may make use of previously tested routine to allow the creation of the data that is to be passed to the routine under test.

The test data and drivers required by the other routines are omitted for the sake of brevity. The listing of the complete program is given in LISTING-4.11.

**LISTING-4.11**

Using Routines

```
program HandlingDates;
{*******************************************************}
{* PROGRAM          : HandlingDates                     *}
{* AUTHOR           : Patricia Stamp                    *}
{* DATE             : 11/7/1998                         *}
{* VERSION          : 0.1                               *}
{* DESCRIPTION      : Allows the user to manipulate dates*}
{*                          in various ways             *}
{* HARDWARE         : PC Compatible                     *}
{* SOURCE           : Borland Pascal V7.0               *}
{*******************************************************}
uses WinCrt;
{*** program constant ***}
const
   QUIT = 5;
{*******************************************************}
{*                Date routines definitions            *}
{*******************************************************}
{*** Leap year routine ***}
function IsLeapYear(y : integer): boolean;
begin
   {*** Check pre-condition met ***}
   if y < 1600 then
        halt;
   IsLeapYear := (y mod 4 = 0)and(y mod 100 <> 0)or
                                               (y mod 400 = 0);
end;

{*** Calculate the days in a given month ***}
function DaysInMonth(m : integer): integer;
begin
   {*** Check pre-condition met ***}
   if (m < 1) or (m > 12) then
        halt;
   {*** If its April, June, September or November, return 30 ***}
   if (m = 4)or(m = 6)or(m = 9)or(m = 11)then
        DaysInMonth := 30
   {*** If its February, return 28 ***}
   else if(m = 2) then
        DaysInMonth := 28
   {*** Otherwise return 31 ***}
   else
        DaysInMonth := 31;
end;

{*** Read date from keyboard ***}
procedure GetDate(var day, month, year : integer);
var
   instring : string;
   x, y     : integer;   {Used to move the cursor}
   valid    : boolean;   {Validity of date}
   maxdays  : integer;   {Max. days in month}
   post     : integer;
   err      : integer;   {Error flag for Val}
begin
   day := 0;
   month := 0;
   year := 0;
   x := WhereX;
   y := WhereY;
   repeat
        valid := false;
        {*** Read date as a string ***}
        GotoXY(x,y);
        write('Enter date: ','          '#8#8#8#8#8#8#8#8#8#8);
        readln(instring);
        {*** Separate it into the component parts ***}
        {** IF no separator THEN re-enter date**}
```

**Continued on next page**

**LISTING-4.11**
(continued)

Using Routines

```
      post := Pos('/',instring);
      if post = 0 then
          continue;
      {** IF the day component is numeric THEN re-enter date **}
      Val(Copy(instring,1,post-1),day,err);
      if err <> 0 then
          continue;
      {** Remove day part from string **}
      Delete(instring,1,post);
      {** Find month part and convert to a number **}
      post := Pos('/',instring);
      if post = 0 then
          continue;
      Val(Copy(instring,1,post-1),month,err);
      if err <> 0 then
          continue;
      Delete(instring,1,post);
      Val(instring,year,err);
      if err <> 0 then
          continue;
      if (month < 1)or(month > 12) then
          continue;
      if (year < 1600) then
          continue;
      maxdays := DaysInMonth(month) + integer((month = 2) and
                                            (IsLeapYear(year)));
      if (day < 1)or(day > maxdays)then
          continue;
      valid := true;
  until valid;
end;


{*** Convert date to days ***}
function DateToJulian(d,m,y : integer): longint;
var
  temp : double;
begin
  temp := y + (m - 2.85) / 12;
  DateToJulian := Trunc(Int(Int(Int(367.0 * temp) - Int(temp)
                                      - 0.75 * Int(temp) + d)

      -0.75*2.0) + 1721115.0);
end;


{** Convert days to date ***}
procedure JulianToDate(v : double; var day, month, year :
integer);
var
  t1, t2, y1, m1 : double;
begin
  t1 := (v - 1721119.0) + 2.0;
  y1 := Int((t1 - 0.2) / 365.25);
  t2 := t1 - int(365.25 * y1);
  m1 := Int((t2-0.5)/30.6);
  day := Trunc(t2 - 30.6 * m1 + 0.5);
  year := Trunc(y1 + integer(m1 > 9));
  month := Trunc(m1 + 3 - (integer(m1 > 9) * 12));
end;


{*** Give day of week date fell on ***}
function DateToDayofWeek(day,month,year : integer): integer;
var
  M, CY, C, Y, temp : integer;
begin
  M    := (month + 9) mod 12 + 1;
  CY   := year - M div 11;
  C    := CY div 100;
```

**Continued on next page**

**LISTING-4.11**
(continued)

Using Routines

```
  Y    := CY mod 100;
  temp := Trunc(2.6 * M - 0.2);
  DateToDayOfWeek := (((temp + day + Y + Y div 4 + C div 4 - 2
  ↳* C) mod 7 + 7) mod 7);
end;


{*** Display day's name ***}
procedure DisplayDayofWeek(daycode : integer);
begin
  {*** Check pre-condition met ***}
  if (daycode < 0) or (daycode > 6) then
      halt;
  case daycode of
      0: writeln('Sunday');
      1: writeln('Monday');
      2: writeln('Tuesday');
      3: writeln('Wednesday');
      4: writeln('Thursday');
      5: writeln('Friday');
      6: writeln('Saturday');
  end
end;


{**********************************************************}
{*              Other routines definitions               *}
{**********************************************************}
{*** Display menu options ***}
procedure DisplayMenu;
begin
  writeln('MENU':39);
  writeln('1 - Days between dates');
  writeln('2 - Add days to date');
  writeln('3 - Subtract days from date');
  writeln('4 - Day of week');
  writeln('5 - QUIT\n');
  write('Enter option (1 to 5) : ');
end;


{*** Get menu option ***}
procedure GetOption(var opt : integer);
begin
  readln(opt);
  while(opt < 1)or(opt > QUIT) do
  begin
      writeln('Invalid option');
      writeln('Must be in the range 1 to ',QUIT);
      readln(opt);
  end
end;


{*** Execute option ***}
procedure ProcessOption(opt : integer);
var
  d1, d2, m1, m2, y1, y2, days :integer;{Local variables to hold}
                                        {day, month & year values}
  temp : double;
  ch   : char;      {Holds key pressed}
  dow  : integer;
begin
  case opt of
      1:  {Difference between two dates}
          begin
              {*** Get Dates ***}
              GetDate(d1,m1,y1);
```

**Continued on next page**

**LISTING-4.11**
(continued)

Using Routines

```
                GetDate(d2,m2,y2);
                {*** Display difference ***}
                writeln('There are ',Abs(DateToJulian(d1,m1,y1)
                     - DateToJulian(d2,m2,y2)), ' days between ',
                     d1, '/', m1, '/',y1, ' and ', d2, '/', m2,
                     '/', y2);
                {*** Press any key to continue ***}
                ch := ReadKey;
            end;
        2:  {Add days to date}
            begin
                {*** get date and days to be added ***}
                GetDate(d1,m1,y1);
                write('Enter number of days : ');
                readln(days);
                {*** Convert to Julian date and add days ***}
                temp := DateToJulian(d1,m1,y1) + days;
                {*** Convert result to date ***}
                JulianToDate(temp,d2,m2,y2);
                {*** Display result ***}
                writeln(d1, '/', m1, '/', y1, ' + ', days,
                     ' days is ', d2, '/', m2, '/', y2);
                {*** Press any key to continue ***}
                ch := ReadKey;
            end;
        3:  {Subtract days from date}
            begin
                {*** get date and days to be subtracted ***}
                GetDate(d1,m1,y1);
                write('Enter number of days : ');
                readln(days);
                {*** Convert to Julian date and subtract days ***}
                temp := DateToJulian(d1,m1,y1) - days;
                {*** Convert result to date ***}
                JulianToDate(temp,d2,m2,y2);
                {*** Display result ***}
                writeln(d1, '/', m1, '/', y1, ' - ', days,
                     ' days is ', d2, '/', m2, '/', y2);
                {*** Press any key to continue ***}
                ch := ReadKey;
            end;
        4:  {Determine date's day of week}
            begin
                {*** Get date ***}
                GetDate(d1,m1,y1);
                dow := DateToDayofWeek(d1,m1,y1);
                {*** Display result ***}
                write(d1,'/',m1,'/',y1,' falls on a ');
                DisplayDayofWeek(dow);
                {*** Press any key to continue ***}
                ch := ReadKey;
            end
  end
end;


{*****************************************}
{*            main program               *}
{*****************************************}

var
  option : integer;    {Menu option entered}
begin
  repeat
      ClrScr;
      DisplayMenu;
      GetOption(option);
      ProcessOption(option);
  until option = QUIT;
end.
```

**Activity 4.20**

Enter and test the program in LISTING-4.11.

# Completing the Program

It is important that the final program matches every aspect of the design, otherwise we have not created the product as specified.

One thing is missing from this case study: the routines *DateToDayOfWeek* and *DateToJulian* both specify a pre-condition that the three integer parameters form a valid date. This has not been tested within the code.

Unfortunately, this test cannot be coded in one or two lines. Hence, it has been decided to create another routine as detailed in the mini-spec below:

**NAME** : IsValidDate
**PARAMETERS**
  **IN** : day, month, year : INTEGER
  **OUT** : valid : BOOLEAN
  **IN/OUT** : None
**PRE-CONDITION** : None

**DESCRIPTION** : Returns *true* if *day, month, year* forms a valid date, otherwise *false* is returned.

**OUTLINE LOGIC** :

```
Set valid to true
IF month outside the range 1 to 12 THEN
    Set valid to false
ENDIF
IF day < 1 or > days in month THEN
    Set valid to false
ENDIF
IF year < 1600 THEN
    Set valid to false
ENDIF
```

**Activity 4.21**

Code and test *IsValidDate* as a function.

Include calls to this routine in *DateToDayOfWeek* and *DateToJulian* to check that their pre-conditions are met.

Of course, these changes have an effect on the structure diagram which is now updated as shown in FIG-4.15.

**FIG-4.15**

Updated Structure Diagram

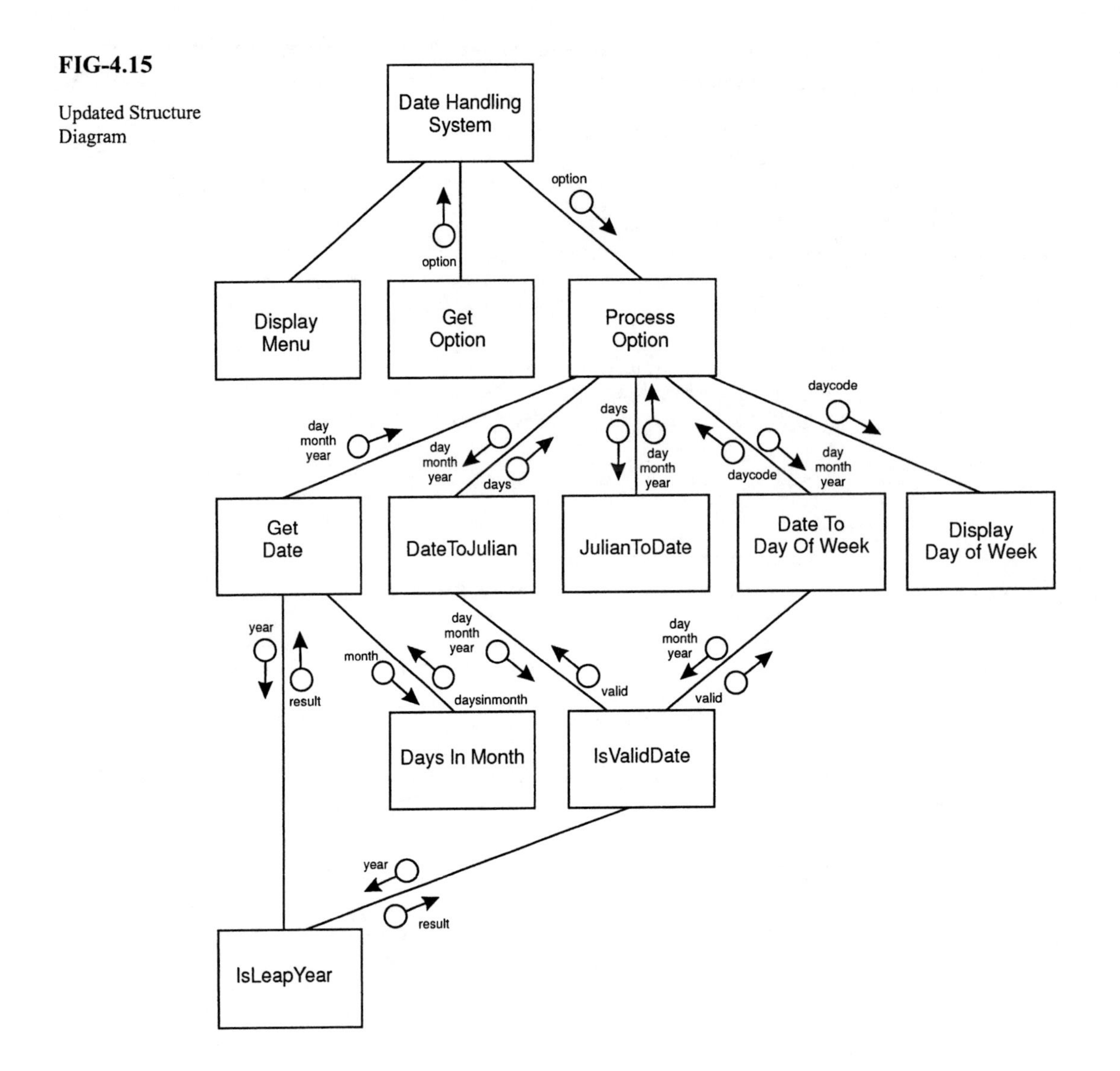

# PASCAL UNITS

## Introduction

The people at Borland have supplied us with many different procedures and functions. However, when we use these routines we don't have to copy their source code into our program; all that is required is that we include the appropriate unit in our code. So, if we want to make use of `ClrScr`, we need to include the statement

```
uses Crt;
```

if you're using the DOS based product.

```
uses WinCrt;
```

in our program.

As well as using the Borland units, we can construct our own and use these in subsequent programs.

The most obvious advantage to using units is that it becomes unnecessary to include the source code for those routines in every program that uses them.

### What is a Unit?

A Unit is similar to a program: it may contain `const` and other declarations as well as code for various procedures and functions.

Like a program, Units can be compiled, creating a machine code file. But, unlike programs, a Unit cannot be executed. Instead, Units are included in other Pascal programs (by employing the `uses` statement). Such units can be given to other programmers who are then free to include them in their own programs. However, since the Unit is in machine code, they cannot get access to the original source code and hence, there is no chance of the Unit's code being tampered with.

## Creating a Unit

Units normally consist of a group of related functions and procedures.

These would first be tested to ensure they are correct and then imported into a Unit source file.

### The Format of a Unit

A Unit consists of two main parts:

the Interface section
and the Implementation section

Declaring user-defined types is dealt with in the next chapter.

The Interface section can contain `const` and `type` declarations, as well as routine headings.

Any of the items stated in this section can then be accessed by any program using that Unit.

The Implementation section normally only contains the code for each of the procedures and functions whose headings appear in the Interface section. However, it may contain other `const`, `type` and routine definitions. Items that appear only in the Implemenation section cannot be accessed by others using the Unit.

The general structure of a Unit is shown in FIG-4.16.

**FIG-4.16**

A Pascal Unit's Structure

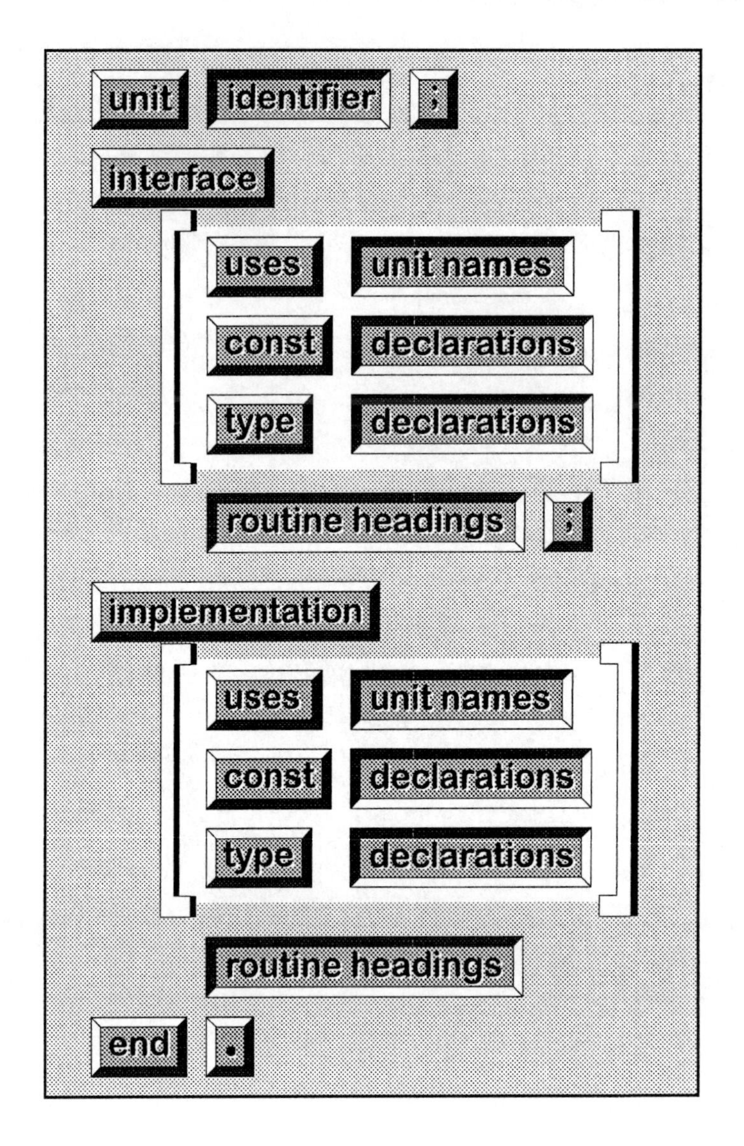


### An Explanation of FIG-4.16

| | |
|---|---|
| `unit` | A Unit must start with the keyword `unit` rather than `program`. |
| `identifier` | This is the name of the Unit. This MUST be the same name as the file in which the Unit is to be saved (but without the extension). Hence a Unit called *Dates* must be saved in a file called *Dates.pas*. |
| `interface` | This marks the start of the section that defines what parts of the Unit are visible to other programs that use the Unit. |
| `implementation` | This is the section of code contining details that are not visible to users of the Unit. It also contains the definitions of the routines whose headings appear in the interface section. |

## Producing the Unit

LISTING-4.12 below is a Unit constructed from the Date routines of the case study.

**LISTING-4.12**

Creating a Unit

```
unit Dates;


interface

{*** Unit constant ***}
const
  QUIT = 5;

{*** Routine headings ***}
function IsLeapYear(y : integer): boolean;
function DaysInMonth(m : integer): integer;
procedure GetDate(var day, month, year : integer);
function DateToJulian(d,m,y : integer): longint;
procedure JulianToDate(v : double; var day, month, year :
integer);
function DateToDayofWeek(day,month,year : integer): integer;
procedure DisplayDayofWeek(daycode : integer);



implementation


{*** USES required to implement routines ***}
uses WinCrt;
{***********************************************************}
{*               Date routines definitions                 *}
{***********************************************************}

{************************}
{***  Hidden routine ***}
{************************}

{*** Check for valid date ***}
function IsValidDate(d,m,y : integer): boolean;
var
  valid : boolean;
begin
  valid := true;
  if (m < 1 ) or (m > 12) then
      valid := false;
  if (d < 1) or (d > DaysInMonth(m) +
                     Integer((m = 2) and (IsLeapYear(y)))) then
      valid := false;
  if y < 1600 then
      valid := false;
  IsValidDate := valid;
end;


{**************************}
{   Visible routines      *}
{**************************}

{*** Leap year routine ***}
function IsLeapYear(y : integer): boolean;
begin
  IsLeapYear := (y mod 4 = 0) and (y mod 100 <> 0)
                or (y mod 400 = 0);
end;
```

**Continued on next page**

**LISTING-4.12**
(continued)

Creating a Unit

```
{*** Calculate the days in a given month ***}
function DaysInMonth(m : integer): integer;
begin
  {*** Check pre-condition met ***}
  if (m < 1) or (m > 12) then
      halt;
  {*** If its April, June, September or November, return 30 ***}
  if (m = 4)or(m = 6)or(m = 9)or(m = 11)then
      DaysInMonth := 30
  {*** If its February, return 28 ***}
  else if(m = 2) then
      DaysInMonth := 28
  {*** Otherwise return 31 ***}
  else
      DaysInMonth := 31;
end;

{*** Read date from keyboard ***}
procedure GetDate(var day, month, year : integer);
var
  instring : string;
  x, y     : integer;   {Used to move the cursor}
  valid    : boolean;   {Validity of date}
  maxdays  : integer;   {Max. days in month}
  post     : integer;
  err      : integer;   {Error flag for Val}
begin
  day := 0;
  month := 0;
  year := 0;
  x := WhereX;
  y := WhereY;
  repeat
      valid := false;
      {*** Read date as a string ***}
      GotoXY(x,y);
      write('Enter date: ','          '#8#8#8#8#8#8#8#8#8#8);
      readln(instring);
      {*** Separate it into the component parts ***}
      {** IF no separator THEN re-enter date**}
      post := Pos('/',instring);
      if post = 0 then
          continue;
      {** IF the day component is numeric THEN re-enter date **}
      Val(Copy(instring,1,post-1),day,err);
      if err <> 0 then
          continue;
      {** Remove day part from string **}
      Delete(instring,1,post);
      {** Find month part and convert to a number **}
      post := Pos('/',instring);
      if post = 0 then
          continue;
      Val(Copy(instring,1,post-1),month,err);
      if err <> 0 then
          continue;          Delete(instring,1,post);
      Val(instring,year,err);
      if err <> 0 then
          continue;
      if (month < 1)or(month > 12) then
          continue;
      if (year < 1600) then
          continue;
      maxdays := DaysInMonth(month)
                 + integer((month = 2)and(IsLeapYear(year)));
      if (day < 1)or(day > maxdays)then
          continue;
      valid := true;
  until valid;
end;
```

**Continued on next page**

**LISTING-4.12**
(continued)

Creating a Unit

```
{*** Convert date to days ***}
function DateToJulian(d,m,y : integer): longint;
var
   temp : double;
begin
   {*** Check pre-condition ***}
   if not IsValidDate(d,m,y) then
       halt;
   temp := y + (m - 2.85) / 12;
   DateToJulian := Trunc(Int(Int(Int(367.0 * temp) - Int(temp)
                 - 0.75 * Int(temp) + d)- 0.75*2.0) + 1721115.0);
end;


{** Convert days to date ***}
procedure JulianToDate(v : double;
                                  var day, month, year : integer);
var
   t1, t2, y1, m1 : double;
begin
   t1 := (v - 1721119.0) + 2.0;
   y1 := Int((t1 - 0.2) / 365.25);
   t2 := t1 - int(365.25 * y1);
   m1 := Int((t2-0.5)/30.6);
   day := Trunc(t2 - 30.6 * m1 + 0.5);
   year := Trunc(y1 + integer(m1 > 9));
   month := Trunc(m1 + 3 - (integer(m1 > 9) * 12));
end;


{*** Give day of week date fell on ***}
function DateToDayofWeek(day,month,year : integer): integer;
var
   M, CY, C, Y, temp : integer;
begin
   {*** Check pre-condition ***}
   if not IsValidDate(day,month,year) then
       halt;
   M    := (month + 9) mod 12 + 1;
   CY   := year - M div 11;
   C    := CY div 100;
   Y    := CY mod 100;
   temp := Trunc(2.6 * M - 0.2);
   DateToDayOfWeek := (((temp + day + Y + Y div 4 + C div 4 - 2
                                   * C) mod 7 + 7) mod 7);
end;


{*** Display day's name ***}
procedure DisplayDayofWeek(daycode : integer);
begin
   {*** Check pre-condition met ***}
   if (daycode < 0) or (daycode > 6) then
       halt;
   case daycode of
       0: writeln('Sunday');
       1: writeln('Monday');
       2: writeln('Tuesday');
       3: writeln('Wednesday');
       4: writeln('Thursday');
       5: writeln('Friday');
       6: writeln('Saturday');
   end
end;


end.
```

Once complete, the Unit must be compiled (not run) to create the compiled Unit. In this case, it will have the name Dates.TPU.

# Using a Unit

With the Unit now compiled, it can be used in any program, just as we use the Units supplied by Borland.

The short program below makes use of the new *Dates* Unit:

```
program UnitTest;
uses WinCrt, Dates;          {uses both Dates and WinCrt}
var
    d,m,y : integer;
begin
    ClrScr;
    GetDate(d,m,y);
    DisplayDayOfWeek(DateToDayOfWeek(d,m,y));
end.
```

**Activity 4.22**

Create the Dates Unit on your own machine and change the case study program as given in LISTING-4.11 to use this Unit.

# Summary

- **A Pascal Unit** is a collection of constants, types and routines.

- **A Pascal Unit contains** two main sections:

    An Interface Section
    An Implementations Section

- **The Interface section** declares other Units, constants, types and routine headings. All of these can be accessed by any other program that uses the Unit.

- **The Implementation section** contains the code for the routines whose headings appear in the Interface section. Other Units, constants, types and routines may be defined here. These will not be accessible by other programs using the Unit.

- **The Unit name** should match the Unit file name. Hence, a Unit beginning

    ```
    unit Dates
    ```

    should be saved in a file called

    *Dates.pas*

- **Units must be compiled** to create a machine code version of the routines it holds. This will be held in a file with the extension *.tpu*. Hence, when compiled *Dates.pas* will create the file

    *Dates.tpu*

- **To use the Unit** in another program, include its name in the program's `uses` statement.

# SOLUTIONS

## Activity 4.1

```
program Act04_01;
uses WinCrt;

var
    c : integer ; {for loop counter}
begin
    {*** Display heading ***}
    ClrScr;
    writeln('Number      Square Root');
    {*** Display numbers and square roots ***}
    for c:= 1 to 20 do
        writeln(c:4,' ':10,Sqrt(c):0:2);
end.
```

## Activity 4.2

a) Valid. s1 = trip
b) Valid. s2 = tone
c) Valid. s1 = titoep
d) Invalid. The middle parameter must be a variable.
e) Valid. s2 = towe

## Activity 4.3

```
program Act04_03;
uses WinCrt;

var
    c : integer;     {Loop counter}
begin
    {*** Seed generator ***}
    Randomize;
    {*** Generate and display 6 numbers ***}
    for c := 1 to 6 do
        write(random(49) + 1:3);
    writeln;
end.
```

## Activity 4.4

1.

```
program Act04_01;
uses WinCrt;

var
    words : string;
begin
    {*** Get text ***}
    ClrScr;
    write('Enter text : ');
    readln(words);
    {*** Display its length ***}
    writeln(words,'        contains ',
    ↳Length(words),' characters');
end.
```

2.

```
program Act04_02;
uses WinCrt;

var
    text1 : string; {Main string}
    text2 : string; {Substring}
    post  : integer;     {Position of match}
begin
    {*** Get text ***}
    ClrScr;
    write('Enter text : ');
    readln(text1);
    {*** Get substring ***}
    write('Enter second string : ');
    readln(text2);
    {*** Delete all occurrences of 2nd string ***}
    post := Pos(text2,text1);
    while post <> 0 do
    begin
        Delete(text1,post,Length(text2));
        post := Pos(text2,text1);
    end;
    {*** Display modified string ***}
    writeln(text1);
end.
```

3.

```
program Act04_03;
uses WinCrt;

var
    words     : string;      {Text entered}
    wordscopy : string;      {Copy of text}
    post      : integer;     {Position of space}
    count     : integer;     {Count of spaces}
begin
    {*** Set count to zero ***}
    count := 0;
    {*** Get text ***}
    ClrScr;
    write('Enter text : ');
    readln(words);
    {*** make copy of string ***}
    wordscopy := words;
    post := Pos(' ',wordscopy);
    while post <> 0 do
    begin
        Inc(count);
        Delete(wordscopy,post,1);
        post := Pos(' ',wordscopy);
    end;
    writeln(words,'       contains ',count + 1,
    ↳' words');
end.
```

4.

```
program Act04_04;
uses WinCrt;

var
    text1   : string;    {Main string}
    txtcopy : string;    {Copy of text1}
    text2   : string;    {Substring}
    post    : integer;   {Position of match}
    count   : integer;   {No. of matches}
begin
    {*** Set count to zero ***}
    count := 0;
    {*** Get text ***}
    ClrScr;
    write('Enter text : ');
    readln(text1);
    {***Make copy of string ***}
    txtcopy := text1;
    {*** Get substring ***}
    write('Enter second string : ');
    readln(text2);
    {*** Find all copies of 2nd string ***}
    post := Pos(text2,txtcopy);
    while post <> 0 do
    begin
        Inc(count);
        Delete(txtcopy,post,Length(text2));
        post := Pos(text2,txtcopy);
    end;
    {*** Display count ***}
    writeln(text1, '    contains ', text2,
    ↳'    ',count,' times');
end.
```

5.

```
program Act04_04;
uses WinCrt;

var
    text1   : string;    {Main string}
    replace : string;    {Replacement string}
    find    : string;    {Find string}
    post    : integer;   {Position of match}
    count   : integer;   {No. of matches}
begin
    {*** Set count to zero ***}
    count := 0;
    {*** Get text ***}
    ClrScr;
    write('Enter text : ');
    readln(text1);
```

**Continued on next page**

## Activity 4.4 (continued)

```
5. (continued)

    {*** Get substring ***}
    write('Find what : ');
    readln(find);
    write('Replace with : ');
    readln(replace);
    {*** Replace all copies find with replace ***}
    post := Pos(find,text1);
    while post <> 0 do
    begin
        Inc(count);
        Delete(text1,post,Length(find));
        Insert(replace,text1,post);
        post := Pos(find,text1);
    end;
    {*** Display final string ***}
    writeln(text1);
end.
```

## Activity 4.5

The code changes are in a larger font

```
program Act05_01;
uses WinCrt;

var
    count   : integer;   {Count of chars entered}
    datain  : string[2]; {Chars entered}
    ch      : char;      {Current character read}
begin
    {*** Issue prompt ***}
    Clrscr;
    write('Enter string : ');
    {*** Set count to zero ***}
    count := 0;
    {*** Set input string to empty ***}
    datain := '';
    {*** Read character from keyboard ***}
    ch := readkey;
    {*** WHILE character not ENTER DO ***}
    while ch <> #13 do
    begin
        {***IF char char AND count < 10 THEN ***}
        if (ch >= 'A') and
        (ch <= 'Z') and
        (count < 10) then
        begin
            {*** Display character ***}
            write(ch);
            {*** Add the char to input string ***}
            datain := datain + ch;
            {*** Add 1 to count ***}
            inc(count);
        end;
        {*** Read character from keyboard ***}
        ch := readkey;
    end;
    writeln;
    readkey;
    DoneWinCrt;
end.
```

Pressing the backspace character has no effect.

## Activity 4.6

```
program Act06_01;
uses WinCrt;

var
    count   : integer;   {Count of chars entered}
    datain  : string[2]; {Chars entered}
    ch      : char;      {Current chars read}
begin
    {*** Issue prompt ***}
    Clrscr;
    write('Enter string : ');
    {*** Set count to zero ***}
    count := 0;
    {*** Set input string to empty ***}
    datain := '';
    {*** Read character from keyboard ***}
    ch := readkey;
    {*** WHILE character not ENTER DO ***}
    while ch <> #13 do
    begin
        {***IF char numeric AND count < 3 THEN ***}
        if (ch >= '0') and (ch <= '9') and
        ↳(count < 3) then
        begin
            {*** Display character ***}
            write(ch);
            {*** Add the char to input string ***}
            datain := datain + ch;
            {*** Add 1 to count ***}
            inc(count);
        end
        {*** IF backspace and count > 0 THEN ***}
        else if (ch = #8) and (count > 0) then
        begin
            {*** Delete last character ***}
            write(#8' '#8);
            Delete(datain,Length(datain),1);
            Dec(count);
        end;
        {*** Read character from keyboard ***}
        ch := readkey;
    end;
    writeln;
    readkey;
    DoneWinCrt;
end.
```

## Activity 4.7

No solution required.

## Activity 4.8

No solution required.

## Activity 4.9

```
program Act09_01;
uses WinCrt;

procedure Box;
var
    c : integer;
begin
    {*** Draw top of box ***}
    writeln('**********');
    {*** Draw vertical lines ***}
    for c := 1 to 8 do
        writeln('*        *');
    {*** Draw bottom line ***}
    writeln('**********');
end;

begin
    {*** Clear Screen ***}
    ClrScr;
    {*** Draw box ***}
    Box;
end.
```

## Activity 4.10

```
1.

program Act10_01;
uses WinCrt;

procedure Box(size : integer);
var
    c : integer;
begin
    {*** Draw top of box ***}
    for c := 1 to size do
        write('*');
    writeln;
    {*** Draw vertical lines ***}
    for c := 1 to size - 2 do
        writeln('*',' ':size-2,'*');
    {*** Draw bottom line ***}
    for c := 1 to size do
        write('*');
    writeln;
end;
```

**Continued on next page**

## Activty 4.10 (continued)

```
1. (continued)

begin
    {*** Clear Screen ***}
    ClrScr;
    {*** Draw box ***}
    Box(20);
end.
```

```
2.

program Act10_02;
uses WinCrt;

procedure DisplaydayOfWeek(d : integer);
begin
    case d of
        0 : writeln('Sunday');
        1 : writeln('Monday');
        2 : writeln('Tuesday');
        3 : writeln('Wednesday');
        4 : writeln('Thursday');
        5 : writeln('Friday');
        6 : writeln('Saturday')
    end
end;

var
    day : integer;
begin
    ClrScr;
    write('Enter number (0 to 6) : ');
    readln(day);
    DisplayDayOfWeek(day);
end.
```

## Activity 4.11

The local variables created as:

*width*
*shape*
*count*

When the routine is called, such as in the code
`Line(30,'=');`

the first value, 30, is copied to the local variable specified first in the parameter list (i.e. *width*). '=' is copied to *shape*.

## Activity 4.12

```
1.

program Act12_01;
uses WinCrt;

procedure Box(size : integer; shape : char);
var
    c : integer;
begin
    {*** Draw top of box ***}
    for c := 1 to size do
        write(shape);
    writeln;
    {*** Draw vertical lines ***}
    for c := 1 to size - 2 do
        writeln(shape,' ':size-2,shape);
    {*** Draw bottom line ***}
    for c := 1 to size do
        write(shape);
    writeln;
end;


begin
    {*** Clear Screen ***}
    ClrScr;
    {*** Draw box ***}
    Box(20,'_');
end.
```

```
2.

program Act12_02;
uses WinCrt;

procedure VertLine(height : integer; shape :
char);
var
    c : integer; {Loop counter}
begin
    {*** Display first char ***}
    write(shape);
    for c := 1 to height do
    begin
        GotoXY(whereX-1,whereY+1);
        write(shape);
    end;
end;

begin
    {*** Clear Screen ***}
    ClrScr;
    {*** Draw vertical line ***}
    VertLine(5,'|');
end.
```

## Activity 4.13

```
1.


program Act13_01;
uses WinCrt;

procedure DateToDayOfWeek(day,month,year :
integer; var dow : integer);
var
    M, CY, C, Y, temp : integer;
begin
    M    := (month + 9) mod 12 + 1;
    CY   := year - M div 11;
    C    := CY div 100;
    Y    := CY mod 100;
    temp := Trunc(2.6 * M - 0.2);
    dow  := ((temp + day + Y + Y div 4 + C div
    ↳4 - 2 * C) mod 7 + 7) mod 7;
end;


var
    d, m, y, dow : integer; {Date and day of week}
begin
    {*** Get date ***}
    write('Enter date (dd mm yyyy) : ');
    readln(d,m,y);
    DayOfWeek(d,m,y,dow);
    {*** Display day of week ***}
    writeln(dow);
end.
```

```
2.

program Act13_02;
uses WinCrt;

procedure Power(x, y : real ; var result : real);
begin
    result := exp(y * ln(x))
end;

var
    no1, no2, ans : real;
begin
    {*** Get numbers ***}
    write('Enter x and y : ');
    readln(no1,no2);
    {*** Calculate power ***}
    Power(no1,no2,ans);
    {*** Display result ***}
    writeln(no1:0:2,' raised to the power ',
    ↳no2:0:2,' is ',ans:0:2);
end.
```

## Activity 4.14

```
program Act14_01;
uses WinCrt;

procedure AddLSD(l1,s1,d1,l2,s2,d2 : integer;
↳var l3,s3,d3 : integer);
var
    totalpence : integer;
begin
    totalpence := (l1 + l2) * 240
    ↳+ (s1 + s2) * 12 + d1 + d2;
    d3 := totalpence mod 12;
    s3 := totalpence div 12;
    l3 := s3 div 20;
    s3 := s3 mod 20;
end;


var
    p1, s1, d1, p2, s2, d2, tp, ts, td : integer;
begin
    {*** Get first amount ***}
    write('Enter first amount  : ');
    readln(p1, s1, d1);
    {*** Get second amount ***}
    write('Enter second amount : ');
    readln(p2, s2, d2);
    AddLSD(p1,s1,d1,p2,s2,d2,tp,ts,td);
    {*** Display result ***}
    writeln('£',tp,':',ts,':',td);
end.
```

## Activity 4.15

```
program Act15_01;
uses WinCrt;

procedure RemoveSpaces(var s : string);
var
    post : integer;
begin
    {*** Find a space ***}
    post := Pos(' ',s);
    {*** WHILE space found DO ***}
    while post <> 0 do
    begin
        {*** Delete it ***}
        Delete(s,post,1);
        {*** Find next space ***}
        post := Pos(' ',s);
    end
end;

var
    st : string;
begin
    {*** Get string ***}
    write('Enter text  : ');
    readln(st);
    {*** Remove spaces ***}
    RemoveSpaces(st);
    {*** Display result ***}
    writeln(st);
end.
```

## Activity 4.16

1.

```
program Act16_01;
uses WinCrt;

function DateToDayOfWeek(day,month,year :
↳integer): integer;
var
    M, CY, C, Y, temp : integer;
begin
    M    := (month + 9) mod 12 + 1;
    CY   := year - M div 11;
    C    := CY div 100;
    Y    := CY mod 100;
    temp := Trunc(2.6 * M - 0.2);
    DayOfWeek  := ((temp + day + Y + Y div 4
    ↳+ C div 4 - 2 * C) mod 7 + 7) mod 7;
end;


var
    d, m, y : integer; {Date}
begin
    {*** Get date ***}
    write('Enter date (dd mm yyyy) : ');
    readln(d,m,y);
    {*** Display day of week ***}
    writeln(DateToDayOfWeek(d,m,y));
end.
```

2.

```
program Act16_02;
uses WinCrt;

function Power(x, y : real): real;
begin
    Power := exp(y * ln(x))
end;


var
    no1, no2, ans : real;
begin
    {*** Get numbers ***}
    write('Enter x and y : ');
    readln(no1,no2);
    {*** Display result ***}
    writeln(no1:0:2,' raised to the power ',
    ↳no2:0:2,' is ',Power(no1,no2):0:2);
end.
```

3.

```
program Act16_03;
uses WinCrt;

function Twice(nbr: integer): integer;
begin
    Twice := nbr * 2;
end;


var
    no1 : integer;
begin
    {*** Get number ***}
    write('Enter value : ');
    readln(no1);
    {*** Display result ***}
    writeln(no1,' doubled is ', Twice(no1));
end.
```

## Activity 4.17

```
program Act17_01;
uses WinCrt;

procedure DisplaydayOfWeek(d : integer);
begin
    {*** Exit if pre-condition not met ***}
    if (d<0) or (d > 6) then
        halt;
    case d of
        0 : writeln('Sunday');
        1 : writeln('Monday');
        2 : writeln('Tuesday');
        3 : writeln('Wednesday');
        4 : writeln('Thursday');
        5 : writeln('Friday');
        6 : writeln('Saturday')
    end
end;

var
    day : integer;
begin
    ClrScr;
    write('Enter number (0 to 6) : ');
    readln(day);
    DisplayDayOfWeek(day);
end.
```

## Activity 4.18

1.

```
program Act18_01;
uses WinCrt;

function SecLargest(n1,n2,n3,n4 : integer):
integer;
var
```

**Continued on next page**

## Activity 4.18 (continued)

1. (continued)

```
    largest, second : integer;
begin
    if n1 > n2 then
    begin
        largest := n1;
        second := n2;
    end
    else
    begin
        largest := n2;
        second := n1;
    end;
    if n3 > largest then
    begin
        second := largest;
        largest := n3;
    end
    else if n3 > second then
        second := n3;
    if n4 > largest then
    begin
        second := largest;
        largest:= n4;
    end
    else if n4 > second then
        second := n4;
    SecLargest := second;
end;

var
    no1, no2, no3, no4 : integer;
begin
    ClrScr;
    write('Enter four numbers : ');
    readln(no1, no2, no3, no4);
    writeln('Second largest value is : '
    ↳,SecLargest(no1,no2,no3,no4));
end.
```

2.

```
program Act18_02;
uses WinCrt;

function ClassifyChar( ch : char): integer;
begin
    {*** IF alphabetic THEN ***}
    if (ch >= 'A') and (ch <= 'Z') then
        {*** IF vowel THEN ***}
        if (ch = 'A') or (ch = 'E') or
        ↳(ch = 'I') or (ch = 'O') or (ch = 'U')
        ↳then
            {*** Return 1 ***}
            Classify := 1
        else
            {*** ELSE return 2 ***}
            Classify := 2
    else
        {*** ELSE return 3 ***}
        Classify := 3
end;

var
    ch : char;
begin
    {*** Read character ***}
    ClrScr;
    write('Enter character : ');
    readln(ch);
    {*** Display result ***}
    case ClassifyChar(ch) of
        1: writeln('Vowel');
        2: writeln('Consonant');
        3: writeln('Non-alphabetic');
    end
end.
```

3.

```
program Act18_03;
uses WinCrt;

function IsLeapYear(y : integer): boolean;
begin
    {*** IF div by 4 or 400, not 100 THEN ***}

    if (y mod 4 = 0) and (y mod 100 <> 0)or
        (y mod 400 = 0)
    then
        {*** Leap year ***}
        IsLeapYear := true
    else
        {*** ELSE not Leap year ***}
        IsLeapYear := false;
end;

var
    year : integer;
begin
    {*** Read year ***}
    ClrScr;
    write('Enter year : ');
    readln(year);
    {*** Call routine and display result ***}
    if IsLeapYear(year) then
        writeln('Leap year')
    else
        writeln('Non-leap year');
end.
```

4.

```
program Act18_04;
uses WinCrt;

function DaysInMonth(m : integer): integer;
begin
    {*** IF Apr, Jun, Sep or Nov THEN ***}
    if (m = 4) or (m = 6) or (m = 9) or
    ↳(m = 11)
    then
        {*** return 30 ***}
        DaysInMonth := 30
    else if m = 2 then
    {*** ELSE IF Feb THEN return 28***}
        DaysInMonth := 28
    else
        {*** ELSE return 31 ***}
        DaysInMonth := 31;
end;

var
    month : integer;
begin
    {*** Read month ***}
    ClrScr;
    write('Enter month : ');
    readln(month);
    {*** Display result ***}
    writeln('Month ', month, ' has ',
    ↳DaysInMonth(month), ' days')
end.
```

5.

```
program Act18_05;
uses WinCrt;

{*** Leap year routine ***}
function IsLeapYear(y : integer): boolean;
begin
    IsLeapYear := (y mod 4 = 0)and
    ↳(y mod 100 <> 0)or(y mod 400 = 0);
end;


{*** Calculate the days in a given month ***}
function DaysInMonth(m : integer): integer;
begin
    {*** Check pre-condition met ***}
    if (m < 1) or (m > 12) then
        halt;
    {*** If its April, June, September ***}
    {*** or November, return 30 ***}
    if (m = 4)or(m = 6)or(m = 9)or(m = 11)then
        DaysInMonth := 30
    {*** If it's February, return 28 ***}
    else if m = 2 then
        DaysInMonth := 28
    {*** Otherwise return 31 ***}
    else
        DaysInMonth := 31;
end;


procedure GetDate(var day, month, year :
integer);
var
```

**Continued on next page**

## Activity 4.18 (continued)

5. (continued)

```
    instring : string;
    x, y     : integer; {Used to move cursor}
    valid    : boolean; {Validity of date}
    maxdays  : integer; {Max. days in month}
    post     : integer;
    err      : integer; {Error flag for Val}
begin
    x := WhereX;
    y := WhereY;
    repeat
        valid := false;
        {*** Read date as a string ***}
        GotoXY(x,y);
        write('Enter date: ',
              '              '#8#8#8#8#8#8#8#8#8#8#8#8#8#8);
        readln(instring);
        {*** Separate it into component parts ***}
        {** IF no separator THEN continue **}
        post := Pos('/',instring);
        if post = 0 then
            continue;
        {** IF day is not numeric THEN continue **}
        Val(Copy(instring,1,post-1),day,err);
        if err <> 0 then
            continue;
        {** Remove day part from string **}
        Delete(instring,1,post);
        {** IF no separator THEN continue **}
        post := Pos('/',instring);
        if post = 0 then
            continue;
        {** IF month not numeric THEN continue **}
        Val(Copy(instring,1,post-1),month,err);
        if err <> 0 then
            continue;
        {** Remove month part from string **}
        Delete(instring,1,post);
        {** IF year not numeric THEN continue **}
        Val(instring,year,err);
        if err <> 0 then
            continue;
        {*** IF month not 1 to 12 THEN continue ***}
        if (month < 1)or(month > 12) then
            continue;
        {*** IF year before 1600 THEN continue ***}
        if (year < 1600) then
            continue;
        {*** IF days invalid THEN continue ***}
        maxdays := DaysInMonth(month) +
        integer((month = 2)and(IsLeapYear(year)));
        if (day < 1)or(day > maxdays)then
            continue;
        {*** Date valid ***}
        valid := true;
    until valid;
end;


var
    d, m, y : integer;
begin
    ClrScr;
    GetDate(d,m,y);
    writeln(d,'/',m,'/',y);
end.
```

6.

```
program Act18_06;
uses WinCrt;
function DateToJulian(d,m,y : integer): longint;
var
    temp : double;
begin
    temp := y + (m - 2.85) / 12;
    DateToJulian := Trunc(Int(Int(Int(367.0 * temp) -
Int(temp) - 0.75 * Int(temp) + d)
        -0.75*2.0) + 1721115.0);
end;

var
    day, month, year : integer;
    result : double;
begin
    write('Enter date : ');
    readln(day,month,year);
    result := DateToJulian(day,month,year);
    writeln(day,'/',month,'/',year,
' is ',result:0:0,' days since 1/1/4713BC');
end.
```

7.

```
program Act18_07;
uses WinCrt;

function DateToJulian(d,m,y : integer): longint;
var
    temp : double;
begin
    temp := y + (m - 2.85) / 12
    DateToJulian := Trunc(Int(Int(Int(367.0*temp)
    ↳- Int(temp) - 0.75 * Int(temp) + d)
    ↳-0.75*2.0) + 1721115.0);
end;

{** Convert days to date ***}
procedure JulianToDate(v : double; var day,
month, year : integer);
var
    t1, t2, y1, m1 : double;
begin
    t1 := (v - 1721119.0) + 2.0;
    y1 := Int((t1 - 0.2) / 365.25);
    t2 := t1 - int(365.25 * y1);
    m1 := Int((t2-0.5)/30.6);
    day := Trunc(t2 - 30.6 * m1 + 0.5);
    year := Trunc(y1 + integer(m1 > 9));
    month := Trunc(m1 + 3 - (integer(m1 > 9)*12));
end;


var
    day, month, year : integer;
    result : double;
begin
    write('Enter date : ');
    readln(day,month,year);
    result := DateToJulian(day,month,year);
    JulianToDate(result+1,day,month,year);
    writeln('Next day is ',day,'/',month,'/',year);
end.
```

8.

```
program Act18_08;
uses WinCrt;

function Reverse(no1 : longint): longint;
var
    temp : longint;
begin
    {*** Set result to zero ***}
    temp := 0;
    {*** WHILE no1 not zero DO ***}
    while no1 <> 0 do
    begin
        {*** Add last digit of no1 to result ***}
        temp := temp * 10 + no1 mod 10;
        {*** Remove last digit from number ***}
        no1 := no1 div 10;
    end;
    {*** Return result ***}
    Reverse := temp;
end;

var
    nbr : longint;
begin
    {*** Read value ***}
    ClrScr;
    write('Enter number : ');
    readln(nbr);
    {*** Display result ***}
    writeln(nbr,' reversed is ',Reverse(nbr))
end.
```

## Activity 4.19

The various results that can be returned by the routine are:

Pre-condition not met
28
30
31

## Activity 4.20

No solution required.

## Activity 4.21

```
program Act21_01;
uses WinCrt;

function IsLeapYear(y : integer): boolean;
begin
    IsLeapYear := (y mod 4 = 0)and(y mod 100 <> 0)
    or↳(y mod 400 = 0);
end;

function DaysInMonth(m : integer): integer;
begin
    {*** Check pre-condition met ***}
    if (m < 1) or (m > 12) then
        halt;
    {*** If its Apr, Jun, Sep or Nov, return 30 ***}
    if (m = 4)or(m = 6)or(m = 9)or(m = 11)then
        DaysInMonth := 30
    {*** If its February, return 28 ***}
    else if(m = 2) then
        DaysInMonth := 28
    {*** Otherwise return 31 ***}
    else
        DaysInMonth := 31;
end;

function IsValidDate(d,m,y : integer): boolean;
var
    valid : boolean;
begin
    valid := true;
    if (m < 1 ) or (m > 12) then
        valid := false;
    if (d < 1) or (d > DaysInMonth(m)+
    ↳Integer((m = 2) and (IsLeapYear(y))))
    then
        valid := false;
    if y < 1600 then
        valid := false;
    IsValidDate := valid;
end;


{*** Driver for IsValidDate ***}
var
    day, month, year : integer;
begin
    ClrScr;
    write('Enter date : ');
    readln(day, month, year);
    if IsValidDate(day,month,year) then
        writeln('Valid date')
    else
        writeln('Invalid date');
end.
```

The routines *DateToDayOfWeek* and *DateToJulian* should begin with the line

```
    if not IsValidDate(d,m,y) then
        halt;
```

changing the parameter names as appropriate.

## Activity 4.22

No solution required.

CHAPTER 5

# Data Structures

**This chapter covers the following topics:**

Array Constants

Array Parameters

Bit Maniuplation Operators

Dynamic Space Allocation

Enumerated Types

How `var` parameters Really Work

Multidimensional Arrays

One-dimensional Arrays

Open Arrays

Ordinal Types

Pointer Variables

Range Checking

Record Structure Definitions

Sets

Strings as Arrays

Subranges

The `with` Statement

Type Definitions

# DATA TYPES

## Existing Types

In the second chapter we met the basic data types. Briefly we might divide these into the following categories:

Numeric types
```
integer
real
```
Non-numeric types
```
char
string
boolean
```

Other types such as `longint` and `double` are simply variations on `integer` and `real` types.

### Ordinal Types

However, rather than divide the types as numeric and non-numeric, a second way of classifying them is as ordinal and non-ordinal types.

An ordinal type is one in which the order of the values is specified. That is, we can state what value comes before and after any given value. For example, integers are ordinal since starting with one integer value, say 12, we can state which value comes before it, 11, and which after, 13.

The same is also true for `char` values (although you have to look up the ASCII table in APPENDIX A to tell what comes before and after characters such as a comma.

Booleans are another ordinal type. They are deemed to have the order *false, true.*

However, real values and strings are not ordinal. Reals are not ordinal since it is impossible to state exactly which value comes before and after a number like 5.17. You might be tempted to say 5.18 follows 5.17, but what about 5.171 or 5.1701 etc. Strings are rather more obvious, since asking what comes after a string such as 'Hello' doesn't make much sense.

To summarise, we can classify existing types as follows:

Ordinal types
```
integer
char
boolean
```
Non-ordinal
```
real
string
```

In fact, we've already met some routines that are designed to work on ordinal types such as `Ord`, `Pred` and `Succ`.

> **Activity 5.1**
>
> Is the `longint` type ordinal?

# Enumerated Types

If none of the existing types suit your purposes, Pascal allows you to define your own types and then declare variables of that type. This is done within a `type` statement. For example, we might require variables designed to hold an applicant's marital status: *single, married, separated, divorced,* or *widowed.* We could achieve this by first defining a *Status* type in which we list the possible values for variables of this type

```
type
    Status = (single, married, separated, divorced, widowed);
```

and then defining variables of that type in the `var` statement.

```
var
    maritalstatus : Status;
```

Finally, we can assign to this variable one of the values specified for the type. For example:

```
maritalstatus := single;
```

It is important to note that the value being assigned is not a string. Hence, it would be invalid to attempt the statement

```
maritalstatus := 'single';
```

or, indeed, to try assigning any value not specified in the `type` declaration.

These types, in which a list of possible values is specified, are known as enumerated types.

The format for declaring an enumerated type is shown in FIG-5.1.

**FIG-5.1**

Enumerated Types

value list

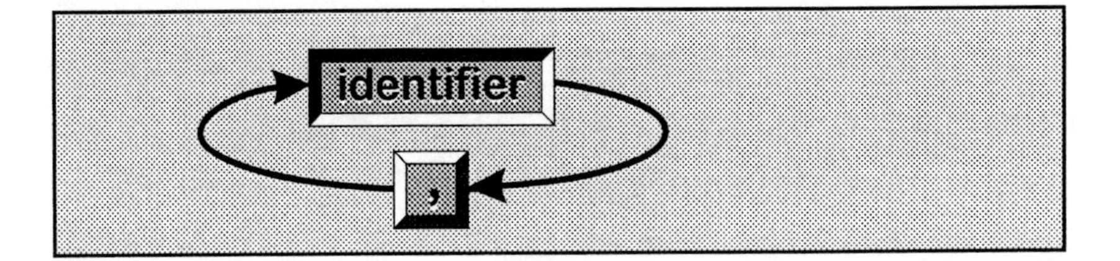


> **Activity 5.2**
>
> Create new types for the following range of values:
>
> 1. Days = *Sunday* through *Saturday.*
>
> 2. Months = *Jan* through *Dec* (use only the first three letters of every month).

Type declarations appear before `var` statements, but can be before or after `const` statements. It's also possible to place a type declaration with a routine, but that would mean that variables of that type could only be defined within that routine. By placing a `type` statement at the start of your program (before the code for routines) then variables of that type can be defined anywhere in the program.

There are some restrictions on enumerated types, and these are:

Variables of this type cannot have their values displayed
e.g. `writeln(maritalstatus);` is invalid

The values for such variables cannot be read in
e.g. `readln(maritalstatus);` is invalid

At this point you must be wondering what use enumerated types can be put to.

They have several benefits over using integer codes or strings. They have the advantage over strings of requiring much less storage space. Enumerated values are held within the machine's memory as an integer value. Hence, the value *single* would be stored as 0, *married* as 1, etc.

Also, using such types can often make a program more readable than making use of numeric codes. For example, the line

```
if maritalstatus = married then
```

is easier to understand than

```
if maritalstatus = 1 then
```

This assumes *maritalstatus* has been declared as an integer.

where you need to remember that 1 is the code for *married.*

Enumerated types are also ordinal, so, if a program contained the code

```
var
    today : Days;
begin
    today := Monday;
```

we could move *today* on to *Tuesday* using the statement

```
Inc(today);
```

It's also possible to create an enumerated variable without defining a type. For example, we can write

```
var
    house : (detached, semi, terraced, flat);
```

and then assign the variable values from the list specified.

```
house := semi;
```

This approach should probably be avoided since such variables cannot be passed as parameters to routines. For, although it would be valid to define a routine with the heading

```
function MyFunct(x : Status):integer;
```

the heading

```
function MyFunct(x : (single, married, separated)): integer;
```

would be invalid since parameters must have a specific type.

## Converting to and from Enumerated Types

Enumerated variables can be assigned a value by using a line such as

```
today := Days(1);
```

which is equivalent to

```
today := Monday;
```

Here, the value to be assigned is stated by giving the type name and the position in that set of values of the one to be assigned. All you have to remember is that enumerated types start at zero. For example, *Days(0)* is *Sunday*.

The function `Ord`, which we've used previously, will return the ordinal value of an enumerated variable's value. Hence, assuming the line

```
today := Sunday;
```

has been executed, a program will display 0 in response to the line

```
writeln(Ord(today));
```

## Enumerated Types and Control Structures

Because a user-defined enumerated type is an ordinal type, a variable of this type can be used as a `for` loop counter. For example, the program in LISTING-5.1 uses such a variable to run through the season of the year.

**LISTING-5.1**

An Enumerated `for` Loop

```
program EnumTypes;
uses WinCrt;

{*** Declare enumerated type ***}
type
  Seasons = (Winter, Spring, Summer, Fall);

var
  time : Seasons;          {loop counter}

begin
  {***FOR each season DO ***}
  for time := Winter to Fall do
      {*** Display its ordinal value ***}
      writeln('This is season ',Ord(time));
end.
```

It's also possible to use the values given in an enumerated type declaration as labels in a `case` statement. This allows code such as:

```
case time of
    Winter       : writeln('Cold');
    Spring, Fall : writeln('Warm');
    Summer       : writeln('Hot');
end;
```

**Activity 5.3**

Enter and run the program in Listing-5.1.

Change the code so that the seasons are displayed as 1 to 4 rather than 0 to 3.

Using a `case` statement, modify the program's output so that the season names are displayed rather than the numeric values.

## Range Checking

The last value of type *Days* is *Saturday*. So if we execute the line

```
today := Saturday;
```

and then attempt a statement such as

```
Inc(today);
```

or

```
tomorrow := Succ(today);
```

what will be the result?

You might think the program will terminate, just as it would when attempting to find the square root of a negative number. In fact, this is not normally the case. Instead, the program will continue and a statement such as

```
writeln (Ord(tomorrow));
```

would return the value 7, something that should not be possible.

The problem is that Pascal will not normally check that the value of a variable stays within a permitted range. To do so would require additional checks every time an assignment was made, and this would slow the program.

However, it is possible to include such **range checking** within your program by including the compiler directive

```
{$R+}
```

This instructs the compiler to insert the additional code necessary to check that any value assigned to a variable lies within an acceptable range for that variable. This directive can be placed at any point in your program. Only those lines of code that follow the directive are affected; no checking is done on preceding lines.

Such checking can also be switched off using the directive:

```
{$R-}
```

This allows us to have the checking switched on for only part of the program.

As a general rule, range checking may be included during testing, but should be removed before compiling the completed program.

LISTING-5.2 demonstrates the use of such testing.

**LISTING-5.2**

Using Range Checking

```
program EnumTypes;
uses WinCrt;

type
  Seasons = (Winter, Spring, Summer, Fall);

var
  time    : Seasons;
  entered : integer;
begin
  ClrScr;
  writeln('Enter season');
  writeln('1 - for winter');
  writeln('2 - for spring');
  writeln('3 - for summer');
  writeln('4 - for fall');
  readln(entered);
  {*** Switch on range check ***}
  {$R+}
  {*** Error if entered not 1 to 4 ***}
  time := Seasons(entered-1);
  {*** Range checking off ***}
  {$R-}
  case time of
      Winter : writeln('It''s Winter');
      Spring : writeln('It''s Spring');
      Summer : writeln('It''s Summer');
      Fall   : writeln('It''s Fall');
  end;
end.
```

**Activity 5.4**

Enter the above program.

Run the program entering a value of 2.

Run it again. This time enter 5.

# Subranges

Another possibility when declaring a variable is to state that its value should lie within a limited range. Hence, instead of the declaration

```
var
    month : integer;
```

for a variable that is only meant to have a value between 1 and 12, we can write

```
var
    month : 1..12;
```

This technique works for any ordinal type, including user-defined enumerated types. Hence, we might write

```
working : Monday..Friday;
spring  : Mar..May;
```

Disjoint ranges are not allowed, making the following statements invalid:

```
winter : Dec,Jan..Feb;
vowels : 'A','E','I','O','U';
```

As with enumerated types, sub-ranges can be defined using types:

```
type
    MonthRange = 1..12;
var
    month : MonthRange;
```

Again, the compiler will not check that your variables stay within the range specified unless you have range checking on (using {$R+}).

# Summary

- **An Ordinal type** is one in which all possible values are known and ordered.
- **Ordinal types are**

```
integer;
char
boolean
```

- **User-defined Enumerated types** are new types defined by the user in which all possible values are stated as part of the type declaration.
- **Internally, enumerated values are stored as integers**, 0 for the first value, 1 for the second, etc.
- **Enumerated variables cannot be read in or displayed.**
- **Enumerated types can be used with various routines** such as `Inc, Dec, Succ, Pred.`
- **Enumerated values can be used in `for` loops and `case` statements.**
- **Range checking** ensures a variable stays within its defined value range.
- **Range checking is switched on** using the compiler directive {$R+} and off using {$R-}
- **Range checking adds extra code** to the compiled program and slows its execution.
- **Variables can be defined to contain values in a specified sub-range** of any ordinal type.
- **Sub-ranges can be defined as a type.**

# ARRAYS

## Problems with Simple Variables

All the variables we have encountered up to this point are known as **simple variables**. A simple variable is capable of holding only a single value. For example,

```
nbr : integer;
```

defines a simple variable *nbr*, which can store a single integer value.

However, there are certain problems which cannot easily be solved using this type of variable. For example, if we need to read in five numbers and then display them, the relevant code might be:

```
var
    no1, no2, no3, no4, no5 : integer;
begin
    write('Enter 5 numbers : ');
    readln(no1, no2, no3, no4, no5);
    writeln(no1:5, no2:5, no3:5, no4:5, no5:5);
```

Although somewhat inelegant, this approach might be acceptable when only five values are used, but would prove more unwieldy if 50 or 100 values were involved.

**Activity 5.5**

Consider possible approaches to tackling the following problems:

1. Read in 20 integer values in the range 1 to 5 and print out how often each value occurred. (e.g. 1 occurred 4 times; 2 occurred 7 times etc.)
2. Read in 15 integer values. Next, read in another value and then display a message saying whether the last value is repeated anywhere in the original 15 values (display FOUND or NOT FOUND as appropriate).

Hopefully, you can see from attempting Activity 5.5 that any solution to these problems is going to be long and cumbersome if simple variables are used.

## One Dimensional Arrays

### What is an Array ?

An array is a collection of **elements** or **cells**. Each of these elements can hold a single data value. That is, an element in an array performs the same role as a simple variable.

All elements of an array are of the same type (i.e. `integer, real, boolean,` etc.).

Like other variables, an array must be given a name. Each element in the array is identified by a unique number known as the element **subscript**.

Visually, we can conceive of an array as shown in FIG-5.2.

**FIG-5.2**

Array Characteristics

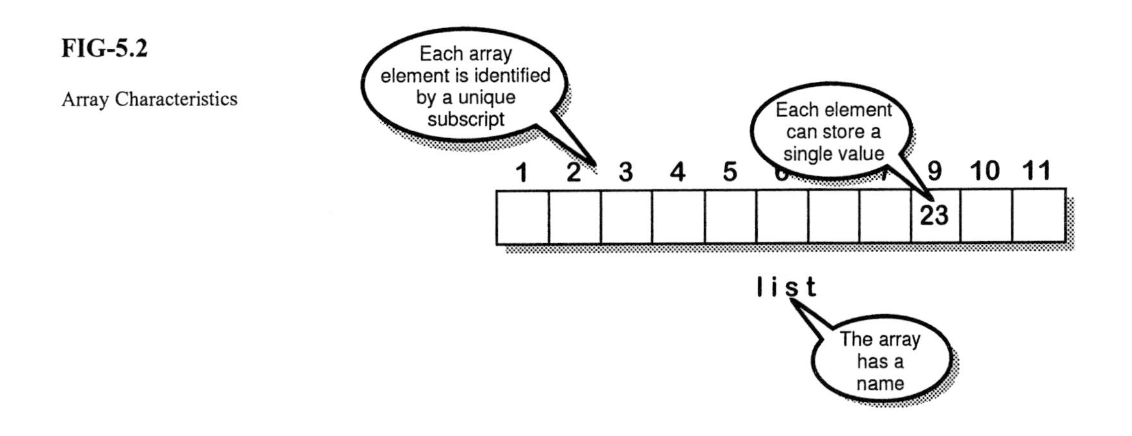


We can summarise the characteristics of an array as:

- It has an identifying name.
- It has a number of elements, the exact number being stated when the array is defined.
- It has a defined type, which specifies the type of values which may be held within the elements of the array.

Each element in an array has :

- A unique integer value identifying its position in the array.
- A value assigned to it which may be changed (as with simple variables).

## Defining Arrays

Arrays are defined in the `var` statement. The definition must include all the details given above. For example, the array shown in FIG-5.2 would be defined as shown in FIG-5.3:

**FIG-5.3**

Defining Arrays

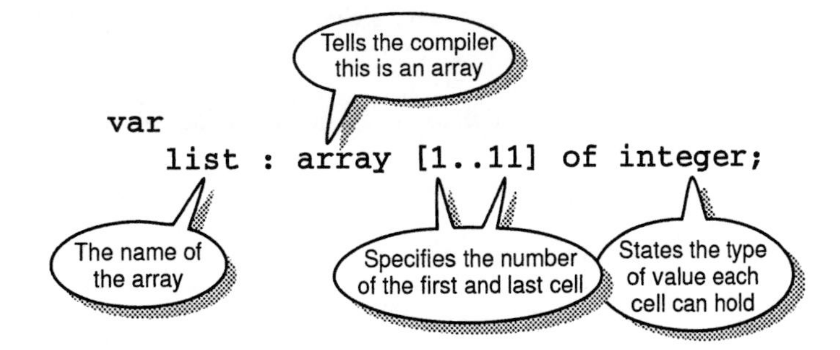


This defines an array called *list* containing eleven elements, each of which can store an integer value. The elements are numbered 1 to 11.

The first element doesn't have to have the subscript 1; any value can be used. Hence, we might define an array as

```
totals : array[-3..5] of real;
```

which would result in an array of 9 elements with a subscript range of -3 to 5.

It's even possible to create arrays that do not use integers for the subscripts; in fact, any ordinal value will do. The following definitions are all valid:

```
    counts : array['A'..'H'] of integer;
    answers : array[false..true] of integer;
```

If a program contains user-defined enumerated types such as

```
type
    Seasons = (Winter, Spring, Summer, Fall);
```

arrays can be declared using values from these types:

```
var
    averagetemp : array[Winter..Fall] of real;
```

The arrays created in the three examples above are shown in FIG-5.4.

**FIG-5.4**

Defining Arrays with

**counts : array['A'..'H'] of integer;**

A B C D E F G H

**answers : array[false..true] of integer;**

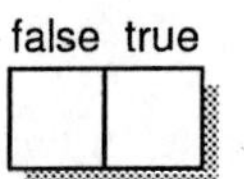


**averagetemp : array[Winter..Fall] of real;**

Winter Spring Summer Fall

> **Activity 5.6**
>
> Write array definitions for the following data items.
>
> 1. An array called *results* which stores exam marks for 15 students.
>
> 2. An array called *weights* which stores 10 weights given in kilograms.

It is also possible to define the structure of an array in a `type` statement:

```
type
    MyArrayType = array[1..11] of integer;
```

and then create a variable of this type:

```
var
    list : MyArrayType;
```

The two methods of defining arrays are shown in FIG-5.5 and FIG-5.6.

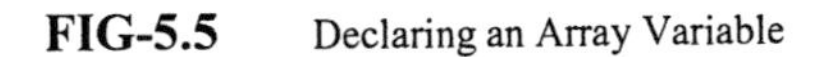

**FIG-5.5** Declaring an Array Variable

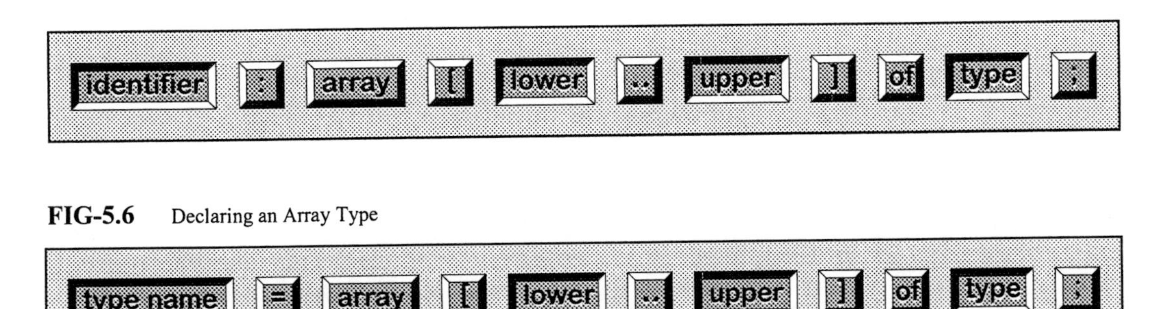


**FIG-5.6** Declaring an Array Type

type name = array [ lower .. upper ] of type ;

## Accessing Arrays

Generally, a program cannot deal with an array as a single entity. Hence, it would be illegal to write

The array *list* is assumed to be defined as

```
var
list;array[1..11]
of integer;
```

```
writeln(list);
```

in the hope of displaying the contents of each element of *list.*

Instead we must access the individual elements of the array by specifying:

- The array name
- The number of the element to be accessed.

Hence, we can assign the value 6 to the third element of the array, using the assignment statement :

```
list[3] := 6;
```

In fact, we may use an array element in any statement where we might use a simple variable of the same type. Table 5.1 lists some English-type statements and the equivalent Pascal code

**TABLE-5.1**

English and Pascal code Equivalents

| English | Pascal Code |
|---|---|
| Read a value into the first cell of *list.* | `readln(list[1]);` |
| Display the value in cell 3 of *list.* | `writeln(list[3]);` |
| Store the value 34 in the last cell in *list* | `list[11] := 34;` |
| Add the contents of cell 5 to cell 7 in *list* | `list[7] := list[7] + list[5]` |
| IF the contents of cell 2 < the contents of cell 3 THEN | `if list[2] < list[3] then` |

This is NOT Structured English as we might use in Outline Logic since its handling of arrays is not precise enough.

Using arrays in Structured English will be dealt with later in this section.

Arrays with non-integer subscripts are accessed with a subscript appropriate to the cell identities. Hence, the array, *averagetemp*, defined as

```
var
    averagetemp : array[Winter..Fall] of real;
```

is accessed with statements such as

```
averagetemp[Summer] := 19.6;
```

**Activity 5.7**

Assuming the declarations

```
var
    counts  : array['A'..'H'] of integer;
    answers : array[false..true] of integer;
```

write the expressions necessary to

a) Set the third cell of *counts* to zero
b) Set the first cell of *answers* to 21.

Pascal makes no attempt to check that the subscript given is a valid one. If the array subscript used is too large, as in

```
list[15] := 45;     {***Invalid subscript***}
```

then unpredictable things will happen as the program attempts to access areas of the computer's memory not allocated to the array. However, checks will be inserted if range checking is on ({$R+}).

If this were all that could be achieved when using arrays, their usefulness would be limited. However, the power of arrays lies in the fact that the subscript may be specified not only as an integer constant, but also as an integer variable or expression. This allows statements such as

```
p := 3;
list[p] := 12;
```

To execute the second assignment statement above, the machine will determine the value of the array subscript variable, *p*, (3), and use that when determining which element of the array is to be accessed. This means that the two statements above are equivalent to:

```
list[3] = 12;
```

The subscript can be given as a constant, variable or expression. Various examples are shown in FIG-5.7 below.

**FIG-5.7**

Variable Subscripts

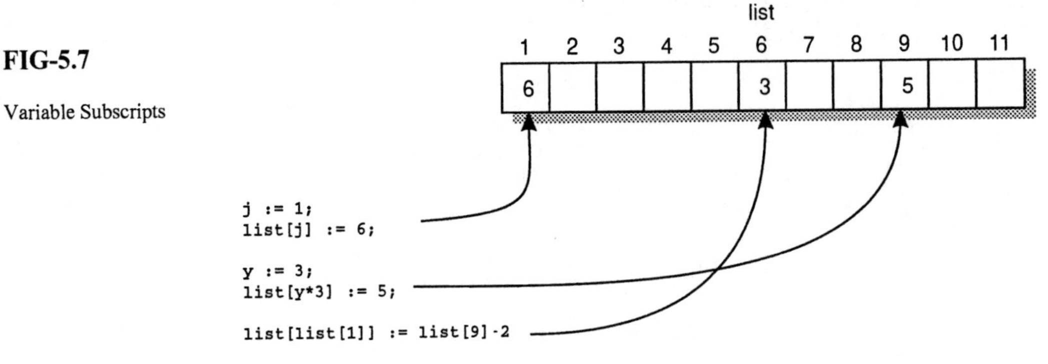

**Activity 5.8**

Assuming the definitions:

```
var
    list : array[1..6] of integer;
    j : integer;
```

and that the elements of *list* contain the values -4,3,9,2,0,12, respectively, state the contents of the array *list* after each of the following statements:

```
list[3] := 7;
j := list[2] + 1;
list[j] := -2;
Inc(j);
list[j] := 3;
j := j + 1;
list[j] := 5;
for j := 1 to 6 do
    list[j] := j*2;
```

## Using Arrays

To get some experience of using arrays to solve real problems, we'll return to the task of reading in five numbers and then displaying them. Using an array, the logic for the program is:

```
FOR 5 times DO
    Read value into next element of array
ENDFOR
FOR 5 times DO
    Display the value in the next element of the array
ENDFOR
```

The coding for this is shown in LISTING-5.3.

**LISTING-5.3**

Using Arrays

```
program Arrays1;
uses WinCrt;

const
  SIZE = 5;
var
  numbers : array[1..SIZE] of integer; {Array holding numbers}
  c       : integer;                      {Loop counter}
begin
  {*** Read in the 5 values ***}
  ClrScr;
  for c := 1 to SIZE do
  begin
      write('Enter number : ');
      readln(numbers[c]);
  end;
  {*** Display the 5 values ***}
  for c := 1 to SIZE do
      writeln(numbers[c]);
end.
```

Notice the use of a constant to define both the size of the array and the number of iterations required in the `for` loops. The advantage of this is that should we require to process 20 numbers rather than 5, the only modification necessary is to change the first line to:

```
SIZE = 20;
```

**Activity 5.9**

Enter and change the program in LISTING-5.3 so that

a) 8 numbers are processed.
b) When entering the numbers the prompt displays a message which includes which number is being entered
(e.g. *Enter number 1 :* , *Enter number 2 :*, etc.)

Looking back at Activity 5.5, we can produce an equally elegant solution for each of the other problems using arrays:

**Problem :** Read in 20 integer values in the range 1 to 5 and display how often each value occurs.

Rather than store the 20 numbers in the array, it is the number of times each value occurs that needs to be placed in the array.

The logic for such a program is:

```
Set all counts to zero
FOR 20 times DO
    Read valid number(1 to 5)
    Add 1 to the appropriate count
ENDFOR
Display counts
```

The implementation of this logic is shown in LISTING-5.4.

**LISTING-5.4**

Counting with Arrays

```
program Arrays2;
uses WinCrt;

var
   counts : array[1..5] of integer; {Array holding counts}
   nbr    : integer; {Holds value entered}
   c      : integer; {Loop counter}
begin
   {*** Set all counts to zero ***}
   for c := 1 to 5 do
       counts[c] := 0;
   {*** FOR 20 times DO ***}
   for c := 1 to 20 do
   begin
       {*** Read in a valid number ***}
       write('Enter number ',c,' : ');
       readln(nbr);
       while (nbr < 1) or (nbr > 5) do
       begin
           writeln('Must be 1 to 5');
           write('Enter number ',c,' : ');
           readln(nbr);
       end;
       {*** Add 1 to the appropriate count ***}
       Inc(counts[nbr]);
   end;
   {*** Display the counts ***}
   for c := 1 to 5 do
       writeln('Total number of ',c,'''s was ', counts[c]);
end.
```

There's one line of the code that may look strange:

```
Inc(counts[nbr]);
```

How does this add 1 to the appropriate count?

The trick is to realise that when *nbr* is 1 then *counts[1]* should be incremented; when *nbr* is 2 then *counts[2]* should be incremented, etc. So the subscript of the element to be incremented is identical to the value of *nbr* and hence, that variable can be used directly to specify the element to be incremented.

The next problem uses an array to search through a list of values. This is such a common requirement in programming that it is dealt with in some detail in a later chapter. Below is one of many ways to tackle the task.

**Problem:** Read in 15 values followed by a final number. Search the first 15 values for one which is equal in value to the final number entered.

The logic for such a program is:

```
Read all 15 values into an array
Get the value to be searched for
Starting at the first value in the array
WHILE value being examined does not match the value being
searched for AND not all values in the array have yet been
examined DO
    Move on to the next value in the array
ENDWHILE
IF a match was found THEN
    Display "Found"
ELSE
    Display "Not found"
ENDIF
```

The corresponding program is given in LISTING-5.5.

**LISTING-5.5**

Searching an Array

```
program Arrays3;
uses WinCrt;

var
  list   : array[1..15] of integer; {Values to be searched}
  nbr    : integer; {Value to be searched for}
  c      : integer; {Loop counter}
  post   : integer; {Position of search in list}
begin
  {*** Read in the 15 values to be searched ***}
  ClrScr;
  for c := 1 to 15 do
  begin
      write('Enter number ',c,' : ');
      readln(list[c]);
  end;
  {*** read value to be searched for ***}
  write('Enter value to be searched for : ');
  readln(nbr);
  {*** Start at the first cell in list ***}
  post := 1;
  {*** WHILE no match found AND not at end of list DO ***}
  while (list[post] <> nbr) and (post < 15) do
      {*** Move to the next value in list ***}
      Inc(post);
  {*** Display message stating if match found ***}
  if list[post] = nbr then
      writeln('FOUND')
  else
      writeln('NOT FOUND')
end.
```

**Activity 5.10**

Enter and run the above program. Check that the correct message appears when a match is found and when it is not.

Modify the code so that when a match is found, the position at which it is found is also displayed.

## Arrays of Strings

It's possible to create an array of any type, including an array of strings. For example, we could make the declaration

```
var
    names : array[1..3] of string;
```

and assign values with statements such as

```
names[1] := 'Liz';
```

and

```
readln(names[2]);
```

**Activity 5.11**

Write the first line of an `if` statement to check if *names[3]* contains the word *John.*

## Array Constants

It's also possible to set up array constants but only as typed constants in which the array's details are also specified. For example:

```
const
    list : array[1..3] of integer = (2,3,4);
```

This can be very useful if you want to display the value of an enumerated type. For although it's not possible to display a enumerated variable's value directly, we can do so by using a string array containing values corresponding to that of the enumerated type. LISTING-5.6 shows an example of this.

**LISTING-5.6**

Constants and Enumerated Types

```
program ConstsandEnum;
uses WinCrt;

type
  Seasons = (Winter, Spring, Summer, Fall);
const
  names : array[Winter..Fall] of string =
                              ('Winter','Spring','Summer','Fall');
var
  time : Seasons;
begin
  for time := Winter to Fall do
      writeln(names[time]);
end.
```

**Activity 5.12**

Write programs to perform the following tasks:

1. Enter 6 numbers; display the numbers in the same order as they were entered; display the numbers in the reverse order (i.e. last number entered displayed first).

```
OUTLINE LOGIC:
    Read numbers into an array
    Display contents of array starting at element one
    Display contents of array starting at element six
```

2. Enter 10 integer values and display only those in the odd numbered elements (i.e. elements 1,3,5,7,9).

```
OUTLINE LOGIC:
    Read numbers into array
    FOR position := 1 TO 9 DO
        IF position is an odd number THEN
            Display the element with that subscript
        ENDIF
    ENDFOR
```

3. Read in 10 characters and display how many E's are in the sequence. Both upper and lower case E's should be counted.

```
OUTLINE LOGIC:
    Set count to zero
    Read in 10 characters
    FOR each character DO
        IF upper case version of character is 'E' THEN
            Add 1 to count
        ENDIF
    ENDFOR
    Display count
```

4. Read in 10 numbers in the range 1 to 50 and display how many fell into each of the categories 1..10, 11..20, 21..30, 31..40, 41..50.

```
OUTLINE LOGIC:
    Set all five counts to zero
    FOR 10 times DO
        Read in a valid number
        Determine which category the number falls into
        Add 1 to the appropriate count
    ENDFOR
    Display each count
```

5. Read in 10 numbers and display the smallest number in the list.

```
OUTLINE LOGIC:
    Read in 10 numbers
    Set smallest equal to the first number
    FOR each remaining number DO
        IF its smaller than smallest THEN
            Set smallest equal to that number
        ENDIF
    ENDFOR
    Display smallest
```

## Arrays as Routine Parameters

Since we can pass every other sort of value to a routine, it should come as no surprise that we're allowed to pass arrays to or from routines.

To pass an array to a procedure or function we begin by specifying the array structure as a type. For example:

```
type
    ArrayType = array[1..20] of integer;
```

This is necessary because every parameter to a routine must be given a specific type in the routine's heading.

Now we can pass such an array to any routine. In the example below, it is passed to a function designed to return the smallest value found within the array:

```
function Smallest(list : ArrayType): integer;
```

The complete code for this routine would be:

```
function Smallest(list:ArrayType): integer;
var
    small : integer; {Smallest value found}
    c     : integer; {Loop counter}
begin
    {*** Assume the first value is the smallest ***}
    small := list[1];
    {*** Search the other elements for smaller values ***}
    for c := 2 to 20 do
        {*** IF smaller value found THEN put it in small ***}
        if list[c] < small then
            small := list[c];
    {*** Return the smallest value ***}
    Smallest := small;
end;
```

> **Activity 5.13**
>
> Write a function similar to *Smallest* that returns the largest value in the array. Call the routine *Largest.*
>
> Write a small program to test your routine.

Passing arrays to procedures is done in exactly the same way. And if we want to return an array from a procedure, as with other types, we need to include the word `var` in the parameter list. The following example is for a routine, *Reverse*, which reverses the order of the values held in an array:

```
procedure Reverse(var list:ArrayType);
```

> **Activity 5.14**
>
> Write and test the procedure *Reverse* using the following logic:
>
> ```
> FOR c := 1 to 7 DO
>     Copy list[c] to temp
>     Copy list[16 - c] to list[c]
>     Copy temp to list[16 - c]
> ENDFOR
> ```

Functions cannot return arrays. The type of value a function can return is restricted to those containing a single value such as integer and real types.

## Open Array Parameters

The problem with the routines *Smallest, Largest* and *Reverse*, is that they can only cope with arrays which have been declared to be of type *ArrayType*. Therefore, it would not be possible to call these routines using as a parameter an array of, say, 10 elements.

To do this we would have to write other versions of the routines specifying differing array parameter types. This is obviously wasteful of effort since the logic in each case would not change.

Pascal version 7.0 has introduced the idea of open array parameters. Open array parameters state simply that a parameter is to be an array, but the size of the array is not given. Using this technique we could rewrite the heading of *Smallest* as:

```
function Smallest( list : array of integer): integer;
```

Notice that the parameter, *list*, is not given a specific type, only that it is an integer array. This is to our advantage, because it means that we are allowed to pass an integer array of any size or type to the function. However, when we come to code the routine we have a problem - how are we to discover the size of the actual array passed so that we can adjust the details of the `for` loop to ensure that every element of the array is accessed?

To our rescue come two standard functions we haven't met yet; `High` and `Low`. These routines can be used on any ordinal type to determine the highest and lowest values that can be stored in variables of that type.

When used with an ordinal type `High` returns the largest value that can be stored. Hence, assuming the declaration

```
var
    v : integer;
```

then the expression

```
High(v)
```

returns the value 32767, that being the highest value that can be stored in the integer variable.

Unusually, `High` can also be called using the type name as an argument:

```
High(integer)
```

Used with a user-defined enumerated type, it will return the highest value available. The expression

```
type
   Seasons =
(Winter,Spring,
Summer, Fall);
```

```
High(Seasons)
```

returns *Fall.*

Used with an array, `High` returns the subscript of the last element of the array. Therefore, assuming we have declared the following

```
var
    numbers : array[1..20] of integer;
    counts  : array[1..5] of integer;
```

then

```
High(numbers)
```

returns 20 and

```
High(counts)
```

returns 5.

Things change slightly when `High` is used within a routine on an open array parameter. So, if we were to pass the array *numbers* to the function *Smallest*, and that routine contained the code

```
function Smallest(list : array of integer): integer;
begin
    writeln(High(list));
```

it would display 19, while passing *counts* to the same function would display the value 4.

*High* deals with open array parameters by returning the number of elements in the array minus 1.

*Low* performs a related operation, returning the lowest value that an ordinal type can store, or, in the case of arrays, returning the lowest subscript of an array. Used on open array parameters, `Low` always returns zero.

The two routines are defined formally below.

| | |
|---|---|
| **Prototype** : | `function High(X): varies with X` |
| **Unit** : | System |
| **Pre-condition:** | *X* must be ordinal or an array type |
| **Description** : | *X* is a variable or a type. High returns a value based on the type of *X*:<br>Ordinal type the highest value in that type<br>Array type the highest subscript of the array<br>String type the declared size of the string<br>Open array number of elements - 1 |

| | |
|---|---|
| **Prototype** : | `function Low(X): varies with X` |
| **Unit** : | System |
| **Pre-condition:** | *X* must be ordinal or an array type |
| **Description** : | *X* is a variable or type. Low returns a value based on the type of *X*:<br>Ordinal type the lowest value in that type<br>Array type the lowest subscript of the array<br>String type returns 0<br>Open array returns 0 |

The program shown in LISTING-5.7 highlights the use of open arrays in combination with `High` to access every element of an array.

**LISTING-5.7**

Using Open Arrays

```
program openArrays;
uses WinCrt;

{*** Procedure to double each element of an array ***}
procedure Twice(var list : array of integer);
var
  c : integer;
begin
  {*** Elements zero to High(list) ***}
  for c := 0 to High(list) do
       list[c] := list[c]*2;
end;



var
  {*** Arrays to be used ***}
  nos : array[0..4] of integer;
  more : array [0..8] of integer;
  c : integer;       {Loop counter}
begin
  {*** Initialise arrays ***}
  for c := 0 to 4 do
       nos[c] := c;
  for c := 0 to 8 do
       more[c] := c+3;
  {*** Call routine with both arrays ***}
  Twice(nos);
  Twice(more);
  {*** Display values in array ***}
  ClrScr;
  for c := 0 to 4 do
       writeln(nos[c]);
  writeln;
  for c := 0 to 8 do
       writeln(more[c]);
end.
```

**Activity 5.15**

Enter and test the program in LISTING-5.7.

Change the subscripts of the arrays *nos* and *more*. *nos* should be changed to [5..12] and *more* to [-2..5].

Change the `for` loops in the main program to account for the new array sizes.

Run the program and examine the results.

The final results from Activity 5.14 are very revealing. Although the arrays now have varying subscript ranges, the procedure *Twice* continues to assume that the first element of the array passed has a subscript of zero. The program continues to give the correct results because open array parameters are always treated within the routine to which they are passed as if their subscripts begin with element zero.

**Activity 5.16**

Rewrite the function *Smallest*, so that it takes an open array as a parameter.

# Multi-Dimensional Arrays

## Declaring Multi-Dimensional Arrays

If a student sits 6 exams, then an array containing 6 elements could be used to store this information:

```
var
    marks : array[1..6] of integer;
```

However, if there are 8 students, we would need 8 such arrays in order to contain all the data. This is achieved with the definition:

```
var
    marks : array[1..8, 1..6] of integer;
```

Literally, this defines 8 copies of a 6 element array.

**FIG-5.8**

A 2D Array

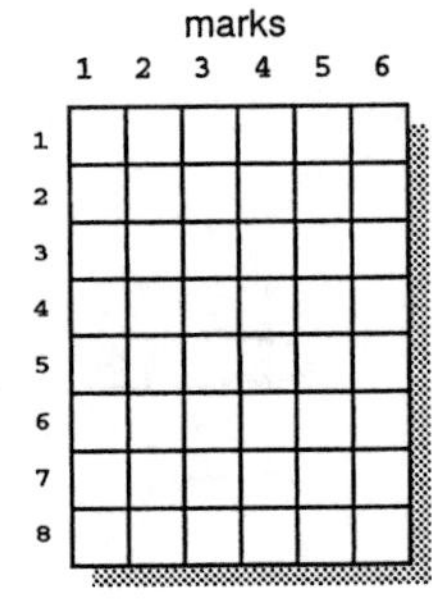


The resulting data structure is a **two-dimensional array** (see FIG-5.8).

There are many situations which call for two-dimensional arrays. For example, a chess board is easily represented by an 8 by 8 array, while a class timetable could be held as a 5 by 7 array, representing 7 subjects taught over 5 days.

These two-dimensional structures are often referred to as **matrices**.

Such arrays can be defined directly, as in the example above, or separately as a type. This second option would be required if the array was being passed as a parameter to a routine.

**Activity 5.17**

Write Pascal definitions for the following integer arrays represented by the diagrams below. In each case, assume that the array is named *matrix*.

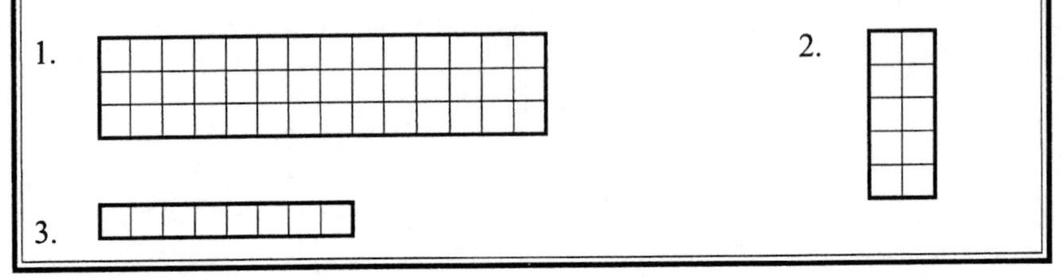


## Accepting the Array

**FIG-5.9** Accessing a Two-Dimensional Array

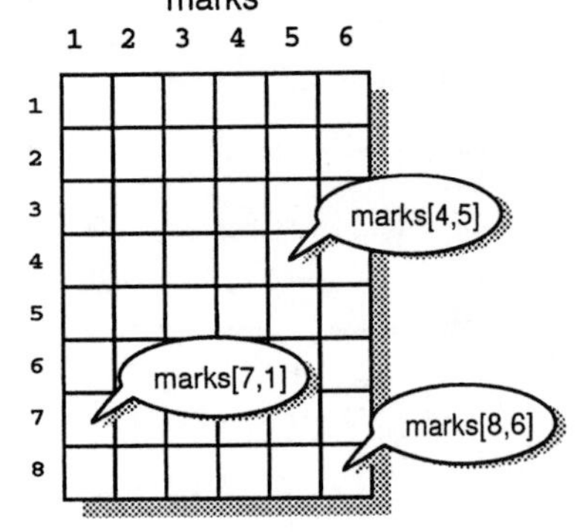


To access an individual element in the array, we must give the array name and the row and column numbers (see FIG-5.9).

To read in the six marks for each of the 8 students, we employ the following logic

```
FOR each student DO
  FOR each mark DO
    Read mark into appropriate element of marks
  ENDFOR
ENDFOR
```

A more program-like logic would be:

```
FOR student := 1 TO 8 DO
    FOR exam := 1 TO 6 DO
        Read valid mark into marks[student,exam]
    ENDFOR
ENDFOR
```

The program in LISTING-5.8 demonstrates this technique.

**LISTING-5.8**

Using a Two-Dimensional Array

```
program MultiDArrays;
uses WinCrt;

var
  marks : array[1..8,1..6] of integer;
  col, row : integer;
begin
  ClrScr;
  {*** FOR each student DO ***}
  for row := 1 to 8 do
  begin
      {*** Read in 6 marks ***}
      writeln('Student ',row);
      for col := 1 to 6 do
      begin
          write('Enter mark ',col,' : ');
          readln(marks[row,col]);
      end;
  end;
  {*** Display results ***}
  ClrScr;
  writeln('RESULTS');
  for row := 1 to 8 do
  begin
      for col := 1 to 6 do
          write(marks[row,col]:3);
      writeln;
  end;
end.
```

## Typed Constants Again

To create a two-dimensional typed constant array, the values are nested within parentheses. For example, a 4 row - 2 column array constant is defined as:

```
const
    matrix : array[1..4,1..2] of integer =
                              ((8,4),(1,1),(2,0),(5,5));
```

**Activity 5.18**

With an array, *matrix[1..4,1..4]*, use nested `for` loops to set up the array in the following ways:

| | | | |
|---|---|---|---|
| 1 | 2 | 3 | 4 |
| 5 | 6 | 7 | 8 |
| 9 | 10 | 11 | 12 |
| 13 | 14 | 15 | 16 |

| | | | |
|---|---|---|---|
| 1 | 5 | 9 | 13 |
| 2 | 6 | 10 | 14 |
| 3 | 7 | 11 | 15 |
| 4 | 8 | 12 | 16 |

| | | | |
|---|---|---|---|
| 16 | 15 | 14 | 13 |
| 12 | 11 | 10 | 9 |
| 8 | 7 | 6 | 5 |
| 4 | 3 | 2 | 1 |

### Higher Dimensions

There are situations in which even two-dimensional arrays are inadequate. For example, if we want to store the minimum and maximum temperatures every hour for a 365 day period, we need an array which is 365 by 24 by 2.

Such arrays can be defined by extending the existing definition format. Hence, we can define an array to hold temperatures as:

```
var
    temp : array[1..365,1..24,1..2] of real;
```

Defining typed constants with higher dimensions simply means the use of more parentheses. For example:

```
const
    arr : array[1..3,1..2,1..4] of integer =
    (
        (
            (1,3,2,3),(1,1,1,1)
        ),
        (
            (1,8,9,7),(6,5,4,3)
        ),
        (
            (0,0,0,0),(6,6,6,6)
        )
    );
```

We can extend our definitions to an almost unlimited number of dimensions, although it is unusual to require more than three.

## Using Arrays in Structured English

When an algorithm calls for arrays, one possibility is to use general terms such as

```
Add value to list
```

or

```
Find position of value in list
```

Often, as the algorithm's detail becomes fuller, array subscripting may be required, and in such cases, Pascal's own syntax can be used:

```
Add value to list[5]
```

## Summary

- **An array is** a sequence of elements. Each element can hold a single value. Each value in an array is of the same type.
- **Arrays can be declared directly** as a variable or by first declaring an array type.
- **Elements in an array are numbered** according to the bounds specified in the array declaration.

- **Each element is identified** by the array name followed by a subscript enclosed in square brackets.

- **Typed constant arrays can be declared.**

- **The array subscript can be given as a constant, variable or expression.**

```
e.g.    list[4];        //*** Constant
        list[no];       //*** Variable
        list[no+2];     //*** Expression
```

# STRING VARIABLES

## Strings as Arrays

We have already encountered string variables. So far we have treated them as if they were simple variables just like integers and reals. However, this is not the case. Strings are actually implemented as `char` arrays.

What makes strings different from both simple variables and arrays is that we can treat them as either a single entity or access individual characters. Hence, with statements such as

These statements assume the declaration
```
var
  words : string;
```

```
readln(words);
```

and

```
words := 'Mary had a little lamb';
```

we treat the variable as a single entity.

However, it is also possible to access individual characters within a string variable using array subscripting. So the expression

```
words[1]
```

gives us access to the first character in the string.

Using this feature we could count the number of E's in a string using the following code:

The *Length* function was described on page 162.

```
count := 0;
for c := 1 to Length(words) do
    if words[c] = 'E' then
        Inc(count);
```

## How Strings are Stored

The compiler has a problem to solve when it reserves space for a string variable - how many bytes should be allocated? We know that each character occupies one byte of memory, but since the compiler doesn't know how many characters are to be stored in a string variable as it converts the Pascal code to machine code, it handles the problem of storage by allocating exactly 256 bytes to a string variable. This means that if a program contains the declaration

```
var
    words : string;
```

then space is allocated as shown in FIG-5.10.

**FIG-5.10**

The Structure of Strings



Notice that the elements are numbered 0 to 255.

Initially, the contents of the string are undefined. However, once we execute a statement such as

```
words := 'Hello there';
```

this data is stored over elements 1 to 11 of the variable.

If we next ask the machine to display the contents of the string with a statement such as

```
writeln(words);
```

there's another problem to be solved - which parts of the string's space contain meaningful data and which is unused? In this example, the data is held in elements 1 to 11 and the contents of only those cells should be displayed. The compiler knows this by keeping a count of the occupied part of the string in element zero. Since the array is designed to hold characters and element zero requires to hold a number, the software gets round this by storing the character whose ASCII code is 11 (see FIG-5.11).

**FIG-5.11**

Storing a String

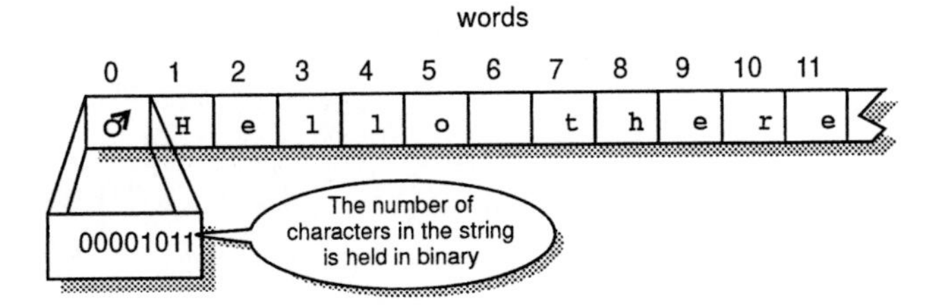


With this information, displaying the contents of the string is easy: the compiler simply employs the following logic:

```
for c := 1 to Ord(words[0]) do
    write(words[c]);
```

If a change is made to the contents of a string, for example,

```
words := 'Goodbye';
```

the machine handles the necessary changes to the string and the count (see FIG-5.12).

**FIG-5.12**

Changing a String

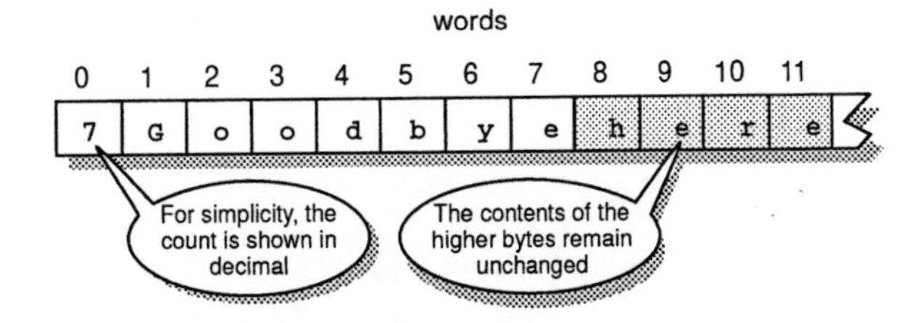


The format of a string variable allows us to store up to 255 characters, but often this will be much more than we require. To reduce the storage allocated to a string variable, we state the maximum number of characters to be stored as part of the string variable's declaration:

```
var
    words : string[20];
```

This example reserves 21 bytes of space: room for 20 characters plus the count in element zero.

Obviously, this allows us to create programs that occupy less memory space. If you attempt to store a string which is too long to fit the allocated space, the right-most characters will be lost. Hence, the following code

```
var
words : string[5];

words := 'ABCDEF';
```

results in *words* containing only *ABCDE.*

## String Operations

In the previous chapter we encountered routines such as `Insert` and `Delete` as well as the + operator which joins strings.

These operations also handle the updating of the count in element zero of the string. Making your own changes to a string may not have the effect you require unless you remember to change the count appropriately.

So, whereas changing a character in a string is relatively easy (the example below changes all E's in a string to X's)

```
for c := 1 to Length(words) do
    if words[c] = 'E' then
        words[c] := 'X';
```

changing the length of the string with a statements such as

```
words := 'ABCD';
words[5] := 'E';
```

will have no apparent effect, since, although element 5 now contains an E, the count in element zero is still at 4, so displaying the string will still show ABCD. To include the extra character we need to add the statement:

```
Inc(words[0]);
```

Even here we have to remember that words[0] must be treated as a character. Attempting to write

```
words[0] := words[0] + 1;
```

would give rise to a compilation error.

Of course, all this could be avoided by using the available operator

```
words := words + 'E';
```

which would update the count as part of the operation.

Control characters such as *newline* and *return* may be inserted in a string by using their ASCII code value. Hence if we write

#10 is the newline character

```
words := 'Hello' + #10+'there';
```

and display the result, we get

```
Hello
     there
```

As you see, the *newline* character moves the cursor vertically down to the next line. To move to the start of that new line we need to include the *return* character:

#13 is the return character

```
words := 'Hello'+#10+#13+'there';
```

**Activity 5.19**

Write routines to perform the following:

1. Reverse the contents of a string. Hence, 'ABC' would be returned as 'CBA'.

2. Capitalise the words in a sentence.

3. Find the last occurrence in a string of a specified character.

## Arrays of Strings

If we need to store something such as a list of names, then the way to do this is to create an array of strings. This can be achieved with a statement such as

```
var
    names : array[1..10] of string[30];
```

which allows 10 names of up to 30 characters each.

We can access individual names with code such as:

```
for c := 1 to 10 do
begin
    write('Enter name : ');
    readln(names[c]);
end;
```

Individual letters of a name can be accessed by treating the structure as a two-dimensional array. Hence the first letter of the third name is accessed with the expression:

```
names[3,1]
```

**Activity 5.20**

1. Write a program to read in 10 names and display how many surnames begin with an 'H'.

```
Outline Logic:

  Set count to zero
  Read 10 names
  FOR each name DO
      Find the last space in the name
      IF the character following that space is 'H' THEN
          Add 1 to count
      ENDIF
  ENDFOR
  Display count
```

2. Write a program that reads in an array of 10 strings and displays the longest string found in the array.

## String Array Constants

We can set up a list of strings as typed constants. The example below shows how this is done:

```
const
   names : array[1..5] of string[20] =
               ('Spock','Scotty','Bones','Jean Luc','Data');
```

## Strings as Parameters

The default string type can be defined as a parameter using the same style as for other standard types. For example:

```
function MyFunct(s:string):integer;
```

However, if you are using smaller strings or string arrays, then these must be declared in a `type` statement

```
type
   ShortString = string[10];
   NameList = array[1..10] of string[30];
```

which can then be used in routine headings:

```
function MyFunct2(v : ShortString): boolean;
procedure Update(var list : NameList);
```

**Activity 5.21**

Write a procedure that takes a string of 30 characters containing a name (forename followed by surname) and places the surname first. Hence, when passed *Liz Heron*, the routine returns *Heron Liz*.

## Entering Strings at the Keyboard

When reading a string's value from the keyboard you might expect to be allowed to type in up to 255 characters. However, this doesn't take into account the limited size of the keyboard buffer. As a result, only 126 characters can be entered.

## Longer Strings

If we need strings that contain more than 255 characters then we need to use a new data type introduced in Borland Pascal Version 7.0. This new structure is explained later in this chapter in the section titled Pointers.

# Summary

- **Strings store up to 255 characters.**
- **Less storage can be used** if the maximum string size is included in the definition.
- **Strings can be treated as** simple variables or arrays of characters.
- **Individual characters can be accessed** using a subscript. The first character is in position 1.

- **Element zero of a string** is used to hold a count of the number of characters in the string.
- **Standard routines** automatically modify the string counter as appropriate.
- **To access individual characters in an array of strings** treat the structure as a two-dimensional array.
- **When using anything other than standard strings as parameters**, define the new structure as a type.
- **A maximum of 126 characters can be read from the keyboard**.
- **Strings of more than 255 characters** require a different data type.

# RECORD STRUCTURES

## Introduction

An array is only useful when the data items to be stored are all of the same type. Where the collection of data items is of differing types, another data structure is required. This is known as a **record**. A record is a collection of individual data items or **fields**. Each data item may be of any type.

## Defining a Record Structure

If we wanted to retain the identity code, sex and score of a student who had taken part in an aptitude test, then we might declare this collection of information using the following Structured English :

```
TYPE
    IQType =
        RECORD
            idcode  : INTEGER
            sex     : CHAR
            score   : INTEGER
        ENDRECORD
```

This acts as a blueprint for any subsequent variables of this type. For example:

```
st1,st2 :  IQType
```

In Pascal, such record structures are defined within a `type` statement. The keyword `record` is used to mark the beginning of the fields defined within the record structure. Hence, the above structure is defined in Pascal as:

Note the use of `end` to mark the termination of the structure. This is one of only two situations in Pascal where `end` is used without a matching `begin`.

```
type
    IQType =
    record
        idcode : integer;
        sex;   : char;
        score  : integer;
    end;
```

We can then declare variables of this type:

```
var
    st1, st2 : IQType;
```

The resulting allocation of memory space is shown in FIG-5.13.

**FIG-5.13**

Record Structures

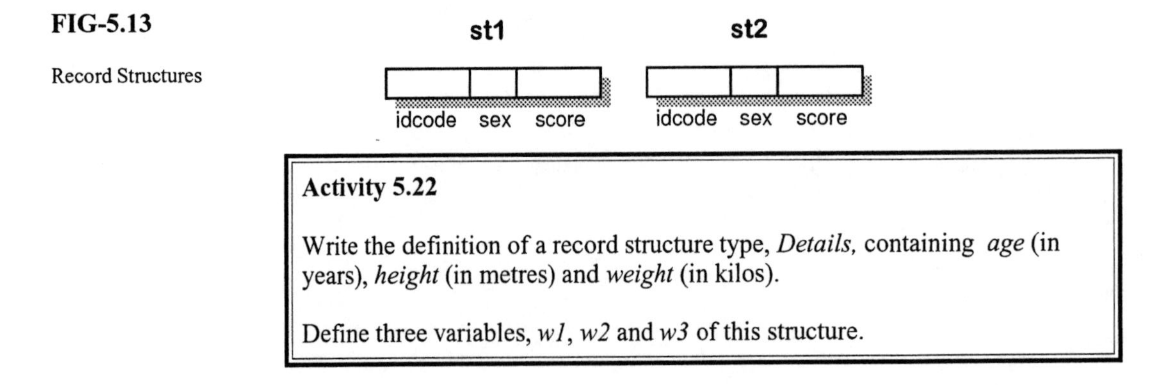


**Activity 5.22**

Write the definition of a record structure type, *Details*, containing *age* (in years), *height* (in metres) and *weight* (in kilos).

Define three variables, *w1*, *w2* and *w3* of this structure.

Record structures are often used even when the data they contain are of the same type - a situation in which we might normally think of using arrays. For example, time information might be held in a record structure defined as

```
type
    TimeType =
    record
        hrs  : integer;
        mins : integer;
        secs : integer;
    end;
```

since this allows us to give a name to each component in the data; something that isn't possible when using an array.

# Record Fields

## Accessing Fields

A field within a structure variable can be accessed using the field selector operator (.).

Hence, assuming the definition

```
var
    st1, st2 : IQType;
```

we can access the *score* field in *st1* using the term

```
st1.score
```

A record field can be employed at any point in the program where it would be legal to use a simple variable of the same type. For example:

```
st1.score := 120;

writeln(st1.score);

readln(st1.score);

if st1.score > 100 then
```

The following program (LISTING-5.9) makes use of record variables in determining the average aptitude score for two students. The program uses the following logic:

```
Read details of first student
Read details of second student
Calculate average score
Display average score
```

**LISTING-5.9**

Using Records

```
program List09;
uses WinCrt;

type
  IQType =
  record
      idcode : integer;
      sex    : char;
      score  : integer
  end;

var
  st1, st2 : IQType;      {Student records}
  average  : real;        {Average score}
begin
  ClrScr;
  {*** Get details of first student ***}
  write('Enter ID of first student : ');
  readln(st1.idcode);
  write('Enter sex : ');
  readln(st1.sex);
  write('Enter score : ');
  readln(st1.score);
  {*** Get details of second student ***}
  write('Enter ID of second student : ');
  readln(st2.idcode);
  write('Enter sex : ');
  readln(st2.sex);
  write('Enter score : ');
  readln(st2.score);
  {*** Calculate average ***}
  average := (st1.score + st2.score) / 2;
  {*** Display average score ***}
  writeln('Average score is ',average:0:1);
end.
```

**Activity 5.23**

Using the record type *Details* defined in Activity 5.22, write a program to determine the height of the tallest of three people.

## Field Types

Record fields may be arrays or other structures, as well as user-defined types. For example, if we want to hold the score achieved by a student in each of six exams we could declare the structure:

```
type
   StudentDetails =
   record
       idcode : integer;
       sex    : char;
       score  : array[1..6] of integer; {Array in record}
end;
```

Assuming *st1* is a variable of this new type, the resulting structure is shown in FIG-5.14.

**FIG-5.14**

Declaring an Array within a Record

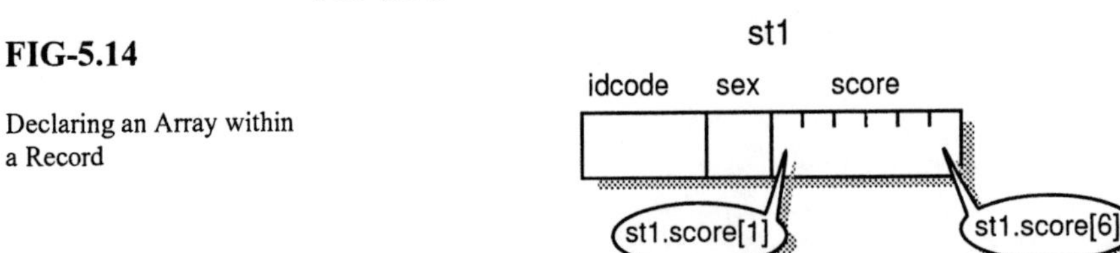

To access this array, we use statements such as

```
st1.score[1] := 79;
```

which sets the first *score* in record *st1* to 79.

> **Activity 5.24**
>
> Add a *name* field of up to 30 characters within the definition of *StudentDetails* as given above.

A common requirement is to store a date. Although this might be held using a simple string variable, because we often require to access the day, month and year components of a date separately, it is often more appropriate to use a record structure such as:

```
type
    DateType =
    record
        day   : 1..31;
        month : 1..12;
        year  : word;
    end;
```

Where a date is required as part of a larger record, then the result is a **nested structure**. For example, to add the date of birth to our student record the new declaration would be:

```
type
    StudentDetails =
    record
        idcode : integer;
        name   : string[30];
        dob    : DateType;
        sex    : char;
        score  : array[1..6] of integer;
    end;
```

Assuming the definition

```
var
    st1 : StudentDetails;
```

we can access the *dob* fields components using the terms

```
st1.dob.day
st1.dob.month
```

and

```
st1.dob.year
```

The structure is shown in FIG-5.15.

**FIG-5.15**

Sub-records

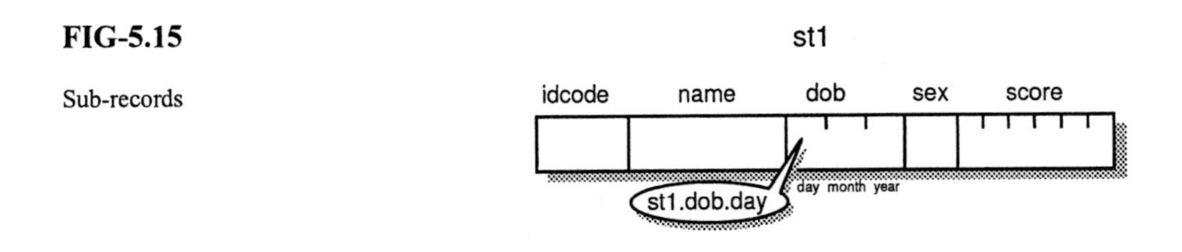

The format for declaring a record structure type is shown in FIG-5.16.

**FIG-5.16**

Record Declaraton Format

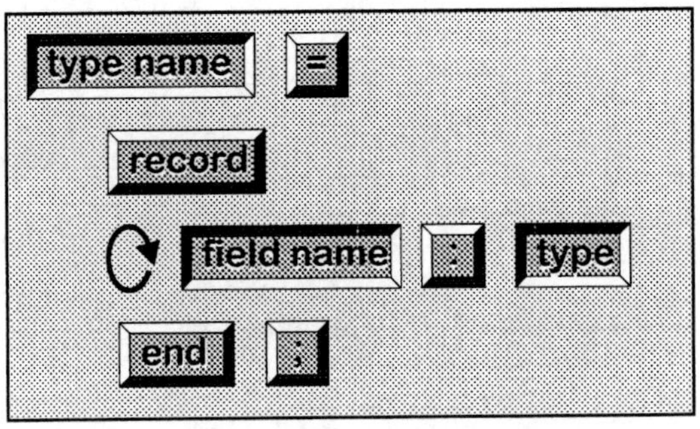

type name =

record

field name : type

end ;

## Record Constants

A record structure can also be used when declaring a typed constant. So, using *StudentDetails* as the structure required we can make the declaration:

```
const
    rec : StudentDetails = (idcode:1234; name:'Liz Heron';
        ↳dob:(day:26; month:10; year:1961); sex:'F';
        ↳score:(12,67,87,91,56,23));
```

This is a complex definition and worth a second look. You will notice that each field has to be named; this is followed by a colon and the value to be assigned to the field. In the case of *dob*, which is itself a record, its own fields are named and assigned values, this is all within an inner set of parentheses. The final field, *score*, being an array, has the value to be assigned to each element held within another set of parentheses.

**Activity 5.25**

A program contains the declarations

```
type
    TimeType =
    record
        hrs : 0..23;
        mins   : 0..59;
        secs : 0..59
    end;
    DateType =
    record
        day   : 1..31;
        month : 1..12;
        year  : word;
    end;
    Event =
    record
        desc : string;
        date : DateType;
        time : TimeType;
    end;
```

Define a constant of type *Event* which contains the following information:
'Moon landing',20/7/1969,10:56:00.

## Copying Record Structures

Like arrays, it's usually not possible to treat a record variable as a single entity. This means that statements such as the `readln` below

```
var
    st1 : StudentDetails;

    readln(st1);
```

are not permissible. Instead, the fields of the structure must be accessed one at a time. For example:

```
readln(st1.idcode);
```

However, there is one exception to this rule: when copying the contents of one record structure to another of the same type, this can be achieved by a single assignment statement. Hence, we might copy the contents of one *StudentDetails* record to another with the statement

```
st1 := st2;
```

## Pascal's `with` Statement

It can be rather tedious having to continually type in a record name every time one of its fields is to be accessed. For example, assuming the declaration

```
var
    newrec : StudentDetails;
```

reading values into each field of the record would involve the code below

```
readln(newrec.idcode);
readln(newrec.name);
readln(newrec.sex);
    .
    .
```

However this can be shortened by using Pascal's `with` statement. This allows us to specify a record structure whose name is to be assumed when fields are specified. Hence, if we write

```
with newrec do
begin
    readln(idcode);
    readln(name);
    readln(sex);
        .
end;
```

the assumption is that all fields mentioned are those belonging to *newrec*.

It's possible to specify more than one record structure in a single `with` statement. Therefore, if our program contains the definitions

```
type
    TimeType =
    record
        hrs  : 0..23;
        mins : 0..59;
        secs : 0..59
    end;
```

```
    DateType =
    record
        day   : 1..31;
        month : 1..12;
        year  : word;
    end;

var
    timerec : TimeType;
    daterec : DateType;
```

then we could use the following with statement to access fields in both records

```
with timerec, daterec do
begin
    writeln(day,'/',month,'/',year);
    writeln(hrs,':',mins,':',secs);
end;
```

You must ensure that no ambiguity arises. If the different record structures had some fields with identical names, then the compiler would not be able to identify which field was to be accessed. In such a case, the full name, including the record variable name, would have to be used.

If there is only a single statement within a `with` structure, `begin` and `end` may be omitted. For example:

```
with daterec do
    writeln(day,'/',month,'/',year);
```

The format of the `with` statement is given in FIG-5.17.

**FIG-5.17**

The `with` Statement

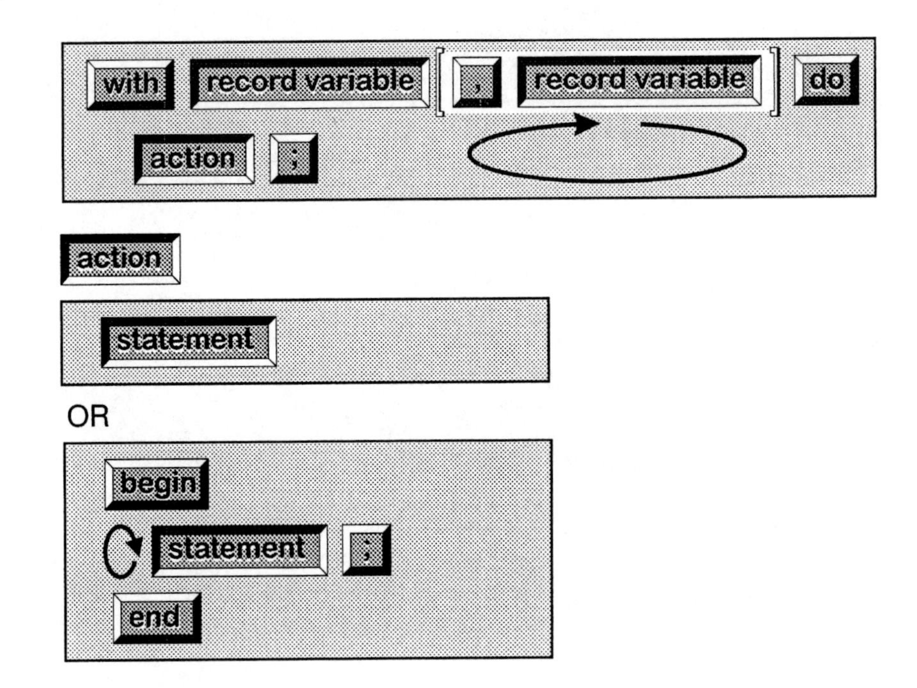

# Records as Parameters

Passing a structure to or from a routine involves the same techniques used to pass simple types such as integer and real values. For values being passed into a routine, simply specify the parameter name and type in the routine heading. For example, to pass a *StudentDetails* record to a function, *HighestMark*, the relevant heading would be:

```
function HighestMark(st : StudentDetails): integer;
```

If the structure is being returned, a procedure must be used since function cannot return complex structures. For example:

```
procedure Update(var st : StudentDetails);
```

# Arrays of Records

If we need to retain the details of several students, then one possibility is to define an array of records. This is done with a definition such as:

```
studentlist : array[1..7] of StudentDetails;
```

To access a specific student's record the array name and element number must be specified. For example:

```
studentlist[5]
```

To access a field within that record we need the field selector operator and the field name:

```
studentlist[5].dob.day
```

(see FIG-5.18)

**FIG-5.18**

Arrays of Records

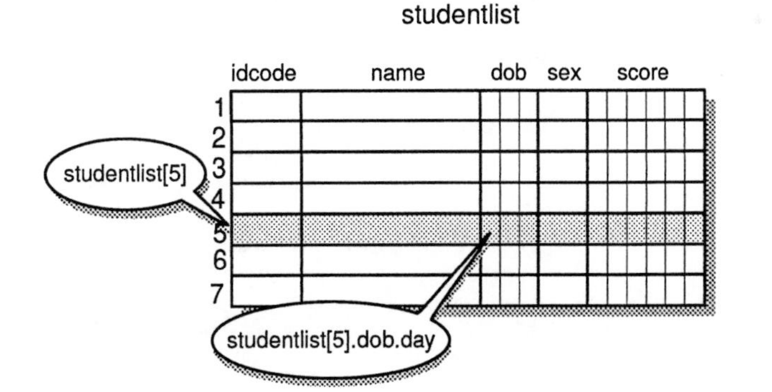


> **Activity 5.26**
>
> Write a program using a record structure which reads in the *account number*, *name*, *address* and *balance* of five bank customers. The name should be sub-divided into *surname*, *first name* and *initials*; the address should be divided into *first line*, *second line*, *third line*, *town*, *district* and *post code*.
>
> The five records are to be held in an array.
>
> The balance in each record should then be increased by 5% and the full details of the five updated records displayed on the screen.

## Summary

- **A record is a collection of fields.**
- **Pascal uses the term** `record` to declare a record structure.
- **The items within a record** are often referred to as **fields** of the record.
- **The commonest format** when defining a `record` is:

```
type
   typename =
   record
      field1 : type;
      field2 : type;
      .
      fieldn : type
   end;
```

- **Use the type when defining variables**

```
variable1, variable2 : typename...
```

- **To initialise the fields** of a record variable use a typed constant:

```
const
   variable:typename=(field1:value1, field2:value2...)
```

- **To access a record field**:

```
simple type          variable_name.field_name
array element        variable_name.array_name[subscript]
sub-record field     variable_name.field_name.field_name
```

- **Record structures can be passed** into a function or procedure.
- **Record structures can only be returned** by procedures.
- **Access a field within an array of records using the format:**

```
array_name[subscript].field_name
```

- **To copy one record variable to another** of the same type, use the normal assignment command:

```
rec_var1 = rec_var2;
```

# SETS

## Introduction

There are times when we want a variable to be assigned more than one value at the same time. For example, we might want a variable named *fontstyle* to take on the values *italic* and *bold* to indicate that the style of some text is to be bold italic.

If we wanted a variable to reflect which days of the week we were at work we might want to set that variable to *Monday, Tuesday, Wednesday, Thursday* and *Friday*.

Of course, if we had to, we could make do with the structures we have, possibly using an array or a string to store this information. However, Pascal offers a more useful alternative - a set variable.

A **set** is a collection of related items. Perhaps a group of characters or values from a user-defined enumerated type. If we declare a set variable then it may be assigned any number of values from the appropriate set.

## Declaring Set Variables

We can declare a set variable as:

```
var
    letters : set of char;
```

Notice that the keywords `set of` are used along with the basic type (here that is `char`).

Pascal imposes a few limits: the underlying set must be an ordinal type and cannot contain more than 256 different values. So, although it's alright to define a set of characters, the definition

```
var
    numbers : set of integer;
```

would not be allowed, since the type `integer` has more than 256 possible values.

However, it is possible to define a subrange of integers

```
var
    numbers : set of 1..12;
```

as long as none of the values are higher than 255.

As usual, an alternative way of creating sets is to first create a type

```
type
    LetterSet = set of char;
```

and then create variables of that type

```
var
    letters : LetterSet;
```

This approach is required if the variables are involved in parameter passing.

The next example shows how to create a set type based on a previous defined enumerated type:

```
type
    Days = (Sunday, Monday, Tuesday, Wednesday, Thursday,
            ↳Friday, Saturday);
    DaysSet =  set of Days;

var
    working : DaysSet;
```

Sets cannot be based on non-ordinal types such as `real` and `string`.

**Activity 5.27**

Define an enumerated type, *Months = (Jan .. Dec)* and using this, create a new type, *MonthSet*, defined as a set of months.

Just as it is possible to define a set based on a subrange of integers, so we can have sets which are subranges of enumerated types:

```
type
    SummerSet = set of Jun..Aug;
```

The format for defining set types is shown in FIG-5.19.

**FIG-5.19**

Defining a Set Type

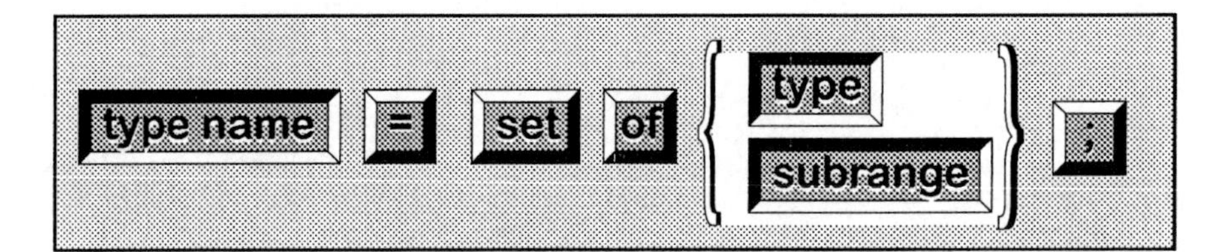


# Assigning Values to Set Variables

Set variables can be assigned values using the normal assignment command.

The variables are assigned any set of values from the range defined for them.

If the program contains the definition

```
var
    working : DaysSet;
```

then the variable *working* can be assigned any set constructed from *DaysSet.*

Be careful though, we can't write something like

```
working := Friday;
```

since the right-hand side of this expression is not a set, but a single value.

Set constants are always enclosed in square brackets, so the correct assigment would be

```
working := [Friday];
```

And if we want more than one value in the set we can write:

```
working := [Monday, Wednesday, Friday];
```

If a contiguous range of values are to be assigned, rather than write the long-winded

```
working := [Monday, Tuesday, Wednesday, Thursday];
```

we can write

```
working := [Moday..Thursday];
```

To assign an empty set to the variable, use empty brackets:

```
working := [ ];
```

Values cannot be duplicated within a set. Hence, it is not valid to write

```
working := [Monday, Wednesday, Monday];
```

# Set Operators

## in

We can test for a specific value within a set using the keyword `in`. For example,

```
if Wednesday in working then
```

will return *true* if *Wednesday* is in the set assigned to *working,* otherwise it will return *false.*

The `in` operator is most often used with `char` and `integer` values. Hence, instead of discovering if the `char` variable *ch* holds a vowel, using the statement

```
if (ch = 'A') or (ch = 'E') or (ch = 'I') or (ch = 'O') or
   (ch = 'U') then
```

we can write the much shorter

```
if ch in ['A','E','I','O','U'] then
```

**Activity 5.28**

Write an `if` statement to discover if the integer variable *month*, has a value corresponding to a month with 30 days (i.e. if *month* is 4,6,9 or 11).

If we wanted to test if *ch* was a consonant, then instead of writing

```
if ch not in ['A','E','I','O','U'] then
```

which common English usage might suggest, we have to write the more awkward

```
if not (ch in ['A','E','I','O','U'] )then
```

The parentheses are necessary because `not` has a higher priority than `in` and this must be overridden.

## Set Equality

We can test if two sets contain exactly the same values using the equality operator (=). This returns *true*, if the sets are identical, otherwise *false* is returned.

For example:

```
if working = [Monday,Wednesday] then
```

## Set Inequality

The inequality operator (<>) returns *true* if the sets are different, and if equal, *false* is returned.

This assumes *available* is a variable of type *DaysSet*

For example:

```
if working <> available then
```

## Set Union

Two sets can be joined using the set union operator (+). For example,

```
var
    d1,d2,d3 : DaysSet;
begin
    d1 := [Monday,Wednesday];
    d2 := [Monday,Friday];
    d3 := d1 + d2;
```

sets *d3* equal to *[Monday, Wednesday, Friday]*. Note that since no duplication is allowed, *Monday* appears only once in *d3*.

## Set Intersection

The set intersection operator (*) creates as a result the common elements of two sets. For example,

```
d3 := d1 * d2;
```

sets *d3* to *[Monday]* since this is the only common element of the two sets *d1* and *d2*.

## Set Difference

The elements in one set but not in another can be found by using the set difference operator (-). So

```
d3 := d1 - d2;
```

returns the set of values which are in *d1* but not in *d2* (i.e.*[Wednesday]*). Note that this is a different result from

```
d3 := d2 - d1;
```

which returns *[Friday]*.

## Sub-Set

We can test if the elements of one set are all included in a second set by using the operators <= and >=. Hence, having executed the code

```
var
    d1, d2 : days;
begin
    d1 := [Monday,Wednesday];
    d2 := [Monday..Friday];
```

the code

```
if d1 <= d2 then
```

will return *true* since all the elemnts of *d1* are also in *d2*. In other words, *d1* is a sub-set of *d2*.

The code

```
if d1 >= d2 then
```

tests if all the elements of *d2* are included in *d1*. This would give the result *false*.

The empty set, [ ], is a sub-set of all sets, so the code

```
if [] <= d1 then
```

would return *true*.

Borland Pascal version 7.0 includes two routines for operating on sets. These are described below:

**Prototype** : `procedure Exclude(var s : set of T; v:T)`
**Unit** : System
**Pre-condition**: None

**Description** : Removes item *v* from the set *s*. *s* can be a set of any type. *v* must be an element of that type.

**Example** :

```
var
    y : set of char;
begin
    y := ['M','T','W'];
    Exclude(y,'T');          {y = ['M','W']}
```

**Prototype** : `procedure Include(var s: set of T; v : T)`
**Unit** : System
**Pre-condition**: None

**Description** : Adds item *v* to the set *s*. *s* can be a set of any type.

**Example** :

```
var
    y : set of char;
begin
    y := ['M','T','W'];
    Include(y,'F');     {y = ['M','T','W','F']}
```

As you can see, these routines have a similar effect to the operators - and +. However, the routines generate more efficient machine code in the compiled program.

**Activity 5.29**

Previously, in Chapter 4, we created a program to accept a maximum number of uppercase letters from the keyboard. Using this as the basis of a new routine, create a function called *GetData* which conforms to the following mini-spec:

| | | | |
|---|---|---|---|
| NAME | : | GetData | |
| PARAMETERS | | | |
| IN | : | allowable | : KeySet |
| | | max | : Integer |
| IN/OUT | : | None | |
| OUT | : | entered | : String |
| PRE-CONDITION | : | *allowabled* is not empty AND *max* > 0. | |
| DESCRIPTION | : | The routine returns a string, *entered*, constructed from characters entered by the user. Only characters from the set specified by *allowable* are accepted.<br>No more than *max* characters are accepted.<br>Input should terminate when ENTER is pressed.<br>Pressing the backspace key should delete the last character entered.<br>Accepted characters should be displayed on the screen as they are entered.<br>Keys not specified in *allowable* should be ignored. | |

OUTLINE LOGIC :

```
Set count to zero
Set entered to empty
Read character from keyboard
WHILE character is not ENTER DO
    IF
        character in allowable AND
        count < max :
            Display character
            Add character to entered
            Add 1 to count
        character=backspace AND count > 0 :
            Remove last char from screen
            Remove last char from entered
            Subtract 1 from count
    ENDIF
    Read character from keyboard
ENDWHILE
Move cursor to a new line
```

You will need to create a set type called *KeySet*, that is defined as `set of char`.

Remember to check that the pre-condition is met at the start of the routine. If the pre-condition is not met, exit the routine returning an empty string.

When complete, write a test driver for the routine and hence test the routine.

# Summary

- **Sets can contain several values** of an ordinal type.
- **A set can contain a maximum of 256 values.**
- **No value within a set can have an ordinal value of more than 255.**
- **Sets can be constructed from types and subranges.**
- **Set constants** are enclosed in square brackets.
- **The following set operators** are available:

```
in
+
-
*
=
<>
<=
>=
Exclude
Include
```

# BIT MANIPULATORS

## Introduction

We saw in the first chapter how values are stored in binary within the computer. The bits that make up a byte or integer value can be manipulated directly using various **bit manipulation operators**. These are explained below.

## Bit Complement Operator (`not`)

This unary operator inverts the bits of a value, giving a result in which the 1's of the original value are replaced by zeros and the original zeros by 1's. A typical piece of code might be:

```
var
    nos, ans : byte;
begin
    nol := $4D;
    ans := not nos;
```

*ans* will then contain the value $4D_{16}$ (see FIG-5.20).

**FIG-5.20**

Bit Complement

Starting Value | 0 | 1 | 0 | 0 | 1 | 1 | 0 | 1 |

Operation : not

Result | 1 | 0 | 1 | 1 | 0 | 0 | 1 | 0 |

> **Activity 5.30**
>
> What is the result of the expressions
> 1. not $7C09
> 2. not 196
>
> Give your results in both hexadecimal and binary.

## Shift Left Operator (`shl`)

This allows us to move a value a specified number of bits to the left. For example:

```
    nol := $B2;
    ans := nol shl 3;
```

The result of this example is shown in FIG-5.21.

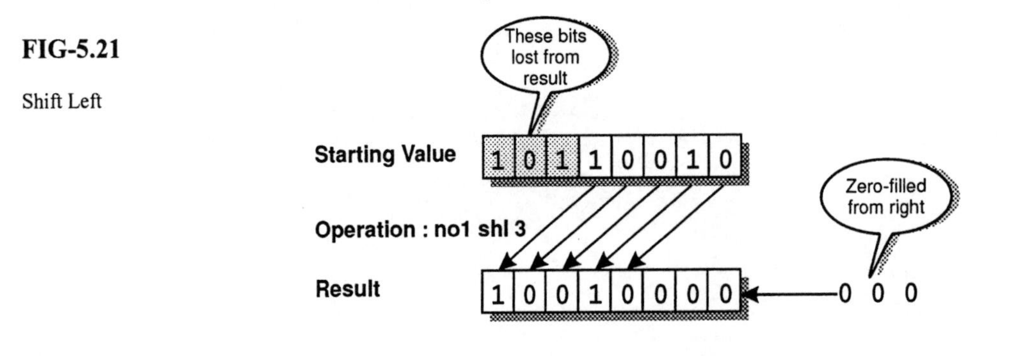


**FIG-5.21**

Shift Left

Note that the left-hand bits of the original value are lost, while the right-hand bits are zero-filled.

The shift left operator can be used as an efficient way of multiplying a value by any power of 2. Hence, to multiply a value by 8 ($2^3$), we simply move the value 3 places to the left.

It can also be used to determine the value of a specific bit. For example, if we want to find out if the third bit (counting from the right) of an integer variable contains a 1, we can simply shift the value 3 places to the left and test if the result is less than zero (remembering that a 1 in the left-most bit of a signed integer will result in the contents being interpreted as a negative value).

**Activity 5.31**

Write a procedure, *ShowBinary*, which displays the contents of an integer value in binary.

OUTLINE LOGIC:

```
FOR each bit DO
    IF value is negative THEN
        Display '1'
    ELSE
        Display '0'
    ENDIF
    Shift value one place to left
ENDFOR
```

## Shift Right Operator (shr)

This operator, rather obviously, moves a value a specified number of places to the right. This is a good way of performing integer division by any power of 2. Hence, to divide the contents of *nol* by 16 ($2^4$) we need merely write:

```
ans := nol shr 4;
```

The effects of this operation are shown in FIG-5.22.

**FIG-5.22**

Shift Right

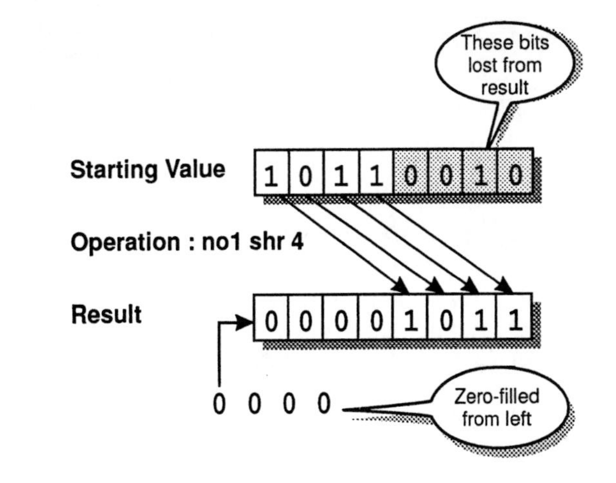

## Bit-wise AND (and)

This operator AND's the bits of two values. A bit in the result is 1 if the corresponding operand bits are both 1, otherwise the result bit is zero. A typical statement might be:

```
ans := nol and $04;
```

The second value specified in this, and the remaining operations, is often referred to as a **mask**, since it can be used to mask or filter out parts of a value. For example, suppose we want to know if bit 3 of a `char` variable contains a 1. One way to do this is to copy only bit 3 of the variable into a second variable and if this result is zero then the original bit 3 was also zero. To stop the other bits of the original value being copied across to the result we use the bit-AND operator with a mask value of $04 (see FIG-5.23).

**FIG-5.23**

Bit-wise AND

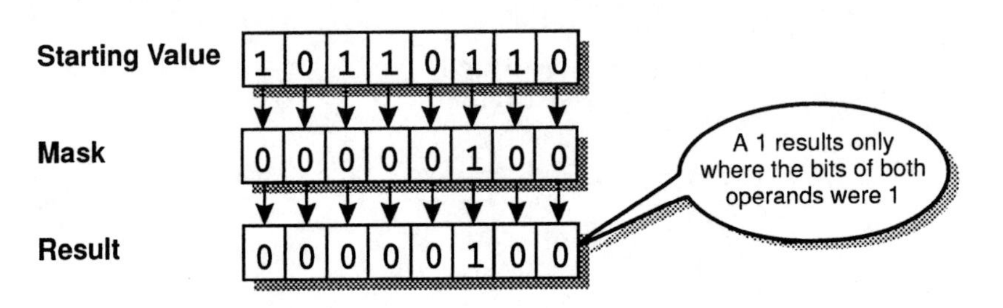


## Bit-wise OR (or)

This operator OR's the bits of two values, giving a result of 1 where either or both of the corresponding operand bits are 1, otherwise giving a zero. A typical statement would be:

```
ans := nol or $OF;
```

The result of the above example is shown in FIG-5.24.

**FIG-5.24**

Bit-wise OR

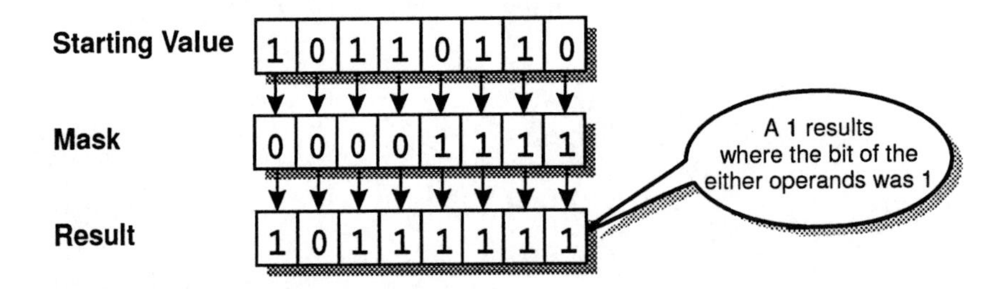


## Bit-wise Exclusive OR (xor)

A given bit in the result is set to 1 if the corresponding bits in the two operands are of differing values (0, 1 or 1,0); a result of zero is given where both bits are the same (0,0 or 1,1). A typical statement might be:

```
ans := nol xor no2;
```

An example is shown in FIG-5.25.

**FIG-5.25**

Exclusive OR

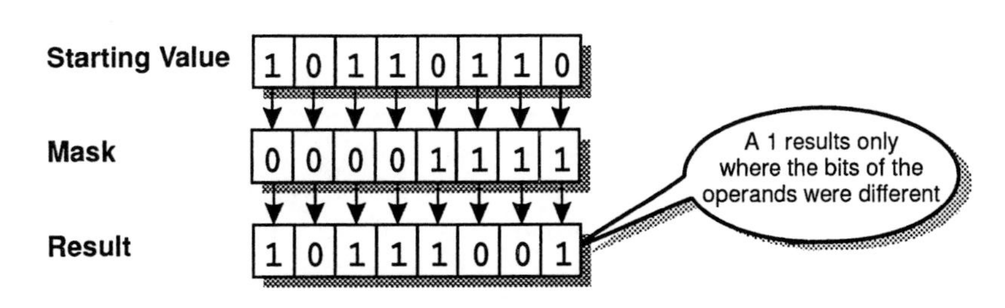


> **Activity 5.32**
>
> 1. Write down the result of the operation
>    01011101 XOR 01110000
>
> 2. Exclusive OR the result of 1) above with the same value as before (01110000).

The result from the above Activity highlights an important feature of the exclusive OR operation: performing XOR twice produces the original value. This characteristic is used in various programming situations.

# Summary

- **Bit operators** manipulate the bits of integer values.

- The following operators are available:

```
not
shl
shr
and
or
xor
```

# POINTERS

## Introduction

**FIG-5.26**
Allocating Memory

2000 letter

**Main Memory**

When we define a variable, it is allocated one or more bytes in the computer's memory. This, in effect, associates each variable with a unique address within that memory. Hence, the definition

```
var
    letter : char;
```

might allocate the memory location at address 2000 to the variable *letter* (see FIG-5.26).

**FIG-5.27**
Allocating More Memory

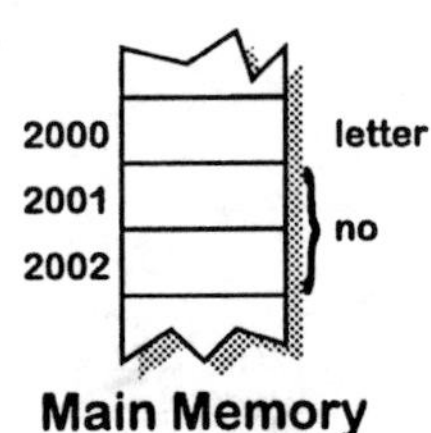


Where a variable is allocated two or more bytes, the variable is identified by the address of the first byte allocated to it. For example, if the definition

```
var
    letter : char;
    no     : integer;
```

results in the space allocation shown in FIG-5.27, then the variable *no* is associated with the address 2001.

### The Address Of Operator, @

The address allocated to a variable can be determined using the address of operator, @. For example, while we can display the contents of *no* with the statement

```
writeln(no);
```

we might be able to display the address of the first byte allocated to *no* using the statement

```
writeln(@no);
```

but Pascal won't allow us to display addresses directly, so we need to cast the address to a long integer first

```
writeln(longint(@no));
```

in order to display the address of the variable.

Assuming the addresses in FIG-5.27, the above statement would result in the value 2001 being displayed. However, in practice, there is no way of knowing in advance the exact memory locations allocated by the compiler to a variable.

## Pointer Variables

### What is a Pointer?

As well as variables to hold numeric and character values, Pascal allows us to create variables designed to hold memory addresses. These are known as **pointer variables**, since their contents is an integer value representing the address of some location in memory and, hence, they can be thought of as pointing to (or referencing) a memory location.

Since addresses are simply integers (e.g. 2001), you may be tempted to assume that normal integer variables could be used to hold this information, but pointer variables have their own unique set of operations and are treated differently from other variable types by the compiler.

### Defining Pointers

Like any other variable, a pointer must be defined. A variable is identified as a pointer, by preceding its type with a caret symbol (^). For example:

```
var
    cptr : ^char;
```

This identifies *cptr* as a pointer and also the type of value expected at the location pointed to by the variable. Hence we may read the above definition as

*cptr* is a pointer to a `char` value.

or

*cptr* will contain an address of `char` value

> **Activity 5.33**
>
> Write the definition necessary to create variables *iptr1* and *iptr2* which are pointers to `integer` values and *fptr* which references a `real` value.

## Using Pointers

### Allocating a Value to a Pointer

If we assume a program begins with the definitions

```
var
    letter : char;          {simple char variable}
    no     : integer;       {simple integer variable}
    cptr   : ^char;         {pointer to a char value}
    iptr   : ^integer;      {pointer to an integer value}
```

**FIG-5.28**

Allocating Pointer Space

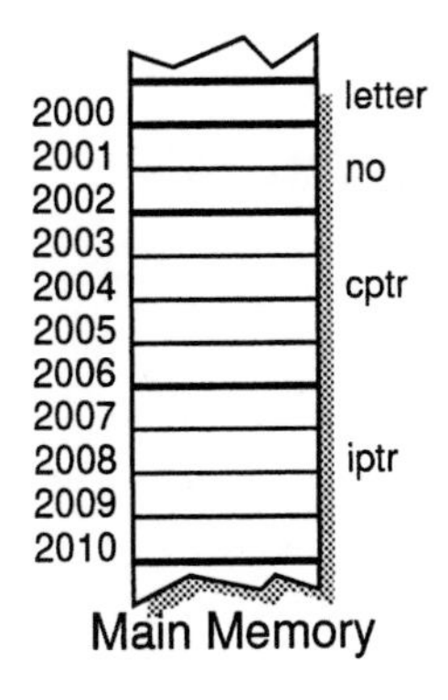


then the memory allocated by the compiler might be as shown in FIG-5.28, with each pointer being allocated 4 bytes.

For clarity we may simplify this diagram to show only each variable and its start address (see FIG-5.29)

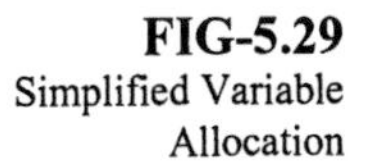

**FIG-5.29**
Simplified Variable Allocation

2000 letter
2001 no
2003 cptr
2007 iptr
Memory Allocated

**Activity 5.34**

Draw a simplified memory allocation diagram for the following declaration:

```
var
    rnol   : real;
    rptr   : ^real;
    lno    : longint;
    lptr   : ^longint;
```

Assume space is allocated in sequential order, beginning at location 3010.

**FIG-5.30**
Allocating Addresses

2000 A letter
2001 65 no
2003 2000 cptr
2007 2001 iptr
Memory Allocated

While program assignments such as

```
letter := 'A';
no := 65;
```

result in values being stored in the simple variables *letter* and *no*, the pointer variables can be allocated the addresses of *letter* and *no* using the statements

```
cptr := @letter;
iptr := @no;
```

**FIG-5.31**
Referencing: Generalised Form

cptr letter
iptr no

The results of these four statements are shown in FIG-5.30.

Note that we must allocate the address of a `char` value to the `char` pointer and an `integer` value to the `integer` pointer, otherwise an error will occur.

Since, in practice, we are unlikely to know the actual addresses involved when variables are allocated memory space, we can show that *cptr* references *letter* and *iptr* points to *no* using the more abstract style shown in FIG-5.31.

## Dereferencing a Pointer

Once a pointer contains a valid address, it can be used to access the data at that address. This is known as **dereferencing**.

To access the contents of the referenced address, we used the pointer name followed by a caret. Hence, the statement

```
writeln(longint(cptr))
```

would display the address in *cptr* while the statement

```
writeln(cptr^)
```

will display the contents held at the address pointed to by *cptr* (i.e. 'A').

In this context, the caret is known as the **indirection operator**.

The program in LISTING-5.10 demonstrates these statements.

Dereferencing can be used in any situation where a normal variable name might be used. This allows statements such as

```
no := 12;
```

to be replaced by

```
iptr^ := 12;
```

**LISTING-5.10**

Using Pointers

```
program Pointers1;
uses WinCrt;
var
  no     : integer;
  letter : char;
  iptr   : ^integer;
  cptr   : ^char;
begin
  {***Store values in the normal variables ***}
  no := 12;
  letter := 'A';
  {*** Store the addresses of those variables in pointers ***}
  iptr := @no;
  cptr := @letter;
  {*** Display the contents of the pointers ***}
  writeln('iptr contains the address ', longint(iptr));
  writeln('cptr contains the address ', longint(cptr));
  {*** Display contents of addresses referenced by pointers ***}
  writeln('Data at the address referenced by iptr is ',iptr^)
  writeln('Data at the address referenced by cptr is ',cptr^);
end.
```

TABLE-5.2 gives several examples showing normal variable statements and the dereferenced equivalents.

**TABLE-5.2**

Pointer Equivalents

| Standard Commands | Pointer Equivalent |
|---|---|
| `no := no + 1;` | `iptr^ := iptr^ + 1;` |
| `readln(letter) ;` | `readln(cptr^);` |
| `if letter= 'A' then` | `if cptr^ = 'A' then` |
| `writeln(10 - no) ;` | `writeln(10 - iptr^);` |
| `for no := 1 to 5 do` | `for iptr^ := 1 to 5 do` |

**Activity 5.35**

The following program reads in two numbers and assigns the smaller value to *answer*.

```
program pointers2;
uses WinCrt;
var
  no1, no2, answer : integer;
begin
  write('Enter two numbers ');
  readln(no1, no2);
  if no1 < no2 then
     answer := no1
  else
     answer := no2;
  writeln('The smaller value is ', answer)
end.
```

**Continued on next page**

**Activity 5.35** (continued)

Type in the program and run it.

Now, add three integer pointers, *p1, p2* and *p3*.

Immediately after the `begin` statement, set these pointers to contain the address of *no1, no2* and *answer* respectively.

Next, replace the remaining statements of the program that make direct references to the three integer variables with the corresponding statement containing a dereferenced pointer. For example,

```
answer := no1;
```

is replaced by

```
p3^ := p1^;
```

Finally, rerun the program to check that the same results are obtained.

## Initialising Pointers

To indicate that a pointer variable does not contain an address, we can assign it the value NIL. For example:

```
iptr := NIL;
```

**FIG-5.32**

Null Pointer Symbol

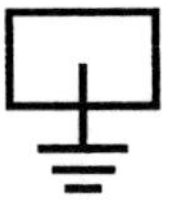

The graphical representation of an empty pointer is shown in FIG-5.32.

Two or more pointer variables may reference the same address. Hence, assuming the definitions

```
var
    no             : integer;
    iptr1, iptr2   : ^integer;
```

both pointers can reference *no* by using the statements

```
iptr1 := @no;
iptr2 := @no;
```

or

```
iptr1 := @no;
iptr2 := iptr1;
```

**FIG-5.33**
Referencing the same Address

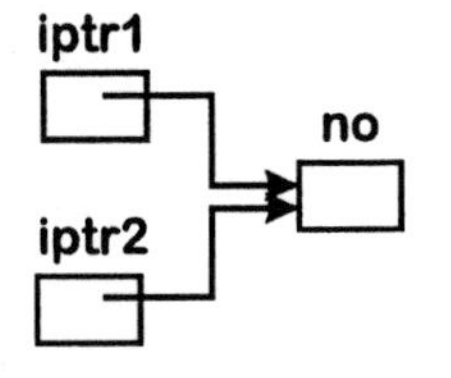


This last method copies the contents of one pointer variable (*iptr1*) to another (*iptr2*), with the result that both then contain the same address (see FIG-5.33).

**Activity 5.36**

Write the `if` statement necessary to check if two integer pointers, *iptra* and *iptrb*, reference:

1. the same address.
2. the same value (possibly held at different locations).

# Dynamic Space Allocation

## New

Since pointer dereferencing can be used to replace a variable name in a program, the final stage in this process is to eliminate the need to define the normal variable in the first place. This approach is useful since it allows us to reserve memory space as and when required; once the space is no longer needed, it can be deallocated, thereby being freed for other purposes later in the program.

Variable space can be allocated and referenced by a pointer using the `New` command. Assuming the definition

```
var
    iptr : ^integer;
```

we can allocate space for a variable value using the statement

```
New(iptr);
```

Allocating data space in this way is known as **dynamic space allocation.**

Executing `New` performs two tasks:

1. It allocates space for a variable of the type specified by the pointer argument.
2. It changes the pointer argument to reference the variable created.

The effects of the command are shown in FIG-5.34.

**FIG-5.34**

Dynamic Space Allocation

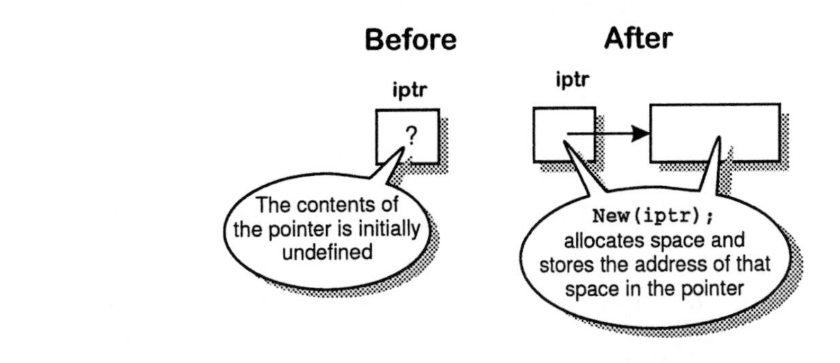
Before
After
iptr
?
The contents of the pointer is initially undefined
iptr
New(iptr);
allocates space and stores the address of that space in the pointer

Notice that the allocated space does not have a name as normal variables do. This means that the only method of accessing the space created is via the pointer. Hence the statement

```
iptr^ := 12;
```

would be required to store the value 12 in the dynamically allocated space (see FIG-5.35).

**FIG-5.35**

Assigning a Value to Dynamic Space

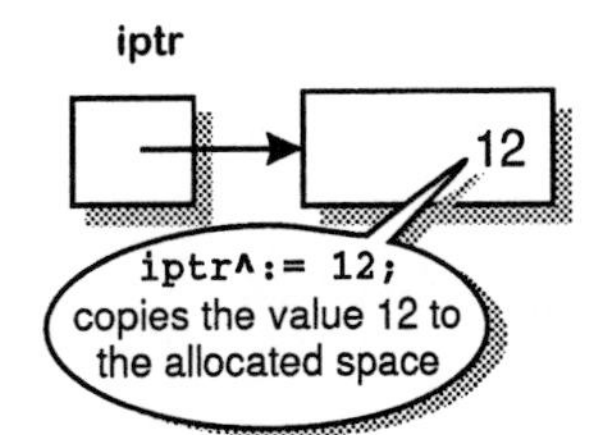
iptr
12
iptr^:= 12;
copies the value 12 to the allocated space

If we were to modify the contents of a pointer variable then we would lose all means of accessing the dynamically allocated space which it had previously referenced. In the following example, access to the area created by the `New(ptr1)` statement is lost by the subsequent `ptr1 := ptr2;` statement:

```
var
    ptr1, ptr2 : ^integer;
begin
    {***Allocate space ***}
    New (ptr1);
    New (ptr2);
    {*** Lose address of first space ***}
    ptr1 := ptr2;
```

With no pointers referencing a dynamically allocated variable it is impossible to access that variable space (see FIG-5.36).

**FIG-5.36**

Unreachable Space

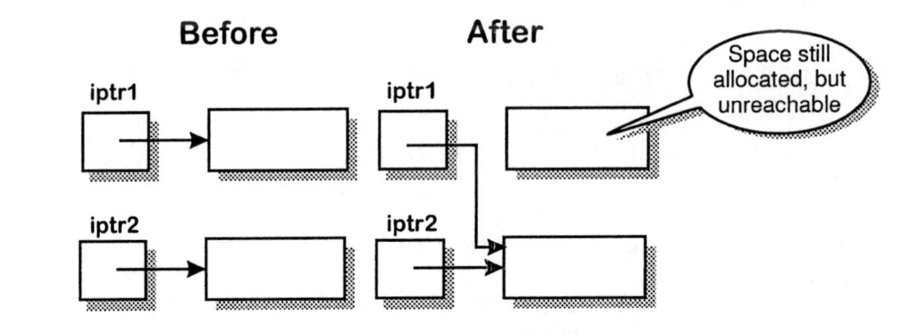


## Dispose

The space assigned to normal variables is deallocated at the end of their lifetime (see Chapter 4), but dynamically allocated space remains allocated until it is deallocated with the `Dispose` command. To delete the space referenced by *ptr1* use

```
Dispose(ptr1);
```

This deallocates the space but does not modify the contents of the pointer variable. It is important to deallocate space when it is no longer required, otherwise there is a danger, when large amounts of memory are dynamically allocated, of running out of memory space.

Once the space has been deallocated, attempting to dereference the pointer will result in a run-time error. For example, the following code would cause a program to terminate:

```
program pointers3;
uses WinCrt;
var
    p : ^integer;
begin
    New(p);
    writeln(longint(p));
    Dispose (p);               {Space deallocated}
    writeln(longint(p));       {Pointer contents unchanged}
    p^ := 12;                  {Invalid attempt at dereferencing}
end.
```

To avoid this situation, it is good policy to follow the `Dispose` statement by a command to reset the pointer involved to NIL:

```
Dispose(ptr1);
ptr1 := NIL;
```

**Activity 5.37**

Assuming a program contains the following code:

```
var
  ptr1,  ptr2  : ^integer;
  no1          : integer;
begin
  New(ptr1);
  New(ptr2);
```

which of the following statements are valid.

a) `readln(ptr1^);`
b) `writeln(ptr2);`
c) `no1 := ptr1 + ptr2;`
d) `ptr1 := ptr2;`

Explain the effect of any valid statement.

## Pointers To Records

As well as using pointers to reference simple variables, they can also be used on record structures.

For example, if we have defined the record structure

```
type
    StudentDetails =
    record
        idcode : integer;
        name   : string[30];
        dob    : DateType;
        sex    : char;
        score  : array(1. .6] of integer
    end;
```

then we can define a pointer to this type with the definition

```
var
    recptr : ^StudentDetails;
```

and dynamically create space for a record with

```
New(recptr);
```

and then access that space via the pointer with statements such as

```
readln (recptr^.name)
readln (recptr^.dob.day);
recptr^.score[3] := 35;
```

```
DateType =
record
   day : 1..31;
   month : 1..12;
   year : word
end;
```

**Activity 5.38**

Write a program to dynamically allocate space for a *DateType* value (as defined earlier) and read in and display the contents of this space.

## Reserving Blocks of Memory

A simple variable can hold only one value; an array can hold many values. Rather than dynamically allocate space for just one integer or real value, we can reserve space for many such values. In other words, we can dynamically allocate space for an array.

To do this we start by declaring an array type:

```
type
    ListType = array[1..50] of integer;
```

Next, we need a pointer variable for this type:

```
var
    ptr : ^ListType;
```

Now the memory must be allocated:

```
New(ptr),
```

Finally, we can access the elements of our dynamically allocated array using the dereferenced pointer and subscripting. For example:

```
ptr^[1] := 12;
ptr^[2] := 20;
writeln(ptr^[1], ' ', ptr^[2]);
```

> **Activity 5.39**
>
> Use the technique described above to dynamically create a 5 element integer array. Read values into the array and then display them.

# The Truth About `var` Parameters

In the last chapter, the effect of using a `var` parameter was explained (see page 179). That explanation, although describing the consequences of using a `var` parameter, did not show the actual mechanism employed by the compiler. In fact, `var` parameters are implemented using pointers.

Looking again at the *Smaller* procedure described in the last chapter (and shown again here in LISTING-5.11), we can see exactly how `var` parameters operate.

**LISTING-5.11**

Implementing `var` Parameters

```
program ReturningValues;
uses WinCrt;
{************************************}
{*      Procedure definition        *}
{************************************}
procedure Smaller(no1, no2 : integer; var ans : integer);
begin
  if no1 < no2 then
      ans := no1
  else
      ans := no2;
end;
{************************************}
{*        main program              *}
{************************************}
```

**Continued on next page**

**LISTING-5.11**
(continued)

Implementing `var` Parameters

```
var
  n1, n2, result : integer;
  ch             : char;

begin
  {*** Read in the two values ***}
  ClrScr;
  write('Enter two numbers : ');
  readln(n1, n2);
  {*** Determine the smaller value ***}
  Smaller(n1,n2,result);
  {*** Display result ***}
  writeln('The two numbers were ', n1, ' and ', n2);
  writeln('The smaller value is ', result);
  {*** Close window when key pressed ***}
  ch := ReadKey;
  DoneWinCrt;
end.
```

When the procedure *Smaller* is called, local variables are created for the parameters. However, any `var` parameters are created as pointers which are then used to store the address of the corresponding actual parameters (see FIG-5.37).

**FIG-5.37**

Handling `var` Parameters

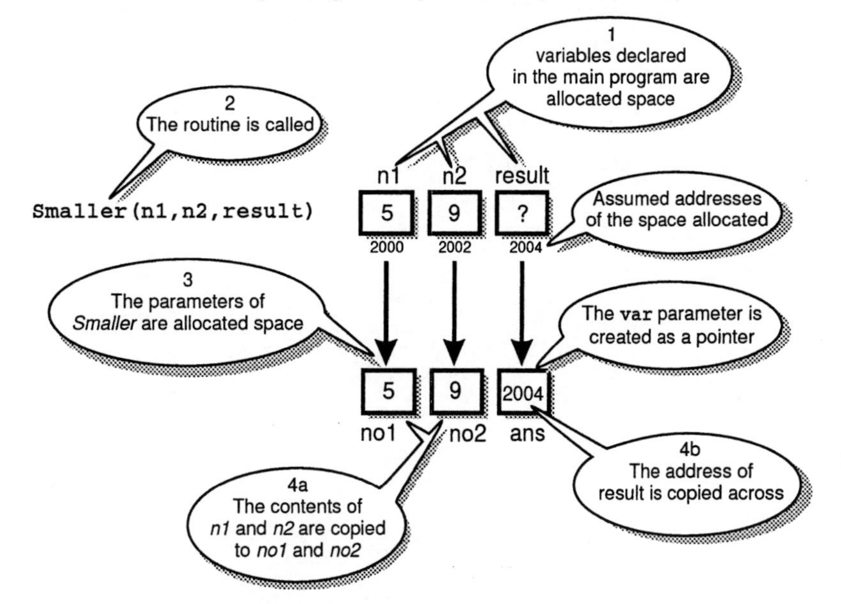


Another step is required by the compiler in order to use this `var` parameter correctly -it has to modify the code we have created!

Although *Smaller* contains the code

```
if no1 < no2 then
    ans := no1
else
    ans := no2;
```

for this to make sense, the compiler has to change the code to

```
if no1 < no2 then
    ans^ := no1
else
    ans^ := no2;
```

thereby dereferencing the pointer parameter it has created.

This code change doesn't affect the source code that we have created, rather, the appropriate changes are inserted as the program is translated into machine code. Don't be tempted to make the changes yourself within the source code, as this will only create compilation errors.

`var` parameters are often referred to as **pass by reference** parameters, while others are called **pass by value** parameters

## Other Reasons for using `var` Parameters

The assumption till now has been that we use `var` parameters when we want to return a value from a routine, but there is another reason to use them. Let's assume we've written a new version of *Smaller* that returns the smallest value in a 200 element array. We could start such a program with the definition

```
type
    BigArrayType = array(1..200] of integer;
```

and the declaration of a variable of this type

```
var
    numbers : BigArrayType;
```

The definition for *Smallest* would be:

```
procedure Smaller(list : BigArrayType; var ans : integer)
var
    c     : integer;
    small : integer;
begin
    {*** Assume first element is smallest ***)
    small := list[1]
    {*** Find anything smaller ***}
    for c := 2 to 200 do
        if list[c] < small then
            small := list[c];
    {*** Return result ***}
    ans := small;
end;
```

When the routine is called, a local variable called *list* will be created. This will be a 200 element array, and hence, requires a considerable amount of memory space. In addition, every value held in *numbers* will have to be copied into the corresponding element of *list*. This will take some time, slowing down the execution of the program.

Alternatively, we could define *Smaller* with two `var` parameters:

```
procedure Smaller(var list : BigArrayType; var ans : integer);
```

As a result of this, when the routine is called, *list* will be created as a pointer to *numbers* in the main program. This means the only space allocated is that required by a single pointer, and the data copied across will be the address of *numbers*. This will give us a much more efficient routine.

But there is one drawback: as a `var` parameter, should the routine accidentally contain code which changes *list* in any way, the contents of *numbers* will be effected.

Ideally, we'd like the best of both situations: the efficiency of using `var` parameters and a check on any accidental changes. Borland Pascal version 7.0 has introduced this ability by allowing the declaration of `const` parameters.

```
procedure Smaller(const list : BigArrayType; var ans : integer);
```

This makes *list* a pointer as before, but will signal an error if any attempt is made to change the contents of *list* within the routine.

## Functions and var Parameters

By using `var` parameters we can persuade a function to return a value and update one or more of its parameters at the same time.

Why might we want to do this? The usual reason to create `var` parameters in a function is to help with error conditions. For example, the `Sqrt` function which is part of the *System* Pascal Unit, will terminate your program if you try to find the square root of a negative number. Perhaps it would be better if it simply returned some indicator to say it had been unsuccessful and then we could code our program to deal with the problem appropriately. Of course, this means we want to return two values returned by the routine: the square root and a success indicator. And, although we could do this with a procedure, there are times where a function would be more useful. The program in LISTING-5.12 demonstrates the use of this technique.

The *SquareRoot* function returns the square root of the argument and also a success indicator; the main program then uses that indicator to display the result or an error message as required.

**LISTING-5.12**

Functions and `var` Parameters

```
program Functvar;
uses WinCrt;

function SquareRoot(var v : real) :boolean;
begin
  {*** IF negative THEN return false ***}
  if v < 0 then
  begin
      SquareRoot := false;
      exit;
  end;
  {*** ELSE calculate square root and return true ***}
  v := Sqrt(v);
  SquareRoot := true;
end;



var
  nbr, temp : real;
begin
  {*** Get number ***}
  ClrScr;
  write('Enter number ');
  readln(nbr);
  {*** Make copy ***}
  temp := nbr;
  {*** Display message as required ***}
  if SquareRoot(temp) then
      writeln('The square root of ',nbr:0:2,' is ',temp:0:2)
  else
      writeln('Cannot find the square root of a negative number')
end.
```

This has introduced you to the basic concepts of the pointer and dynamic space allocation. In later chapters we'll see how these features can be used to create powerful new data structures.

# Summary

- **The address of operator (@)** can be used to access the start address of a simple variable.

- **A pointer variable** contains an address.

- **A pointer to data** is defined using the format

```
var
    variable : ^type;
```

- **The indirection operator (^)** can be used to access the data at the address held in a pointer variable.

- **The term NIL** may be used to assign a value to a pointer variable, which is taken to mean that the pointer references no valid address.

- **Dynamic variable space can be allocated** using `New`.

- **Dynamic space can be deallocated** using `Dispose`.

- **`var` parameters** are implemented as pointers.

- **Functions can have `var` parameters** and hence return more than one value.

# CASE STUDY

## The Problem

A program is required which reads in up to 20 students' details. The details can be listed at the user's request and may be sorted if required. The details held for each student are:

- a unique identity code
- name
- sex
- scores for exactly 6 exams

## Clarification

The user is to be presented with a menu of options. These options will be:

1. Enter a student's details
2. Sort the student list
3. Display the student list
4. Quit

Where the sort option is chosen, the user can select to sort on either the student's identity code or surname.

## The Algorithm

A basic logic used is:

```
1.  REPEAT
2.      Display menu
3.      Get option
4.      Process option
5.  UNTIL QUIT option chosen
```

The process option step can be further detailed to:

```
4.  Process option
    4.1     IF
    4.2         option is Enter Student's Details:
    4.3             Get student's details
    4.4             Add student's details to list
    4.5         option is Sort:
    4.6             Display sort options
    4.7             Get sort option
    4.8             Sort on option chosen
    4.9         option is Display:
    4.10            Display all students' details
    4.11        option is Quit:
    4.12            Clear data from list
    4.13    ENDIF
```

This represents a sufficiently detailed solution to allow us to begin a more detailed design of our system.

# The Data Structure

The information for one student can be held in a structure declared in Pascal as:

```
type
    StudentDetails =
    record
        idcode : integer;
        name   : string[30];
        sex    : char;
        score  : array[1..6] of integer;
    end;
```

In order to accommodate the information of 20 students, we require an array of such records:

```
data : array[1..20] of StudentDetails;
```

However, we also need to keep track of how many students' details have been entered, and for this a count must be maintained. Since this count has such a close relation to the array, it would be good policy to reflect this relationship by grouping the two values together:

```
ListType =
record
    data  : array[1..20] of StudentDetails;{All students' details}
    count : integer;       {Number of students in list}
end;
```

### A Final Adjustment

Rather than reserve space for all 20 records, some of which may never by used, a more memory efficient approach would be to allocate space for each student's details as and when the need arises. To achieve this we need to define the array, *data*, as a series of pointers:

```
ListType =
record
    data  : array[1..20] of ^StudentDetails;
    count : integer;
end;
```

# The Mini-Specifications

By examining the outline logic for the system we can identify most of the routines needed. These are given below in the form of Mini-Specs.

| | | |
|---|---|---|
| **NAME** | : | GetOption |
| **PARAMETERS** | | |
| **IN** | : | None |
| **OUT** | : | option : INTEGER |
| **IN/OUT** | : | None |
| **PRE-CONDITION** | : | None |
| **DESCRIPTION** | : | Accepts users menu option from keyboard. |
| **OUTLINE LOGIC** | : | `Display "Enter option : "`<br>`Read option` |

| | | |
|---|---|---|
| **NAME** | : | ProcessOption |
| **PARAMETERS** | | |
| **IN** | : | option : INTEGER |
| **OUT** | : | None |
| **IN/OUT** | : | None |
| **PRE-CONDITION** | : | None |

**DESCRIPTION** : Performs the action requested by user.
Option 1 allows new data to be entered for one student.
Option 2 sorts the list.
Option 3 lists all the students' details.
Option 4 quits the system.

**OUTLINE LOGIC** :

```
IF
    option = 1:
        Get student's details
        Add details to list
    option = 2:
        Display sort menu
        Get user option
        Sort list according to option
    option = 3:
        Display all students' details
    option = 4:
        Clear data from list
 ENDIF
```

| | | |
|---|---|---|
| **NAME** | : | DisplayMenu |
| **PARAMETERS** | | |
| **IN** | : | None |
| **OUT** | : | None |
| **IN/OUT** | : | None |
| **PRE-CONDITION** | : | None |

**DESCRIPTION** : Displays the main options available.

**OUTLINE LOGIC** :

```
Clear the screen
Display "   Menu"
Display "1 - Enter student's details"
Display "2 - Sort students' list"
Display "3 - List students' details"
Display "4 - QUIT"
```

| | | |
|---|---|---|
| **NAME** | : | DisplaySortMenu |
| **PARAMETERS** | | |
| **IN** | : | None |
| **OUT** | : | None |
| **IN/OUT** | : | None |
| **PRE-CONDITION** | : | None |

**DESCRIPTION** : Displays the list of options available for sort.

**OUTLINE LOGIC** :

```
Display "1 - Sort on idcode"
Display "2 - Sort on surname"
```

| | | |
|---|---|---|
| **NAME** | : | GetStudentDetails |
| **PARAMETERS** | | |
| **IN** | : | None |
| **OUT** | : | stdtls : StudentDetails |
| **IN/OUT** | : | None |
| **PRE-CONDITION** | : | None |
| **DESCRIPTION** | : | Accepts a single student's details from the keyboard into *stdtls*. |
| **OUTLINE LOGIC** | : | see below |

```
Get the student's idcode
Get student's name
Get student's sex
Get student's score for all 6 exams
```

| | | |
|---|---|---|
| **NAME** | : | AddToList |
| **PARAMETERS** | | |
| **IN** | : | stdtls : StudentDetails |
| **OUT** | : | ind :BOOLEAN |
| **IN/OUT** | : | stlist : ListType |
| **PRE-CONDITION** | : | None |
| **DESCRIPTION** | : | Adds *stdtls* to the end of the list *stlist* if space is available. Sets *ind* to *true* if the *stdtls* was added to *stlist* else sets *ind* to *false*. |
| **OUTLINE LOGIC** | : | see below |

```
IF stlist not full THEN
    Allocate space using the first free
    pointer element in stlist.data
    Copy stdtls to the space allocated
    Increment stlist.count
    Set ind to true
ELSE
    Set ind to false
ENDIF
```

| | | |
|---|---|---|
| **NAME** | : | SortOnId |
| **PARAMETERS** | | |
| **IN** | : | None |
| **OUT** | : | None |
| **IN/OUT** | : | stlist : ListType |
| **PRE-CONDITION** | : | None |
| **DESCRIPTION** | : | Sorts the data in *stlist* according to *idcode*. |
| **OUTLINE LOGIC** | : | see below |

```
FOR pass := 1 TO st.count-1 DO
    FOR p := 1 TO st.count-pass DO
        IF idcode in st.data[p]
            and idcode in st.data[p+1]
            in wrong order
        THEN
            swap position of records
        ENDIF
    ENDFOR
ENDFOR
```

**NAME** : SortOnSurname
**PARAMETERS**
  **IN** : None
  **OUT** : None
  **IN/OUT** : stlist : ListType
**PRE-CONDITION** : None

**DESCRIPTION** : Sorts the data in *stlist* according *surname*

**OUTLINE LOGIC** :

```
FOR pass := 1 TO st.count-1 DO
    FOR p := 1 TO st.count-pass DO
        IF surname in st.data[p]
            and surname in st.data[p+1]
            in wrong order
        THEN
            swap position of records
        ENDIF
    ENDFOR
ENDFOR
```

**NAME** : DisplayList
**PARAMETERS**
  **IN** : stlist : ListType
  **OUT** : None
  **IN/OUT** : None
**PRE-CONDITION** : None

**DESCRIPTION** : Lists the details of each entry in *stlist*.

**OUTLINE LOGIC** :

```
Display headings
FOR each entry in stlist DO
    Display its details
ENDFOR
```

**NAME** : DeleteDetails
**PARAMETERS**
  **IN** : None
  **OUT** : None
  **IN/OUT** : stlist : ListType
**PRE-CONDITION** : None

**DESCRIPTION** : Deletes all of the space allocated for the records referenced by the elements of *stlst.data*.
This empties the list.

**OUTLINE LOGIC** :

```
FOR each element of stlist.data DO
    deallocate the referenced space
    Reset the pointer to NIL
ENDFOR
Set the stlist.count to zero.
```

| | | |
|---|---|---|
| **NAME** | : | StudentSystem |
| **PARAMETERS** | | |
| **IN** | : | None |
| **OUT** | : | None |
| **IN/OUT** | : | None |
| **PRE-CONDITION** | : | None |
| **DESCRIPTION** | : | Allows students' details to be entered, sorted and listed. The user specifies which option is required. The sort may be on the identity number or surname. |
| **OUTLINE LOGIC** | : | REPEAT<br>    Display menu<br>    Get option<br>    Process option<br>UNTIL QUIT option chosen |

**Activity 5.40**

Draw a structure diagram for this system showing the calling relationship between the functions defined above.

# Program Listing

**LISTING-5.13**

Maintaining a List

```
program StudentList;
{*******************************************}
{* PROGRAM     : Student Details List      *}
{* AUTHOR      : Patricia Stamp            *}
{* DATE        : 15/8/1998                 *}
{* VERSION     : 0.1                       *}
{* DESCRIPTION : Allows up to 20 students' *}
{*               details to be entered and *}
{*               stored. Records can be    *}
{*               sorted on idcode or surname *}
{* HARDWARE    : PC Compatible             *}
{* SOURCE      : Borland Pascal V7.0       *}
{*******************************************}
uses WinCrt;
{***Main menu quit value ***}
const
  QUIT = '4';
{*** Student record structure ***}
type
  StudentDetails =
  record
      idcode  : integer;
      name    : string[30];
      sex     : char;
      score   : array[1..6] of integer;
  end;
{*** List structure ***}
  ListType =
  record
      data : array[0..19] of ^StudentDetails;
      count    : integer;
  end;
```

**Continued on next page**

**LISTING-5.13**
(continued)

Maintaining a List

```
{** Add new record to List ***}
function AddToList( sd : StudentDetails; var stlst : ListType)
:boolean;
begin
  {*** IF list full, return from routine ***}
  if stlst.count = 20 then
  begin
      AddToList := false;
      exit;
  end;
  {*** Create space for record ***}
  New(stlst.data[stlst.count]);
  {*** Copy record into allocated space ***}
  stlst.data[stlst.count]^ := sd;
  Inc(stlst.count);
  AddToList := true;
end;


{*** Delete dynamic space ***}
procedure DeleteDetails(var stlst : ListType);
var
  j : integer;
begin
  {*** Delete area referenced by each pointer ***}
  for j := 0 to stlst.count-1 do
  begin
      Dispose(stlst.data[j]);
      stlst.data[j] := NIL;
  end;
  {*** Reset count to zero ***}
  stlst.count := 0;
end;


{*** Display list of student details ***}
procedure DisplayList(stlst : ListType);
var
  j, exam : integer;
begin
  {*** Display headings ***}
  writeln('STUDENTS'' DETAILS LIST' :45);
  writeln;
  writeln('ID              NAME              SEX          SCORES');
  {***FOR each record in list DO ***}
  for j := 0 to stlst.count - 1 do
  begin
      {**Display its details **}
      write(stlst.data[j]^.idcode,'    ',stlst.data[j]^.name,
      ' ':26 - Length(stlst.data[j]^.name));
      write(stlst.data[j]^.sex,' ':3);
      for exam := 1 to 6 do
          write(stlst.data[j]^.score[exam]:4);
      writeln;
  end
end;


{***  Display main menu ***}
procedure DisplayMenu;
begin
  ClrScr;
  writeln('MENU':42);
  writeln('1 - Enter student''s details');
  writeln('2 - Sort student list');
  writeln('3 - List students'' details');
  writeln('4 - QUIT');
end;
```

**Continued on next page**

**LISTING-5.13**
(continued)

Maintaining a List

```
{*** Display options for sort key ***}
procedure DisplaySortMenu;
begin
  writeln('SORT' :18);
  writeln(' 1 - On Student''s Id');
  writeln(' 2 - On Student''s surname');
end;


{*** Get a student's details ***}
procedure GetStudentDetails (var sd : StudentDetails);
var
  j : integer;
begin
  ClrScr;
  {***Get student's id ***}
  write('Enter student''s id : ');
  readln(sd.idcode);
  {*** Get student's name ***}
  write('Enter student''s name : ');
  readln(sd.name);
  {*** Get student's sex ***}
  write('Enter student''s sex : ');
  readln(sd.sex);
  {*** Get marks for six tests ***}
  writeln('Enter student''s marks');
  for j := 1 to 6 do
  begin
      write('Score for test ',j,' : ');
      readln(sd.score[j]);
      while (sd.score[j] < 0) or (sd.score[j] > 100)do
      begin
          write('Score must be between 0 and 100 : ');
          readln(sd.score[j]);
      end;
  end;
end;


{*** Get user's option ***}
function GetOption: char;
var
  op : char;
begin
  write('Enter option : ');
  readln(op);
  GetOption := op;
end;


{*** Sort Students' Records on Idcode ***}
procedure SortOnld(var stlst :ListType);
var
  temp : StudentDetails;
  times, comp : integer;
begin
  {*** Sort Pointers ***}
  for times := 1 to stlst.count - 1 do
      for comp := 0 to stlst.count-2 do
          {** If wrong order swap position **}
          if stlst.data[comp]^.idcode >
              stlst.data[comp + 1]^.idcode
          then
          begin
              temp := stlst.data[comp]^;
              stlst.data[comp]^ := stlst.data[comp+1]^;
              stlst.data[comp+1]^ := temp;
          end
end;
```

**Continued on next page**

**LISTING-5.13**
(continued)

Maintaining a List

```
{*** Sort Students' Records on Surname ***}
procedure SortOnSurname(var stlst : ListType);
var
  temp : StudentDetails;
  times, comp : integer;
begin
  {*** Sort Pointers ***}
  for times := 1 to stlst.count - 1 do
      for comp := 0 to stlst.count-2 do
          {** If wrong order swap position of pointers **}
          if Copy(stlst.data[comp]^.name,
              Pos(' ',stlst.data[comp]^.name),
              Length(stlst.data[comp]^.name)-
              Pos(' ',stlst.data[comp]^.name)) >
              Copy(stlst.data[comp + 1]^.name,
              Pos(' ',stlst.data[comp + 1]^.name),
              Length(stlst.data[comp + 1]^.name) -
              Pos(' ',stlst.data[comp + 1]^.name))
          then
          begin
              temp := stlst.data[comp]^;
              stlst.data[comp]^ := stlst.data[comp + 1]^;
              stlst.data[comp + 1]^ := temp;
          end
end;


{*** Execute user's option ***}
procedure ProcessOption(op : char);
const
  studentlist : ListType=(); {Contains all students' details}
var
  sd : StudentDetails; {Details of an individual}
  ops : char;
begin
  {***Execute option chosen ***}
  case op of
      '1': {*** Add a new student to list ***}
              begin
                  GetStudentDetails (sd);
                  if not AddToList(sd, studentlist) then
                      writeln('Table full');
              end;
      '2': {*** Sort list ***}
              begin
                  {** Get sort key **}
                  DisplaySortMenu;
                  ops := GetOption;
                  {** Call correct sort routine **}
                  if ops = '1' then
                      SortOnId(studentlist)
                  else
                      SortOnSurname(studentlist)
              end;
      '3': (*** Display contents of list ***)
              begin
                  ClrScr;
                  DisplayList(studentlist);
                  writeln('Press any key to continue');
                  ReadKey;
              end;
      '4': {*** Delete allocated space ***}
              DeleteDetails(studentlist)
  end
end;
```

**Continued on next page**

**LISTING-5.13**
(continued)

Maintaining a List

```
  var
  list : ListType;
  option : char;
begin
  ClrScr;
  repeat
      DisplayMenu;
      option := GetOption;
      ProcessOption(option);
  until option = QUIT;
end.
```

**Activity 5.41**

1. How does the mini-spec for *AddToList* differ from its implementation? Make the required changes to the code to correct this error.

2. Modify the above program to ensure that non-numeric and out-of-range values entered for the *option*, *mark* and *idcode* are correctly handled.

# SOLUTION TO TASKS

## Activity 5.1

`longint` is an ordinal type since we know the order of every possible value.

## Activity 5.2

```
1.  type
        Days = (Sunday, Monday, Tuesday, Wednesday,
            Thursday, Friday, Saturday);

2.  type
        Months = (Jan, Feb, Mar, Apr, May, Jun,
                  Jul, Aug, Sep, Oct, Nov, Dec);
```

## Activity 5.3

The first modification adds one to the output:

```
program enumTypes;
uses WinCrt;

{*** Declare enumerated type ***}
type
    Seasons = (Winter, Spring, Summer, Fall);

var
    time :  Seasons;    {loop counter}
begin
    {*** FOR each season DO ***}
    for time    := Winter to Fall do
        {*** Display its ordinal value ***}
        writeln('This is season ', Ord(time)+1);
end.
```

The `case` statement outputs the season names:

```
program enumTypes;
uses WinCrt;

(*** Declare enumerated type ***)
type
Seasons = (Winter, Spring, Summer, Fall);

var
    time : Seasons; {loop counter}
begin
    {*** FOR each season DO ***}
    for time := Winter to Fall do
        (** Display as a string ***)
        case time of
            Winter  : writeln('Winter');
            Spring  : writeln('Spring');
            Summer  : writeln('Summer');
            Fall    : writeln('Fall');
    end;
end.
```

## Activity 5.4

The first run should output the phrase *It's spring*.

The second run should cause an execution error.

## Activity 5.5

```
1.  Set all counts to zero
    FOR 20 times DO
        Read a number
        IF
            number = 1
                Add 1 to first count
            number = 2:
                Add 1 to second count
            etc.

2.  Read 15 values into variables n1, n2, n3 etc.
    Read in search value
    IF
        search value = n1:
            Display "Found"
        search value = n2:
            Display "Found"
        etc
    ELSE
        Display "Not found"
    ENDIF
```

## Activity 5.6

```
1.  results : array[1..15] of integer;

2.  weights : array[1..10] of real
```

## Activity 5.7

```
1.  counts['C'] := 0;

2.  answers[false]:= 21;
```

## Activity 5.8

| Statement | Array contents |
|---|---|
| Initial contents | -4,3,9,2,0,12 |
| list[3] := 7; | -4,3,7,2,0,12 |
| list[j] := -2;(j=4) | -4,3,7,-2,0,12 |
| list[j] := 3; (j=5) | -4,3,7,-2,3,12 |
| list[j] := 5; (j=6) | -4,3,7,-2,3,5 |
| for j := 1 to 6 do list[j] := j * 2; | 2,4,6,8,10,12 |

## Activity 5.9

a) Only the value of SIZE needs to be changed. However, the comments should also be modified to give an accurate description of the program.

```
program Arrays1a;
uses WinCrt;

const
    SIZE = 8;
var
    numbers : array[1..SIZE] of integer;
                        {Array holding numbers}
    c       : integer;  {Loop counter}
begin
    {*** Read in the 8 values ***}
    ClrScr;
    for c := 1 to SIZE do
    begin
        write('Enter number : ');
        readln(numbers[c]);
    end;
    {***Display the 8 values ***}
    for c := 1 to SIZE do
        writeln(numbers[c]);
end.
```

b) The change required is to display the value of the `for` loop counter as part of the prompt.

**Continued on next page**

## Activity 5.9 (continued)

```
program Arrays1b;
uses WinCrt;

const
    SIZE = 8;
var
    numbers : array[1..SIZE] of integer;
                        {Array holding numbers}
    c       : integer; {Loop counter}
begin
    {*** Read in the 9 values ***}
    ClrScr;
    for c := 1 to SIZE do
    begin
        write('Enter number ',c,' : ');
        readln(numbers[c]);
    end;
    {*** Display the 9 values ***}
    for c := 1 to SIZE do
        writeln (numbers[c]);
end.
```

## Activity 5.10

The program should operate correctly.
To show the position at which the match is found we need to display the value of *post*

```
if list[post] = nbr then
    writeln('FOUND at location ', post)
else
    writeln('NOT FOUND');
```

## Activity 5.11

The line required is

```
if names[3] = 'John' then
```

## Activity 5.12

```
1.

program Act12_01;
uses WinCrt;

const
    SIZE = 6;
var
    list : array[1..SIZE] of integer;
                        {Contains values}
    c    : integer;     {Loop counter}
begin
    {*** Read in numbers ***}
    ClrScr;
    for c := 1 to SIZE do
    begin
        write('Enter number ',c,' : ');
        readln(list[c]);
    end;
    {*** Display in same order as entered ***}
    writeln('Same order');
    for c := 1 to SIZE do
        writeln(list[c]);
    {***    Display in reverse order ***}
    writeln('Reverse order');
    for c := SIZE downto 1 do
        writeln(list[c])
end.

2.
program Act12_02;
uses WinCrt;

const
    SIZE = 10;
var
    list : array[1..SIZE] of integer;
                        {Contains values}
    c    : integer; {Loop counter}
begin
    {*** Read in numbers ***}
    ClrScr;
    for c := 1 to SIZE do
    begin
        write('Enter number ',c,' : ');
        readln(list[c]);
    end;
    {*** Display odd elements ***}
    for c := 1 to SIZE do
        if Odd(c) then
            writeln(c,' ',list[c]);
end.
```

The last **for** loop would be safer as a I to SIZE loop. This would ensure that if SIZE were an odd number, the logic would still hold.

```
3.

program Act12_03;
uses WinCrt;

const
    SIZE = 10;
var
    list : array[1..SIZE] of char;
                        {Contains values}
    c    : integer;     {Loop counter}
    count: integer;     {Count of E's}
begin
    {*** Set count to zero ***}
    count := 0;
    {*** Read in characters ***}
    ClrScr;
    for c := 1 to SIZE do
    begin
        write('Enter character ',c,' : ');
        readln(list[c]);
    end;
    {*** Count E's ***}
    for c := 1 to SIZE do
        if Upcase(list[c]) = 'E' then
            Inc(count);
    {*** Display count ***}
    writeln('There are ', count,' E''s')
end.

4.

program Act12_04;
uses WinCrt;

const
    SIZE = 5;
var
    counts  : array[1..SIZE] of integer;
                        {Contains values}
    c       : integer;  {Loop counter}
    nbr     : integer;  {Current number entered}
    cat     : integer;  {Numbers category}
begin
    {*** Set counts to zero ***}
    for c := 1 to SIZE do
        counts[c] := 0;
    {** Read in numbers ***}
    ClrScr;
    for c := 1 to 10 do
    begin
        write('Enter number (1 to 50): ');
        readln(nbr);
        {*** Determine category ***}
        cat := (nbr - 1) div 10 + 1;
        Inc(counts[cat]);
    end;
    {*** Display counta***}
    for c := 1 to SIZE do
        writeln('Numbers in the range ',
        (c - 1) * 10,' - ',c * 10,' : ',
        counts[c]);
end.

5.

program Act12_05;
uses WinCrt;
const
    SIZE = 10;
var
    list     : array[1..SIZE] of integer;
                        {Contains values}
    c        : integer; {Loop counter}
    smallest : integer; {Smallest value in list}
```

**Continued on next page**

## Activity 5.12 (continued)

```
begin
    {*** Read in numbers ***}
    ClrScr;
    for c := 1 to SIZE do
    begin
        write('Enter number ',c,' : ');
        readln(list[c]);
    end;
    {*** Set smallest to first number entered ***}
    smallest := list[1];
    {*** Search remainder for smaller values ***}
    for c := 2 to SIZE do
        if list[c] < smallest then
            smallest := list[c];
    {*** display smallest found ***}
    writeln('Smallest value is ', smallest);
end.
```

## Activity 5.13

```
program Act13_01;
uses WinCrt;

const
    SIZE = 10;

type
    ArrayType = array[1..SIZE] of integer;


function Largest(list:ArrayType) : integer;
var
    large : integer; {largest value found}
    c     : integer; {Loop counter}
begin
    {*** Assume first value is largest ***}
    large := list[1];
    {*** Search remainder for larger value ***}
    for c := 2 to SIZE do
        if list[c] > large then
            large := list[c];
    {*** Return largest value ***}
    Largest := large;
end;


var
    numbers : ArrayType;{Values to be searched}
    c       : integer;  {Loop counter}
begin
    {*** Read in the values ***}
    ClrScr;
    for c := 1 to SIZE do
    begin
        write('Enter value ',c,' : ');
        readln (numbers[c]);
    end;
    {*** Display result ***}
    writeln('Largest value entered was ',
                Largest(numbers))
end.
```

## Activity 5.14

```
program Act14_01;
uses WinCrt;
const
    SIZE = 10;
type
    ArrayType = array[1..SIZE] of integer;


procedure Reverse(var list : arrayType);
var
    c     : integer; {Loop counter}
    temp  : integer; {Holds value when swapping}
begin
    {*** Swap first half of array with second ***}
    for c := 1 to SIZE div 2 do
    begin
        temp := list[c];
        list[c] := list[SIZE + 1 - c];
        list[SIZE + 1 - c] := temp;
    end;
end;

var
    numbers : ArrayType; {Values to be searched}
    c       : integer;   {Loop counter}
    begin
        {*** Read in the values ***}
        ClrScr;
        for c := 1 to SIZE do
        begin
            write('Enter value ',c,' : ');
            readln(numbers[c]);
        end;
        {*** Reverse numbers ***}
        Reverse(numbers);
        {*** Display result ***}
        for c := 1 to SIZE do
            writeln(numbers[c]);
end.
```

## Activity 5.15

```
program Act15_01;
uses WinCrt;

{*** Procedure to double each element of an
array ***}
procedure Twice(var list : array of integer);
var
    c : integer;
begin
    {*** Elements zero to High(list) ***}
    for c := 0 to High(list) do
        list[c] := list[c] * 2;
end;

var
    {*** Arrays to be used ***}
    nos  : array[1..12] of integer;
    more : array[-2..5] of integer;
    c    : integer; {Loop counter}
begin
    {*** Initialise arrays ***}
    for c := 5 to 12 do
        nos[c] := c;
    for c := -2 to 5 do
        more[c] := c + 3;
    {*** display original contents ***}
    for c := 5 to 12 do
        writeln(nos[c]);
    writeln;
    for c := -2 to 5 do
        writeln(more[c]);
    writeln('Press any key to continue ');
    ReadKey;
    {*** Call routine with both arrays ***}
    Twice(nos);
    Twice(more);
    {*** Display values in array ***}
    for c := 5 to 12 do
        writeln(nos[c]);
    writeln;
    for c := -2 to 5 do
        writeln(more[c]);
end.
```

## Activity 5.16

```
program Act16_01;
uses WinCrt;

{*** Smallest - open array version ***}
function Smallest(list: array of integer) :
integer;
var
    small : integer; {Smallest value found}
    c     : integer; {Loop counter}
begin
    {*** Assume first value is the smallest ***}
    small := list[0];
    {*** Search for smaller values ***}
    for c := 1 to High(list) do
        {*** IF found THEN place in small ***}
        if list[c] < small then
            small := list[c];
    {*** Return the smallest value ***}
    Smallest := small;
end;
```

**Continued on next page**

## Activity 5.16 (continued)

```
var
    numbers : array[2..7] of integer;
                        {Values to be searched}
    c       : integer;  {Loop counter}
begin
    {*** Read in the values ***}
    ClrScr;
    for c := 2 to 7 do
    begin
        write('Enter value : ');
        readln (numbers[c]);
    end;
    {*** display smallest ***}
    writeln('Smallest value was ',Smallest(numbers));
end.
```

## Activity 5.17

```
1.
matrix : array[1..13,1..3] of integer;

2.
matrix : array[1..2,1..5) of integer;

3.
matrix : array[1..8] of integer;
```

## Activity 5.18

```
1.
program Act18_01;
uses WinCrt;
var
    matrix   : array[1..4,1..4] of integer;
    row, col : integer;
begin
    {*** Assign Values ***}
    for row := 1 to 4 do
        for col := 1 to 4 do
            matrix[row,col] := (row-1) * 4 + col;
    {*** Display values ***}
    for row := 1 to 4 do
    begin
        for col := 1 to 4 do
            write(matrix[row,col]:4);
        writeln;
    end;
end.

2.
program Act18_02;
uses WinCrt;
var
    matrix   : array[1..4,1..4] of integer;
    row, col : integer;
begin
    {*** Assign Values ***}
    for row := 1 to 4 do
        for col := 1 to 4 do
            matrix[row,col] := (col-1) * 4 + row;
    {*** Display values ***}
    for row := 1 to 4 do
    begin
        for col := 1 to 4 do
            write(matrix[row,col]:4);
        writeln;
    end;
end.

3.
program Act18_03;
uses WinCrt;
var
    matrix   : array[1..4,1..4] of integer;
    row, col : integer;
begin
    {*** Assign Values ***}
    for row := 1 to 4 do
        for col := 1 to 4 do
            matrix[row,col] := 16 -((row-1) * 4 + col-1);
    {*** Display values ***}
    for row := 1 to 4 do
    begin
        for col := 1 to 4 do
            write(matrix[row,col]:4);
        writeln;
    end;
end.
```

## Activity 5.19

```
1.

program Act19_01;
uses WinCrt;

procedure ReverseString(var s : string);
var
    c    : integer;
    temp   : char;
begin
    for c := 1 to Length(s) div 2 do
    begin
        temp := s[c];
        s[c] := s[Length(s) - c + 1];
        s[Length(s) - c + 1] := temp;
    end
end;

var
    str : string;
begin
    ClrScr;
    write('Enter string : ');
    readln(str);
    writeln(str);
    ReverseString(str);
    writeln(str)
end.
```

```
2.

procedure Capitalise(var s : string);
var
    c : integer;
begin
    {*** Capitalise first character ***}
    s[1] := UpCase(s[1]);
    {*** Capitalise every char after a space ***}
    for c := 2 to Length(s) do
        if s[c - 1] = ' ' then
            s[c] := UpCase(s[c]);
end;

var
    str : string;
begin
    ClrSCr;
    write('Enter string : ');
    readln(str);
    writeln(str);
    Capitalise(str);
    writeln(Str)
end.
```

```
3.

function LastOccur(ch : char; s : string)
                            : integer;
var
    c : integer;
begin
    for c := Length(s) downto 1 do
        if s[c] = ch then
            break;
    LastOccur := c;
end;

var
    str : string;
    ch : char;
begin
    ClrScr;
    write('Enter string : ');
    readln(str);
    write('Enter character : ');
    readln(ch);
    writeln(str);
    writeln('Last occurrence of ',ch,
    ' is at position ', LastOccur(ch, str));
end.
```

## Activity 20

1.

```
program Act20_01;
uses WinCrt;

function LastOccur(ch : char; s : string)
                                  : integer;
var
    c : integer;
begin
    for c := Length(s) downto 1 do
        if s[c] = ch then
            break;
    LastOccur := c;
end;

var
    names : array[1..10] of string[30]; {names}
    c     : integer;    {Loop counter}
    count : integer;    {No. of surnames }
                        {starting with 'H'}
begin
    ClrScr;
    {*** Set count to zero ***}
    count := 0;
    {*** Read in names ***}
    for c := 1 to 10 do
    begin
        write('Enter name ',c,' : ');
        readln(names[c]);
    end;
    {*** FOR each name DO ***}
    for c := 1 to 10 do
        {*** IF H after last space, inc count ***}
        if UpCase(names[c,LastOccur(' ',names[c])
                                  +1])='H' then
            Inc(count);
    {*** Display result ***}
    writeln(count,' surnames began with ''H''');
end.
```

2.

```
program Act20_02;
uses WinCrt;

var
    messages : array[1..10] of string[30];
    c        : integer; {Loop counter}
    post     : integer; {position of longest string}
    size     : integer; {length of longest string}
begin
    ClrScr;
    {*** Read in strings ***}
    for c := 1 to 10 do
    begin
        write('Enter text ',c,' : ');
        readln(messages[c]);
    end;
    {*** assume first is longest ***}
    size := Length(messages[1]);
    post := 1;
    {*** FOR remaining messages DO ***}
    for c := 2 to 10 do
        {*** IF message longer record details ***}
        if Length(messages[c]) > size then
        begin
            size := Length(messages[c]);
            post := c;
        end;
    {*** Display result ***}
    writeln('Longest string is ',messages[post],
        ' which contains ', size,' characters');
end.
```

## Activity 5.21

```
program Act21_01;
uses WinCrt;

function LastOccur(ch : char; s : string)
                                  : integer;
var
    c : integer;
begin
    for c := Length(s) downto 1 do
        if s[c] = ch then
            break;
    LastOccur := c;
end;


procedure SurnameFirst( var s : string);
var
    post : integer;
            {Position of first letter of surname}
begin
    {*** Surname starts after last space ***}
    post := LastOccur(' ',s)+1;
    {*** Rebuild as surname+space+other names ***}
    s := Copy(s,post,Length(s)-post+1) + ' '
                              + Copy(s,1,post-2);
end;

var
    name     : string[30]; {name}
begin
    ClrScr;
    {*** Read in name ***}
    write('Enter name : ');
    readln(name);
    SurnameFirst(name);
    writeln('Name : ',name);
end.
```

## Activity 5.22

```
type
    Details =
    record
        age    : integer;
        height : real;
        weight : real;
    end;

var
    w1, w2, w3 : Details;
```

## Activity 5.23

```
program Act23_01;
uses WinCrt;
type
    Details =
    record
        age    : integer;
        height : real;
        weight : real;
    end;

{*** Gets details of a single record ***}
procedure GetDetails(var w : Details);
begin
    write('Enter age : ');
    readln(w.age);
    write('Enter height (metres) : ');
    readln(w.height);
    write('Enter weight (kilos) : ');
    readln(w.weight);
end;

var
    w1, w2, w3 : Details;
    highest    : real;
begin
    {*** read details of all three records ***}
    ClrScr;
    GetDetails(w1);
    GetDetails(w2);
    GetDetails(w3);
    {*** Find highest ***}
    highest := w1.height;
    if w2.height > highest then
        highest := w2.height;
    if w3.height > highest then
        highest := w3.height;
    {*** display result ***}
    writeln('Highest persion is ', highest:0:2,
                              ' metres tall');
end.
```

## Activity 5.24

```
type
    StudentDetails =
    record
        idcode : integer;
        name   : string[30];
        sex    : char;
        score  : array[1..6] of integer;
    end;
```

## Activity 5.25

```
const
    lunar : Event = (desc:'Moon landing';
            date:(day:20; month:7; year:1969);
            time(hrs:10; mins:56; secs:0));
```

## Activity 5.26

```
program Act26_01;
uses WinCrt;
type
    NameType =
    record
        surname : string[20];
        first   : string[20];
        initials: string[8];
    end;
    AddressType =
    record
        firstline  : string[30];
        secondline : string[30];
        thirdline  : string[30];
        town       : string[18];
        district   : string[18];
        postcode   : string[10];
    end;
    AccountType =
    record
        accno      : integer;
        name       : NameType;
        address    : AddressType;
        balance    : real
     end;

procedure GetAccountDetails(var a : AccountType);
begin
    with a do
    begin
        write('Enter first name : ');
        readln(name.first);
        write('Enter any other intials : ');
        readln(name.initials);
        write('Enter surname : ');
        readln(name.surname);
        writeln('Enter three lines of address : ');
        readln(address.firstline);
        readln(address.secondline);
        readln(address.thirdline);
        write('Enter town : ');
        readln(address.town);
        write('Enter district : ');
        readln(address.district);
        write('Enter post code : ');
        readln(address.postcode);
        write('Enter balance : ');
        readln(balance);
    end;
end;

procedure AddInterest(var v : real);
begin
    v := v *1.05;
end;

procedure DisplayAccount(a : AccountType);
begin
    writeln(a.accno);
    with a.name do
        writeln(surname,' ',first,' ',initials);
    with a.address do
    begin
        writeln(firstline);
        writeln(secondline);
        writeln(thirdline);
        writeln(town);
        writeln(district);
        writeln(postcode);
    end;
    writeln(a.balance:8:2);
end;

var
    list : array[1..5] of AccountType;
    c    : integer;      {loop counter}
begin
    for c := 1 to 5 do
    begin
        ClrScr;
        GetAccountDetails(list[c]);
    end;
    for c := 1 to 5 do
        AddInterest(list[c].balance);
    for c := 1 to 5 do
    begin
        DisplayAccount(list[c]);
        write('Press any key to continue');
        ReadKey;
    end;
end.
```

## Activity 5.27

```
type
    Months = (Jan, Feb, Mar, Apr, May, Jun,
            Jul, Aug, Sep, Oct, Nov, Dec);

    MonthSet = set of Months;
```

## Activity 5.28

```
if month in [4,6,9,11] then
```

## Activity 5.29

```
program Act29_01;
uses WinCrt;

type
    KeySet = set of char;

{*** Get Data from Keyboard ***}
function GetData(allowed : KeySet; max :
integer):string;
const
    ENTER = #13;
    BACKSPACE = #8;
var
    ch     : char;       {char from keyboard}
    count  : integer;    {chars entered}
    result : string;     {Contains the characters
                         ↳typed in}
begin
    {*** Check pre-conditions ***}
    if (allowed = []) or (max<=0) then
    begin
        GetData := '';
        exit;
    end;
    {*** Set result to empty & count to zero ***}
    result := '';
    count := 0;
    {*** Read a character ***}
    ch := ReadKey;
    {*** WHILE return key not pressed DO ***}
    while ch <> ENTER do
    begin
        {*** IF allowed char & not full THEN ***}
        if (ch in allowed) AND (count < max)then
        begin
            {*** Display char & add to result ***}
            write(ch);
            result := result + ch;
            Inc(count);
        end
        {*** IF delete & result not empty ***}
        else if (ch = BACKSPACE)
            AND (count > 0)
        then
        begin
            {*** Remove last char ***}
            write(#8,#32,#8);
            Delete(result,length(result),1);
            Dec(count);
        end;
        {*** Read another character ***}
        ch := ReadKey;
    end;
    writeln;
        GetData := result;
end;


var
    result : string;
begin
    ClrScr;
    write('Enter data : ');
    result := GetData(['0'..'9'],3);
    writeln('result is ',result);
end.
```

## Activity 5.30

1.

```
$7C09 in binary is 0111 1100 0000 1001
Inverted gives     1000 0011 1111 0110
In hex this is       8    3    F    6
```

2.

```
196 in binary is   1100 0100
Inverted gives     0011 1011
In Hex this is       3    B
```

## Activity 5.31

```
program Act31_01;
uses WinCrt;

procedure Binary(v : integer);
var
    c : integer;     {Loop counter}
begin
    for c := 1 to 16 do
    begin
        if v < 0 then
            write('1')
        else
            write('0');
        v := v shl 1;
    end;
end;

var
    nbr : integer;
begin
    ClrScr;
    write('Enter value : ');
    readln(nbr);
    Binary(nbr);
end.
```

## Activity 5.32

1.

0101 1101
0111 0000    XOR
0010 1101    =

2.

0111 0000    XOR
0101 1101    =

**NOTE**: By performing XOR twice we arrive back at the original value.

## Activity 5.33

```
var
    iptr1, iptr2 : ^integer;
    fptr         : ^real;
```

## Activity 5.34

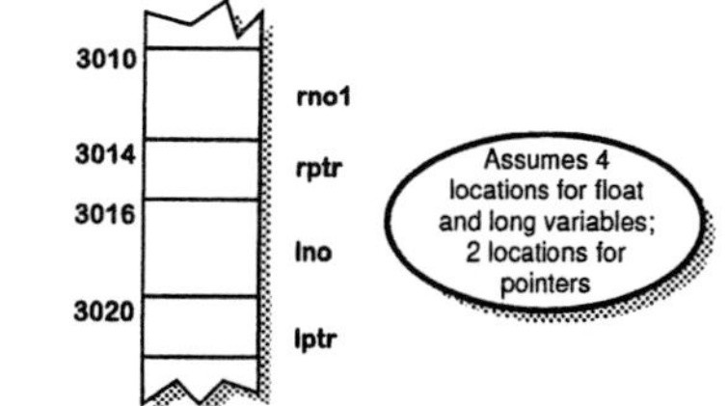


**Main Memory**

## Activity 5.35

```
program Act35_01;
uses WinCrt;
var
    no1, no2, answer : integer;
    p1, p2, p3 : ^integer;
begin
    p1 := @no1;
    p2 := @no2;
    p3 := @answer;

    write('Enter two numbers : ');
    readln(p1^, p2^);
    if p1^ < p2^ then
        p3^ := p1^
    else
        p3^ := p2^;
    writeln('The smaller value is ',p3^);
end.
```

## Activity 5.36

1.

```
if iptr1 = iptr2 then
```

2.

```
if iptr1^ = iptr2^ then
```

## Activity 5.37

a) Valid. Reads a value into the space referenced by *ptr1*.

b) Invalid.

c) Invalid.

d) Valid. *ptr1* references the same address as *ptr2*.

## Activity 5.38

```
program Act38_01;
uses WinCrt;
type
    DateType =
    record
        day   : 1..31;
        month : 1..12;
        year  : word
    end;

var
    Dptr : ^DateType;
begin
    New(Dptr);
    write('Enter date : ');
    with Dptr^ do
    begin
        readln(day, month, year);
        writeln(day,'/',month,'/',year);
    end;
end.
```

## Activity 5.39

```
program Act39_01;
uses winCrt;

type
    ArrayType = array[1..5] of integer;

var
    Aptr : ^ArrayType;
    c : integer;
begin
    New(Aptr);
    ClrScr;
    {$R+}
    for c := 1 to 5 do
    begin
        write('Enter value ',c,' : ');
        readln(Aptr^[c]);
    end;
    for c := 1 to 5 do
        writeln(Aptr^[c]);
end.
```

## Activity 5.40

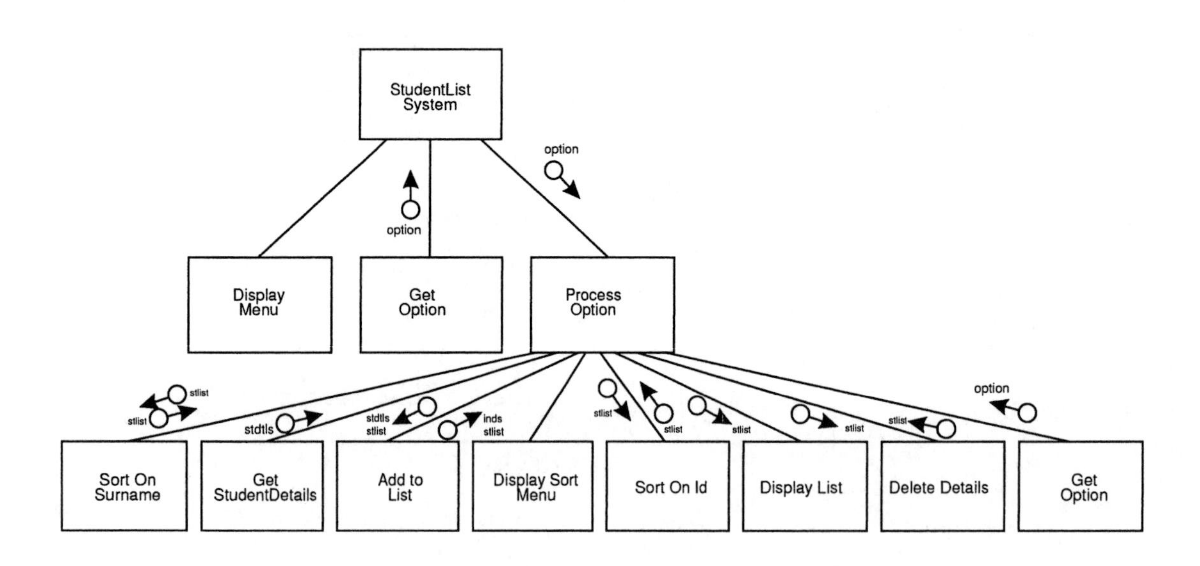


## Activity 5.41

1. Although the overall effect of AddToList agrees with the description, the program code does not match the Outline Logic given in the Mini-Spec. To achieve this we need to recode the routine as:

```
function AddToList( sd : StudentDetails; var
stlst : ListType) :boolean;
begin
    {*** IF list full, return from routine ***}
    if stlst.count < 20 then
    begin
        {*** Create space for record ***}
        New(stlst.data[stlst.count]);
        {*** Copy record into allocated space ***}
        stlst.data[stlst.count]^ := sd;
        Inc(stlst.count);
        AddToList := true;
    end
else
    AddToList := false;
end;
```

2. To ensure that only valid data is entered, use the *GetData* routine designed in Activity 5.29 to ensure only keys within the required set are accepted. In addition, use a `while` loop when getting the marks. For example:

```
temp := GetData(['0'..'9'],3);
val(temp,sd.score[j],err);
while sd.score[j] > 100 do
begin
    write('Invalid mark 0 - 100 : ');
    temp := GetData(['0'..'9'],3);
    val(temp,sd.score[j],err);
end;
```

*temp* is a string; *err* an integer

CHAPTER 6

# File Handling

## This chapter covers the following topics:

Appending to a File

Dealing with Error Conditions

Deleting Records

File Variables

Inserting Records

Outputting to the Printer

Random Access

Standard File-Handling Routines

Text Files

Typed Files

Updating Records

Writing to a File

# TEXT FILES

## Introduction

Data held exclusively within the variables of a program is going to be lost when that program is terminated. Hence, it is normal to store important data which is likely to be required at a later date in a more permanent form. This means using disk files in which information can be held indefinitely.

The text file is the simplest of all files. A program writes information to a text file in much the same way as it would write data to the computer screen.

## Declaring a File Variable

To use a disk file we must first declare a file variable in our `var` statement. This is where we tell the program what type of file we intend to use. For text files, we declare the file variable to be of type `text`. Hence, we might write

```
var
    myfile : text;
```

to declare the file.

## Linking the File Variable to a File Name

Although our program is going to call the file *myfile* (because of the declaration given above), the operating system names files using a different convention. In DOS that format is yyyyyyyy.xxx, so a file might be named *report.dat*, for example.

Before we can use a file in our program, we need to tie together the name used in the program (*myfile*) and the name used by the operating system (we'll assume its to be *report.dat*). This is done using the `assign` statement:

```
assign(myfile,'C:\REPORT.DAT');
```

Notice that when stating the name used by the operating system, path information may be included (if it isn't, then the file is assumed to be in the current directory).

From now on, the program will only ever refer to the file by its program name, *myfile*.

The general structure for the `assign` instruction is shown in FIG-6.1.

**FIG-6.1**

The `assign` Statement

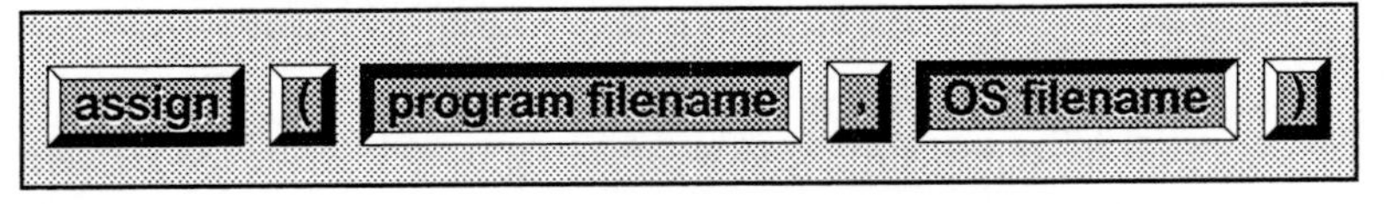


where

| | |
|---|---|
| `program filename` | is a file variable declared within a `var` statement. |
| `OS filename` | is a string containing the name and location of the file as used within the operating system. |

## Opening the File

The final task to be done before using the file is to open it. When opening a file we must specify whether we intend to write to the file or read from it. If we are going to write information to the file, it is opened using the `rewrite` statement:

```
rewrite(myfile);
```

If the file already exists on the disk, its current contents are erased, ready for new data to be written to it; if the file does not exist, it is created by the operating system.

## Writing to the File

Now that the file is ready for use, we can write data to it. This is done by using the `write` and `writeln` statements. A statement such as

```
write('Hello  world');
```

will output its data to the screen. To have the data sent to a file instead, we need to add the name of the file at the start of the parentheses:

```
write(myfile,'John Jakes');
```

This time, nothing will appear on the screen.

## Closing the File

Once a program has finished with a file, that file must be closed. This is done using the statement:

```
close(myfile);
```

## Bringing It all Together

The program in LISTING-6.1 brings all these bits together to write the text *Hello world* to a file:

**LISTING-6.1**

Outputting to a Text File

```
program List6_1;
uses WinCrt;
var
  myfile : text;
begin
  assign(myfile,'c:\report.dat');
  rewrite(myfile);
  write(myfile,'John Jakes');
  close(myfile);
end.
```

**Activity 6.1**

Type in and run the program given in LISTING-6.1.

Using a simple text editor, examine the contents of the file *C:\report.dat.*

## Using `write` and `writeln`

All the options available to us when writing to the screen also apply to outputting to a file. This means that it's possible to output constants, variables or expressions to the file and that a single output statement can output several values.

> **Activity 6.2**
>
> Add the following statements to your previous program:
>
> ```
> write(myfile,22,'M');
> ```
>
> Run the program and examine the output.

In the next program (LISTING-6.2) the data written to the file is held in variables.

**LISTING-6.2**

Outputting Several Values

```
program List6_2;
uses WinCrt;

var
  myfile : text;     {File variable}

  name : string;     {Name of student}
  age  : integer;    {Age of student}
  sex  : char;       {Sex of student}

begin
  {*** Prepare the file ***}
  assign(myfile,'c:\report.dat');
  rewrite(myfile);
  {*** Read the data from the keyboard ***}
  write('Enter name : ');
  readln(name);
  write('Enter age  : ');
  readln(age);
  write('Enter sex  : ');
  readln(sex);
  {*** Write data to file ***}
  write(myfile,name,age,sex);
  {*** Close file ***}
  close(myfile);
end.
```

> **Activity 6.3**
>
> Enter and run the above program, examining the contents of the data file created. Use the data 'John Jakes', 22 and 'M' as the data.

When examining the contents of *report.dat*, you'll see that the data it contains has been squeezed together giving:

```
John Jakes22M
```

This shouldn't come as a surprise since this is how it would have appeared if we'd sent the data to the screen. However, it would be better if we could distinguish between the three items when viewing the file.

As with screen output, we can use field sizes to adjust the layout of the data held in our file. Hence, the output of the program in LISTING-6.2 could be made more readable with the line:

```
write(myfile,name:20, age:3,sex:2);
```

**Activity 6.4**

Change the program created for Activity 6.3 to include field size as shown above.

Rerun the program using the same data as before.

Has the contents of the file been affected by this change?

**Activity 6.5**

Now change the `assign` statement to read

```
assign(myfile,'C:\report2.dat');
```

and remove the final `write` statement, replacing it with the lines

```
writeln(myfile,name);
writeln(myfile,age);
writeln(myfile,sex);
```

Now, run the program again using the same data.

What differences exist between the contents of the two files, *report.dat* and *report2.dat?*

# Reading from a Text File

Often we will output to a text file with the intention of later sending the file to the printer or using it within a text editor. However, it is also possible to create a Pascal program that reads from a text file. To read from a file we need to open it using the `reset` command rather than `rewrite`. Hence, to read from *report.dat* our program would contain the statement

```
reset(myfile);
```

then the program uses the `readln` statement to read data from the file into specified variables. The `readln` statement is modified from its standard form by including the filename:

```
readln(myfile, name);
```

The program in LISTING-6.3 attempts to read back from *report.dat* a value for the variable *name.*

**LISTING-6.3**

Reading from a Text File

```
program List6_3;
uses WinCrt;

var
  myfile : text;      {File variable}
  name : string;      {Name of student}
  age  : integer;     {Age of student}
  sex  : char;        {Sex of student}
```

**Continued on next page**

**LISTING-6.3**
(coninued)

Reading from a Text File

```
begin
   {*** Prepare the file ***}
   assign(myfile,'c:\report.dat');
   {*** Open the file for reading ***}
   reset(myfile);
   {*** Read the data from the file ***}
   readln(myfile, name);
   {*** Display the data read ***}
   writeln(name);
   {*** Close the file ***}
   close(myfile);
end.
```

**Activity 6.6**

Enter and run the above program.

Is the name correctly displayed on the screen?

Our problem in trying to read the data back from the file is caused by the fact that all three items of data are stored in a single line of text. That is, there is no return character between each item. If we are to read separate items of data back from a text file it is best to make sure we insert a *return* character between each item of data when writing to the file in the first place. This we can do by replacing the `write` statements with `writeln` statements as we did in Activity 6.5.

**Activity 6.7**

Modify your program from Activity 6.6 so that it opens the file *Report2.dat* rather than *Report.dat.*

Is the name correctly displayed this time?

Add lines to the program to read the *age* and *sex* values from the file. Also display the values read to these variables.

**Activity 6.8**

Write a program that reads from the keyboard values for the maximum and minimum temperatures (in Celsius) for 7 consecutive days (starting with the data for Sunday). The program should then read the file and display the average temperature for each day.

OUTLINE LOGIC:

```
Open file for writing
FOR 7 times DO
    Read in min and max temperatures for day
    Write temperatures to file
ENDFOR
Close file
```

**Continued on next page**

**Activity 6.8** (continued)

```
Open file for reading
FOR 7 times DO
    Read the max and min temperatures from the file
    Calculate the average for the day
    Display day of week and average temperature
ENDFOR
Close the file
```

# Appending to a File

If we open a text file that already contains data then that data will normally be lost if we write to the file. However, we can open a file using the term `append` rather than `rewrite`. As the term suggests, this allows new data to be added after the file's existing contents. Hence if *myfile* contains the data *John Jakes, 22, M* and we wish to add the new information *Liz Heron, 37, F* we can use the statements:

```
append(myfile);
writeln(myfile,'Liz Heron');
writeln(myfile,37);
writeln(myfile,'F');
```

# Outputting to the Printer

Although the idea may seem strange, we can also treat the printer as a text file. Of course, in this case we can only output to the file.

Borland have done most of the hard work required to use the printer as a text file. All we need to do is include the *Printer* unit in our `uses` clause

```
uses WinCrt, Printer;
```

and then declare a file variable named *Lst*:

```
var
    Lst : Text;
```

There is no need to assign or rewrite the file variable, instead we can write directly to it with statements such as:

```
writeln(Lst,'hello world');
```

**Activity 6.9**

Modify the program from Activity 6.8 so that the data is read from the file and written to the printer.

OUTLINE LOGIC:

```
Open file for reading
FOR 7 times DO
    Read the max and min temperatures from the file
    Calculate the average for the day
    Write day of week and average temp to the printer
ENDFOR
Close the file
```

# Summary

- When using a file, **a file variable must be declared.**
- **The filename used within a program must be tied to an operating system file name.** This is done using the `assign` statement.
- **A file is opened for writing** using the `rewrite` statement.
- **Files opened using** `rewrite` are automatically created if they do not already exist.
- **Existing files opened using** `rewrite` have their current contents destroyed by the opening process.
- **Files are written to** using `write` or `writeln`.
- **Files must be closed** before the program terminates. This is done using the `close` statement.
- **When a file is to be read**, open it using `reset`.
- **Data is read from a file using** the `read or readln` statements.
- **Text files contain** data in ASCII code format.
- **Output can be directed to the printer** using the *Printer* unit and the filename *Lst.*
- **Data can be added to the existing contents** of a text file if it is opened using `append`.

# TYPED FILES

## Introduction

Text files are of limited use for storing data that we intend to interrogate later. A second option is to create **typed** files.

A typed file is one in which we store data of a specific type. To use a typed file we declare a file variable in which we state the type of values held in the file. Hence, if we want a file to contain a list of integers, we declare the file variable using the statement:

```
var
    myfile      : file of integer;
```

Other valid examples include declarations such as:

```
    myfile2     : file of double;
    myfile3     : file of string;
```

It is more likely that we will want to use a typed file to store the contents of record variables. For example if we had declared the structure:

```
type
    StudentDetails =
    record
        idcode  : integer;
        name    : string[30];
        sex     : char;
        score   : array[1..6] of integer;
    end;
```

We can then write records of this structure to a file by declaring a file variable which is designed to hold such structures:

```
var
    myfile : file of StudentDetails;
```

The general format for declaring a typed file variable is given in FIG-6.2.

**FIG-6.2**

Declaring Typed File Variables

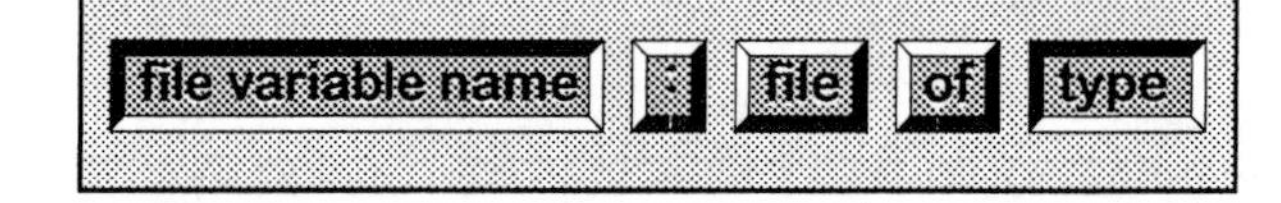


## Writing to the File

We'll also need a record variable into which the data must be placed before it can be written to the file:

```
var
    myfile  : file of StudentDetails;
    myrec   : StudentDetails;
```

Now the main program consists of the logic:

```
Open the file for writing
Read details of a record from the keyboard
Write the details to the file
Close the file
```

This logic is implemented in LISTING-6.4.

**LISTING-6.4**

Writing to a Typed File

```
program List6_4;
uses WinCrt;
type
  StudentDetails =
  record
      idcode    : integer;
      name      : string[30];
      sex       : char;
      score     : array[1..6] of integer;
  end;
var
  c        : integer;                    {Loop counter}
  myfile   : file of StudentDetails;
  myrec    : StudentDetails;
begin
  {*** Open the file ***}
  assign(myfile,'C:\students.dat');
  rewrite(myfile);
  {*** Read the student's details ***}
  ClrScr;
  write('Enter id code : ');
  readln(myrec.idcode);
  write('Enter name : ');
  readln(myrec.name);
  write('Enter sex (M/F) : ');
  readln(myrec.sex);
  for c := 1 to 6 do
  begin
      write('Enter score ',c,' : ');
      readln(myrec.score[c]);
  end;
  {*** Write to file ***}
  write(myfile,myrec);
  {*** Close file ***}
  close(myfile);
end.
```

When writing to a typed file don't use `writeln` since this would attempt to insert a return character in the file after the record details have been written. This would cause problems later.

**Activity 6.10**

Enter and run the above program. Use the data 128, 'John Jakes', 'M', 0,8,16,32,64,0.

## Data Storage Format

Typed files write data to the disk in a different way from text files. The best way to understand what's going on is to look at the contents of the file using the debug command from DOS.

**Activity 6.11**

Enter DOS mode and type in the command
   DEBUG C:\REPORT.DAT
This tells DEBUG to load the contents of our file into memory.
Now the DEBUG hyphen prompt appears.

**Continued on next page**

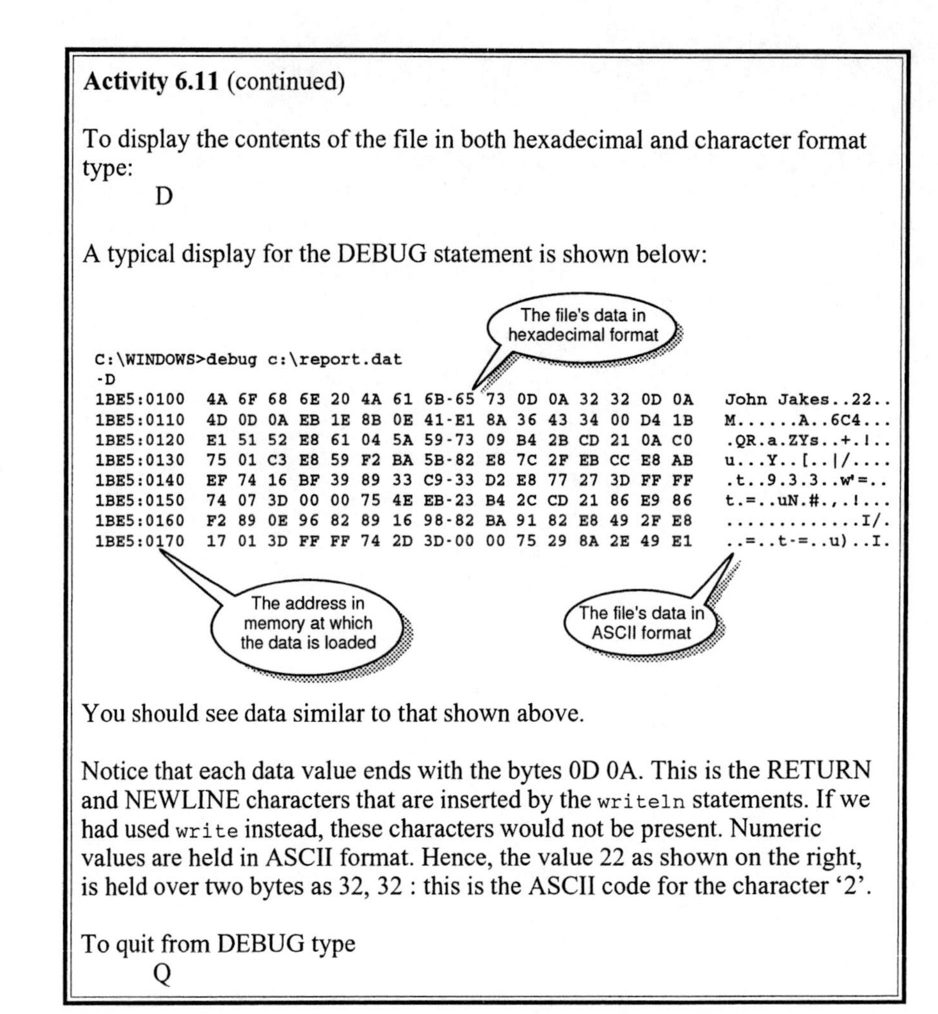

**Activity 6.11** (continued)

To display the contents of the file in both hexadecimal and character format type:

D

A typical display for the DEBUG statement is shown below:

```
C:\WINDOWS>debug c:\report.dat
-D
1BE5:0100  4A 6F 68 6E 20 4A 61 6B-65 73 0D 0A 32 32 0D 0A   John Jakes..22..
1BE5:0110  4D 0D 0A EB 1E 8B 0E 41-E1 8A 36 43 34 00 D4 1B   M......A..6C4...
1BE5:0120  E1 51 52 E8 61 04 5A 59-73 09 B4 2B CD 21 0A C0   .QR.a.ZYs..+.!..
1BE5:0130  75 01 C3 E8 59 F2 BA 5B-82 E8 7C 2F EB CC E8 AB   u...Y..[..|/....
1BE5:0140  EF 74 16 BF 39 89 33 C9-33 D2 E8 77 27 3D FF FF   .t..9.3.3..w'=..
1BE5:0150  74 07 3D 00 00 75 4E EB-23 B4 2C CD 21 86 E9 86   t.=..uN.#.,.!...
1BE5:0160  F2 89 0E 96 82 89 16 98-82 BA 91 82 E8 49 2F E8   .............I/.
1BE5:0170  17 01 3D FF FF 74 2D 3D-00 00 75 29 8A 2E 49 E1   ..=..t-=..u)..I.
```



You should see data similar to that shown above.

Notice that each data value ends with the bytes 0D 0A. This is the RETURN and NEWLINE characters that are inserted by the `writeln` statements. If we had used `write` instead, these characters would not be present. Numeric values are held in ASCII format. Hence, the value 22 as shown on the right, is held over two bytes as 32, 32 : this is the ASCII code for the character '2'.

To quit from DEBUG type

Q

DEBUG shows random characters beyond the file data.

When we perform debug on *c:\students.dat* we can see that the data is held in quite different ways (see FIG-6.3)

**FIG-6.3**

Formatted Storage

```
C:\         debug c:\students.dat
-d
1BE5:0100  80 00 0A 4A 6F 68 6E 20-4A 61 6B 65 73 00 00 00   ...John Jakes...
1BE5:0110  00 00 00 00 00 00 00 00-00 00 00 00 00 00 00 00   ................
1BE5:0120  00 4D 00 00 08 00 10 00-20 00 40 00 00 00 0A C0   .M...... .@.....
1BE5:0130  75 [illegible] C3 [illegible] BA 5B-82 E8 7C 2F EB [illegible]   u...Y..[..|/....
1BE5:0140  [illegible] 16 [illegible] 33 C9-33 D2 E8 77 27 3D [illegible]   .t..9.3.3..w'=..
1BE5:0150  [illegible] 07 3D 00 [illegible] 4E EB-23 B4 2C CD 21 86 [illegible]   t.=..uN.#.,.!...
1BE5:0160  F2 89 0E 96 82 89 16 98-82 BA 91 82 E8 49 2F E8   .............I/.
1BE5:0170  17 01 3D FF FF 74 2D 3D-00 00 75 29 8A 2E 49 E1   ..=..t-=..u)..I.
```

idcode
name
sex
score[1]
score[6]

This time the numeric fields are much less obvious. No ASCII characters are shown for those fields *(idcode* and *score)*. However, if we look at the hexadecimal values we see that the *idcode* is stored as 80 00. To make sense of this we must first reverse the order of the bytes, giving 00 80. This is simply a quirk of the Intel microprocessor, which stores numbers in reverse byte order, a fact that must be reflected in the data file. If we now convert the hexadecimal value 0080 to decimal we get 128 - the value of the *idcode*.

In fact, formatted files hold their data in the same format as used within the variables of the program. So when we write the contents of *myrec* to the file, the program simply copies the binary contents of that variable to the file. This explains the contents of *name*, with the character count at the start (0A) and the random bytes at the end, after the meaningful data (in this case, the bytes are zero-filled).

# Reading from a Typed File

We read the data back from a typed file in much the same way as we did with a text file. The data needs to be read from the file into a record variable of the appropriate type. The program in LISTING-6.5 reads the student's details from the existing file and displays it on the screen.

**LISTING-6.5**

Reading from a Formatted File

```
program List6_05;
uses WinCrt;

type
  StudentDetails =
  record
      idcode   : integer;
      name     : string[30];
      sex      : char;
      score    : array[1..6] of integer;
  end;
var
  c        : integer;                 {Loop counter}
  myfile   : file of StudentDetails;
  myrec    : StudentDetails;

begin
  {*** Open the file ***}
  assign(myfile,'C:\students.dat');
  reset(myfile);
  {*** Read the student's details ***}
  read(myfile,myrec);
  {*** Display the details on the screen ***}
  ClrScr;
  with myrec do
  begin
      writeln('Id code : ',idcode);
      writeln('Name : ',name);
      writeln('Sex : ',sex);
      for c := 1 to 6 do
          writeln('Score ',c,' : ',score[c]);
  end;
  {*** Close file ***}
  close(myfile);
end.
```

# Dealing with Multiple Records

If we are going to store information such as a student's details, it is likely that we will want to write many records to our file. This is simply done by putting the core part of the operation within an iterative structure of some kind. In the example given in LISTING-6.6 records are written to the file until an *idcode* of zero is entered; this terminates the program. It employs the following logic:

```
Open file for writing
Read idcode
WHILE idcode not zero DO
    Read remaining student's details
    Write record to file
    Read next idcode
ENDWHILE
Close file
```

**LISTING-6.6**

Writing Several Records to a File

```
program List6_06;
uses WinCrt;


type
  StudentDetails =
  record
      idcode    : integer;
      name      : string[30];
      sex       : char;
      score     : array[1..6] of integer;
  end;



var
  c        : integer;    {Loop counter}
  myfile   : file of StudentDetails;
  myrec    : StudentDetails;


begin
  {*** Open the file ***}
  assign(myfile,'C:\students.dat');
  rewrite(myfile);
  {*** Read the student's idcode ***}
  ClrScr;
  write('Enter id code : ');
  readln(myrec.idcode);
  {*** WHILE idcode not zero DO ***}
  while myrec.idcode <> 0 do
  begin
      {*** Read remaining details ***}
      write('Enter name : ');
      readln(myrec.name);
      write('Enter sex (M/F) : ');
      readln(myrec.sex);
      for c := 1 to 6 do
      begin
          write('Enter score ',c,' : ');
          readln(myrec.score[c]);
      end;
      {*** Write to file ***}
      write(myfile,myrec);
      ClrScr;
      {*** Read next idcode ***}
      write('Enter id code : ');
      readln(myrec.idcode);
  end;
  {*** Close file ***}
  close(myfile);
end.
```

When we want to read the data back from the file, we have an added problem: how many records are there to be read? If we read too few, then we won't access some of the data; if we try to read too many, then an error will occur as we try to read past the end of the file's data.

Luckily, Pascal has a function called *Eof* which returns *true* when we have reached the end of the data in the file. When a file is opened in Pascal, a file position indicator is automatically maintained by the program. This acts rather like the screen cursor, indicating the position in the file of the next character to be read. When this position indicator passes the end of the file, *Eof* returns *true*. The definition of the routine is given below.

| | | |
|---|---|---|
| **Prototype** | : | `function Eof(F:filetype):boolean` |
| **Unit** | : | System |
| **Pre-condition**: | | File *F* should be open for reading. |
| **Description** | : | Returns *true* if the file position indicator has passed the last byte of data within the file, otherwise *false* is returned. |
| **Example** | : | `while not Eof(myfile) do begin read(myfile,myrec); writeln(myrec.name); end;` |

The program in LISTING-6.7 reads back and displays the students' data stored by the program in LISTING-6.6. It uses the logic:

```
Open file for reading
WHILE end of file not reached DO
    Read a student's record from the file
    Write record's details to the screen
ENDWHILE
Close file
```

**LISTING-6.7**

Reading Records from a Typed File

```
program List6_07;
uses WinCrt;

type
  StudentDetails =
  record
      idcode   : integer;
      name     : string[30];
      sex      : char;
      scores   : array[1..6] of integer;
  end;


var
  c        : integer;    {Loop counter}
  myfile   : file of StudentDetails;
  myrec    : StudentDetails;


begin
  {*** Open the file ***}
  assign(myfile,'C:\students.dat');
  reset(myfile);
  {*** WHILE not end of file DO ***}
  while not Eof(myfile) do
  begin
      {*** Read a  record from file ***}
      read(myfile,myrec);
      {*** Display record's details ***}
      with myrec do
      begin
          write(idcode:5,name:20,sex:2);
          for c := 1 to 6 do
              write(scores[c]:4);
          writeln;
      end
  end;
  {*** Close file ***}
  close(myfile);
end.
```

**Activity 6.12**

Enter and run the programs in LISTING-6.6 and LISTING-6.7.

Modify the first program so that all input is done using the *GetData* function written in the previous chapter.

Modify the second program so only the details of students with an average of under 50 are displayed.

## Random Access

When we write information to a file, each new record is placed immediately after the last; when we subsequently read information from that file, the records are read one by one in the same order in which they were written. However, there are occasions when we want to go directly to a record without accessing the preceding one (in much the same way as we might want to go to track 5 on a CD without playing the first four).

When a typed file is opened, the file position indicator references the first record - known as record zero (see FIG-6.4).

**FIG-6.4**

Initial Value of the File Position Indicator

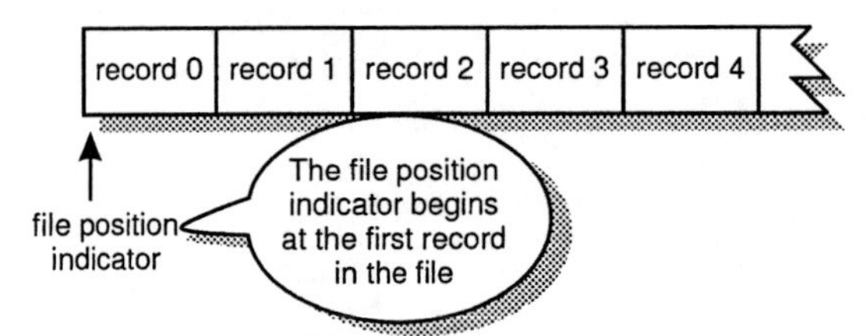


Each time a `read` statement is executed, the file position moves on to the next record (see FIG-6.5).

**FIG-6.5**

The Indicator moves on after a Record is Read

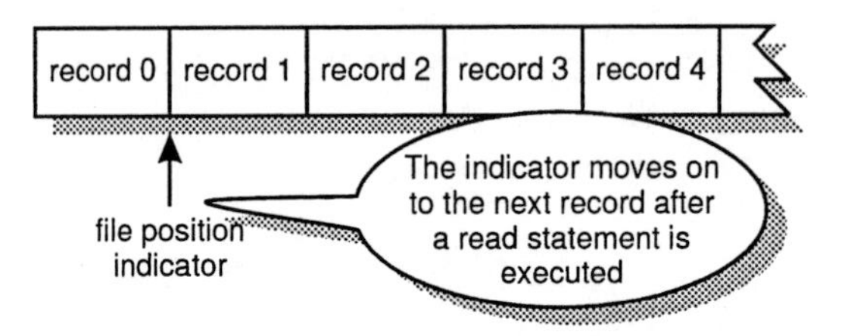


We can control the movement of the file position indicator using the `Seek` procedure described below:

| | | |
|---|---|---|
| **Prototype** | : | `procedure Seek(F:filetype; recno : integer)` |
| **Unit** | : | System |
| **Pre-condition**: | | *F* should be open. |
| **Description** | : | Positions the file position indicator of file *F* to record number *recno*. |
| **Example** | : | `seek(myfile,0); {Moves to the first record}`<br>`seek(myfile,2); {Moves to the third record}` |

The program in LISTING-6.8 demonstrates the use of random file access. The program uses the following logic:

```
Open file for reading
Read position of required record from keyboard
WHILE not terminate program option DO
    Seek record
    Read record
    Display its details
    Read position of required record
ENDWHILE
Close file
```

**LISTING-6.8**

Using Random Access

```
program List6_08;
uses WinCrt;

type
  StudentDetails =
  record
      idcode   : integer;
      name     : string[30];
      sex      : char;
      score    : array[1..6] of integer;
  end;


var
  c        : integer;    {Loop counter}
  post     : integer;    {Position of rec to be read}
  myfile   : file of StudentDetails;
  myrec    : StudentDetails;

begin
  {*** Open the file ***}
  assign(myfile,'C:\students.dat');
  reset(myfile);
  {*** Read position of req'd record ***}
  ClrScr;
  write('Position of record req''d (-1 to end): ');
  readln(post);
  {*** WHILE not terminate value DO ***}
  while post <> -1 do
  begin
      {*** Seek record ***}
      Seek(myfile, post - 1);
      {*** Read record ***}
      read(myfile,myrec);
      {*** Display record ***}
      writeln('RECORD AT POSITION ',post);
      with myrec do
      begin
          write(idcode:5,name:25,sex:2);
          for c := 1 to 6 do
              write(score[c]:4);
          writeln;
      end;
      {*** Get position of next record req'd ***}
      write('Position of record req''d (-1 to end) : ');
      readln(post);
  end;
end.
```

If we assume the user will enter 1 if they want to access the first record in the file, we need to subtract one from the value of *post* before applying the *seek* procedure.

**Activity 6.13**

Enter and run the program in LISTING-6.8.

What happens if you attempt to read from an invalid position?

# Dealing With Errors

As you can see from the results of the last Activity, using files can cause problems.

We could help overcome that particular problem if we knew how many records were in the file. This can be achieved using the function *FileSize* which returns the number of records in a file.

| | | |
|---|---|---|
| **Prototype** | : | `function FileSize(F:filetype): longint` |
| **Unit** | : | System |
| **Pre-condition** | : | *F* should be open. |
| **Description** | : | Returns the number of records or items within a file. If the file is empty, zero is returned. |
| **Example** | : | `Seek(myfile, FileSize(myfile))` ↳`{Moves to end of file}`<br>`writeln(FileSize(myfile)){Displays no. of recs}` |

Using this we can make the program in LISTING-6.8 a little friendlier by replacing the line

```
write('Position of record req''d (-1 to end): ');
```

with

```
write('Position required 1 to ',FileSize(myfile),' or -1 : ');
```

Of course, this only helps by giving the user more information, it won't stop invalid positions being entered and causing a runtime error.

We can get more control over the program by turning off automatic I/O checking. This is done using the compiler command {$I-} within your program. Dealing with any subsequent problems encountered during input/output operations becomes the responsibility of the programmer - the program will no longer terminate automatically.

The programmer can check for such errors by making a call to the function *IOResult* immediately after any I/O operation such as `read` or `write`. *IOResult* is described below.

| | | |
|---|---|---|
| **Prototype** | : | `function IOResult : integer` |
| **Unit** | : | System |
| **Pre-condition** | : | I/O checking should be off. |
| **Description** | : | Returns zero if the previous I/O statement performed correctly, otherwise a negative value is returned. |
| **Example** | : | see below |

```
{$I-}
seek(myfile,post - 1);
read(myfile,myec);
if IOResult <> 0 then
    writeln('Invalid position')
```

Typical errors include:

Disk write error
File not open
File not open for output

I/O checking can be turned on again using {$I+}.

The program in LISTING-6.9 is a revised version of the one already given in LISTING-6.8 to include error checking. The program's logic is:

```
Switch off I/O checking
Open file for reading
IF IO error THEN
    Display error message
    Terminate program
ENDIF
Read position of required record from keyboard
WHILE not terminate program option DO
    Seek record
    Read record
    IF IO error THEN
        Display error message
    ELSE
        Display record's details
    ENDIF
    Read position of required record
ENDWHILE
Close file
Turn on I/O checking
```

**LISTING-6.9**

Using IOResult

```
program List6_09;
uses WinCrt;

type
  StudentDetails =
  record
      idcode    : integer;
      name      : string[30];
      sex       : char;
      score     : array[1..6] of integer;
  end;
var
  c             : integer;    {Loop counter}
  post          : integer;    {Position of rec to be read}
  myfile        : file of StudentDetails;
  myrec         : StudentDetails;
begin
  {*** Switch off I/O checking ***}
  {$I-}
  {*** Open the file ***}
  assign(myfile,'C:\students.dat');
  reset(myfile);
  {*** IF IO error display error message and terminate ***}
  if IoResult <> 0 then
  begin
      writeln('Could not open file');
      halt;
  end;
  {*** Read position of req'd record ***}
  ClrScr;
  write('Position req''d 1 to ',FileSize(myfile),' or -1 : ');
  readln(post);
  {*** WHILE not terminate value DO ***}
  while post <> -1 do
  begin
```

**Continued on next page**

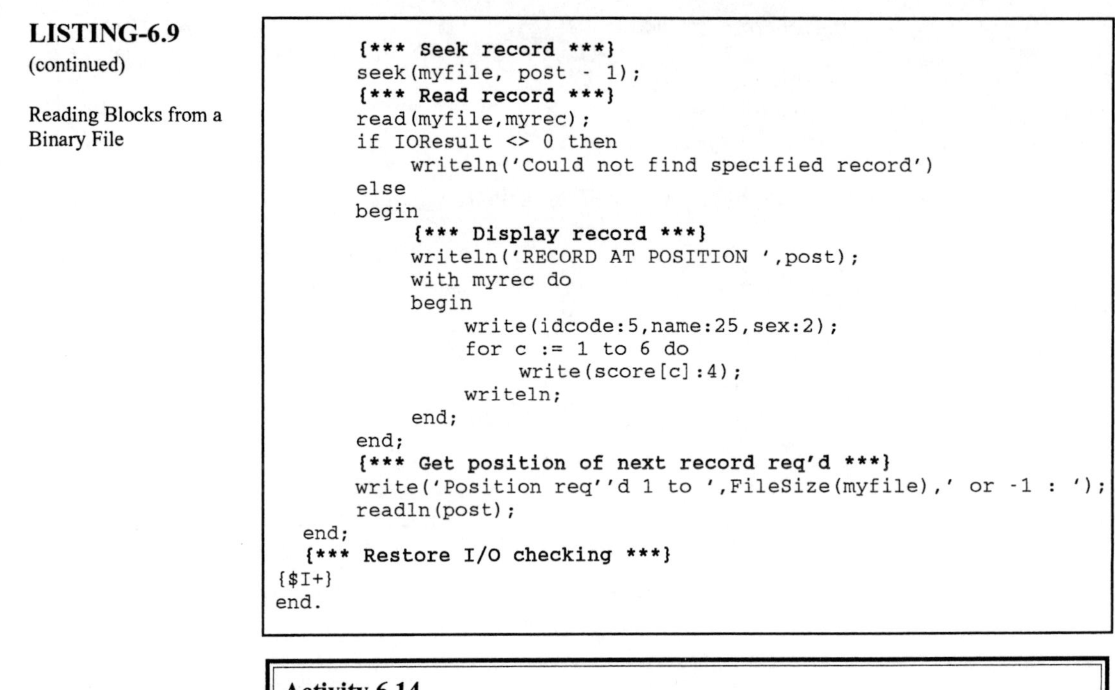

**LISTING-6.9**
(continued)

Reading Blocks from a Binary File

```
        {*** Seek record ***}
        seek(myfile, post - 1);
        {*** Read record ***}
        read(myfile,myrec);
        if IOResult <> 0 then
            writeln('Could not find specified record')
        else
        begin
            {*** Display record ***}
            writeln('RECORD AT POSITION ',post);
            with myrec do
            begin
                write(idcode:5,name:25,sex:2);
                for c := 1 to 6 do
                    write(score[c]:4);
                writeln;
            end;
        end;
        {*** Get position of next record req'd ***}
        write('Position req''d 1 to ',FileSize(myfile),' or -1 : ');
        readln(post);
    end;
    {*** Restore I/O checking ***}
{$I+}
end.
```

**Activity 6.14**

Make these changes to your program and test its ability to handle errors.

# Updating Files

The contents of most files will need to be changed periodically. There are only three basic operations required when files are updated:

Adding new records
Modifying existing records
Deleting records

## Adding a Record

If we want to write to a typed file, we mustn't open it using the `rewrite` statement since this will only result in the existing data being lost. Instead, we need to open the file using the `reset` statement. When used with a text file, `reset` only allows data to be read from a file, but in the case of typed files, both reading and writing are permitted.

So, if we assume a record is to be added to the end of the existing data, we can do that by using the following logic:

```
Open the file for updating (using reset)
Move the file position indicator to the end of the file
Read the new record's details from the keyboard
Write the new record to the file
Close the file
```

> **Activity 6.15**
>
> Modify the program you created in Activity 6.12 based on LISTING-6.6 so that new records can be added after the existing data.
>
> Add I/O error handling to the code.

Adding records at any other position in a file is not really practical. We cannot persuade the file to move records aside in the way that a word processor's text moves to allow new characters to be inserted between existing ones. Instead, we need to copy the existing records from the file into a new file, inserting the additional record into the new file at the appropriate point (see FIG-6.6).

**FIG-6.6**

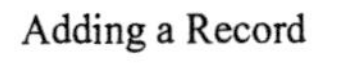
Adding a Record

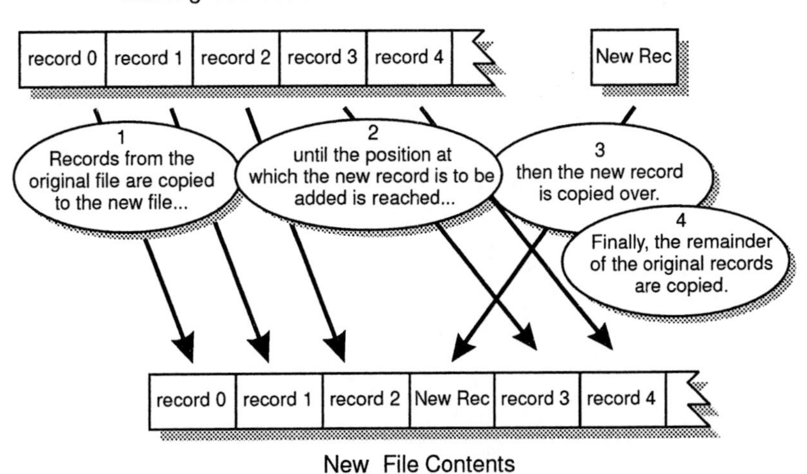


## Modifying a Record

To change the contents of a record, we must first read the record from the file into some record variable; next we need to modify the required field(s), and, finally, the record must be written back to the file.

When a file is opened in reset mode, writing to a file will place the new record in the position specified by the file indicator. The tricky bit in updating a record is to realise that by reading a record we move the file position indicator on to the next record and, hence, it must be moved back before we attempt to write the updated record to the file. These steps are shown in FIG-6.7.

**FIG-6.7** Updating a Record

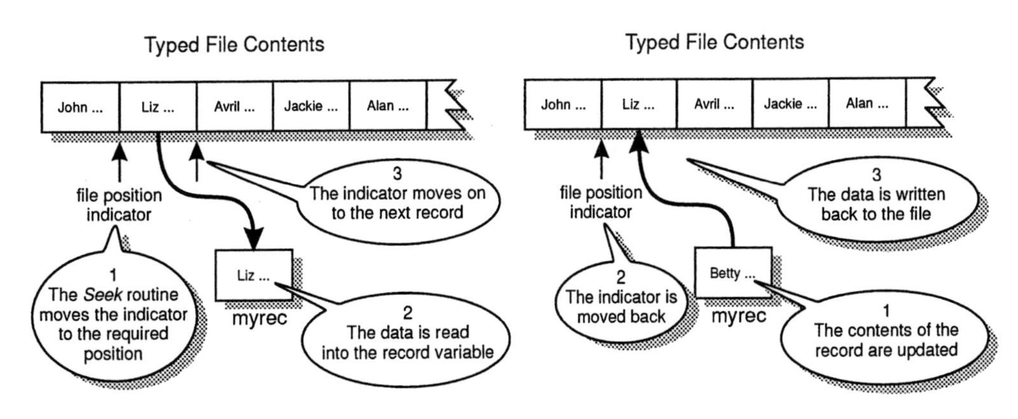

In order to move the file position indicator back to the previous record we need to know its current position. We can discover this by using another function, *FilePos*, described below:

| | | |
|---|---|---|
| **Prototype** | : | `function FilePos(F:filetype): longint` |
| **Unit** | : | System |
| **Pre-condition**: | | *F* should be open. |
| **Description** | : | Returns the current position of the file indicator. |
| **Example** | : | `Seek(myfile, FilePos(myfile)-1); {Moves to previous rec}` |

The program in LISTING-6.10 allows the user to change the name in a specified record in STUDENTS.DAT. The program's logic is:

```
Open file for updating (using reset)
Calculate and display the number of records in the file
Get the position of the record to be changed
WHILE number not -1 DO
    Seek record
    IF found THEN
        Display record
        Get new name
        Update name field in record
        Move file pointer back to the record just read
        Write updated record to file
    ELSE
        Display error message
    ENDIF
    Get the number of the record to be changed
ENDWHILE
Close file
```

**LISTING-6.10**

Updating Records

```
program List6_10;
uses WinCrt;

type
  StudentDetails =
  record
      idcode   : integer;
      name     : string[30];
      sex      : char;
      score    : array[1..6] of integer;
  end;

var
  post     : integer;         {Position of record to be changed}
  c        : integer;         {Loop counter}
  myfile   : file of StudentDetails;
  myrec    : StudentDetails;
  newname  : string[30]; {Contains the new name}

begin
  {*** Open the file for updating ***}
  assign(myfile,'C:\students.dat');
  reset(myfile);
  {*** Calculate and display the number of records in file ***}
  writeln('File contains ',FileSize(myfile),' records');
  {*** Get position of the record to be changed ***}
  write('Enter position of record to be changed (-1 to end) : ');
  readln(post);
```

**Continued on next page**

**LISTING-6.10**
(continued)

Updating Records

```
{*** WHILE number not -1 DO ***}
  while post <> -1 DO
  begin
       {*** Seek record ***}
       {$I-}
       Seek(myfile,post - 1);
       read(myfile,myrec);
       {*** IF found THEN ***}
       if IOResult = 0 then
       begin
            {*** Display record ***}
            with myrec do
            begin
                 write(idcode:5,name:20,sex:2);
                 for c := 1 to 6 do
                      write(scores[c]:4);
                 writeln;
            end;
            {*** Get new name ***}
            write('Enter new name : ');
            readln(newname);
            {*** Update name field in record ***}
            myrec.name := newname;
            {*** Move file indicator back to record just read ***}
            Seek(myfile,FilePos(myfile) - 1);
            {*** Write updated record to file ***}
            write(myfile,myrec);
       end
       else
            {*** Display error message ***}
            writeln('Invalid record position');
       {*** Get position of the record to be changed ***}
       write('Enter position of record to change (-1 to end) : ');
       readln(post);
  end;
  {*** Close file ***}
  close(myfile);
  {$I+}
end.
```

**Activity 6.16**

Write a menu driven program for your *StudentDetails* file which allows you to add new records, display a specific record, display all records or modify a record. Assume only scores can be modified.
Your program should make use of routines already written. These include: *DisplayMenu; GetOption* and *GetData*.

## Deleting a Record

The usual way to delete a record from a file is to make a new copy of the file in which the record to be deleted has been omitted. Such a program would use the logic:

```
Open old file for reading
Open new file for writing
Get position of record to be deleted
WHILE not at end of original file DO
    Read a record from file
    IF not record to be deleted THEN
        Write the record to the new file
    ENDIF
ENDWHILE
Close both files
Delete old file
Rename new file to that given to the original file
```

You can see from the logic that after the files are closed, near the end of the description, the old file is erased and the new one given the name of the old one. This is necessary so that the other programs we have already written will continue to operate correctly. After all, our previous programs expect the data to be in a file named *C:\students.dat*, so we must make sure this is still true after deleting a record from the file.

There are two routines available to help with these operations: *Erase* which erases a file from disk; and *Rename* which renames a file. The two routines are described below:

| | |
|---|---|
| **Prototype** : | `procedure Erase(var F:filetype)` |
| **Unit** : | System |
| **Pre-condition**: | *F* should be closed. |
| **Description** : | The file associated with *F* is deleted. |
| **Example** : | `assign(myfile, 'C:\students.dat');`<br>`Erase(myfile);`<br>`{C:\students.dat is deleted}` |

| | |
|---|---|
| **Prototype** : | `procedure Rename(var F:filetype; newname;string)` |
| **Unit** : | System |
| **Pre-condition**: | *newname* must not be an existing file name.. |
| **Description** : | The file associated with *F* is renamed as *newname.* |
| **Example** : | `{*** Renames c:\student2.dat as c:\copy.dat ***}`<br>`assign(myfile2,'C:student2.dat');`<br>`Rename(myfile2, 'C:\copy.dat');` |

The program in LISTING-6.11 deletes a record from a given position in a file.

**LISTING-6.11**

Deleting a Record

```
program List6_11;
uses WinCrt;

type
  StudentDetails =
  record
      idcode   : integer;
      name     : string[30];
      sex      : char;
      score    : array[1..6] of integer;
  end;

var
  post     : integer;         {Position of record to be changed}
  c        : integer;         {Loop counter}
  oldfile  : file of StudentDetails; {Existing file}
  newfile  : file of StudentDetails; {New copy of file}
  myrec    : StudentDetails;
  newname  : string[30]; {Contains the new name}
```

**Continued on next page**

**LISTING-6.11**
(continued)

Deleting a Record

```
begin
  {*** Open the old file for reading ***}
  assign(oldfile,'C:\students.dat');
  reset(oldfile);
  {*** Open new file for writing ***}
  assign(newfile,'C:\student2.dat');
  rewrite(newfile);
  {*** get position of record to be deleted ***}
  writeln('Old file contains ',FileSize(oldfile),' records');
  write('Enter position of record to be deleted : ');
  readln(post);
  {*** WHILE number not end of old file DO ***}
  while not Eof(oldfile) DO
  begin
      {*** Read a record from old file ***}
      if FilePos(oldfile) + 1 = post then
          read(oldfile, myrec)
      else
      begin
          read(oldfile,myrec);
          write(newfile,myrec);
      end;
  end;
  {*** Close files ***}
  close(oldfile);
  close(newfile);
  {*** Erase old file ***}
  Erase(oldfile);
  {*** Rename new file to that of old ***}
  Rename(newfile,'C:\students.dat');
end.
```

This approach to deleting records in a file can be rather time consuming if the file is a large one and records are removed frequently. An alternative approach is to simply mark records for deletion without actually removing them. The program in LISTING-6.12 allows records to be marked for deletion. The program employs the following logic:

```
Open file for updating
Get position in file of record to be deleted
WHILE position not -1 DO
    Find required record
    Change idcode field to DELETED indicator
    Get position in file of record to be deleted
ENDWHILE
    Close file
```

**LISTING-6.12**

Marking Deleted Records

```
program List6_12;
uses WinCrt;
const
  DELETED = -1; {Value used to denote a deleted record}
type
  StudentDetails =
  record
      idcode   : integer;
      name     : string[30];
      sex      : char;
      score    : array[1..6] of integer;
  end;
var
  post     : integer;        {Position of record to be changed}
  c        : integer;        {Loop counter}
  myfile   : file of StudentDetails; {Existing file}
  myrec    : StudentDetails;
  newname  : string[30]; {Contains the new name}
```

**Continued on next page**

**LISTING-6.12**

(continued)

Marking Deleted Records

In this example the value -1 in the *idcode* is used to indicated a deleted record.

```
begin
  {*** Open the file for updating ***}
  assign(myfile,'C:\students.dat');
  reset(myfile);
  {*** get position of record to be deleted ***}
  writeln('File contains ',FileSize(myfile),' records');
  write('Enter position of rec to be deleted(-1 to end): ');
  readln(post);
  {*** WHILE post not -1 DO ***}
  while post <> -1 do
  begin
      {*** Find required record ***}
      seek(myfile,post - 1);
      {*** Change idcode to DELETED ***}
      read(myfile,myrec);
      myrec.idcode := DELETED;
      seek(myfile,post - 1);
      write(myfile,myrec);
      {*** Read position of next record to be deleted ***}
      write('Enter position of rec to be deleted(-1 to end): ');
      readln(post);
  end;
  {*** Close files ***}
  close(myfile);
end.
```

**Activity 6.17**

Type in and test the program in LISTING-6.12.

Examine the contents of the file by re-running the program given in LISTING-6.7.

Although the listing program is useful to ensure that the deleted *idcode* has been inserted properly, any program designed to display the contents of a file in which records are marked as deleted will have to omit those records when displaying the contents of the file.

Modify the program in LISTING-6.7 so that only records whose *idcode* is not -1 are displayed.

However, this approach for handling deleted records still requires us to develop a program which can be used periodically to physically remove the records marked for deletion from the file. We now need a second program which copies those records not marked for deletion into another file.

The Structure English description of such a program is:

```
Open original file for reading
Open new file for writing
WHILE not EOF DO
    Read a record from original file
    IF record read is not marked for deletion THEN
        Write record to new file
    ENDIF
ENDWHILE
Close both files
Delete the original file
Rename the new file
```

**Activity 6.18**

Write a program based on the Structured English given above. By using a string variable as the second parameter of any `assign` statements in your program, include the ability for the user to specify the name of the source file being copied.

Include I/O checking within your program.

# Summary

- **Typed files store items all of the same type.**
- **Typed files hold their information** in the same format as variables in memory.
- **Typed files are declared** using the format:

```
filename : file of type of data in file
```

- **Typed files are often used to store records.**
- **Files maintain a file position indicator.**
- **The file position indicator** is used by both read and write statements to determine the next record to be accessed.
- ***Eof*** returns *true* if the file position indicator has reached the end of the file.
- The file position indicator can be moved using the ***Seek*** function.
- ***FileSize*** returns the number of items within a file.
- ***FilePos*** returns the position of the file indicator. Zero is returned if the indicator is at the start of the file.
- **I/O errors checking** can be switched off using `{$I-}` and on using `{$I+}`.
- **When I/O error checking is off**, the program will not terminate when an I/O error occurs.
- ***IOResult*** is a function which returns the value generated by the preceding I/O statement.
- ***IOResult* returns zero** if the previous I/O statement is executed correctly.
- **Records can be added** to the end of a file's existing data by

  Opening the file using `reset`
  Moving the file position indicator to the end of the file
  Writing the new record to the file

- **Records can be updated** by

  Opening the file using `reset`
  Moving the file position indicator to the required record
  Reading the record

Modifying the data fields
Moving the file position indicator back to the original record
Writing the record back to the file

- **Records can be deleted** by copying all other records to a new version of the file.

# CASE STUDY

## The Problem

When we need to examine the contents of a text file it's easy enough to load it into a text editor. Looking at binary files is a different problem since all its numeric values will appear as random ASCII characters if we examine it in an editor.

Normally, we need to write specific programs to display the contents of binary files, with a different program for each record format. However, a more useful program would allow us to enter the format of the record and use this to interpret and display the contents of the file.

## Clarification

We require a program which will display the contents of any binary file by allowing us to specify that file's record structure which is then used when displaying the contents of the file.

We will assume a maximum record size of 80 characters and no more than 20 fields in each record.

## The Algorithm

Although the implementation of this program uses some unusual code, the logic behind it is quite simple and is given in the algorithm below:

```
Set up a general record variable
Get the filename
Display possible field types
Get type of first field
WHILE not end of fields DO
    IF field is a string THEN
        Get length of string
    ENDIF
    Record field's type and size
    Get type of next field
ENDWHILE
Calculate size of record in bytes
FOR each field in record DO
    Set pointer to start of field position in general record
ENDFOR
Open file for reading
Read data into record variable
WHILE not EOF DO
    FOR each field pointer DO
        Cast pointer to filed type
        Display contents of field
    ENDFOR
    Read data into record variable
ENDWHILE
Close files
```

The program is given in LISTING-6.13.

**LISTING-6.13**

Viewing Typed Files

```
program DisplayingFiles;
uses WinCrt;

type
  KeySet = set of char;

{*** Get Data from Keyboard ***}
function GetData(allowed : KeySet; max : integer):string;
const
  ENTER = #13;
  BACKSPACE = #8;
var
  ch     : char;         {char from keyboard}
  count  : integer;      {chars entered}
  result : string;       {Contains the characters typed in}
begin
  {*** Check pre-conditions ***}
  if (allowed = []) or (max<=0) then
  begin
      GetData := '';
      exit;
  end;
  {*** Set result to empty and count to zero ***}
  result := '';
  count := 0;
  {*** Read a character ***}
  ch := ReadKey;
  {*** WHILE return key not pressed DO ***}
  while ch <> ENTER do
  begin
      {*** IF allowed char & result not full THEN ***}
      if (ch in allowed) AND (count < max)then
      begin
          {*** Display char and add to result ***}
          write(ch);
          result := result + ch;
          inc(count);
      end
      {*** ELSE if delete & result not empty ***}
      else if (ch = BACKSPACE) AND (count > 0) then
      begin
          {*** Remove last char ***}
          write(#8,#32,#8);
          delete(result,length(result),1);
          dec(count);
      end;
      {*** Read another character ***}
      ch := readkey;
  end;
  writeln;
        GetData := result;
end;

{*** Displays menu string & returns no. of options in menu ***}
function DisplayMenu(m : string):integer;
var
  count : integer; {Option count}
  c     : integer; {Loop counter}
begin
  {*** Display the menu string ***}
  writeln(m);
  {*** Count number of options by ***}
  {*** counting return characters in string ***}
  count:=0;
  for c:= 1 to Length(m) do
      if m[c]=#13 then
          Inc(count);
  DisplayMenu := count;
end;
```

**Continued on next page**

**LISTING-6.13**
(continued)

Viewing Typed Files

```
{*** Get option chosen by user ***}
function GetOption(max : integer):integer;
var
  opstr : string[3];    {Option as string}
  op    : integer;      {option as integer}
  err   : integer;      {Error flag for Val}
begin
  {*** Read option ***}
  write('Enter option : ');
  opstr := GetData(['0'..'9'],2);
  val(opstr, op,err);
  {*** WHILE invalid, re-read ***}
  while(op < 1) or (op > max) do
  begin
      write(#7'?:');
      opstr := GetData(['0'..'9'],2);
      val(opstr,op,err);
  end;
  GetOption := op;
end;


const
  typesize  : array[0..3] of integer = (1,2,1,4);
                          {Size of string/int/char/real}
var
  filename  : string[20];   {Name of file to be read}
  rec       : string[80];   {Storage space for one record}
  fieldinfo : array[0..10,0..1]of integer;
                          {Type and size of up to 10 fields}
  fieldptr  : array[0..10] of pointer;
                          {Ptrs to starting loc of each field}
  size      : integer;    {Actual size of a single record}
  refile    : file;       {File variable}
  option    : integer;    {Menu option chosen}
  recsize   : integer;    {Size of record}
  c         : integer;    {Loop counter}
  offset    : integer;    {Position of field within record}
  noofops   : integer;    {No. of options in menu}
  fields    : integer;    {Loop counter}
  err       : integer;    {Error flag for Val}
begin
  {*** Get the filename ***}
  ClrScr;
  write('Enter the name of the file to be opened : ');
  filename := GetData(['A'..'Z','a'..'z','.',':','\'],30);
  {*** Display possible field types ***}
  writeln('Enter the next field''s type');
  noofops := DisplayMenu('1 - String'#13#10'2 - int'#13#10
          '3 - char'#13#10'4 - real'#13#10'5 - QUIT'#13#10);
  {*** Get user's choice ***}
  option := GetOption(noofops);
  {*** WHILE not end of fields DO ***}
  fields := 0;
  while option <> 5 do
  begin
      {*** Record field type and size ***}
      fieldinfo[fields][0]:=option;
      fieldinfo[fields][1]:=typesize[option-1];
      {*** IF its a string THEN ***}
      if option = 1 then
      begin
          {*** Get its length ***}
          write('enter size of string : ');
          val(GetData(['0'..'9'],2),size,err);
          fieldinfo[fields][1]:= size + 1;
      end;
      {*** Get next field type ***}
      option:= GetOption(noofops);
```

**Continued on next page**

**LISTING-6.13**
(continued)

Viewing Typed Files

```
        Inc(fields);
    end;
    {*** Calculate record size ***}
    recsize := 0;
    for c := 0 to fields - 1 do
        recsize := recsize + fieldinfo[c][1];
    writeln('Record size = ',recsize);
    {*** Set pointers for each field ***}
    offset:=0;
    for c:=0 to fields - 1 do
    begin
        fieldptr[c] := @rec[offset];
        offset := offset + fieldinfo[c][1];
    end;
    {*** Open file ***}
    assign(refile,filename);
    reset(refile,recsize);
    {*** Read a record ***}
    while not Eof(refile) do
    begin
        BlockRead(refile,rec,1);
        {*** Interpret and display record's data ***}
        for c:=0 to fields - 1 do
            case fieldinfo[c,0] of
                1:  {*** Display string ***}
                    write(string(fieldptr[c]^),' ');
                2:  {*** Display int *** }
                    write(integer(fieldptr[c]^),' ');
                3:  {*** Display char ***}
                    write(char(fieldptr[c]^),' ');
                4:  {*** Display real ***}
                    write(real(fieldptr[c]^),' ');
            end;
    end;
    writeln;
    {*** Close file ***}
    close(refile);
end.
```

This program uses a few techniques that have not been explained previously.

We'll start by looking at an array declaration:

```
fieldptr   : array[0..10] of pointer;
```

The purpose of this array is to hold pointers to the start of each field in the record read from the file. The idea is depicted visually in FIG-6.6.

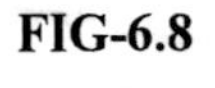

**FIG-6.8**

Referencing the Fields of a Record

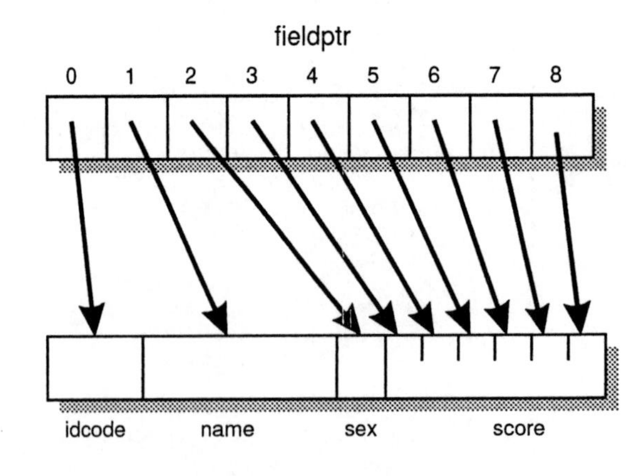

Notice, however, that the word `pointer` is used to define the array's type rather than a specific value such as `^char`. The term `pointer` is used when we want to define pointers but not the type of value they will reference. This is needed here since each of the pointers will reference different field types within the record.

Later, when we need to dereference these pointers, we must cast them to an appropriate type with statements such as:

```
write(integer(fieldptr[c]^),' ');
```

The next problem is, how do we define the file variable? Since we don't know in advance what type of records are in the file, we can't complete the `file of` term used in the file variable declaration. Luckily, Pascal allows us to define an untyped file, where we treat the contents of the file as blocks of bytes, the structure of those bytes being undefined. We create such a file variable with the statement:

```
refile : file;
```

To tell the program how many bytes are in each data block we use an extended form of the `reset` command:

```
reset(refile,recsize);
```

The second parameter of this command gives the number of bytes in a block.

Finally, we need a instruction to read from the file. In an untyped file, this is done using the `BlockRead` instruction:

```
BlockRead(refile,rec,1);
```

This specifies the file (*refile*), a variable to hold the data read (*rec*), and the number of blocks to be read (1).

**Activity 6.19**

Enter the program in LISTING-6.13 and test it using *student.dat*.

# SOLUTIONS

### Activity 6.1

No solution required.

### Activity 6.2

No solution required.

### Activity 6.3

No solution required.

### Activity 6.4

There should now be additional spaces within the file.

### Activity 6.5

Each data item of *report2.dat* should be on a separate line.

### Activity 6.6

All the data written to the file is read into the single variable, *name*.

### Activity 6.7

This time the name is read correctly.

### Activity 6.8

```
program Act08_01;
uses WinCrt;
const
    day : array[0..6] of string[9]=
        ('Sunday','Monday','Tuesday','Wednesday',
         'Thursday','Friday','Saturday');
var
    myfile   : text;    {Text file}
    c        : integer; {Loop counter}
    min, max : integer; {Daily min/max temps}
    average  : real;    {Average daily temp}
begin
    {*** Open file for writing ***}
    assign(myfile,'C:temp.dat');
    rewrite(myfile);
    {*** Get data and write to file ***}
    ClrScr;
    for c := 1 to 7 do
    begin
        write('Enter min : ');
        readln(min);
        write('enter max : ');
        readln(max);
        writeln(myfile,min,' ',max);
    end;
    {*** Re-open file for reading ***}
    close(myfile);
    reset(myfile);
    {*** Display results ***}
    writeln(' ':10,' Max  Min  Average');
    for c := 1 to 7 do
    begin
        readln(myfile,min,max);
        average := (min + max) / 2;
        write(day[c-1]:10);
        writeln(min:3,'  ',max:3,' ':4,average:4:1);
    end;
    {*** close file ***}
    close(myfile);
end.
```

### Activity 6.9

```
program Act09_01;
uses WinCrt, Printer;
const
    day : array[0..6] of string[9]=
    ('Sunday','Monday','Tuesday','Wednesday',
     'Thursday','Friday','Saturday');
var
    myfile   : text;    {Text file}
    c        : integer; {Loop counter}
    min, max : integer; {Daily min/max temps}
    average  : real;    {Average daily temp}
begin
    {*** Open file for reading ***}
    assign(myfile,'C:temp.dat');
    reset(myfile);
    {*** Display results ***}
    writeln(Lst,' ':10,' Max  Min');
    for c := 1 to 7 do
    begin
        readln(myfile,min,max);
        average := (min + max)/2;
        write(Lst,day[c-1]:10);
        writeln(Lst,min:3,'  ',max:3,'  ',
                                  average:0:1);
    end;
    {*** close file ***}
    close(myfile);
end.
```

### Activity 6.10

No solution required.

### Activity 6.11

No solution required.

### Activity 6.12

1.

```
program List12_01;
uses WinCrt;
type
    StudentDetails =
    record
        idcode : integer;
        name   : string[30];
        sex    : char;
        score  : array[1..6] of integer;
    end;
    KeySet = set of char;

{*** Get Data from Keyboard ***}
function GetData(allowed : KeySet;
                     max : integer):string;
const
    ENTER = #13;
    BACKSPACE = #8;
var
    ch     : char;      {char from keyboard}
    count  : integer;   {chars entered}
    result : string;    {Contains chars typed in}
begin
    {*** Check pre-conditions ***}
    if (allowed = []) or (max<=0) then
    begin
        GetData := '';
        exit;
    end;
    {*** Set result to empty & count to zero ***}
    result := '';
    count := 0;
    {*** Read a character ***}
    ch := ReadKey;
    {*** WHILE return key not pressed DO ***}
    while ch <> ENTER do
    begin
```

**Continued on next page**

```
        {*** IF allowed char & not full THEN ***}
        if (ch in allowed) AND (count < max)then
        begin
            {*** Display char & add to result ***}
            write(ch);
            result := result + ch;
            inc(count);
        end
        {*** ELSE if delete & result not empty ***}
        else if (ch=BACKSPACE) AND (count>0) then
        begin
            {*** Remove last char ***}
            write(#8,#32,#8);
            delete(result,length(result),1);
            dec(count);
        end;
        {*** Read another character ***}
        ch := readkey;
    end;
    writeln;
    GetData := result;
end;

var
    c      : integer;   {Loop counter}
    myfile : file of StudentDetails;
    myrec  : StudentDetails;
    err    : integer;        {Parameter for Val}
    temp   : string[1];      {Sex as string}
begin
    {*** Open the file ***}
    assign(myfile,'C:\students.dat');
    rewrite(myfile);
    {*** Read the student's idcode ***}
    ClrScr;
    write('Enter id code : ');
    Val(GetData(['0'..'9'],4),myrec.idcode,err);
    {*** WHILE idcode not zero DO ***}
    while myrec.idcode <> 0 do
    begin
        {*** Read remaining details ***}
        write('Enter name : ');
        myrec.name := GetData(['A'..'Z','a'..'z',
                          ' ','.','-'],30);
        write('Enter sex (M/F) : ');
        temp := GetData(['M','F'],1);
        myrec.sex := temp[1];
        for c := 1 to 6 do
        begin
            write('Enter score ',c,' : ');
            Val(GetData([')'..'9'],3),
                              myrec.score[c],err);
        end;
        {*** Write to file ***}
        write(myfile,myrec);
        ClrScr;
        {*** Read next idcode ***}
        write('Enter id code : ');
        Val(GetData(['0'..'9'],4),myrec.idcode,err);
    end;
    {*** Close file ***}
    close(myfile);
end.
```

2.

```
program List12_02;
uses WinCrt;

type
    StudentDetails =
    record
        idcode : integer;
        name   : string[30];
        sex    : char;
        score  : array[1..6] of integer;
    end;

var
    c       : integer;  {Loop counter}
    myfile  : file of StudentDetails;
    myrec   : StudentDetails;
    total   : integer;  {Total of student's scores}
    average : real;     {Student average}

begin
    {*** Open the file ***}
    assign(myfile,'C:\students.dat');
    reset(myfile);
    {*** WHILE not end of file DO ***}
    while not eof(myfile) do
    begin
        {*** Read a  record from file ***}
        read(myfile,myrec);
        {*** calculate average ***}
        total := 0;
        for c := 1 to 6 do
            total := total + myrec.score[c];
        average := total / 6;
        if average < 50 then
            {*** Display record's details ***}
            with myrec do
            begin
                write(idcode:5,name:20,sex:2);
                for c := 1 to 6 do
                    write(score[c]:4);
                writeln;
            end
    end;
    {*** Close file ***}
    close(myfile);
end.
```

## Activity 6.13

The program will terminate if an attempt to read from an invalid position is performed.

## Activity 6.14

No solution required.

## Activity 6.15

```
program Act15_01;
uses WinCrt;

type
    StudentDetails =
    record
        idcode  : integer;
        name    : string[30];
        sex     : char;
        score   : array[1..6] of integer;
    end;

var
    c : integer;    {Loop counter}
    myfile : file of StudentDetails;
    myrec : StudentDetails;
begin
    {*** Turn off I/O checking ***}
    {$I-}
    {*** Open the file ***}
    assign(myfile,'C:\students.dat');
    reset(myfile);
    if IOResult <> 0 then
    begin
        writeln('Error opening file ');
        halt;
    end;
    {*** Move to the end of the file ***}
    seek(myfile, FileSize(myfile));
    {*** Read the student's idcode ***}
    ClrScr;
    write('Enter id code : ');
    readln(myrec.idcode);
    {*** WHILE idcode not zero DO ***}
    while myrec.idcode <> 0 do
    begin
        {*** Read remaining details ***}
        write('Enter name : ');
        readln(myrec.name);
        write('Enter sex (M/F) : ');
        readln(myrec.sex);
        for c := 1 to 6 do
        begin
            write('Enter score ',c,' : ');
            readln(myrec.scores[c]);
        end;
        {*** Write to file ***}
        write(myfile,myrec);
        ClrScr;
        {*** Read next idcode ***}
        write('Enter id code : ');
        readln(myrec.idcode);
    end;
    {*** Close file ***}
    close(myfile);
end.
```

## Activity 6.16

```
program Act16_01;
uses WinCrt;

const
    QUIT = 5;
type
    StudentDetails =
    record
        idcode : integer;
        name   : string[30];
        sex    : char;
        score  : array[1..6] of integer;
    end;

    KeySet = set of char;

{*** Get Data from Keyboard ***}
function GetData(allowed : KeySet;
                        max : integer) :string;
const
    ENTER = #13;
    BACKSPACE = #8;
var
    ch     : char;           {char from keyboard}
    count  : integer;        {chars entered}
    result : string;         {Characters typed in}
begin
    {*** Check pre-conditions ***}
    if (allowed = []) or (max<=0) then
    begin
        GetData := '';
        exit;
    end;
    {*** Set result to empty and count to zero ***}
    result := '';
    count := 0;
    {*** Read a character ***}
    ch := ReadKey;
    {*** WHILE return key not pressed DO ***}
    while ch <> ENTER do
    begin
        {*** IF allowed & result not full THEN ***}
        if (ch in allowed) AND (count < max)then
        begin
            {*** Display char & add to result ***}
            write(ch);
            result := result + ch;
            inc(count);
        end
        {*** ELSE if delete & result not empty ***}
        else if (ch=BACKSPACE) AND (count>0) then
        begin
            {*** Remove last char ***}
            write(#8,#32,#8);
            delete(result,length(result),1);
            dec(count);
        end;
        {*** Read another character ***}
        ch := readkey;
    end;
    writeln;
    GetData := result;
end;


{*** Display menu options ***}
procedure DisplayMenu;
begin
    writeln('MENU':39);
    writeln('1 - Add a new record');
    writeln('2 - Display a specific record');
    writeln('3 - Display all records');
    writeln('4 - Modify a record');
    writeln('5 - QUIT\n');
    write('Enter option (1 to 5) : ');
end;


{*** Get menu option ***}
procedure GetOption(var opt : integer);
begin
    readln(opt);
    while(opt < 1)or(opt > QUIT) do
    begin
        writeln('Invalid option');
        writeln('Must be in the range 1 to ',QUIT);
        readln(opt);
    end
end;
```

```
{*** Execute option ***}
procedure ProcessOption(opt : integer);
var
    myfile : file of StudentDetails;
    strec  : StudentDetails;
    ch     : char;
    c      : integer;     {Loop counter}
    post   : integer;     {Position of record}
    err    : integer;     {Parameter for Val}
    temp   : string[1];   {String for sex}
    change : integer;     {Score to be changed}
begin
    assign(myfile,'c:\students.dat');
    case opt of
       1:  {add new record}
           begin
               {*** Read the student's idcode ***}
               write('Enter id code : ');
               Val(GetData(['0'..'9'],4),
                          strec.idcode,err);
               write('Enter name : ');
               strec.name := GetData(['A'..'Z',
                   'a'..'z',' ','.','-'],30);
               write('Enter sex (M/F) : ');
               temp := GetData(['M','F'],1);
               strec.sex := temp[1];
               for c := 1 to 6 do
               begin
                   write('Enter score ',c,' : ');
                   Val(GetData([')'..'9'],3),
                       strec.score[c],err);
               end;
               {*** Open file ***}
               reset(myfile);
               {*** Move to end of the file ***}
               seek(myfile, FileSize(myfile));
               {*** Write to file ***}
               write(myfile,strec);
               {$I+}
               {*** Close file ***}
               close(myfile);
           end;
     2:   {display specific record}
          begin
               reset(myfile);
               {$I-}
               write('Position req''d 1 to ',
                    FileSize(myfile),' : ');
               Val(GetData(['0'..'9'],2),post,err);
               Seek(myfile,post - 1);
               read(myfile,strec);
               if IOResult <> 0 then
                   writeln('Record not found')
               else
                   with strec do
                   begin
                       write(idcode:5,name:20,sex:2);
                       for c := 1 to 6 do
                           write(score[c]:3,' ');
                       writeln;
                   end;
               {$I+}
               close(myfile);
               {*** Press any key to continue ***}
               ch := ReadKey;
          end;
     3:   {Display all records}
          begin
               reset(myfile);
               while not Eof(myfile) do
               begin
                   read(myfile,strec);
                   with strec do
                   begin
                       write(idcode:5,name:20,sex:2);
                       for c := 1 to 6 do
                           write(score[c]:3,' ');
                       writeln;
                   end;
               end;
               close(myfile);
               {*** Press any key to continue ***}
               ch := ReadKey;
          end;
     4:   {Modify a record}
          begin
               {*** Find record ***}
               reset(myfile);
               {$I-}
               write('Position req''d 1 to ',
                    FileSize(myfile),' : ');
               Val(GetData(['0'..'9'],2),post,err);
               Seek(myfile,post - 1);
               read(myfile,strec);
               {*** and display it ***}
               if IOResult <> 0 then
```

**Continued on next page**

## Activity 6.16 (continued)

```
                    writeln('Record not found')
                else
                begin
                    with strec do
                    begin
                        write(idcode:5,name:20,sex:2);
                        for c := 1 to 6 do
                            write(score[c]:3,' ');
                        writeln;
                    end;

                    write('Which score (1 - 6 ) : ');
                    Val(GetData(['0'..'6'],1),
                            change,err);
                    write('Enter the new value : ');
                    Val(GetData([')'..'9'],3),
                        strec.score[change],err);
                    {*** move back in file **}
                    Seek(myfile, FilePos(myfile)-1);
                    {*** Update record ***}
                    write(myfile,strec);
                end;
                {$I+}
                close(myfile);
            end
    end
end;

var
    op : integer;
begin
    repeat
        DisplayMenu;
        GetOption(op);
        ProcessOption(op);
    until op = QUIT;
end.
```

## Activity 6.17

```
program List17_01;
uses WinCrt;

type
    StudentDetails =
    record
        idcode : integer;
        name   : string[30];
        sex    : char;
        score  : array[1..6] of integer;
    end;

var
    c      : integer;   {Loop counter}
    myfile : file of StudentDetails;
    myrec  : StudentDetails;

begin
    {*** Open the file ***}
    assign(myfile,'C:\students.dat');
    reset(myfile);
    {*** WHILE not end of file DO ***}
    while not eof(myfile) do
    begin
        {*** Read a  record from file ***}
        read(myfile,myrec);
        {*** Display record's details ***}
        with myrec do
        begin
            {*** IF rec not deleted, display it ***}
            if idcode <> -1 then
            begin
                write(idcode:5,name:20,sex:2);
                for c := 1 to 6 do
                    write(scores[c]:4);
                writeln;
            end
        end
    end;
    {*** Close file ***}
    close(myfile);
end.
```

## Activity 6.18

```
program Act18_01;
uses WinCrt;

type
    StudentDetails =
    record
        idcode  : integer;
        name    : string[30];
        sex     : char;
        score   : array[1..6] of integer;
    end;

var
    oldfile : file of StudentDetails;
                            {Existing file}
    newfile : file of StudentDetails;
                            {New copy of file}
    myrec   : StudentDetails;
    newname : string[30];
                            {Contains new name}

begin
    {*** Open the old file for reading ***}
    assign(oldfile,'C:\students.dat');
    reset(oldfile);
    {*** Open new file for writing ***}
    assign(newfile,'C:\student2.dat');
    rewrite(newfile);
    {*** WHILE number not end of old file  DO ***}
    while not Eof(oldfile) DO
    begin
        {*** Read a record from old file ***}
        read(oldfile, myrec);
        {*** IF it's not deleted, copy it ***}
        if myrec.idcode <> -1 then
            write(newfile,myrec);
    end;
    {*** Close files ***}
    close(oldfile);
    close(newfile);
    {*** Erase old file ***}
    Erase(oldfile);
    {*** Rename new file to that of old ***}
    Rename(newfile,'C:\students.dat');
end.
```

## Activity 6.19

No solution required.

CHAPTER 7

# A Software Project

## This chapter covers the following topics:

A Complete Software Project

Data Dictionary

Data Flow Diagrams

Functional Specification

Requirements Analysis

Reviewing the Development Life Cycle

Statement Of Requirements

Systems Specification

# CREATING A SOFTWARE SYSTEM

## Introduction

In this chapter we're going to bring together all of the knowledge we have acquired over the previous chapters to design, code, and test a complete software system. Along the way we'll come across new techniques often used in the earlier stages of the process.

Before we start on the system, it's worth having another look at the main stages involved in creating a new system. This is shown in FIG-7.1 shown below.

**FIG-7.1**

The Development Life Cycle

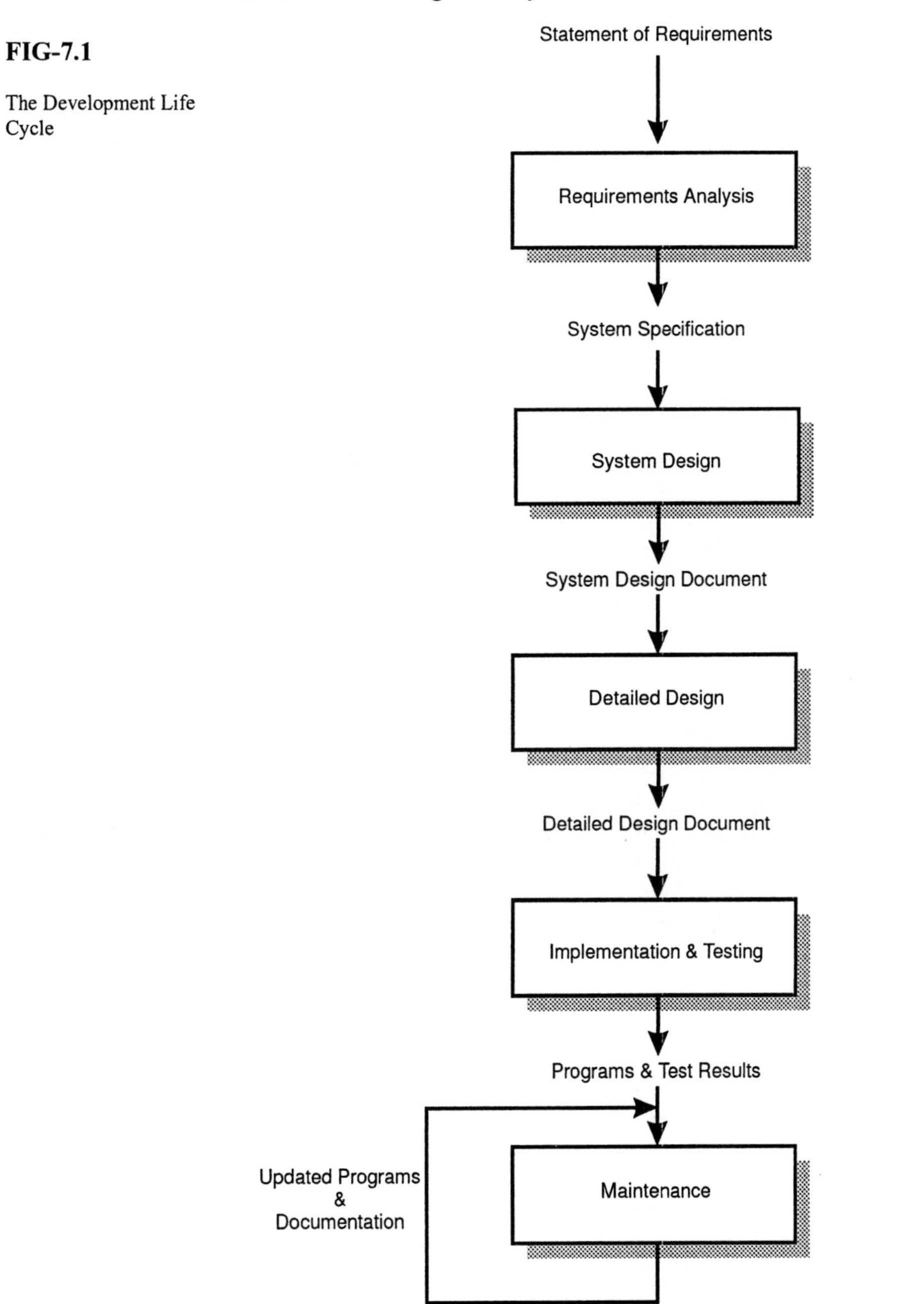

# A Statement of Requirements

As a software designer, your most likely starting point when creating a new system will be with a written request from a customer which outlines the system requirements. This document supplied is known as the **statement of requirements**.

The statement of requirements will be written in English, using terms and phrases from the customer's environment. For example, if the system is one involving stock control, the document is likely to include terms such as *minimum stock level, re-order level, cost price, selling price, lead time, etc.*

The length of the statement of requirements may be anything from a few pages to several volumes depending on the complexity of the system required.

The purpose of the statement of requirements is to detail what the proposed system is required to do. In addition, it also specifies any **constraints** to be placed upon the system or the development of the system. For example, a constraint might be : the system must execute on a machine with a 64Kbytes main memory, or the system must respond to any command within 1 second or the system must be completed within 2 years, etc.

The following is an extract from a statement of requirements.

> *When the LIST BOOKINGS command is entered, the system will prompt the user for the period to be listed. The user will then enter start and finish dates which represent the period for which bookings have to be listed. If any of the dates entered are more than one year from the present date or if the start date is after the finish date, then an error message will be issued and the user prompted to enter acceptable dates.*
>
> *The system should respond to the entry of valid dates by listing the names, addresses, type of room and period of booking for all transactions which fall wholly or partly within the period specified. If there have been no bookings for the period then a message to this effect should be displayed. All responses must be made within a maximum time of 3 seconds.*

Notice that the description contains information on what the system is to do (e.g.*the system is to produce an error message if an invalid date is entered).* These are the **functional requirements** of the system. Additionally, there is a limitation on the system (*that it must respond within 3 seconds*). This is a constraint or, as it is sometimes called, a **non-functional requirement**.

**Activity 7.1**

Examine the following extract from a statement of requirements.
List the functional requirements and constraints.

*A computer system is used to monitor the temperature of a house. Each room contains a temperature sensor, connected to the computer.*
*The system should monitor and display the temperatures of each room. If the temperature goes above 60°C in any room an alarm should be sounded.*
*For statistical purposes, the temperature of each room is to be recorded every hour on a 3.5inch floppy disk. The monitoring program must occupy no more than 10K of memory.*

# Requirement Analysis

From the statement of requirements the software engineer has to extract the functions and constraints of the system to be developed. This task is known as **requirements analysis**. Since some of the details contained in the statement of requirements usually require clarification, this stage will almost certainly entail further fact finding discussions with the customer. There may also be a need for the software engineer to gain an insight into the overall operation of any existing system which performs the same function as the new one.

Requirement analysis is the most difficult part of the development life cycle and the part most likely to introduce problems and errors.

## Why is Requirement Analysis Difficult?

There are several reasons :

1. Requirement analysis involves two groups: the customers and the designers. While one is an expert in software engineering techniques, probably with little knowledge of the application area, the other is an expert in the application with little knowledge of software system. Hence there is a **language gap** between the two parties.
2. The statement of requirements will almost certainly be a flawed document in several respects:
   a) Functional requirements and constraints will be intermingled. It is most unusual to find a statement of requirements which is structured neatly into functions and constraints.

   b) The statement of requirements will contain ambiguities. Since English will be used to describe the requirements it is almost inevitable that certain sections of the description will be open to differing interpretations.
   When the designer's interpretation differs from the customer's intended meaning serious problems are going to arise if this is not corrected at the earliest possible stage.
   **Example**
   *The screen is to display the name and price shares in quoted companies. If the price decreases then it will be shown in red; if it increases it will be shown in blue; otherwise the display is in white.*
   This could be interpreted as:
   i) the share's price is shown in red, blue or white
   ii) the full details of the company are to be in blue, red or white

   c) Design and implementation directives are included.
   A design directive is a statement about design decisions, which should normally not be considered at this early stage in the development.
   **Example**
   *The students' details are to be held in an array using the student's number as the key field.*

   An **implementation directive** gives instructions on certain aspects of the system which should normally be left until the implementation stage. For example, the programming language to be used may be specified.

Normally, such directives should be avoided. Since the customer is not an expert in software design he should not be imposing such restrictions. If such restrictions are included, the designer should attempt to have them removed from the statement of requirements. However, there are circumstances when such directives should be included - for example, where a new system has to interact with an existing system - in which case design and implementation decision made during the creation of the earlier system will inevitably impinge on the new one.

d) There will be omissions from the statement of requirements. For all but the smallest system it is extremely easy to leave out necessary details.

**Example**

*When the user types in a student identity number the system will display, either on the screen or a printer, the name of each unit which the student has entered and passed.*

**Activity 7.2**

What are the two omissions in the example above?

e) The amount of detail given may vary from function to function. For example, a stock control system may contain the statement :

*The system should record all units passed by students*

along with statements such as

*The PRINT-PASSES command should display on a VDU the code for each unit a given student has achieved. The unit numbers should be in ascending order*

The first statement is quite superficial; the second more specific.

# The System Specification Document

The purpose of requirement analysis is to produce the **system specification document**. This describes, in a full and unambiguous way, the functions and constraints of the system. The document will be produced by the designer from a combination of information gleaned from the statement of requirements and from follow-up interviews with the customer. It may be necessary to conduct several interviews before a full system specification is produced.

The guiding principle in producing a system specification is that the flaws and omissions of the statement of requirements should be corrected.

For a commercial product, the developer will include some additional details in the system specification. These are likely to include:

- A description of any training to be offered by the developer to the customer.
- The support to be offered by the developer. For example, what support will be offered in correcting errors which come to light after the customer has accepted the system.
- Details of acceptance testing — that is, those tests which are to be carried out on the system by the customer and the developer before the system is accepted.

A system specification for a small project consists of four main sub-sections:

1. A **Data Flow Diagram** (DFD) showing how data flows through the system and is changed by the system. This gives an overview of the operations and data involved in the system.

2. A description of the main items of data used or created by the system (this can be determined from the DFD). This is called the **Data Dictionary**.

3. A description of the operations or functions the system is to perform. This is called the **Functional Specification**. The first version of this can be derived from the customer's statement of requirements, subsequent interviews and the DFD.

4. The other section of the system specification is the constraints or Non-Functional Specifications. These details come from the statement of requirements and interviews.

## Data Flow Diagrams

In order to achieve an overall picture of a large and complex system, software engineers often employ a Data Flow Diagram (DFD) to act as a road-map for the data and actions that are used within a system. This is a graphical method of showing how data is created and transformed within a system. FIG-7.2 illustrates how the task of making a cup of tea might be shown using a DFD.

**FIG-7.2**

Making Tea

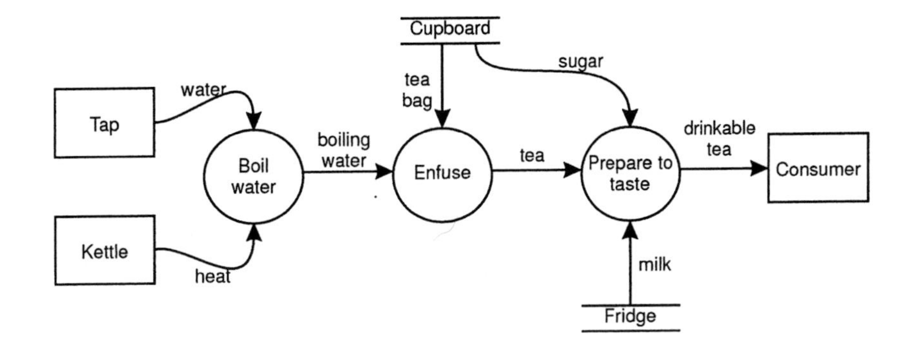


**This simple example shows the main features of DFDs:**

The rectangle represents people or things outside the system being designed. These either supply items (water or heat in the above example) or receive the product of the system (drinkable tea). The supplier is known as a **source**; the receiver as a **sink**. Collectively these are termed **external entities**.

boiling water

The solid lines represent the physical material or data being passed through the system. The arrows show the direction of flow. The line is labelled with the name of the item involved.

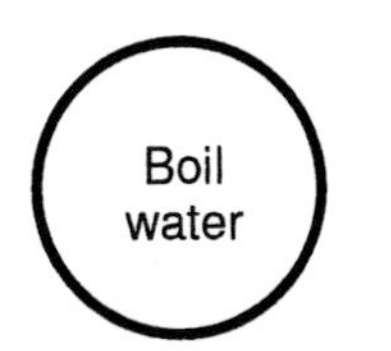


Circles represent a **process** (sometimes called a **transform**). A process transforms the item(s) arriving at it into the item(s) leaving (so water and heat arrive at the *Boil water* process and *boiling water* is produced by the process). Processes are described using a verb. Values passed into a process are called **input flows** while those leaving are called **output flows**.

Cupboard

The parallel lines represent a **store**. A store indicates items which are held by the system for later use. In this case, the *tea bags, sugar* and *milk* will have been placed in the stores by some earlier activity (shopping).

From the DFD we can determine that water and heat are used to create boiling water, which is then used in conjuction with a tea bag extracted from the cupboard to make tea; this tea is then adjusted to taste by adding milk and sugar as required to produce the final, drinkable tea which is passed to the consumer.

**Two points to note:**

1. The physical transfer of unchanged items within the system are not shown. For example, we do not show the transfer of the boiling water from kettle to tea pot.

2. No indication is given of items which may in the end not be used. For example, in creating drinkable tea we may decide not to add milk and sugar, nevertheless, because there is a possibility that they will be used, they need to be included in the diagram.

**Activity 7.3**

Create a DFD for washing clothes. This should involve *washing, spin drying, final drying* and *ironing*. Items should include *water, heat, powder* and *steam.*

Of course, any system being created to run on a computer will involve the processing of data and so the corresponding DFDs show data items on their flow lines. The DFD in FIG-7.3 shows the stages involved in using a cash dispenser.

**FIG-7.3**

DFD for a Simplified ATM System

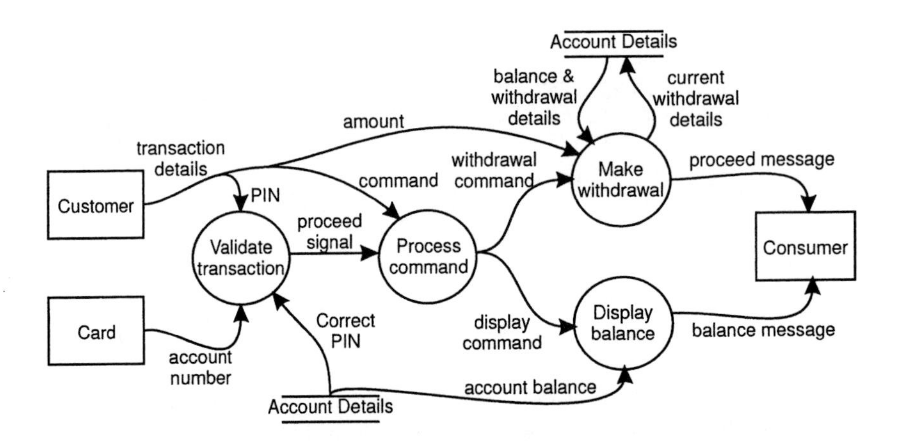


This example introduces some new concepts:

The line labelled *transaction* details splits into three parts. These, *command, PIN* and *amount* represent the component parts of *transaction*.

The store, *Account Details,* occurs in two places within the diagram. This repetition is simply to eliminate crossed lines in the DFD.

Information is read from the *Account Details* store; getting the current balance and details of previous withdrawals that day (to make sure the daily limit is not passed).

But data is also written to this store, updating the balance and withdrawal details after the withdrawal has been allowed.

It is not the purpose of this text to give a full and complete description of DFDs. However, the short description given above should give you the basic grounding necessary to make sense of a Data Flow Diagram.

## Data Dictionary

The data dictionary holds a formal definition of all the data items used by a system. Each item may be accompanied by a description of what it represents; how it is calculated and any constraints placed on the range of values it may take. These items of data will be identified from the system's DFD and the Statement of Requirements received from the customer.

Where a data item is exactly one character long, such as could be the case with an item, sex, designed to hold the sex of a person by storing an 'M' or 'F', then this would be represented as:

```
sex = 'M'|'F'
```

The vertical line ( | ) represents the term OR. Hence, we may read the above definition as:

*The data item called* sex *can be given the value 'M' or 'F'.*

If we intended to store the full word within sex it would be defined as:

```
sex = 'Male'|'Female'
```

> **Activity 7.4**
>
> Write a data dictionary entry for a data item called *Title* that is to contain one of the following possibilities: *Mr, Mrs, Miss, Ms, Dr, Rev, Prof.*

Of course, often a data item will not be assigned such specific values. For example, the PIN number used in the ATM is exactly 4 numeric digits in length but these could be any four digits. Since it isn't very practical to write

```
PIN = '0001'|'0002'|'0003'| etc.
```

we need a briefer approach.

To do this we start by defining the range of values allowed for any one digit within the PIN. This could be written as

Notice that numeric values do not have to appear within quotes.

```
0|1|2|3|4|5|6|7|8|9
```

but can be more briefly given as

```
0|..|9
```

with the intervening digits between 0 and 9 implied by the .. symbol.

Next we have to state that a PIN value is made up of exactly four such digits. This is written as:

```
4(0|..|9)4
```

The first 4 represents the minium number of digits that must appear in a valid PIN value; the last 4 represents the maximum number of digits that may appear. Since a PIN value must be exactly four digits, both the minimum and maximum digits allowed are set to four. Hence, the final definition is:

```
PIN = 4(0|..|9)4
```

This tells us that a PIN value must consist of exactly four characters and that each character must be numeric.

If *Surname* was an item of data within a system, we might define it as:

```
Surname = 1('A'|..|'Z')12
```

**Activity 7.5**

Assuming the above definition of *Surname,* which of the following are invalid values for *Surname?*

*X*
*ABC*
*Smith*
*O'DONNELL*
*BELLERTHORPES*
*Smythe-Brown*

As you can see, our definitions have to be carefully considered. To allow all of the above surnames, our new definition would be:

```
Surname =1('A'|..|'Z'|'a'|..|'z'|'-'|''')14
```

These definitions are often referred to as a data item's **picture.**

When defining the picture for a money item such as *Account Balance* we need an extra feature to descibe the pounds, decimal point and pence structure of such an item. To describe the pounds part we only have to decide on the maximum digits. We'll settle on 9 - that allows hundreds of millions! Therefore the pounds component can be given the picture:

```
1(0|..|9)9
```

The decimal point can only be one specific character, so we get a picture of:

```
'.'
```

The pence, which must be exactly two digits, can be defined as:

```
2{0|..|9)2
```

Finally, to describe *Account Balance,* we need to put all three parts together:

```
Account Balance = 1(0|..|9)9 + '.' + 2(0|.|9)2
```

The plus sign ( + ) signifies the joining of the component parts.

> **Activity 7.6**
>
> Write a data dictionary definition for *Post Code*. Assume a post code consists of a single letter followed by two numeric digits, a space, one numeric digit and two letters (letters are always in uppercase).

The picture used for *Account Balance* could be used for any other data item that involves money. However, it's a bit of a chore to have to rewrite such a complex picture several times. An alternative is to define a data type (rather than a data item) and then define items to be of that type. For example, we could create the definition

```
MoneyType       =    1{0|..|9}9+'.'+2{0|..|9}2
```

and then define *Account Balance* as

```
Account Balance = MoneyType
```

> **Activity 7.7**
>
> Write a type definition called *NumericDigit* which allows a single numeric digit and then rewrite *MoneyType* using *NumericDigit* where appropriate.

Some data items are equivalent to a record structure containing several distinct, but related data fields. For example, we can see from FIG-7.3 that *Transaction Details* consists of *PIN*, *command* and *amount*. A data item which is constructed from several other, separate data items is called a **composite data structure**. *Transaction Details* would therefore be defined in the data dictionary as:

```
Transaction Details = PIN + command + amount
```

Each of the items that made up the definition of *Transaction Details* would then be defined separately:

```
PIN          = 4(0|..|9)4
command      = withdrawal|display
amount       = MoneyType
```

Notice that *command* is shown as *withdrawal* or *display*, but these terms are not within quotes. Quotes would imply that the actual words *withdrawal* or *display* had to be entered, whereas the reality is that a single button representing one of these commands will be pressed, hence we show the values in a method similar to those within user-defined enumerated type.

From the DFD for the ATM we can identify the following data items:

Account Balance
Account Number
Amount
Balance & Withdrawal Details
Balance Message
Command
Correct PIN
Current Withdrawal Details
Display Command
PIN
Proceed signal
Proceed Message
Withdrawal Command

Each of these items must be defined in terms of the type of values it may contain and the maximum number of characters in that value.

Some data items may be left empty. For example, if a form contained a box labelled *Maiden Name*, no details would be entered by males or single females. We define such a field with a minimum of zero characters:

```
Maiden Name =  0{'A'|..|'Z'|'a'|..|'z'|'-'|'''}20
```

As was stated earlier, the Data Dictionary may contain additional, descriptive information. For each data item there will be an English description of what that data item represents.

**Example**

| | | |
|---|---|---|
| Month | = | 1{DigitType}2 |
| Description | : | Represents the month of the year (as a numeric value). |

Sometimes the definition of the data item is not restrictive enough. For example, using *Month* as defined above, that data item could contain values such as 0, 00, or 99 since these all fall within the scope of the definition. Obviously, these are not intended to be valid values for this data item.

What is required is to impose further restrictions on the possible values that *Month* can assume. This is achieved by adding a constraint.

**Example 1**

| | | |
|---|---|---|
| Month | = | 1{DigitType}2 |
| Description | : | Represents the month of the year (as a numeric value). |
| Constraint | : | Month must lie between 1 and 12 inclusive. |

**Example 2**

| | | |
|---|---|---|
| Hours Worked | = | 1{Digit}3 + '.' + Digit |
| Description | : | Gives the number of hours worked this week to the nearest 1/10th of an hour. |
| Constraint | : | The value given cannot be greater than 100.0. |

Remember, constraints are only required where the original definition of the data item is not restrictive enough.

Many of the data items supplied to a computerised system are entered via the computer keyboard, but others are calculated by the computer itself. For example, where a system produces details of wages due, the *number of hours worked* and the *rate of pay per hour* may be entered manually but the *gross wage* due to the employee will be calculated by the computer.

Where a data item's value is to be calculated by the computer, the data dictionary will contain a description of how its value is derived. This is defined as the formula for the data item. For example;

Gross Pay = 1{Digit}4 + '.' + 2{Digit}2
Description : Gives the gross pay of the employee for the week.
Formula : *HoursWorked x PayRate*

A guideline to follow when creating an entry in the data dictionary is that items which are to be input will contain a definition, description and possibly a constraint (if the definition has to be qualified). Values which are calculated will contain a definition, description and formula.

## Functional Specifications

The functional specification should specify WHAT the system should do. It should NOT define HOW the system is to go about achieving these objectives.

As the project progresses, more and more detail of what the system is to do in any given set of circumstances must be written down. Decisions about the correct actions to be carried out are based on the information in the system specification. So it is important to include all the details that will be necessary to answer any questions which may arise at later stages in the project.

To aid readability the functional specification should be partitioned. This allows the material to be read a section at a time. For example:

**Section 5 Hotel Invoice calculation**

The system should calculate the basic cost of a room for the period and produce an addressed invoice.

5.1 The PRINTINVOICE option. The number of days is calculated as the number of days between the arrival date and the leaving date + 1. Single rooms cost £20 per day and doubles £35 per adult. Children are charged at £12 per day irrespective of the room type. Any discount is then subtracted before VAT is calculated.

5.2 The DISCOUNT option. This allows an amount to be entered for a given customer which will be subtracted from the cost of the room.

5.3 The CANCELLATION option. This produces a letter acknowledging cancellation of a booking. It includes details of a cancellation charge. The charge is 10% if cancelled at least 8 weeks before the arrival date and 50% if 4 weeks or less before arrival.

**Section 6 Statistical Analysis**

The system should give statistical information on bookings and costs.

6.1 The BOOKINGS option. This produces a calendar for the current year showing, for each room, the days on which it is booked.

6.2 The ACCOUNTS option. This produces the total income and expenditures for each month of the current year.

Splitting the specification up in this fashion not only aids readability but it also eases the later task of design.

The functional specification should also include details of error conditions which may arise and how they are to be dealt with. For example:

| |
|---|
| 8.1 The number of items in stock will be reduced by the number ordered by the customer. If this results in the *items in stock* figure falling below zero an error message will be issued; the number ordered will be adjusted to match the number in stock before the order, and the number in stock set to zero. |

The functional specification should also be understandable by the customer. Therefore it is important that the specification is written in terms that the customer can understand, since he will need to read and approve its contents.

## Non-Functional Specifications

Non-functional specifications include information on:

**The Hardware Requirements**
This gives details of the hardware required by the new system. For example, *a PC-compatible with 64Mbytes of main memory; 10Gbytes of backing storage and a250Mbyte ZIP drive is to be used to run the system.*

**The Performance Characteristics**
This might include details of the maximum response time for an enquiry or the maximum number of records with which the system must be able to cope.

**Security Issues**
This includes details of how information is to be protected from unauthorised access and accidental/malicious corruption. Recovery procedures from error situations will also be specified.

**Resource and Management Issues**
This will detail such items as cost, time, personnel and hardware requirements to construct the system.

## Other Parts of the System Specification

As mentioned earlier, the system specification can include details of training, support and acceptance tests for the new system. The first two of these will not concern us here. However, it is important to consider, from the start, what testing should be carried out by the customer before the system is acceptable. For any system the testing required will be considerable and in a large commercial system will occupy several volumes.

What follows is a small sample of the type of detail included in such a document.

Assuming we have already defined the functional requirements of a stock control system as:

***1. Increasing stock***

*1.1 The NEW command. This allows details of a previously unstocked item to be added to the information held. The user will enter a stock number, stock description, number in stock and cost per item for the new item. If the stock number entered is already used for some other item an error message will be produced. The number in stock and cost per item must both be greater than zero, otherwise an error message is produced.*

*1.2 The ADD command. This allows the stock level of an existing stock item to be increased. The user will enter the stock code and the number of items to be added. The amount entered will be added to the corresponding stock level. If the stock number does not match an existing item, an error message will be displayed.*

***2. Decreasing Stock***

*2.1 The REMOVE command. The user will enter the stock number and the number of items to be removed. The corresponding record's stock level will be reduced by the specified amount. If the stock number does not match any existing stock record, an error message will be displayed. If the amount of stock to be taken is greater than the number in stock, an error message is given.*

then the test document would contain details such as:

**The NEW Command**

Test 1
When a stock number is entered which is not already recorded, the user may go on to enter the remainder of the information for the new entry.

Test 2
When an existing stock number is entered, an error message is displayed and the user may enter another stock number.

Test 3
When the cost per item is entered, any value greater than zero is accepted.

Test 4
When the number in stock is entered as zero or less, an error message is delivered.

Test 5
When the cost per item is entered as zero or less, an error message is issued.

Test 6
When a valid stock number, stock description, number in stock and cost per item is entered, this information is correctly added to the existing stock records.

**The ADD command**

Test 1
When a valid stock number and quantity are entered, the appropriate record is correctly updated.

Test 2
When a stock number which does not already exist is entered, an error message is issued.

Test 3
When the quantity to be added is zero or less, an error message is issued.

**The REMOVE command**

Test 1
When a valid stock number is entered and the quantity to be removed is less than or equal to the quantity in stock, the appropriate record is correctly updated.

Test 2
When a stock number which does not already exist is entered, an error message is issued.

Test 3
When the quantity to be removed, which is entered by the user, is greater than the quantity in stock, an error message is issued.

More general tests may be specified. For example, the system may be required to produce the same results as an existing manual system when fed with data for a specified period; there may be a requirement for the system to deal correctly with large volumes of data (many problems concerning insufficient storage space may show up in this test).

Once the customer has satisfied himself that the specification reflects the system he requires and that the testing to be performed is acceptable, the document is formally **signed off** by the customer. Normally, no changes can be made from this point without the customer agreeing to additional costs being incurred.

# Summary

To produce a system specification for a simple system, use the following steps:

- From the statement of requirements and any additional information obtained, create a Data Flow Diagram (DFD).

- Using the DFD, create a Data Dictionary.
  - The entries should be kept in alphabetical order.
  - The names given in the Data Dictionary must match those of the DFD (although the Data Dictionary may contain additional entries).
  - Each entry represents a data item or data type.
  - A data item may be of a simple or composite structure.
  - Items within a composite structure must, themselves, be defined.

- Create a functional specification.
  - This should be in sections.
  - As a rule-of-thumb, create one section for each transform in the DFD.
  - Create an additional section to deal with any inputs required by the system.

- Use information in the statement of requirements to create the non-functional specifications.

- Define the tests required for acceptance testing.

# STUDENT RECORD SYSTEM

## Introduction

In the remainder of this chapter we're going to put everything that has gone before - design and programming - into practice. What follows is the complete documentation for a small system for maintaining a file of student records.

## Background Information

A private educational institute wishes to maintain a set of computerised student records. The institute already owns an old PC-compatible machine with laser printer and this is the hardware on which the new software is to be run.

## Statement Of Requirements

The institute has supplied the following statement of requirements:

*The institute maintains records of all current students. The maximum number of students at any one time is around 50. Each student is allocated a unique idcode. In addition, the name and sex of each student is recorded. During their stay at the institute, students sit a total of 6 exams. These exams are averaged out and students graduate based on this average. Students with an average of 0 to 45 fail; an average of 50 to 100 gains a pass. Those with a score of 46 to 49 may appeal and will, after due consideration, be graded as a pass or fail.*

*The computer system is required to allow the maintenance of these records. The following operations will be required:*

- *Adding new records.*
- *Deleting existing records.*
- *Modifying record details. Only the name and marks will be modified.*
- *Adding the results of a specific exam to all the students.*

*Also, the following reports are required:*

- *A listing of all students currently in the institute.*
- *Details of one specific record.*
- *A listing of all students of a specific sex.*
- *Listings of students' results: one for each category, pass, fail and appeal.*

While reading the statement of requirements (possibly several times) the software designer will create a list of questions to ask the customer. These questions are used to clear up any points arising from the inadequacy of the statement of requirements and/or the designer's lack of knowledge in the application area.

Having read the above statement of requirements the designer arranges an interview with the institute's owner. Part of a possible interview is given below:

*When a new student's details are added, will all the details be available?*

Obviously we'll have their personal details and the idcode is taken from a list held by the secretary, but the student won't have sat any exams at that point.

*Is that always the case?*

Well, I suppose it is possible that a student that dropped out could return, in which case, any results achieved previously would still hold. In fact, I think that did happen once.

*Do the students have to sit all six exams before they can be graded?*

Yes.

*No exceptions?*

None.

*How are exams scored? Marks out of 100? Grade A, B or C? Or what?*

Exams are always scored from 0 to 100.

*Do all students sit a particular exam at the same time?*

Yes.

*So, you'll want to enter the results of a particular exam all at one go?*

Yes. Well, except if anyone's off ill. They'll sit the exam later.

*So you need to miss out some of the marks when they're entered, and fill those ones in later?*

Yes.

The information gained from questioning the customer would, of course, be recorded as the interview progressed. With the aid of this additional information and the original statement of requirements, the designer will then produce the system specification.

If the need arises, the designer will question the customer further while producing the system specification.

The designer must never make decisions at this stage without consultation with the customer. It is still an all too common fault for companies to produce software which does not meet the customer's requirements.

# System Specification

## Overview

The system is to record details of students within the institute. Details can be modified later. Reports are required based on these details.

## Data Flow Diagram

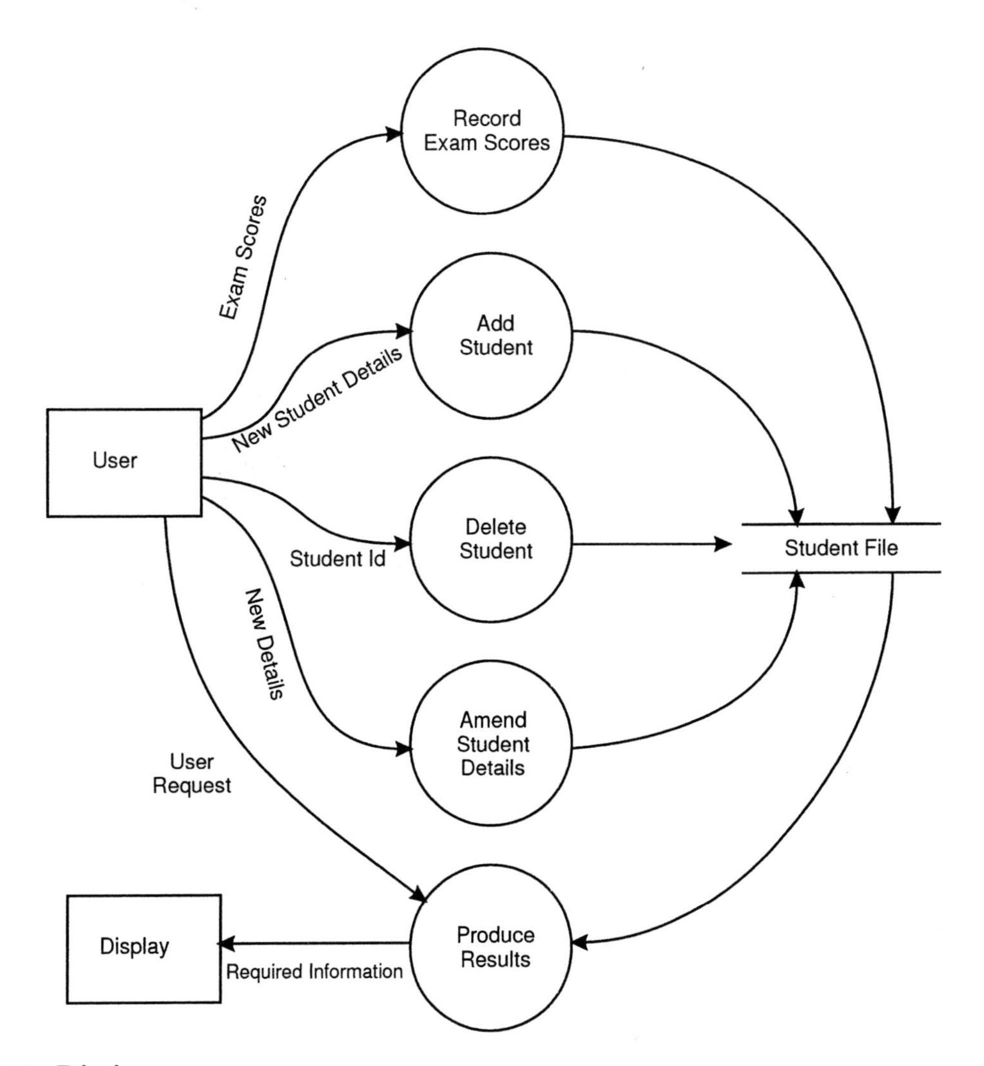


## Data Dictionary

From the DFD, and taking into account the requirements of the system, the designer can produce the Data Dictionary in which the data items are defined.

In producing a Data Dictionary, the designer will probably start by defining the structure and contents of any composite data items. For example:

**StudentDetailsType** = **Idcode + Name + Sex + Score**
Description: Details of a single student.

He will then continue by defining the component parts of the item. In the above case, all the items in the composite structure.

**Idcode** = **1{0|..|9}5**
Description: Student's identification code. Each student is given a unique value.

**Name** = **1{'A'|..|'Z','a'|..|'z'|'.'|'-'|'∇'|'''}30**
Description: Student's name.

| | | |
|---|---|---|
| **Sex** | = | **1{'M'\|'F'}1** |
| Description | | Student's sex. |
| **Score** | = | **5{ScoreType}5** |
| Description | | Student's scores for exactly 5 exams. |
| **ScoreType** | = | **-1\|..\|100** |
| Description | | Student's score type. |
| Constraint | | Most have a value in the range 0 to 100. |
| **Student File** | = | **0{StudentDetailsType}100** |
| Description | | Holds the details of every student. |
| **ExamScores** | = | **1{ScoreType}100** |
| Description | | Set of exam scores for every student. |
| **New Student Details** | = | **1{StudentdetailsType}1** |
| Description | | Details of a new student to be added to the file. |
| **Student Id** | = | **1{0\|..\|9}5** |
| Description | | Idcode of student whose record is to be deleted. |
| **New Details** | = | **UpdatedId + (NewName \| (ScoreNo + NewScore))** |
| Description | | Details required to change the name or score of a specified student. |
| **UpdatedId** | = | **1{0\|..\|9}5** |
| Description | | Idcode of student whose details are to be changed. |
| **NewName** | = | **1{'A'\|..\|'Z','a'\|..\|'z'\|'.'\|'-'\|'∇'\|'''}30** |
| Description | | New name to be given to existing student. |
| **ScoreNo** | = | **1{1\|..\|5}1** |
| Description | | Number of exam to be modified. |
| **NewScore** | = | **ScoreType** |
| Description | | Replacement score. |
| **User Request** | = | **1\|..\|7** |
| Description | | Indicates which item of required information the user wants. |
| **Required Information** | = | **StudentList\|SingleStudent\|Passed\|Failed\|Appeal\|AllMales\|AllFemales** |
| Description | | Various report details available to the user. |
| **StudentList** | = | **0{StudentDetailsType}100** |
| Description | | List of all information held in Student File. |
| **SingleStudent** | = | **StudentDetailsType** |
| Description | | Details of a single, specified student. |
| **Passed** | = | **0{Idcode + Name}100** |
| Description | | Idcode and name of every student who has passed the exams. |

**Failed** = **0{Idcode + Name}100**
Description: Idcode and name of every student who has failed the exams.

**Appeal** = **0{Idcode + Name}100**
Description: Idcode and name of every student who can appeal the exam's result.

**AllMales** = **0{StudentDetailsType}100**
Description: List of all male students.

**AllFemale** = **0{StudentDetailsType}100**
Description: List of all female students.

Once all the data items have been defined, the contents of the data dictionary can be re-arranged into alphabetical order. This will aid easy referencing at later stages in the project.

## FUNCTIONAL SPECIFICATIONS

We can use the DFD to help section the Functional Specification: one section for each of the transforms.

### General

The system will allow updating of a students' file and create various reports from the information held within that file.

### 1 Adding a Student

1.1 *Entering the student's idcode.* A prompt will be given to enter the student's idcode. If no idcode is entered, an error message will be displayed and the user made to enter a non-blank idcode.

1.2 *Entering the student's name.* A prompt will be given to enter the student's name. If no name is entered, an error message will be displayed and the user made to enter a non-blank name.

1.3 *Entering the student's sex.* A prompt will be given to enter the student's sex. If any value other than 'M' or 'F' is entered, an error message will be displayed and the user made to enter a valid value.

1.4 *Entering the student's scores.* A prompt will be given to enter each of the student's scores If the value entered is outside the range -1 to 100, then an error message will be displayed and the user made to re-enter the value. The value -1 is used when no score is available.

1.5 *Updating the file.* If the idcode given matches an existing record an error message will be displayed and the operation abandoned. If the idcode does not match an existing record, the new record is added to the end of the existing data.

### 2 Recording Exam Scores

2.1 *Entering the exam number.* A prompt will be given to enter the exam number. If the value entered is outside the range 1 to 5, then an error message will be displayed and the user made to re-enter the value.

2.2 *Entering the Exam Score.* For each student held in the Student File whose mark for the specified exam has not yet been entered, a prompt will be given to enter the exam mark. If the value entered is outside the range -1 to 100, then an error message will be displayed and the user made to re-enter the value. The value -1 is used when no score is available. Each mark entered will be recorded within the corresponding student's record.

**3 Deleting a Students Details**

3.1 *Entering the idcode of the student to be deleted.* A prompt will be given to enter the idcode of the student to be deleted. If no idcode is entered, an error message will be displayed and the user made to enter a non-blank idcode.

3.2 *Deleting the record.* If the idcode given matches an existing one, the record of the specified student will be removed from the file. If there is no match, an error message will be given and the operation abandoned.

**4 Amending a Student's Details**

4.1 *Specifying which amendment.* A prompt will be given to enter the type of modification to be made. Either the name or a score can be changed. If the option chosen is not valid, an error message will be given and the user made to enter a valid choice.

4.2 *Entering the idcode of the student to be modified.* A prompt will be given to enter the idcode of the student to be modified. If no idcode is entered, an error message will be displayed and the user made to enter a non-blank idcode.

4.3 *Displaying the existing record.* If the idcode given matches an existing record, that record will be displayed; otherwise an error message will be displayed and the operation abandoned.

4.4 *Changing the student's name.* A prompt will be given to enter the student's name. If no name is entered, an error message will be displayed and the user made to enter a non-blank name.

The record will be updated to contain the new name.

4.5 *Changing a student's mark.* A prompt will be given to enter the exam number. If the value entered is outside the range 1 to 5, then an error message will be displayed and the user made to re-enter the value.

A prompt will be given to enter the student's score for the specified exam If the value entered is outside the range -1 to 100, then an error message will be displayed and the user made to re-enter the value. The value -1 is used when no score is available.

The specified record will be updated to contain the new score.

**5 Producing Results**

5.1 *Selecting the required report.* A prompt will be given to enter the type of report to be displayed. These are selected from full listing, specific record, students passing, students failing, students appealing, all females, all males.

5.2 *Full listing.* This lists the complete contents of the file.

5.3 *Specific record.* A prompt will be given to enter the idcode of the record to be displayed. If a match is found within the student file then the details of that record are displayed. If no match is found, then an error message will be displayed and the operation abandoned.

5.4 *Students passing.* A list of the idcode and name of every student who has gained a pass is displayed. A student passes if the average of the 5 exam marks is 50 or over.

5.5. *Students failing.* A list of the idcode and name of every student who has failed is displayed. A student fails if the average of the 5 exam marks is less than 46.

5.6. *Students appealing.* A list of the idcode and name of every student who can appeal their result is displayed. A student can appeal if the average of the 5 exam marks is between 46 and 49.

5.7. *Male students* . A list of the full details of every male student is displayed.

5.8. *Female students* . A list of the full details of every female student is displayed.

**NON-FUNCTIONAL SPECIFICATIONS**

**Hardware**

The system must run on a PC-compatible. Output will be to a laser printer.

**Performance Characteristics**

Response from the system should appear to be instantaneous to the user.

**Security**

Since no information is held permanently on the system, no security is necessary.

**Resource and Management**

The system is to be completed for delivery within 8 weeks of the date of acceptance by the customer. The cost will be £1000.00.

Note that the system specification includes details of what constitutes an error condition and what action is to be carried out when an error condition occurs. These actions should be agreed with the customer who requested the software.

The system specification will be validated by comparing it with the statement of requirements and the answers given at the interview to ensure that there are no errors or omissions.

This case study will be used throughout this package to illustrate the points raised in each chapter. By the time you have completed the teaching package you will have followed the invoicing through from a statement of requirements to a completed system.

## Structure Diagram

Routines from other units are not shown.

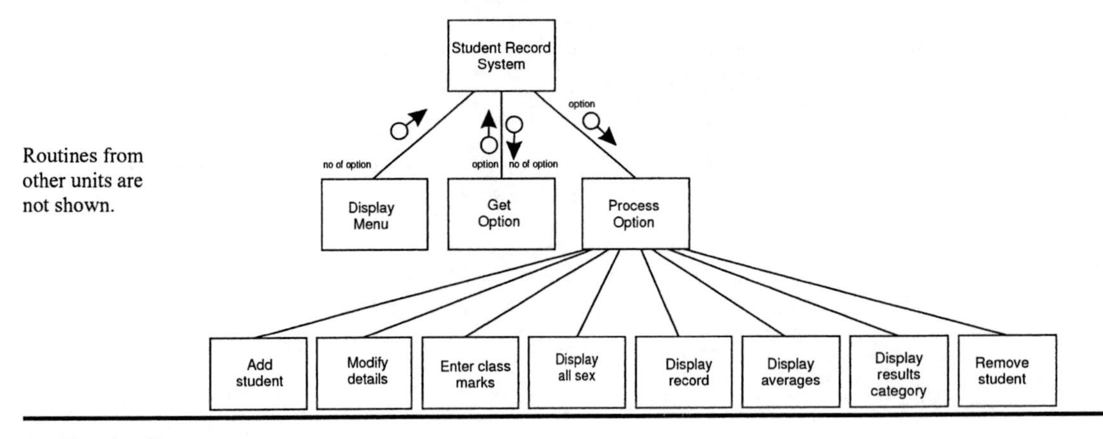


# Mini-Specs

## Routines in Auxiliary Unit

| | | |
|---|---|---|
| **NAME** | : | GetData |
| **PARAMETERS** | | |
| **IN** | : | allowed : KeySet<br>max : integer |
| **OUT** | : | None |
| **IN/OUT** | : | result : string |
| **PRE-CONDITION** | : | None |
| **DESCRIPTION** | : | Accepts and displays up to *max* characters. Each character must come from the set *allowed.* Backspace can be used to delete the last character accepted. Input is terminated when the enter key is pressed. Invalid and surplus characters are ignored.<br>*result* returns a string of all characters accepted and in the same order.<br>The enter key is not part of the returned string. |
| **OUTLINE LOGIC** | : | see below |

```
Empty result
Set count to zero
Read a charcater
WHILE character not ENTER DO
    IF
        allowed and not full :
            Display character
            Increment count
        backspace and not empty:
            Delete char from screen
            Delete char from result
            Decrement count
    ENDIF
    Read a character
ENDWHILE
Move cursor to new line
```

| | | |
|---|---|---|
| **NAME** | : | DisplayMenu |
| **PARAMETERS** | | |
| **IN** | : | m : string |
| **OUT** | : | result : integer |
| **IN/OUT** | : | None |
| **PRE-CONDITION** | : | None |
| **DESCRIPTION** | : | Displays the string *m* containing a list of menu options. Each option must be followed by a return/newline character pair.<br>*result* contains the number of menu options given in the string. |
| **OUTLINE LOGIC** | : | see below |

```
Display m
Set count to zero
FOR each character in m
    IF its a RETURN THEN
        Increment count
    ENDIF
ENDFOR
```

| | | |
|---|---|---|
| **NAME** | : | GetOption |
| **PARAMETERS** | | |
| **IN** | : | max : integer |
| **OUT** | : | result : integer |
| **IN/OUT** | : | None |
| **PRE-CONDITION** | : | 0 <= *max* <= 99 |
| **DESCRIPTION** | : | Allows the user to enter an integer value in the range 1 to *max*. *result* returns the value entered. |
| **OUTLINE LOGIC** | : | see below |

```
Read result
WHILE result outside range 1 to max DO
    Beep
    Read result again
ENDWHILE
```

## Routines in Students Unit

| | | |
|---|---|---|
| **NAME** | : | GetExamMark |
| **PARAMETERS** | | |
| **IN** | : | None |
| **OUT** | : | result : integer |
| **IN/OUT** | : | None |
| **PRE-CONDITION** | : | None |
| **DESCRIPTION** | : | Reads a value in the range -1 to 100.<br>This value is returned in *result.*<br>A value of -1 used to represent no exam score. |
| **OUTLINE LOGIC** | : | see below |

```
REPEAT
    Get value for result
UNTIL result in the range -1 to 100
```

| | | |
|---|---|---|
| **NAME** | : | GetStudentDetails |
| **PARAMETERS** | | |
| **IN** | : | None |
| **OUT** | : | sd : StudentDetails |
| **IN/OUT** | : | None |
| **PRE-CONDITION** | : | None |
| **DESCRIPTION** | : | Gets and validates the details for a single student, the details of which are returned in *sd.* |
| **OUTLINE LOGIC** | : | see below |

```
Get idcode
Get name
Get sex
FOR each score DO
    Read in a value between -1 and 100
ENDFOR
```

| | | |
|---|---|---|
| **NAME** | : | DisplayStudent |
| **PARAMETERS** | | |
| **IN** | : | sd : StudentDetails |
| **OUT** | : | None |
| **IN/OUT** | : | None |
| **PRE-CONDITION** | : | None |
| **DESCRIPTION** | : | displays the contents of *sd.* |
| **OUTLINE LOGIC** | : | see below |

```
Display idcode, name and sex
FOR each score DO
    Display it
ENDFOR
Move cursor to new line
```

**NAME** : CalcAverage
**PARAMETERS**
  **IN** : sd : StudentDetails
  **OUT** : result : integer
  **IN/OUT** : None

**PRE-CONDITION** : None

**DESCRIPTION** : Calculates the average for the scores in *sd*. If any score is set at -1 (not yet entered) then *result* is set to -1, otherwise, *result* is calculated as the total of the 6 scores / 6

**OUTLINE LOGIC** :

```
Set total to zero
FOR each score DO
    IF its not been entered THEN
        Set result to -1
        Exit routine
    ENDIF
    Add score to total
ENDFOR
Set result to total / 6 rounded to
                nearest integer
```

## Routines in the Main Program File

**NAME** : StudentResultsSystem
**PARAMETERS**
  **IN** : None
  **OUT** : None
  **IN/OUT** : None

**PRE-CONDITION** : None

**DESCRIPTION** : Allows the user to add, delete and modify student records. Records can have the name or score fields modified. Various reports are available:
  List details of all students in the file
  List details of a specified student
  List of all male or female students
  List of all student averages
  List of students obtaining a pass grade
  List of students who have failed
  List of students who may appeal their result

**OUTLINE LOGIC** :

```
REPEAT
    Clear screen
    Display menu
    Get user option
    Execute specified option
UNTL exit chosen
```

| | | |
|---|---|---|
| **NAME** | : | ExecuteOption |
| **PARAMETERS** | | |
| **IN** | : | op : integer |
| **OUT** | : | None |
| **IN/OUT** | : | None |
| **PRE-CONDITION** | : | None |
| **DESCRIPTION** | : | Executes the option specified by *op*. Options are |

1 Add a new student
2 Modify a student's details
3 Enter marks for an exam
4 Display all records
5 Display all females
6 Display all males
7 Display a specified record
8 Display averages
9 Display failed
10 Display appeals
11 Display passed
12 Remove a record
13 Exit program

**OUTLINE LOGIC** :

```
IF
    op=1 : Add Student
    op=2 : Modify record
    op=3 : Enter marks
    op=4 : Display all records
    op=5 : Display details of all females
    op=6 : Display details of all males
    op=7 : Display specified record
    op=8 : Display average for every
                student
    op=9 : Display details of failed
                students
    op=10: Display details of all appeal
                students
    op=11: Display details of all
                passed students
    op=12: Remove a specified record
ENDIF
```

| | | |
|---|---|---|
| **NAME** | : | AddStudent |
| **PARAMETERS** | | |
| **IN** | : | None |
| **OUT** | : | None |
| **IN/OUT** | : | None |
| **PRE-CONDITION** | : | None |
| **DESCRIPTION** | : | Reads a record's details from the keyboard. If it doesn't match any existing record the new record is added to the end of the file, otherwise an error message is displayed. |

**OUTLINE LOGIC** :

```
Open the student file
Read details of new record
Read record from file
WHILE idcode not same as new rec and
        not eof
DO
    Read a record
ENDWHILE
IF idcodes match THEN
    Display error message
ELSE
    Add new rec to file
ENDIF
Close file
```

| | | |
|---|---|---|
| **NAME** | : | EnterClassMark |
| **PARAMETERS** | | |
| **IN** | : | None |
| **OUT** | : | None |
| **IN/OUT** | : | None |
| **PRE-CONDITION** | : | None |
| **DESCRIPTION** | : | Allows the marks for a specific exam to be entered for every student. If a student already has a mark for that exam, no new mark is entered. |

**OUTLINE LOGIC** :

```
Get exam number (1 to 6)
Open file
FOR each student DO
    Read record from file
    IF no mark recorded for exam THEN
        Read mark
        Update record
    ENDIF
ENDFOR
Close file
```

| | | |
|---|---|---|
| **NAME** | : | ModifyStudentRecord |
| **PARAMETERS** | | |
| **IN** | : | None |
| **OUT** | : | None |
| **IN/OUT** | : | None |
| **PRE-CONDITION** | : | None |
| **DESCRIPTION** | : | Modifies either the name or a score in a specified record. The updated record is written back to the file. |
| **OUTLINE LOGIC** | : | |

```
Get idcode of rec to change
Open file
Attempt to find matching record
IF found THEN
    Display menu of options
    Get choice
    IF
        choice=1:  Get new name
                   Update record
        choice=2:  Get which exam
                   Get score
                   Update record
        choice=3:  Exit routine
    ENDIF
    Write record back to file
    Close file
ELSE
    Display not found message
ENDIF
```

| | | |
|---|---|---|
| **NAME** | : | DisplayAllSex |
| **PARAMETERS** | | |
| **IN** | : | sx : char |
| **OUT** | : | None |
| **IN/OUT** | : | None |
| **PRE-CONDITION** | : | sx = 'M','F' or 'A' |
| **DESCRIPTION** | : | Displays details of students of a specified sex. If *sx* is 'A', all records are displayed. |
| **OUTLINE LOGIC** | : | |

```
Open file
WHILE not eof DO
    Read a record
    IF record of correct sex THEN
        display it
    ENDIF
ENDWHILE
Close file
```

| | | |
|---|---|---|
| **NAME** | : | DisplayAverages |
| **PARAMETERS** | | |
| **IN** | : | None |
| **OUT** | : | None |
| **IN/OUT** | : | None |
| **PRE-CONDITION** | : | None |
| **DESCRIPTION** | : | Displays the idcode, name and average score of every student. If a student has not yet sat all six exams, then an appropriate message is displayed. |
| **OUTLINE LOGIC** | : | see below |

```
Open file
WHILE not eof DO
    read a record
    Calculate average
    IF student has sat all exams THEN
        Display idcode, name and average
    ELSE
        Display idcode, name and message
    ENDIF
ENDWHILE
Close file
```

| | | |
|---|---|---|
| **NAME** | : | DisplayResultCategory |
| **PARAMETERS** | | |
| **IN** | : | cat : char |
| **OUT** | : | None |
| **IN/OUT** | : | None |
| **PRE-CONDITION** | : | cat = 'P','F' or 'A' |
| **DESCRIPTION** | : | List the records that have averages that fall into the specified category given in *cat*. |
| **OUTLINE LOGIC** | : | see below |

```
Write report heading
Open file
WHILE not eof DO
    Read a record
    Calculate its average
    IF
        average 0 to 45 and cat = 'F':
            Display record
        average 46 to 49 and cat = 'A':
            Display record
        average 50 or over and cat = 'P':
            Display record
    ENDIF
ENDWHILE
Close file
```

| | | |
|---|---|---|
| **NAME** | : | DisplayRecord |
| **PARAMETERS** | | |
| **IN** | : | None |
| **OUT** | : | None |
| **IN/OUT** | : | None |
| **PRE-CONDITION** | : | None |
| **DESCRIPTION** | : | Displays the details of a specified record. |
| **OUTLINE LOGIC** | : | |

```
Open the file
Get idcode of record to be displayed
Read a record
WHILE not match and not eof DO
    Read a record
ENDWHILE
IF match THEN
    Display record
ELSE
    Display error message
ENDIF
Close file
```

| | | |
|---|---|---|
| **NAME** | : | RemoveStudent |
| **PARAMETERS** | | |
| **IN** | : | None |
| **OUT** | : | None |
| **IN/OUT** | : | None |
| **PRE-CONDITION** | : | None |
| **DESCRIPTION** | : | Removes a speciified record from the file by marking its idcode as -1. |
| **OUTLINE LOGIC** | : | |

```
Open the file
Get idcode of record to be deleted
Read a record
WHILE not match and not eof DO
    Read a record
ENDWHILE
IF match THEN
    Change idcode to -1
    Write updated record back to file
ELSE
    Display error message
ENDIF
Close file
```

## Creating White Box Test Data

Each of the routines that have been designed for the system will have test data created for it. However, any routine which has been lifted from a previous project, or from an existing Pascal Unit, is assumed to be working correctly and may be safely ignored as far as testing is concerned.

As you will appreciate by now, testing can require a considerable amount of work and generates a large amount of documentation. Rather than list all of the tests for this system (which would take several pages) the flavour of the task is shown by describing the test requirements for **ModifyStudentRecord.**

## Black Box Test Data

### Responses:

The name is changed
The student's mark for a specified exam is changed
The record is not modified

### Equivalence classes

1. Valid idcode ; new name
2. Valid idcode; valid exam number; valid score
3. Invalid idcode

### Test Data

The student file is assumed to contain the following records

```
1234 Liza Heron   F   78   65   79   89   97   67
2222 John Farrell M   65   86   69   71   58   59
```

### Data Entered

| Class | Test data | Expected Results |
|---|---|---|
| 1 | 1234, Liz Farrell | Name changed |
| 2 | 2222, 3, 96 | 3rd score changed to 96 |
| 3 | 4444 | No change to file |

# Program Listing

## Code in Auxiliary Unit

**LISTING-7.1**

Students' Records System

```
unit Auxiliary;

interface

type
  KeySet = set of char;

function GetData(allowed : KeySet; max : integer):string;
function DisplayMenu(m:string): integer;
function GetOption(max:integer):integer;


implementation
uses WinCrt;
{*** Get Data from Keyboard ***}
function GetData(allowed : KeySet; max : integer):string;
const
  ENTER = #13;
  BACKSPACE = #8;
var
  ch    : char;          {char from keyboard}
  count : integer;       {chars entered}
  result : string;       {Contains the characters typed in}
begin
  {*** Set result to empty and count to zero ***}
  result := '';
  count := 0;
  {*** Read a character ***}
  ch := ReadKey;
  {*** WHILE return key not pressed DO ***}
  while ch <> ENTER do
  begin
       {*** IF allowed char & result not full THEN ***}
       if (ch in allowed) AND (count < max)then
       begin
            {*** Display char and add to result ***}
            write(ch);
            inc(count);
            result := result + ch;
       end
       {*** ELSE if delete & result not empty ***}
       else if (ch = BACKSPACE) AND (count > 0) then
       begin
            {*** Remove last char ***}
            write(#8,#32,#8);
            dec(count);
            delete(result,length(result),1);
       end;
       {*** Read another character ***}
       ch := readkey;
  end;
  writeln;
  GetData := result;
end;

{*** Display menu ***}
function DisplayMenu(m:string): integer;
var
  count : integer;       {No. of items in menu}
  c     : integer;       {Loop counter}
begin
  {*** Display menu ***}
  writeln(m);
  {*** Count options in menu ***}
  count := 0;
```

**Continued on next page**

**LISTING-7.1**
(continued)

Students' Records
System

```
  for c := 1 to length(m) do
      if m[c] = #13 then
          inc(count);
  {*** Return number of items in menu ***}
  DisplayMenu := count;
end;


{*** Get user's option ***}
function GetOption(max:integer):integer;
var
  opstr : string[2];     {Option chosen as string}
  op    : integer;       {Menu option chosen}
  err   : integer;      {Convertion flag}
begin
  {*** Read option ***}
  write('Enter option : ');
  opstr := GetData(['0'..'9'],2);
  val(opstr,op,err);
  {*** WHILE invalid DO ***}
  while (op < 1) or (op > max) do
  begin
      {*** re-read ***}
      opstr := GetData(['0'..'9'],2);
      val(opstr,op,err);
  end;
  {*** Return option ***}
  GetOption := op;
end;


end.
```

## Code in Students Unit

**LISTING-7.1**
(continued)

Students' Records
System

```
Unit Students;


interface
{********************************************}
{*** StudentDetails Data Type Declarations ***}
{********************************************}
{*** Data ***}
 type
  StudentDetails =
  record
      idcode : integer;
      name   : string[30];
      sex    : char;
      score  : array[1..6] of integer;
  end;

{*** Operations ***}
function GetExamMark : integer;
procedure GetStudentDetails(var sd: StudentDetails);
procedure DisplayStudent(sd:StudentDetails);
function CalcAverage(sd : StudentDetails) : integer;




implementation
uses auxiliary;
{***Operations ***}
```

**Continued on next page**

**LISTING-7.1**
(continued)

Students' Records System

```
{*** Get exam mark -1 to 100 ***}
function GetExamMark : integer;
var
  result : integer; {Holds exam mark}
  err    : integer; {Parameter for Val}
begin
  repeat
      Val(GetData(['0'..'9','-'],3),result,err)
  until (err = 0) and (result >= -1) and (result <= 100);
  GetExamMark := result;
end;


{*** Read Student details ***}
procedure GetStudentDetails(var sd: StudentDetails);
var
  c    : integer;   {Loop counter}
  err  : integer;   {Parameter for Val}
  temp : string[1]; {Stores sex - must be in string}
begin
  {*** Get idcode ***}
  {** Read up to 5 digits **}
  write('Enter id code : ');
  Val(GetData(['0'..'9',' '],5),sd.idcode,err);
  {*** Get name ***}
  write('Enter name : ');
  sd.name := GetData(['A'..'Z','a'..'z',' ','.','-',''''],29);
  {*** Get sex ***}
  write('Enter sex : ');
  temp := GetData(['F','M','f','m'],1);
  sd.sex := upcase(temp[1]);
  {*** Get six scores ***}
  for c := 1 to 6 do
  begin
      write('Enter score ',c,' : ');
      sd.score[c] := GetExamMark;
  end
end;


{*** Display student details ***}
procedure DisplayStudent(sd:StudentDetails);
var
  c : integer; {Loop counter}
begin
  {*** Display idcode, name and sex ***}
  write(sd.idcode:4,'  ',sd.name,'
':20-length(sd.name),sd.sex:3,'   ');
  {*** Display scores ***}
  for c := 1 to 6 do
      write(sd.score[c]:4);
  {*** Move to a new line ***}
  writeln;
end;


function CalcAverage(sd : StudentDetails) : integer;
var
  c     : integer; {Loop counter}
  total : integer; {Total of 6 scores}
begin
  {*** Set total to zero ***}
  total := 0;
  {*** FOR each score DO ***}
  for c := 1 to 6 do
  begin
      {*** IF score not entered, return -1 ***}
      if sd.score[c] = -1 then
      begin
```

**Continued on next page**

LISTING-7.1
(continued)

Students' Records System

```
            CalcAverage := -1;
            exit;
        end;
        {*** otherwise add score to total ***}
        total := total + sd.score[c];
    end;
    {*** Return average ***}
    CalcAverage := Round(total/6);
end;

end.
```

## Code in the Main File

LISTING-7.1
(continued)

Students' Records System

```
program StudentsSystem;
uses WinCrt, Auxiliary, Students;
const
  NL = #13#10;

{*** Add student record to file ***}
procedure AddStudent;
var
  strec : StudentDetails ; {Holds details of record to be added}
  exrec : StudentDetails ; {Holds record read from file}
  stfile : file of StudentDetails; {Student file}
begin
  {*** prepare file **}
  assign(stfile, 'C:\students.dat');
  reset(stfile);
  {*** Get details of new record ***}
  GetStudentDetails(strec);
  {*** Check idcode doesn't match existing record ***}
  exrec.idcode := -1;
  while not eof(stfile) do
  begin
      read(stfile,exrec);
      {*** IF there is a match, exit routine ***}
      if exrec.idcode = strec.idcode then
      begin
          close(stfile);
          writeln('New record''s id matches existing record');
          writeln('Add failed. Press any key to continue');
          ReadKey;
          exit;
      end;
  end;
  {*** Add record to file ***}
  write(stfile,strec);
  {*** Close file ***}
  close(stfile);
  writeln('Record added. Press any key to continue');
  ReadKey;
end;

{*** Get mark for every student ***}
procedure EnterClassMark;
var
  exrec  : StudentDetails ; {Holds record read from file}
  stfile : file of StudentDetails; {Student file}
  examno : integer; {Value to be assigned for exam}
  err    : integer; {Parameter for Val}
begin
  {** Get exam numbner ***}
  write('Which exam (1-6) : ');
  Val(GetData(['1'..'6'],1),examno,err);
```

**Continued on next page**

**LISTING-7.1**
(continued)

Students' Records System

```
   {*** prepare file ***}
   assign(stfile, 'C:\students.dat');
   reset(stfile);
   {*** WHILE not eof DO ***}
   while not eof(stfile) do
   begin
       {*** Read student record ***}
       read(stfile,exrec);
       {*** IF no mark entered already THEN ***}
       if exrec.score[examno] = -1 then
       begin
           {*** Get student's score and update record ***}
           write('Exam ',examno,' Mark for ',exrec.name,':');
           exrec.score[examno] := GetExamMark;
           {*** Update record ***}
           Seek(stfile,FilePos(stfile)-1);
           write(stfile,exrec);
       end;
   end;
   {*** Close file ***}
   close(stfile);
   write('Press any key to continue');
   ReadKey;
end;


{*** Modify name or score ***}
procedure ModifyStudentRecord;
var
   exrec    : StudentDetails; {Rec read from file}
   stfile   : file of StudentDetails;
   modid    : integer;   {Id of record to be modified}
   examno   : integer;   {No. of score to be changed}
   newscore : integer;   {New score}
   err      : integer;   {Parameter for Val}
   op       : integer;   {Option chosen from menu}
   noofopts : integer;   {Number of options in menu}
begin
   {*** Get student idcode ***}
   write('Enter idcode of record to be modified : ');
   Val(GetData(['0'..'9'],5),modid,err);
   {*** prepare file **}
   assign(stfile, 'C:\students.dat');
   reset(stfile);
   {*** Find matching record ***}
   read(stfile,exrec);
   while (exrec.idcode <> modid) and (not eof(stfile)) do
       read(stfile,exrec);
   {*** IF match found THEN ***}
   if exrec.idcode = modid then
   begin
       {*** Display modification menu ***}
       noofopts := DisplayMenu('1 - Modify name'+NL+
                  '2 - Modify a score'+NL+
                  '3 - Return to main menu'+NL);
       {*** Get user selection ***}
       op := GetOption(noofopts);
       {*** Execute option ***}
       case op of
           1 : {Modify name}
               begin
                   write('Enter new name : ');
                   exrec.name := GetData(['A'..'Z','a'..'z',
                                     '.','''','-',' '],29);
               end;
```

**Continued on next page**

**LISTING-7.1**
(continued)

Students' Records System

```
            2 : {Modify score}
                begin
                    write('Which exam (1-6) : ');
                    Val(GetData(['1'..'6'],1),examno,err);
                    newscore := GetExamMark;
                    exrec.score[examno] := newscore;
                end;
            3 : {Return to main menu}
                    exit;
        end;
        {*** Update record ***}
        Seek(stfile,FilePos(stfile)-1);
        write(stfile,exrec);
    end
    else
        {*** ELSE Error message ***}
        writeln('Record not found');
    {*** Close file ***}
    close(stfile);
    write('Press any key to continue');
    ReadKey;
end;


{*** Display records of specific sex or all ***}
procedure DisplayAllSex(sx : char);
var
    exrec  : StudentDetails ; {Holds record read from file}
    stfile : file of StudentDetails; {Student file}
begin
    {*** IF pre-condition not met THEN exit ***}
    if not(UpCase(sx) in ['M','F','A']) then
        exit;
    {*** prepare file ***}
    assign(stfile, 'C:\students.dat');
    reset(stfile);
    {*** Display all records that meet criteria ***}
    while not eof(stfile) do
    begin
        read(stfile,exrec);
        if ((UpCase(exrec.sex) = UpCase(sx))or(Upcase(sx)='A'))
                                 and(exrec.idcode <> -1) then
            Displaystudent(exrec);
    end;
    {*** Close file ***}
    close(stfile);
    write('Press any key to continue');
    ReadKey;
end;



{*** Display student averages ***}
procedure DisplayAverages;
var
    exrec  : StudentDetails ; {Holds record read from file}
    stfile : file of StudentDetails; {Student file}
    average : integer; {Average score}
begin
    {*** Write Report title ***}
    writeln ('STUDENT AVERAGES');
    {*** prepare file ***}
    assign(stfile, 'C:\students.dat');
    reset(stfile);
    {*** WHILE not eof ***}
```

**Continued on next page**

**LISTING-7.1**
(continued)

Students' Records System

```
  while not eof(stfile) do
  begin
      {*** Read a record ***}
      read(stfile,exrec);
      {*** IF not marked as deleted THEN ***}
      if exrec.idcode <> -1 then
      begin
          {*** Calculate average ***}
          average := CalcAverage(exrec);
          {*** Display details ***}
          write(exrec.idcode:6,'   ',exrec.name:31,'   ');
          if average <> -1 then
              writeln(average:3)
          else
              writeln('Some scores still to be entered');
      end;
  end;
  {*** Close file ***}
  close(stfile);
  writeln('Press any key to continue');
  ReadKey;
end;

{*** Display records in a specified results category ***}
procedure DisplayResultCategory(cat : char);
var
  exrec  : StudentDetails ; {Holds record read from file}
  stfile : file of StudentDetails; {Student file}
  average : integer; {Average score}
begin
  {*** IF pre-condition not met exit ***}
  if not (cat in ['P','F','A']) then
      exit;
  {*** Display category heading ***}
  write('The following students have ');
  case cat of
      'F' : writeln('FAILED');
      'A' : writeln('APPEALED');
      'P' : writeln('PASSED');
  end;
  {*** prepare file ***}
  assign(stfile, 'C:\students.dat');
  reset(stfile);
  {WHILE not eof DO ***}
  while not eof(stfile) do  begin
      {*** Read a record ***}
      read(stfile,exrec);
      {IF its not marked as deleted THEN ***}
      if exrec.idcode <> -1 then
      begin
          {*** Display category if all marks entered ***}
          average := CalcAverage(exrec);
          case average of
              0..45 : if cat = 'F' then
                           writeln(exrec.idcode:6,'   ',
                               exrec.name:31,'   ',average:3);
              46..49: if cat = 'A' then
                           writeln(exrec.idcode:6,'   ',
                               exrec.name:31,'   ',average:3);
              50..100: if cat = 'P' then
                           writeln(exrec.idcode:6,'   ',
                               exrec.name:31,'   ',average:3);
          end;
      end;
  end;
  {*** Close file ***}
  close(stfile);
  writeln('Press any key to continue');
  ReadKey;
end;
```

**Continued on next page**

**LISTING-7.1**
(continued)

Students' Records System

```
{*** Display a specified record ***}
procedure DisplayRecord;
var
  exrec  : StudentDetails ; {Details of record read from file}
  disid  : integer ;        {Idcode of record to be displayed}
  stfile : file of StudentDetails; {Student file}
  err    : integer;         {Parameter for Val}
begin
  {*** prepare file ***}
  assign(stfile, 'C:\students.dat');
  reset(stfile);
  {*** Get idcode of record to delete ***}
  write('Enter idcode of record to be displayed : ');
  Val(GetData(['0'..'9'],5),disid,err);
  {*** WHILE not eof DO ***}
  while not eof(stfile) do
  begin
      read(stfile,exrec);
      {*** IF there is a match THEN display record***}
      if exrec.idcode = disid then
      begin
          DisplayStudent(exrec);
          {*** Close file ***}
          close(stfile);
          writeln('Press any key to continue');
          ReadKey;
          exit;
      end;
  end;
  {*** close file ***}
  close(stfile);
  writeln('Record not found. Press any key to continue');
  ReadKey;
end;


{*** Delete a specified student record ***}
procedure RemoveStudent;
var
  exrec  : StudentDetails ; {Details of record read from file}
  delid  : integer ;        {Idcode of record to be deleted}
  stfile : file of StudentDetails; {Student file}
  err    : integer;         {Parameter for Val}
begin
  {*** prepare file ***}
  assign(stfile, 'C:\students.dat');
  reset(stfile);
  {*** Get idcode of record to delete ***}
  write('Enter idcode of record to be removed : ');
  Val(GetData(['0'..'9'],5),delid,err);
  {*** WHILE not eof DO ***}
  while not eof(stfile) do
  begin
      {*** read a record ***}
      read(stfile,exrec);
      {*** IF match THEN mark as deleted and exit***}
      if exrec.idcode = delid then
      begin
          exrec.idcode := -1;
          Seek(stfile,FilePos(stfile)-1);
          write(stfile,exrec);
          {** Close file **}
          close(stfile);
          writeln('Record removed. Press any key to continue');
          ReadKey;
          exit;
      end;
  end;
```

**Continued on next page**

**LISTING-7.1**
(continued)

Students' Records System

```
  {*** close the file ***}
  close(stfile);
  writeln('Record not found. Press any key to continue');
  ReadKey;
end;



{*** Executes option chosen by user ***}
procedure ExecuteOption(op : integer);
var
  studentrec : StudentDetails;
  studentfile : file of StudentDetails;
begin
  case op of
      1:  {Add new student}
          AddStudent;
      2:  {Modify details}
          ModifyStudentRecord;
      3:  {Enter exam marks for whole class}
          EnterClassMark;
      4:  {Display all records}
          DisplayAllSex('A');
      5:  {Display all females}
          DisplayAllSex('F');
      6:  {Display all male}
          DisplayAllSex('M');
      7:  {Display a specific record}
          DisplayRecord;
      8:  {Display average for every student}
          DisplayAverages;
      9:  {Display failed}
          DisplayResultCategory('F');
      10: {Display appeals}
          DisplayResultCategory('A');
      11: {Display passed}
          DisplayResultCategory('P');
      12: {Remove student}
          RemoveStudent;
  end;
end;



var
  numofmenuoptions : integer;
  userchoice       : integer;
begin
  repeat
      ClrScr;
      numofmenuoptions := DisplayMenu(
              '1 -Add student'+NL+
              '2 -Modify details'+NL+
              '3 -Enter class marks'+NL+
              '4 -Display all'+NL+
              '5 -Display females'+NL+
              '6 -Display males'+NL+
              '7 -Display record'+NL+
              '8 -Display averages'+NL+
              '9 -Display failed'+NL+
              '10-Display appeal'+NL+
              '11-Display passed'+NL+
              '12-Remove student'+NL+
              '13-QUIT'+NL);
      userchoice := GetOption(numofmenuoptions);
      ExecuteOption(userchoice);
  until userchoice = numofmenuoptions;
  DoneWinCrt;
end.
```

**Activity 7.8**

There are several differences between the specification and the implementation. List any you can find.

Modify the program so that a filename may be specified by the user at start of program.

Write a second program to remove the records marked as deleted within the students' file.

# SOLUTIONS

## Activity 7.1

**Functional Specifications**

The System is to monitor the temperature of each room.

The system is to display the temperature of each room.

An alarm should be sounded if the temperature goes above 60°C in any room.

Once per hour, the temperature in each room is to be recorded.

**Non-functional Specifications**

A 3.5 inch disk is to be used when saving the weekly temperature.

The program must occupy no more than 10Kbytes of memory.

## Activity 7.2

There is no mention of how the user is to choose between printer and screen output.

There is no mention of what is to be done if an unrecognised student identity is entered.

## Activity 7.3

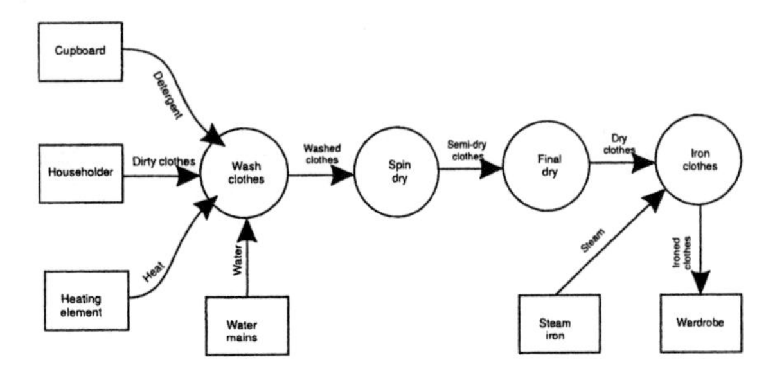


## Activity 7.4

Title = 'Mr'|'Mrs'|'Miss'|'Ms'|'Dr'|'Rev'|'Prof'

## Activity 7.5

| | | |
|---|---|---|
| X | - | valid |
| ABC | - | valid |
| Smith | - | invalid (lowercase letters) |
| O'DONNELL | - | invalid (apostrophe) |
| BELLERTHORPES | | invalid (too long) |
| Smythe-Brown | - | invalid (lowercase, hyphen) |

## Activity 7.6

Post Code = 1{'A'|..'Z'}1+2{0|..|9}2 + '∇' + 1{0|..|9}1 + 2{'A'|..'Z'}2

You could include lowercase letters as well.

## Activity 7.7

NumericDigit = 0|..|9

MoneyType = 1{NumericDigit}9 + '.' +
2{NumericDigit}2

## Activity 7.8

The final program lists every student along with their average. This operation was not defined in the System Specification.

If the filename is to be given by the user, we need to define a global string variable:

```
var
    filename ; string;
```

and allow the user to enter a value for this at the start of the program.

```
procedure GetFilename;
begin
    ClrScr;
    write(' Enter name of the file holding student details : ');
    readln(filename);
end;

begin
    GetFilename;
    repeat
        ClrScr;
            .
            .
```

```
uses WinCrt;

type
    StudentDetails =
    record
        idcode  : integer;
        name    : string[30];
        sex     : char;
        score   : array[1..6] of integer;
    end;

var
    c        : integer;                {Loop counter}
    oldfile  : file of StudentDetails;  {Existing file}
    newfile  : file of StudentDetails;  {New copy of file}
    myrec    : StudentDetails;
begin
    {*** Open the old file for reading ***}
    assign(oldfile,'C:\students.dat');
    reset(oldfile);
    {*** Open new file for writing ***}
    assign(newfile,'C:\student2.dat');
    rewrite(newfile);
```

## Activity 7.8 (continued)

```
    {*** WHILE number not end of old file DO ***}
    while not eof(oldfile) DO
    begin
        {*** Read a record from old file ***}
        read(oldfile, myrec)
        {*** IF its not marked for deletion THEN***}
        if myrec.idcode <> -1 then
            {*** Write it to new file ***}
            write(newfile,myrec);
    end;
    {*** Close files ***}
    close(oldfile);
    close(newfile);
    {*** Erase old file ***}
    Erase(oldfile);
    {*** Rename new file to that of old ***}
    Rename(newfile,'C:\students.dat');
end.
```

# CHAPTER 8
# Tables

**This chapter covers the following topics:**

- Abstract Data Types
- Bubble Sort
- Comparing Search Efficiency
- Comparing Sort Efficiency
- Direct Access Tables
- Hash Tables
- Insertion Sorts
- Linear Searching Techniques
- Non-Linear Searching
- Selection Sorts
- Simple Tables
- Table Efficiency

# ABSTRACT DATA TYPES

## Introduction

### Concrete Data Types

This range of values assumes a 16 bit integer.

Most languages have built-in data types. For example, Pascal has `integer`, `real` `char` and `string` types. The data type of a variable determines what type and range of values may be held in that variable. Hence, we know that an `integer` value may hold any value between -32,768 and +32,767. In addition, a variable's type also determines what operations can be performed on the variable. In the case of `integer` variables, we can perform operations such as addition, subtract, multiplication, and integer division, as well as comparisons using <, >, =, etc.

From this informal description we can produce a definition for data types:

*A data type defines not only the type and range of values which may be held in a variable of that type, but also the set of operations which may be performed on it.*

The data types available within a programming language are known as **concrete data types**.

### Abstract Data Types

During the design of most software systems the need for new data types, which are not part of the final programming language, will be highlighted. For example, we might identify the need to record weights in terms of pounds and ounces. Such weights will have to be read in and displayed. In addition, we might need to add, subtract or compare weights.

One way to handle these requirements is to define a new data type containing *pounds* and *ounces* data components with *ReadIn, Display, Add, Subtract* and *Compare* operations.

A vital part of the specifications of such a data structure is that no details of how the structure is to be implemented must be given. This abstraction ensures that the description can remain a simple one and also allows the programmer, who will later implement the new data type, complete freedom in the method chosen when coding the design requirements. Data structures defined in this way are known as **abstract data structures**.

## Designing Abstract Data Types

In the initial stages of the design, we will want to describe the data components and operations of our new data type. The purpose of an abstract data type is to describe the data type without specifying any details of how the data components and operations should be implemented in the target programming language.

The general format for describing an abstract data type is:

```
ADT new_data_type_name IS
    DATA
        description of the data components
    OPERATIONS
        description of each operation
END ADT
```

**Data**

This area contains a description of the data values held and where necessary the range of values which may be assigned.

**Operations**

Each operation is described separately in mini-spec format containing the headings:

```
NAME
PARAMETERS
    IN
    OUT
    IN/OUT
PRE-CONDITION
POST-CONDITION
```

The POST-CONDITIONS describes the state of the data type after the operation is complete. We might think of this as a description of what happens when the operation is performed.

## A Weight ADT

Let's assume a software system under design identifies the need to record imperial weights given in pounds and ounces. The system will need to be able to read in, add, subtract and display such weights.

A final operation will be to set a weight variable to a specific value by supplying two integer values representing the pounds and ounces values to be assigned.

From this informal description we can now write the specification for a *Weight* abstract data type:

**ADT Weight IS**

```
Data
    A weight is stored in terms of pounds and ounces, where pounds can
    be any non-negative integer value and ounces has an integer value
    between 0 and 15 inclusive.

Operations
    NAME               :   ReadIn
    PARAMETERS
        IN             :   None
        OUT            :   w : Weight
        IN/OUT         :   None
    PRE-CONDITION      :   None
    POST-CONDITION     :   w is assigned a value entered from the
                           keyboard.

    NAME               :   Display
    PARAMETERS
        IN             :   w:Weight
        OUT            :   None
        IN/OUT         :   None
    PRE-CONDITION      :   None
    POST-CONDITION     :   The value in w is displayed on the screen.
```

NAME : SetWeight
PARAMETERS
IN : npnds : INTEGER
noz :INTEGER
OUT : w : Weight
IN/OUT : None
PRE-CONDITION : $0 \leq npnds$ AND $0 \leq noz \leq 15$
POST-CONDITION : *w* is set to *npnds* pounds, *noz* ounces.

NAME : Add
PARAMETERS
IN : w2 : Weight
OUT : None
IN/OUT : w : Weight
PRE-CONDITION : None
POST-CONDITION : $w = w + w2$

NAME : Subtract
PARAMETERS
IN : w2 : Weight
OUT : None
IN/OUT : w : Weight
PRE-CONDITION : $w2 \leq w$
POST-CONDITION : $w = w - w2$

This ensures that the result cannot be negative

NAME : Compare
PARAMETERS
IN : w1 : Weight
w2 : Weight
OUT : result : INTEGER
IN/OUT : None
PRE-CONDITION : None
POST-CONDITION : if *w1*< *w2* then *result* is 1;
if *w2*< *w1* then *result* is 2;
if *w1* = *w2* then *result* is zero.

**END ADT**

**Activity 8.1**

Write an ADT definition for a *Distance* type which can record distances in yards, feet and inches (12 inches = 1 foot; 3 feet = 1 yard).
The operations required are the same as for the *Weight* type.

# Implementation

## Implementing WeightType

When the designer has completed his work, the description of the new *Weight* data type will be passed to the programmer who has the task of implementing the type in a programming language.

The programmer should have complete freedom in the method of implementation chosen. He is likely to try and find an approach which will result in the shortest, clearest and fastest code with the minimum of storage space requirements. Usually, however, not all of these goals are attainable.

First we begin by defining the data components. These might reflect exactly the structure suggested by the design:

```
type
    Weight =
    record
        pounds : integer;
        ounces : integer;
    end;
```

Next, the operations must be coded. Again, the programmer has complete freedom but must ensure that the name and parameters of the operations match those given in the abstract design.

Often this will be done by first adding Outline Logic to the mini-spec. So for example, the expanded mini-spec for *Add* might be

| | | |
|---|---|---|
| NAME | : | Add |
| PARAMETERS | | |
| IN | : | w2 : Weight |
| OUT | : | None |
| IN/OUT | : | w : Weight |
| PRE-CONDITION | : | None |
| POST-CONDITION | : | *w* = *w* + *w2* |
| OUTLINE LOGIC | : | Calculate the total ounces in *w*<br>Calculate the total ounces in *w2*<br>Add these results to get the grand total<br>Produce the pounds in result by calculating [grand total / 16]<br>Produce the ounces in the result by calculating grand total modulo 16 |

After the outline logic is complete, coding and testing of each operation can proceed. Each routine should, where possible, be tested separately using the strategies we developed in earlier chapters. Unfortunately, space restrictions make that impractical here. However, the complete code for the new data type and a test driver is given in Listing-8.1.

**LISTING-8.1**

Implementing an Abstract Data Type

```
program WeightsDataType;
uses crt;

{*************************************}
{***       Subsidiary Routines     ***}
{***           and types           ***}
{*************************************}
{*** Types ***}
{*** Set of allowable input characters ***}
type
  KeySet = set of char;

{*** Get Data from Keyboard ***}
function GetData(allowed : KeySet; max : integer):string;
const
   ENTER = #13;
```

**Continued on next page**

**LISTING-8.1**
(continued)

Implementing an Abstract Data Type

```
  BACKSPACE = #8;
var
  ch     : char;            {char from keyboard}
  count  : integer;         {chars entered}
  result : string;          {Contains the characters typed in}
begin
  {*** Set result to empty and count to zero ***}
  result := '';
  count := 0;
  {*** Read a character ***}
  ch := readkey;
  {*** WHILE return key not pressed DO ***}
  while ch <> ENTER do
  begin
      {*** IF allowed char & result not full THEN ***}
      if (ch in allowed) AND (count < max)then
      begin
          {*** Display char and add to result ***}
          write(ch);
          inc(count);
          result := result + ch;
      end
      {*** ELSE if delete & result not empty ***}
      else if (ch = BACKSPACE) AND (count > 0) then
      begin
          {*** Remove last char ***}
          write(#8,#32,#8);
          dec(count);
          delete(result,length(result),1);
      end;
      {*** Read another character ***}
      ch := readkey;
  end;
  writeln;
  GetData := result;
end;


{***************************************}
{*** Weight Data Type Declarations ***}
{***************************************}
{*** Data ***}
type
  Weight =
  record
      pounds : integer;
      ounces : integer;
  end;

{*** Operations ***}

{*** Read weight ***}
procedure ReadIn(var w : Weight);
var
  temp    : string[9];  {Temporary storage for chars entered}
  lbs,oz  : string[7];  {Holds weight components}
  err     : integer;    {Flag indicating success of string to
int conversion}
begin
  {*** Get weight ***}
  {** Read up to 7 digits **}
  temp := GetData(['0'..'9',' '],7);
  {** Convert to numeric weight **}
  lbs := copy(temp,1,pos(' ',temp)-1);
  oz := copy(temp,pos(' ',temp)+1,length(temp)-pos(' ',temp)+1);
  val(lbs,w.pounds,err);
  val(oz,w.ounces,err);
```

**Continued on next page**

**LISTING-8.1**
(continued)

Implementing an Abstract Data Type

```
  {***WHILE ounces invalid DO ***}
  while(w.ounces>15) do
  begin
      {*** Sound alarm ***}
      write(#7);
      temp := GetData(['0'..'9',' '],7);
      {** Convert to numeric weight **}
      lbs := copy(temp,1,pos(temp,' '));
      oz := copy(temp,pos(temp,' ')+1,length(temp)-
                                          pos(temp,' ')+1);
      val(lbs,w.pounds,err);
      val(oz,w.ounces,err);
  end;
end;


{*** Compare two weights ***}
function Compare(w1,w2:Weight):integer;
var
  totaloz1, totaloz2 : integer;
begin
  {*** Convert each weight to ounces ***}
  totaloz1 := w1.pounds * 16 + w1.ounces;
  totaloz2 := w2.pounds * 16 + w2.ounces;
  {*** IF w1 < w2 THEN set returned value to 1 ***}
  if totaloz1 < totaloz2 then
      Compare := 1;
  {*** IF w2 < w1 THEN set returned value to 2 ***}
  if totaloz2 < totaloz1 then
      Compare := 2;
  {*** IF w1 = w2 THEN set returned value to 0 ***}
  if totaloz1 = totaloz2 then
      Compare := 0;
end;


{*** Display weight ***}
procedure Display(w:Weight);
begin
  {*** Display the weight ***}
  writeln(w.pounds,'lbs ',w.ounces,' oz');
end;


{*** Set weight ***}
procedure SetWeight(nlbs,noz:integer; var w: Weight);
begin
  {*** IF parameters invalid THEN exit ***}
  if (nlbs<0)OR(noz<0)OR(noz>15) then
      exit;
  {*** Assign to weight ***}
  w.pounds := nlbs;
  w.ounces := noz;
end;


{*** Add to weight ***}
procedure Add(var w1:Weight; w2:Weight);
var
  totaloz : integer;
begin
  {*** Convert combined weights to ounces ***}
  totaloz := (w1.pounds + w2.pounds) * 16 + w1.ounces +
                                              w2.ounces;
  {*** Convert back to lbs and oz ***}
  w1.pounds := totaloz div 16;
  w1.ounces := totaloz mod 16;
end;
```

**Continued on next page**

**LISTING-8.1** (continued)

Implementing an Abstract Data Type

```
{*** Subtract from weight ***}
procedure Subtract(var w1:Weight; w2:Weight);
var
  totaloz1, totaloz2 : integer;
begin
  {*** IF w1 < w2 THEN exit ***}
  if (Compare(w1,w2)= 1) then
      exit;
  {*** Convert each weight to ounces ***}
  totaloz1 := w1.pounds * 16 + w1.ounces;
  totaloz2 := w2.pounds * 16 + w2.ounces;
  {*** Subtract second weight's ounces from first ***}
  totaloz1 := totaloz1 - totaloz2;
  {*** Convert result to lbs and oz ***}
  w1.pounds := totaloz1 div 16;
  w1.ounces := totaloz1 mod 16;
end;

{*** Test Weight type ***}
var
  w1,w2 : Weight;
begin
  clrscr;
  write('Enter weight (pounds ounces) : ');
  ReadIn(w1);
  SetWeight(12,3,w2);
  write('w1 has the value ');
  Display(w1);
  writeln;
  write('w2 has the value ');
  Display(w2);
  writeln;
  writeln('Perform add');
  Add(w1,w2);
  write('w1 has the value ');
  Display(w1);
  writeln;
  write('w2 has the value ');
  Display(w2);
  writeln;
  writeln('Perform invalid subtract');
  Subtract(w2,w1);
  write('w1 has the value ');
  Display(w1);
  writeln;
  write('w2 has the value ');
  Display(w2);
  writeln;
  writeln('Perform valid subtract');
  Subtract(w1,w2);
  write('w1 has the value ');
  Display(w1);
  writeln;
  write('w2 has the value ');
  Display(w2);
  writeln;
  writeln('Perform compare');
  case Compare(w1,w2) of
      1: writeln('w1 is smaller');
      2: writeln('w2 is smaller');
      0: writeln('Both weights are equal')
  end;
end.
```

**Activity 8.2**

Code and test the *ReadIn, Display, Set* and *Add* operations for *Distance* data type.

## An Alternative Implementation

Of course, the programmer is free to implement an Abstract Data Type in any way. For example, an alternative approach to coding *Weight* type might be to begin with the data component declaration:

```
type
   Weight =
   record
      value : real;
   end;
```

With this method, the ounces component of a weight would be stored as a fraction of a pound. Hence, 5 lbs 4 oz would be held in *value* as 5.25.

Obviously, this will have an effect on how the operations of the data structure are to be coded. Some will be easier to implement. For example, *Add* can now be written as:

```
procedure Add(var w1: Weight; w2:Weight);
begin
   w1.value := w1.value + w2.value;
end;
```

Others will become more complex:

```
procedure Display(w:Weight);
begin
   write(Trunc(w.value), ' lbs ', Trunc(Frac(w.value)*16+0.5),
                                                      ' oz');
end;
```

However, irrespective of the implementation, the parameters of the operations must remain the same.

**Activity 8.3**

Create an ADT for an abstract data type named *StudentDetails*. The data components of this type are: *idcode* (integer), *name, sex, score* ( 6 integers).

The operations are:

| | |
|---|---|
| *GetStudentDetails* | Reads values for all the details from the keyboard. |
| *DisplayStudent* | Displays the value of each data component on the screen. |
| *ModifyName* | Changes the value of the name field to a new specified value. |
| *ModifyScore* | Changes the value assigned to a single score. |
| *CompareId* | Compares the *idcode* values of two *StudentDetails* variables and returns 1 if the first is less than the second; 2 if the second is less than the first; and zero if they are both equal. |

**Activity 8.4**

Implement and test the *StudentDetails* data type. Use the function *GetData* implemented in the Routines chapter when coding the *GetStudentDetails* operation.

# Summary

- **A Data Type** is defined by the set of values it may be assigned and the operations which can be performed on those values.

- **Concrete Data Types** are those data types built-in to a language.

- **Abstract Data Types** (ADT) are user-designed types without any details of how they are to be implemented.

- **The definition of an abstract data type** is given in the form:

```
ADT type_name IS
    Data
        Description of the data components
    Operations
        Description of each operation
END ADT
```

- **Each operation is defined** using a mini-spec.

- **Abstract Data Types** are implemented using concrete data types.

- **The programmer is free to use any implementation method** but aims for efficiency.

- **Operation names and parameters** must not be changed during the implementation stage.

# SIMPLE TABLES

## Introduction

It is often necessary to maintain a list of data within the computer's main memory. The advantage of this approach over reading records one at a time from a disk file is simply that of speed: accessing information held in memory is many hundreds of times faster than trying to get at the same data held on disk. Of course, disk storage is still required for long-term storage and where there is too much data to be held within main memory.

Where a collection of data exists, it is likely that the value in one or more of the record fields will be unique. Such a field can be used as the record's key. For example, in our student records disk file (see previous chapter), the value of the *idcode* field was unique for each student.

This data list, using a key field to identify each entry, is often known as a **table**.

## Designing a Table

Tables, like most data collections, require three basic operations:

- Insertion of new entries
- Deletion of existing entries
- Modification of existing entries

With these come some requirements for additional functions such as:

- Creating an empty table
- Finding a specific entry in the table
- Displaying the contents of the table

Using a table of *StudentDetails* entries, we'll create a formal definition of an abstract data type:

**ADT StudentTable IS**

Data

A list of StudentDetails values. The *idcode* field of *StudentDetails* is to be used as the key field and must be unique to each entry.

Operations

```
    NAME                 :   CreateTable
    PARAMETERS
        IN               :   None
        OUT              :   t : StudentTable
        IN/OUT           :   None
    PRE-CONDITION        :   None
    POST-CONDITION       :   t is empty.

    NAME                 :   AddToTable
    PARAMETERS
        IN               :   sd:StudentDetails
        OUT              :   None
```

| | | |
|---|---|---|
| IN/OUT | : | t : StudentTable |
| PRE-CONDITION | : | *sd.idcode* does not match any in *t* AND *t* is not full. |
| POST-CONDITION | : | *sd* is added to *t.* |
| | | |
| NAME | : | DeleteFromTable |
| PARAMETERS | | |
| IN | : | key : INTEGER |
| OUT | : | None |
| IN/OUT | : | t : StudentTable |
| PRE-CONDITION | : | *key* matches an idcode in *t.* |
| POST-CONDITION | : | The entry whose idcode is equal to *key* is removed from *t.* |
| | | |
| NAME | : | DisplayTable |
| PARAMETERS | | |
| IN | : | t : StudentTable |
| OUT | : | None |
| IN/OUT | : | None |
| PRE-CONDITION | : | None |
| POST-CONDITION | : | The contents of *t* are displayed on the screen. |
| | | |
| NAME | : | GiveRecord |
| PARAMETERS | | |
| IN | : | key : INTEGER<br>t : StudentTable |
| OUT | : | sd : StudentDetails |
| IN/OUT | : | None |
| PRE-CONDITION | : | *key* must match an idcode value in *t.* |
| POST-CONDITION | : | *sd* contains a copy of the entry in *t* whose idcode field has the value *key.* |
| | | |
| NAME | : | UpdateRecord |
| PARAMETERS | | |
| IN | : | sd : StudentDetails |
| OUT | : | None |
| IN/OUT | : | t : StudentTable |
| PRE-CONDITION | : | The idcode in *sd* should match an existing entry in *t.* |
| POST-CONDITION | : | The record *st* replaces the entry with the same idcode in *t.* |
| | | |
| NAME | : | IsFull |
| PARAMETERS | | |
| IN | : | t : StudentTable |
| OUT | : | result : BOOLEAN |
| IN/OUT | : | None |
| PRE-CONDITION | : | None |
| POST-CONDITION | : | If *t* is full, *result* is set to *true.*<br>If *t* is not full, *result* is set to *false.* |

**END ADT**

# Implementing a Table

## Data Components

We start by deciding on how to implement the data part of our structure. As we saw from the Weight data type, how we hold the data affects the coding of the operations that follow, so we should bear this in mind when choosing a structure. We may even have to modify the structure at a later stage if coding certain operations proves to be difficult or inefficient using our first data model.

One of the simplest ways of implementing a table is to hold the data in an array of records. Hence, we could declare a table structure for our student details as:

```
const
    SIZE = 20;


type

    StudentDetails =
    record
        idcode : integer;
        name   : string[30];
        sex    : char;
        score  : array[1..6] of integer;
    end;


    StudentTable =
    record
        count : integer;
        list  : array[0..SIZE-1] of StudentDetails;
    end;
```

The number of elements required in the array *(list)* would be determined by the analysis of the system which should reveal the maximum number of entries required.

We need to maintain a count of how many entries are held in *list* at any time and this is the purpose of the *count* field. This count will help us determine, amongst other things, when the table is full.

## Operations

### Creating An Empty Table

The Outline Logic for the *CreateTable* operation is:

```
Set t.count to zero
```

Note, that there is no need to empty the contents of the array, *list*.

The code for the Pascal routine is:

```
procedure CreateTable(var t:StudentTable);
begin
    {*** Set table count to zero ***}
    t.count := 0;
end;
```

The effect of the routine is shown graphically in FIG-8.1.

**FIG-8.1**

An Empty StudentTable Variable

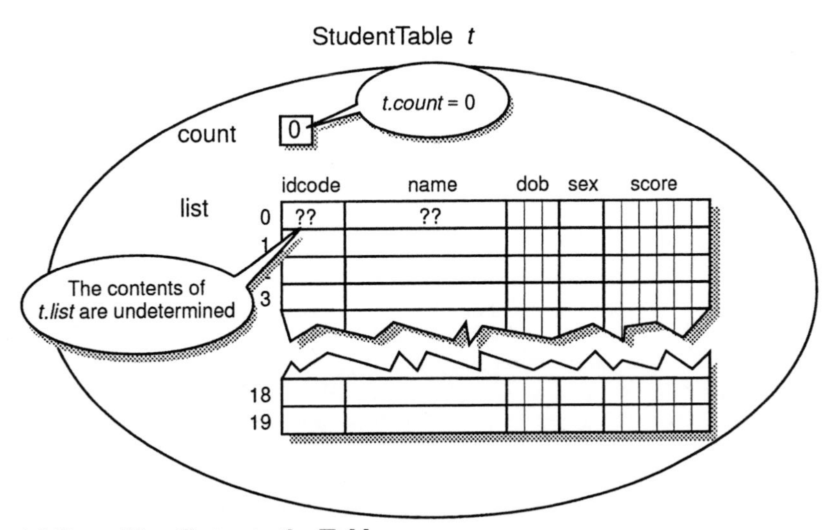

## Adding a New Entry to the Table

Before looking at the logic behind this operation, we can see the effect of adding two new entries to our table in FIG-8.2.

**FIG-8.2**

Adding records to the Table

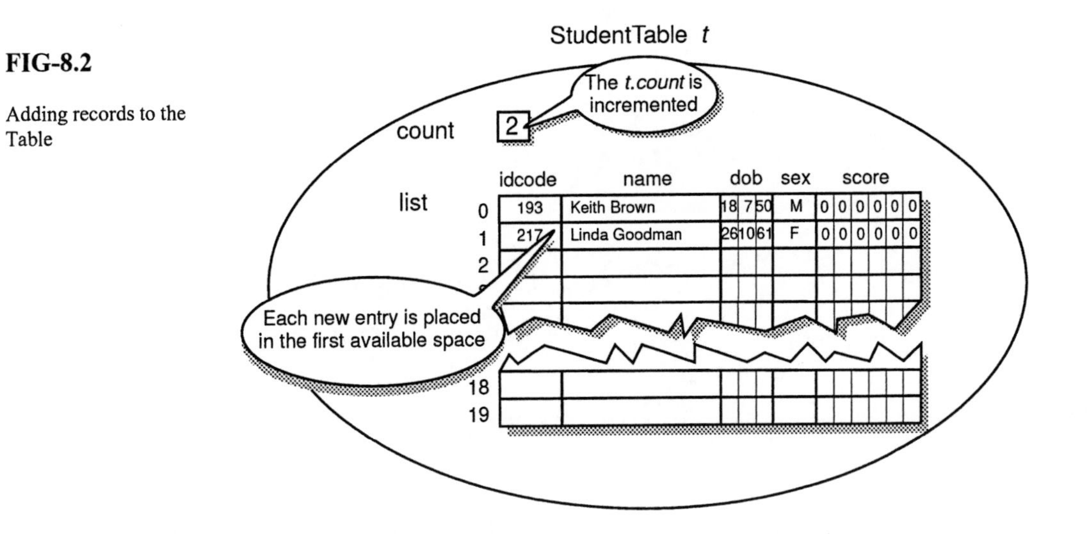


Note the two effects of each *Add* operation:

- The new entry is added at the first empty position in the table.
- The *count* field is incremented after each record is inserted.

The lines of code necessary for each of the effects are:

```
t.list[t.count] := sd;      {Places st in first empty position}
inc(t.count);               {Adds 1 to t.count}
```

It's important that we don't try to insert a new record which contains the same *idcode* number as an existing record in the table so, when describing the *Add* operation, we need to include a pre-condition stating that a record with the same key must not already exist. Another condition we need to check for before inserting a record is that the table is not already full. Hence, before we can code the *Add* routine, we'll need to produce the *IsFull* function (as defined in the ADT). The coding for this simple routine is:

```
function IsFull(var t:StudentTable):boolean;
begin
    {*** IF count is equal to the size of the list THEN ***}
    if t.count = SIZE then
        {*** return true ***}
        IsFull := true
    else
        {*** ELSE return false ***}
        IsFull := false;
end;
```

It would also be useful to create an auxiliary function which detects if the new record's *idcode* matches an existing one. We'll call this new routine *IsAt* and design it to return the position in table containing a match for a specified *idcode* value; if there is no match, it will return -1.

The description of the new function doesn't belong in the design of the ADT as it has only been created to aid the coding of other operations.

In order to determine if the key is already in the list we're going to have to search the list. Searching is such an important operation that we'll dedicate a section of this chapter to that task, but for the moment we'll use the simplest approach which can be described informally as:

```
Start at the beginning of the list
Compare the idcode value of each entry in the list until a match
is found or the last record in the list is reached.
IF a match was found THEN
    result is the position at which a match was found
ELSE
    result is -1
ENDIF
```

or more formally as

```
Set position to 0
WHILE t.list[position].idcode not equal req'd key
    AND position < count-1
DO
    Increment post
ENDWHILE
IF t.list[position].idcode=req'd key THEN
    result := position
ELSE
    result := -1
ENDIF
```

> **Activity 8.5**
>
> Create an *IsAt* function based on the description above.

Using this new function, we can return to the coding of the *Add* routine:

```
procedure AddToTable(sd:StudentDetails; var t:StudentTable);
begin
    {*** IF idcode matches existing one or table full THEN ***}
    if (IsAt(sd.idcode,t) <> -1) or (IsFull(t)) then
        {*** exit routine ***}
        exit;
    {*** Add student's details to end of table ***}
    t.list[t.count] := sd;
    {*** Increment count ***}
    inc(t.count);
end;
```

Any good application programmer using a *StudentTable* data structure in his program, will write code in such a way as to check the success of the *AddToTable* routine. After all, we can see from *AddToTable* that it will fail if the *idcode* field in the record to be added matches any already in the table or if the table is full.

To check for this, the programmer makes a conditional call to *AddToTable* :

```
if (IsAt(sd.idcode,t)<> -1) and (not IsFull(t)) then
    AddToTable(sd,t)
else
begin
    writeln('Key already exists. Record not added');
    writeln('Press any key to continue');
    readkey;
end;
```

But this is very inefficient code since *IsAt* will be executed twice if the record is successfully added to the table: once in the `if` statement before *AddToTable* is called, and again inside *AddToTable* itself. How can we avoid this? A simple way to get round this problem is to make *AddToTable* a function that returns some indicator of its success. Such a change needs to be reflected in a reworking of the ADT's definition of that operation. The new descriptor would be:

| | | |
|---|---|---|
| NAME | : | AddToTable |
| PARAMETERS | | |
| IN | : | sd : StudentDetails |
| OUT | : | success : BOOLEAN |
| IN/OUT | : | t : StudentTable |
| PRE-CONDITIONS | : | None |
| POST-CONDITIONS | : | If *t* is full or *sd.idcode* matches an idcode in *t* *success* is set to *false* and *t* is unchanged, otherwise *sd* is added to *t* and *success* is set to *true*. |

Now we can create code to match the new definition:

Note that the routine has been changed from a procedure to a function.

Nevertheless, IN/OUT parameters are still possible.

```
function AddToTable(sd:StudentDetails; var t:StudentTable):boolean;
begin
    {*** IF idcode matches existing one or table full THEN ***}
    if (IsAt(sd.idcode,t) <> -1) or (IsFull(t)) then
    begin
        {*** Return false ***}
        AddToTable := false;
        exit;
    end;
    {*** Add student's details to end of table ***}
    t.list[t.count] := sd;
    {*** Increment count ***}
    inc(t.count);
    {*** Return true ***}
    AddToTable := true
end;
```

This allows the application programmer to write more succinct code such as:

```
if not AddToTable(sd,t) then
begin
    writeln('Key already exists. Record not added');
    writeln('Press any key to continue');
    readkey
end
```

**Displaying the Contents of StudentTable**

It would be useful if we could check that the operations we've created so far perform correctly. To do that, we need to be able to display the contents of the table, so the next operation to code is *DisplayTable*, the Outline Logic of which is:

```
IF table empty THEN
    Display "Table empty"
ELSE
    FOR post := 0 TO t.count - 1 DO
        Display t.list[post]
    ENDFOR
ENDIF
```

> **Activity 8.6**
>
> Create a menu-driven program, to operate on a *StudentTable* structure, which contains all of the routines described so far:
> *CreateTable*
> *IsFull*
> *IsAt*
> *AddToTable*
> *DisplayTable*
>
> Check that the program operates correctly when attempting to:
> Display an empty table.
> Add a record containing a duplicate *idcode* field.
> Add a record to a full table.

**Returning an Entry**

Often the application programmer will want to retrieve a specific entry from the table. This may be in order to examine the contents of some of the fields or to display its contents.

> **Activity 8.7**
>
> Write an updated version of the mini-spec for *GiveRecord* which returns a *success* indicator. Success is *true* if the required record is retrieved from the table, otherwise it is *false.*

> **Activity 8.8**
>
> Add the *GiveRecord* function to your *StudentTable* program.

**Deleting a Record**

We may need to remove a record from the table because it has been entered in error or because the student has left the course.

Removing the last record in the list isn't really a problem: all we have to do is reduce the count by one (we don't even need to remove the record's data from the list). But when the record being erased is at some other position in the table, then there's a bit more involved. The stages required are shown in FIG-8.3.

Like the *Add* operation, it will be worth going back to the original design and adding a success/fail indicator to the operation. The new mini-spec being:

| | | |
|---|---|---|
| NAME | : | DeleteFromTable |
| PARAMETERS | | |
| IN | : | key : INTEGER |
| OUT | : | success : BOOLEAN |
| IN/OUT | : | t : StudentTable |
| PRE-CONDITION | : | None |
| DESCRIPTION | : | If *key* matches any idcode in *t* then *success* is set to *false* and *t* is unchanged, otherwise the entry whose idcode field is equal to *key* is removed from *t* and *success* is set to *true.* |

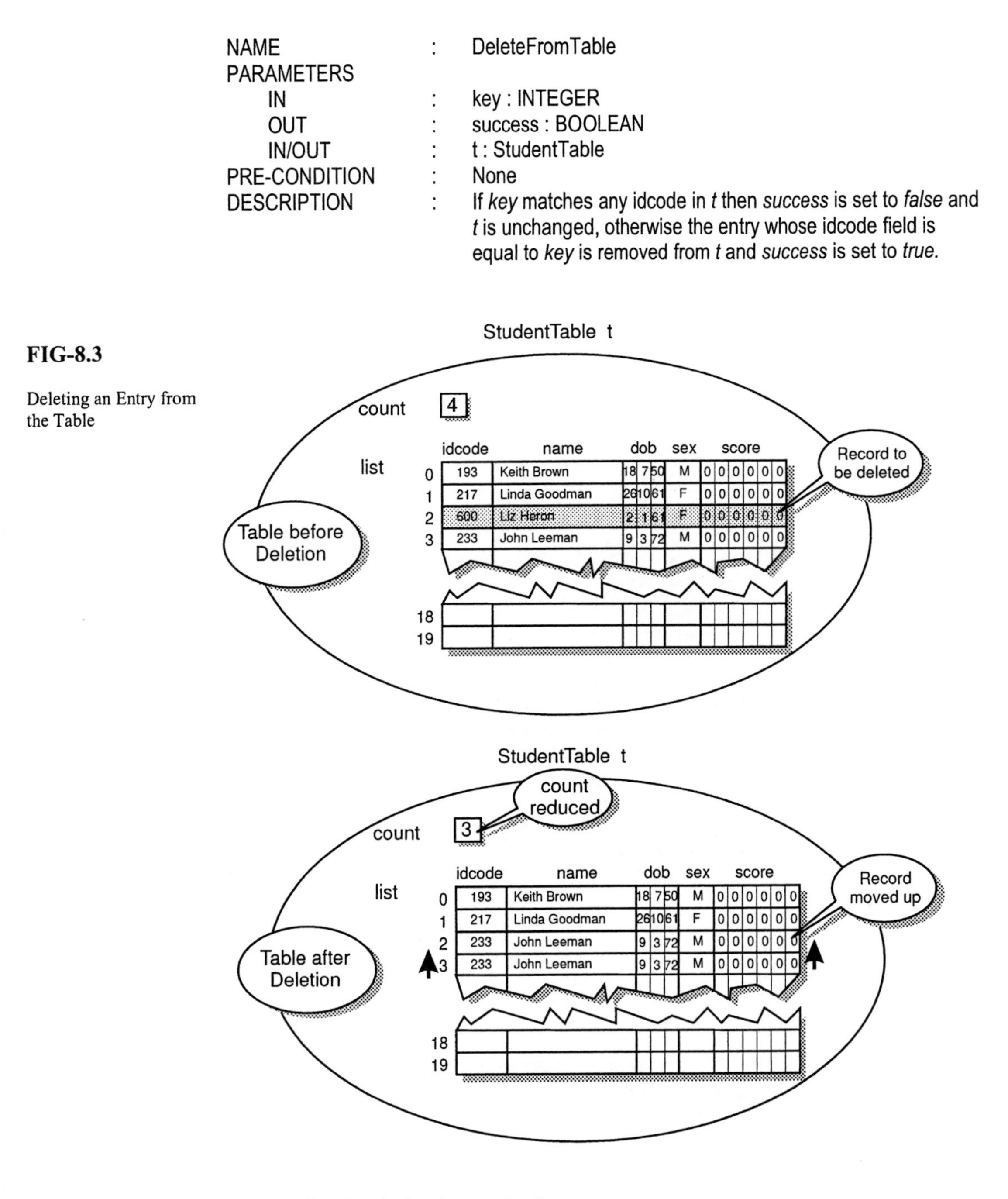


**FIG-8.3**

Deleting an Entry from the Table

The Outline Logic for the routine is

```
Find position of record to be deleted
IF record not found THEN
    Set success to false
ELSE
    Move all records below the one to be
    deleted up one position in the list
    Decrement the count
    Set success to true
ENDIF
```

and the Pascal code is:

```
function DeleteFromTable(key:integer; var t:StudentTable):boolean;
var
    post : integer;     {Position of match in table}
    c    : integer;     {Loop counter}
begin
    {*** Attempt to find matching idcode in table ***}
    post := IsAt(key,t);
    {*** IF not found THEN ***}
    if post = -1 then
    begin
        {*** Return false ***}
        Delete := false;
        exit
    end;
    {*** Move remaining entries up ***}
    for c := post+1 to t.count do
        t.list[c-1] := t.list[c];
    {*** Decrement the number of entries in table ***}
    dec(t.count);
    {*** Return true to indicate delete was successful ***}
    Delete := true;
end;
```

### Modifying a Record

There are many reasons which may cause us to change the contents of a record once it has been stored in the table. For example, we may start off with no scores recorded and later need to enter such information. The only restriction in allowing changes is that it is not good policy to allow the key field (in this case, the *idcode* field) to be changed; where this is necessary, use the *DeleteFromTable* operation to remove the original record, and then insert a new record containing the required *idcode* value. This ensures that there is no possibility of ending up with two records with the same key in the table.

See Activity 8.3 for the StudentDetails data type.

Changing the contents of any field in a single *StudentDetails* record is an operation properly defined within the *StudentDetails* ADT; for example, we have already defined *ChangeName* and *ChangeScore* operations. So, the only operation required to be defined for *StudentTable* is one which allows us to overwrite a record whose *idcode* matches one already in the table. This allows the application program to employ the following strategy to update a table entry:

```
Get the required record from the table (using GiveRecord)
Make changes to this copy (using ModifyName or ModifyScore)
Write the copy back to the table (using UpdateRecord)
```

As with other operations, we'll start by modifying the definition of *UpdateRecord* so that it returns a success/fail indicator:

| | | |
|---|---|---|
| NAME | : | UpdateRecord |
| PARAMETERS | | |
| IN | : | sd : StudentDetails |
| OUT | : | success : BOOLEAN |
| IN/OUT | : | t : StudentTable |
| PRE-CONDITION | : | None |
| POST-CONDITION | : | If the idcode of *sd* matches an entry in *t*, then *sd* replaces the entry with the same idcode in *t* and *success* is set to *true*, otherwise *success* is set to *false*. |

The corresponding function is:

```
function UpdateRecord(sd:StudentDetails;
                                    var t:StudentTable):boolean;
var
    post : integer;     {Position of match in table}
begin
    {*** Attempt to find matching idcode in table ***}
    post := IsAt(sd.idcode,t);
    {*** IF not found THEN ***}
    if post = -1 then
    begin
        {*** Return false ***}
        UpdateRecord := false;
        exit
    end;
    {*** update entry and return success indicator ***}
    t.list[post] := sd;
    UpdateRecord := true
end;
```

> **Activity 8.9**
>
> Add the *UpdateRecord* operation to your table program.
>
> By adding the *StudentDetail* operations created in Activity 8.3, allow either the name or a score to be modified.

## Other Operations on the Table

As well as changing the contents of the table, we may want to retrieve information held in the table or generate statistical data. For example, we might require an operation to return the number of students of a specified sex or a list of the *idcode* values of all students with an average score of at least 50.

It may be that we cannot predict all the operations required by the application programmer. The solution to this problem is to include operations to return a specific record from the table, then the application program can interrogate the entry's data in any way necessary.

Now, we already have a *GiveRecord* operation, but that is not sufficient. For example, to determine the total number of females in the table using *GiveRecord*, the *idcode* value of each entry would have to be supplied in order to retrieve the data from the table and this is impractical. When every entry in the table needs to be examined, the best approach is to define another operation which returns a specific entry in the table. The difference between *GiveRecord* and this new routine (let's call it *GiveRecordAt*) is that the new routine returns a record based on its position in the table rather than on its *idcode* value.

The mini-spec for the new routine is:

| | | |
|---|---|---|
| NAME | : | GiveRecordAt |
| PARAMETERS | | |
| IN | : | post : INTEGER<br>t : StudentTable |
| OUT | : | sd : StudentDetails<br>success : BOOLEAN |
| IN/OUT | : | None |
| PRE-CONDITIONS | : | None |
| POST-CONDITIONS | : | If *post* lies between 1 and the number of entries<br>*t* then *sd* returns the entry at position *post* in *t* and |

*success* is set to *true*, otherwise an empty record is returned and *success* is set to *false*.

The code for this routine is simply:

```
function GiveRecordAt(post : integer; var t:StudentTable;
                          var sd:StudentDetails):boolean;
const
    emptyrec :StudentDetails = (idcode:0;name:'EMPTY';
                                sex:' ';score:(0,0,0,0,0,0));
begin
    {*** IF no match THEN ***}
    if (post < 1) or (post > t.count) then
    begin
        {*** Return empty record and false ***}
        sd := emptyrec;
        GiveRecordAt := false
    end
    else
    begin
        {*** ELSE return specified record and true ***}
        sd := t.list[post-1];
        GiveRecordAt := true
    end;
end;
```

**Activity 8.10**

Create a final version of your *StudentTable* program containing all of the operations defined so far.

Add a *NoOfSex* operation which returns the number of students of a given sex. Check for an invalid sex parameter which should result a count of -1.

# Summary

- **A table** is a list of composite values.
- One or more fields in the composite value is used as **the key field**.
- **Key field values should be unique** to each table entry.
- **The basic operations** required of a table are:

  Adding a new entry
  Deleting an entry
  Modifying an entry

- **A table may be implemented** as a sequential array of records.
- **Adding an entry**. One option is to add a new entry at the end of the occupied area of the table.
- **Deleting an entry**. This will mean moving all entries 'below' the one being removed.
- **Modifying an entry**. This allows an entry within the table to be overwritten with a record containing the same key value.

- It can be useful to design these operations in such a way as to return a value which indicates the success or fail of the operation when called.

- The main table operations give rise to **additional operations** such as:

    IsFull
    IsAt
    Display
    GiveRecord

# SEARCHING

## Introduction

In implementing the insert, delete and modify operations for a table, you should have noted that each requires the table to be searched for an appropriate entry in the list. This task is so common, that much time and effort has gone into developing efficient methods of searching and into ways of measuring the efficiency of these methods.

### Implementation Efficiency and Searching

If a table contains thousands of items then the speed of any search operation can be a major influence on the way in which that table is implemented.

The main factors which are considered when determining the efficiency of a search technique are:

1. Average number of comparisons required to determine if the required value is in the list being searched.
2. The complexity of the routine required to code the search method.

## Linear Searching Techniques

A linear search technique is one where each entry in the list is searched in turn until the possibility of a match is determined.

There are several search techniques which fall into this class.

### Serial Searching

In a serial search the list of values being searched are not held in key field order.

For example, let's assume we want to search a *StudentTable* structure containing the values shown in FIG-8.4.

**FIG-8.4**

The Table to be Searched

Only the *idcode* field is shown since it is the only part of the table involved in the search process.

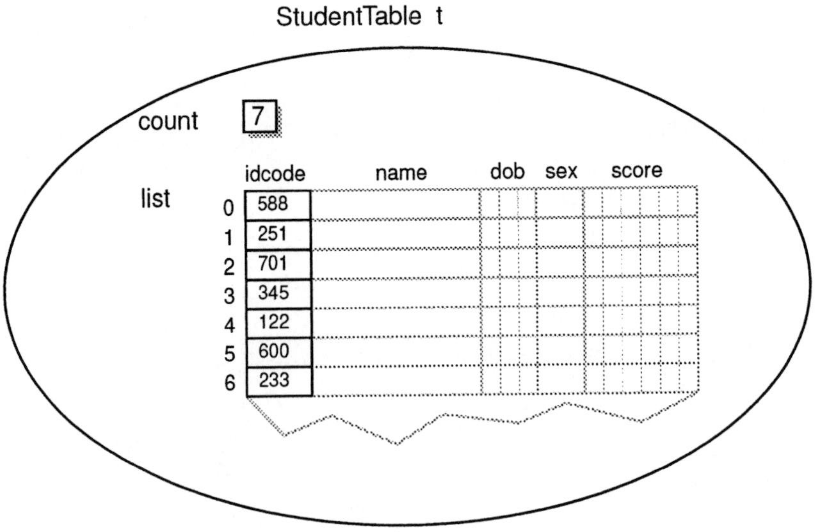

StudentTable t

count 7

list

| | idcode | name | dob | sex | score |
|---|---|---|---|---|---|
| 0 | 588 | | | | |
| 1 | 251 | | | | |
| 2 | 701 | | | | |
| 3 | 345 | | | | |
| 4 | 122 | | | | |
| 5 | 600 | | | | |
| 6 | 233 | | | | |

The search progresses by comparing the *idcode* field in each table entry in turn with the required key value. When a match is found the search terminates. We can formalise this algorithm as:

```
Starting at the beginning of the table
WHILE current entry's idcode not equal to req'd key
   AND not at end of table
DO
   Move to next entry in the table
ENDWHILE
IF the idcode of the current table entry = req'd key THEN
   found is TRUE
ELSE
   found is FALSE
ENDIF
```

FIG-8.5 shows the search path taken when searching the student table for an *id* value of 122.

**FIG-8.5**

Performing a Serial Search

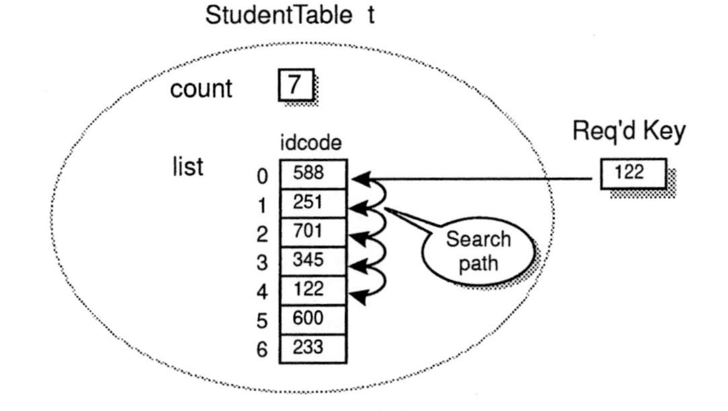


As already stated, one criteria used when judging the efficiency of a search method is the average number of comparisons required to find a match.

Using a serial search, the number of comparisons required before finding the matching entry equals the position of the required entry in the list.

| so | 122 requires | 5 comparisons before being found |
|---|---|---|
| | 701 requires | 3 comparisons |
| | etc. | |

Assuming that each entry in the list has an equal probability of being the one required, then the average number of comparisons is given by:

*Total number of comparisons required to search for each entry in the list separately* divided by *the total number of entries in the list.*

Alternatively, since the number of comparisons increases linearly, the average number of comparisons =

$$\frac{\text{Minimum number of comparisons} + \text{Maximum number of comparisons}}{2}$$

For the table in FIG-8.5 this would give us a result of

$(1 + 7)/ 2 = 4$

> **Activity 8.11**
>
> What would be the average number of comparisons required if the list contained:
> a) 255 entries
> b) N entries

What if the entry we were looking for was not in the table? For example, FIG-8.6 shows the search path for the *idcode* value 181.

**FIG-8.6**

Serial Searching - No match Found

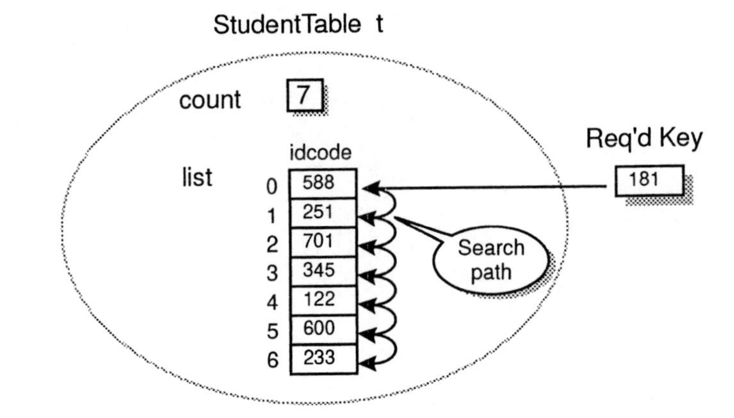


We can see from the diagram that the whole table must be searched before we can be sure that no match exists.

In the above example, that means 7 comparisons. For a table containing *N* entries, then *N* comparisons would be required.

The Serial Search algorithm as used in *IsAt* was coded as:

```
function IsAt(key:integer; var t:StudentTable):integer;
var
    post : integer;
begin
    {*** Move to the start of the list ***}
    post := 0;
    {*** Move through list until match found or end reached ***}
    while(t.list[post].idcode <> key) and (post < t.count-1) do
        inc(post);
    {*** IF match found THEN ***}
    if t.list[post].idcode = key then
        {*** Return position of match ***}
        IsAt := post
    else
        {*** ELSE return -1 ***}
        IsAt := -1
end;
```

We have stated that the efficiency of the search depends on the average number of comparisons required, but another factor is the efficiency of the coded algorithm. The most critical part of the algorithm is the search loop

```
while(t.list[post].idcode <> key) and (post < t.count-1) do
    inc(post);
```

since all other parts of the routine are executed only once, while the coding within the loop may be executed many times (depending on the size of list to be searched and the position of the required value).

There are three components to the loop in *IsAt*. These are:

```
t.list[post].idcode <> key
post < t.count - 1
inc(post)
```

Each of these components will take some portion of time to execute. Let's assume the following timings:

| | |
|---|---|
| `t.list[post].idcode <> key` | 3 time units |
| `post < t.count-1` | 2 time units |
| `inc(post)` | 1 time unit |

Accessing an array element is a relatively slow process, while incrementing is very fast.

In a table containing 10,000 entries (i.e. N = 10,000), the average search time to find a key match would be:

(10000 + 1)/2 * 6 = 30003 units of time

And, where there is no match, the search time would be:

10000*6 = 60000 units of time

If we can reduce this time then obviously the algorithm will be more efficient.

**Activity 8.12**

What is the purpose of the condition *post* < *t.count-1* in the algorithm?

We can only be rid of this condition from the code if we can be certain that a match for the required key will be found within the table. And the only way we can be certain of that is to add it ourselves!

Before starting the search, we can add the required key at the first empty position in the table (this assumes that at least one empty position exists). FIG-8.7 shows the results of such a technique when searches for both matched and unmatched keys are performed.

Notice that where a matching key already existed in the table, it is the first occurrence of the key that is found (not our inserted copy) but where the key did not originally exist in the table, the search stops at the matching key inserted at the end of the table. This gives us the strategy for the new algorithm:

```
Add copy of req'd key to end of table
Starting at beginning of table
WHILE no match found DO
    move to next position in table
ENDWHILE
If match found at inserted key position THEN
    result is -1
ELSE
    result is position where match found
ENDIF
```

By eliminating *position* < *t.count-1* the execution time of the algorithm becomes:

| | |
|---|---|
| Average search for match = (10000 + 1)/2 * 4 | = 20002 |
| Search for non-match = 10001 * 4 | = 40004 |

**FIG-8.7**

Adding the Search key to the Table

**NOTE**: To ensure there will always be space for the extra entry in the table we should create the table with SIZE+1 elements in the array.

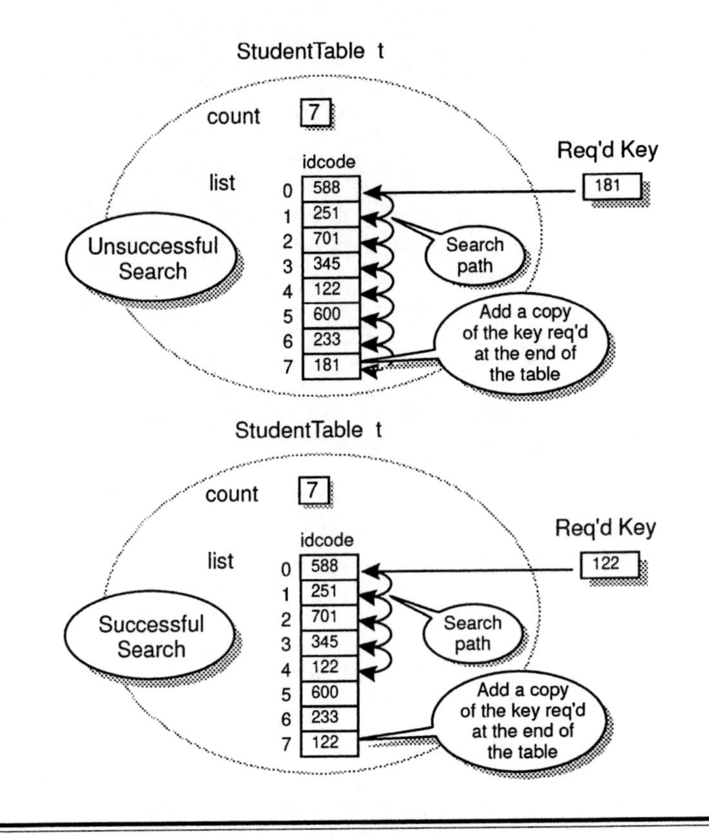


> **Activity 8.13**
>
> Code this new version of *IsAt* and add it to your *StudentTable* program.

So is this more efficient? That depends: making a copy of the *idcode* value in the table will take time, and the table has to be made one element larger to ensure there is always one free space in which to place this copy. However, if the table is a large one, chances are we will have a faster search method using this new approach. However, for our small table, we'll ignore this approach from now on.

## Sequential Searching

Can we improve the efficiency of the search by arranging the entries in order?

For example, FIG-8.8 shows the search path to find value 251 within a sorted table.

**FIG-8.8**

Sequential Searching

Using this technique on a sorted list is known as Sequential Searching.

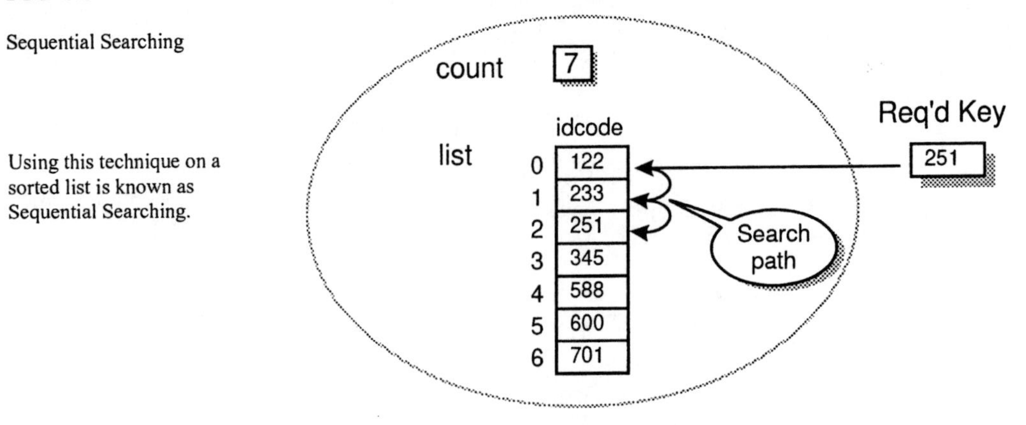

The number of comparisons required to find 251 was 3, whereas searching for 122 would have required 1 comparison and searching for 701 would have required 7 comparisons. In other words, the number of comparisons required is given by the position of the required entry in the list. These figures match those achieved by the serial search.

So the average number of comparisons to find a match is the same as that for the serial search - there has been no improvement in the figures by sorting the list to be searched.

Now let us look for a value which is not in the list, say 219 (see FIG-8.9).

**FIG-8.9**

Unsuccessful Search of a Sorted Table

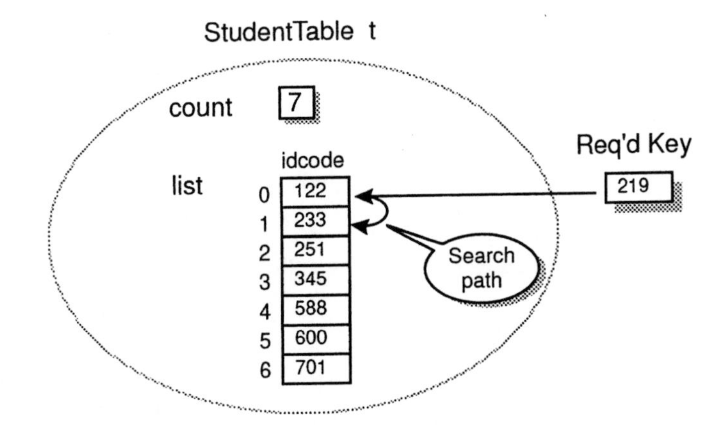


Notice that it is not necessary to search the whole list since, as soon as we reach an entry with an *idcode* value greater than the one we seek, there is no possibility of a match being found further along the list.

Three comparisons were required to establish that key 219 was not present. If 219 had been in the list it would have been in position 3. We can generalise this to produce the rule:

> *When a value is not present in a sorted list, the number of comparisons required to determine this fact is equal to the position in the list at which that value would have been placed.*

**Activity 8.14**

Using the table in FIG-8.9, how many comparisons would be required to determine if the following *idcode* values existed in the table:

a) 100
b) 599
c) 800

At best, when searching for an unmatched key, the number of comparisons required is 1, and, at worst, is equal to the number of entries in the table (5 in the example above).

Hence the average number of comparisons required when searching for a value which is not in the list is :

(min comps + max comps) / 2
= ( 1 + 7 ) / 2
= 4

For a list of $N$ elements we get:

$$(1+N)/2$$

Using a sorted table, we can rewrite the logic for *IsAt* as:

```
Starting at beginning of table
WHILE idcode of current entry < req'd key
    AND not at end of table
DO
    move to next position in table
ENDWHILE
If match found THEN
    result is position where match found
ELSE
    result is -1
ENDIF
```

Should we maintain a sorted table? First, we can see that only when searching for unmatched keys does a sorted list offer an improvement on our search efficiency. So, unless a large number of searches will be for unmatched values, the improvement is of little significance. And, as usual, there is a price to be paid for maintaining a sorted table: we need to modify the *Add* routine so that new records are added at the appropriate position in the table (we'll look at this in detail later).

## Estimated Entry

The search methods described above are fairly obvious approaches. But how good are they? For example, confronted with a telephone directory (which is an ordered list), would we use a sequential search? If we did, it would take a very long time to find John Smith's phone number.

When we want to find an entry in the phone book, we make an initial guess about where in the book we are going to find the entry and begin searching from there. If this initial guess results in us starting at an entry which is before the one we're looking for, we search forward through the book until we find a match or until we pass the place where the entry should have been.

On the other hand, if we start at a name placed after the required value, we search backwards through the book until we find a match or until we pass where the name should be.

The main problem of such an algorithm is how to make the initial guess. That depends on several factors including:

The key value's type (usually numeric or alphabetic)
The length of the list being searched

The StudentTable *t* is sorted on a numeric key, *idcode*, while a telephone directory is sorted on an alphabetic key - surname.

Let's assume that all the *idcode* values in our students' table lie in the range 100 to 999. If we also assume these values are allocated on an apparently random basis, then 1/9 of all keys should be in the 100-199 range, 1/9 in the 200-299 range etc.

This means that for a table containing 20 elements we would expect the first 20/9 elements to contain *idcode* in the range 100 - 199; the next 20/9 elements to contain idcodes in the range 200 - 299, etc.

To translate a key into a position in the table we need to use formula:

[ x ] means the largest integer values less than or equal to

[(key's most significant digit - 1)*20/9 +0.5]

So if we were looking for a match for the value 820 we should start looking at position [(8-1) * 20/9+0.5] which is element 16 (see FIG-8.10).

**FIG-8.10**

The Estimated-Entry Search

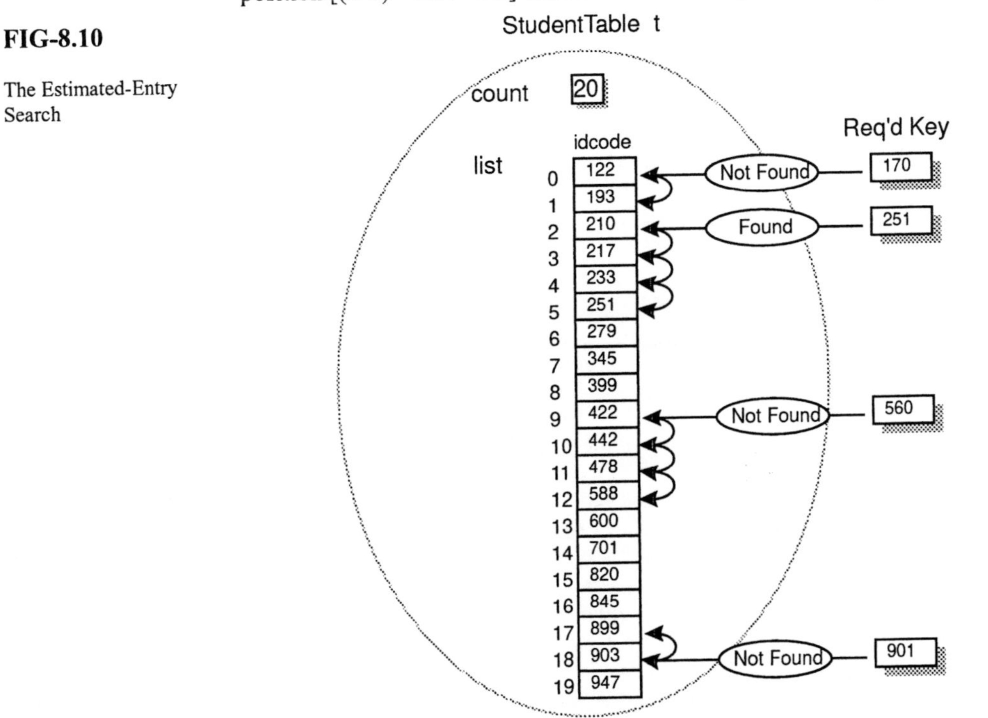


The efficiency of this method depends to a great extent on the effectiveness of the initial starting position. However, it can be seen from the example that this method seems much quicker than any previous technique.

If the values in the list are changed in such a way as to give an unbalanced distribution, then the efficiency drops (see FIG-8.11).

**FIG-8.11**

Estimated-Entry with a Biased Key Range

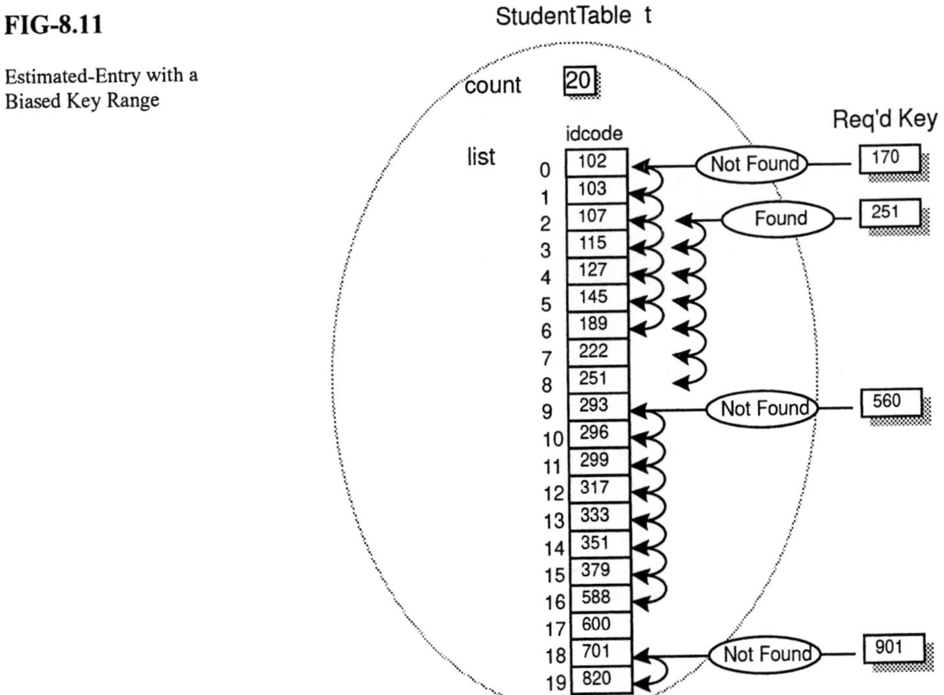

The number of comparisons required has increased because our entry point into the table, which was based on there being an average of 1/9*20 entries in each key range 100 - 199, 200 - 299 etc., gives a poor estimate of the required value's actual position.

Even if the algorithm appears to work well initially it may become less efficient as records are added and deleted from the table, hence changing the spread of values.

However, even for a relatively poor algorithm, the estimated entry approach tends to give better figures for the average number of comparisons required than any of the previous methods.

# Non-linear Searching

## The Binary Search

The initial guess method seems to give the best search method so far. However, if we return to the every day searching situation of using a telephone directory it is obvious that, in practice, the method employed is none of those described previously.

If the guess at where in the book the entry we require is likely to be is a poor one, then we make other estimates based on each preceding estimate. So if we are looking for SMITH in the directory and the first page we open at (say page 340) contains McELROY then we know that SMITH is somewhere further on and make our next guess accordingly (between page 341 and the end of the directory). If that results in opening at TAYLOR (on page 612) then our next guess is made between the pages containing McELROY and TAYLOR (between pages 341 and 611) etc.

The next computer searching technique to be examined uses this "divide and conquer" strategy and is known as the **binary search**.

The search uses the following algorithm:

```
Starting at the middle of the occupied area of the table
WHILE no match AND search area not empty DO
    IF entry's idcode is less than req'd key THEN
        Eliminate top half of table from search area
    ELSE
        Eliminate bottom half of table from search area
    ENDIF
    Examine the middle entry in the search area
ENDWHILE
IF search area is empty THEN
    found := -1
ELSE
    found := 0
ENDIF
```

FIG-8.12 shows the strategy in practice for a 15 entry table. The steps involved in searching for key 442 are:

1. Compare the middle entry (at position 7) with the required key.
2. Since the key at position 7 (345) is smaller than the required key, we can eliminate the top half of the table (positions 0 to 7) because they contain values smaller than the one required.
3. We are left with positions 8 to 14 in the search area. The middle of these is position 11 which is compared with the required key.
4. This time the key examined (478) is too large. Hence, positions 11 to 14 can be eliminated as they contain *idcode* values

which are too large.
5. Now only elements 8 to 10 remain in the search area. Element 9 is used in the next comparison.
6. Since it is too small, positions 8 and 9 are eliminated.
7. Only element 10 remains, and on this comparison a match is found.

**FIG-8.12**

The Binary Search

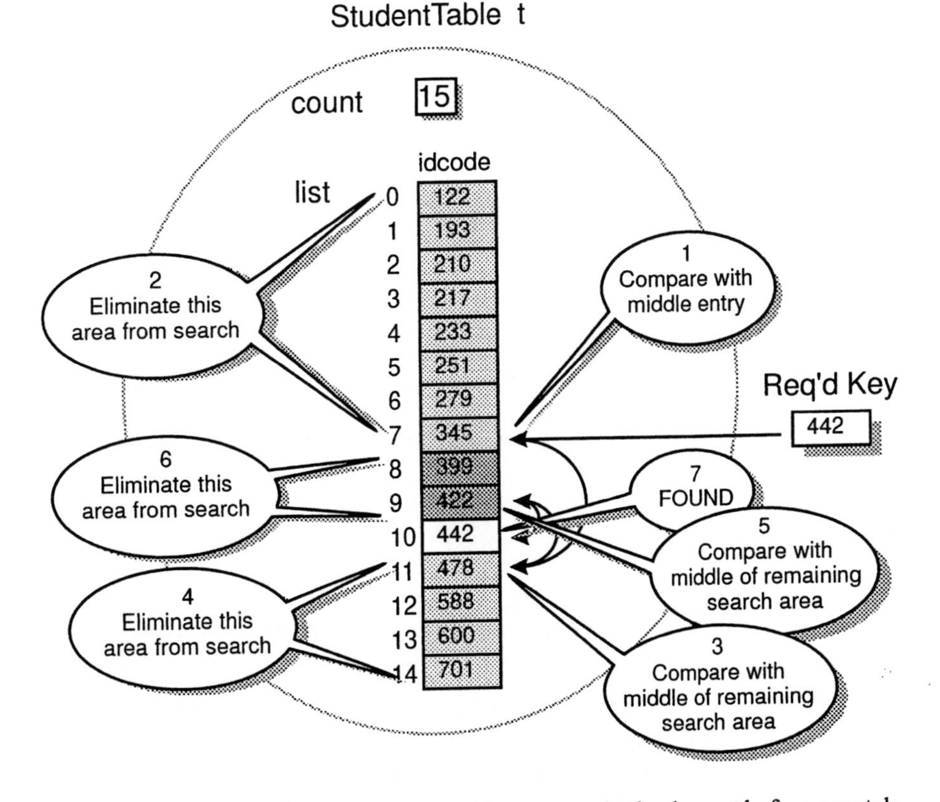


In this example we had to reduce the search area to a single element before a match was found, but if we had been searching for *idcode* 345 it would have been found after only 1 comparison, and 478 after 2 comparisons.

**Activity 8.15**

1. List the number of comparisons required to reach each of the entries in the table using the binary search approach.

2. How many entries in the table can be found after:
   a) 1 comparison?
   b) 2 comparisons?
   c) 3 comparisons?
   d) 4 comparisons?

3. What is the average number of comparisons required to find an entry?

From the results of Activity 8.15 you can see that the maximum number of comparisons required to find an entry is 4. This seems to be the most effective search method so far.

From the example, we see that the worst search case occurs when we have to reduce the search area to a single entry. Generally, how many comparisons does this require?

If we begin with a table of $N$ entries, after 1 comparison (assuming a match is not found) there will be $N/2$ entries remaining in the search area (since we will have halved the search area). After the next comparison, there will be $N/4$ entries remaining (again a halving of the search area).

**Activity 8.16**

How many entries remain after:
a) 3 comparisons?
b) 4 comparisons?

If we write the numbers 2,4,8,16 as powers of 2, we get

$$2 = 2^1$$
$$4 = 2^2$$
$$8 = 2^3$$
$$16 = 2^4$$

Using this notation in stating the size of the search area:

| No of comparisons | Size of search area |
|---|---|
| 1 | $N/2^1$ |
| 2 | $N/2^2$ |
| 3 | $N/2^3$ |
| 4 | $N/2^4$ |

we can see that the size of the search area is related to the number of comparisons made. Hence we can generalise and say that after $x$ comparisons, the size of the search area is $N/2^x$ elements.

Now, after a number of comparisons (say $p$) we must reach a stage where the search area has been reduced to one element (i.e. when $N/2^p = 1$). At that point (if not earlier) we will discover if a match exists or not. So the maximum number of comparisons required for a list of $N$ elements is $p$ when $N/2^p = 1$. This can be re-arranged to give:

$$p = \log_2 N$$

The value $\log_2 N$ will not always give an integer result, whereas the maximum number of comparisons must obviously be an integer. So to get the final result we need to modify our formula to:

$$\text{maximum comparisons} = [\log_2 N+1]$$

**Activity 8.17**

Using the formula above, calculate the maximum number of comparisons for a table of size:
a) 15
b) 16
c) 1,000
d) 10,000

The maximum comparisons required to find a match is also the number of comparisons required to discover that a key is not in the table.

One way to calculate the average number of comparisons (rather than the maximum) has already been shown in Activity 8.15. Since such a calculation would be long and tedious for a list of any significant length, an approximation can be obtained using the formula:

$$\text{Average comparisons} = (\log_2 N) - 1$$

where $N$ is the number of entries in the table.

The accuracy of this approximation increases as $N$ becomes large.

## Implementing the Binary Search

Assuming we are willing to maintain a sorted table, the binary search approach seems to be the approach to use when coding our *IsAt()* function.

To indicate which part of the table remains in the search area, we need to maintain two indicator variables, *lowest* and *highest*. These hold the lowest and highest element numbers still in the search area. Hence, at the start of our search, in a table containing 15 entries, *lowest* would contain the value zero and *highest* 14. The middle of the search area can be found using the formula:

```
[(lowest+highest) /2]
```

> **Activity 8.18**
>
> List the values of *lowest* and *highest*, during the search shown in FIG-8.12.

The detailed logic and code for the new version of *IsAt()* is given below:

**Outline Logic:**

```
lowest := 0
highest := t.count
mid := (lowest+highest)/2
WHILE not a match AND search area not empty DO
    IF table's idcode < req'd key THEN
        lowest := mid+1
    ELSE
        highest := mid -1
    ENDIF
    mid := (lowest+highest)/2
ENDWHILE
IF search area not empty THEN
    post := mid
ELSE
    post = -1
ENDIF
```

**Code:**

```
function IsAt(key :integer; var t : StudentTable):integer;
var
    lowest, mid, highest : integer;
                          {extremes and middle of search area}
begin
    {*** Search area is the occupied part of the table ***}
    lowest := 0;
    highest := t.count-1;
    {*** Mid entry is half way ***}
    mid := (lowest + highest) div 2;

    {*** WHILE no match found & search area not empty DO ***}
    while (t.list[mid].idcode <> key) and (lowest <= highest) do
```

```
    begin
        {*** IF the mid entry's idcode < required key THEN ***}
        if t.list[mid].idcode < key then
            {*** Eliminate the top end of the search area ***}
            lowest := mid + 1
        else
            {*** ELSE eliminate the bottom end ***}
            highest := mid - 1;
        {*** Calculate the mid point of the new search area ***}
        mid := (lowest + highest) div 2;
    end;
    {*** ENDWHILE ***}
    {*** IF key found (i.e. search area not empty) THEN ***}
    if lowest <= highest then
        {*** Return last mid-point - it is position of match ***}
        IsAt := mid
    else
        {*** ELSE return -1 to indicate no match found ***}
        IsAt := -1;
end;
```

**Activity 8.19**

Update your *StudentTable* program to include this version of *IsAt*.
(Ensure the table entries are sorted by adding them in the correct order.)

# A Final Comparison

A comparison of the Sequential and Binary searches (see TABLE-8.1) shows that, using only this criteria, the Binary Search is an obviously superior method.

**TABLE-8.1**

Comparison of Sequential and Binary Searching

| Size of List | Average number of comparisons (seq) | (binary) |
|---|---|---|
| 10 | 5.5 | 2.9 |
| 100 | 50.5 | 5.8 |
| 1000 | 500.5 | 9.0 |
| 10000 | 5000.5 | 12.4 |

However, the search loop of the Binary Search is more complex which implies that each comparison will require more time than with the earlier methods.

If the time taken for one iteration of the sequential search is $t_s$ and the time for the Binary search $t_b$ then the average time for a binary search must be less than that for the sequential search to make it worthwhile. That is:

$$t_b(\log_2 N - 1) < t_s((N+1)/2)$$

In practice this point occurs long before the list reaches 100 elements.

# Choosing An Implementation

The discussion on searching should highlight the sort of thing a designer has to take into consideration when choosing the method of implementation for a data structure:

If an array is to be used, should the values contained in that array be held in order (even if the application does not require it) since this will allow faster search methods to be employed (i.e. the Binary Search)?

The price that must be paid for maintaining an ordered list is the effort of inserting and deleting entries in such a list. These operations involve moving existing entries about within the array to create space for a new entry or to remove an entry. This movement will take a long time (in computer terms) and hence degrade the efficiency of the program.

Generally, the programmer may decide on a sorted array if the number of new entries and deletions are expected to be small (and hence minimise the amount of data movement involved) but if many such insertions and deletions are expected some other method will probably be chosen.

# Summary

- **Search method efficiency** is determined by

  the average number of comparisons required to find a given value
  the efficiency of the algorithm used to implement the method

- **Linear search methods** include

  Serial search
  Sequential Search
  Estimated entry Search

- **The Binary Search is a non-linear method**.

# DIRECT ACCESS TABLES

## Introduction

As we've seen from the analysis of the techniques, both ordered and unordered tables give relatively poor performance when searched. Even the best method, Binary Search, suffers from the overhead of having to maintain a sorted list.

When minimising search time is our top priority, one method of achieving this is to use a direct access table. A direct access table contains a position for every possible key value. For example if the *idcode* field in our *StudentTable* contained values between 0 and 999 the table would have 1000 elements (see FIG-8.13).

**FIG-8.13**

Creating a Direct Access Table

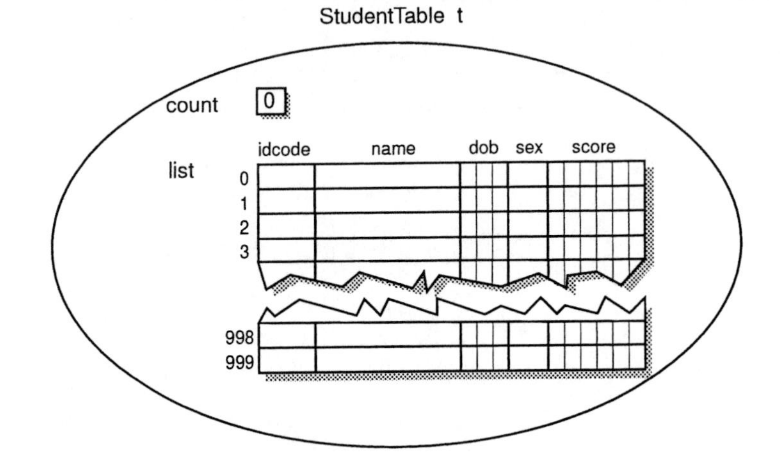


The code for this structure would be:

```
StudentTable =
record
    count : integer;
    list  : array[0..99] of StudentDetails;
end;
```

New entries to the table are inserted at the position in the table which corresponds to their key value. Hence, if we added records for students 1, 3, and 998 then the table would be as shown in FIG-8.14.

**FIG-8.14**

Adding Records to a Direct Access Table

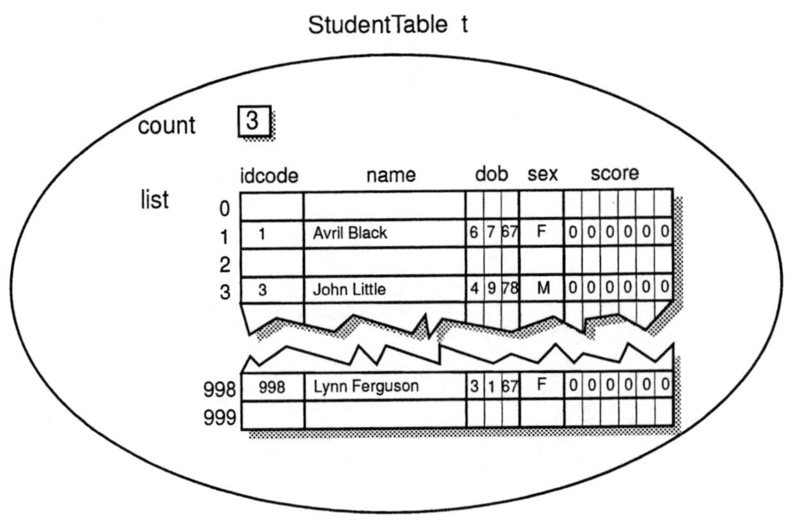

Notice that there is no requirement to store the actual *idcode* field since the record's position in the table is the same as its *idcode* value. This would allow us to redefine the table's structure and omit the *idcode* field from the array's record structure.

# Implementation

Since we need to differentiate between an occupied and unoccupied position in the table's array, the *CreateTable()* function will have to set each entry in the array to some value corresponding to "empty".

We might do this by setting the *name* field to blank with the code:

```
procedure CreateTable(var t:StudentTable);
var
    c : integer;    {Loop counter}
begin
    {*** Set the count to zero ***}
    t.count := 0;
    {*** Set each name to an empty string ***}
    for c := 0 to 999 do
        t.list[c].name := '';
end;
```

The code for *IsAt* now becomes trivial. To find a record, we simply examine the position in the table corresponding to the student's *idcode.* If there's an entry, the routine returns the position in the table of the matching record; if not, -1 is returned.

This means we have reduced the number of comparisons required to find an entry in the table to 1. In other words, we can access the required entry directly; hence the name: **Direct Access Table**.

**Activity 8.20**

1. Write the code for *IsAt* function using the strategy described above.
   HINT: If the name field is empty the required record is not in the table.

2. Write the *DeleteFromTable* function for removing an entry in the table.
   HINT: You need to reset the name field to an empty string.

We have created the ultimate in fast access tables. And there are several advantages:

- The key field does not need to be saved
- Access to a record is immediate with no searching
- Inserting and deleting a record does not involve moving any of the other entries

So why isn't this the way all tables are implemented? Unfortunately, direct access tables have one overwhelming drawback: the size of the array. Our table requires 1000 entries, and if we don't have many students, only a few elements of the array will ever be occupied. For a six-digit numeric key, we'd need 1,000,000 entries and for a 30 character key field, such as *name*, we'd need more storage than any computer's memory is capable of holding.

# HASH TABLES

## Introduction

The **hash table** is a structure which attempts to gain the fast access characteristic of direct access tables without the corresponding large storage requirements. To achieve this, the hash table is created with an array which is approximately 50% larger than the number of records it is likely to hold and the key field of any new records is transformed (or hashed) to give the position in the table where the record should be stored.

For example, assume we need to store information on five students in a table containing 20 positions. One way of deciding where in the table each record should be placed is to store the record in the position corresponding to the last digit of the *idcode* number. So, if we assume the data for the five students is

```
1162   Keith Brown    M   61 21 32 11 21 19
7914   Linda Goodman  F   45 67 21 34 23 12
2635   James Allen    M   10 12 16 13 18 14
2937   Carol Wight    F   65 45 53 37 41 57
1329   Fiona Black    F   87 79 65 45 62 16
```

then the position of the records in the hash table would be as shown in FIG-8.15.

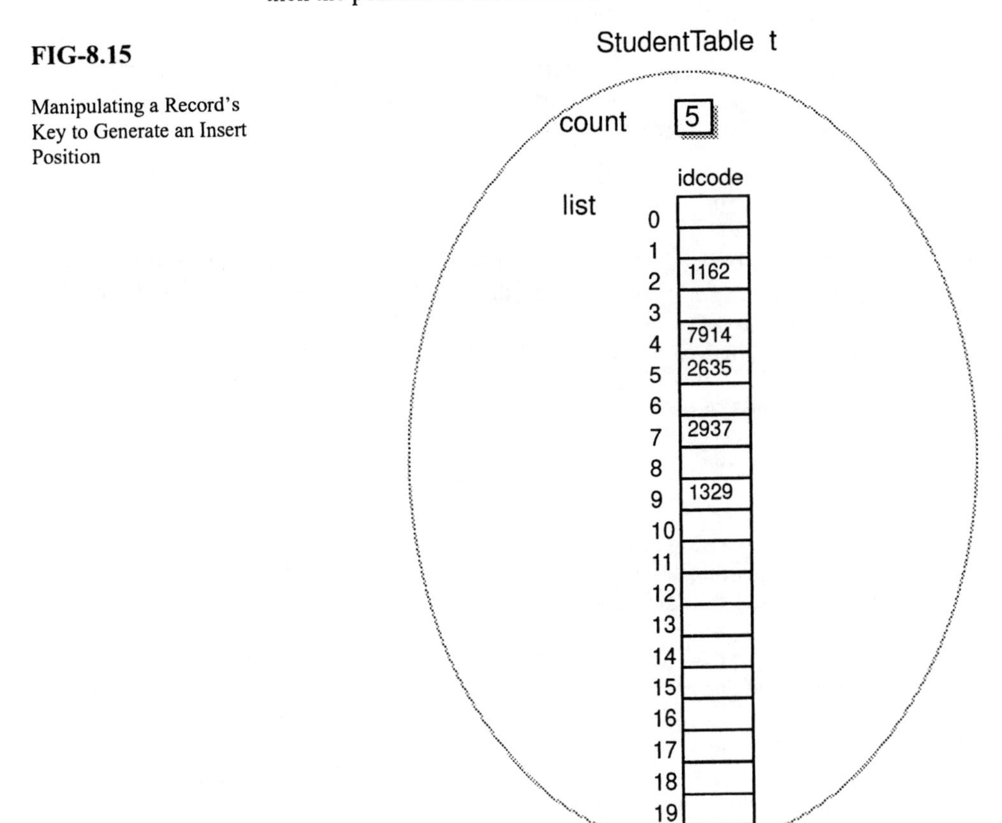


**FIG-8.15**

Manipulating a Record's Key to Generate an Insert Position

Unlike direct access tables, we have to store the key field since the position of the record is not identical to the key.

This isn't a very good method of deciding where to place the entries since only positions 0 to 9 will ever be occupied. It's important therefore that we choose a good hashing algorithm. Some of the more popular are described below.

# Key Transformation Algorithms

The main criteria in choosing a method of key transformation is that the entries should spread as evenly as possible throughout the table and not cluster in one area. Secondly, the time taken to carry out the translation should be kept to a minimum.

## Modular Division

In this technique, the key is divided by the number of elements in the table and the remainder is taken as the position. For example, assuming the use of a table with 17 elements (numbered 0 to 16) then an entry with key 615 would have its position calculated as:

key modulo table size
= 615 MOD 17
= 3

It can be shown (but we will not do so here!) that the best results are obtained when division is by a prime number. That is, the number of elements in the table should be a prime number.

Modular Division is one of the best general purpose hashing algorithms.

## Folding

In this method the key is divided into separate segments, with each segment having the same number of digits as contained in the index of the last element of the table (e.g. if the last position in a table is 999, the key would be split into three-digit segments). These segments are added together to give a result in the range of the table length. For example, assuming a table size of 100 (0 to 99) and a 6 digit key, then for the key value 242586 we get

242586 = 24 + 25 + 86
= 135
= position 35 (the most-significant digit is ignored)

For a larger table, the key is split into larger sections. For example, assuming a table size of 1000 (0 to 999), the result for the same key (242586) is:

242586 = 242 + 586
= 828
= position 828

**Activity 8.21**

Using FOLDING, find the position for key 102438 in a
a) 100 element table
b) 1000 element table

## Mid-Square

Using this method, the key is squared and a group of digits from the middle of the result are used to specify the position. The size of the group is decided by the number of elements in the table. For example, assuming a table of 100 elements and a 4 digit key, then for the key 4573 we get the result:

$$4573^2 = 20912329$$
$$= \text{position } 12 \text{ (taken from the middle 2 digits)}$$

If the table contained 1000 elements, then the address would have been 912 or 123 depending on which group of digits were chosen (it is obviously important to be consistent).

## Hashing String Fields

So far the key fields to be hashed have been numeric ones. This isn't an unreasonable assumption since many computer systems do use numeric keys. However, this is not always the case. For example, a National Insurance number contains both letters and numbers, while a small table might even use a person's name as the key field. The simplest way to handle such fields is simply to convert part of the field to a numeric value which can then be hashed using one of the methods described above. For example, in a small table using a client's name as the key field, we might take the first 4 bits of the first letter and the first 4 bits of the last letter in the name to create a single 8 bit numeric value (giving values in the range 0 to 255) which can then be hashed to lie within the table size.

**Activity 8.22**

Write the code necessary to create such an 8-bit value from a string.
HINT: you may find the remainder operator useful.

# Handling Collisions

FIG-8.16 shows where various records are stored using the hashing algorithm *idcode* modulo 17.

**FIG-8.16**

Using Modular Division Hashing

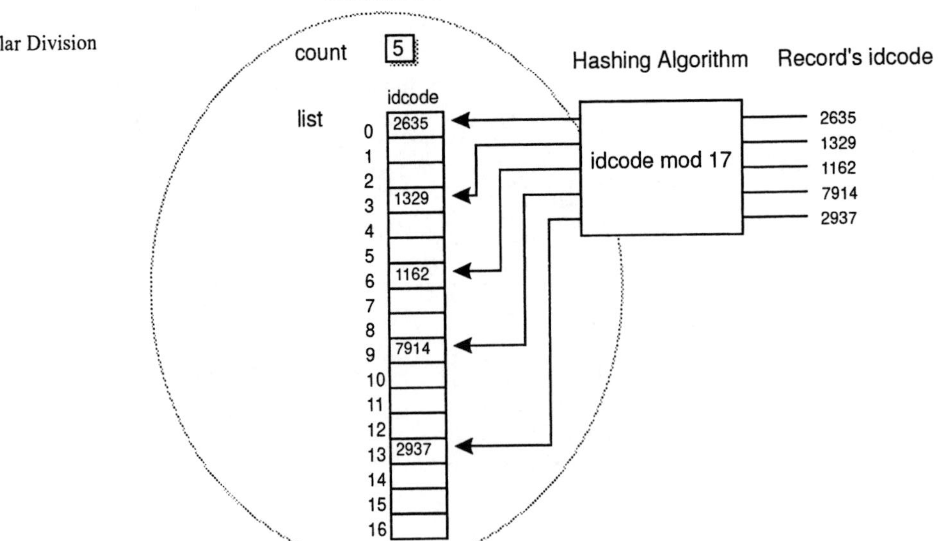

> **Activity 8.23**
>
> Using the same hashing algorithm, calculate the insertion points for the records whose *idcode* values are:
>
> 8838
> 6627
> 4895
> 1995

The last value in Activity 8.23 highlights the problem with hashing. What happens when two or more keys hash to the same position in the table?

When a new record hashes to an already occupied location, we have a **collision**. The simplest way to deal with this situation is to insert the new record in the first empty space available (see FIG-8.17).

**FIG-8.17**

Handling Collisions

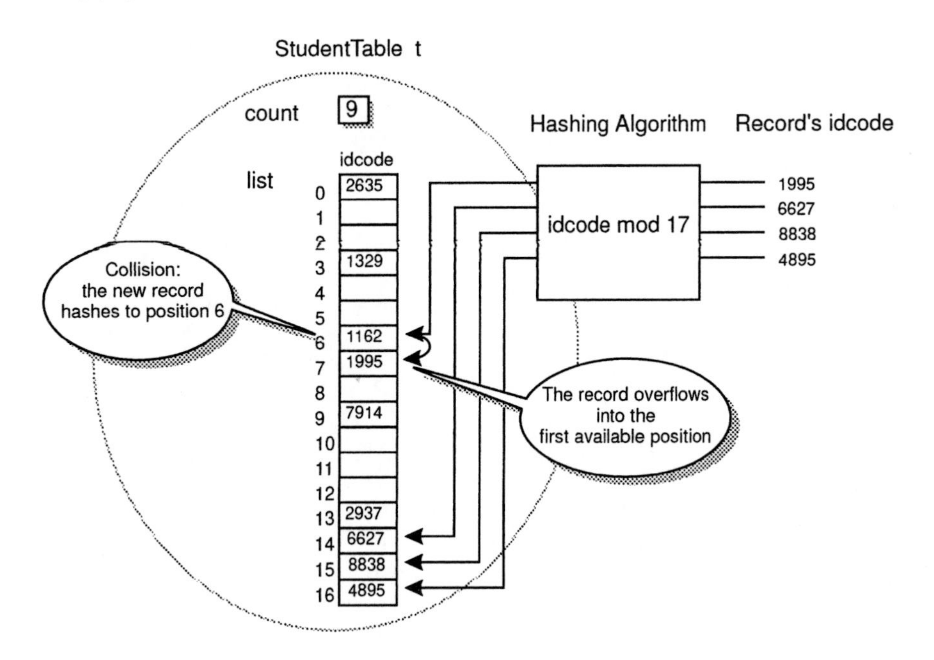


This approach to handling collisions is known as **linear probing** and the displaced record is said to have **overflowed**.

If a record cannot find an overflow position before the end of the list is reached, searching continues at the start of the list. For example, if the record with *idcode* 1765 were to be inserted in the table shown in FIG-8.17, its initial hash position would be 14, and, this being occupied, locations 15, 16, 0 and 1 would be probed to find an empty table element.

We can describe the logic required to add an entry to the hash table as:

```
Hash record's key to find insert position
WHILE position occupied DO
    move to next position
ENDWHILE
```

This assumes the table is not full and, when the end of the table is reached, the next position is the start of the table.

# Implementation

Our hash table will contain records of *StudentDetails* type. The *list* component of the table consists of 17 elements (too small to gain any practical advantage from hashing but large enough to demonstrate the theory of hash tables).

## Defining the StudentTable

The only difference in the declaration of the table's structure from earlier versions is that, from what's been said already, it will be more efficient to make sure that the list component's size is a prime number. In this case 17. This gives us the declaration:

```
const
    SIZE = 20;


type

    StudentDetails =
    record
        idcode : integer;
        name   : string[30];
        sex    : char;
        score  : array[1..6] of integer;
    end;


    StudentTable =
    record
        count : integer;
        list  : array[0..SIZE-1] of StudentDetails;
    end;
```

## Creating the Table

Like the direct access table, we need to mark every element in the list as empty, as well as setting the *count* field to zero. This time, we'll use the value 0 in the *idcode* field to indicate an empty position.

So, assuming the global definition

```
const
    EMPTY = 0;
```

we can code this routine as

```
procedure CreateTable(var t:StudentTable);
var
    c : integer;    {Loop counter}
begin
    {*** Set count to zero ***}
    t.count := 0;
    {*** Set all key fields to empty ***}
    for c := 0 to SIZE-1 do
        t.list[c].idcode := EMPTY;
end;
```

## Creating the Hash Function

Since transforming the record's key field will be such a common occurrence, this can be written as a separate function:

```
function Hash(key:integer):integer;
begin
    Hash := key mod SIZE
end;
```

In other tables, with non-numeric keys, the hashing algorithm will obviously be adjusted appropriately.

## Adding an Entry to the Table

To add a new student we need to make sure that the *idcode* value is not already in the table. If it isn't, then we need to calculate where in the table the new record needs to be placed.

As with our earlier table, we'll start by creating an *IsAt* function. This needs to look through the table for a match. Finding a match is easy: we just hash the key and use the same strategy employed to insert the record in the first place. But how do we know a record isn't in the table? We could search the whole table, but that would negate many of the advantages of the hash table. Instead, we need only look at the section of the table in which the record should have been placed.

The mini-spec for the routine is similar to that for the standard table:

| | | |
|---|---|---|
| NAME | : | IsAt |
| PARAMETERS | | |
| IN | : | key : INTEGER<br>t : StudentTable |
| OUT | : | post : INTEGER |
| IN/OUT | : | None |
| PRE-CONDITION | : | None. |
| POST-CONDITION | : | Returns in *post* the position in *t* of the record whose *idcode* value is *key*. Where no match exists, *post* is set to -1. |

The Outline Logic for the routine is:

```
Calculate starting position by hashing key
WHILE no match AND position not EMPTY
  AND complete table not searched
DO
    Move to next position in the table
ENDWHILE
IF id at stopping position is equal to key THEN
    Set post to stopping position
ELSE
    Set post to -1
ENDIF
```

From this we get the code:

```
function IsAt(key:integer; var t:StudentTable):integer;
var
    post  : integer;    {Position in table of required entry}
    start : integer;    {The starting position of the search}
begin
    {*** Hash to where record should be ***}
    start := Hash(key);
    post := start;
    {*** WHILE no match or empty position reached DO ***}
    while (t.list[post].idcode <> key) and
    ↳(t.list[post].idcode <> EMPTY) do
    begin
        {*** Move to next position in table ***}
        post := (post+1) mod SIZE;
        {*** IF all entries searched, give up ***}
        if post = start then
```

NOTFOUND is a named constant assigned the value -1

```
            break;
      end;
      {*** IF not successful THEN, return -1 ***}
      if(t.list[post].idcode <> key)then
          IsAt := NOTFOUND
      else
          {*** ELSE return position of record ***}
          IsAt := post;
end;
```

The function contains the line

```
post := (post+1) mod SIZE ;
```

which is a shorter, if more obscure, way of writing

```
if post < SIZE-1 then
    inc(post)
else
    post := 0;
```

We can then make use of *IsAt* to make sure any *AddToTable* operation does not allow two or more entries to contain the same *idcode* value.

The mini-spec for the *AddToTable* operation is:

| | | |
|---|---|---|
| NAME | : | AddToTable |
| PARAMETERS | | |
| IN | : | sd : StudentDetails |
| OUT | : | success : BOOLEAN |
| IN/OUT | : | t : StudentTable |
| PRE-CONDITION | : | None |
| POST-CONDITION | : | If *t* is full or *sd.idcode* matches an idcode in *t*, *success* is set to *false* and *t* is unchanged, otherwise *sd* is added to *t* and *success* is set to *true*. |

The Outline Logic is:

```
IF table is full OR st.idcode matches an entry in t THEN
    success := 0
ELSE
    Calculate insert position by hashing st.idcode
    WHILE no match AND position occupied DO
        move to next position
    ENDWHILE
    Insert new record at position
    Increment count
    success:=1
ENDIF
```

The code for this is:

```
function AddToTable(sd:StudentDetails; var t:StudentTable)
                                                    :boolean;
var
    post : integer;    {Position in table of record}
begin
    {*** IF idcode matches existing one or table full THEN ***}
    if (IsAt(sd.idcode,t) <> NOTFOUND) or (IsFull(t)) then
    begin
        {*** Return false ***}
        AddToTable := false;
        exit;
    end;
    {*** Find insert position ***}
    {** Hash key **}
```

```
    post := Hash(sd.idcode);
    {** Linear probe until available position found **}
    while(t.list[post].idcode <> EMPTY) do
        post := (post+1) mod SIZE;
    {*** Add student's details to table ***}
    t.list[post] := sd;
    {*** Increment count ***}
    inc(t.count);
    {*** Return true ***}
    AddToTable := true;
end;
```

## Displaying the Table

Since much of the table will be empty, the display function must look at each position in the table displaying only the contents of occupied positions. This requires the logic:

```
Starting at the first position in the table
REPEAT
    IF the position is occupied THEN
        Display its contents
    ENDIF
UNTIL the end of the table is reached
```

## Returning a Single Table Entry

Previously, we had two functions for returning a single record: *GiveRecord* and *GiveRecordAt*. However, the second of these, designed to return the entry at a specified position in the table is of little use in this situation where the position of an entry cannot be easily predicted. The mini-spec for *GiveRecord* is repeated below.

| | | |
|---|---|---|
| NAME | : | GiveRecord |
| PARAMETERS | | |
| IN | : | key : INTEGER<br>t : StudentTable |
| OUT | : | sd : StudentDetails<br>success: INTEGER |
| IN/OUT | : | None |
| PRE-CONDITION | : | None |
| POST-CONDITION | : | If *key* matches the idcode of an entry in *t*, *success* is set to *true* and *sd* returns a copy of the matching record from *t*. If *key* does not match, *success* is set to *false* and *sd* holds an empty record. |

When using a hash table, the Outline Logic for *GiveRecord* is:

```
Calculate position of req'd record
IF found THEN
    sd := t.list[position]
    success := true
ELSE
    success := false
ENDIF
```

**Activity 8.24**

Based on the logic given above, produce the code for *GiveRecord.*

## Deleting a Table Entry

It's much easier to delete a record from a hash table than from serial and sequential tables. This is because there is no need to move any of the other entries in the table when deleting from a hash table. All we need to do is to find the required entry and place a marker in its key field.

The question is, what sort of marker? Perhaps we should simply mark it with an EMPTY value. At first sight, this might seem a reasonable choice, since, once deleted, the record's position will be free to take a new entry. But there's a major problem: if we mark a deleted record as EMPTY, the search procedure may fail (see FIG-8.18).

**FIG-8.18**

Breaking the Search Path

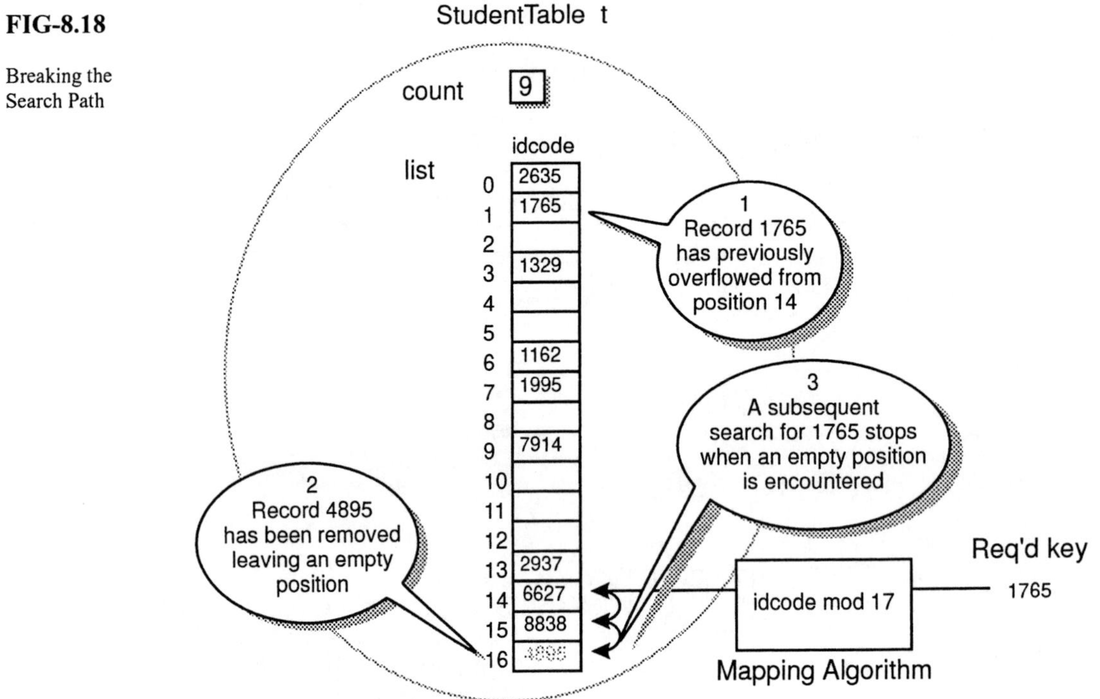


To avoid this problem, we need to use a distinct marker for deleted records. This way, the search algorithm won't stop too early.

There's one final tweak to get the whole thing working: the *AddToTable* function needs to change from

```
while t.list[post].idcode <> EMPTY do
```

to

```
while( t.list[post].idcode <> EMPTY) and
                              (t.list[post].idcode <> DELETED) do
```

which allows us to insert new entries at deleted as well as empty positions in the table.

**Activity 8.25**

Create a hash table implementation of *StudentTable*.

# An Alternative Method of Dealing with Overflow

## Problems With Linear Probing

For a hash table to be efficient, it is important that we keep the number of comparisons required to find an entry to a minimum. If the required entry has not overflowed, then the number of comparisons required during a search will be 1. However, if overflow has occurred this figure will increase. The actual figure depends on the length of the search path through the table.

Linear probing, the method of overflow that we dealt with above, has some problems in this area. You can see from FIG-8.19 that if several entries hash to the same position in a table, they follow the same route when searching for an empty position. This situation obviously leads to a reduction in the efficiency of the search and needs to be eliminated.

**FIG-8.19**

Overflowing in the Footsteps of Others

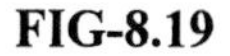

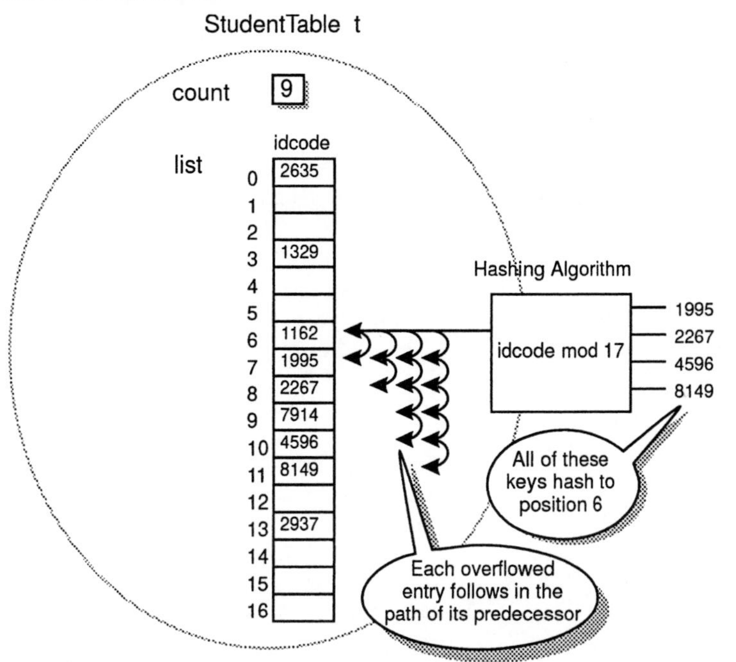


The second method of overflow we are going to examine attempts to eliminate this *following in the footsteps* of previous synonyms which linear probing suffers from.

## Double Hashing

This technique is similar to linear probing, but instead of probing the next element of the table when a collision occurs, double hashing calculates a step size which is then used to calculate the next position to be probed. For example, if a new entry such as 8149 hashes to an occupied position 6 in our table then a step size is calculated. Assuming a step size of 11, the table would be probed for an empty (or deleted) element at positions 0 ((6+11) mod 17), 11, 5 , 16, etc. until an insert position is found (see FIG-8.20).

**FIG-8.20**

Using an Overflow Step Size

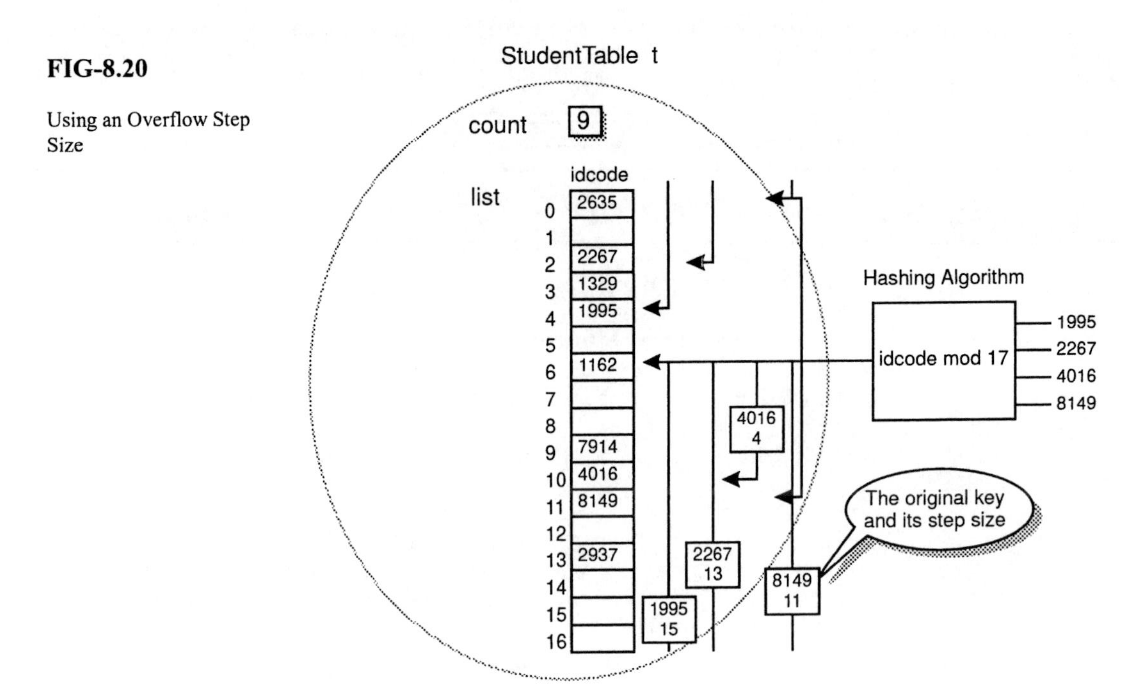


**Calculating the step Size**

To calculate the step size, the original key is transformed using a second (different) hashing algorithm.

To be effective the second hashing algorithm must have the following characteristics:

1. It must not return a step size of zero.
   Obviously, with a step size of zero the search position would be unchanged from the original hash position.

2. It should not return a value which divides exactly into the length of the table.
   This would mean that not all elements of the table could be probed. (e.g. if a table had 8 elements and a new entry which mapped to position 6 overflowed using a step size of 2, then the elements which could be probed are 8,2,4,6,8,2... etc. ). This problem is easily solved by making the number of positions in the table a prime number and the step size some lesser value.

3. It must return a different step size for keys which are synonyms under the first hashing algorithm. For example, keys 1995 and 4016 both map to position 6, but under the second hash algorithm they should have differing step sizes say 15, and 4. This restriction is necessary otherwise overflowing entries will still follow each other's 'footsteps' in a search for an insert position.

A good second transformation algorithm for a table containing N elements is:

(N-2) - (key MOD (N-2))

In our example N = 17, so the step size is calculated as:

15 - (key MOD 15)

Using this double hashing approach, the *Add* operation would be coded using the logic:

```
IF new entry's idcode matches an existing one OR table full THEN
    Set success to zero
ELSE
    Transform the key to get insert position
    IF position in table is not empty or deleted THEN
        Calculate step size by hashing new entry's key
        (using second hash algorithm)
        REPEAT
            Calculate next position as
                        (current position + step size)MOD SIZE
        UNTIL table position empty or deleted
    ENDIF
    Insert new entry
    Add 1 to count
    Set success to 1
ENDIF
```

**Activity 8.26**

Modify your hash table program to use Double Hashing overflow.

# Hash Table Efficiency

The hash table gives a very small average number of comparisons when searching. When the table is around 50% full, the average number of comparisons required is approximately 1.625. Also, this value does not vary with the size of the table but rather with the percentage occupied. Hence, a table which has 200 elements and is 50% full, will have the same average number of comparisons when searching as one which has 5000 elements and is 50% full. Double hashing gives a slight improvement in the average over linear probing. When the table is over 70% full the average climbs rapidly and the best solution is to rehash all the entries into a larger table.

# Summary

- **A hash table** is designed to give fast access to entries without excessive storage requirements.
- **The key field of the record is hashed** using a mapping algorithm to determine the point of insertion within the table.
- **Modular division** is the commonest method of hashing.
- **Synonyms** are keys which hash to the same value.
- **A collision** occurs when a record attempts insertion at a position already occupied.
- **A record overflows** into some other position in the table when the required insert position is already occupied.
- **Linear probing** searches forward one position at a time for an insert point.
- **Double hashing** calculates a step size when choosing the next position to be examined as a possible insert position.

■ **Double hash algorithm must**:

Not give a zero step size
Not give a step size which divides exactly into the table size
Not produce the same step size for all synonyms

# SORTING

## Introduction

Sorting is the act of arranging a list of items into a specific order. Typical examples of sorted information include:

- The entries in a telephone directory which have been sorted into alphabetic order of the subscriber's name.
- A football league table which has been sorted according to the points gained by each team.
- The entries in a bank statement which have been sorted in order of date of transaction.

Consider a set of records held by a bookseller giving details of the items in stock. Such a record could have the following structure:

```
BookRec =
RECORD
    Isbn    : INTEGER
    Title   : STRING
    Author  : STRING
    InStock : INTEGER
ENDRECORD
```

If the books are to be arranged in order of the author's name, then the field, *Author*, is said to be the record's **sort key**.

The sort key is defined as the set of characters within a record that is used to determine the order during the sorting process. This is sometimes simply referred to as the key. A key can consist of:

Part of a field
A single field
or Several fields

### Sort Order

Sorting may arrange the data in either ascending or descending order. Ascending order is, by far, the more commonly used of the two organisations.

**Activity 8.27**

Write down the order of the following records after sorting them in ascending order using the Author field as the sort key.

| ISBN | TITLE | AUTHOR | QTY |
|---|---|---|---|
| 330 | Childhood's End | A.C.Clarke | 8 |
| 708 | Janissaries | J.Pournelle | 6 |
| 586 | Hiero's Journey | S.E.Lanier | 3 |
| 090 | 2001 | A.C.Clarke | 7 |
| 911 | A Martian Odyssey | S.G.Weinbaum | 1 |
| 569 | 2010 | A.C.Clarke | 2 |
| 255 | I,Robot | I.Asimov | 4 |

Since there are three books by A.C.Clarke in the data given in Activity 8.27, any arrangement of these three records would conform to the definition of a sorted list.

To define a unique order for the above records, the sort key specified must incorporate one or more additional fields. For example, the sort key could be *Author* followed by *Isbn*. That is, the sort can be thought of as the action of sorting the books by *Author* then for records with the same author, the *Isbn* is used to determine their order. The term used is **sorting on *Isbn* within *Author.***

Using *Author/Isbn* would give the Clarke books an order of:

```
090 2001                A.C.Clarke 7
330 Childhood's End     A.C.Clarke 8
569 2010                A.C.Clarke 2
```

In this situation, *Author* is termed the **major key**; *Isbn* is the **minor key**.

In practice, the sorting algorithm concatenates the fields that make up the key into a single string that is then used as the sort key.

A key made up of non-contiguous fields is known as a **split-key**.

### Why Sort?

Some of the main reasons for sorting data are:

- The order in which items are stored often has a profound effect on the speed and simplicity of the algorithms that manipulate them.

  *Example*
  The binary search requires data to be in key field order.

- So that the output can be presented in a useful and meaningful form.

  *Example*
  Sales figures could be sorted to show
  a) Sales by branch
  b) Sales by item
  c) Sales by date

- So that calculations that require data in a particular order can operate efficiently.

  *Example*
  Sales forecasting would require sales data to be in chronological order.

- To facilitate the retrieval of information.

  *Example*
  Telephone directories would be difficult to use if not sorted by name.

## Types of Sorts

There are two main classes of sorts:

**Internal sorts**. The data to be sorted is held entirely within the main memory of the machine. Obviously, this can only be used if the amount of data is relatively small.

**External sorts**. The data to be sorted is held on backing store. A batch of records from the data is read into main memory from backing store. These records are then sorted using internal sorting techniques and then written to a new file on backing store. This process continues until all of the original data has been read in, sorted and written to various files on disk (or tape). These files are then merged to form a single sorted file. We'll be looking at this in more detail later.

We will examine internal sorts only in this chapter.

Generally, internal sorts are faster than external sorts since all records to be sorted are held in main memory, the access to which is much faster than backing store access. The data is normally held in an array of records.

### Types of Internal Sorts

Internal sorts may be sub-divided into 3 groups:

**Selection sorts**. These scan an unsorted list repeatedly, selecting the record with the smallest key on each scan through the list. The record selected is then added to the sorted list.

**Insertion sorts**. Each record in the unsorted list is taken in turn, starting at the first, and inserted into the correct position in a sorted list.

**Exchange sorts**. The keys of two records are compared and if the records are out of order with respect to each other they exchange positions. This process is repeated until the whole list is sorted.

## The Selection Sorts

### Simple Selection

This is possibly the simplest of all sort algorithms, being little more complicated than just finding the minimum value in a list.

We begin with two lists (in this case, we'll continue to use tables). One of the lists contains the records to be sorted (let's call it *t1*); the other (*t2*) is empty. Now, *t1* is scanned from start to finish in search of the record containing the lowest key. Once identified, this record is copied to the first empty position in *t2*. To ensure that the same record is not picked on the next pass through *t1*, each record transferred to t2 is erased from the unsorted list. This is usually achieved by replacing the key field with a value greater than any possible for a valid key.

These three steps constitute one **pass** of the sort and are shown in FIG-8.21.

The steps are repeated until all records have been transferred.

**FIG-8.21**

Simple Selection Sort

Step 1: Find the smallest key in t1

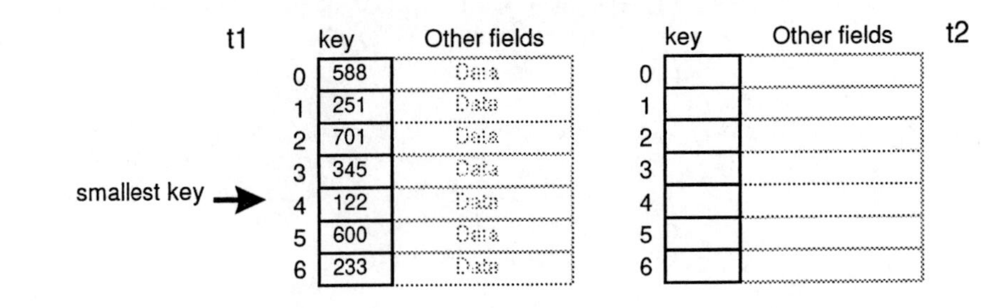


Step 2: Transfer the record to t2

| t1 | key | Other fields | | t2 | key | Other fields |
|---|---|---|---|---|---|---|
| 0 | 588 | Data | | 0 | 122 | Data |
| 1 | 251 | Data | | 1 | | |
| 2 | 701 | Data | | 2 | | |
| 3 | 345 | Data | | 3 | | |
| 4 | 122 | Data | | 4 | | |
| 5 | 600 | Data | | 5 | | |
| 6 | 233 | Data | | 6 | | |

Step 3: Delete the transferred record from t1

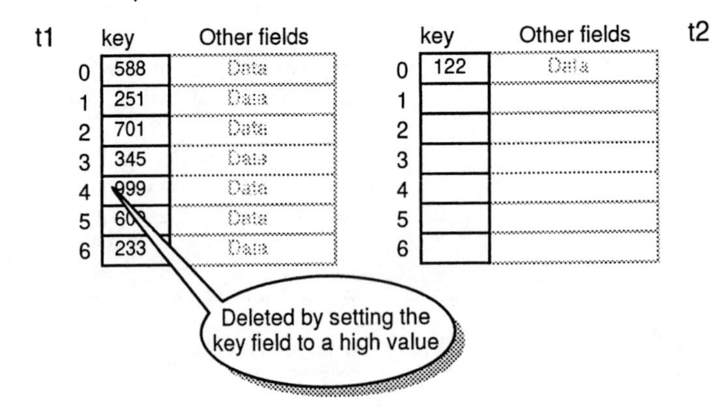


**Activity 8.28**

How many passes will be required before all 7 records shown in FIG-8.21 are transferred?

The number of passes required by a sort is one of the characteristics used to determine the efficiency of the sort.

The Simple Selection sort performed on a list of *N* entries can be described in Structured English as:

```
FOR N passes DO
    Find the smallest key in the unsorted list
    Copy the corresponding record to the first empty position
     in the sorted list
    Delete the record from the unsorted list
ENDFOR
```

**Activity 8.29**

Using the *StudentTable* structure created in Activity 8.19:

a) Create a function *SmallestAt* which returns the position of the smallest *idcode* in a *StudentTable* variable.

b) Create a sort operation which will copy the contents of one table in sorted order to another.

HINT: Use 32,767 when setting a record's *idcode* to a high value.

We need to discover a few more facts before deciding the efficiency of this sort method.

**Activity 8.30**

1. To sort a list of *N* elements, how many record storage elements are required?
2. How many comparisons are required to find the minimum key in the unsorted list during
   a) Pass 1
   b) Pass 2
   c) Pass *N*
3. What is the total number of comparisons carried out during the whole sorting process ?
4. How many record movements are there on each pass?
5. How many record movements does the sort require in total?

To summarise, when deciding on the efficiency of a sorting technique the following factors are taken into account:

- The storage requirements
- The total number of comparisons involved
- The total number of record movements required

## Selection With Exchange

The big problem with the Simple Selection sort that we looked at earlier was the space requirement: 2*N* record positions to sort *N* records. The obvious refinement is to reduce this to a single list of records so only *N* locations are required. In the Selection with Exchange sort, the minimum key in the list is found as before. However, this time the record involved is not moved to a different list but is swapped with the record at the top of the list. The process is shown in FIG-8.22.

This is the end of pass 1 and at this point we have the record with the smallest key in the first position (element 0) in the list. This means that only elements 2 and upwards have still to be sorted.

In the second pass we again search for the smallest key but only in the unsorted portion of the list (i.e. elements 1 to 6). When the smallest key in that array is found its record is exchanged with the record at the second position in the list. Now, only elements 2 through 6 are unsorted. This continues until the search area is reduced to the last two records in the list. When the smallest of these two is found and repositioned then, as a consequence, the last record must be in the correct position also. FIG-8.23 shows the progression of the sort.

**FIG-8.22**

Selection with Exchange - The First Pass

Step 1: Find the smallest key in t1

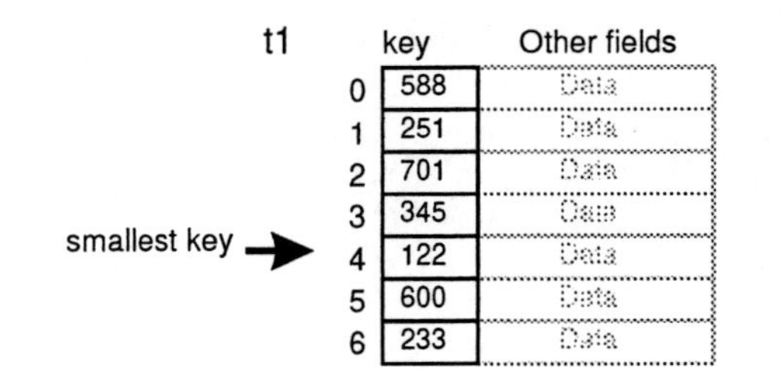


Step 2: Swap the first and smallest records

Before (t1):

| | key | Other fields |
|---|---|---|
| 0 | 588 | Data |
| 1 | 251 | Data |
| 2 | 701 | Data |
| 3 | 345 | Data |
| 4 | 122 | Data |
| 5 | 600 | Data |
| 6 | 233 | Data |

After (t1):

| | key | Other fields |
|---|---|---|
| 0 | 122 | Data |
| 1 | 251 | Data |
| 2 | 701 | Data |
| 3 | 345 | Data |
| 4 | 588 | Data |
| 5 | 600 | Data |
| 6 | 233 | Data |

**FIG-8.23**

Selection with Exchange - Subsequent Passes

Pass 2:

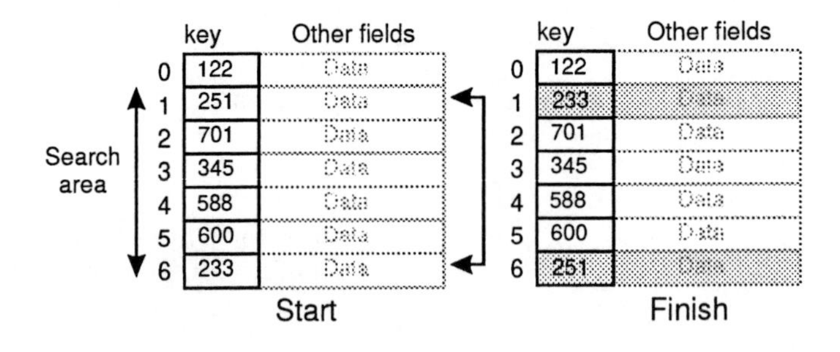

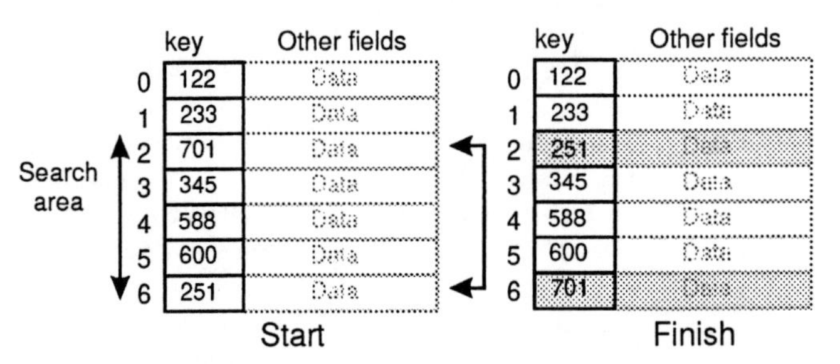

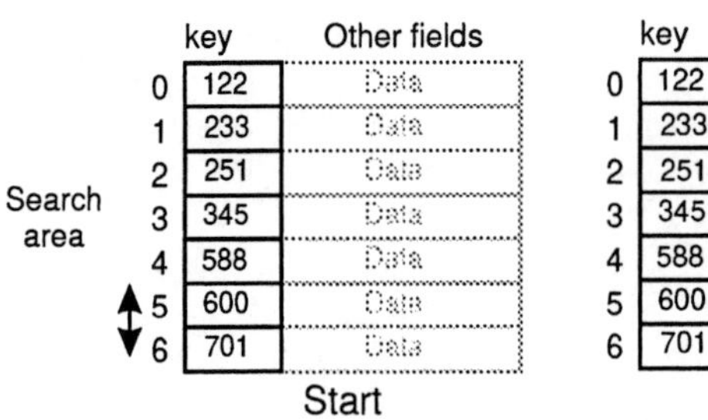


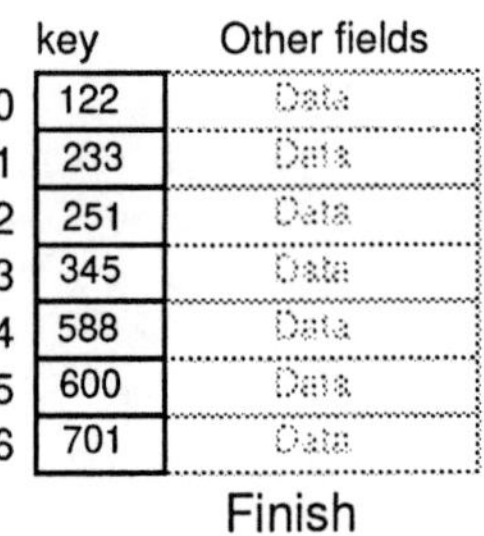

Since the last two elements sort on the final pass only 6 passes were required to sort the 7 element list in the example above. When a list containing *N* elements is sorted using this technique *N*-1 passes are required.

Note that the list contains a sorted area at the beginning of the list that grows larger by at least one record on each pass (2 on the last pass) and an unsorted area that correspondingly decreases on each pass. However, it is possible that, depending on the original ordering of the records, the sort may be completed in fewer passes. In the previous example, the sort was complete after only 3 passes.

The sort can be described in Structured English as:

```
FOR N-1 PASSES DO
    Find the smallest key in the unsorted part of the list
    Swap its record with the one at the top of the unsorted area
ENDFOR
```

**Activity 8.31**

1. How many comparisons are required to find the minimum key for a list of *N* elements on:
    a) Pass 1
    b) Pass 2
    c) Pass 3
    d) Pass *N*-1
2. What is the total number of comparisons required?
3. How many record movements are performed on each pass?
4. How many movements are performed in total?

**Activity 8.32**

Change the sort operation written in Activity 8.29 to use the Selection with Exchange sort method.

If we compare the statistics of the two Selection sorts we can see that while one has a smaller number of moves, the other has a smaller number of comparisons. These are the elements which are going to affect the execution time of the sort. But which takes the longest to perform, a compare or a move?

The answer is - it depends. It depends on the length of the key and the length of the record. Keys will be compared a word at a time, so integer keys can be compared quickly, while a 15 digit character key will take longer. Also, record movement will depend on the length of the record. Obviously a 50 character record can be moved more quickly than a 500 character record.

However, if a record is short (less than 100 characters) and the key is only a word or two long, then the time taken to perform a comparison can be taken as approximately equal to the time to move a record.

In that case, if we want to make a comparison of the likely execution time of two sort methods, then this can be achieved by adding the total number of moves and the total number of comparisons for each and comparing the figures.

The only time that the Simple Selection sort is the more efficient is when the records being moved are large, in which case the time taken to execute a move is much greater than the time required for a comparison. But since you'll need 2*N* locations, the chances are you'll run out of space!

# The Insertion Sorts

## Simple Insertion

In the **Simple Insertion** sort, like the Simple Selection sort, two lists are used. One list contains the unsorted records, the other is initially empty. The records of the unsorted list are transferred one at a time, working from the start of the unsorted list to the second list. This second list is maintained in order at all times. This requirement usually involves moving records about within the second list. The first stages of the sort are shown in FIG-8.24.

**FIG-8.24**

The Simple Insertion Sort

Starting Condition: Copy the first record in t1 to t2

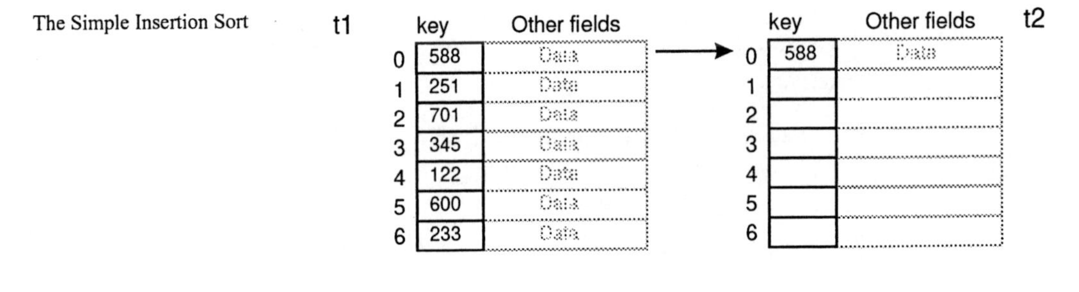


Step 1: Using the next record in t1, determine its insert point in t2

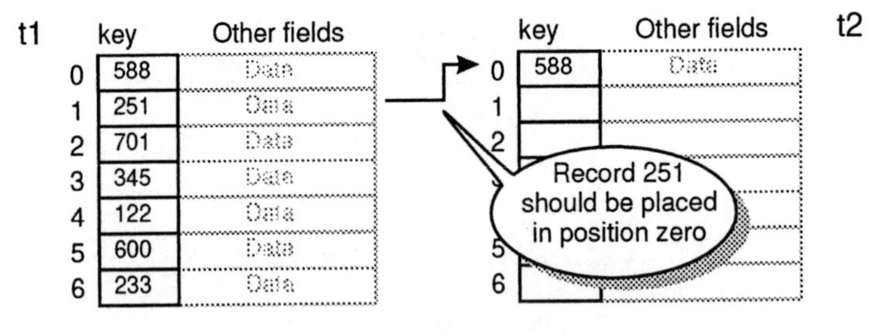


Step 2: Create a gap in t2 for the new record from t1

t1

| | key | Other fields |
|---|---|---|
| 0 | 588 | Data |
| 1 | 251 | Data |
| 2 | 701 | Data |
| 3 | 345 | Data |
| 4 | 122 | Data |
| 5 | 600 | Data |
| 6 | 233 | Data |

t2

| | key | Other fields |
|---|---|---|
| 0 | | |
| 1 | 588 | Data |
| 2 | | |
| 3 | | |
| 4 | | |
| 5 | | |
| 6 | | |

Record moved down to create gap

Step 3: Insert new record from t1

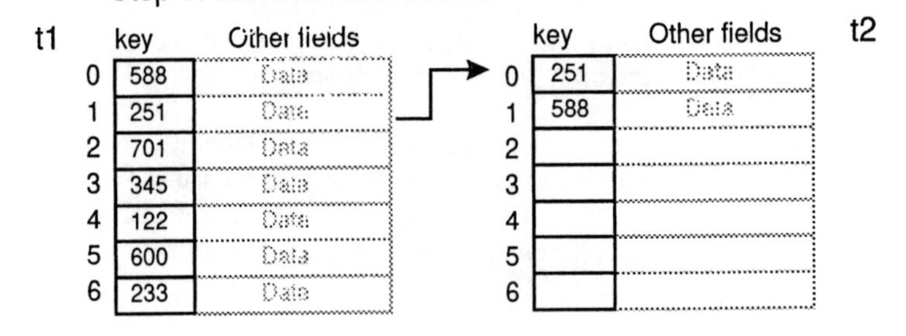

Steps 1 to 3 make up a single pass of the sort. Since the first record of t1 is simply copied across to t2, at the beginning of the sort, only 6 passes are required to sort the 7 records. Hence a list of *N* records requires *N-1* passes.

The sort Outline Logic is:

```
Move the first record to the sorted list
FOR N-1 passes DO
    Find the insert point in the sorted list for the next record
    Move the necessary records in the sorted list to make room
    for the new record
    Copy record from unsorted to sorted list
ENDFOR
```

The code for this is:

```
procedure InsertionSort(var t1,t2:StudentTable);
var
    pass    : integer;     {Current sort pass}
    placeat : integer;     {Insert point for record}
    post    : integer;     {Loop counter}
begin
    {*** Insert first record ***}
    t2.list[0] := t1.list[0];
    t2.count := 1;
    {*** FOR each remaining record DO ***}
    for pass := 1 to t1.count - 1 do
    begin
        {*** Find insert point ***}
        placeat := InsertAt(t1.list[pass].idcode,t2);
        {*** Move down lower records ***}
        for post := t2.count - 1 downto placeat do
            t2.list[post+1] := t2.list[post];
        {***Insert new record ***}
        t2.list[placeat] := t1.list[pass];
        inc(t2.count);
    end
end;
```

The auxiliary function, *InsertAt*, is coded as:

```
function InsertAt(id:integer; var t:StudentTable):integer;
var
    post : integer;    {Position id should be inserted}
begin
    {*** Start from beginning of table ***}
    post := 0;
    {*** WHILE keys are smaller and not at end of table DO ***}
    while (t.list[post].idcode < id) and (post < t.count) do
        {*** Move to next entry ***}
        inc(post);
    {*** Return insert position ***}
    InsertAt := post;
end;
```

Although the example earlier shows the data to be sorted held in an array, the Insertion sort is often used when sorting an incomplete set of data. For example, if transactions are being entered at a keyboard at random intervals for an application which requires the transactions to be in sorted order at all times (perhaps for easy interrogation), then the Insertion sort is ideal since it does not require the complete set of data to be present before sorting is commenced. This is not true of other sorting methods.

**Activity 8.33**

Modify your Table program's *AddToTable* operation to maintain a sorted table

As has been already stated, the number of comparisons and moves required by a sort gives an indication of its efficiency. However, these figures are not as easy to calculate for the Simple Insertion sort since they can vary. For example, FIG-8.25 shows the possible range of comparisons and moves involved when inserting a new entry in the sorted list.

**FIG-8.25**

Simple Insertion - The Range of Comparisons and Moves

**Minimum Comparisons - Maximum Moves**

Record to be Inserted

Sorted List

key Other fields key Other fields

122 Data

251 Data 122 Data
588 Data 251 Data
600 Data 588 Data
701 Data 600 Data
701 Data

One comparison to find insert position

Search Move

Five moves required

**Maximum Comparisons - Minimum Moves**

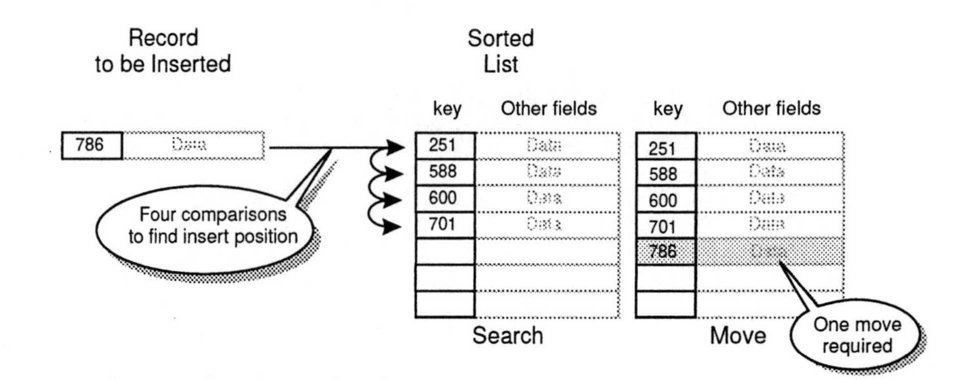


This requires us to talk in terms of the minimum and maximum moves and comparisons which can arise during each pass.

**Activity 8.34**

1. Assuming a list contains $N$ records, state the minimum and maximum moves and comparisons required during:
   a) Pass 1
   b) Pass 2
   c) Pass 3
   d) Pass $N$-1
2. What is the average number of moves and comparisons required to complete the sort?

It is in the nature of this sort that the better the original order of the list, the more comparisons (but less moves) there will be. Conversely, the worse the original order, the fewer comparisons and more moves. So the sort is slightly better at dealing with a source list which is already quite well ordered.
Finally, if we assume that a comparison and move take the same amount of time, then the moves and comparisons can be combined to give a figure of approximately $N^2/2$

## Insertion With Exchange Sort

Just as we improved the simple selection sort by restricting the memory requirements to one list, so the Simple Insertion can be improved in the same way. When using only one list we can think of it as consisting of sorted and unsorted areas.

At the beginning of the sort, the sorted area occupies only the first element of the list but with each pass more and more of the list becomes sorted. Initially the first entry in the list is considered to be in the sorted area. The keys of the first and second records are compared. If the records are in the wrong order they are exchanged. At this point the sorted area is two records in length. Now the key of the third record is compared in turn with each of those in the sorted area (starting at record 2 and working backwards) until a key less than that of record 3 is encountered or the start of the list is reached. Record 3 is inserted at that point. The process continues until the whole list is sorted. FIG-8.26 shows the sort in action.

**FIG-8.26**

Selection with Exchange

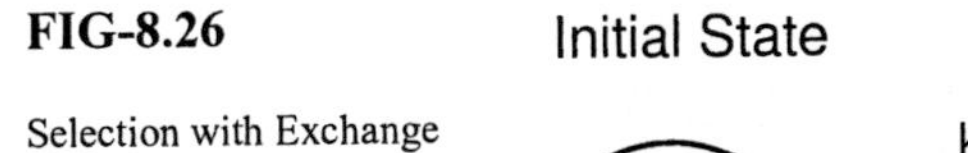


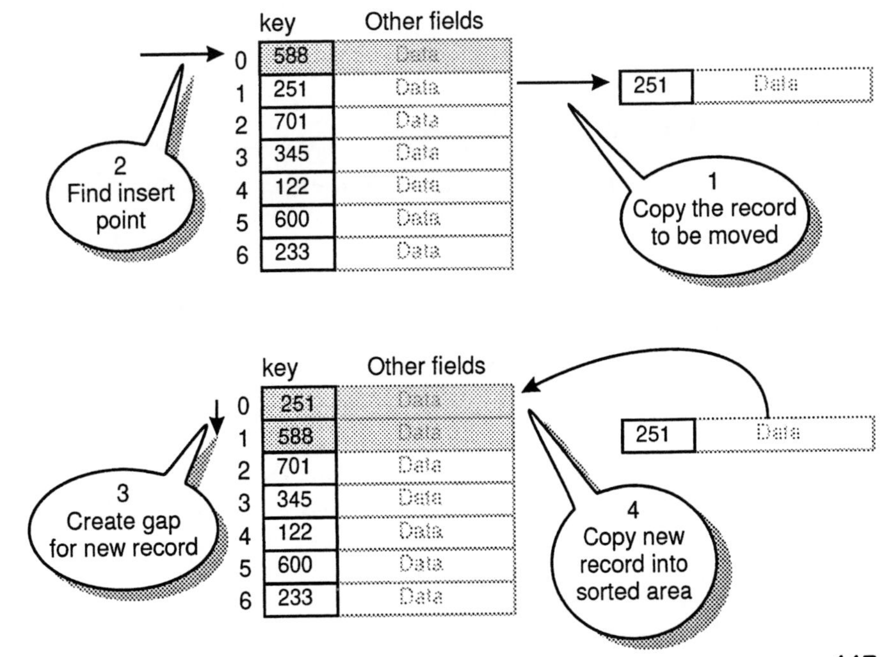

The logic of the Insertion with Exchange sort is:

```
FOR N-1 passes DO
    Make a copy of the record to be inserted
    Find the insert position in the unsorted area
    Create space for the new record in the sorted area
    Insert record at appropriate point
ENDFOR
```

For the *StudentTable* structure we can code this as

```
procedure InsertionWithExchangeSort(var t:StudentTable);
var
    pass    : integer;          {Current pass of sort}
    sd      : StudentDetails;   {Student record copy}
    placeat : integer;          {Insert position for record}
    post    : integer;          {Loop counter}
begin
    for pass := 1 to t.count - 1 do
    begin
        {*** Copy record ***}
        sd := t.list[pass];
        {*** Find insertion point ***}
        placeat := InsertAt(sd.idcode,t,pass);
        for post := pass -1 downto placeat do
            t.list[post + 1] := t.list[post];
        {*** Insert new record ***}
        t.list[placeat] := sd;
    end
end;
```

This makes use of a modified *InsertAt* function which examines only a specified area of the table:

```
function InsertAt(id:integer; var t:StudentTable;
                                        max:integer):integer;
var
    post : integer;
begin
    {*** Start at the beginning of the table ***}
    post := 0;
    {*** Search specified area for insert point ***}
    while (t.list[post].idcode < id) and (post < max) do
        inc(post);
    {*** Return insert point ***}
    InsertAt := post;
end;
```

# The Exchange Sorts

The classification of sorting methods is seldom entirely clear-cut. Both the *Selection with Exchange* and the *Insertion with Exchange* sorts can be viewed in some ways as exchange sorts. However, there is classification of sorting techniques whose dominant characteristic is the comparison of two items and, if they are not in order with respect to each other, an exchange is made.

This comparison and possible exchange is repeated as the list of records is scanned. The scan may work from top to bottom or vice versa. There are also some variations where the direction of the scan alternates from pass to pass.

This classification contains the largest number of sorting algorithms, only the Bubble sort and its main variations are examined here.

**FIG-8.27**

The Bubble Sort

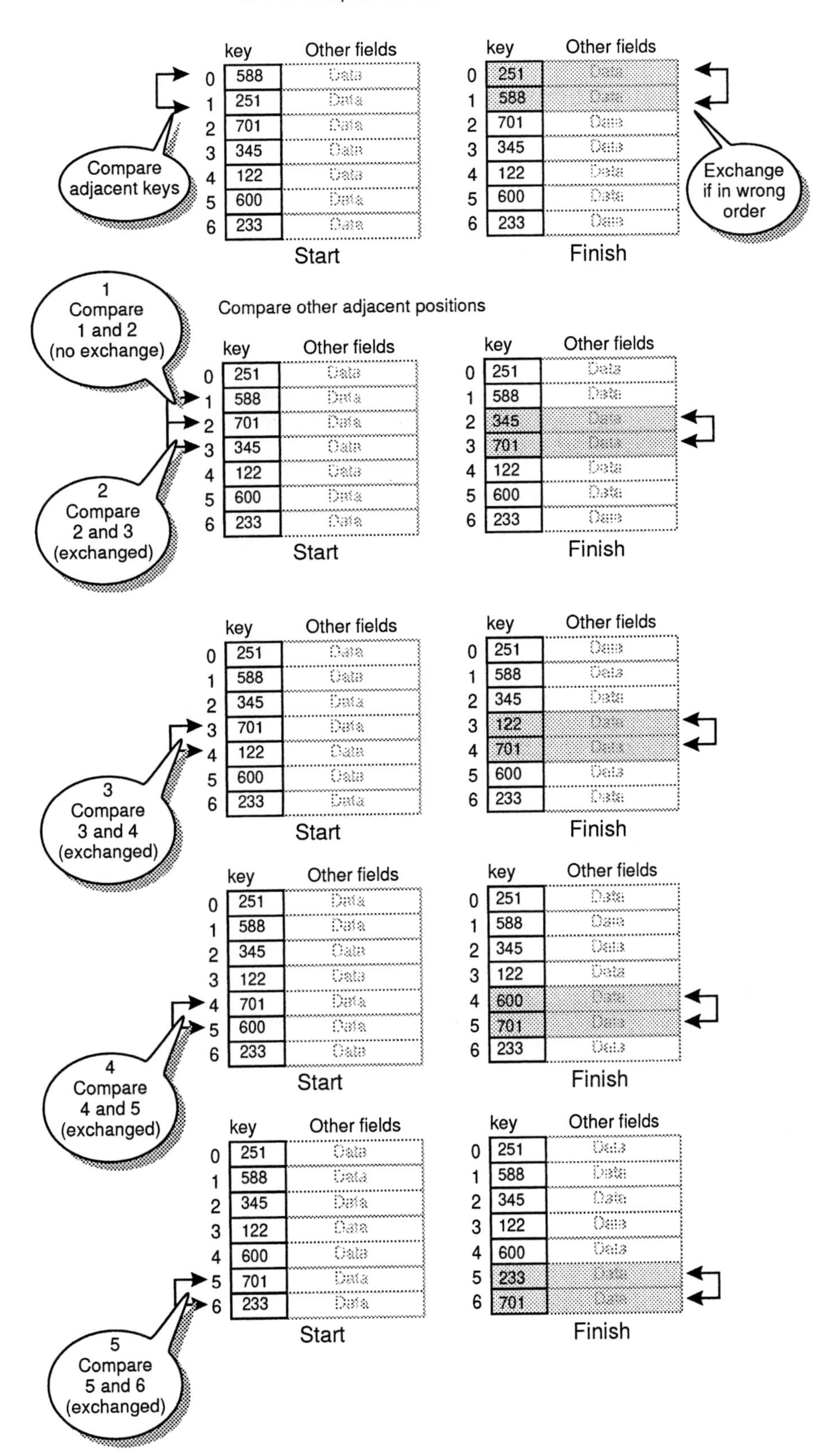

### The Bubble Sort

In the Bubble sort the keys of adjacent records are compared and where necessary the records exchange positions.

FIG-8.27 shows the first pass of a Bubble sort.

Note that by the end of the first pass, the record with the largest key has sunk to the bottom of the list. Again, we can think of the list containing a sorted area (this time at the bottom of the list) and an unsorted area. During the second pass we need only compare the records in the unsorted area (elements 0 to 5). When the second pass is complete, the record in the unsorted area with the largest key will have been moved to element 5 in the list, hence increasing the size of the sorted area by one.

**Activity 8.35**

1. Assuming a list of $N$ records is to be sorted using the Bubble sort, state the number of comparisons and maximum moves required during:
   a) Pass 1
   b) Pass 2
   c) Pass 3
   d) Pass $N$ - 1
2. State the total number of comparisons and the average number of moves required to complete the sort.

The Bubble sort's algorithm can be described in Structured English as:

```
FOR N-1 passes DO
    Starting at the beginning of the list
    FOR number of records in the unsorted area of list -1 DO
        IF the next two records are out of order THEN
            Exchange them
        ENDIF
    ENDFOR
ENDFOR
```

A routine to perform the Bubble sort on a *StudentTable* variable is given below.

```
procedure BubbleSort(var t1:StudentTable);
var
    sd        : StudentDetails;    {Holds copy of record}
    pass,post : integer;           {Loop counters}
begin
    {*** FOR N-1 passes DO ***}
    for pass := 1 to t1.count - 1 do
        {*** FOR each record in the unsorted list DO ***}
        for post := 0 to t1.count - pass-1 do
            {*** IF wrong order THEN exchange records ***}
            if t1.list[post].idcode > t1.list[post+1].idcode then
            begin
                sd := t1.list[post+1];
                t1.list[post+1] := t1.list[post];
                t1.list[post] := sd;
            end;
end;
```

## Comparison of Sorts

TABLE-8.2 shows the average figures for sorting a list of 20 records using various sorting methods.

**TABLE-8.2**

Comparing Sorts

| Sort | Comparisons | Moves | Total |
|---|---|---|---|
| Selection with Exchange | 190 | 29 | 219 |
| Insertion with Exchange | 95 | 114 | 209 |
| Bubble | 190 | 285 | 475 |

The above table highlights how poor the Bubble sort is; the Insertion sort coming out best.

The Insertion sort's figures can be improved by using the Binary search during the scan of the sorted portion of the list.

Generally, sorts are compared on three standards:

1) Execution time.
   This is a function of the number of moves and comparisons which is affected by the order of the data.
2) Storage requirements.
3) The ease of implementation.

For short lists points 2) and 3) tend to be the most important but for longer lists and sorts which are to be executed often then factor 1) tends to be the most dominant.

# Summary

- **Sorting involves** ordering data according to some data field(s).
- **Sorting may be required** for the presentation of data or the efficient processing of data.
- **Sorts may be classified** as either internal or external.
- **Internal sorts** hold all the data within the computer's memory
- **External sorts** hold the data on back storage.
- **Internals sorts may be subdivided** into *Selection*, *Insertion* and *Exchange* sorts.
- **Selection sorting** involves finding the data with the lowest key and inserting it at the end of a list.
- **Insertion sorting** takes records in any order and adds them at the correct position in a sorted list.
- **Only Insertion sorts** may be used when not all the data is available at the start of the sort.
- **Exchange sorting** involves comparing two keys and swapping the position of the data if the keys are not in order.
- **Sort processes are compared** using the amount of storage space required, the number of comparisons, and the number of moves.

# CASE STUDY

## The Problem

Although a hash table gives very fast access to its data, any such structure is always limited in size to the amount of memory available.

An alternative is to create the hash table on disk,where we are restricted only by the much larger capacity of the disk and get the bonus of having a permanent copy of our data.

## Clarification

In this program we are simply going to create an alternative way of implementing *StudentTable*. All operations and their parameters must remain the same as before otherwise our original design will be compromised.

## Implementing the Data Type

### Data

We need to declare both a *StudentDetails* type and a *StudentTable* type. Whereas the *StudentDetails* declaration is unchanged:

```
type
    StudentDetails =
    record
        idcode : integer;
        name   : string[30];
        sex    : char;
        score  : array[1..6] of integer;
    end;
```

the declaration for *StudentTable* is simply a renaming of a FILE type:

```
type
    StudentTable = file of StudentDetails;
```

### Operations

Although, as we will see, it is possible to write the existing operations of a *StudentTable* data type without violating the formal design definitions, it will be necessary to add two new operations: *OpenTable* and *CloseTable* which open and close the file used to hold the *StudentTable* structure.
These two operations are defined below:

| | | |
|---|---|---|
| NAME | : | OpenTable |
| PARAMETERS | | |
| IN | : | filename:STRING |
| OUT | : | t : StudentTable |
| IN/OUT | : | None |
| PRE-CONDITION | : | None |
| POST-CONDITION | : | Opens a disk file named *filename* in which the contents of *t* is stored. |

| | | |
|---|---|---|
| NAME | : | CloseFile |
| PARAMETERS | | |
| IN | : | t : StudentTable |
| OUT | : | None |
| IN/OUT | : | None |
| PRE-CONDITION | : | t has previously been opened |
| POST-CONDITION | : | Close the file holding the contents of t. |

The main program follows a simple menu driven logic:

```
Open table
REPEAT
    Display menu
    Get user option
    Execute option
UNTIL option is QUIT
Close table
```

# Program Code

**Listing-8.2**

Hashing to Disk

```
program HashFiles;
uses wincrt;
{*****************************************************}
{* PROGRAM      :    Disk Hash Table                 *}
{* AUTHOR       :    Patricia Stamp                  *}
{* DATE         :    25/6/1998                       *}
{* VERSION      :    0.1                             *}
{* DESCRIPTION  :    Creates a disk-based hash table *}
{* HARDWARE     :    PC Compatible                   *}
{* SOURCE       :    Borland Pascal v7.0             *}
{*****************************************************}

{**********************************************}
{***      Subsidiary Routines and Types     ***}
{**********************************************}
 type
  KeySet = set of char;

{*** Get Data from Keyboard ***}
function GetData(allowed : KeySet; max : integer):string;
const
  ENTER = #13;
  BACKSPACE = #8;
var
  ch    : char;           {char from keyboard}
  count : integer;        {chars entered}
  result : string;        {Contains the characters typed in}
begin
  {*** Set result to empty and count to zero ***}
  result := '';
  count := 0;
  {*** Read a character ***}
  ch := readkey;
  {*** WHILE return key not pressed DO ***}
  while ch <> ENTER do
  begin
      {*** IF allowed char & result not full THEN ***}
      if (ch in allowed) AND (count < max)then
      begin
          {*** Display char and add to result ***}
          write(ch);
          inc(count);
          result := result + ch;
      end
```

**Continued on next page**

**Listing-8.2**
(continued)

Hashing to Disk

```
        {*** ELSE if delete & result not empty ***}
        else if (ch = BACKSPACE) AND (count > 0) then
        begin
            {*** Remove last char ***}
            write(#8,#32,#8);
            dec(count);
            delete(result,length(result),1);
        end;
        {*** Read another character ***}
        ch := readkey;
    end;
    writeln;
    GetData := result;
end;


{**********************************************}
{*** StudentDetails Data Type Declarations ***}
{**********************************************}
{*** Data ***}
type
   StudentDetails =
   record
       idcode : integer;
       name   : string[30];
       sex    : char;
       score  : array[1..6] of integer;
end;



{***Operations ***}

{*** Read Student  details ***}
procedure GetStudentDetails(var sd: StudentDetails);
var
   temp : string[30];      {Temp storage for data entered}
   err  : integer;         {string to number conversion status}
   c    : integer;         {Loop counter}
begin
   {*** Get idcode ***}
   {** Read up to 5 digits **}
   write('Enter id code : ');
   temp := GetData(['0'..'9',' '],5);
   {** Convert to numeric distance **}
   val(temp,sd.idcode,err);
   {*** Get name ***}
   write('Enter name : ');
   sd.name := GetData(['A'..'Z','a'..'z',' ','.','-',''''],29);
   {*** Get sex ***}
   write('Enter sex : ');
   temp := GetData(['F','M','f','m'],1);
   sd.sex := upcase(temp[1]);
   {*** Get six scores ***}
   for c := 1 to 6 do
   begin
       write('Enter score ',c,' : ');
       temp := GetData(['0'..'9'],3);
       val(temp,sd.score[c],err);
       while(sd.score[c] > 100) do
       begin
           write('#7');
           temp := GetData(['0'..'9'],3);
           val(temp,sd.score[c],err);
       end
   end
end;
```

**Continued on next page**

**Listing-8.2**
(continued)

Hashing to Disk

```
{*** Display student details ***}
procedure DisplayStudent(sd:StudentDetails);
var
  c : integer; {Loop counter}
begin
  {*** Display idcode, name and sex ***}
  write(sd.idcode:4,'  ',sd.name,'
':20-length(sd.name),sd.sex:3,'   ');
  {*** Display scores ***}
  for c := 1 to 6 do
      write(sd.score[c]:4);
  {*** Move to a new line ***}
  writeln;
end;


{*** Compare Student idcodes ***}
function CompareId(sd1,sd2:StudentDetails):integer;
begin
  if sd1.idcode < sd2.idcode then
      CompareId := 1;
  if sd2.idcode < sd1.idcode then
      CompareId := 2;
  if sd1.idcode = sd2.idcode then
      CompareId := 0;
end;



{*** Modify a student's name ***}
procedure ModifyName(newname:string; var sd:StudentDetails);
begin
  sd.name := newname;
end;


{*** Modify a student's score ***}
procedure ModifyScore(scoreno,newscore : integer; var
sd:StudentDetails);
begin
  {*** IF score number or mark is invalid THEN exit routine ***}
  if (scoreno < 1) or (scoreno > 6) or (newscore < 0)
                                   or (newscore > 100) then
      exit;
  {*** Set specified score to new value ***}
  sd.score[scoreno] := newscore;
end;

{****************************************************}
{***  END StudentDetails Data Type Declaration   ***}
{****************************************************}




{***********************************************}
{***  StudentTable Data Type Declarations   ***}
{***********************************************}
{*** Data ***}
const
  SIZE = 17;
  EMPTY = 0;
  DELETED = -1;
  NOTFOUND = -1;

type
  StudentTable = file of StudentDetails;
```

**Continued on next page**

**Listing-8.2**
(continued)

Hashing to Disk

```
{*** Operations ***}

{*** Check if table is full ***}
function IsFull(var t:StudentTable):boolean;
var
  sd : StudentDetails;  {Copy of record read}
begin
  {*** Move to the start of the file ***}
  seek(t,0);
  {*** WHILE not at end of file DO ***}
  while not eof(t) do
  begin
      {*** Read a record ***}
      read(t,sd);
      {*** If it's empty or deleted THEN return false ***}
      if (sd.idcode = EMPTY) or (sd.idcode = DELETED) then
      begin
          IsFull := false;
          exit;
      end;
  end;
  {*** Table is full, return true ***}
  IsFull := true;
end;



{*** Hash key to give insert position ***}
function Hash(key:integer):integer;
begin
  Hash := key mod SIZE
end;



{*** Find position of entry in table ***}
function IsAt(key:integer; var t:StudentTable):integer;
var
  post  : integer;         {Position in table of required entry}
  start : integer;         {The starting position of the search}
  sd    : StudentDetails; {Copy of record read}
begin
  {*** Hash to where record should be ***}
  start := Hash(key);
  post := start;
  {*** WHILE its no match or empty position reached DO ***}
  seek(t,post);
  read(t,sd);
  while (sd.idcode <> key) and (sd.idcode <> EMPTY) do
  begin
      {*** Move to next position in table ***}
      post := (post+1) mod SIZE;
      seek(t,post);
      read(t,sd);
      {*** IF all entries searched, give up ***}
      if post = start then;
          {break; *************************************}
  end;
  {*** IF not successful THEN, return -1 ***}
  if(sd.idcode <> key)then
      IsAt := NOTFOUND
  else
      {*** ELSE return position of record ***}
      IsAt := post;
end;
```

**Continued on next page**

**Listing-8.2**
(continued)

Hashing to Disk

```
{*** Create empty table ***}
procedure CreateTable(var t:StudentTable);
const
   EMPTYREC : StudentDetails =
          (idcode:EMPTY;name:'';sex:' ';score:(0,0,0,0,0,0));
var
   c  : integer;          {Loop counter}
begin
   {*** Fill the file with empty records ***}
   seek(t,0);
   for c := 1 to SIZE do
       write(t,EMPTYREC);
end;



{*** Add a student's details to the table ***}
function AddToTable(sd:StudentDetails; var
t:StudentTable):boolean;
var
   post  : integer;          {Position in table of record}
   start : integer;          {Start position for record search}
   strec : StudentDetails;   {Copy of record read from file}
begin
   {*** IF the idcode matches existing one or table full THEN ***}
   if (IsAt(sd.idcode,t) <> NOTFOUND) or (IsFull(t)) then
   begin
       {*** Return false ***}
       AddToTable := false;
       exit;
   end;
   {*** Find insert position ***}
   {** Hash key **}
   start := Hash(sd.idcode);
   post := start;
   {** Linear probe until available position found **}
   seek(t,post);
   read(t,strec);
   while(strec.idcode <> EMPTY) and (strec.idcode <> DELETED)do
   begin
       post := (post + 1) mod SIZE;
       {** or, if none then return false **}
       if post = start then
       begin
           AddToTable := false;
           exit;
       end;
       seek(t,post);
       read(t,strec);
   end;
   {*** Write new record to file ***}
   seek(t,post);
   write(t,sd);
   {*** Return true ***}
   AddToTable := true;
end;



{*** Display contents of table *** }
procedure DisplayTable(var t: StudentTable);
var
   sd    : StudentDetails;   {Copy of record read from file}
   count : integer;          {Number of valid records read}
```

**Continued on next page**

**Listing-8.2**
(continued)

Hashing to Disk

```
begin
  {*** No valid records read yet ***}
  count := 0;
  {*** Read first record in the file ***}
  seek(t,0);
  read(t,sd);
  {*** Display heading ***}
  writeln(' ':23,'STUDENT TABLE CONTENTS');
  writeln(' Id ','Name':10,'            Sex          Scores');
  {*** Display and count records in the table ***}
  while not eof(t) do
  begin
      read(t,sd);
      if (sd.idcode <> EMPTY) and (sd.idcode <> DELETED) then
      begin
          DisplayStudent(sd);
          inc(count);
      end;
  end;
  {*** IF no records displayed THEN give table empty message ***}
  if count = 0 then
      writeln('Table is empty');
end;



{*** Returns a specified entry in the table ***}
function GiveRecord(key:integer; var t:StudentTable;
                               var sd:StudentDetails): boolean;
const
  emptyrec :StudentDetails =
          (idcode:0;name:'EMPTY';sex:' ';score:(0,0,0,0,0,0));
var
  post : integer;   {Position of required record in file}
begin
  {*** Attempt to locate record ***}
  post := IsAt(key,t);
  {*** IF found THEN ***}
  if post <> NOTFOUND then
  begin
      {*** Return record found and true ***}
      seek(t,post);
      read(t,sd);
      GiveRecord := true;
  end
  else
  begin
      {*** ELSE return an empty record and false ***}
      sd := emptyrec;
      GiveRecord := false;
  end;
end;



{*** Delete a specified record ***}
function DeleteFromTable(key:integer; var
t:StudentTable):boolean;
var
  post : integer;            {Position of match in table }
  c    : integer;            {Loop counter}
  sd   : StudentDetails;     {Record read from file}
begin
  {*** Attempt to find matching idcode in table ***}
  post := IsAt(key,t);
```

**Continued on next page**

**Listing-8.2**
(continued)

Hashing to Disk

```
  {*** IF not found THEN ***}
  if post = NOTFOUND then
  begin
      {*** Return false ***}
      DeleteFromTable := false;
      exit;
  end;
  {*** Delete by setting key field ***}
  {** read record from file **}
  seek(t,post);
  read(t,sd);
  {** Change idcode in record **}
  sd.idcode := DELETED;
  {** Write record back to file **}
  seek(t,post);
  write(t,sd);
  {*** Return true ***}
  DeleteFromTable := true
end;



{*** Modify an existing record ***}
function UpdateRecord(sd:StudentDetails; var
t:StudentTable):boolean;
var
  post : integer;   {Position of match in table }
begin
  {*** Attempt to find matching idcode in table ***}
  post := IsAt(sd.idcode,t);
  {*** IF not found THEN ***}
  if post = NOTFOUND then
  begin
      {*** Return false ***}
      UpdateRecord := false;
      exit
  end;
  {*** update entry and return success indicator ***}
  seek(t,post);
  write(t,sd);
  UpdateRecord := true
end;



{*** Determine number of given sex ***}
function NoOfSex(sex:char; var t:StudentTable):integer;
var
  count   : integer;          {Count of same sex entries}
  sexcopy : char;             {Sex being searched for}
  c       : integer;          {Loop counter}
  sd      : StudentDetails;   {Copy of record read}
begin
  {*** Start count at zero ***}
  count := 0;
  {*** Change selection to uppercase ***}
  sexcopy := upcase(sex);
  {*** IF its not M or F THEN return zero ***}
  if (sexcopy <> 'F') and (sexcopy <> 'M') then
  begin
      NoOfSex := 0;
      exit;
  end;
  {*** Starting at the beginning of the file ***}
  seek(t,0);
  {*** FOR each record in the file ***}
```

**Continued on next page**

**Listing-8.2**
(continued)

Hashing to Disk

```
    for c := 0 to SIZE-1 do
    begin
        read(t,sd);
        {*** IF its the required sex THEN add 1 to count ***}
        if(sd.idcode <> EMPTY) and (sd.idcode <> DELETED) then
            count := count + integer(sd.sex = sexcopy);
    end;
    {*** Return count ***}
    NoOfSex := count;
end;



{*** Open table's file ***}
procedure OpenTable(filename:string; var t:StudentTable);
begin
    {*** Try to open existing file ***}
    assign(t,filename);
    {$I-}
    reset(t);
    {*** IF it doesn't exist THEN create it ***}
    if IOResult <> 0 then
        rewrite(t);
    {$I+}
end;



{*** Close table's file ***}
procedure CloseTable(var t:StudentTable);
begin
    close(t);
end;


{*********************************************}
{***  END StudentTable Type Declaration   ***}
{*********************************************}



{*********************************************}
{***          Other Routines              ***}
{*********************************************}

{*** Display menu ***}
function DisplayMenu(m:string): integer;
var
    count : integer;      {No. of items in menu}
    c     : integer;      {Loop counter}
begin
    {*** Display menu ***}
    writeln(m);
    {*** Count options in menu ***}
    count := 0;
    for c := 1 to length(m) do
        if m[c] = #13 then
            inc(count);
    {*** Return number of items in menu ***}
    DisplayMenu := count;
end;
```

**Continued on next page**

**Listing-8.2**
(continued)

Hashing to Disk

```
{*** Get user's option ***}
function GetOption(max:integer):integer;
var
  opstr : string[2];      {Option chosen as string}
  op    : integer;        {Menu option chosen}
  err   : integer;        {Convertion flag}
begin
  {*** Read option ***}
  write('Enter option : ');
  opstr := GetData(['0'..'9'],2);
  val(opstr,op,err);
  {*** WHILE invalid DO ***}
  while (op < 1) or (op > max) do
  begin
      {*** Sound bell and re-read ***}
      writeln(#7);
      opstr := GetData(['0'..'9'],2);
      val(opstr,op,err);
  end;
  {*** Return option ***}
  GetOption := op;
end;



{*** Execute menu option chosen ***}
procedure ExecuteOption(opt:integer; var t:StudentTable);
var
  sd       : StudentDetails;     {Copy of record from file ***}
  c        : integer;            {Loop counter}
  key      : integer;            {Idcode of record to be processed}
  b        : boolean;            {Value returned by some functions}
  ch       : char;               {Holds the key}
  sex      : char;               {Sex query variable}
  err      : integer;            {String-to-number error status}
  temp     : string[30];         {Keys entered from keyboard}
  examno   : integer;            {Exam number when changing score}
  exammark : integer;            {Replacement score}
begin
  case opt of
      1: {*** Create empty table ***}
         CreateTable(t);
      2: {*** Add a new record ***}
         begin
              {** Get student's details **}
              GetStudentDetails(sd);
              {** Add to table **}
              b := AddToTable(sd,t);
         end;
      3: {*** Change name ***}
         begin
              {** Get idcode of record to be changed **}
              write('Enter idcode of record : ');
              temp := GetData(['0'..'9'],4);
              val(temp,key,err);
              {** IF record not retrieved THEN display message**}
              if not GiveRecord(key,t,sd) then
              begin
                   writeln('Record not found');
                   ch := readkey;
              end
              else
              {** ELSE **}
              begin
                   {** get new name **}
                   write('Enter new name : ');
                   temp := GetData(['a'..'z','A'..'Z',' ',
                                        '.','-',''''],29);
```

**Continued on next page**

**Listing-8.2**
(continued)

Hashing to Disk

```
                {** and modify the existing record **}
                ModifyName(temp,sd);
                {** before writing back to file **}
                b:=UpdateRecord(sd,t);
            end
        end;
    4:  {*** Change score ***}
        begin
            {** Get the idcode of the record to be changed **}
            write('Enter idcode of record : ');
            temp := GetData(['0'..'9'],4);
            val(temp,key,err);
            {** IF record not found THEN display message **}
            if not GiveRecord(key,t,sd) then
            begin
                writeln('Record not found');
                ch := readkey;
            end
            else
            {** ELSE **}
            begin
                {** Get exam score details **}
                write('Enter exam number : ');
                temp := GetData(['1'..'6'],1);
                val(temp,examno,err);
                write('Enter new mark : ');
                temp := GetData(['0'..'9'],3);
                val(temp,exammark,err);
                while (exammark > 100) do
                begin
                    writeln(#7);
                    temp := GetData(['0'..'9'],3);
                    val(temp,exammark,err);
                end;
                {** and update record ***}
                ModifyScore(examno,exammark,sd);
                {** before writing back to file **}
                b := UpdateRecord(sd,t);
            end
        end;
    5:  {*** Count no. of given sex ***}
        begin
            {** Get sex required **}
            write('Enter sex (F or M) : ');
            temp := GetData(['M','F'],1);
            sex := temp[1];
            {** Display the result **}
            writeln('There are ',NoOfSex(sex,t),
                                    ' students of that sex');
            ch:=readkey;
        end;
    6:  {*** Return specific record ***}
        begin
            {** Get idcode of record to be retrieved **}
            write('Enter record id : ');
            temp := GetData(['0'..'9'],4);
            val(temp,key,err);
            {** IF record retrieved THEN display details **}
            if GiveRecord(key,t,sd) then
            begin
                {** Display heading **}
                writeln(' ':23,'STUDENT TABLE CONTENTS');
                writeln(' Id ','Name':10,
                        '                Sex           Scores');
                {*** and record ***}
                DisplayStudent(sd);
                ch:=readkey;
            end
```

**Continued on next page**

**Listing-8.2**
(continued)

Hashing to Disk

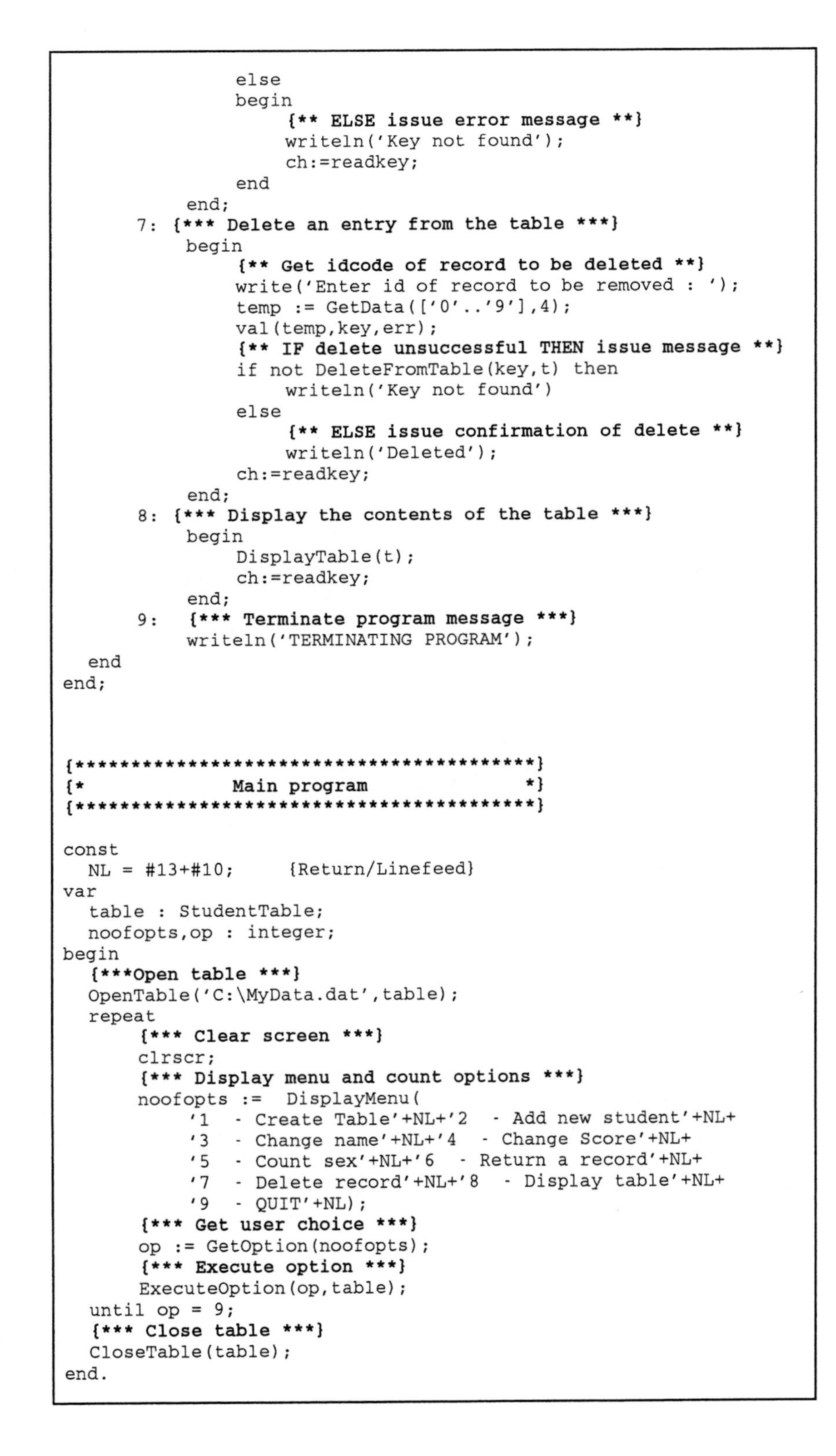

```
                else
                begin
                    {** ELSE issue error message **}
                    writeln('Key not found');
                    ch:=readkey;
                end
            end;
        7: {*** Delete an entry from the table ***}
            begin
                {** Get idcode of record to be deleted **}
                write('Enter id of record to be removed : ');
                temp := GetData(['0'..'9'],4);
                val(temp,key,err);
                {** IF delete unsuccessful THEN issue message **}
                if not DeleteFromTable(key,t) then
                    writeln('Key not found')
                else
                    {** ELSE issue confirmation of delete **}
                    writeln('Deleted');
                ch:=readkey;
            end;
        8: {*** Display the contents of the table ***}
            begin
                DisplayTable(t);
                ch:=readkey;
            end;
        9:  {*** Terminate program message ***}
            writeln('TERMINATING PROGRAM');
  end
end;


{*****************************************}
{*            Main program             *}
{*****************************************}

const
  NL = #13+#10;     {Return/Linefeed}
var
  table : StudentTable;
  noofopts,op : integer;
begin
  {***Open table ***}
  OpenTable('C:\MyData.dat',table);
  repeat
      {*** Clear screen ***}
      clrscr;
      {*** Display menu and count options ***}
      noofopts :=  DisplayMenu(
          '1  - Create Table'+NL+'2  - Add new student'+NL+
          '3  - Change name'+NL+'4  - Change Score'+NL+
          '5  - Count sex'+NL+'6  - Return a record'+NL+
          '7  - Delete record'+NL+'8  - Display table'+NL+
          '9  - QUIT'+NL);
      {*** Get user choice ***}
      op := GetOption(noofopts);
      {*** Execute option ***}
      ExecuteOption(op,table);
  until op = 9;
  {*** Close table ***}
  CloseTable(table);
end.
```

# SOLUTIONS

## Activity 8.1

ADT Distance is

DATA
A distance is stored in terms of yards, feet and inches. Where yards can be any non-negative integer value, feet has an integer value between 0 and 2, and inches has an integer value between 0 and 11.

OPERATIONS

| | | |
|---|---|---|
| NAME | : | Read |
| PARAMETERS | | |
| IN | : | None |
| OUT | : | d:Distance |
| IN/OUT | : | None |
| PRE-CONDITION | : | None |
| POST-CONDITION | : | *d* is assigned a value entered from the keyboard. |

| | | |
|---|---|---|
| NAME | : | Display |
| PARAMETERS | | |
| IN | : | d:Distance |
| OUT | : | None |
| IN/OUT | : | None |
| PRE-CONDITION | : | None |
| POST-CONDITION | : | The value of *d* is displayed on the screen. |

| | | |
|---|---|---|
| NAME | : | SetWeight |
| PARAMETERS | | |
| IN | : | nyards : INTEGER<br>nfeet : INTEGER<br>ninches : INTEGER |
| OUT | : | None |
| IN/OUT | : | d : Distance |
| PRE-CONDITION | : | *nyards*≥0 AND 0≤*nfeet*≤2 AND 0≤*ninches*≤11 |
| POST-CONDITION | : | *d* is set to *nyards* yards, *nfeet* feet *ninches* inches |

| | | |
|---|---|---|
| NAME | : | Add |
| PARAMETERS | | |
| IN | : | d2 : Distance |
| OUT | : | None |
| IN/OUT | : | d : Distance |
| PRE-CONDITION | : | None |
| POST-CONDITION | : | *d* = *d* + *d2* |

| | | |
|---|---|---|
| NAME | : | Subtract |
| PARAMETERS | | |
| IN | : | d2 : Distance |
| OUT | : | None |
| IN/OUT | : | d : Distance |
| PRE-CONDITION | : | *d2*≤*d* |
| POST-CONDITION | : | *d* = *d* - *d2* |

| | | |
|---|---|---|
| NAME | : | Compare |
| PARAMETERS | | |
| IN | : | d1 : Distance<br>d2 : Distance |
| OUT | : | result : INTEGER |
| IN/OUT | : | None |
| PRE-CONDITION | : | None |
| POST-CONDITION | : | if *d1*<*d2* then result is 1;<br>if *d2*<*d1* then result is 2;<br>if *d1* = *d2* then result is zero. |

END ADT

## Activity 8.3

ADT StudentDetails is

DATA
A student's details are stored in terms of the student's idcode,name,sex and the scores achieved on six tests. The test scores should lie in the range 0 to 100.

OPERATIONS

| | | |
|---|---|---|
| NAME | : | GetStudentDetails |
| PARAMETERS | | |
| IN | : | None |
| OUT | : | sd:StudentDetails |
| IN/OUT | : | None |
| PRE-CONDITION | : | None |
| POST-CONDITION | : | Values for each components of *sd* are assigned from the keyboard |

| | | |
|---|---|---|
| NAME | : | DisplayStudent |
| PARAMETERS | | |
| IN | : | sd : StudentDetails |
| OUT | : | None |
| IN/OUT | : | None |
| PRE-CONDITION | : | None |
| POST-CONDITION | : | The contents of *sd* are displayed on the screen. |

| | | |
|---|---|---|
| NAME | : | ModifyName |
| PARAMETERS | | |
| IN | : | newname : String |
| OUT | : | None |
| IN/OUT | : | sd : StudentDetails |
| PRE-CONDITION | : | None |
| POST-CONDITION | : | The contents of the name field in *sd* are changed to *newname*. |

| | | |
|---|---|---|
| NAME | : | ModifyScore |
| PARAMETERS | | |
| IN | : | markno : INTEGER<br>newmark : INTEGER |
| OUT | : | None |
| IN/OUT | : | sd : StudentDetails |
| PRE-CONDITION | : | 1≤*markno*≤6 AND 0≤newmark≤100 |
| POST-CONDITION | : | The *markno*$^{th}$ score in *sd* is changed to *newmark*. |

| | | |
|---|---|---|
| NAME | : | CompareId |
| PARAMETERS | | |
| IN | : | sd1 : StudentDetails<br>sd2 : StudentDetails |
| OUT | : | result : INTEGER |
| IN/OUT | : | None |
| PRE-CONDITION | : | None |
| POST-CONDITION | : | If the idcode of *sd1* < idcode of *sd2* then *result* = 1<br>If the idcode of *sd2* < idcode of *sd1* then *result* = 2<br>If the idcode of *sd1* = idcode of *sd2* then *result* = 0 |

END ADT

## Activity 8.4

The routines *GetData, DisplayMenu* and *GetOption* are assumed to be in a Pascal Unit named *Auxiliary*. This saves repeating the code for these often-used routines.

```
program Act4_01;
uses winCrt, Auxiliary;

{*********************************************}
{*** StudentDetails Data Type Declarations ***}
{*********************************************}
{*** Data ***}
 type
    StudentDetails =
    record
        idcode : integer;
        name   : string[30];
        sex    : char;
        score  : array[1..6] of integer;
    end;

{***Operations ***}

{*** Read Student  details ***}
procedure GetStudentDetails(var sd:
StudentDetails);
var
    temp : string[30];  {Storage for data entered}
    err  : integer;     {Parameter for Val}
    c    : integer;     {Loop counter}
begin
    {*** Get idcode ***}
    {** Read up to 5 digits **}
    write('Enter id code : ');
    temp := GetData(['0'..'9',' '],5);
    {** Convert to numeric distance **}
    val(temp,sd.idcode,err);
    {*** Get name ***}
    write('Enter name : ');
    sd.name := GetData(['A'..'Z','a'..'z','
','.','-',''''],29);
    {*** Get sex ***}
    write('Enter sex : ');
    temp := GetData(['F','M','f','m'],1);
    sd.sex := upcase(temp[1]);
    {*** Get six scores ***}
    for c := 1 to 6 do
    begin
        write('Enter score ',c,' : ');
        temp := GetData(['0'..'9'],3);
        val(temp,sd.score[c],err);
        while(sd.score[c] > 100) do
        begin
            write('#7');
            temp := GetData(['0'..'9'],3);
            val(temp,sd.score[c],err);
        end
    end
end;


{*** Display student details ***}
procedure DisplayStudent(sd:StudentDetails);
var
    c : integer; {Loop counter}
begin
    {*** Display idcode, name and sex ***}
    write(sd.idcode:4,'  ',sd.name,
        ' ':20-length(sd.name),sd.sex:3,'    ');
    {*** Display scores ***}
    for c := 1 to 6 do
        write(sd.score[c]:4);
    {*** Move to a new line ***}
    writeln;
end;


{*** Compare Student idcodes ***}
function
CompareId(sd1,sd2:StudentDetails):integer;
begin
    if sd1.idcode < sd2.idcode then
        CompareId := 1;
    if sd2.idcode < sd1.idcode then
        CompareId := 2;
    if sd1.idcode = sd2.idcode then
        CompareId := 0;
end;


{*** Modify a student's name ***}
procedure ModifyName(newname:string; var
sd:StudentDetails);
begin
    sd.name := newname;
end;

{*** Modify a student's score ***}
procedure ModifyScore(scoreno,newscore : integer;
var sd:StudentDetails);
begin
    {*** IF score no or mark is invalid, exit ***}
    if (scoreno < 1) or (scoreno > 6) or
          newscore < 0) or (newscore > 100)
    then
        exit;
    {*** Set specified score to new value ***}
    sd.score[scoreno] := newscore;
end;

{*********************************************}
{***  END StudentDetails Type Declaration  ***}
{*********************************************}


{***********************************}
{*       other routines            *}
{***********************************}

{*** Execute menu option chosen ***}
procedure ExecuteOption(opt : integer;
              var sd : StudentDetails);
const
    TESTREC : StudentDetails =
        (idcode:1234;name:'Liz Heron'; sex:'F';
                       score:(9,7,2,1,11,27));
var
    ch       : char;          {key pressed}
    sex      : char;          {sex inquiry}
    err      : integer;       {Parameter for Val}
    temp     : string[30];    {keyboard entry}
    examno   : integer;       {Exam no. (1 to 6)}
    exammark : integer;       {new exam score }
begin
    case opt of
        1: {*** Read new details ***}
            begin
                GetStudentDetails(sd);
            end;
        2: {*** Change name ***}
            begin
                {** get new name **}
                write('Enter new name : ');
                temp := GetData(['a'..'z','A'..'Z'
                      ,' ','.','-',''''],29);
                {** & modify the existing record **}
                ModifyName(temp,sd);
            end;
        3:  {*** Change score ***}
            begin
                {** Get exam score details **}
                write('Enter exam number : ');
                temp := GetData(['1'..'6'],1);
                Val(temp,examno,err);
                write('Enter new mark : ');
                temp := GetData(['0'..'9'],3);
                Val(temp,exammark,err);
                while (exammark > 100) do
                begin
                    writeln(#7);
                    temp := GetData(['0'..'9'],3);
                    val(temp,exammark,err);
                end;
                ModifyScore(examno,exammark,sd);
            end;
        4:  {*** Compare Idcodes ***}
            begin
                case CompareId(sd,TESTREC) of
                    0:  {*** Same idcodes ***}
                        writeln('Idcodes match');
                    1: {*** sd < TESTREC ***}
                        writeln('Your idcode < '+
                        ' test rec (1234)');
                    2: {*** sd > TESTREC ***}
                        writeln('Your idcode > '+
                        'test rec (1234)');
                end;
                ch := readkey;
            end;
        5:  {*** Display record ***}
            begin
                {** Display heading **}
                writeln(' ':18,'STUDENT RECORD '+
                              CONTENTS');
                writeln(' Id ','Name':10,
      '              Sex               Scores');
                {*** and record ***}
                DisplayStudent(sd);
                ch:=readkey;
            end;
```

**Continued on next page**

## Activity 8.4(continued)

```
        6:  {*** Terminate program message ***}
            writeln('TERMINATING PROGRAM');
    end
end;

{*****************************************}
{*             Main program              *}
{*****************************************}



const
    NL = #13+#10;
var
    sd          : StudentDetails;
    noofopts,op : integer;
begin
    repeat
      clrscr;
      noofopts :=   DisplayMenu('1  - Read record'
                    +NL+'2  - Change name'+NL+
                    '3  - Change Score'+NL+
                    '4  - Compare idcodes'+NL+
                    '5  - Display record'+NL+
                    '6  - QUIT'+NL);
      op := GetOption(noofopts);
      ExecuteOption(op,sd);
    until op = 6;
end.
```

## Activity 8.6

It is assumed that the *StudentDetails* type and related operations are held in a Unit called *Students*.

```
program SimpleTable;
uses WinCrt, Auxiliary, Students;
const
    SIZE = 20;
    NL =#13+#10;

{*********************************}
{*  StudentTable Data Type       *}
{*********************************}

{*** Data ***}
type
    StudentTable =
    record
        count : integer;
        list  : array[0..SIZE-1] of StudentDetails ;
    end;

{*** Operations ***}

procedure CreateTable(var t : StudentTable);
begin
    {*** set table count to zero ***}
    t.count := 0;
end;

function IsFull(var t : StudentTable) : boolean;
begin
    {*** IF count = SIZE-1 THEN ***}
    if t.count = SIZE then
        {*** return true ***}
        IsFull := true
    else
        {*** ELSE return false ***}
        IsFull := false;
end;

function IsAt(key : integer; var t :
StudentTable) : integer;
var
    post : integer;
begin
    {*** Search for match ***}
    post := 0;
    while (t.list[post].idcode <> key) and
        (post < t.count - 1)
    do
        post := post + 1;
    {*** IF found, return its position ***}
    if t.list[post].idcode = key then
        IsAt := post
    else
        {*** ELSE return -1 ***}
        IsAt := -1
end;

function AddToTable(sd : StudentDetails;
          var t : StudentTable) : boolean;
begin
    {*** IF idcode matches existing entry or table
full THEN ***}
    if(IsAt(sd.idcode,t)<> -1) or (IsFull(t)) then
    begin
        {*** return false ***}
        AddToTable := false;
        exit;
    end;
    {*** Add record to table ***}
    t.list[t.count] := sd;
    {*** Increment count ***}
    Inc(t.count);
    {*** Return true ***}
    AddToTable := true;
end;


procedure DisplayTable(var t : StudentTable);
var
    post, c : integer;
begin
    if t.count = 0 then
        writeln('Table is empty')
    else
    begin
        writeln('STUDENT TABLE CONTENTS':50);
        writeln;
        writeln('  Id ','Name':12,
'                Sex            Scores');
        for post := 0 to t.count - 1 do
            with t.list[post] do
            begin
                write(idcode:5,'   ',name,
                ' ':30-Length(name),sex,' ');
                for c := 1 to 6 do
                    write(score[c]:4);
                writeln;
            end;
    end
end;



procedure ExecuteOption(opt : integer; var t :
StudentTable);
var
    sd    : StudentDetails;
    no, c : integer;
    ch    : char;
    key   : integer;
    err   : integer;
    post  : integer;
begin
    case opt of
        1:
              CreateTable(t);
        2:
            begin
                GetStudentDetails(sd);
                AddToTable(sd,t);
            end;
        3:
            begin
                DisplayTable(t);
                ch := ReadKey;;
            end;
        4:
            begin
                if IsFull(t) then
                    writeln('Table is full')
                else
                    writeln('table is not full');
                ch := ReadKey;
            end;
        5:
            begin
                write('Enter key required : ');
                Val(GetData(['0'..'9'],4),key,err);
                post := IsAt(key,t);
                if post <> -1 then
                    writeln(key,' at position ',post)
                else
                    writeln('No match found');
                ch := Readkey;
            end;
        6:
            writeln('TERMINATING PROGRAM');
    end
end;
```

**Continued on next page**

## Activity 8.6 (continued)

```
var
    table :     StudentTable ;
    noofopts, op : integer;
begin
    CreateTable(table);
    repeat
        ClrScr;
        noofopts := DisplayMenu(
                '1-Create Table'
                +NL+'2-Add new student'
                +NL+'3-Display Table'
                +NL+'4-Check if full'
                +NL+'5-Check for match'
                +NL+'6-QUIT'+NL);
        op := GetOption(noofopts);
        ExecuteOption(op,table);
    until op = noofopts;
end.
```

## Activity 8.7

The ADT operation's definition is modified to:

```
NAME            :   GiveRecord
PARAMETERS
    IN          :   key : INTEGER
                    t : StudentTable
    OUT         :   success : BOOLEAN
                    st : StudentDetails
    IN/OUT      :   None
PRE-CONDITION   :   None
POST-CONDITION  :   If key matches an idcode
                    in t, then st contains
                    a copy of the entry in t
                    whose idcode is key and
                    success is set to true.
                    If key does not match
                    an entry in t, st
                    contains an idcode of -1
                    and success is set to
                    false.
```

## Activity 8.8

```
function GiveRecord(post : integer;
                    var t : StudentTable;
                    var sd : StudentDetails)
                            : boolean;
begin
    if (post<1) or (post > t.count)then
        GiveRecord := false;
    sd := t.list[post - 1];
    GiveRecord := true;
end;
```

## Activity 8.9

The new *UpdateRecord* routine is coded as

```
function UpdateRecord(sd:StudentDetails;
                var t:StudentTable):boolean;
var
    post : integer; {Position of match in table }
begin
    {*** Attempt to find match in table ***}
    post := IsAt(sd.idcode,t);
    {*** IF not found THEN ***}
    if post = -1 then
    begin
        {*** Return false ***}
        UpdateRecord := false;
        exit
    end;
    {*** update entry and return true ***}
    t.list[post] := sd;
    UpdateRecord := true
  end;
```

To execute this we need to update the *ExecuteOption* routine as follows

```
procedure ExecuteOption(opt : integer;
        var t : StudentTable);
var
    sd      : StudentDetails;
    no, c : integer;
    ch    : char;
    key      : integer;
    err      : integer;
    post     : integer;
    nops     : integer;
    op       : integer;
    newscore : integer;
begin
    case opt of
        1:
                CreateTable(t);
        2:
            begin
                GetStudentDetails(sd);
                AddToTable(sd,t);
            end;
        3:
            begin
                DisplayTable(t);
                ch := ReadKey;;
            end;
        4:
            begin
                if IsFull(t) then
                    writeln('Table is full')
                else
                    writeln('table is not full');
                ch := ReadKey;
            end;
        5:
            begin
                write('Enter key to be search for : ');
                Val(GetData(['0'..'9'],4),key,err);
                post := IsAt(key,t);
                if post <> -1 then
                    writeln(key,' at position ',post)
                else
                    writeln('No match found');
                ch := ReadKey;
            end;
        6:
            begin
                write('Key of record to be changed : ');
                Val(GetData(['0'..'9'],4),key,err);
                post := IsAt(key,t);
                if post = -1 then
                begin
                    writeln('No match found');
                    ch := ReadKey;
                    exit;
                end;
                GiveRecord(key, t,sd);
                repeat
                    write('Current contents ');
                    DisplayStudent(sd);
                    nops := DisplayMenu
                        ('1-Change name'+NL+
                        '2-Change score'+NL+
                        '3-Return to main menu'
                        +NL);
                    op := GetOption(nops);
                    case op of
                        1:
                            begin
                                write('New name : ');
                                sd.name := GetData
                                (['A'..'Z','a'..'z',
                                ' ','.','''','-'],30);
                            end;
                        2:
                            begin
                                write('Score to change (1-6):');
                                Val(GetData(['1'..'6'],1),
                                            post,err);
                                write('New score (0-100):');
                                Val(GetData(['0'..'9'],3),
                                        newscore,err);
                                while (newscore < 0) or
                                      (newscore > 100)
                                do
                                begin
                                   write('0-100. Re-enter:');
                                   Val(GetData(['0'..'9'],3),
                                          newscore,err);
                                end;
                                sd.score[post] := newscore;
                            end;
                    end;
                until op = 3;
                UpdateRecord(sd,t);
            end;
        7:
            writeln('TERMINATING PROGRAM');
    end
end;
```

The main program's *DisplayMenu* call would now include an extra option:

```
noofopts := DisplayMenu(
                  '1  - Create Table'+NL+
                  '2  - Add new student'+NL+
                  '3  - Display Table'+NL+
                  '4  - Check if full'+NL+
                  '5  - Check for match'+NL+
                  '6  - Update record'+NL+
                  '7  - QUIT'+NL);
```

## Activity 8.10

To test all of the routines so far we need to start by including *GiveRecordAt* and *NoOfSex*. The code for these routines is given below:

```
function GiveRecordAt(post : integer;
            var t : StudentTable;
            var sd : StudentDetails) : boolean;
const
    emptyrec : StudentDetails =
            (idcode:0;name:'EMPTY';sex:' '
                    ;score:(0,0,0,0,0,0));
begin
    {*** IF no match THEN ***}
    if (post<1) or (post > t.count) then
    begin
        {*** Return empty rec and false ***}
        sd := emptyrec;
        GiveRecordAt := false;
    end
    else
    begin
        {*** ELSE return req'd record & true ***}
        sd := t.list[post - 1];
        GiveRecordAt := true;
    end;
end;
```

```
function NoOfSex(sex : char; var t :
StudentTable): integer;
var
    sd    : StudentDetails;
    count : integer;
    Sxx   : char;
    c     : integer;
begin
    Sxx := Upcase(sex);
    if(Sxx <> 'F') and (Sxx <> 'M')then
        NoOfSex := -1
    else
    begin
        count := 0;
        for c :=1 to t.count do
        begin
            GiveRecordAt(c,t,sd);
            count := count + integer(sd.sex = Sxx);
        end;
        NoOfSex := count;
    end
end;
```

Next, we need to change the final options in *ExecuteOption*

```
 7:
    begin
        write('Male or female (M/F) : ');
        temp := GetData(['M','F','m','f'],1);
        sx := temp[1];
        writeln('Students of that sex : ',
                         NoOfSex(sx,t));
        ch := ReadKey;
    end;
 8: writeln('TERMINATING PROGRAM');
```

And, finally, the main program's menu has to add as option 7, *Students of a specified sex*.

## Activity 8.11

a) 126     i.e. (1+255)/2
b) (1+N)/2

## Activity 8.12

This condition tests for the end of the entries being reached without finding a match.

## Activity 8.13

The new version of *IsAt* is :

```
function IsAt(key : integer; var t :
StudentTable) : integer;
var
    post : integer;
begin
    {*** Copy rerq'd key to end of table ***}
    t.list[t.count].idcode := key;
    {*** Search for match ***}
    post := 0;
    while (t.list[post].idcode <> key) do
        post := post + 1;
    {*** IF found at end of table, return -1 ***}
    if post = t.count then
        IsAt := -1
    else
        {*** ELSE return post ***}
        IsAt := post
end;
```

Otherwise, the program is unchanged.

## Activity 8.14

a) 1
b) 6
c) 7

## Activity 8.15

1. The number of comparisons required to reach each key in the table is

| Key | Comparisons |
|---|---|
| 122 | 4 |
| 1 93 | 3 |
| 210 | 4 |
| 217 | 2 |
| 233 | 4 |
| 251 | 3 |
| 279 | 4 |
| 345 | 1 |
| 399 | 4 |
| 422 | 3 |
| 442 | 4 |
| 478 | 2 |
| 588 | 4 |
| 600 | 3 |
| 701 | 4 |

2. a) 1
   b) 2
   c) 4
   d) 8

3. ((1*1)+(2*2)+(4*3)+(8*4))/15
   = 3.27

## Activity 8.16

a) 1
b) None

## Activity 8.17

a) 4
b) 5
c) 10
d) 14

## Activity 8.18

| | lowest | highest |
|---|---|---|
| Initially | 0 | 15 |
| After 1 comp | 8 | 15 |
| After 2 | 8 | 10 |
| After 3 | 10 | 10 |

## Activity 8.19

The new version of *IsAt* is:

```
function IsAt(key :integer; var t :
StudentTable):integer;
var
    lowest, mid, highest : integer;
            {extremes and middle of search area}
begin
    {*** Search area is occupied part of table ***}
    lowest := 0;
    highest := t.count-1;
    {*** Mid entry is half way ***}
    mid := (lowest + highest) div 2;
    {*** WHILE no match & recs to search DO ***}
    while (t.list[mid].idcode <> key) and (
            lowest <= highest)
    do
    begin
        {*** IF mid entry's < req'd key THEN ***}
        if t.list[mid].idcode < key then
            {*** Eliminate the top end ***}
            lowest := mid + 1
        else
            {*** ELSE eliminate bottom end ***}
            highest := mid - 1;
        {*** Calc new mid point ***}
        mid := (lowest + highest) div 2;
    end;
    {*** IF key found THEN ***}
    if lowest <= highest then
        {*** Return position of match ***}
        IsAt := mid
    else
      {*** ELSE return -1 for no match found ***}
        IsAt := -1;
end;
```

All other code remains unchanged.

## Activity 8.20

```
1.
function IsAt(key : integer;
        var t : StudentTable) : integer;
begin
    if t.list[key].name <> '' then
        IsAt := key
    else
        IsAt := -1;
end;
```

```
2.
function DeleteFromTable(key : integer;
        var t : StudentTable) : boolean;
begin
    if t.list[key] <> '' then
    begin
        t.list[key].name := '';
        DeleteFromTable := true
    end
    else
        DeleteFromTable := false;
end;
```

## Activity 8.21

```
a)  10 + 24 + 38 = 72
b)  102 + 438 = 540
```

## Activity 8.22

Assuming the string to be manipulated is in a field called key then we can create an 8-bit numeric value using the code

```
value := ((Ord(key[0]) and $0F) shl 4) +
         (Ord(key[Length(key)]) and $0F)
```

## Activity 8.23

| Key | Position |
|---|---|
| 8838 | 15 |
| 6627 | 14 |
| 4895 | 16 |
| 1995 | 6 |

## Activity 8.24

No change is required to this routine; only the function responsible for finding the table entry (*IsAt*) requires modification.

```
function GiveRecord(key : integer;
         var t :StudentTable ;
         var sd : StudentDetails): boolean;
var
    post : integer;
begin
    post := IsAt(key,t);
    if post <> -1 then
    begin
        sd := t.list[post];
        GiveRecord := true;
    end
    else
        GiveRecord := false;
end;
```

## Activity 8.25

```
program HashTables1;
uses WinCrt, Auxiliary, Students;
const
    NL = #13+#10;

{*********************************************}
{***  StudentTable Data Type Declarations  ***}
{*********************************************}
{*** Data ***}
const
    SIZE = 17;
    EMPTY = 0;
    DELETED = -1;
    NOTFOUND = -1;
```

**Continued on next page**

## Activity 8.25(continued)

```
type
    StudentTable =
    record
        count : integer;
        list  : array[0..SIZE-1] of StudentDetails;
    end;

{*** Operations ***}

{*** Check if table is full ***}
function IsFull(var t:StudentTable):boolean;
begin
    {*** IF count is equal to the size of the list
THEN ***}
    if t.count = SIZE then
        {*** return true ***}
        IsFull := true
    else
        {*** ELSE return false ***}
        IsFull := false;
end;



{*** Hash key to give insert position ***}
function Hash(key:integer):integer;
begin
    Hash := key mod SIZE
end;

{*** Find position of entry in table ***}
function IsAt(key:integer; var
t:StudentTable):integer;
var
    post  : integer;    {Post of required entry}
    start : integer;    {Starting post of search}
begin
    {*** Hash to where record should be ***}
    start := Hash(key);
    post := start;
    {*** WHILE no match or empty position DO ***}
    while (t.list[post].idcode <> key)
            and (t.list[post].idcode <> EMPTY)
    do
    begin
        {*** Move to next position in table ***}
        post := (post+1) mod SIZE;
        {*** IF all entries searched, give up ***}
        if post = start then
            break;
    end;
    {*** IF not successful THEN, return -1 ***}
    if(t.list[post].idcode <> key)then
        IsAt := NOTFOUND
    else
        {*** ELSE return position of record ***}
        IsAt := post;
end;



{*** Create empty table ***}
procedure CreateTable(var t:StudentTable);
var
    c : integer;     {Loop counter}
begin
    {*** Set count to zero ***}
    t.count := 0;
    {*** Set all key fields to empty ***}
    for c := 0 to SIZE-1 do
        t.list[c].idcode := EMPTY;
end;


{*** Add a student's details to the table ***}
function AddToTable(sd:StudentDetails;
                    var t:StudentTable):boolean;
var
    post : integer; {Position in table of record}
begin
    {*** IF match or table full THEN ***}
    if (IsAt(sd.idcode,t) <> NOTFOUND)
            or (IsFull(t))
    then
    begin
        {*** Return false ***}
        AddToTable := false;
        exit;
    end;
    {*** Find insert position ***}
    {** Hash key **}
    post := Hash(sd.idcode);
    {** Linear probe until post found **}
    while(t.list[post].idcode <> EMPTY)
        and (t.list[post].idcode <> DELETED)do
        post := (post+1) mod SIZE;
    {*** Add student's details to table ***}
    t.list[post] := sd;
    {*** Increment count ***}
    inc(t.count);
    {*** Return true ***}
    AddToTable := true;
end;


{*** Display contents of table *** }
procedure DisplayTable(var t: StudentTable);
var
    c,k:integer;
begin
    {*** IF table empty THEN ***}
    if t.count = 0 then
        {*** Display empty message ***}
        writeln('Table is empty')
    else
        {*** ELSE display contents ***}
    begin
        {** Display heading **}
        writeln(' ':23,'STUDENT TABLE CONTENTS');
        writeln(' Id ','Name':10,
        '              Sex            Scores');
        {** Display occuppied positions**}
        for c := 0 to SIZE-1 do
            with t.list[c] do
                if (idcode <> EMPTY) and
                    (idcode <> DELETED)
                then
                    DisplayStudent(t.list[c]);
    end
end;



{*** Returns a specified entry in the table ***}
function GiveRecord(key:integer;
    var t:StudentTable; var sd:StudentDetails)
                                : boolean;
const
    emptyrec :StudentDetails =
        (idcode:0;name:'EMPTY';
        sex:' ';score:(0,0,0,0,0,0));
var
    post : integer;
begin
    {*** Attempt to locate record ***}
    post := IsAt(key,t);
    {*** IF found THEN ***}
    if post <> NOTFOUND then
    begin
        {*** Return record found and true ***}
        sd := t.list[post];
        GiveRecord := true;
    end
    else
    begin
        {*** ELSE return empty rec and false ***}
        sd := emptyrec;
        GiveRecord := false;
    end;
end;


{*** Delete a specified record ***}
function DeleteFromTable(key:integer;
                var t:StudentTable):boolean;
var
    post : integer;     {Position of match in table }
    c : integer;        {Loop counter}
begin
    {*** Find matching idcode in table ***}
    post := IsAt(key,t);
    {*** IF not found THEN ***}
    if post = -1 then
    begin
        {*** Return false ***}
        DeleteFromTable := false;
        exit;
    end;
    {*** Delete: key field to empty & dec count***}
    t.list[post].idcode := EMPTY;
    Dec(t.count);
    DeleteFromTable := true
end;
```

**Continued on next page**

## Activity 8.25(continued)

```
{*** Modify an existing record ***}
function UpdateRecord(sd:StudentDetails;
        var t:StudentTable):boolean;
var
    post : integer; {Position of match in table }
begin
    {*** Find matching idcode in table ***}
    post := IsAt(sd.idcode,t);
    {*** IF not found THEN ***}
    if post = NOTFOUND then
    begin
        {*** Return false ***}
        UpdateRecord := false;
        exit
    end;
    {*** update entry & return true ***}
    t.list[post] := sd;
    UpdateRecord := true
end;



{*** Determine number of given sex ***}
function NoOfSex(sex:char;
            var t:StudentTable):integer;
var
    count   : integer;  {Count of same sex}
    sexcopy : char;     {Sex being searched for}
    c       : integer;  {Loop counter}
begin
    count := 0;
    sexcopy := upcase(sex);
    if (sexcopy <> 'F') and (sexcopy <> 'M') then
    begin
        NoOfSex := 0;
        exit;
    end;
    for c := 0 to SIZE-1 do
        if(t.list[c].idcode <> EMPTY)
            and (t.list[c].idcode <> DELETED)
        then
            count := count +
                integer(t.list[c].sex = sexcopy);
    NoOfSex := count;
end;
{*******************************************}
{***  END StudentTable Type Declaration  ***}
{*******************************************}

procedure ExecuteOption(opt : integer;
                        var t : StudentTable);
var
    sd       : StudentDetails;
    no, c    : integer;
    ch       : char;
    key      : integer;
    err      : integer;
    post     : integer;
    nops     : integer;
    op       : integer;
    newscore : integer;
    sx       : char;
    temp     : string[1];
begin
    case opt of
        1:
            CreateTable(t);
        2:
            begin
              GetStudentDetails(sd);
              AddToTable(sd,t);
            end;
        3:
            begin
              DisplayTable(t);
              ch := ReadKey;;
            end;
        4:
            begin
              if IsFull(t) then
                writeln('Table is full')
              else
                writeln('table not full');
              ch := ReadKey;
            end;
        5:
            begin
              write('Required key : ');
              Val(GetData(['0'..'9'],4),
                        key,err);
              post := IsAt(key,t);
              if post <> -1 then
                writeln(key,' at position ',
                    post)
              else
                writeln('No match found');
            ch := Readkey;
        end;
    6:
        begin
          write('Required key : ');
          Val(GetData(['0'..'9'],4),key,err);
          post := IsAt(key,t);
          if post = -1 then
          begin
              writeln('No match found');
              ch := ReadKey;
              exit;
          end;
          GiveRecord(key, t,sd);
          repeat
              write('Current contents ');
              DisplayStudent(sd);
              nops := DisplayMenu
                    ('1-Change name'+NL+
                     '2-Change score'+NL+
                     '3-Return to main menu'
                        +NL);
              op := GetOption(nops);
              case op of
                  1:
                      begin
                          write('New name : ');
                          sd.name :=
                           GetData(['A'..'Z',
                          'a'..'z',' ','.',
                          '''','-'],30);
                  2:
                      begin
                          write('Score to chang(1-6):');
                          Val(GetData(['1'..'6'],1),
                              post,err);
                          write('New score(0-100):');
                          Val(GetData(['0'..'9'],3),
                                 newscore,err);
                          while (newscore < 0) or
                              (newscore > 100)
                          do
                          begin
                            write('0-100. Re-enter:');
                            Val(GetData(['0'..'9'],3),
                                   newscore,err);
                          end;
                          sd.score[post] := newscore;
                      end;
                  end;
          until op = 3;
          UpdateRecord(sd,t);
        end;
    7:{*** Delete an entry from the table ***}
        begin
            write('Id of record to be removed : ');
            Val(GetData(['0'..'9'],4),key,err);
            if not DeleteFromTable(key,t) then
                writeln('Key not found')
            else
                writeln('Deleted');
            ch:=readkey;
        end;
    8:
        begin
          write('Male or female (M/F) : ');
          temp := GetData(['M','F','m','f'],1);
          sx := temp[1];
          writeln('Students of that sex : ',
                        NoOfSex(sx,t));
          ch := ReadKey;
        end;

    9:
        writeln('TERMINATING PROGRAM');
    end
  end;
{*****************************************}
{*            Main program               *}
{*****************************************}
var
    table : StudentTable;
    noofopts,op : integer;
begin
    CreateTable(table);
    repeat
      clrscr;
      noofopts :=   DisplayMenu(
        '1  - Create Table'+NL+'2  - Add new student'+NL+
        '3  - Display Table'+NL+'4  - Check if full'+NL+
        '5  - Check for match'+NL+'6  - Update record'+NL+
        '7  - Delete record'+NL+'8  - No of given sex'+NL+
        '9  - QUIT'+NL);
      op := GetOption(noofopts);
      ExecuteOption(op,table);
    until op = noofopts;
end.
```

Activity 8.26

Few changes are required to the previous program. These are:

1. The definition of a *StepSize* function:

```
function StepSize(key : integer) : integer;
begin
    StepSize := (SIZE - 2)-(key mod (SIZE - 2));
end;
```

2. An update to the *AddToTable* operation:

```
{*** Add a student's details to the table ***}

function AddToTable(sd:StudentDetails;
                var t:StudentTable):boolean;
var
    post : integer; {Position in table of record}
    step : integer; {Step size used for overflow}
begin
    {*** IF idcode matches or table full THEN ***}
    if (IsAt(sd.idcode,t) <> NOTFOUND)
            or (IsFull(t))
    then
    begin
        {*** Return false ***}
        AddToTable := false;
        exit;
    end;
    {*** Find insert position ***}
    {** Hash key **}
    post := Hash(sd.idcode);
    {** IF collision THEN Double hash **}
    if(t.list[post].idcode <> EMPTY) and
        (t.list[post].idcode <> DELETED)
    then
    begin
        step := StepSize(sd.idcode);
        while (t.list[post].idcode <> EMPTY)
            and (t.list[post].idcode <> DELETED)
        do
            post := (post + step) mod SIZE;
    end;
    {*** Add student's details to table ***}
    t.list[post] := sd;
    {*** Increment count ***}
    Inc(t.count);
    {*** Return true ***}
    AddToTable := true;
end;
```

3. An update to *IsAt* function:

```
{*** Find position of entry in table ***}
function IsAt(key:integer;
                var t:StudentTable):integer;
var
    post  : integer;  {Post of required entry}
    start : integer;  {Starting post of search}
    step  : integer;  {Step size when overflowing}
begin
    {*** Hash to where record should be ***}
    start := Hash(key);
    post := start;
    {*** IF no match found and not empty THEN ***}
    if (t.list[post].idcode <> key) and
        (t.list[post].idcode <> EMPTY)
    then
    begin
        {*** Calculate step size ***}
        step := StepSize(key);
        {*** WHILE no match and not empty DO ***}
        while (t.list[post].idcode <> key)
            and (t.list[post].idcode <> EMPTY)
        do
        begin
            {*** Move to next post in table ***}
            post := (post + step) mod SIZE;
            {*** IF all searched, give up ***}
            if post = start then
                break;
        end;
    end;
    {*** IF not successful THEN, return -1 ***}
    if(t.list[post].idcode <> key)then
        IsAt := NOTFOUND
    else
        {*** ELSE return position of record ***}
        IsAt := post;
end;
```

# Activity 8.27

The important point here is not to be fooled into sorting on the surname. The computer will treat the name field as a simple string when organising the data.

The final result will give the records in the order

330
090
569
255
708
589
911

Since the first three records have the same author, these can be given in any order.

# Activity 8.28

7. One for each record transferred.

# Activity 8.29

```
a)
function SmallestAt(var t : StudentTable) :
integer;
var
    post : integer; {Post of smallest idcode}
    c    : integer;      {Loop counter}
begin
    {*** IF table empty, return -1 ***}
    if t.count = 0 then
    begin
        SmallestAt := -1;
        exit;
    end;
    {*** Search for smallest idcode ***}
    post := 0;
    for c := 1 to t.count - 1 do
        if t.list[c].idcode<t.list[post].idcode
        then
            post := c;
    {*** Return position of smallest ***}
    SmallestAt := post;
end;
```

```
b)
procedure SelectionSort(var t1,t2:StudentTable);
const
    HIGHVALUE = 32767; {High key value}
var
    pass : integer;    {Sort pass}
    post : integer; {position of lowest idcode}
begin
    for pass := 1 to t1.count do
    begin
        post := SmallestAt(t1);
        t2.list[pass-1] := t1.list[post];
        t1.list[post].idcode := HIGHVALUE;
    end;
    t2.count := t1.count;
end;
```

# Activity 8.30

1. 2N
2. a) N-1
   b) N-1
   c) N-1
3. N(N-1)     i.e. Passes * Comparisons per pass
4. 1
5. N

## Activity 8.31

1. a) N-1
   b) N-2
   c) N-3
   d) 1 i.e. N - (N-1)
2. N(N-1)/2 i.e. Passes * Average comparisons per pass
3. 3
4. 3(N-1)

## Activity 8.32

Since we only want to search a restricted area of the table for the smallest key, we begin by rewriting *SmallestAt* to specify the area of the table to be searched:

```
function SmallestAt(var t : StudentTable;
                    start : integer) : integer;
var
    post : integer;     {Post of smallest idcode}
    c    : integer;     {Loop counter}
begin
    {*** IF table empty, return -1 ***}
    if t.count = 0 then
    begin
        SmallestAt := -1;
        exit;
    end;
    {*** Search for smallest idcode ***}
    post := start;
    for c := start + 1 to t.count - 1 do
        if t.list[c].idcode < t.list[post].idcode then
            post := c;
    {*** Return position of smallest ***}
    SmallestAt := post;
end;
```

```
procedure SelectionWithExSort
                    (var t : StudentTable);
const
    HIGHVALUE = 32767; {High key value}
var
    pass : integer;     {Sort pass}
    post : integer; {position of lowest idcode}
    st   : StudentDetails;
begin
    for pass := 1 to t.count do
    begin
        post := SmallestAt(t, pass-1);
        st := t.list[pass-1];
        t.list[pass-1] := t.list[post];
        t.list[post] := st;
    end;
end;
```

## Activity 8.33

We need to start by adding the *InsertAt* function which will be needed by the new version of *AddToTable*.

```
function InsertAt(id : integer; var t :
StudentTable) : integer;
var
    post : integer; {Post id to be inserted}
begin
    {*** Start at the beginning of the table ***}
    post := 0;
    {*** WHILE keys < id & not end of table DO ***}
    while (t.list[post].idcode < id ) and (post <
t.count) do
        Inc(post);
    {*** Return insert position ***}
    InsertAt := post;
end;

function AddToTable(sd : StudentDetails; var t :
StudentTable) : boolean;
var
    placeat : integer; {Insert position}
    post    : integer; {Loop counter}
begin
    {*** IF idcode matches existing entry or table
full THEN ***}
    if(IsAt(sd.idcode,t)<> -1) or (IsFull(t)) then
    begin
        {*** return false ***}
        AddToTable := false;
        exit;
    end;
    {*** Determine insert point ***}
    placeat := InsertAt(sd.idcode,t);
    {*** Move lower records ***}
    for post := t.count - 1 downto placeat do
        t.list[post + 1] := t.list[post];
    {*** Add record to table ***}
    t.list[placeat] := sd;
    {*** Increment count ***}
    Inc(t.count);
    {*** Return true ***}
    AddToTable := true;
end;
```

## Activity 8.34

1.

| | Moves Min | Moves Max | Comparisons Min | Comparisons Max |
|---|---|---|---|---|
| a) | 1 | 2 | 1 | 1 |
| b) | 1 | 3 | 1 | 2 |
| c) | 1 | 4 | 1 | 3 |
| d) | 1 | N | 1 | N-1 |

2. Min moves total = N-1
   max moves total = (N-1)(N+2)/2
   Av. moves = $(N^2+3N-4)/4$

   Min comparisons total = N-1
   Max comparisons total = N(N-1)/2
   Av. comparisons = $(N^2+N-2)4$

## Activity 8.35

1. a) Comparisons: N-1 Max moves : 3(N-1)
   b) Comparisons: N-2 Max moves : 3(N-2)
   c) Comaprisons: N-3 Max moves : 3(N-3)
   d) Comparisons: 1 Max moves : 3
2. Total comparisons : N(N-1)/2
   Total av. moves : 3N(N-1)/4

Chapter 9

# Dynamic Linear Types

**This chapter covers the following topics:**

Defining a Node

Doubly Linked Lists

Problems with Fixed Size Storage

Queues

Stacks

# LINKED LISTS

## The Problem with Arrays

We have already seen that it is possible to define a pointer to any data type. For example, we might create a pointer to an `integer` value using the definition

```
iptr : ^integer;
```

One of the advantages of using pointers is that we are free to create and destroy data as and when required using the `New` and `Dispose` commands.

Of course, with only one pointer, we can only reference a single item of data. What if we want to reference several data items using pointers?

One way to tackle this is to create an array of pointers (see the Case Study in the previous chapter). This approach is acceptable if we know in advance the maximum number of data items to be created since we need to specify the size of the array (see FIG-9.1).

**FIG-9.1**

An Array of Pointers

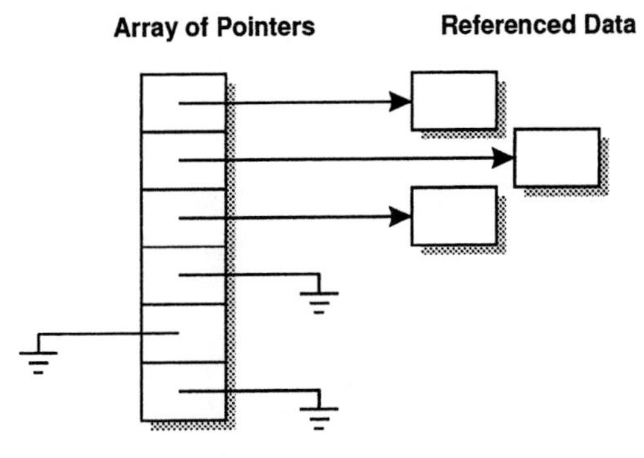


But when the number of items involved cannot be predicted this technique is of little use. What we need is some way of increasing the number of pointers available as our storage requirements grow. This is the purpose of a **linked list**.

## Creating a Linked List

### Adding a pointer field to a Structure

A standard structure might be declared as

```
type
    Data =
    record
        // data fields declared here
    end;
```

The idea behind a linked list is to combine the pointer and the data in a single structure. Hence, the new structure could be:

Node is the usual term for a component of a linked list.

```
type
    Node =
    record
        value : Data;
        next  :^Node;
    end;
```

Unfortunately, Pascal won't allow the *next* field to be defined as a pointer to a *Node* since the definition of *Node* is not complete at that point. Instead, we need to employ a more roundabout approach by first defining a *Node* pointer type:

```
type
    NodePointerType = ^Node;
```

and then using this to define *next:*

```
    Node =
    record
        value : Data;
        next  : NodePointerType;
    end;
```

## Manipulating a Linked List

How does this help us create a collection of data unlimited in size? The easiest way to see how this approach solves our problem is to follow a specific example. Let's assume that our declarations are

```
type
    Data =
    record
        no:integer;
    end;

    NodePointerType = ^Node;

    Node =
    record
        value : Data;
        next  : NodePointerType;
    end;
```

and that our program has defined a pointer to this structure:

```
start : NodePointerType;
```

We can create space and store a value using the instructions

```
New(start);
start^.value.no := 12;
start^.next := NIL;
```

This situation is shown in FIG-9.2.

**FIG-9.2**

Pointer to a Node

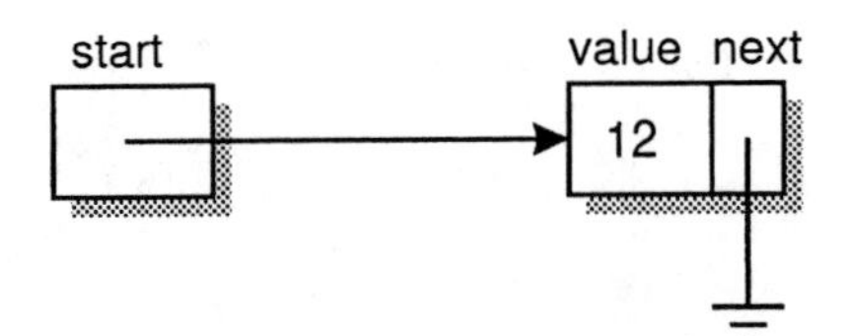


> **Activity 9.1**
>
> What expressions are required to reference the following parts of the node?
>
> a) *value*
>
> b) *next*

Notice that, as well as creating space for our data, we have also created another pointer (*start^.next*). Now, when a second item of data needs to be stored, we can use this newly created pointer as a reference to the second data item:

```
New(start^.next);
start^.next^.value.no = 53;
start^.next^.next = NIL;
```

This gives us the situation shown in FIG-9.3.

**FIG-9.3**

Pointing to the next Node

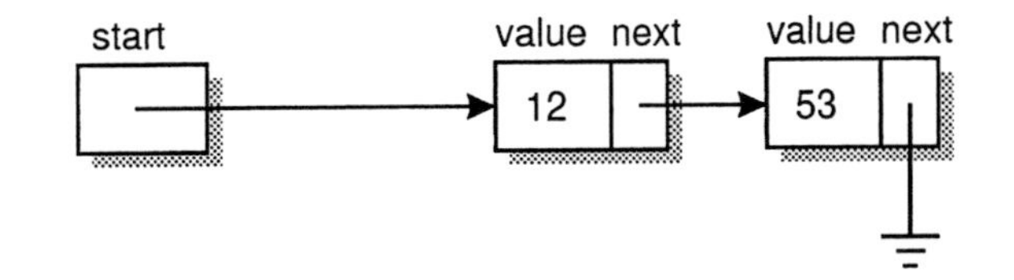


This linking together of the data components gives rise to the data structure's name: **linked list**. Continuing with this approach will allow us to create a list of any length (ignoring the fact that we may run out of memory). However, we are in danger of being overwhelmed by the syntax: to add a third node to the list the instruction would be

```
New(start^.next^.next);
```

with subsequent nodes requiring even more awkward terms.

We can solve this by introducing two additional *Node* pointers, *temp* and *current*. The first pointer, *temp*, is used when creating a new node; the second, *current*, moves along the existing list until it references the final node. We can then create a new node, insert data in the node, and link it to the list using the instructions

The logic assumes there is at least one existing node in the list.

```
//*** Create node ***
New(temp);
//*** Place data in node ***
temp^.value.no := 99;
temp^.next := NIL;
//*** Find the end of the list ***
current := start;
while(current^.next <> NIL)
    current := current^.next;
//*** Add new node to list ***
current^.next := temp;
```

The steps described above are shown in FIG-9.4.

**FIG-9.4**

Adding a Node to the end of the List

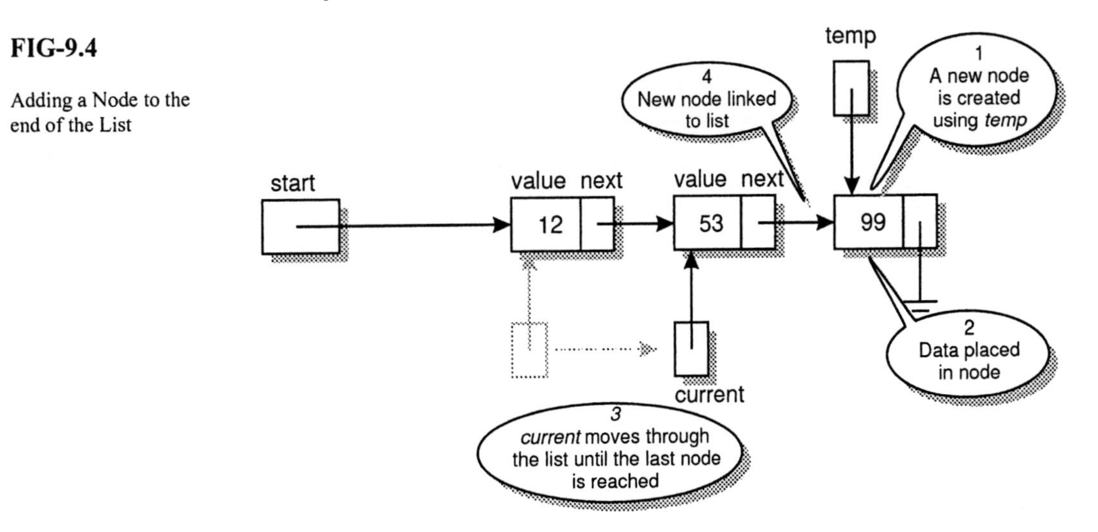

# Creating a Linked List Data Structure

Now that we've examined the general approach to the problem, we need to design the components of a linked list in such a way as to allow us to go on and define variables of this type on which we can perform operations such as adding and removing data.

## The Data Components

We need to begin by defining the structure of the data held in each node. For the purpose of this example, we'll keep it simple and use a single short string:

```
type
    Data =
    record
        FText : string[31];
    end;
```

Of course, the actual construct used will depend on the data to be held in the list.

**Activity 9.2**

Write a new declaration for *Data* which contains the following information:

```
idcode : integer
name   : string[30]
sex    : char
score  : array[1..6]of integer
```

Once *Data* has been declared, we need to declare *NodePointerType* and *Node*:

```
NodePointerType = ^Node;

Node =
record
    value : Data;
    next  : NodePointerType;
end;
```

**Activity 9.3**

Why is the *next* pointer a *NodePointerType* type rather than a *^Data* type?

Finally, we need to declare the linked list structure itself. From the previous diagrams, we can see that only the *start* pointer exists when the list is empty, so we might define the linked list structure as:

```
List =
record
    start : NodePointerType;
end;
```

But, as in other lists, it is often useful to maintain a count of the number of items held, so we'll expand the declaration to include a count:

```
List =
record
    start : NodePointerType;
    count : integer;
end;
```

> **Activity 9.4**
>
> What changes will be required to the design of *Node* and *List* in order to accommodate the *Data* definition produced in Activity 9.2?

## The Operations Required

There are several basic operations normally used with a list of data; these are defined informally overleaf:

| | |
|---|---|
| **CreateList** | : Creates an empty list. |
| **Len** | : Returns the number of items in the list. |
| **IsEmpty** | : Returns *true* if the list is empty, otherwise returns *false*. |
| **AddAt** | : Adds new data at a specified point in the list. |
| **DeleteFrom** | : Removes the node at a specified point in the list. |
| **Head** | : Returns the first data at the front of the list. The list itself is unaffected by this operation. |
| **Tail** | : Removes the first node from the list. |
| **DisplayList** | : Displays all the data in the list. |
| **DeleteList** | : Removes all data from the list. |

We'll now look at each of these operations in more detail.

### CreateList

The list parameter used throughout these descriptions is named *seq*.

This routine simply initialises the list by setting the *start* pointer to NIL and *count* to zero (see FIG-9.5).

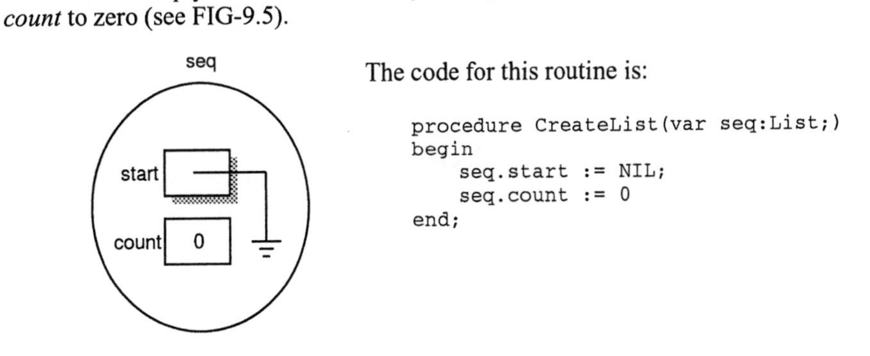


**FIG-9.5**

Initialising the List

The code for this routine is:

```
procedure CreateList(var seq:List;)
begin
    seq.start := NIL;
    seq.count := 0
end;
```

### Len

This routine returns the number of nodes in the list. All that is required is to return the value of *count*. The code is:

```
function Len(seq:List):integer;
begin
    Len := seq.count
end;
```

## IsEmpty

This function returns the value 1 if the list is empty, otherwise it returns zero. Code for this routine is:

```
function IsEmpty(seq:List) : boolean;
begin
    IsEmpty := (seq.count = 0)
end;
```

## AddAt

This routine inserts a new node at any specified position in the list. For example, in a list currently containing 3 nodes, the new node can be placed at positions 1,2,3 or 4. If the position specified is outside this range then we have an invalid situation and the operation cannot be performed. One method of dealing with an error condition such as this is to return a value indicating the success or failure of the operation. Assuming the position of the new node is specified by the parameter *post*, then the code necessary to detect an invalid position is:

```
if (post < 1)or(post > Len(seq)+1) then
begin
    AddAt := false;
    exit;
end;
```

*post* is the position in the list at which the new node is to be placed.

If the insert position is valid, we need to create a new node and transfer the new data to it. This requires the code:

```
New(temp);
temp^.value := item;    //item contains the new data
temp^.next  := NIL;
```

FIG-9.6 shows the state of a list at this point.

**FIG-9.6**

Creating a New Node

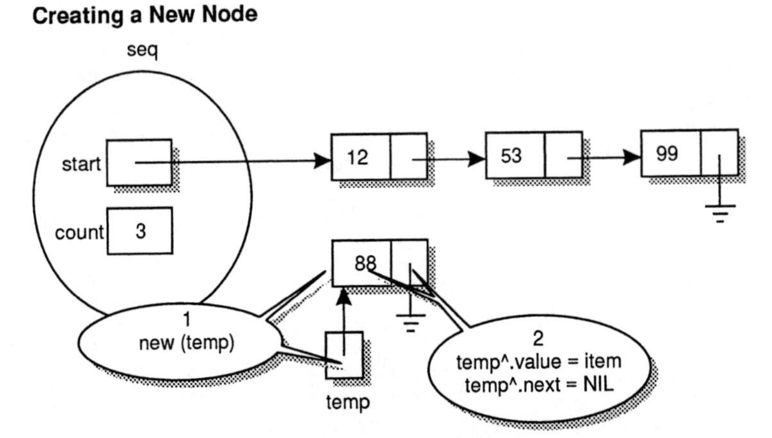


Once the new node has been created it must be inserted into the existing list. In doing this there are two distinct circumstances which have to be dealt with:

1. If the new value is to be placed at the beginning of the list, then the value in start must be changed. The code for this option is:

```
if post = 1 then
begin
    temp^.next := seq.start;
    seq.start  := temp;
end
```

FIG-9.7 shows the consequences of this code.

**FIG-9.7**

Inserting at the Start of the List

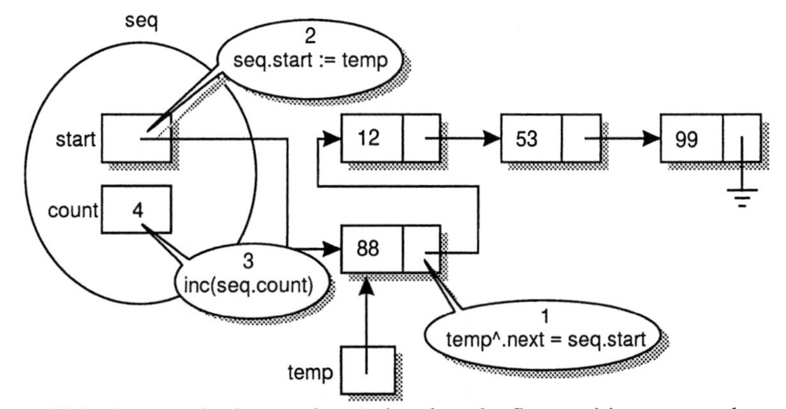


2. If the insert point is anywhere other than the first position, we need to find the insert point in the list and adjust the pointers in the surrounding nodes to insert the new value.

This second situation needs to be looked at in greater detail. To find the insert point for the new node we employ two pointers, *current* and *previous*, which move along the linked list until *current* references the node at the insert position and *previous*, the preceding node. The code for this is:

The variable *c* must be declared at the start of the routine.

```
previous := NIL;
current := seq.start;
for c := 2 to post do
begin
    previous := current;
    current := current^.next;
end
```

For example, if we want to insert a new node at position 3, *current* would reference the third node and *previous* the second. Next, we have to break the existing links and splice in the new node. This is done with the code:

```
previous^.next := temp;
temp^.next := current;
```

FIG-9.8 shows the main stages in this operation.

**FIG-9.8**

Inserting a Node within the List

**Inserting a New Node within the List**

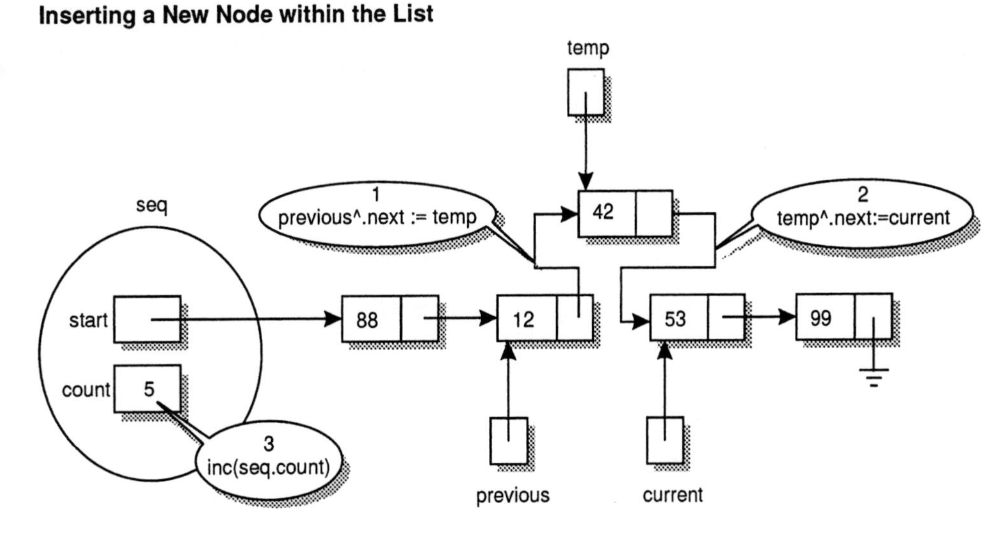

Wherever the new node is added, *count* has to be incremented:

```
Inc(seq.count);
```

The final task is to return a value indicating the success of the operation:

```
AddAt := true;
```

The complete code for the *InsertAt* function is:

```
function AddAt(item:Data;post:integer ;var seq:List) : boolean;
var
    current, previous, temp : NodePointerType;
    c : integer;
begin
    {*** IF invalid position THEN exit with false ***}
    if(post < 1) or (post > Len(seq) + 1) then
        AddAt := false;
    {*** Create space for new node ***}
    New(temp);
    {*** Place data in node ***}
    temp^.value := item;
    temp^.next  := NIL;
    {*** IF placed at start, update main pointer***}
    if post = 1 then
    begin
        current := seq.start;
        seq.start := temp;
        temp^.next := current;
    end
    else
    {*** ELSE find insert position ***}
    begin
        previous := NIL;
        current := seq.start;
        for c := 2 to post do
        begin
            previous := current;
            current := current^.next;
        end;
        {** Link new node into chain **}
        previous^.next := temp;
        temp^.next := current;
    end;
    {*** Add 1 to count ***}
    Inc(seq.count);
    AddAt:= true;
end;
```

### DeleteFrom

This routine shares some code with the previous routine: again, we need to check that the specified position is valid with the code

```
if(post < 1)or(post > Len(seq)) then
begin
    DeleteFrom := false;
    exit;
end;
```

and, if everything is okay, we need to distinguish between

a) deleting the first node

and

b) deleting any other node.

Removing the first node involves changing the value of *start* and deleting the node. This requires the code:

```
current   := seq.start;
seq.start := current^.next;
Dispose(current);
```

Deleting any other node involves referencing that node and its predecessor using the pointers *current* and *previous*. The node is then removed from the list by making *previous^.next* bypass it and then deleting the required node. The code for this is:

```
//*** Find required node ***
previous := NIL;
current  := seq.start;
for c := 2 to post do
begin
    previous := current;
    current  := current^.next;
end;
//*** Adjust node pointer to bypass deleted node ***
previous^.next := current^.next;
//*** Delete node ***
dispose(current);
```

Finally, the count must be decremented.

The two situations are illustrated in FIG-9.9.

**FIG-9.9**

Deleting a Node

**OPTION 1 : Deleting the first node**

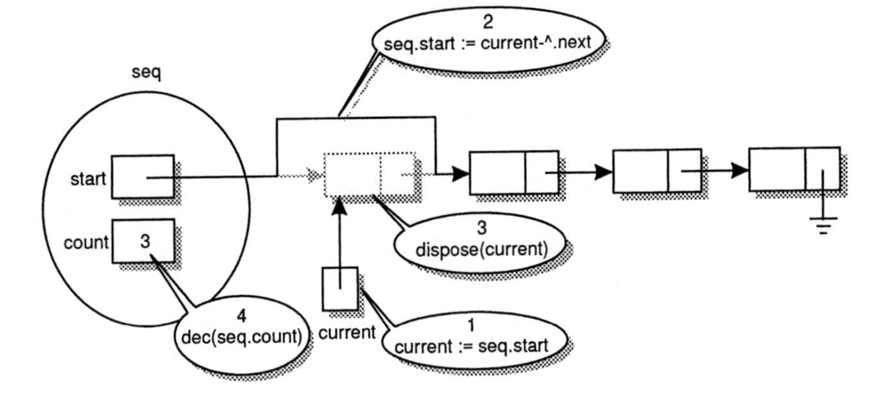


**OPTION 2 - Deleting other nodes**

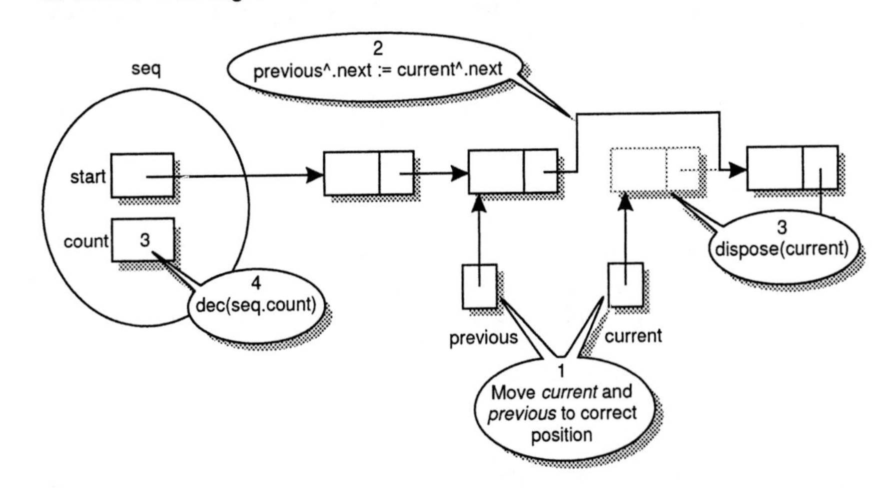

The complete code is:

```
function DeleteFrom(post:integer; var seq:List) : boolean;
var
    current, previous : NodePointerType;
    c : integer;
begin
    {*** IF invalid position THEN exit with false ***}
    if(post < 1) or (post > Len(seq))then
        DeleteFrom := false;
    {*** IF first node update main pointer***}
    if post = 1 then
    begin
        current    := seq.start;
        seq.start := current^.next;
        Dispose(current);
    end
    else
    {*** ELSE find delete position ***}
    begin
        previous := NIL;
        current  := seq.start;
        for c := 2 to post do
        begin
            previous := current;
            current  := current^.next;
        end;
        {** Remove node from chain **}
        previous^.next := current^.next;
        Dispose(current);
    end;
    {*** Subtract 1 from count ***}
    Dec(seq.count);
    DeleteFrom := true;
end;
```

### Head

This routine returns the data held in the first node of the list. It can only be performed if there is at least one node in the list, hence, we must begin by checking that the list is not empty. Where the list is empty, the program itself, rather than just this routine, is terminated. The code for the function is:

```
procedure Head(seq:List;var front:Data);
begin
    {*** IF the list is empty then terminate the program ***}
    if IsEmpty(seq)  then
    begin
        write('Invalid operation - Head');
        halt;
    end;
    {*** Return the first value in the list ***}
    front := seq.start^.value;
end;
```

The instruction `halt` is responsible for ending the program.

### Tail

The purpose of the operation is to remove the first node from the list. Like *Head*, this routine cannot operate if the list is empty and needs a similar check at the start of the routine. All being well, we can remove the first node using the previously defined *DeleteFrom* function:

```
procedure Tail(var seq:List);
begin
    {*** If list empty, terminate program ***}
    if IsEmpty(seq) then
    begin
        writeln('Invalid operation - Tail');
        halt;
    end;
    {*** Else delete the first node ***}
    DeleteFrom(1,seq);
end;
```

**DisplayList**

This routine displays all the data held in the list using the code:

```
procedure DisplayList(seq:List);
var
    current : NodePointerType;
    c       : integer;
begin
    {*** Point to first node in list ***}
    current := seq.start;
    {*** For each node ***}
    for c := 1 to Len(seq) do
    begin
        {*** Display its contents ***}
        writeln(current^.value.Ftext);
        {*** Move on to the next node ***}
        current := current^.next;
    end
end;
```

**DeleteList**

You might be tempted to think that this routine is identical to *CreateList* and only requires the *start* pointer to be set to NIL and *count* to zero. However, if we were to do this, the nodes of the list would still be allocated, and hence continue to reduce the amount of memory available. To avoid this we need to go through the list deleting each node in turn. One method of doing this is:

```
procedure EmptyList(var seq:List);
begin
    while not IsEmpty(seq) do
        DeleteFrom(1,seq);
end;
```

**Activity 9.5**

Which of the routines defined above would need to be changed if the *Data* component of a node was declared as:

```
Data =
record
    idcode : integer;
    name   : string[30];
    sex    : char;
    score  : array[1..6] of integer;
end;
```

A complete program using each of the operations on a list is given in LISTING-9.1.

**Program Logic:**

```
Create a list
REPEAT
    Display menu
    Get option
    Execute option
UNTIL option is QUIT
Empty the list
```

**Program Code:**

**LISTING-9.1**

Implementing a List type as a Linked List

```
program ListDataStructure;
uses WinCrt;

{**************************}
{*** Type declarations ***}
{**************************}
type
  Data =
  record
      Ftext : string[21];
  end;

  NodePointerType = ^Node;

  Node =
  record
      value : Data;
      next  : NodePointerType;
  end;

  List =
  record
      start : NodePointerType;
      count : integer;
  end;

{****************************}
{*** Routine definitions ***}
{****************************}

{*** Get length of list ***}
function Len(seq:List):integer;
begin
  Len := seq.count;
end;

{*** Check for empty list ***}
function IsEmpty(seq:List):boolean;
begin
  IsEmpty :=( seq.count=0);
end;

{*** Create a new list ***}
procedure CreateList(var seq:List);
begin
  seq.start := NIL;
  seq.count := 0;
end;

{*** Add new data at a specified position in the list ***}
function  AddAt(item:Data;post:integer ;var seq:List):boolean;
var
  current, previous, temp:NodePointerType;
  c : integer;
begin
```

**Continued on next page**

**LISTING-9.1**
(continued)

Implementing a List type as a Linked List

```
  {*** IF invalid position THEN exit with zero ***}
  if(post < 1) or (post > Len(seq) + 1)then
      AddAt := false;
  {*** Create space for new node ***}
  new(temp);
  {*** Place data in node ***}
  temp^.value := item;
  temp^.next := NIL;
  {*** IF placed at start update main pointer***}
  if post = 1 then
  begin
      current := seq.start;
      seq.start := temp;
      temp^.next := current;
  end
  else
  {*** ELSE find insert position ***}
  begin
      previous := NIL;
      current := seq.start;
      for c := 2 to post do
      begin
          previous := current;
          current := current^.next;
      end;
      {** Link new node into chain **}
      previous^.next := temp;
      temp^.next := current;
  end;
  {*** Add 1 to count ***}
  inc(seq.count);
  AddAt := true;
end;


{*** Delete node from specified position ***}
function DeleteFrom(post:integer; var seq:List):boolean;
var
  current, previous : NodePointerType;
  c : integer;
begin
  {*** If invalid position, exit routine ***}
  if(post < 1) or (post > Len(seq)) then
      DeleteFrom := false;
  {*** IF first node update main pointer***}
  if post = 1 then
  begin
      current := seq.start;
      seq.start := current^.next;
      dispose(current);
  end
  else
  {*** ELSE find delete position ***}
  begin
      previous := NIL;
      current := seq.start;
      for c := 2 to post do
      begin
          previous := current;
          current := current^.next;
      end;
      {** Remove node from chain **}
      previous^.next := current^.next;
      dispose (current);
  end;
  {*** Subtract 1 from count ***}
  dec(seq.count);
  DeleteFrom := true;
end;
```

**Continued on next page**

**LISTING-9.1**
(continued)

Implementing a List type as a Linked List

```
{*** Return first item in list ***}
procedure Head(seq:List;var front:Data);
begin
   {*** If list is empty, terminate program ***}
   if IsEmpty(seq)  then
   begin
       write('Invalid operation - Head');
       halt(1);
   end;
   {*** Return first value in list ***}
   front := seq.start^.value;
end;

{*** Remove first item from list ***}
procedure Tail(var seq:List);
begin
   {*** If the list is empty, terminate the program ***}
   if IsEmpty(seq) then
   begin
       writeln('Invalid operation - Tail');
       halt(1);
   end;
   {*** Delete first item from list ***}
   DeleteFrom(1,seq);
end;

{*** Display contents of list ***}
procedure DisplayList(seq:List);
var
   current : NodePointerType;
   c       : integer;
begin
   {*** Reference first element of list ***}
   current := seq.start;
   {*** For each value in the list do ***}
   for c := 1 to Len(seq) do
   begin
       {*** Display value ***}
       writeln(current^.value.Ftext);
       {*** Move to next node ***}
       current := current^.next;
   end
end;

{*** Remove all entries in the list ***}
procedure EmptyList(var seq:List);
begin
   while not IsEmpty(seq) do
       DeleteFrom(1,seq);
end;

{*** Return the position of a specified value ***}
function IsAt(d:Data; seq:List):integer;
var
   nptr : NodePointerType;
   post : integer;
begin
   {*** If the list is empty, return zero ***}
   if Len(seq) = 0 then
       IsAt := 0;
   {*** Search list until match found or end of list reached ***}
   post := 1;
   nptr := seq.start;
   while (nptr <> NIL) and (nptr^.value.Ftext <> d.Ftext) do
   begin
       nptr := nptr^.next;
       inc(post);
   end;
```

**Continued on next page**

**LISTING-9.1**
(continued)

Implementing a List type as a Linked List

```
  {*** If match found then, return list position ***}
  if nptr <> NIL then
      IsAt := post
  else
      {*** Else return zero ***}
      IsAt := 0;
end;


{****************************************}
{*      Additional Routines            *}
{****************************************}


{*** Display the menu; return number of options in menu ***}
function DisplayMenu(Ftext:string):integer;
var
  total : integer;
  c     : integer;
begin
  {*** Display options ***}
  clrscr;
  writeln('MENU'#13);
  writeln(Ftext);
  {*** Count the number of options ***}
  total := 0;
  for c := 1 to length(Ftext) do
      if Ftext[c] = #13 then
          inc(total);
  {*** Return option count ***}
  DisplayMenu := total;
end;


{*** Get the user's menu choice ***}
function GetOption(max:integer):integer;
var
  sopt : string[3];
  opt  : integer;
  err  : integer;
begin
  {*** Get option as string ***}
  write('Enter option : ');
  readln(sopt);
  {*** Convert it to an integer **}
  val(sopt,opt,err);
  {*** While option is invalid do ***}
  while(opt < 1) or (opt > max) or (err <> 0)do
  begin
      {*** Display error and re-enter ***}
      writeln('Invalid option');
      readln(opt);
  end;
  {*** Return option ***}
  GetOption := opt;
end;

{*** Execute the chosen option ***}
procedure ExecuteOption(opt:integer; var seq:List);
var
  val  : Data;
  post : integer;
begin
  case (opt) of
          {*** Create an empty list ***}
      1:  EmptyList(seq);
```

**Continued on next page**

**LISTING-9.1**
(continued)

Implementing a List type as a Linked List

```
            {*** Add a new value ***}
        2:  begin
                write('Enter value to be added : ');
                readln(val.Ftext);
                write('Add where (1 to ',(Len(seq)+1),') : ');
                readln(post);
                AddAt(val,post,seq);
            end;
            {*** Delete an entry ***}
        3:  if not IsEmpty(seq) then
            begin
                write('Delete from where (1 to ',Len(seq),') : ');
                readln(post);
                DeleteFrom(post,seq);
            end
            else
            begin
                writeln('The list is empty');
                readkey;
            end;
            {*** Display first value in list ***}
        4:  if not IsEmpty(seq) then
            begin
                Head(seq,val);
                writeln('First in list is : ',val.Ftext);;
                readkey;
            end
            else
            begin
                writeln('List is empty');
                readkey;
            end;
            {*** Remove first value from list ***}
        5:  if not IsEmpty(seq) then
                Tail(seq)
            else
            begin
                writeln('List is empty');
                readkey;
            end;
            {*** Display length of list ***}
        6:  begin
                writeln('The list contains ',Len(seq),' values');
                readkey;
            end;
            {*** Determine if list is empty ***}
        7:  begin
                if IsEmpty(seq) then
                    writeln('List is empty')
                else
                    writeln('List is not empty');
                readkey;
            end;
            {*** Remove all entries from list ***}
        8:  EmptyList(seq);
            {*** Display contents of list ***}
        9:  begin
                clrscr;
                writeln('CONTENTS OF LIST');
                DisplayList(seq);
                readkey;
            end;
    end
end;
```

**LISTING-9.1**
(continued)

Implementing a List type as a Linked List

```
var
   seq : List;
   option, noofoptions : integer;
begin
   repeat
        noofoptions:=DisplayMenu('1. - Create List'#13#10
             +'2. - AddAt'#13#10'3. - DeleteFrom'+#13#10
             +'4. - Head'#13#10'5. - Tail'#13#10'6. - Length'#13#10
             +'7. - IsEmpty'+#13#10'8. - Empty'#13#10
             +'9. - Display'#13#10'10 - QUIT'#13);
        option := GetOption(noofoptions);
        ExecuteOption(option, seq);
   until option = noofoptions;
   EmptyList(seq);
   writeln('PROGRAM TERMINATED');
   readkey;
end.
```

**Activity 9.6**

1. Enter the above program and test it.

2. Add two new routines to the *List* structure:
   a) **IsAt** - returns the first position in the list of a specified value. If the value is not present, zero is returned.
   b) **Give** - returns the value at a specified position in the list. The routine should return an undefined value if the position specified is invalid.

# Creating Other Structures - The Stack

The **stack** is a simplified type of list in which value can only be added and removed from the front of the list. We can compare a stack to a pile of books: additional books are placed on top of the pile, with books also being removed from the top (see FIG-9.10).

**FIG-9.10**

Adding and Removing from a Stack

Books are removed from the top
Books are added to the top

Several operations are defined for stacks:

| | |
|---|---|
| **CreateStack** | Creates an empty stack. |
| **Push** | Adds a value to the 'top' of the stack. |
| **Top** | Returns the value at the top of the stack. The stack itself remains unchanged.<br>This routine should not be called if the stack is empty. |
| **Pop** | Removes the top element from the stack. No value is returned by the stack.<br>This routine should not be called if the stack is empty. |
| **EmptyStack** | Removes all elements from an existing stack. |
| **DisplayStack** | Displays the contents of the stack. |

Rather than write the complete code for this data structure we can assemble our new data structure from our existing *List* structure. This will allow us to produce reliable software in the shortest possible time.

We begin by declaring a *List* field within the *Stack* structure:

```
Stack=
record
    seq : List;
end;
```

Now we can construct our new operations from existing ones. For example, *CreateStack* can be coded as:

```
procedure CreateStack(var s:Stack)
begin
    CreateList(s.seq);
end;
```

And the *Push* operation can be coded just as simply:

```
procedure Push(Data v; var s:Stack)
begin
    AddAt(v,1,s.seq);
end;
```

**Activity 9.7**

Write the code necessary to implement *Top* and *Pop* operations.
HINT: These should use the *Head* and *Tail* functions of the *List* structure.

# Creating Other Structures - The Queue

A queue is another type of restricted list. In a queue items are added at one end and deleted from the other. Queues occur all too frequently in real life: at gas stations, in the supermarket and at bus stops. The queue is often referred to as a **first in - first out** structure, since the first value placed in the queue is also the first to be removed (see FIG-9.11).

**FIG-9.11**

Adding and Removing from a Queue

Cars are removed from the front
Cars are added at the rear of the queue

The following operations are defined for a Queue:

| | |
|---|---|
| **CreateQueue** | Creates an empty queue. |
| **InsertQ** | Adds a value to the end of the queue. |
| **Front** | Returns the first value in the queue. The queue is unaffected by this operation. |
| **DeleteQ** | Removes the value at the front of the queue. The queue must not be empty. |
| **IsEmptyQ** | Returns 1 if the queue is empty, otherwise returns zero. |
| **LengthQ** | Returns the number of items in the queue. |
| **EmptyQueue** | Removes all entries from a queue. |
| **GiveQ** | Returns the value held in a specified element. |

**Activity 9.8**

Write a complete menu driven program to implement a *Queue* data structure as described above.

Make use of the previously coded *List* structure when producing the program.

# Summary

- **A linked list** is constructed from a sequence of nodes.
- **A node** consists of a data component and a pointer to the next node.
- **Linked lists can grow** and shrink as required.
- **A stack** is a list in which values are added and removed at the same end.
- **A queue** is a list in which values are added at one end and removed from the other.

# DOUBLY LINKED LISTS

## What's Wrong with Linked Lists

A linked list in which each node has a single pointer to the next (or sometimes previous) node is called a **singly-linked list**. There are some things that singly-linked lists aren't very efficient at handling. For example, if we needed to display the contents of the list in reverse order we would have to use an algorithm such as:

```
FOR post := number of nodes in list DOWN TO 1 DO
    Start at the beginning of the list
    Move through the list until node at post reached
    Display value in node
ENDFOR
```

Having to move through the list for every value to be displayed is very time-consuming but cannot be avoided with the current list design.

## Two-Way Nodes

By redesigning a node so that it has pointers in both directions, one to the previous node and one to the next, we get a greater flexibility in our design (see FIG-9.12).

**FIG-9.12**

Double Pointer Node

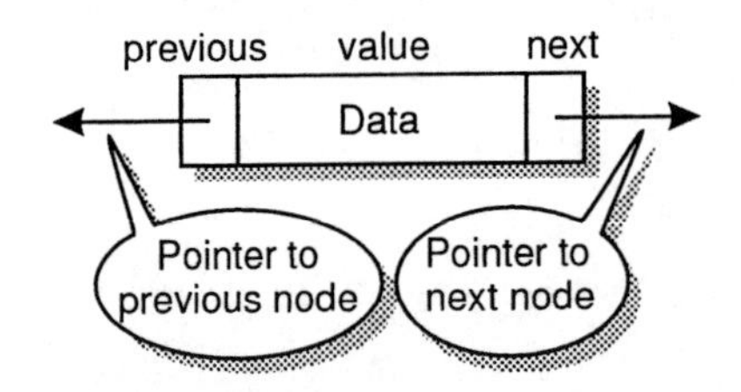


In the case of the first and last nodes, one of the pointer fields will be set to NIL.

**Activity 9.9**

Rewrite the definition of the structure *Node* given previously using this new set up.

**Activity 9.10**

Draw a diagram (in the style of that given in FIG-9.3) showing a list containing three nodes of this new design.

Another aid to the efficiency of our new *List* structure is to maintain a pointer to the final node in the list. This will allow us to go directly to the last node in the list without having to start at the beginning and move through each node in turn until the end is reached. The new declaration for *List* would now be:

```
List =
record
    start  : NodePointerType;
    finish : NodePointerType;
    count  : integer;
end;
```

With the definition of *List* changed, most of the associated functions will also require modification. For example *CreateList* will now be coded as:

```
procedure CreateList(var seq : List);
begin
    with seq do
    begin
        start  := NIL;
        finish := NIL;
        count  := 0;
    end;
end;
```

Some other routines will need even greater changes. For example, when adding a new node we may have to:

a) Change *start* and *finish* (if adding the first node)
b) Change the *start* pointer (if added at the beginning of the list)
c) Change the *finish* pointer (if added at the end of the list)
d) Change *neither* pointer (if inserting somewhere between the first and last node)

**Activity 9.11**

What possible modifications to *start* and *finish* exist when deleting a node?

The new code for *AddAt* now becomes:

```
function AddAt(item : Data; post : integer; var seq :List):
boolean;
var
    current, temp : NodePointerType;
    c : integer;
begin
    {*** If position is invalid exit routine ***}
    if (post < 1) or (post > Len(seq)+1) then
        AddAt := false;
    {*** Create space for new node ***}
    New(temp);
    {*** Place data in node ***}
    temp^.value := item;
    temp^.next := NIL;
    temp^.prev := NIL;
    {*** If first node to be placed in list***}
    if(Len(seq) = 0) then
    begin
        seq.start := temp;
        seq.finish := temp;
    end
    {*** Else if placed at start of list *** }
    else if(post = 1) then
    begin
        current := seq.start;
        seq.start := temp;
        temp^.next := current;
        current^.prev := temp;
    end
    {*** Else if placed at end of list ***}
    else if(post = Len(seq)+1) then
    begin
        current := seq.finish;
        seq.finish := temp;
        temp^.prev := current;
        current^.next := temp;
    end
    else
    begin
        {*** Else find insert position ***}
```

```
        current := seq.start;
        for c := 2 to post do
            current := current^.next;
        {** Link new node into chain **}
        current^.prev^.next := temp;
        temp^.next := current;
        current^.prev := temp;
      end;
      {*** Add 1 to count ***}
      Inc(seq.count);
      AddAt := true;
end;
```

The four options are shown graphically in FIG-9.13 through FIG-9.16.

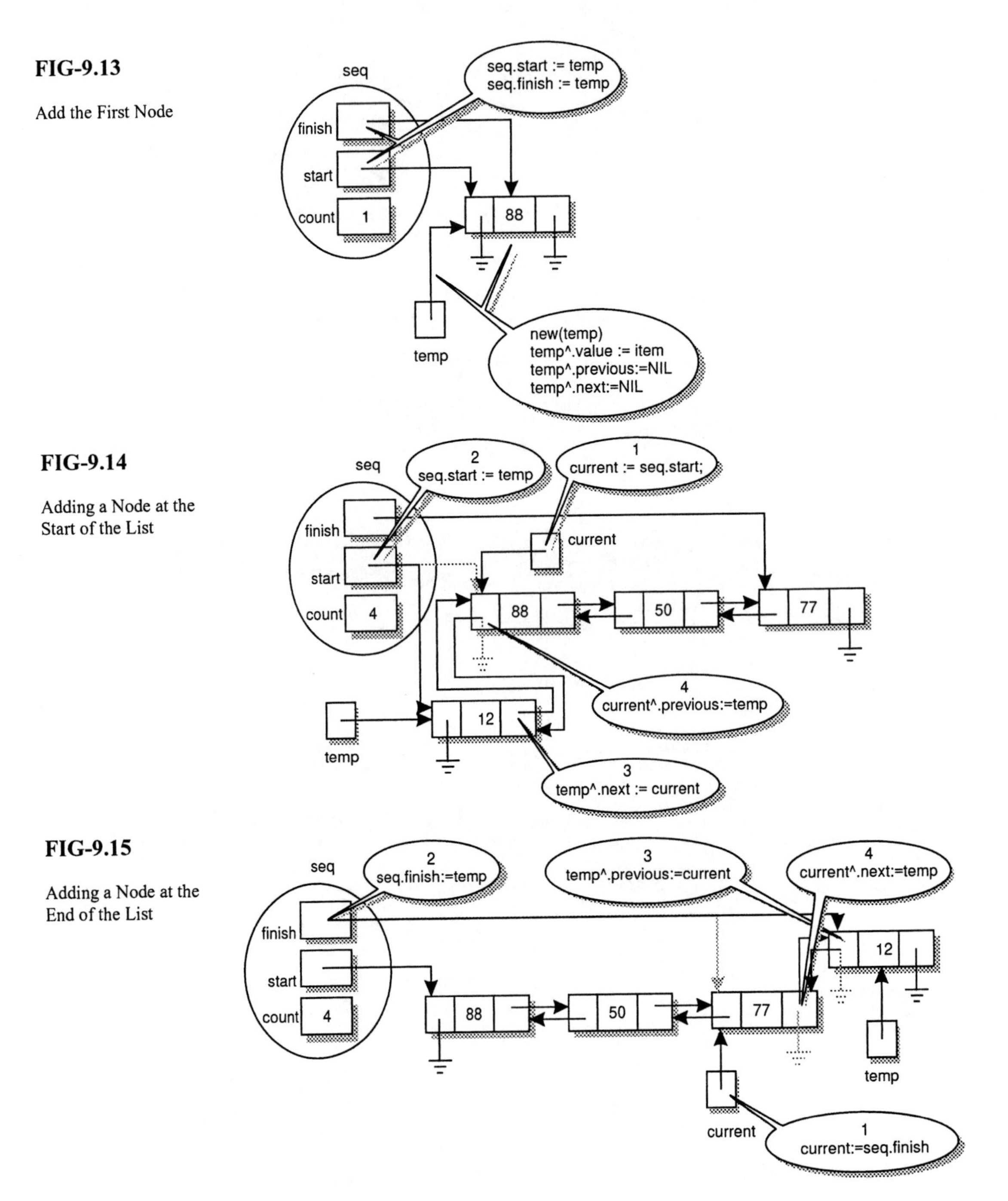


**FIG-9.13**

Add the First Node

**FIG-9.14**

Adding a Node at the Start of the List

**FIG-9.15**

Adding a Node at the End of the List

**FIG-9.16**

Adding a Node Within the List

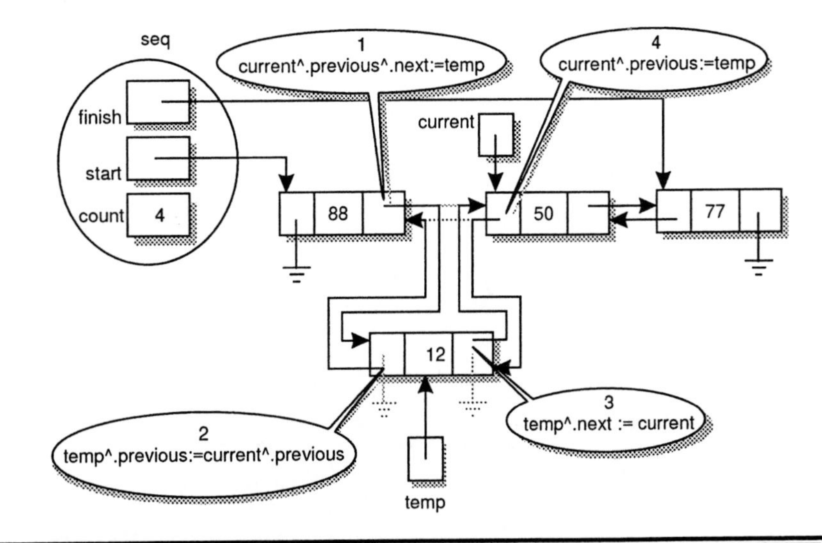


> **Activity 9.12**
>
> Write the code required for a *DeleteFrom* operation.

> **Activity 9.13**
>
> Complete the changes required to implement the List structure as a doubly linked list.

# Summary

- The doubly linked list is constructed from nodes containing two pointers.
- Each node contains a pointer to the previous node and a pointer to the next node.
- Doubly linked lists allow more efficient reverse traversal of the list.
- Using a start and end pointer in a list allows quick access to the final node. This allows an efficient algorithm to be employed when adding to the end of the list.

# CASE STUDY

## The Problem

A program is required to convert an infix expression such as

```
(6 + 3) / 12 - 1
```

to the postfix equivalent

```
6 3 + 12 / 1 - .
```

## An Explanation

We are used to writing arithmetic expressions in which the operators (+, - , * , /, etc.) are placed between the operands (6, 3, 12, etc.); this is called infix notation. However, calculators and computers use notation in which the operator is placed after the two operands on which it is to perform; this is known as **postfix** or **Reverse Polish** notation. Hence, whereas we would write 12 + 3 in standard infix notation, we write 12 3 + in postfix notation. Although postfix expressions may look awkward, they are in fact very efficient. For example, postfix expressions never require the use of parentheses and are evaluated on a simple left-to-right basis.

The downside of postfix notation is that we humans don't like writing in it! But this is a problem easily solved since a relatively simple algorithm can be employed to convert from infix to postfix notation.

## The Algorithm

```
1.  Create an empty stack
2.  Create an empty queue
3.  Read in the infix expression to be converted
4.  Extract the left-most token from the expression
5.  WHILE not at end of expression DO
6.      IF
7.          token is an operand:
8.              Add it to queue
9.          token is '(':
10.             Push it onto stack
11.         token is ')':
12.             Remove value from the stack
13.             WHILE value removed is not '(' DO
14.                 Add value removed to queue
15.                 Remove value from stack stack
16.             ENDWHILE
17.         token is an operator:
18.             REPEAT
19.                 IF stack empty OR token > top of stack THEN
20.                     Push token onto stack
21.                 ELSE
22.                     Remove value from stack
23.                     Add value removed to queue
24.             UNTIL token added to stack
25.     ENDIF
26. ENDWHILE
27. WHILE stack not empty DO
28.     Remove value from stack
29.     Add value removed to queue
30. ENDWHILE
31. Display original expression
32. Display queue
```

**Activity 9.14**

Using the algorithm given, convert the following expressions to postfix notation:

a) 8 + 3 * (6 - 1)
b) ( ( 1 + 2) * 3 / 4) * ( 5 - 6)
c) 1 / ((2 + 3) * (4 - 5))

# The Program

The program (see LISTING-9.2) makes use of three Pascal Units: ListU, StackU and QueueU which contain definitions for List, Stack and Queue data structures respectively. These structures have been implemented as singly linked lists. The data element of the nodes are defined as

```
type
    Data =
        record
            token : string[10];
        end;
```

and other routines have been modified, where necessary, to handle strings.

The data input should consist of numeric operands, and elements of the expression must be separated by a single space character. The program also assumes that the expressions entered are syntactically correct.

**LISTING-9.2**

Infix to Postix

Modified sections of the code are shown in bold.

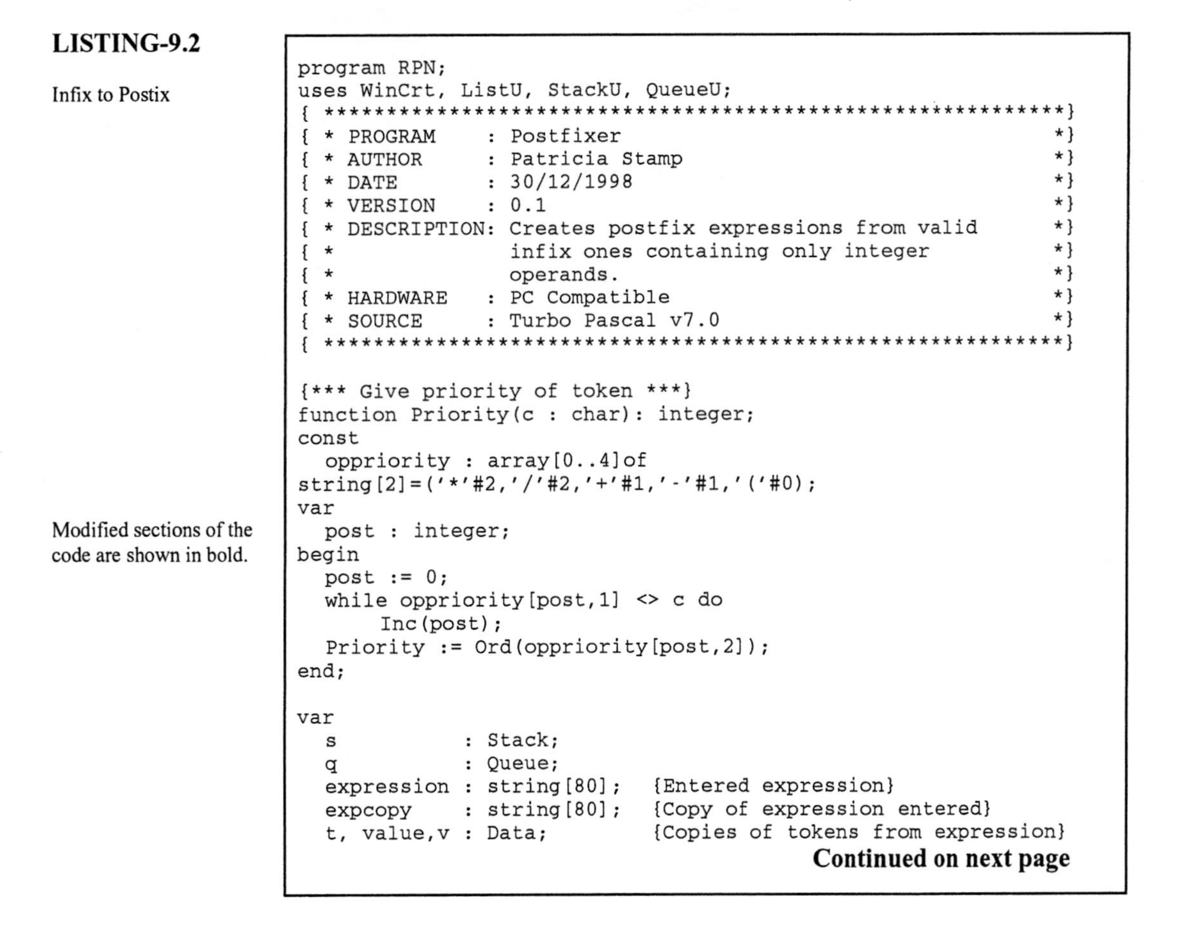

```
program RPN;
uses WinCrt, ListU, StackU, QueueU;
{ ***************************************************************}
{ * PROGRAM     : Postfixer                                       *}
{ * AUTHOR      : Patricia Stamp                                  *}
{ * DATE        : 30/12/1998                                      *}
{ * VERSION     : 0.1                                             *}
{ * DESCRIPTION: Creates postfix expressions from valid           *}
{ *              infix ones containing only integer               *}
{ *              operands.                                        *}
{ * HARDWARE    : PC Compatible                                   *}
{ * SOURCE      : Turbo Pascal v7.0                               *}
{ ***************************************************************}

{*** Give priority of token ***}
function Priority(c : char): integer;
const
  oppriority : array[0..4]of
string[2]=('*'#2,'/'#2,'+'#1,'-'#1,'('#0);
var
  post : integer;
begin
  post := 0;
  while oppriority[post,1] <> c do
      Inc(post);
  Priority := Ord(oppriority[post,2]);
end;

var
  s          : Stack;
  q          : Queue;
  expression : string[80];   {Entered expression}
  expcopy    : string[80];   {Copy of expression entered}
  t, value,v : Data;         {Copies of tokens from expression}
```

**Continued on next page**

**LISTING-9.2**
(continued)

Infix to Postix

```
   post        : integer;       {post of space after token}
   added       : boolean;
   c           : integer;
begin
   {*** Initialise data structures ***}
   CreateStack(s);
   CreateQueue(q);
   {*** Get expression ***}
   ClrScr;
   write('Enter expression : ');
   readln(expression);
   {*** Copy expression and add space ***}
   expcopy := expression+' ';
   {*** Reference first token in expression ***}
   post := Pos(' ',expcopy);
   t.token := Copy(expcopy,1,post-1);
   Delete(expcopy,1,post);
   {*** WHILE not at end of expression DO ***}
   while post <> 0 do
   begin
        {** IF numeric, add to Queue **}
        if t.token[1] in ['0'..'9'] then
             InsertQ(t,q)
        {** IF '(' , add to Stack ** }
        else if t.token[1] = '(' then
             Push(t,s)
        {** IF ')' **}
        else if t.token[1] = ')' then
        begin
             {* Get top value in stack *}
             Top(s, value);
             Pop(s);
             {* WHILE removed value not '(' DO * }
             while value.token <> '(' do
             begin
                  { Add value to queue }
                  InsertQ(value,q);
                  {Get next value from stack}
                  Top(s,value);
                  Pop(s);
             end;
        end
        {*** IF its an operator *** }
        else
        begin
             added := false;
             repeat
                  {*IF stack empty OR current token has a higher *}
                  {* priority than TOP(stack), add token to stack*}
                  if not IsEmptyS(s) then
                       Top(s,v);
                  if (IsEmptyS(s)) or (Priority(t.token[1]) >
Priority(v.token[1]))then
                  begin
                       Push(t,s);
                       added := true;
                  end
                  {* ELSE remove top of stack and place in queue *}
                  else
                  begin
                       Top(s, value);
                       Pop(s);
                       InsertQ(value,q);
                  end;
             until added;
        end;
        {*** Reference next token in expression ***}
        post := Pos(' ',expcopy);
        t.token := Copy(expcopy,1,post-1);
```

**Continued on next page**

**LISTING-9.2**
(continued)

Infix to Postix

```
        Delete(expcopy,1,post);
    end;
    {*** Empty stack onto queue ***}
    while not IsEmptyS(s) do
    begin
        Top(s,v);
        InsertQ(v,q);
        Pop(s);
    end;
    {*** Display original expression ***}
    writeln('Infix expression    : ',expression);
    {*** Display postfix expression ***}
    write('Postfix expression : ');
    for c := 1 to LengthQ(q) do
    begin
        GiveQ(c,q,v);
        write(v.token,' ');
    end;
    writeln;
    readkey;
end.
```

# SOLUTIONS

## Activity 9.1

```
a)  start^.value
b)  start^.next
```

## Activity 9.2

```
type
    Data =
    record
        idcode : integer;
        name   : string[30];
        sex    : char;
        score  : array[1..6] of integer;
    end;
```

## Activity 9.3

*next* references another node (i.e. a structure containing both data and another pointer) rather than just data.

## Activity 9.4

No changes are required. The *value* field in *Node* is of type *Data* - by redefining *Data*, the *Node* structure changes automatically.

## Activity 9.5

Only the *Display* routine needs to be modified to output the fields within *Data*.

## Activity 9.6

1.

No solution required.

2.

Code for *IsAt* :

```
function IsAt(d:Data; seq:List):integer;
var
    nptr :NodePointer;
    post :integer;
begin
    if Len(seq) = 0 then
        IsAt:= 0;
    post := 1;
    nptr := seq.start;
    while (nptr <> NIL) and
            (nptr^.value.token<>d.token)
    do
    begin
        nptr := nptr^.next;
        inc(post);
    end;
    if nptr <> NIL then
        IsAt:= post
    else
        IsAt:= 0;
end;
```

The code for *Give* is:

```
procedure Give(post:integer;seq:List;
                            var result:Data);
var
    nptr : NodePointer;
    c    : integer;
begin
    if(post < 1)or( post > Len(seq)) then
    begin
        writeln('Invalid position - Give');
        halt;
    end;
    nptr := seq.start;
    for c := 1 to post - 1 do
        nptr := nptr^.next;
    result := nptr^.value;
end;
```

## Activity 9.7

Code for *Top*:

```
procedure Top(s:Stack;var v:Data);
begin
    Head(s.seq,v);
end;
```

Code for *Pop:*

```
procedure Pop(var s:Stack);
begin
    Tail(s.seq);
end;
```

## Activity 9.8

1. No solution required.

2. The program uses a unit named *ListU* containing the List data structure.

   Program code:

```
program Queues;
uses WinCrt, Auxiliary, ListU;

type
Queue =
    record
        seq:List;
    end;

{**** Queue operations ***}

procedure CreateQueue(var q:Queue);
begin
    CreateList(q.seq);
end;

function LengthQ(q:Queue):integer;
begin
    LengthQ:= Len(q.seq);
end;

procedure InsertQ(v:Data;var q: Queue);
begin
    AddAt(v,LengthQ(q)+1,q.seq);
end;

procedure Front(q:Queue;var d:Data);
begin
    Head(q.seq,d);
end;

procedure DeleteQ(var q:Queue);
begin
    DeleteFrom(1,q.seq);
end;

function IsEmptyQ(q:Queue):boolean;
begin
    IsEmptyQ:= IsEmpty(q.seq);
end;


procedure EmptyQueue(var q:Queue);
begin
    EmptyList(q.seq);
end;
```

**Continued on next page**

## Activity 9.8 (continued)

```
procedure DisplayQ(q:Queue);
begin
    Display(q.seq);
end;

procedure GiveQ(post:integer; q:Queue;var d:Data);
begin
    Give(post,q.seq,d);
end;

function IsIn(v:Data; q:Queue):boolean;
begin
    if(IsAt(v,q.seq)<>0) then
        IsIn:= true
    else
        IsIn:= false;
end;

{*** Other routines ***}

procedure ExecuteOption(opt:integer; var
q:Queue);
var
    val:Data;
    post:integer;
begin
    case (opt) of
        1:      EmptyQueue(q);
        2:      begin
                    write('Value to be added : ');
                    readln(val.text);
                    Insert(val,q);
                end;
        3:      if not IsEmptyQ(q) then
                begin
                    Delete(q);
                end
                else
                begin
                    writeln('The queue is empty');
                    readkey;
                end;
        4:      if not IsEmptyQ(q) then
                begin
                Front(q,val);
                    writeln('First in queue: ',
                        val.text);
                    readkey;
                end
                else
                begin
                    writeln('The queue is empty');
                    readkey;
                end;
        5:      begin
                    writeln('Queue contains ',
                        LengthQ(q),' values');
                    readkey;
                end;
        6:      begin
                    if IsEmptyQ(q) then
                        writeln('Queue is empty')
                    else
                        writeln('Queue is not empty');
                    readkey;
                end;
        7:      EmptyQueue(q);
        8:      begin
                    clrscr;
                    writeln('CONTENTS OF LIST');
                    DisplayQ(q);
                    readkey;
                end;
    end
end;

const
    NL = #13#10;
var
    q:Queue;
    option, noofoptions:integer;
begin
    repeat
        noofoptions:=DisplayMenu
            ('1. - Create Queue+NL+
            '2. - Add'+NL+'3. - Delete'+NL+
            '4. - Front'+NL+'5. - Length'+NL+
            '6. - IsEmpty'+NL+'7. - Empty'+NL+
            '8. - Display'+NL+'9. - QUIT'+NL);
        option := GetOption(noofoptions);
            ExecuteOption(option, q);
    until option = noofoptions;
    EmptyQueue(q);
    writeln('PROGRAM TERMINATED');
        readkey;
end.
```

## Activity 9.9

```
type
    Node =
record
    prev  : NodePointerType;
    value : Data;
    next  : NodePointerType;
end;
```

## Activity 9.10

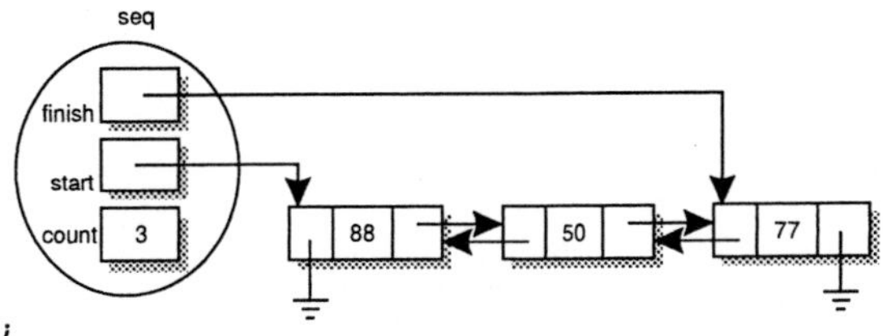

## Activity 9.11

a) Change *start* and *finish* (if deleting the only node in the list)
b) Change *start* (if deleting first node)
c) Change *finish* (if deleting last node)
d) No change (if deleting other than the first or last node)

## Activity 9.12

```
function DeleteFrom(post:integer;
                var seq:List):boolean;
var
    current, previous:NodePointerType;
    c:integer;
begin
    {*** If invalid position or empty, exit ***}
    if(post < 1) or (post > Len(seq))then
    begin
        DeleteFrom:= false;
        exit;
    end;
    {*** IF only node, update both pointers ***}
    if (post = 1) and (Len(seq) = 1) then
    begin
        current := seq.start;
        seq.start := NIL;
        seq.finish := NIL;
    end
    {*** IF first node update start ***}
    else if post = 1 then
    begin
        current := seq.start;
        seq.start := current^.next;
    end
    {*** If last node, update finish ***}
    else if post = Len(seq) then
    begin
        current := seq.finish;
        seq.finish := current^.prev;
    end
    else
    {*** ELSE find delete position ***}
    begin
        previous := NIL;
        current := seq.start;
        for c:=2 to post do
        begin
            previous := current;
            current := current^.next;
        end;
        {** Remove node from chain **}
        previous^.next := current^.next;
    end;
```

Continued on next page

## Activity 9.12 (continued)

```
        {*** Delete node ***}
        Dispose (current);
        {*** Subtract 1 from count ***}
        Dec(seq.count);
        DeleteFrom := true;
end;
```

## Activity 9.13

```
program DLLists;
uses WinCrt, Auxiliary;
type
    Data =
    record
            Ftext:string[21];
    end;
    NodePointerType = ^Node;
    Node =
    record
            prev  : NodePointerType;
            value : Data;
            next  : NodePointerType;
    end;

    List =
    record
            start  : NodePointerType;
            finish : NodePointerType;
            count  : integer;
    end;

function Len(seq : List): integer;
begin
    Len := seq.count;
end;

 procedure CreateList(var seq : List);
 begin
    with seq do
    begin
        start := NIL;
        finish := NIL;
        count := 0;
    end;
 end;

function AddAt(item : Data; post : integer; var
seq :List): boolean;
var
    current, temp : NodePointerType;
    c : integer;
begin
    {*** If position is invalid exit routine ***}
    if (post < 1) or (post > Len(seq)+1)then
          AddAt := false;
    {*** Create space for new node ***}
    New(temp);
    {*** Place data in node ***}
    temp^.value := item;
    temp^.next := NIL;
    temp^.prev := NIL;
    {*** If first node to be placed in list***}
    if(Len(seq) = 0) then
    begin
        seq.start := temp;
        seq.finish := temp;
    end
    {*** Else if placed at start of list *** }
    else if(post = 1) then
    begin
        current := seq.start;
        seq.start := temp;
        temp^.next := current;
        current^.prev := temp;
     end
     {*** Else if placed at end of list ***}
     else if(post = Len(seq)+1) then
     begin
        current := seq.finish;
        seq.finish := temp;
        temp^.prev := current;
        current^.next := temp;
     end
     else
     begin
        {*** Else find insert position ***}
        current := seq.start;
        for c := 2 to post do
            current := current^.next;
        {** Link new node into chain **}
        current^.prev^.next := temp;
        temp^.next := current;
        current^.prev := temp;
     end;
     {*** Add 1 to count ***}
     Inc(seq.count);
     AddAt := true;
end;

function IsEmpty(seq:List):boolean;
begin
    IsEmpty:=(seq.count=0);
end;


function DeleteFrom(post:integer; var
seq:List):boolean;
var
    current, previous:NodePointerType;
    c:integer;
begin
    {*** If invalid position or empty, exit ***}
    if(post < 1) or (post > Len(seq))then
    begin
        DeleteFrom:= false;
        exit;
    end;
    {*** IF only node, update both pointers ***}
    if (post = 1) and (Len(seq) = 1) then
    begin
        current := seq.start;
        seq.start := NIL;
        seq.finish := NIL;
    end
    {*** IF first node update start ***}
    else if post = 1 then
    begin
        current := seq.start;
        seq.start := current^.next;
    end
    {*** If last node, update finish ***}
    else if post = Len(seq) then
    begin
        current := seq.finish;
        seq.finish := current^.prev;
    end
    else
    {*** ELSE find delete position ***}
    begin
        previous := NIL;
        current := seq.start;
        for c:=2 to post do
        begin
            previous := current;
            current := current^.next;
        end;
        {** Remove node from chain **}
        previous^.next := current^.next;
    end;
    {*** Delete node ***}
    Dispose (current);
    {*** Subtract 1 from count ***}
    Dec(seq.count);
    DeleteFrom := true;
end;


procedure Head(seq:List;var front:Data);
begin
    if IsEmpty(seq)  then
    begin
        write('Invalid operation - Head');
        halt;
    end;
    front:=seq.start^.value;
end;


procedure Tail(var seq:List);
begin
    if IsEmpty(seq) then
    begin
        writeln('Invalid operation - Tail');
        halt;
    end;
    DeleteFrom(1,seq);
end;


procedure Display(seq:List);
var
    current:NodePointerType;
   c:integer;
begin
    current:=seq.start;
    for c:=1 to Len(seq) do
    begin
        writeln(current^.value.Ftext);
```

**Continued on next page**

## Activity 9.13 (continued)

```
        current:=current^.next;
    end
end;


procedure EmptyList(var seq:List);
begin
    while not IsEmpty(seq) do
        DeleteFrom(1,seq);
end;


function IsAt(d:Data; seq:List):integer;
var
    nptr:NodePointerType;
   post :integer;
begin
    if Len(seq)=0 then
        IsAt:= 0;

    post := 1;
    nptr := seq.start;
    while (nptr <> NIL) and
            (nptr^.value.Ftext<>d.Ftext)
    do
    begin
        nptr := nptr^.next;
        inc(post);
    end;
    if nptr <> NIL then
        IsAt:= post
    else
        IsAt:= 0;
end;


procedure Give(post:integer; seq:List;
                    var result:Data);
var
   nptr:NodePointerType;
   c:integer;
begin
    if(post < 1)or( post > Len(seq)) then
    begin
        writeln('Invalid position - Give()');
        halt;
    end;
    nptr:=seq.start;
    for c:=1 to post-1 do
        nptr := nptr^.next;
    result:=nptr^.value;
end;


procedure ExecuteOption(opt:integer; var
seq:List);
var
    val:Data;
    post:integer;
begin
    case (opt) of
        1:      CreateList(seq);
        2:      begin
                    write('Value to be added : ');
                    readln(val.Ftext);
                    write('Add where(1 to ',
                            (Len(seq)+1),') : ');
                    readln(post);
                    AddAt(val,post,seq);
                end;
        3:      if not IsEmpty(seq) then
                begin
                    write('Delete from where(1 to ',
                            Len(seq),') : ');
                    readln(post);
                    DeleteFrom(post,seq);
                end
                else
                begin
                    writeln('The list is empty');
                    readkey;
                end;
        4:      if not IsEmpty(seq) then
                begin
                Head(seq,val);
                    writeln('First in list is : ',
                            val.Ftext);
                    readkey;
                end
                else
                begin
                    writeln('List is empty');
                    readkey;
                end;
        5:      if not IsEmpty(seq) then
                    Tail(seq)
                else
                begin
                    writeln('List is empty');
                    readkey;
                end;
        6:      begin
                    writeln('The list contains ',
                        Len(seq),' values');
                    readkey;
                end;
        7:      begin
                    if IsEmpty(seq) then
                        writeln('List is empty')
                    else
                        writeln('List is not empty');
                    readkey;
                end;
        8:      EmptyList(seq);
        9:      begin
                    clrscr;
                    writeln('CONTENTS OF LIST');
                    Display(seq);
                    readkey;
                end;
    end;
end;


const
    NL = #13#10;
var
    seq  :  List;
    option, noofoptions : integer;
begin
    repeat
        noofoptions:=DisplayMenu(
                    '1. - Create List'+NL+
                    '2. - AddAt'+NL+
                    '3. - DeleteFrom'+NL+
                    '4. - Head'+NL+
                    '5. - Tail'+NL+
                    '6. - Length'+NL+
                    '7. - IsEmpty'+NL+
                    '8. - Empty'+NL+
                    '9. - Display'+NL+
                    '10 - QUIT'+NL);
        option := GetOption(noofoptions);
        ExecuteOption(option, seq);
    until option = noofoptions;
    EmptyList(seq);
    writeln('PROGRAM TERMINATED');
    readkey;
end.
```

## Activity 9.14

```
a)  8 3 + 6 1 - *
b)  2 1 + 3 * 4 / 5 6 - *
c)  1 2 3 + 4 5 - * /
```

CHAPTER 10

# Advanced Data Structures

**This chapter covers the following topics:**

- Defing Binary Search Trees
- Deleting from a Tree
- Directed Graphs
- Graph Terminology
- Implementing a Binary Search Tree
- Recursion Definitions
- Recursive Coding
- Shortest Path Algorithm
- Tree Terminology
- Undirected Graphs

# RECURSION

## Introduction

Recursion is a method of describing the solution to a problem in terms of the original problem. Since this explanation may not be immediately enlightening, perhaps an example is in order at this point.

In mathematics the expression 4x3x2x1 is written as 4! (called four factorial). Hence 6! is the short-hand way of writing 6x5x4x3x2x1. Mathematics states that the factorial operation may only be applied to non-negative integer values and that 0! is 1.

Given the problem of producing a solution to the term 4! we may say that the result is:

4x3x2x1 which is 24.

Alternatively, we may write that

4! = 4 x 3!

This last solution has resulted in an answer which itself involves factorials. This is an example of a recursive solution where the result is given in terms of itself. Of course, the solution gives rise to a new question: What is 3!? The answer to which can be written recursively as:

3! = 3 x 2!

We can continue in this manner

2! = 2 x 1!
1! = 1 x 0!

until we reach a point where a specific answer must be given:

0! = 1

Having reached a point where we have an exact result (0! = 1), we can now reverse our way back up through the solution.

Knowing 0! = 1, we can substitute this result in our previous equation:

1! = 1 x 0! = 1 x 1 = 1

Continuing this, we get:

2! = 2 x 1! = 2 x 1 = 2
3! = 3 x 2! = 3 x 2 = 6
4! = 4 x 3! = 4 x 6 = 24

Generally, we may write that the solution to *N*! is:

*N* x (*N*-1)!

# Recursive Functions

## Coding a Recursive Function

We can implement recursion within a programming language by coding a function or procedure which calls itself. For example, we can code a *Factorial* function as simply

```
function Factorial(n : longint): longint;
begin
    if n = 0 then
        Factorial := 1
    else
        Factorial := n * Factorial(n - 1);
end;
```

and test it with

```
var
    nbr : longint;
begin
    ClrScr;
    write('Enter factorial value required (1-13) : ');
    readln(nbr);
    writeln(nbr,'! = ',factorial(nbr));
end.
```

**Activity 10.1**

Type in the above program and test it. Use the trace feature of the debugger to watch which lines of code are executed as the program calculates 4!

## The Characteristics of a Recursive Function

All recursive functions contain three characteristics:

1. A terminating condition which gives a final, non-recursive result and stops execution of the function.

   For example, in *Factorial* the terminating condition is:
   ```
   if n = 0 then
       Factorial := 1;
   ```

2. A self-referencing call in which the function calls itself with a modified argument.

   For example:
   ```
   Factorial := n * Factorial(n - 1)
   ```

   You may recall that within the code of a function we have never used the function name on the right-hand side of an assignment statement before. The reason for this is now clear: when placed to the right of the assignment operator, a function's name is taken to be a recursive call.

3. The argument for this self-referencing call must lead towards the terminating condition being met.

   For example, the argument in the term *Factorial(n-1)* ensures that the condition, $n = 0$ ,will eventually be met.

> **Activity 10.2**
>
> One way to determine the number of items in a list (assuming it is implemented without a *count* component) is to make use of two basic facts:
>
> 1. If the list is empty, then its length is zero.
> 2. If it is not empty, its length is 1 + the length of the tail of the list.
>
> Using this information, and assuming the functions *IsEmpty* and *Tail* are available, write a recursive *Len2* function for a *List* type.

*Len2* returns the number of items in a *List* variable.

## How Recursion Works

FIG-10.1 shows the sequence of calls to *Factorial* using an original function argument of 3.

**FIG-10.1**

Recursive Calls

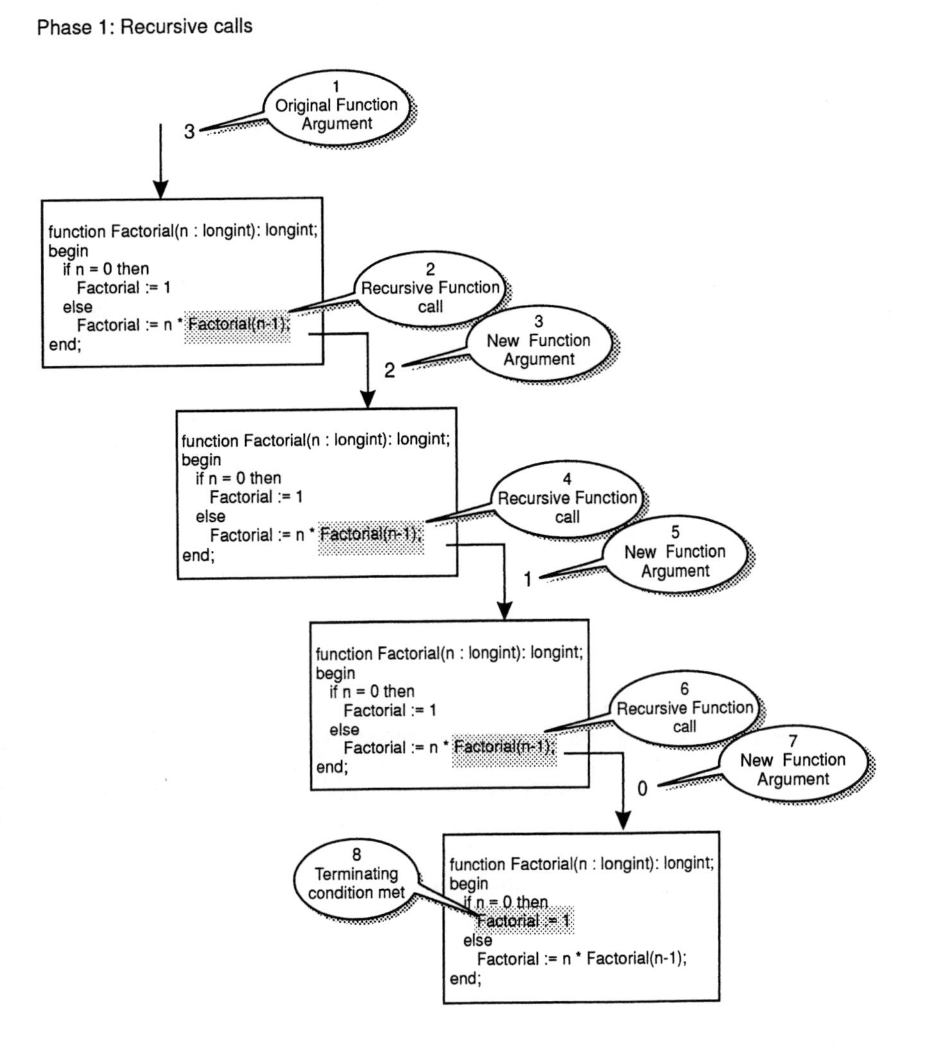


Once the terminating condition has been executed, the returned value is used to complete the expression evaluation in the previous call. This effect ripples back up through the sequence of calls until the result of the original function call can be determined (see FIG-10.2).

**FIG-10.2**

Terminating Recursive Calls

Phase 2: Returning Results

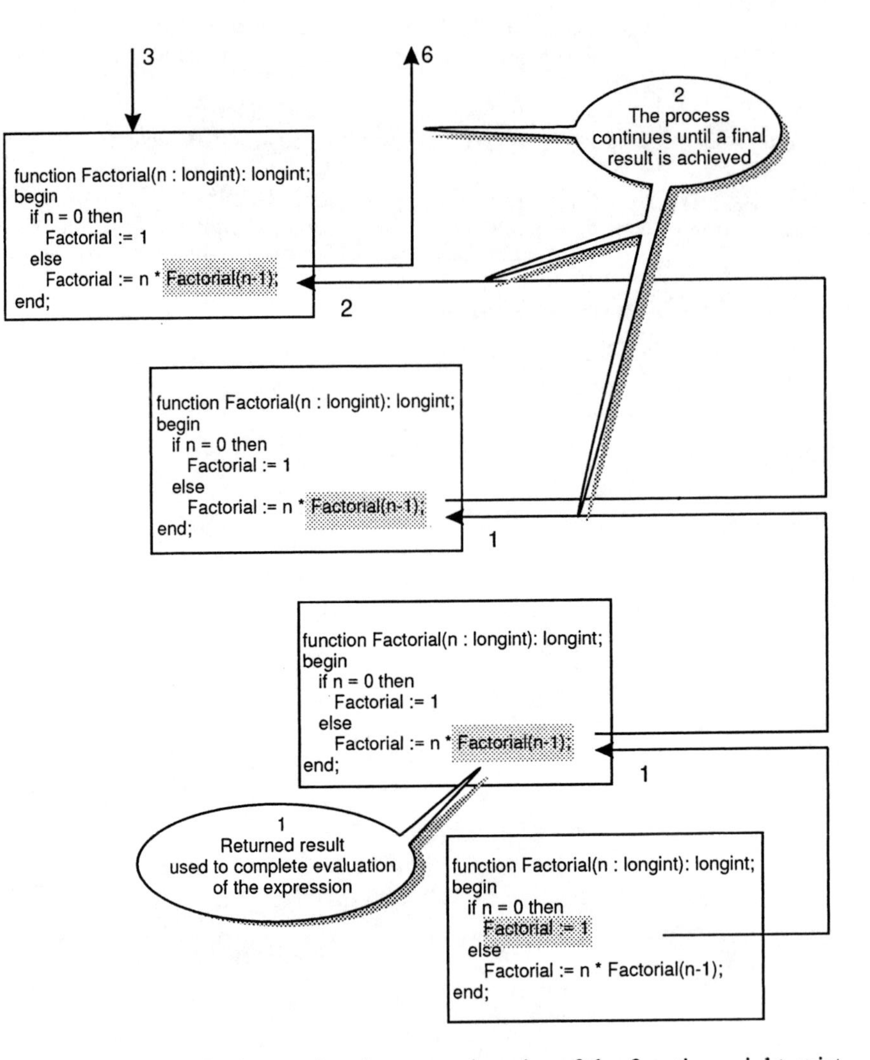


The diagrams give the impression that several copies of the function might exist within the computer's memory during execution of the function. This is not the case. In fact, the machine handles recursion by maintaining a data stack in which the parameters, local variables and return addresses for each call to the routine are held.

This mechanism for handling recursion can consume a great deal of memory. As a result, although recursion can result in very elegant solutions to certain problems, the overheads involved (space and time) mean that it is best avoided when implementing operations.

## More Examples of Recursive Definitions

Even where we choose not to implement a routine recursively, it may still be the best method of defining the logic involved in an operation. For example, if an operation (*CountNeg*) was required to count the number of negative values in a list of integers, we might describe the logic required as:

```
IF IsEmpty(list) THEN
    result := 0
ELSE
    IF Head(list)<0 THEN
        result := 1 + CountNeg(Tail(list))
    ELSE
        result := CountNeg(Tail(list))
    ENDIF
ENDIF
```

*Head* returns the front value in a *List* variable.

Note that this description treats *Head* and *Tail* like functions. This is often the case with descriptive logic since it better resembles the abstract language of mathematics rather than the implementation details of a programming laguage.

It's even possible to have more than one recursive call within an operation. For example, the Fibonacci series is a set of integers which starts with the values 1 and 1; subsequent values are obtained by summing the two previous terms. Hence the sequence continues: 2,3,5,8,13,21, etc.

To find the $n^{th}$ term in the series, we can define an operation, *Fibonacci*, as:

```
IF n<=2 THEN
    result := 1
ELSE
    result := Fibonacci(n-1) + Fibonacci(n-2)
ENDIF
```

**Activity 10.3**

Implement and test the Fibonacci operation as a Pascal function.

**Activity 10.4**

Explain in English the purpose of the following operation:

```
NAME            :  Op1
PARAMETERS
    IN          :  c : INTEGER
    OUT         :  None
    IN/OUT      :  s : LIST
PRE-CONDITION   :  None
POST-CONDITION  :  IF IsEmpty(s) THEN
                       AddAt(1,c,s)
                   ELSE
                       Op1(c,Tail(s))
                   ENDIF
```

*AddAt* adds a value at a specified position in a *List* variable. Hence, *AddAt(1,c,s)* adds the value *c* at the first position in *s*.

## Problems with Recursive Definitions

The main problem with recursive definitions is understanding them! And this is overcome by exposure to many examples. Some computer languages, such as Prolog and Lisp, make extensive use of recursive routines.

Another common pitfall for the unwary is creating recursive definitions which fail to terminate. For example, in the definition below, the routine will fail to terminate because the stopping condition is never met.

```
NAME            :  Sum
PARAMETERS
    IN          :  no: REAL
    OUT         :  sum: REAL
    IN/OUT      :  None
PRE-CONDITION   :  no >= 0
POST-CONDITION  :  IF no = 0 THEN
                       sum := 0
                   ELSE
                       sum := no + Sum(no/2)
```

The routine, *Sum*, is intended to sum the sequence *no* + *no/2* + *no/4* ... +*0* but the expression *no/2* although tending to zero will never reach it and hence the terminating condition, *no* = *0*, is never satisfied.

So, why should we use recursion? Most importantly, recursive definitions allow a more rigorous proof of the correctness of that definition (although such proofs are beyond the scope of this text). A recursive definition also gives a short, but precise description of an operation. The argument for recursive implementation is harder to sustain since it often results in unacceptable overheads. However, even here, it sometimes offers much shorter and more easily tested code.

# Summary

- **A recursive operation** is one which calls itself in describing the solution to that operation.

- **Recursive operations have three main characteristics**

    1. A terminating condition which gives a final, non-recursive result and stops execution of the function.
    2. A self-referencing call in which the function calls itself with a modified argument.
    3. The argument for this self-referencing call must lead towards the terminating condition being met.

- **The correctness of a recursively defined routine** can be proved mathematically.

- **A recursively defined routine need not be implemented recursively**.

- **A recursively implemented routine is usually inefficient** in terms of both execution time and the amount of memory required by the routine.

- **A recursive implementation is used when** non-recursive methods would result in over-complicated code.

# BINARY SEARCH TREES

## Introduction

We have already seen that the linked list is a useful method of implementing a collection of data since it allows the structure to grow or shrink with the amount of data being held. This is a great advantage over earlier implementations using arrays which imposed a fixed size on the amount of data which could be stored. But linked lists have one great disadvantage: interrogation of the structure must be done using simple linear searching techniques. This can lead to unacceptable delays in the execution of some operations when the linked list is a long one.

For data which does not contain a key field or where the existing order of the data is important, we need to live with this problem. On the other hand, with a key field and the discretion of holding the data in any order, we are free to use a greater range of implementation methods. One structure which helps improve search times is the **binary search tree.**

The binary tree is a special form of the general tree structure.

The tree data structure is unlike any of the previous structures we have examined in that the data which it contains is organised in a hierarchical manner. Perhaps the most familiar tree structure is the family, an example of which is shown in FIG-10.3.

**FIG-10.3**

A Family Tree

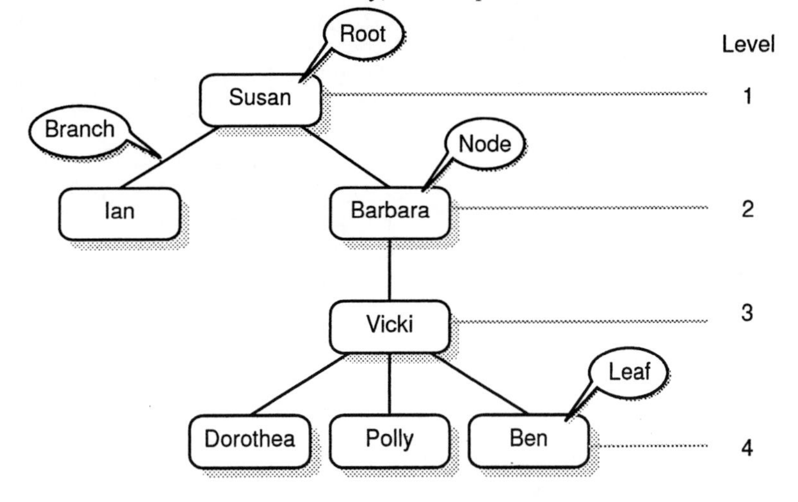


Much of the terminology used in describing tree data structures comes from the vocabulary of both botany and genealogy.

### Tree Terminology

| | |
|---|---|
| **NODE** | A single item of data in a tree is called a node (SUSAN, IAN, POLLY are nodes from the example above). |
| **ROOT** | The top-most node (SUSAN). |
| **BRANCH** | A direct link between one node and another (There is a branch from SUSAN to IAN. There is no branch from BARBARA to BEN.). |

| | |
|---|---|
| **PARENT** | The immediately preceding node. All nodes, except the root, have exactly one parent (VICKI is the parent of POLLY - and also of DOROTHEA and BEN). |
| **CHILD** | An immediately succeeding node. A node may have zero or more children (IAN and BARBARA are the children of SUSAN). |
| **ANCESTOR** | If a node can be reached by following branches upwards through a tree then that node is an ancestor of the node at which you started (BARBARA is an ancestor of BEN. IAN is not an ancestor of BEN). |
| **DESCENDANT** | If a node can be reached by following the branches down through the tree, then that node is a descendant of the node at which you started. |
| **SIBLING** | All nodes which have the same parent (IAN and BARBARA are siblings). |
| **LEAF** | A node which has no children. |
| **LEVEL** | The root of the tree is at level 1; its children are at level 2; its grandchildren at level 2, etc. |
| **HEIGHT** | Each node is at a specific height in the tree. Leaves are at height zero; a leaf's parent has a height of 1, etc. The height of the tree is the height of the root from the lowest leaf. |
| **DEGREE** | A node's degree is equal to the number of children the node has. A leaf's degree is zero. |
| **SUBTREE** | A subtree is part of an existing tree. That is, if we take any node, along with its descendants, the result is another tree which is a subtree of the original tree. |
| **FOREST** | A collection of separate trees is known as a forest.<br>A forest is very similar to a tree, since if we remove the root of a tree, the result is a forest.<br>A forest may also be transformed into a single tree by adding a linking root node. |

## Binary Trees

A binary tree is a restricted form of tree. The restriction being that no node may have more than two branches.

By definition a binary tree may be either:

1. An empty tree (one containing no nodes).

or 2. A structure consisting of a left sub-tree (which is itself a binary tree); a root node ; and a right sub-tree (which is also a binary tree).

FIG-10.4 shows some examples of binary trees.

**FIG-10.4**

Examples of Binary Trees

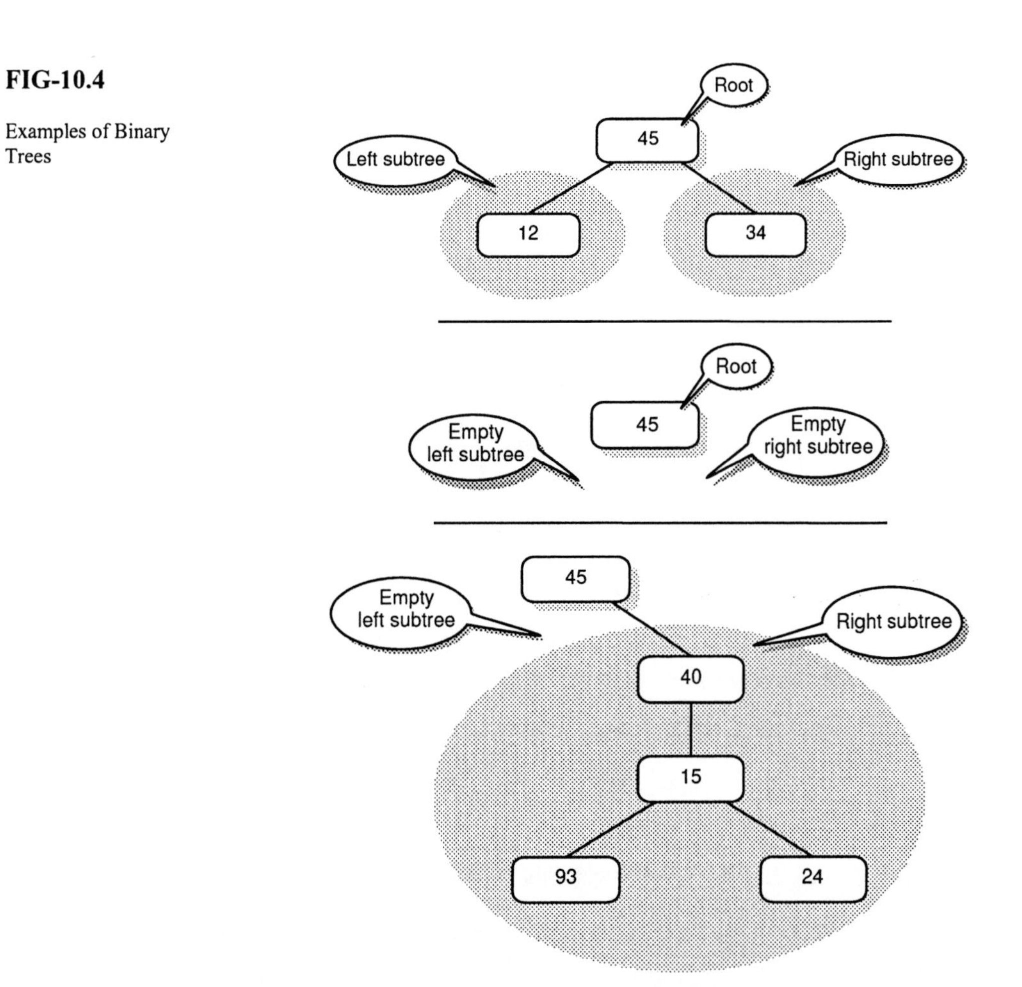


**Activity 10.5**

In the following binary tree

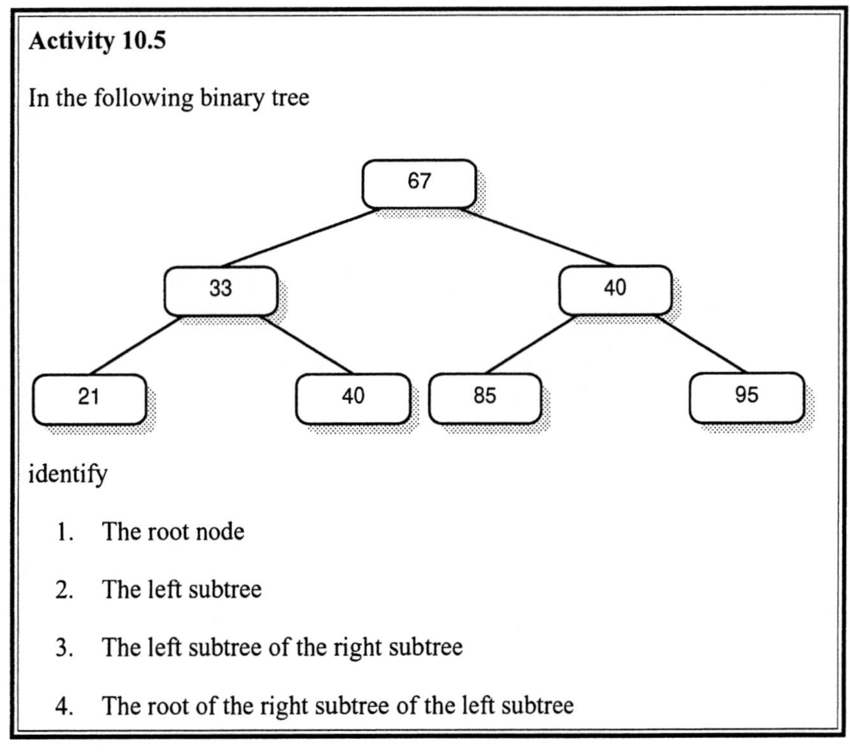


identify

1. The root node
2. The left subtree
3. The left subtree of the right subtree
4. The root of the right subtree of the left subtree

## Binary Search Trees

This tree is a restricted form of binary tree in which all items in the left subtree have a value less than the root node and all values in the right subtree are greater than the root (see FIG-10.5).

**FIG-10.5**

A Binary Search Tree

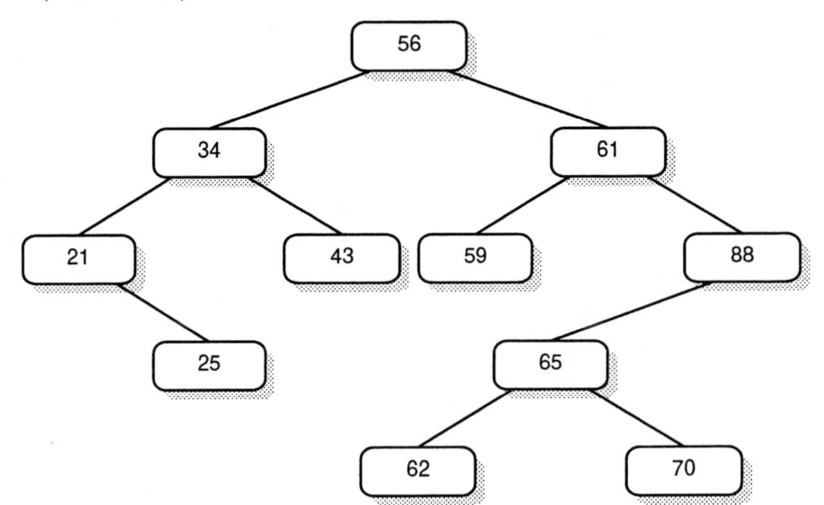


The binary search tree is often referred to as a **BSTree**.

A BSTree is defined as either

1. An empty tree.

or 2. A left BSTree; a root; and a right BSTree.

We can create a Binary Search Tree from a set of values by using the following algorithm:

```
REPEAT
    IF
        the tree is empty:
            Insert new value as tree root
        value to be added < root:
            Using the left subtree and restart this process
        value to be added > root:
            Using the right subtree restart this process
    ENDIF
UNTIL new value inserted
```

**Activity 10.6**

1. Draw a binary search tree from the following values. Assume the values are placed in the tree in the order they are given here.

   65, 12, 45, 23, 96, 44, 21, 53, 72, 88, 75, 10

2. What is the height of the tree created?

The main use of the Binary Search Tree structure is given in its name. It allows a binary search to be performed on data which is not held in physical order.

# Creating a Binary Search Tree

## Defining a BSTree ADT

Although we might reasonably treat a binary tree as simply a method of implementing a table, it can also be considered as a data type in its own right. The following ADT gives an informal description of such a structure.

```
ADT BSTree is

    DATA
        Consists of a finite set of data nodes and a finite set of branches connecting pairs
        of nodes.
        In a non-empty BSTree, there is a single root node which is connected to a left
        BSTree and a right BSTree. All values in the left subtree are less than the value
        of the root; all values in the right subtree are greater than the node.

    OPERATIONS
        NAME              :   CreateBSTree
        PARAMETERS
            IN            :   None
            OUT           :   t : BSTree
            IN/OUT        :   None
        PRE-CONDITION     :   None
        POST-CONDITION    :   t is empty

        NAME              :   IsEmptyTree
        PARAMETERS
            IN            :   t : BSTree
                              result : INTEGER
            OUT           :   None
            IN/OUT        :   None
        PRE-CONDITION     :   None
        POST-CONDITION    :   IF t is empty THEN
                                  result =1
                              ELSE
                                  result =0

        NAME              :   AddToTree
        PARAMETERS
            IN            :   v : Item
            OUT           :   None
            IN/OUT        :   t : BSTree
        PRE-CONDITION     :   None
        POST-CONDITION    :   IF t is empty THEN
                                  insert v as root
                                  ELSE
                                      IF key of v < key of root THEN
                                          AddToTree(v,left subtree of t)
                                      ELSE
                                          IF key of v > key of root THEN
                                              AddToTree(v,right subtree of t)
                                          ELSE
                                              t is unchanged
```

| | | |
|---|---|---|
| NAME | : | Root |
| PARAMETERS | | |
| IN | : | t : BSTree |
| OUT | : | v : Item |
| IN/OUT | : | None |
| PRE-CONDITION | : | *t* not empty |
| POST-CONDITION | : | *v* holds a copy of the root of *t* |

| | | |
|---|---|---|
| NAME | : | DisplayTree |
| PARAMETERS | | |
| IN | : | t : BSTree |
| OUT | : | None |
| IN/OUT | : | None |
| PRE-CONDITION | : | None |
| POST-CONDITION | : | IF *t* not empty THEN<br>DisplayTree(left subtree of *t*)<br>Display contents of root<br>DisplayTree(right subtree of *t*) |

**END ADT**

This time the post-conditions have been given in a much more formal manner than those in earlier chapters. This results in a less ambiguous type of description and can give the programmer a greater insight into a possible approach to implementing the new data type.

**Activity 10.7**

Using the ADT defined above, state:

a) What happens to the tree, *t*, when an attempt is made to add a new value whose key matches an existing entry in the tree?

b) What is the effect of trying to find the root of an empty tree?

# Implementing a Binary Search Tree

## Data

Although the ADT's description of the structure did not included details of the actual data stored in the tree, we'll now have to commit ourselves to what information we want to hold in our structure. For this example, we'll use the *StudentDetails* structure as the data component of a node. So, we begin with the declaration:

```
type
    StudentDetails =
    record
        idcode : integer;
        name   : string[30];
        sex    : char;
        score  : array[1..6]of integer;
    end;

    Data = StudentDetails;
```

Next we have to declare the structure of a single node in the tree. This is constructed from a data area and two pointers. The pointers reference the left and right subtrees (see FIG-10.6).

**FIG-10.6**

A BSTree Node

| Left subtree pointer | Data | Right subtree pointer |
|---|---|---|

The declaration for a node is given as:

```
NodePointerType = ^Node;
Node =
record
    left    : NodePointerType;
    value   : Data;
    right   : NodePointerType;
end;
```

The Binary Search Tree structure is simply a pointer to a node:

```
BSTree = NodePointerType;
```

Once constructed a typical *BSTree* variable will have the form shown in FIG-10.7.

**FIG-10.7**

A Typical BSTree Variable

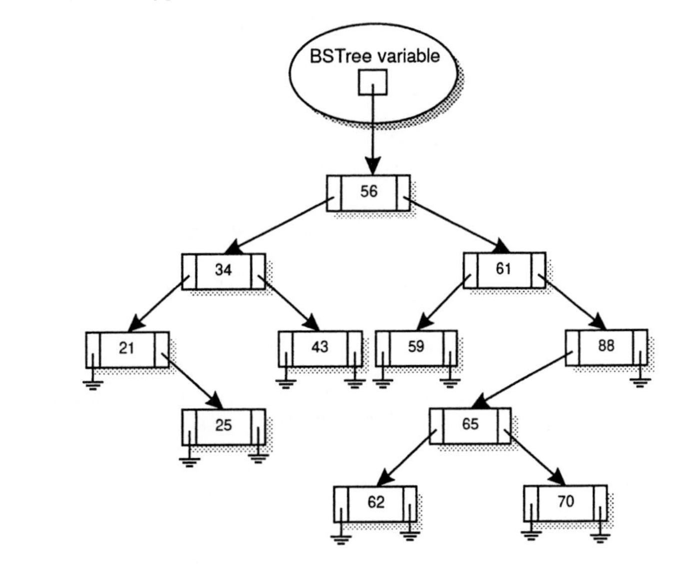


**NOTE**: Only the *idcode* values are shown within the nodes of the tree.

## Operations

The first routine that we need to write is *CreateTree* which sets the tree pointer to NULL:

```
{*** Create an Empty Tree ***}
procedure CreateTree(var t : BSTree);
begin
    {*** Set pointer to root to NIL ***}
    t := NIL;
end;
```

Another routine which can be easily implemented is *IsEmptyTree*:

```
{*** Check if tree empty ***}
function IsEmptyTree(t : BSTree): boolean;
begin
    {*** IF pointer to root is NIL THEN ***}
    if t = NIL then
        {*** Tree is empty ***}
        IsEmptyTree := true
    else
        {***ELSE tree is not empty ***}
        IsEmptyTree := false;
end;
```

Retrieving the root node is also relatively simple, but we need to check that its pre-condition (the tree is not empty ) is met:

```
{*** Get Root of Tree ***}
procedure Root(t : BSTree; var d : Data);
begin
    {*** IF tree is empty THEN ***}
    if IsEmptyTree(t) then
        {*** Exit program ***}
        halt;
    {*** ELSE Return value of root ***}
    d := t^.value;
end;
```

One possible way of implementing the *AddToTree* operation is to use the same recursive approach suggested in the post-condition of the operation:

```
{*** Add new node to tree ***}
procedure AddToTree(v : Data; var t : BSTree);
var
    temp : NodePointerType;
    cpy : Data;
begin
    {*** IF tree is empty THEN ***}
    if IsEmptyTree(t) then
    begin
        {*** Create node ***}
        New(temp);
        temp^.left := NIL;
        temp^.right := NIL;
        temp^.value := v;
        {*** Add node as root ***}
        t := temp;
    end
    else
    begin
        {*** IF new value < root THEN ***}
        Root(t,cpy);
        if v.idcode < cpy.idcode then
            {*** Insert into left subtree ***}
            AddToTree(v,t^.left)
        else
            {*** Insert into right subtree ***}
            AddToTree(v,t^.right);
    end;
end;
```

Now all we have to do is implement the *DisplayTree* operation which, again, follows the logic suggested by its post-condition:

This version of *DisplayTree* only outputs the *idcode* value of each node.

```
{*** Display contents of tree ***}
procedure DisplayTree(t : BSTree);
begin
    {*** IF tree is empty THEN ***}
    if IsEmptyTree(t) then
        {*** Exit routine ***}
        exit;
    {*** Display the left subtree ***}
    DisplayTree(t^.left);
    {*** Display the root ***}
    writeln(t^.value.idcode);
    {*** Display the right subtree ***}
    DisplayTree(t^.right);
end;
```

This code is brought together in LISTING-10.1 which implements a simple tree program.

The program uses the Pascal Units *Auxiliary* and *Students*. From these it makes use of *DisplayMenu, GetOption, GetStudentDetails* and *DisplayStudent.* In addition, *StudentDetails* type is defined within the Students Unit and so is not redefined here.

**LISTING-10.1**

Implementing the Binary Search Tree

```
program BSTreeProg;
uses WinCrt,Auxiliary,Students;

{*****************************************}
{ *** BSTree Data Type Declarations ***}
{*****************************************}
type

  {*** Data ***}

  Data = StudentDetails;

  NodePointerType = ^Node;
  Node =
  record
      left   : NodePointerType;
      value  : Data;
      right  : NodePointerType;
  end;

  BSTree = NodePointerType;

  {*** Operations ***]

{*** Create an Empty Tree ***}
procedure CreateTree(var t : BSTree);
begin
  {*** Set pointer to root to NIL ***}
  t := NIL;
end;



{*** Check if tree empty ***}
function IsEmptyTree(t : BSTree): boolean;
begin
  {*** IF pointer to root is NIL THEN ***}
  if t = NIL then
      {*** Tree is empty ***}
      IsEmptyTree := true
  else
      {***ELSE tree is not empty ***}
      IsEmptyTree := false;
end;



{*** Get Root of Tree ***}
procedure Root(t : BSTree; var d : Data);
begin
  {*** IF tree is empty THEN ***}
  if IsEmptyTree(t) then
      {*** Exit program ***}
      halt;
  {*** ELSE Return value of root ***}
  d := t^.value;
end;



{*** Add new node to tree ***}
procedure AddToTree(v : Data; var t : BSTree);
var
  temp : NodePointerType;
  cpy : Data;
begin
  {*** IF tree is empty THEN ***}
  if IsEmptyTree(t) then
```

**Continued on next page**

**LISTING-10.1**
(continued)

Implementing the Binary Search Tree

```
  begin
      {*** Create node ***}
      New(temp);
      temp^.left := NIL;
      temp^.right := NIL;
      temp^.value := v;
      {*** Add node as root ***}
      t := temp;
  end
  else
  begin
      {*** IF new value < root THEN ***}
      Root(t,cpy);
      if v.idcode < cpy.idcode then
          {*** Insert into left subtree ***}
          AddToTree(v,t^.left)
      else
          {*** Insert into right subtree ***}
          AddToTree(v,t^.right);
  end;
end;


{*** Display contents of tree ***}
procedure DisplayTree(t : BSTree);
begin
  {*** IF tree is empty THEN ***}
  if IsEmptyTree(t) then
      {*** Exit routine ***}
      exit;
  {*** Display the left subtree ***}
  DisplayTree(t^.left);
  {*** Display the root ***}
  DisplayStudent(t^.value);
  {*** Display the right subtree ***}
  DisplayTree(t^.right);
end;
{***********************************}
{*** END BSTree Type Definitions ***}
{***********************************}

procedure ExecuteOption(opt : integer; var t : BSTree);
var
  st : Data;
begin
  case opt of
      1:  CreateTree(t);
      2:  begin
              GetStudentDetails(st);
              AddToTree(st,t);
          end;
      3:  begin
              DisplayTree(t);
              ReadKey;
          end;
      4:  begin
              if IsEmptyTree(t) then
                  writeln('Tree empty')
              else
              begin
                  Root(t,st);
                  writeln('Root''s idcode : ',st.idcode)
              end;
              readkey;
          end;
      5:  writeln('TERMINATING PROGRAM');
  end;
end;
```

**Continued on next page**

**LISTING-10.1**
(continued)

Implementing the Binary Search Tree

```
const
  NL = #13#10;
var
  tree : BSTree;
  noofopts, opt : integer;
begin
  CreateTree(tree);
  repeat
      ClrScr;
      noofopts := DisplayMenu('1 - Create tree'+NL+
                              '2 - Add Node'+NL+
                              '3 - Display'+NL+
                              '4 - Display first value'+NL+
                              '5 - QUIT'+NL);
      opt := GetOption(noofopts);
      ExecuteOption(opt,tree);
   until opt = noofopts;
end.
```

**Activity 10.8**

Enter and test the program in LISTING-10.1. Save it as *Trees.pas*.

Rewrite the *AddToTree* routine using a non-recursive approach.

## Deleting From a Binary Search Tree

There is one basic operation which has been omitted so far in the discussion on BSTrees and that is deletion. Unfortunately, deletion from a tree is not always a simple task. There are three distinct situations which may arise when deleting a node:

**1. The Node to be Deleted has no Children**

Deleting a leaf node is simple since it has no descendants. The node is erased by removing the branch from it to its parent. In Pascal, deletion of a leaf is achieved by removing the allocated node space using `delete`, and setting the left or right pointer (as appropriate) of the leaf's parent to NIL (see FIG-10.8).

**FIG-10.8**

Deleting a Leaf from a BSTree

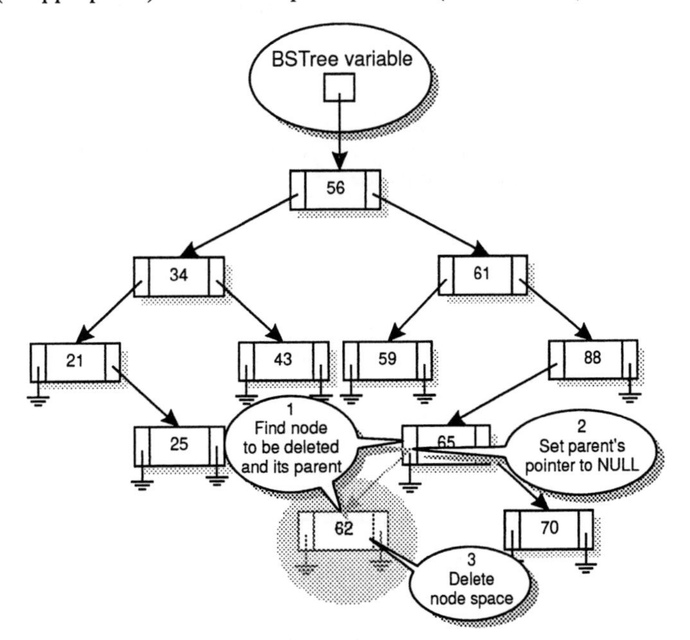

The logic involved required for this operation is:

```
Find the node to be deleted and its parent
Set the parent's left or right pointer (whichever one is
    pointing to the deleted node) to NULL
Dispose of the node to be removed
```

### 2. The Node to be Deleted has a Single Child

When the node to be deleted has a single branch leading from it, its child replaces the deleted item in the tree.

In Pascal this is achieved by linking the parent of the node to be deleted to the child of the node to be deleted. The link is to the *left* or *right* pointer of the parent as appropriate (see FIG-10.9). The logic for this operation is:

**FIG-10.9**

Deleting a Node with a Single Child

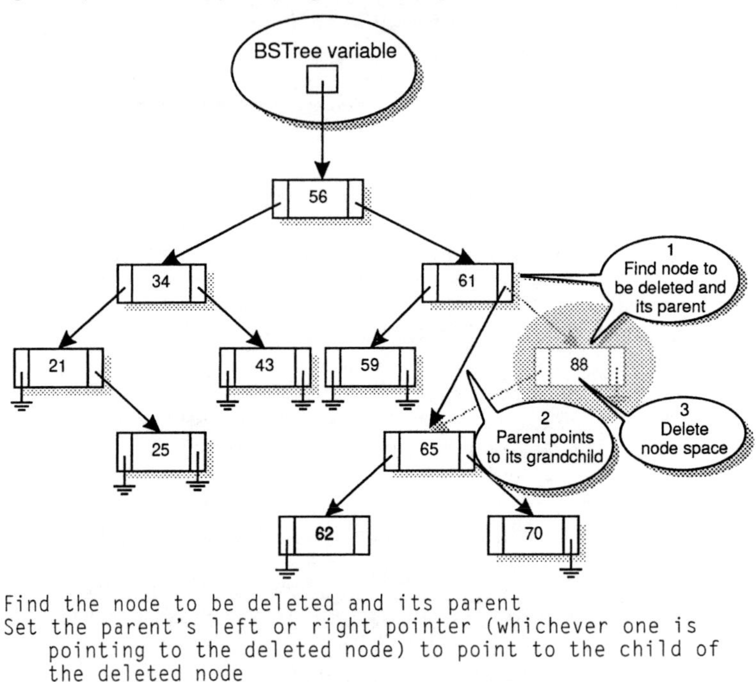


```
Find the node to be deleted and its parent
Set the parent's left or right pointer (whichever one is
    pointing to the deleted node) to point to the child of
    the deleted node
Dispose of the node to be removed
```

### 3. The Node to be Deleted has Two Children

This is the most complex case. Simply deleting the node will split the tree into separate parts (see FIG-10.10), cutting off the descendants of the deleted node from the rest of the tree.

To overcome this problem we do not delete the node containing the value to be removed; we simply overwrite the contents of the node with the data of a descendant. So that the tree's structure will remain substantially the same, the new value must be close to the one just overwritten.

> **Activity 10.9**
>
> Which remaining value is closest to that of the deleted value in FIG-10.9 above?

In fact, it is not necessary for the replacement value to be the closest value to the one deleted. It is only necessary that the replacement value is such that the resulting structure still conforms to the definition of a BSTree (i.e. that all values to the left of the replacement value are less than the replacement value and that those to the right are larger.

**FIG-10.10**

The Problem with Deleting a Two-Child Node

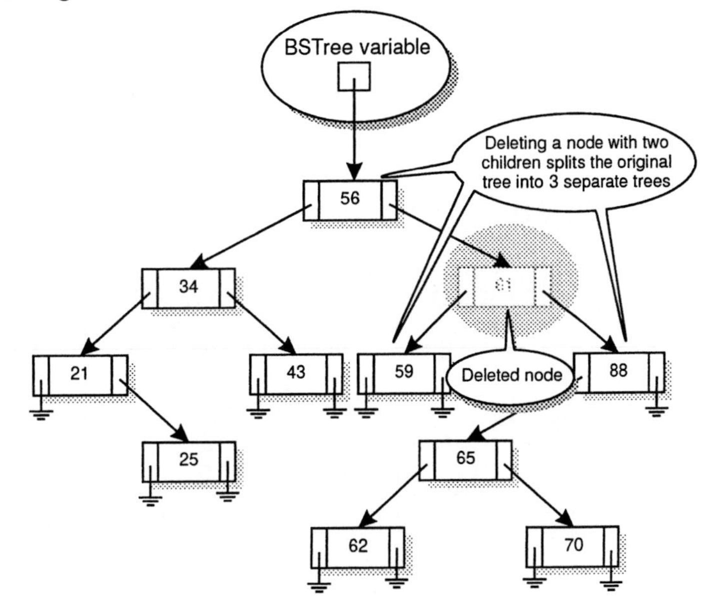


This means that we do not have to search the tree for the nearest value to the one being deleted but need merely employ the following logic:

```
Starting with the subtree for which the value to be deleted
    is the root (we'll call this T1)
Choose the right subtree of T1 (called T2)
Go down through T2 choosing only left subtrees until the left
    subtree is empty
Make a copy of the value found
Delete the node from which the copy was made
Place the copy of the deleted node's data in the root of T1
```

FIG-10.11 gives a graphical representation of the steps involved.

**FIG-10.11**

Deleting a Two-Child Node

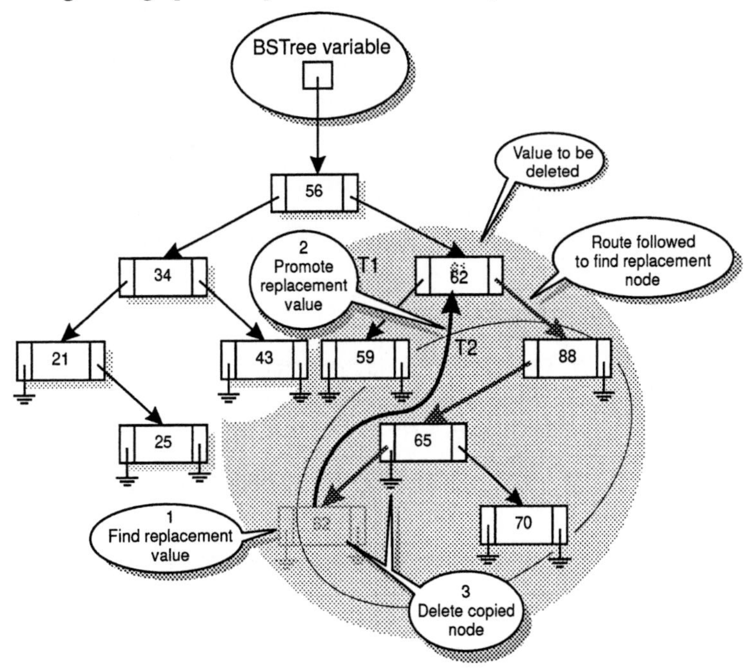

Note that the node actually deleted during this process will either be a leaf (as in FIG-10.11) or a node with a single branch. And, since we have already described how these two cases are dealt with, our approach to deleting a two-child parent is complete.

To code the *DeleteFromTree* operation, we'll need to start by defining something similar to the *IsAt* operation we've used in the past. However, this time we need a routine which returns pointers to both the required node and its parent. We'll call the routine *FindParCh*. The Mini-Spec for this routine is:

| | | |
|---|---|---|
| **NAME** | : | FindParCh |
| **PARAMETERS** | | |
| **IN** | : | key : INTEGER<br>t : BSTree |
| **OUT** | : | success : BOOLEAN<br>par : NODE pointer<br>ch : NODE pointer |
| **IN/OUT** | : | None |
| **PRE-CONDITION** | : | None |
| **POST-CONDITION** | : | *success* is set to zero if *key* does not match any idcode in *t,* otherwise *success* is set to 1. If match found then *ch* holds the address of the node containing a match and *par* holds the address of its parent. |

The code for this routine is:

```
{***Returns pointers to specified node and its parent ***}
function FindParCh(key : integer; t : BSTree;
                   var par, ch : NodePointerType): boolean;
begin
    {*** Set parent to NULL and child to root ***}
    par := NIL;
    ch := t;
    {*** WHILE not end of tree AND no match DO ***}
    while (ch <> NIL) and (ch^.value.idcode <> key) do
    begin
        {*** Current child becomes new parent ***}
        par := ch;
        {*** Child moves down tree ***}
        if key < ch^.value.idcode then
            ch := ch^.left
        else
            ch := ch^.right;
    end;
    {*** Return success indicator ***}
        if ch = NIL then
            FindParCh := false
        else
            FindParCh := true;
end;
```

Once we've found the required node, we need to determine what type of node it is. That is, is it a leaf, single-child or two-child node? This can be decided by examining the left and right pointers of the node. Again, we'll do this by writing another short routine, *NodeType*, which takes a *Node* pointer and returns -1, 0, 1, or 2 representing a NIL pointer, leaf, 1-child node or 2-child node respectively.

```
{*** Return node type ***}
function NodeType(nd :NodePointerType): integer;
begin
    {*** IF nd doesn't reference a node, return -1 **}
```

```
    if nd = NIL then
        NodeType := -1
    {*** IF both node's pointers NIL, its a leaf ***}
    else if (nd^.left = NIL) and (nd^.right = NIL) then
        NodeType := 0
    {*** IF one pointer not NIL then, one child ***}
    else if (nd^.left = NIL) or (nd^.right = NIL) then
        NodeType := 1
    else
        {*** otherwise must be 2 children ***}
        NodeType := 2;
end;
```

> **Activity 10.10**
>
> Add another user option to the program you created in Activity 10.8 which allows the user to find a match for a given key. A display of "FOUND" or "NOT FOUND" should be given as appropriate and where a match is found, its node type should be displayed as "LEAF", "1 - CHILD" or "2 - CHILDREN".

We're now ready to tackle the two simpler delete options: deleting a leaf and single-child node. In fact, these two cases can be combined into a single method. If we examine the logic for both variations (given below), we can see that the only difference lies in what value is assigned to the parent's left or right pointer.

**Deleting a Leaf**

```
Find the node to be deleted and its parent
Set the parent's left or right pointer (whichever one is
    pointing to the node to be deleted) to NIL
Dispose of the node to be deleted
```

**Deleting a Node with a Single Child**

```
Find the node to be deleted and its parent
Set the parent's left or right pointer (whichever one is
    pointing to the node to be deleted) to point to the
    child of the node to be deleted
Dispose of the node to be deleted
```

In the second case, the parent's pointer will be set to point to the child of the node to be deleted. This value will be taken from either the left or right pointer in the node to be deleted.

Where a leaf node is being deleted, the parent's appropriate pointer is set to NIL and this may simply be considered as a copy of the left or right pointer of the node to be deleted as they are both set to NIL (since we are dealing with a leaf).

We can now describe the delete strategy (first two cases only) as

```
Find the node to be deleted and its parent
IF a match is found THEN
    Determine which type of node is to be deleted
        (zero, one or two children)
    IF node to be deleted has less than two children THEN
            Delete leaf or single child node
    ENDIF
ENDIF
```

which is coded as:

```
{*** Deletes a BSTree Node ***}
function DeleteFromTree(key : integer; var t : BSTree) : boolean;
var
    parent, child : NodePointerType;
    grandchild    : NodePointerType;
```

```
begin
    {*** IF a match is found for key THEN ***}
    if FindParCh(key,t,parent,child) then
    begin
        {*** Deal with type of delete ***}
        case NodeType(child) of
            0,1: {*** Delete 1-child node ***}
                begin
                    {***Determine grandchild position - ***}
                    {*** left, right, none ***}
                    if child^.left <> NIL then
                        grandchild := child^.left
                    else
                        grandchild := child^.right;
                    {*** Link grandchild to parent ***}
                    {** Special case for deleting root **}
                    if parent = NIL then
                        t := grandchild
                    else if parent^.left = child then
                        parent^.left := grandchild
                    else
                        parent^.right := grandchild
                end;
        end;
        {*** Deallocate node's space ***}
        Dispose(child);
        DeleteFromTree := true
    end;
    DeleteFromTree := false
end;
```

Notice that the code itself is somewhat more complex than the outline logic suggests since we need to treat deletion of the root as a special case (since it has no parent), and we also need to find out if the grandchild is on the left or right side of the child node.

> **Activity 10.11**
>
> Add this *DeleteFromTree* function to your **Trees** program and test it.

To complete the *DeleteFromTree* operation, we require to be able to handle the removal of nodes with two children. To do that, we need to find and promote a successor to the data being removed. The logic for such a process is:

```
Starting at the right subtree of the node to be deleted
Move down through the left branches of the tree until the
    end is reached
Copy data at that node to the original node
Delete the node from which the data was copied
```

The first three lines of this can be done with the code:

Have another look at FIG-10.11 to see a visual representation of this logic.

```
successor := child^.right;
parent := child;
while successor^.left <> NIL do
begin
    parent := successor;
    successor := successor^.left;
end;
{** Copy data to original node **}
child^.value := successor^.value;
```

To complete the task, we simply need to make *child* and *parent* reference the promoted node and its own parent. After that, we can use the previous code (for deleting a leaf and single child node) to delete this node. The code above already moves the *parent* pointer to the correct position; all that is required to complete the job is the line:

```
            child := successor;
```

We can now complete the code for *DeleteFromTree*:

```
function DeleteFromTree(key : integer; var t : BSTree) : boolean;
var
    parent, child : NodePointerType;
    grandchild    : NodePointerType;
    successor     : NodePointerType;
begin
    {*** IF a match is found for key THEN ***}
    if FindParCh(key,t,parent,child) then
    begin
        {*** Deal with type of delete ***}
        {*** Two child node ***}
        if NodeType(child) = 2 then
        begin
            {** Find successor **}
            successor := child^.right;
            parent := child;
            while successor^.left <> NIL do
            begin
                parent := successor;
                successor := successor^.left;
            end;
            {** Copy data to original node **}
            child^.value := successor^.value;
            {*** Now delete successor's orginal node by ***}
            {*** executing next case option ***}
            child := successor;
        end;
        case NodeType(child) of
            0,1: {*** Delete leaf or 1-child node ***}
                begin
                    {***Determine grandchild position - ***}
                    {*** left, right, none ***}
                    if child^.left <> NIL then
                        grandchild := child^.left
                    else
                        grandchild := child^.right;
                    {*** Link grandchild to parent ***}
                    {** Special case for deleting root **}
                    if parent = NIL then
                        t := grandchild
                    else if parent^.left = child then
                        parent^.left := grandchild
                    else
                        parent^.right := grandchild
                end;
        end;
        {*** Deallocate node's space ***}
        Dispose(child);
        DeleteFromTree := true
    end;
    DeleteFromTree := false
end;
```

**Activity 10.12**

Complete the *DeleteFromTree* operation in your **Trees** program.

# Summary

- **A tree** is a hierarchical structure.
- **A tree is constructed** from nodes and branches.

- **The root** of a tree is the first node in the tree.
- **A leaf** is a node which has no branches.
- **A binary tree** is one in which each node has, at most, two children.
- In **a binary search tree**, all values to the left of any node are less than the value of that node and all values to the right of the node are greater than the value of the node.
- **Binary search trees are used to** allow efficient searching of a collection of data.

# GRAPHS

## Undirected Graphs

### Introduction

A graph, like a tree, is a collection of nodes connected by lines (called **edges**). What differentiates these two structures is that a node may connect back to a previous node (something that cannot happen in a tree).

### Graphs in the Real World

The map below (see FIG-10.12) shows the destinations available from ABC Airlines.

**FIG-10.12**

Flight Routes on a Map

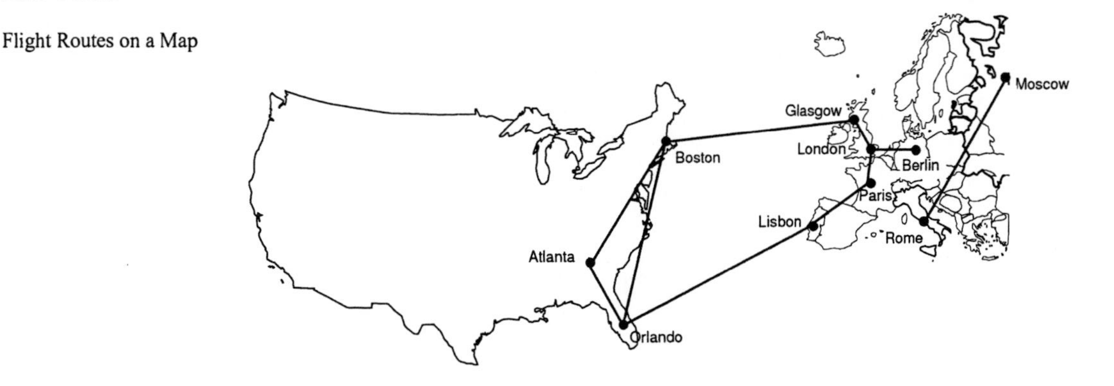


We could use this diagram to select a route from, say, Glasgow to Orlando. But we could equally well use a more abstract form of the diagram to make the same decision (see FIG-10.13).

**FIG-10.13**

A More Abstract Model of the Flight Routes

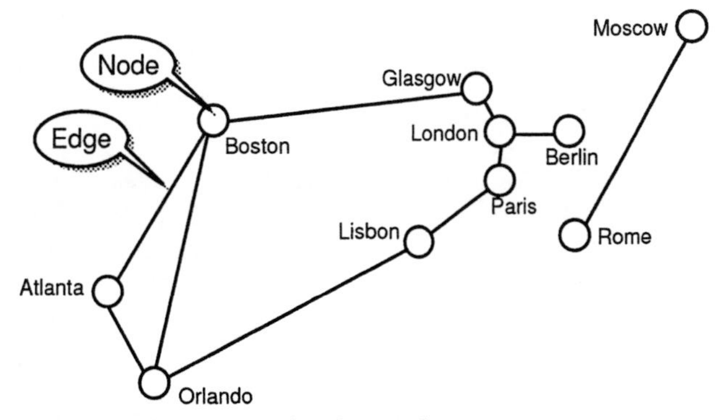


This abstract diagram is an example of a graph.

### Terminology

A graph is constructed from **nodes** (also known as **vertices**) which are connected by **edges**. In the example above, the destinations (*Glasgow, Atlanta, Orlando*, etc.) are the nodes and the edges are the lines connecting the nodes. The nodes at either end are used to identify an edge; for example, one edge is (*Atlanta,Orlando*). Note that the nodes identifying an edge are enclosed in parenthesis. In this case, the order of the nodes is unimportant. Therefore the edge between *Glasgow* and *London* can be identified as (*Glasgow,London*) or (*London,Glasgow*). Later we will see examples of graphs where the order of the nodes is significant when identifying edges.

See FIG-10.13

**Activity 10.13**

List all of the nodes and any five edges in the diagram above.

Nodes at either end of an edge are called **adjacent nodes** (*Boston* is adjacent to *Orlando*). A **path** is the list of nodes that are passed through when travelling from one node to another. One possible path from *Glasgow* to *Orlando* is (*Glasgow,Boston,Atlanta,Orlando*).

A graph is said to be **connected** if there is at least one path from each node to every other node. This is not the case in the graph on the previous page (e.g. there is no path from *Rome* to *Glasgow* - see FIG-10.13).

A **cycle** is a path of at least three different nodes that leads back to the starting node. (*Boston, Atlanta, Orlando, Boston*) is a cycle.

A connected graph that has no cycles is a **tree**. If we start with a connected graph and remove all edges that form cycles but retain connections to all nodes, then we have formed a **spanning tree** (see FIG-10.14).

**FIG-10.14**

Graphs and Spanning Trees

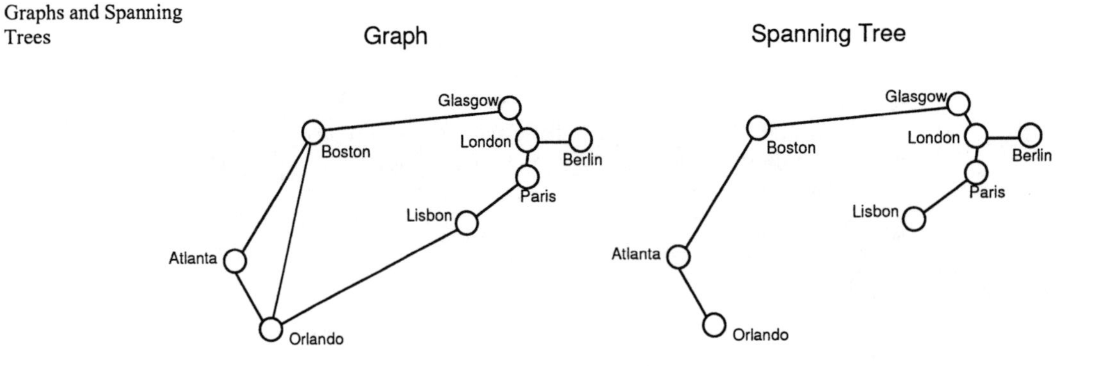


So far we have assumed that the existence of an edge allows movement in both directions between the nodes of that edge. For example, since there is an edge between *Boston* and *Glasgow* it is possible to travel both from *Glasgow* to *Boston* and *Boston* to *Glasgow*. This type of graph is known as an **undirected graph** and the edges are said to be **unordered** since the nodes used in identifying an edge can be specified in any order.

A graph can have any number of nodes but the number of edges on an undirected graph can vary from zero (where none of the nodes are connected) to a maximum value determined by the number of nodes.

In general, if a graph contains $N$ nodes, then the maximum number of edges is given by the formula:

$$N(N-1)/2$$

Where all possible edges are present in a graph, the graph is said to be **complete**. If most of the edges are present then the graph is termed dense while a graph with few edges is called a **sparse graph**.

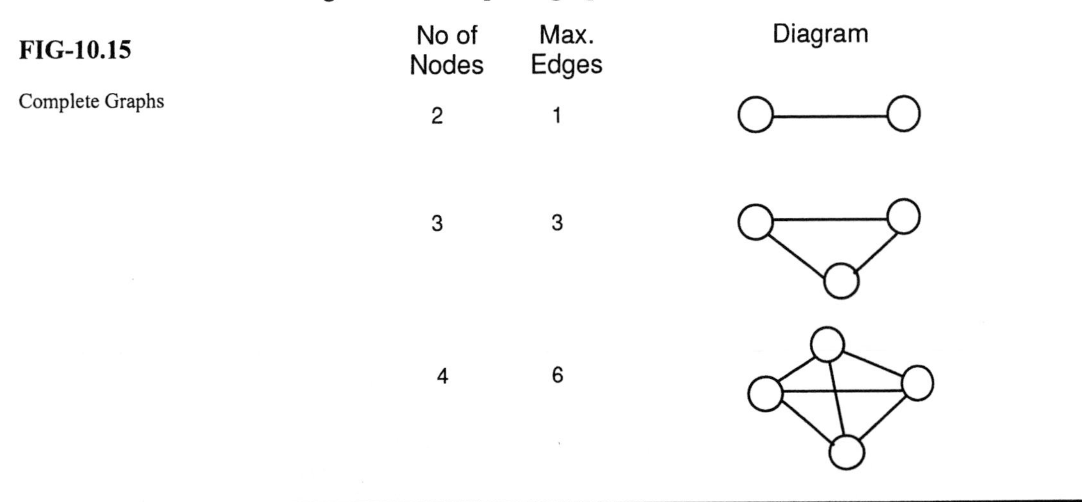

No of Nodes
Max. Edges
Diagram
2
1
3
3
4
6


**FIG-10.15**

Complete Graphs

# Directed Graphs

In a directed graph, edges indicate a one-way connection between nodes. This is shown graphically as an arrowed line (see FIG-10.16).

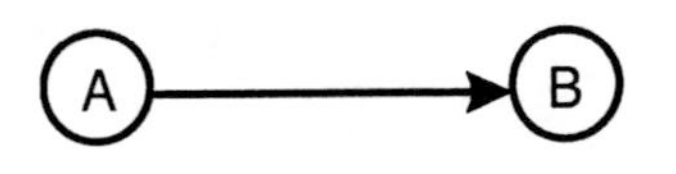


**FIG-10.16**

A One-way Connection in a Directed Graph

Where a connection exists in both directions between nodes then two lines are required (see FIG-10.17).

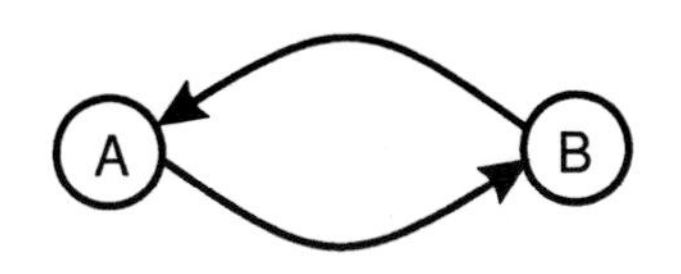


**FIG-10.17**

A Two-way Connection in a Directed Graph

When specifying an edge between a node, A, and another node, B, then the starting node is given first. Hence the edge in FIG-10.16 is identified as (A,B), while those in FIG-10.17 are (A,B) and (B,A).

# Abstract Definition of a Graph

Typical operations for a graph data type differ somewhat from other types we have created so far. As well as the usual requirements to add and remove nodes and edges, we need operations to do such things as determine which nodes are adjacent to a given node, and the shortest paths between two nodes.

**ADT Graph is**

DATA

A set of node identifiers and a set of edges

OPERATIONS

| | | |
|---|---|---|
| NAME | : | CreateGraph |
| PARAMETERS | | |
| IN | : | gt : GraphType |
| OUT | : | g : Graph |
| IN/OUT | : | None |
| PRE-CONDITION | : | None |
| POST-CONDITION | : | *g* is created as an empty graph. *gt* specifies which type of graph is to be created: directed or undirected. |

| | | |
|---|---|---|
| NAME | : | AddNode |
| PARAMETERS | | |
| IN | : | n : Node |
| OUT | : | success : BOOLEAN |
| IN/OUT | : | g : Graph |
| PRE-CONDITION | : | None |
| POST-CONDITION | : | If *n* does not already exist in *g* and *g* is not full, *n* is added to *g* and *success* returns *true*, otherwise *g* is unchanged and *success* returns *false*. |

| | | |
|---|---|---|
| NAME | : | AddEdge |
| PARAMETERS | | |
| IN | : | e : Edge |
| OUT | : | success : BOOLEAN |
| IN/OUT | : | g : Graph |
| PRE-CONDITION | : | None |
| POST-CONDITION | : | If *e* does not already exist in *g* and *g* is not full, *e* is added to *g* and *success* returns *true*, otherwise *g* is unchanged and *success* returns *false*. |

| | | |
|---|---|---|
| NAME | : | DeleteEdge |
| PARAMETERS | | |
| IN | : | e : Edge |
| OUT | : | success : BOOLEAN |
| IN/OUT | : | g : Graph |
| PRE-CONDITION | : | None |
| POST-CONDITION | : | If *e* exists in *g*, it is removed from *g* and *success* returns *true*, otherwise *g* is unchanged and *success* returns *false*. |

| | | |
|---|---|---|
| NAME | : | DeleteNode |
| PARAMETERS | | |
| IN | : | n : Node |
| OUT | : | success : BOOLEAN |
| IN/OUT | : | g : Graph |
| PRE-CONDITION | : | None |
| POST-CONDITION | : | If *n* exists in *g*, then *n* and all edges linked to *n* are removed from *g* and *success* returns *true*, otherwise *g* is unchanged and *success* returns *false*. |

| | | |
|---|---|---|
| NAME | : | AdjacentNodes |
| PARAMETERS | | |
| IN | : | n : Node<br>g : Graph |
| OUT | : | nlist: set of Node |
| IN/OUT | : | None |
| PRE-CONDITION | : | None |
| POST-CONDITION | : | *nlist* contains all nodes adjacent to *n* |

```
NAME            :  IsConnected
PARAMETERS
    IN          :  start : Node
                   end : Node
                   g : Graph
    OUT         :  connected : INTEGER
    IN/OUT      :  None
PRE-CONDITION   :  start and end are valid node names
POST-CONDITION  :  Sets connected to 1 if a path exists between the two
                   nodes start and end, otherwise connected is set to zero.

NAME            :  ShortestPath
PARAMETERS
    IN          :  start : Node
                   end : Node
                   g : Graph
    OUT         :  path : Stack
    IN/OUT      :  None
PRE-CONDITION   :  start and end must be in g
POST-CONDITION  :  path contains, in order, the nodes which make up the
                   shortest path (least edges)between start and end

NAME            :  DisplayGraph
PARAMETERS
    IN          :  g : Graph
    OUT         :  None
    IN/OUT      :  None
PRE-CONDITION   :  None
POST-CONDITION  :  if there are any nodes in g then the contents of g is
                   displayed else no output is produced.
END ADT
```

Note that there is no need to differentiate between directed and undirected graphs at this stage.

# Implementing a Graph

## Data

**FIG-10.18**

Storing Nodes

| | |
|---|---|
| 0 | Glasgow |
| 1 | London |
| 2 | Boston |
| 3 | Atlanta |
| 4 | Orlando |
| 5 | Lisbon |
| 6 | Paris |
| 7 | Berlin |
| 8 | Rome |
| 9 | Moscow |

The data components of a graph consist of a set of nodes and a set of edges.

The node names can be held in a string array (see FIG-10.18).
The simplest way to hold the edges of the graph is in a matrix. Each node is represented by one row and one column. Where two nodes are connected by an edge, the corresponding matrix cell holds the distance between the two nodes. For example, if we assume a distance of 3700 miles between *Glasgow* and *Boston* this connection is represented by placing this value (3700) in the corresponding cells. In an undirected graph, the value is placed in the cells representing both the (*Glasgow,Boston*) and (*Boston,Glasgow*) edges (see FIG-10.19).

**Activity 10.14**

How is the edge between Boston and Atlanta represented if the distance between the two nodes is 1000.

**FIG-10.19**

Representing the Edges

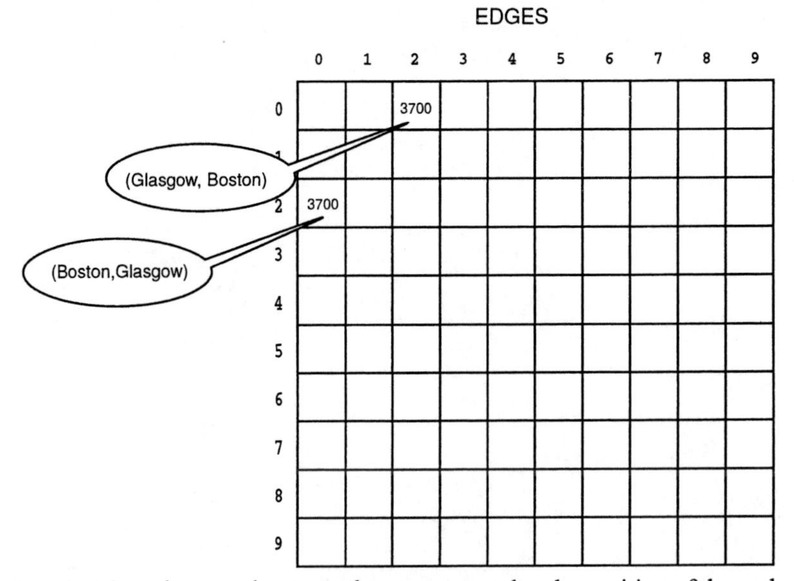


Note that the column and row numbers correspond to the position of the node name in the earlier table. Hence, row 5 and column 5 represent *Lisbon*.

Additionally, it will be useful to maintain a count of the number of nodes in the graph and an indication of the graph type: directed or undirected. All of this can be achieved by the declarations given below.

```
const
    MAXNODES = 10; {max nodes in graph}
type
    GraphType =(directed, undirected);
    Graph =
    record
        count       : integer;      {No. of nodes in graph}
        gtype       : GraphType;    {Directed/undirected}
        nodenames   : array[0..MAXNODES-1]of string[21];
                                    {names of nodes}
        connections : array[0..MAXNODES-1,0..MAXNODES-1]of integer;
                                    {List of edges}
    end;
```

## Operations

### CreateGraph

The first operation, *CreateGraph*, is only required to set the *count* and *gtype* fields of our structure:

```
{*** Create a new graph ***}
procedure CreateGraph(gt:GraphType;var g:Graph);
begin
    g.count := 0;
    g.gtype := gt;
end;
```

### AddNode

This routine requires a new node name to be added to the *nodenames* array. If the name already exists, the structure is unchanged. Additionally, since we've implemented the data structure with fixed-size arrays, we'll also need to check that there is sufficient space for the new entry.

To search the existing node names list, it will be useful to create an auxiliary function, *NodeAt*, which returns the position in *nodenames* of a specified node; where the node does not exist, the function will return -1. This additional function is coded as:

```
{*** Find position of node ***}
function NodeAt(name:string;g: Graph):integer;
var
    post:integer;
begin
    post := 0;
    while (g.nodenames[post] <> name) and (post < g.count) do
        inc(post);
    if g.nodenames[post] = name then
        NodeAt := post
    else
        NodeAt := -1;
end;
```

We're now ready to code the *AddNode* operation:

```
{*** Add a new node to graph ***}
function AddNode(newname:string;var g: Graph):boolean;
begin
    {***IF graph full or name exists THEN exit ***}
    if(g.count = MAXNODES)or(NodeAt(newname,g) <> -1) then
        AddNode := false
    else
    begin
        {*** Copy name to node names list ***}
        g.nodenames[g.count] := newname;
        {*** Increment node count***}
        Inc(g.count);
        AddNode := true;
    end
end;
```

### AddEdge

To add an edge we need to specify the two nodes which the edge is to join and the distance or cost of the edge. For example, if we wish to create an edge between *Glasgow* and *Boston*, with a distance of 3700, the routine must first check that the the two nodes exist and then add the value 3700 to the appropriate cell in the connections matrix (*g.connections[0][2]*). If the graph is undirected, we need to add the corresponding edge (*Boston, Glasgow*) by placing the value 3700 in *g.connections[2][0]* (see FIG-10.19). The code for the routine is:

```
{*** Add new edge ***}
function AddEdge(sn,fn:string;cost:integer;var g:Graph):boolean;
var
    pstart, pend : integer;    {*** Position of nodes in matrix}
begin
    {*** Determine position of nodes ***}
    pstart := NodeAt(sn,g);
    pend := NodeAt(fn,g);
    {*** IF nodes not found THEN return zero ***}
    if(pstart = -1)or(pend = -1) then
        AddEdge := false
    else
    begin
        {*** Add edge ***}
        g.connections[pstart][pend] := cost;
        {*** IF undirected graph THEN add return connection ***}
        if(g.gtype = undirected) then
            g.connections[pend][pstart] := cost;
        AddEdge := true;
    end
end;
```

## DeleteEdge

To remove an edge all that is required is to place a zero in the corresponding cell of the connections matrix. Of course, if the graph is undirected, then two cells are affected.

```
{*** Delete edge ***}
function DeleteEdge(sn,fn:string;var g:Graph):boolean;
var
    pstart, pend : integer;
begin
    {*** Determine position of nodes ***}
    pstart := NodeAt(sn,g);
    pend := NodeAt(fn,g);
    {*** IF nodes not found THEN return false ***}
    if(pstart = -1) or (pend = -1) then
        DeleteEdge := false
    else
    begin
        {*** Set connection to zero ***}
        g.connections[pstart][pend] := 0;
        {*** IF undirect THEN set opposite connection to zero ***}
        if g.gtype = undirected then
            g.connections[pend,pstart] := 0;
        DeleteEdge := true;
    end;
end;
```

## DeleteNode

Removing a node is a much more complex operation since it has a widespread affect on other components in the graph as it is implemented.

For example, FIG-10.20, shows a graph with only four nodes and three connections.

**FIG-10.20**

The Graph before Removing a Node

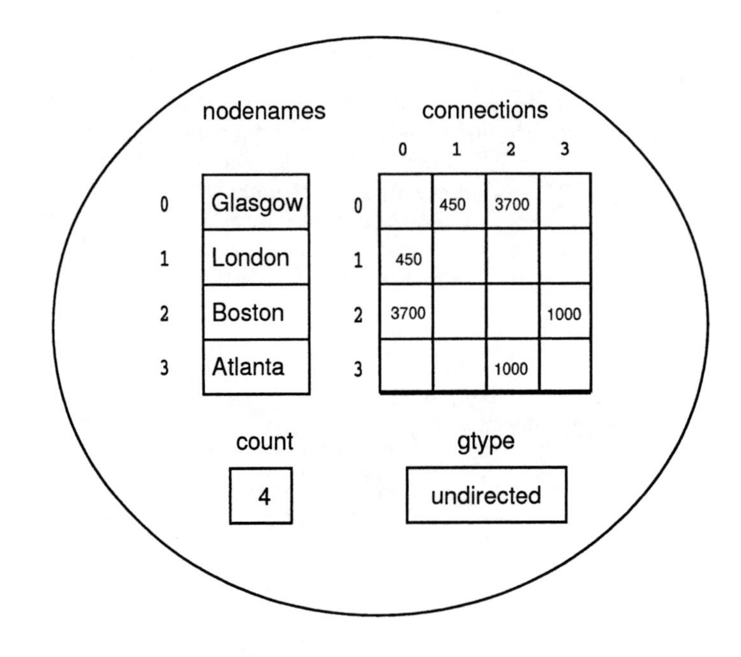


If we remove *London* from the graph, FIG-10.21 shows what changes are required.

As you see, this requires the row and column for *London* to be removed and the contents of subsequent rows and columns to be moved.

**FIG-10.21**

The Graph after a Node has been Removed

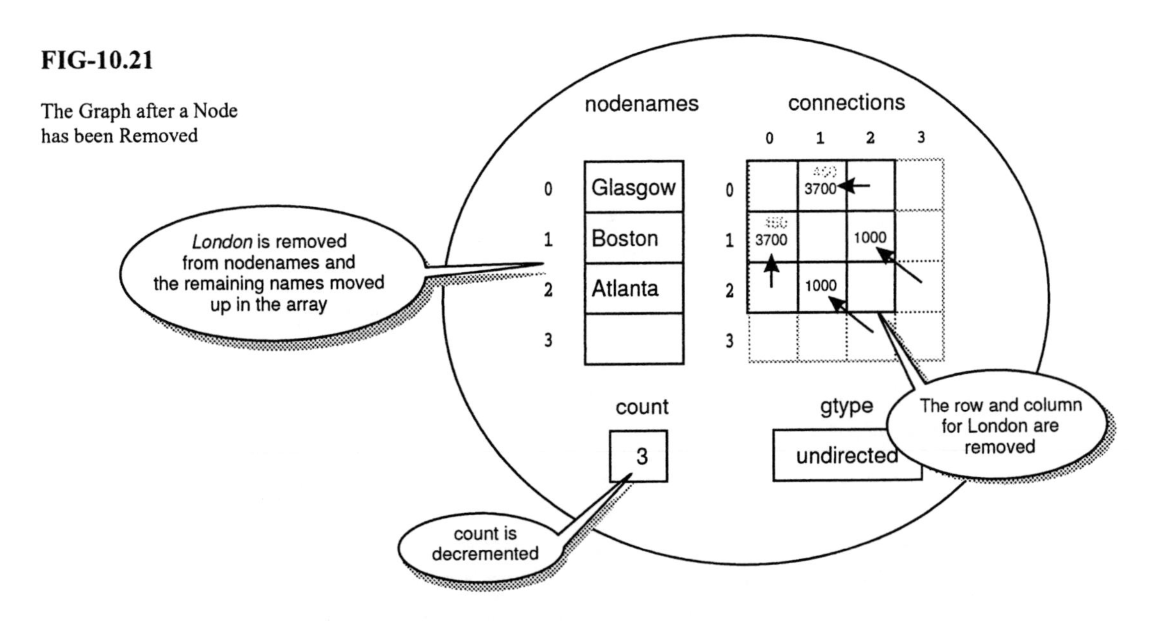


The code required to achieve these changes is:

```
{*** Delete node ***}
function DeleteNode(name:string;var g:Graph):boolean;
var
    nodeno : integer;
    r, c   : integer;
begin
    {** Find node in graph ***}
    nodeno := NodeAt(name,g);
    {*** IF not found, return false ***}
    if nodeno = -1 then
    begin
        DeleteNode := false;
        exit;
    end;
    {*** Remove node name ***}
    for r := nodeno + 1 to g.count - 1 do
        g.nodenames[r - 1] := g.nodenames[r];
    {*** Remove node's row ***}
    for r := nodeno + 1 to g.count - 1 do
        for c := 0 to g.count - 1 do
            g.connections[r-1,c] := g.connections[r,c];
    {*** Reduce count ***}
    Dec(g.count);
    {*** Remove node's column ***}
    for c := nodeno + 1 to g.count do
        for r := 0 to g.count - 1 do
            g.connections[r,c-1] := g.connections[r,c];
    DeleteNode := true;
end;
```

**AdjacentNodes**

To determine which nodes are directly connected to some specified node we need only scan the specified node's row in the connections matrix for non-zero values. The columns in which these non-zero values occur give us, by accessing the corresponding element in the nodenames list, the names of adjacent nodes. For example, FIG-10.22 shows the connections to *Glasgow*.

**FIG-10.22**

Determining Adjacent Nodes

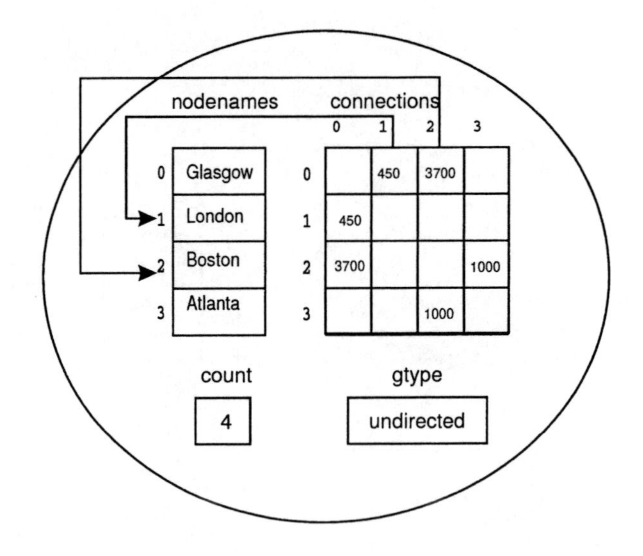


In order to return a list of such nodes a *Queue* variable is used to store the names.

NOTE: the *Data* component of the List data structure (which is used within a Queue) has been redefined as

```
Data =
   record
      FText : string[20];
   end;
```

```
{*** Return adjacent nodes ***}
function AdjacentNodes(name:string; g:Graph;
                                    var adjnodes:Queue):boolean;
var
   post, c : integer;
   d       : Data;
begin
   CreateQueue(adjnodes);
   post := NodeAt(name,g);
   if post = -1 then
   begin
      AdjacentNodes := false;
      exit;
   end;
   for c := 0 to g.count-1 do
      if g.connections[post,c] <> 0then
      begin
         d.Ftext := g.nodenames[c];
         InsertQ(d,adjnodes);
      end;
   AdjacentNodes := true;
end;
```

**IsConnected**

We need to work a bit harder to find out if two specified nodes are connected, since they may be connected indirectly through several nodes. For example, *Glasgow* and *Orlando* are connected via *Boston*.

To determine if a path exists between two nodes we need to start at the first node and move through the other connected nodes until our destination node is arrived at or there are no more nodes to visit. This is called **graph traversal**.

There are two methods of traversing a graph.

One method of visiting each node in a graph is called **depth-first** traversing. This is similar in technique to traversing a tree. Unlike a tree, a graph has no obvious beginning, so to begin a search we must specify a starting node. Let's assume we want to start traversing our graph from *Glasgow* (see FIG-10.23).

**FIG-10.23**

Starting a Depth-First Traversal

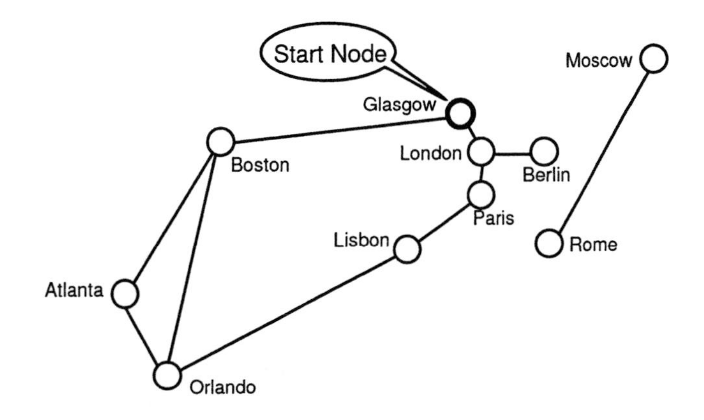


Next, a node adjacent to the first is visited. If there are several adjacent nodes any one will do.

In this case, we'll assume *Boston* is visited (see FIG-10.24).

**FIG-10.24**

Visit a Node Adjacent to Glasgow

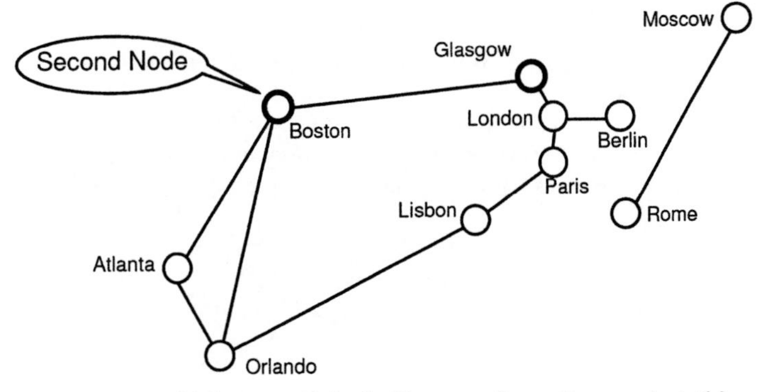


Of course, we could have revisited *Glasgow* from *Boston,* but this would be pointless so it is important to keep note of which nodes have already been visited when traversing the graph.

Next, we visit a node adjacent to *Boston* (see FIG-10.25).

**FIG-10.25**

Visit a Node Adjacent to Boston

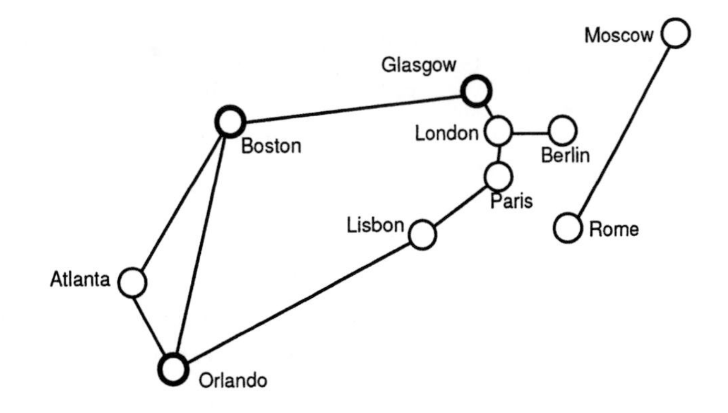


We now move on from *Orlando* to another adjacent node (see FIG-10.26).

**FIG-10.26**

Visit a Node Adjacent to Orlando

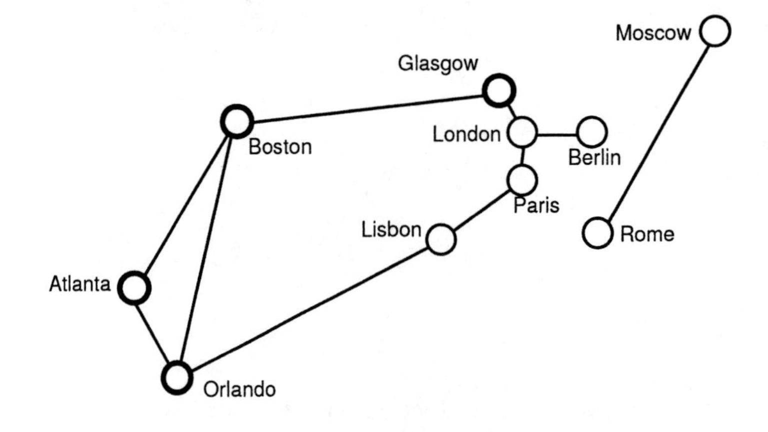


At this stage, we have reached a dead-end. There are no unvisited nodes adjacent to *Atlanta*. In this situation, we begin backtracking along the path we have taken until we find a node which has adjacent nodes which have not yet been visited. Using this strategy, we arrive back at *Orlando* and from there we can move on to *Lisbon.*

From *Lisbon* we move on through *Paris* and *London* until, finally, *Berlin* is reached.

With no further new nodes to be reached from Berlin, we backtrack through *London, Paris,Lisbon,Orlando* and *Boston* to our starting point in *Glasgow* and since none of these have any new nodes to be visited the traversal is complete.

This new routine, which we'll call *DeepSearch*, returns an array indicating which nodes have been visited. Hence, if *Lisbon* (node 5) is visited, element 5 of the array will contain a 1; array elements corresponding to nodes which have not been visited will contain a zero.

The routine parameters specify the start node, the graph to be searched, and returns an indication of the nodes visited.

```
{*** Search graph ***}
procedure DeepSearch(name:string;var g:Graph; var visited:Queue);
var
    temp:Data;
    c:integer;
begin
    temp.Ftext:=name;
    InsertQ(temp,visited);
    for c:=0 to g.count-1 do
    begin
        temp.Ftext:=g.nodenames[c];
        if(g.connections[NodeAt(name,g),c]<>0) then
            if (not(IsIn(temp,visited))) then
                DeepSearch(g.nodenames[c],g,visited);
    end
end;
```

This time, the routine has been coded recursively; it is equally possible to create a non-recursive version using a Stack to hold previously visited nodes.

It's now a simple matter to code *IsConnected* by simply beginning at the starting node (parameter *sn*) and checking the array returned by *DeepSearch* to determine if the destination node (*fn*) has been visited during the search.

```
{*** Check if two nodes are connected ***}
function IsConnected(sn,fn : string; g:Graph):boolean;
var
    visited : Queue;
    temp    : Data;
begin
    CreateQueue(visited);
    DeepSearch(sn,g,visited);
    temp.Ftext := fn;
    if IsIn(temp,visited) then
        IsConnected := true
    else
        IsConnected := false;
end;
```

### ShortestPath

Our final operation, *ShortestPath*, requires a second method of traversal known as **breadth-first** traversal. With this approach we first visit ALL of the nodes adjacent to the starting node. This means that, if we start at *Glasgow*, we visit *Boston* and *London* (see FIG-10.27).

**FIG-10.27**

Visit All Nodes Adjacent to Glasgow

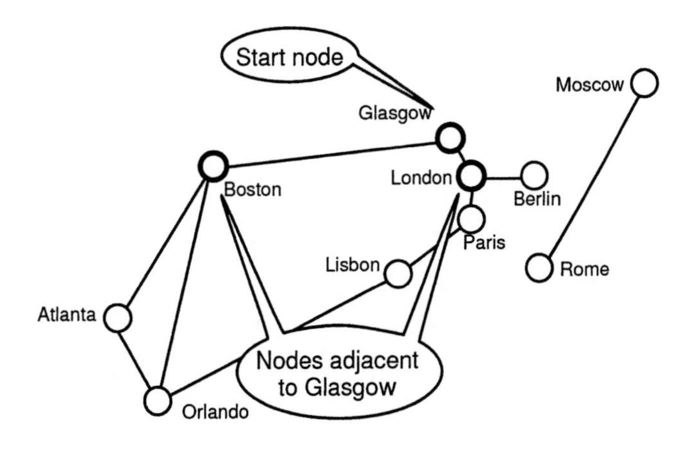


These nodes are, rather obviously, exactly one edge away from the starting node. We can say that there is a distance of one between *Glasgow* and *Boston* and between *Glasgow* and *London*.

For every node which is a distance of one away from our starting node (i.e. *Boston* and *London*) we visit ALL of their adjacent nodes. So from *Boston* we visit *Atlanta* and *Orlando* while from *London* we visit *Paris* and *Berlin* (see FIG-10.28).

**FIG-10.28**

Visit All Nodes at a Distance of Two from Glasgow

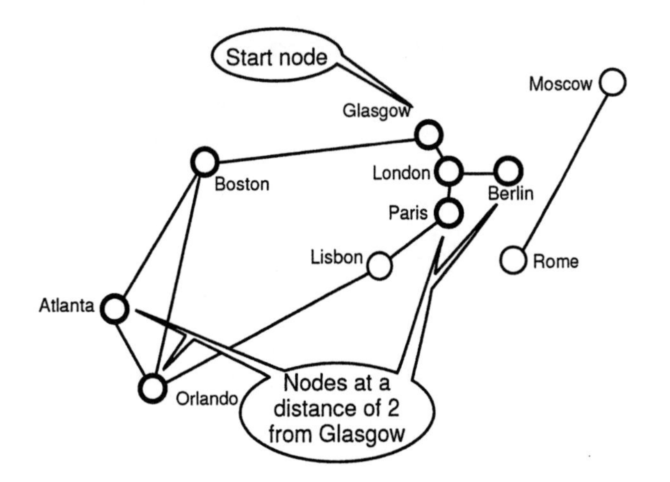

The nodes visited on this second stage (i.e. *Atlanta*, *Orlando*, *Paris* and *Berlin*) have a distance of two from our starting node.

The same strategy is repeated and we visit all unvisited nodes adjacent to *Atlanta*, *Orlando*, *Paris* and *Berlin*. This results in only one new node being visited, *Lisbon*, which has a distance of three from *Glasgow*. Since there are no unvisited nodes adjacent to Lisbon, the search is complete.

That is the principle behind a width-first search but in order to put the theory into practice we need to use a Queue data structure to hold the nodes whose adjacent nodes are still to be visited. We also need an array to hold the distance to a given node from the starting node.

We begin by creating an empty queue and setting each entry in the table of distances to -1. This value represents a non-visited node (see FIG-10.29).

**FIG-10.29**

Initialising a Wide Search

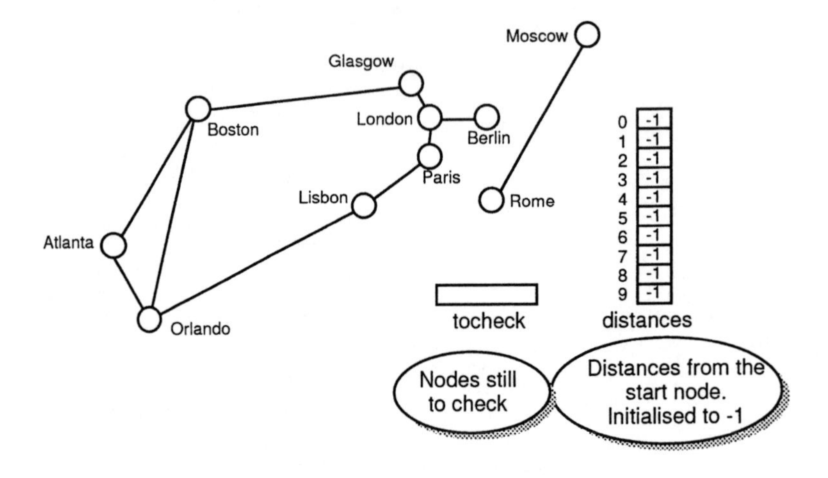


We visit the starting node; place it in the queue and set the distance to node 1 (Glasgow) to zero in the *distances* array(see FIG-10.30).

**FIG-10.30**

The Start Node

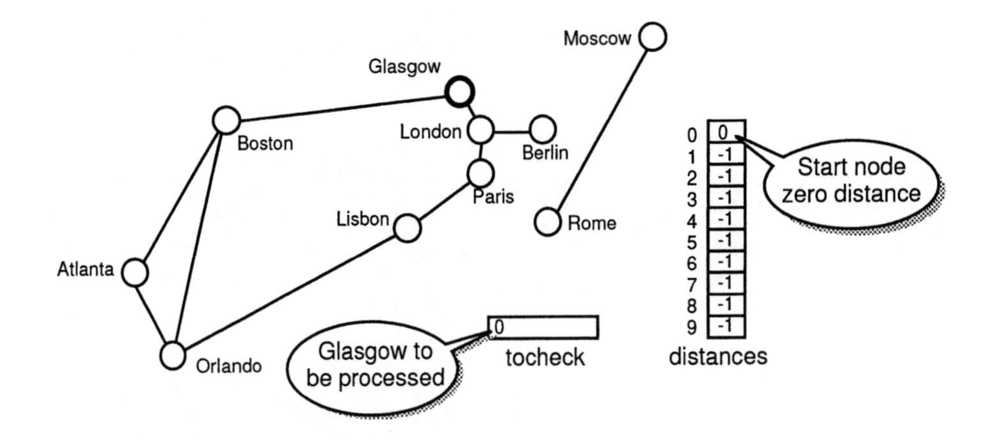


The node at the front of the queue is removed and its adjacent nodes visited. Those visited are added to the queue and their distances set to 1 (see FIG-10.31).

**FIG-10.31**

Process Nodes Adjacent to Glasgow

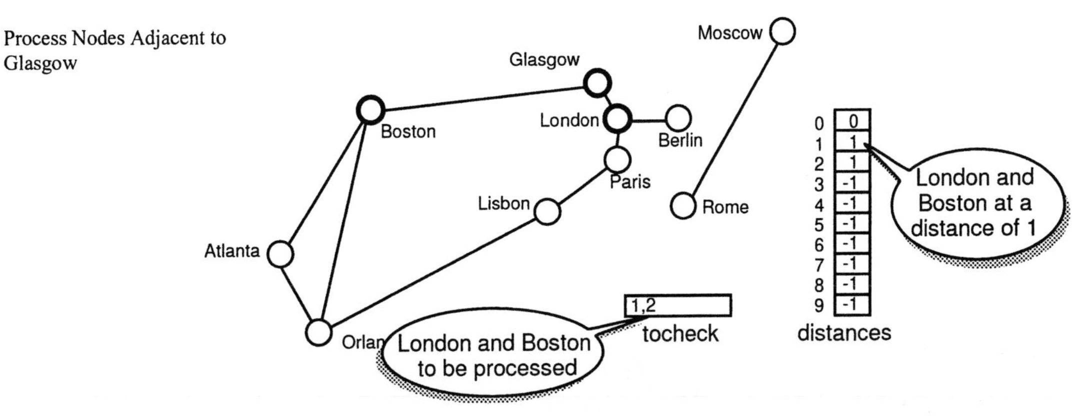


Again we remove the node at the front of the queue; check its distance from the starting node; and visit each of its adjacent nodes. Each node is placed on the queue and its distance from the starting node recorded (see FIG-10.32).

**FIG-10.32**

Process Nodes Adjacent to London

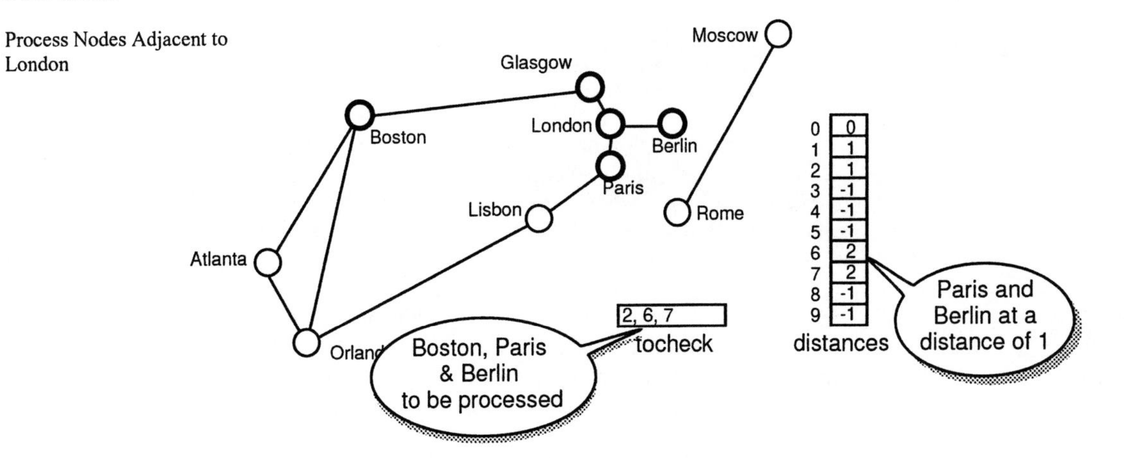


This process continues until the traversal is complete. In the case of the above example, completion of the traversal will result in the distance array containing the values:

| 0 | 1 | 2 | 3 | 4 | 5 | 6 | 7 | 8 | 9 |
|---|---|---|---|---|---|---|---|---|---|
| 0 | 1 | 1 | 2 | 2 | 3 | 2 | 2 | -1 | -1 |

The code for this search routine is given below:

```
procedure WideSearch(nodeno : integer; g : Graph;
                              var distance : distanceType);
var
    tocheck      : Queue;
    v            : Data;
    c            : integer;
    distanceout  : integer;
    city         : Data;
    currentnode  : integer;
    err          : integer;
begin
    {*** Set distances to -1 ***}
    for c := 0 to g.count - 1 do
        distance[c] := -1;
```

```
    {*** Initialise queue ***}
    CreateQueue(tocheck);
    {*** Set distance from start node ***}
    distanceout := -1;
    distance[nodeno] := 0;
    {*** Place start node in queue ***}
    Str(nodeno,v.Ftext);
    InsertQ(v,tocheck);
    {*** WHILE queue not empty DO ***}
    while not IsEmptyQ(tocheck) do
    begin
        {*** Get front of queue ***}
        Front(tocheck,city);
        Val(city.FText,currentnode,err);
        DeleteQ(tocheck);
        {*** IF node further than previous, inc. distanceout ***}
        if distance[currentnode] > distanceout then
            Inc(distanceout);
        {*** Set adjacent node distance and place in queue ***}
        for c := 0 to g.count - 1 do
            if(g.connections[currentnode,c] <> 0) and
                (distance[c] = -1)
            then
            begin
                distance[c] := distanceout + 1;
                Str(c,v.Ftext);
                InsertQ(v,tocheck);
            end;
    end;
    {*** De-allocate space ***}
    EmptyQueue(tocheck);
end;
```

We only require one more step to display the shortest path between two nodes. If we assume we want to travel from *Glasgow* to *Orlando* we can see from the graph that *Orlando* is a distance of two edges from *Glasgow*. But which two edges? To find out we start at *Orlando* and look for an adjacent node which is closer to *Glasgow* (i.e. a node with a distance of one). If there is more than one node which meets this requirement any one will do. Here there is only one - *Boston*. From *Boston* we look for an adjacent node nearer to *Glasgow*. This time it is *Glasgow* itself with a distance of zero. Assuming we have recorded our steps from destination to start node we merely display it in reverse order (*Glasgow, Boston, Orlando*) to give the path from *Glasgow* to *Orlando*. We can describe the logic of this routine as:

```
Determine the distance to all other nodes from the start node
Push the finish node onto an empty stack
Set currentnode to finish node
WHILE not back at start node DO
    Find a node adjacent to the current node which is nearer
     the start node
    Push this node onto the stack
    Make this the currentnode
ENDWHILE
```

From this, we derive the code:

```
{*** Get shortest path between two nodes ***}
procedure ShortestPath(sn, fn : string; g : Graph; var s : Stack);
var
    visited : DistanceType;
    startno : integer;
    endno   : integer;
    c       : integer;
    v       : Data;
    temp    : Data;
    post    : integer;
    currentposition : integer;
    currentdistance : integer;
    q       : Queue;
begin
```

```
    {*** Determine number of start and finish nodes ***}
    startno := NodeAt(sn,g);
    endno   := NodeAt(fn,g);
    CreateStack(s);
    {*** IF nodes invalid OR not connected THEN exit ***}
    if (startno = -1) or (endno = -1) or
        (not IsConnected(sn,fn,g))
    then
        exit;
    {*** Determine distances to all other connected nodes ***}
    WideSearch(startno,g,visited);
    {*** Place end node on empty stack ***}
    v.Ftext := g.nodenames[endno];
    Push(v,s);
    currentposition := endno;
    currentdistance := visited[endno];
    {*** WHILE not back at start node DO ***}
    while currentposition <> startno do
    begin
        {*** Find closer adjacent node and place on stack ***}
        AdjacentNodes(g.nodenames[currentposition],g,q);
        Front(q,v);
        post := NodeAt(v.FText,g);
        while visited[post] >= currentdistance do
        begin
            DeleteQ(q);
            Front(q,v);
            post := NodeAt(v.FText,g);
        end;
        Push(v,s);
        currentposition := post;
        Dec(currentdistance);
        EmptyQueue(q);
    end;
end;
```

**FIG-10.33**

Shortest Path

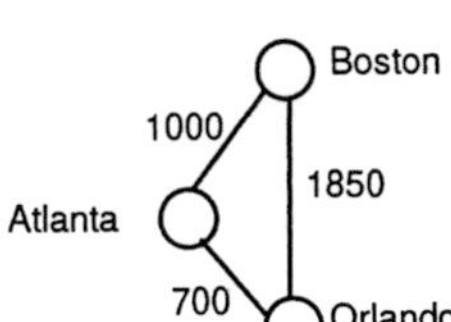


It should be emphasised that the above operation finds the route containing fewest edges between two nodes, not the shortest routine in terms of distance. Hence, for the graph shown in FIG-10.33, the route returned would be *Boston, Orlando* and not *Boston, Atlanta, Orlando* which has the shorter distance.

## DisplayGraph

This routine displays the structure of the graph in the form of a matrix. For example, in the graph in FIG-10.33 above, containing only the *Atlanta*, *Boston* and *Orlando* nodes would produce the output:

GRAPH

| | Atlan | Bosto | Orlan |
|---|---|---|---|
| Atlanta | 0 | 1000 | 700 |
| Boston | 1000 | 0 | 1850 |
| Orlando | 700 | 1850 | 0 |

Note that the columns are identified using only the first 5 characters from the node name; this allows identical column widths in the display.

**FIG-10.34**

A Directed Graph

Boston
1000
1850
Atlanta
700
Orlando

The sample output assumes an undirected graph; for a directed graph such as that in FIG-10.34, the output would be:

GRAPH

| | Atlan | Bosto | Orlan |
|---|---|---|---|
| Atlanta | 0 | 1000 | 0 |
| Boston | 0 | 0 | 1850 |
| Orlando | 700 | 0 | 0 |

The code required for this routine is

```
{*** Display graph ***}
procedure DisplayGraph(g:Graph);
var
    temp:string[6];
    c,k:integer;
begin
    writeln('GRAPH':46,#10#10#13);
    write(' ':22);
    for c:= 0 to g.count-1 do
        write(copy(g.nodenames[c],1,6):7);
    writeln;
    for c:=0 to g.count-1 do
    begin
        write(g.nodenames[c],' ':22-length(g.nodenames[c]));
        for k:=0 to g.count-1 do
            write(g.connections[c,k]:5,'  ');
        writeln;
    end
end;
```

## The Program

At this point we're just about ready to create the complete program. However, to reduce the size of the code, it is worth starting by creating Pascal Units for the *List*, *Stack* and *Queue* data structures. Since we require node names to be held in these structures we'll have to define the *Data* structure as

```
struct Data
{
    char  no[21];
};
```

which will allow us node names of up to 20 characters in length.

The code that follows (see LISTING-10.2) assumes the existence of the Pascal Units *ListU, StackU, QueueU* and *Auxiliary.*

**LISTING-10.2**

Implementing a Graph

```
program GraphU;
uses WinCrt,StackU,QueueU,ListU, Auxiliary;
{***********************************}
{*** Graph Data Type Declarations ***}
{***********************************}
{*** Data ***}
const
  MAXNODES = 12; {Max nodes in graph}
type
  GraphType =(directed, undirected);
  Graph =
  record
      count       : integer;     {No. of nodes in graph}
      gtype       : GraphType;   {Directed/undirected}
      nodenames   : array[0..MAXNODES-1]of string[21];
                                 {names of nodes}
      connections : array[0..MAXNODES-1,0..MAXNODES-1]of integer;
                                 {List of edges}
  end;
  DistanceType = array[0..MAXNODES-1] of integer;
{**********************************}
{*** Graph Routines Definitions ***}
{**********************************}
```

**Continued on next page**

**LISTING-10.2**
(continued)

Implementing a Graph

```
{*** Create a new graph ***}
procedure CreateGraph(gt:GraphType;var g:Graph);
begin
  g.count:=0;
  g.gtype := gt;
end;

{*** Find position of node ***}
function NodeAt(name:string;g: Graph):integer;
var
   post:integer;
begin
  post := 0;
  while (g.nodenames[post] <> name) and (post < g.count) do
      inc(post);
  if g.nodenames[post] = name then
      NodeAt := post
  else
      NodeAt := -1;
end;


{*** Add a new node to graph ***}
function AddNode(newname:string;var g: Graph):boolean;
begin
  {***IF graph full or name exists THEN exit ***}
  if(g.count = MAXNODES)or(NodeAt(newname,g) <> -1) then
      AddNode := false
  else
  begin
      {*** Copy name to node names list ***}
      g.nodenames[g.count] := newname;
      {*** Increment node count***}
      Inc(g.count);
      AddNode := true;
  end
end;


{*** Add new edge ***}
function AddEdge(sn,fn:string;cost:integer;
                                     var g:Graph) : boolean;
var
  pstart, pend : integer;    {*** Position of nodes in matrix}
begin
  {*** Determine position of nodes ***}
  pstart := NodeAt(sn,g);
  pend := NodeAt(fn,g);
  {*** IF nodes not found THEN return zero ***}
  if(pstart = -1)or(pend = -1) then
      AddEdge := false
  else
  begin
      {*** Add edge ***}
      g.connections[pstart][pend] := cost;
      {*** IF undirected graph THEN add return connection ***}
      if(g.gtype = undirected) then
          g.connections[pend][pstart] := cost;
      AddEdge := true;
  end
end;


{*** Delete a node ***}
function DeleteNode(name:string;var g:Graph):boolean;
var
  nodeno : integer;
  r, c   : integer;
begin
```

**Continued on next page**

**LISTING-10.2**
(continued)

Implementing a Graph

```
  {** Find node in graph ***}
  nodeno := NodeAt(name,g);
  {*** IF not found, return false ***}
  if nodeno = -1 then
  begin
      DeleteNode := false;
      exit;
  end;
  {*** Remove node name ***}
  for r := nodeno + 1 to g.count - 1 do
      g.nodenames[r - 1] := g.nodenames[r];
  {*** Remove node's row ***}
  for r := nodeno + 1 to g.count - 1 do
      for c := 0 to g.count - 1 do
          g.connections[r-1,c] := g.connections[r,c];
  {*** Reduce count ***}
  Dec(g.count);
  {*** Remove node's column ***}
  for c := nodeno + 1 to g.count do
      for r := 0 to g.count - 1 do
          g.connections[r,c-1] := g.connections[r,c];
  DeleteNode := true;
end;


{*** Delete an edge ***}
function DeleteEdge(sn,fn:string;var g:Graph):boolean;
var
  pstart, pend : integer;
begin
  {*** Determine position of nodes ***}
  pstart := NodeAt(sn,g);
  pend := NodeAt(fn,g);
  {*** IF nodes not found THEN return false ***}
  if(pstart = -1) or (pend = -1) then
      DeleteEdge := false
  else
  begin
      {*** Set connection to zero ***}
      g.connections[pstart][pend] := 0;
      {*** IF undirect THEN set opposite connection to zero ***}
      if g.gtype = undirected then
          g.connections[pend,pstart] := 0;
      DeleteEdge := true;
  end;
end;


{*** Return adjacent nodes ***}
function AdjacentNodes(name:string; g:Graph;
                              var adjnodes:Queue) : boolean;
var
  post,c : integer;
  d      : Data;
begin
  {*** Create empty queue ***}
  CreateQueue(adjnodes);
  {*** If name not found in graph, return false ***}
  post := NodeAt(name,g);
  if post = -1 then
  begin
      AdjacentNodes := false;
      exit;
  end;
  {*** Check every node, if connected add to queue ***}
  for c := 0 to g.count - 1 do
      if(g.connections[post,c] <> 0)then
```

**Continued on next page**

**LISTING-10.2**
(continued)

Implementing a Graph

```
        begin
            d.Ftext := g.nodenames[c];
            InsertQ(d,adjnodes);
        end;
    AdjacentNodes := true;
end;


{*** Deep Search graph ***}
procedure DeepSearch(name:string;var g:Graph; var
visited:Queue);
var
    temp:Data;
    c:integer;
begin
    temp.Ftext:=name;
    InsertQ(temp,visited);
    for c:=0 to g.count-1 do
    begin
        temp.Ftext:=g.nodenames[c];
        if(g.connections[NodeAt(name,g),c]<>0) then
            if (not(IsIn(temp,visited))) then
            DeepSearch(g.nodenames[c],g,visited);
    end
end;


{*** Wide search graph ***}
procedure WideSearch(nodeno : integer; g : Graph;
                                  var distance : distanceType);
var
    tocheck      : Queue;
    v            : Data;
    c            : integer;
    distanceout  : integer;
    city         : Data;
    currentnode  : integer;
    err          : integer;
begin
    {*** Set distances to -1 ***}
    for c := 0 to g.count - 1 do
        distance[c] := -1;
    {*** Initialise queue ***}
    CreateQueue(tocheck);
    {*** Set distance from start node ***}
    distanceout := -1;
    distance[nodeno] := 0;
    {*** Place start node in queue ***}
    Str(nodeno,v.Ftext);
    InsertQ(v,tocheck);
    {*** WHILE queue not empty DO ***}
    while not IsEmptyQ(tocheck) do
    begin
        {*** Get front of queue ***}
        Front(tocheck,city);
        Val(city.FText,currentnode,err);
        DeleteQ(tocheck);
        {*** IF node further than previous, inc. distanceout ***}
        if distance[currentnode] > distanceout then
            Inc(distanceout);
        {*** Set adjacent node distance and place in queue ***}
        for c := 0 to g.count - 1 do
            if(g.connections[currentnode,c] <> 0) and
                (distance[c] = -1)
            then
            begin
                distance[c] := distanceout + 1;
                Str(c,v.Ftext);
                InsertQ(v,tocheck);
            end;
```

**LISTING-10.2**
(continued)

Implementing a Graph

```
   end;
   {*** De-allocate space ***}
   EmptyQueue(tocheck);
end;


{*** Determine if two nodes are connected ***}
function IsConnected(sn,fn : string; g:Graph):boolean;
var
    visited : Queue;
    temp    : Data;
begin
   {*** Create empty queue ***}
   CreateQueue(visited);
   {*** Fill queue with all connected nodes ***}
   DeepSearch(sn,g,visited);
   {*** IF finish node in queue THEN ***}
   temp.Ftext := fn;
   if IsIn(temp,visited) then
        {*** return true ***}
        IsConnected := true
   else
        {*** ELSE return false ***}
        IsConnected := false;
   {*** Deallocated space in queue ***}
   EmptyQueue(visited);
end;


{*** Get shortest path between two nodes ***}
procedure ShortestPath(sn, fn : string; g : Graph;
                                                  var s : Stack);
var
   visited : DistanceType;
   startno : integer;
   endno   : integer;
   c       : integer;
   v       : Data;
   temp    : Data;
   post    : integer;
   currentposition : integer;
   currentdistance : integer;
   q       : Queue;
begin
   {*** Determine number of start and finish nodes ***}
   startno := NodeAt(sn,g);
   endno   := NodeAt(fn,g);
   CreateStack(s);
   {*** IF nodes invalid OR not connected THEN exit ***}
   if (startno = -1) or (endno = -1) or (
        not IsConnected(sn,fn,g))
   then
        exit;
   {*** Determine distances to all other connected nodes ***}
   WideSearch(startno,g,visited);
   {*** Place end node on empty stack ***}
   v.Ftext := g.nodenames[endno];
   Push(v,s);
   currentposition := endno;
   currentdistance := visited[endno];
   {*** WHILE not back at start node DO ***}
   while currentposition <> startno do
   begin
        {*** Find closer adjacent node and place on stack ***}
        AdjacentNodes(g.nodenames[currentposition],g,q);
        Front(q,v);
        post := NodeAt(v.FText,g);
```

**Continued on next page**

**LISTING-10.2**
(continued)

Implementing a Graph

```
        while visited[post] >= currentdistance do
        begin
            DeleteQ(q);
            Front(q,v);
            post := NodeAt(v.FText,g);
        end;
        Push(v,s);
        currentposition := post;
        Dec(currentdistance);
        EmptyQueue(q);
    end;
end;


{*** Display graph ***}
procedure DisplayGraph(g:Graph);
var
    temp:string[6];
     c,k:integer;
begin
    writeln('GRAPH':46,#10#10#13);
    write(' ':22);
     for c:= 0 to g.count-1 do
        write(copy(g.nodenames[c],1,6):7);
    writeln;
    for c:=0 to g.count-1 do
    begin
        write(g.nodenames[c],' ':22-length(g.nodenames[c]));
        for k:=0 to g.count-1 do
            write(g.connections[c,k]:5,'  ');
        writeln;
    end
end;

{*****************************}
{*** END Graph Definitions ***}
{*****************************}


{*** Execute option chosen from menu ***}
procedure ExecuteOption(opt:integer;var g:Graph);
var
    name:string[21];
    start,finish:string[21];
    adjnodes,visited:Queue;
    cost:integer;
    path : Stack;
begin
    case opt of
        1:CreateGraph(undirected,g);
        2:begin
            write('Enter node name : ');
            readln(name);
            AddNode(name,g);
          end;
        3:begin
            write('Enter start node : ');
            readln(start);
            write('Enter finish node : ');
            readln(finish);
            write('Enter cost of edge : ');
            readln(cost);
            AddEdge(start,finish,cost,g);
          end;
        4:begin
            write('Enter node to be removed : ');
            readln(name);
            DeleteNode(name,g);
          end;
```

**Continued on next page**

**LISTING-10.2**
(continued)

Implementing a Graph

```
        5:begin
            write('Enter start node : ');
            readln(start);
            write('Enter finish node : ');
            readln(finish);
            DeleteEdge(start,finish,g);
          end;
        6:begin
            write('Enter start node : ');
            readln(name);
            write('Enter destination node : ');
            readln(finish);
            if IsConnected(name,finish,g) then
                writeln('Connected')
            else
                writeln('Not connected');
            readkey;
          end;
        7:begin
            write('Enter node : ');
            readln(name);
            CreateQueue(adjnodes);
            AdjacentNodes(name,g,adjnodes);
            DisplayQ(adjnodes);
            readkey;
          end;
        8:begin
            write('Enter start node : ');
            readln(name);
            CreateQueue(visited);
            DeepSearch(name,g,visited);
            DisplayQ(visited);
            readkey;
          end;
        9:begin
            DisplayGraph(g);
            readkey;
          end;
        10:begin
            write('Enter start node : ');
            readln(start);
            write('Enter finish node : ');
            readln(finish);
            ShortestPath(start,finish,g,path);
            DisplayS(path);
            ReadKey;
           end;
        11:writeln('PROGRAM TERMINATED');
  end
end;


const
  NL = #13#10;
var
  g:Graph;
  opt, noofopts:integer;
begin
  CreateGraph(undirected,g);
   repeat
       ClrScr;
       noofopts := DisplayMenu('1 - CreateGraph'+NL+
                     '2 - Add Node'+NL+'3 - Add Edge'+NL+
                     '4 - Remove Node'+NL+'5 - Remove Edge'+NL+
                     '6 - Test for connection'+NL+
                     '7 - List Adjacent Nodes'+NL+
                     '8 - List Connected Nodes'+NL+
                     '9 - Display graph'+NL+
                     '10 - Shortest path'+NL+'11- QUIT'+NL);
```

**Continued on next page**

**LISTING-10.2**
(continued)

Implementing a Graph

```
        opt := GetOption(noofopts);
        ExecuteOption(opt,g);
    until opt=noofopts;
   readkey;
end.
```

# Summary

- **A graph is** constructed from nodes and edges.
- **In an undirected graph**, an edge operates in both directions.
- **In a directed graph**, an edge operates in a single direction.
- **A path** is the list of nodes which are passed through when travelling from one node to another.
- **A connected graph** is one in which a path exists between any node and every other node.

# SOLUTIONS

## Activity 10.1

No solution required.

## Activity 10.2

```
Function Len2(seq : List): integer;
begin
    if IsEmpty(seq) then
        Len2 := 0;
    else
    begin
        Tail(seq);
        Len2 := 1 + Len2(seq);
    end;
end;
```

## Activity 10.3

```
program recursion2;
uses WinCrt;

function Fibonacci(n : integer): longint;
begin
    if n <= 2 then
        Fibonacci := 1
    else
        Fibonacci := Fibonacci(n - 1) +
                                 Fibonacci(n - 2);
end;


var
    nbr : longint;
begin
    ClrScr;
    write('Enter Fibonacci term to be found : ');
    readln(nbr);
    writeln('Term ',nbr,' is ',Fibonacci(nbr));
end.
```

## Activity 10.4

This routine adds the parameter *c* to the end of the List *s*.

## Activity 10.5

1. Root = 67

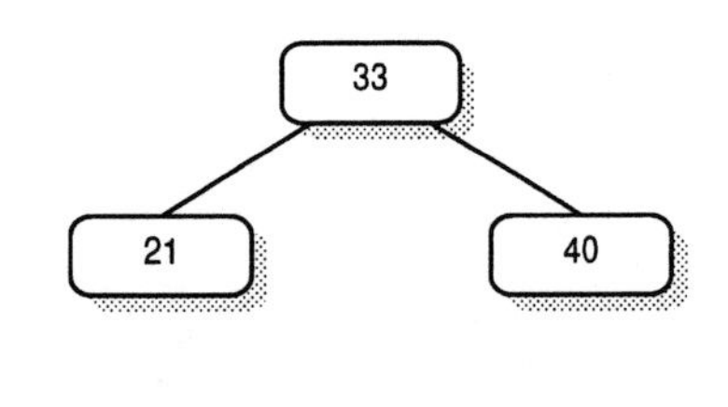


2.

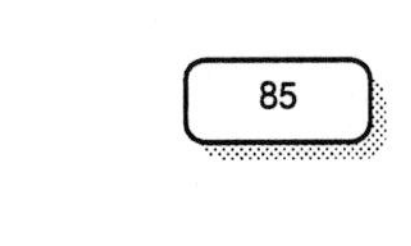


3.

4. 40

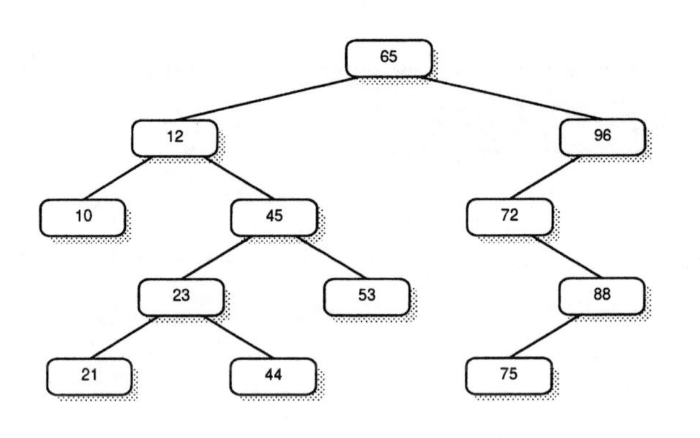


## Activity 10.6

1.

2. 4

## Activity 10.7

a) *t* is unchanged

b) Attempting to find the root of an empty tree will not satisfy the pre-condition of the Root operation and hence the result is undefined (i.e. this is an illegal operation).

## Activity 10.8

```
{*** procedure AddToTree - non-recursive ***}
procedure AddToTree(v : Data; var t : BSTree);
var
    current : NodePointerType;   {Current node }
    parent  : NodePointerType;
    temp    : NodePointerType;   {new node for tree}
begin
     {*** Set current to root ***}
     current := t;
     {*** which as no parent ***}
     parent := NIL;
     {*** WHILE not at bottom of tree DO ***}
     while current <> NIL do
     begin
        {*** Old current becomes parent ***}
        parent := current;
        {*** IF idcode of v < current THEN ***}
        if v.idcode < current^.value.idcode then
            {*** Move down left subtree ***}
            current := current^.left
        else
            {*** ELSE if v>current go down right ***}
            if v.idcode > current^.value.idcode then
                current := current^.right
            else
                {*** ELSE ids match-no changes***}
                exit;
     end;
     {*** Create nodwe and insert data ***}
     New(temp);
     temp^.left := NIL;
     temp^.right := NIL;
     temp^.value := v;
     {*** Link new node to parent ***}
     {** IF tree empty THEN node is root ***}
     if parent = NIL then
        t := temp
     else
        {** ELSE link to parent (left or right)**}
        if v.idcode < parent^.value.idcode then
            parent^.left := temp
```

```
        else
            parent^.right := temp;
    end;}
```

## Activity 10.9

62

## Activity 10.10

The call to *DisplayMenu* must be modified to add the new option to the displayed choices.

Also, an additional case option in *ExecuteOption*. The code for this new option is:

```
5: begin
        write('Enter id of node to be found : ');
        Val(GetData(['0'..'9'],4),key,err);
        FindParCh(key,t,parent,child);
        if child <> NIL then
        begin
            writeln('Found');
            writeln(NodeNames[NodeType(child)]);
        end
        else
            writeln('Not found');
        ReadKey;

            Node *par, *ch;
            cout<<"Enter required key : ";
            cin>>key;
            if(FindParCh(key,t,par,ch))
                cout<<"Found\n";
            else
                cout<<"Not found\n";
            switch(NodeType(ch))
            {
                case -1:
                    cout<<"Invalid node\n";
                    break;
                case 0:
                    cout<<"No children\n";
                    break;
                case 1:
                    cout<<"1 Child\n";
                    break;
                case 2:
                    cout<<"2 Children\n";
                    break;
            }
            getch();
            break;
```

It makes use of the following `const` declaration within *ExecuteOption:*

```
const
    NodeNames : array[0..2] of
        string[8]=('LEAF','CHILD','CHILDREN');
```

## Activity 10.11

No solution required.

## Activity 10.12

No solution required.

## Activity 10.13

Nodes:
- Glasgow
- Boston
- Atlanta
- Orlando
- Lisbon
- Paris
- London
- Berlin
- Rome
- Moscow

Edges:
- (Glasgow,Boston)
- (Glasgow,London)
- (Boston,Atlanta)
- (Boston,Orlando)
- (Atlanta,Orlando)
- (Orlando,Lisbon)
- (Lisbon,Paris)
- (Paris,London)
- (London,Berlin)
- (Rome,Moscow)

## Activity 10.14

The edges matrix would contain the value 1000 in the cells (3,2) and (2,3).

# CHAPTER 11
# Classes and Objects

**This chapter covers the following topics:**

Aggregate Classes

Basic Concepts of Object-Oriented Programming

Constructors

Container Classes

Creating Objects

Data Encapsulation

Defining Classes

Delegation

Destructors

Inheritance

OMT Diagrams

Overriding Class methods

Polymorphism

Private and Public Features

Virtual Methods

# CLASSES and OBJECTS

## Introduction

It is probably true to say that all recent, general-purpose, programming languages use an object-oriented approach. Borland introduced classes and objects in version 5.5 of their Pascal compiler.

So far, we have tackled all the programming exercises using a conventional programming approach. That approach involves breaking a problem down into a series of tasks or processes which are then coded as a group of routines. Object-oriented programming tackles things from a different perspective by identifying the relevant elements, or objects, in a system and defining a solution in terms of the actions that can be carried out by or on those objects.

Since an object-oriented approach is so important, why have we come this far without mentioning it before? The answer is a simple one: although an object-oriented approach is pivotal to using modern languages, we still need to create routines, use control structures and manipulate data; without those abilities we can't get very far in implementing an object-oriented program. However, now we're ready to go!

## What is an Object?

### Real World Objects

Our lives are populated with objects: *computers, books, clouds, words, customers,* etc. Some objects have a physical existence such as *computers* and *books*; others represent roles people or things play such as *customers* or *guard dogs*; yet other objects are incidents such as *a traffic jam* or *enrollment in a class.*

One way to describe an object is to list its characteristics and the operations which can be performed by or on the object. For example, a beach ball is round, has a diameter and colour; it can be inflated, deflated, rolled, bounced, kicked, thrown and burst.

More abstract objects, such as roles and incidents, may be defined in terms of the information required for their description and the operations which can be performed on that information. For example, a bank account might be described in terms of the *name* and *address* of the account holder and the *current balance,* while the operations likely to be performed are *make deposit, make withdrawal, change address,* and *add interest.*

**Activity 11.1**

List the characteristics and operations which could be used in describing:

1. a pencil
2. a date

### Object Classes

We also need to differentiate between a general description of all objects of the same type and specific objects. Hence, *beach ball* is a general term for all similar beach balls and *Elizabeth's beach ball* refers to one specific beach ball. When we identify the characteristics and operations of an item this represents a description of all items of that type. This grouping is known as an **object class** or simply a **class**. An individual item from such a class is called an **object** or an **instance** of that class.

From a programming perspective, we might think of class being equivalent to a type, while an object is equivalent to a variable.

**Activity 11.2**

Identify each of the following as either a class or an object:

1. Dogs
2. Lassie
3. Galaxy class starships
4. The USS Enterprise NCC-1701-D
5. Integers
6. The value 26

## Programming Objects

An object-oriented approach to software analysis and design views a system as a collection of objects and interactions between these objects. In addition, the software itself may introduce the need for additional objects which arise through implementation requirements. For example, we may need to define such objects as *drop-down menus*, *option buttons* and *scrollable data lists*.

Once the objects required in the system have been identified, the relevant characteristics and operations of the classes to which these objects belong are defined.

In the world of object-oriented design, a class's characteristics are known as its **attributes**, while the tasks it can perform are known as its **operations**. Collectively, the attributes and operations are known as the **features** or **members** of the class. For example, if a system uses an imperial weight object, the corresponding imperial weight class could be defined as shown in FIG-11.1.

**FIG-11.1**

The Weight Class

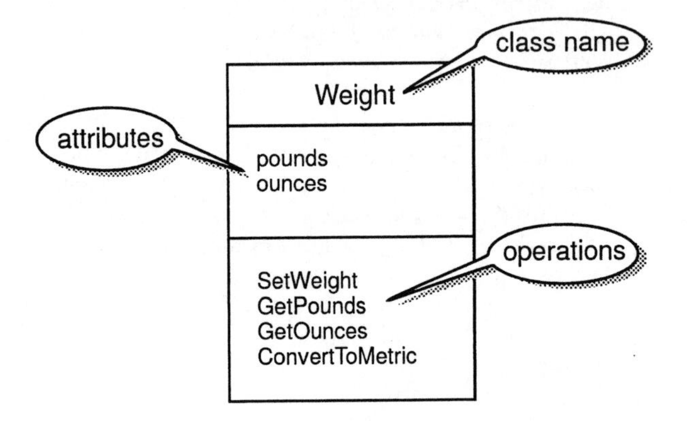


This class definition specifies the name of the class along with its attributes and operations.

FIG-11.1 states that a class, *Weight*, contains two attributes: *pounds* and *ounces*, and four operations: *SetWeight, GetPounds, GetOunces* and *ConvertToMetric.* Each operation requires an explanation and this can be documented in normal Mini-Spec format. Informally, the operations are:

| | |
|---|---|
| **SetWeight** | Sets the attributes to specified values. |
| **GetPounds** | Returns a copy of the value held in the *pounds* attribute. |
| **GetOunces** | Returns a copy of the value held in the *ounces* attribute. |
| **ConvertToMetric** | Converts the imperial weight held in the attributes *pounds* and *ounces* to the metric equivalent in kilograms. |

The class definition will be expanded as the design becomes more detailed to include the attribute types and the parameters of the operations. For example, the operation *SetWeight* requires, as parameters, the new values to be allocated to the class attributes, *pounds* and *ounces*. Hence the *SetWeight* function heading would be written as:

```
SetWeight(newlbs , newoz : INTEGER)
```

On the other hand, the function *ConvertToMetric* has no IN parameters but does return a result and is declared as:

```
ConvertToMetric():REAL
```

Note that the parentheses are retained to emphasise that there are no IN parameters. These are followed by a colon and the type of value returned by the operation.

When defining operation parameters, the attributes of the class are not included since all operations of a class have automatic access to the attributes of that class (see Class Scope later in this chapter).

The more detailed definition of *Weight* class is given in FIG-11.2.

**LISTING-11.2**

Defining a Class

| Weight |
|---|
| pounds : INTEGER<br>ounces : INTEGER |
| SetWeight(lbs, oz : INTEGER)<br>GetPounds():INTEGER<br>GetOunces():REAL<br>ConvertToMetric():REAL |

The class diagrams in this text conform to the UML (Unified Modelling Language)

**Activity 11.3**

Using the box notation shown above, create a definition for a *Distance* class (attributes: *yards, feet* and *inches*) with operations *SetDistance, GetYards, GetFeet, GetInches* and *ConvertToMetric*.

# Classes and Objects in Pascal

## Designing Classes

In Borland Pascal, an object class is defined within `type` declarations using the `object` keyword. The class definition for *Weight* would be:

```
type
    Weight = object
        pounds : integer;
        ounces : integer;

        procedure SetWeight(lbs, oz : integer);
```

```
        function GetPounds:integer;
        function GetOunces:integer;
        function ConvertToMetric:real;
    end;
```

### An Explanation of the Code

It is unfortunate that Borland decided to use the term *object* rather than *class* which would be more appropriate.

```
Weight = object
```

Declares a new object class called *Weight*. This is similar in construct to a `record` statement.

```
pounds : integer;
ounces : integer;
```

The attributes of *Weight* class.

```
procedure SetWeight(lbs, oz ; integer);
function GetPounds:integer;
function GetOunces:integer;
function ConvertToMetric : real;
```

The headings of each of the class's operations. These give the name and parameters required of each operation in the class.

> **Activity 11.4**
>
> Write a class definition, in Pascal, for the *Distance* class which you designed earlier in Activity 11.3.

Within the program, the class definition is followed by the code for each operation. When implemented in code, the operations of a class are referred to as its **methods.**

Those for *Weight* are given below:

```
procedure Weight.SetWeight(lbs, oz : integer);
begin
    {*** IF invalid parameters, exit operation ***}
    if (lbs < 0) or (oz < 0) or (oz > 15) then
        exit;
    {*** otherwise, assign values ***}
    pounds := lbs;
    ounces := oz;
end;


function Weight.GetPounds : integer;
begin
    GetPounds := pounds;
end;


function Weight.GetOunces : integer;
begin
    GetOunces := ounces;
end;


function Weight.ConvertTometric:real;
begin
    ConvertTometric := (pounds * 16 + ounces) * 0.0283495;
end;
```

## An Explanation of the Code

Although similar to normal routine definitions, a class's methods are prefaced by the class name and a full stop. This allows the compiler to recognise these function definitions as the methods of the *Weight* class.

All of this code needs to be placed within a Pascal program. Ultimately, the most useful way to do this is to create a Pascal Unit. The class definition is placed in the `interface` section of the class while the code for each method is placed in the `implementation` section. Hence, the complete *Weight* class would be coded as shown in LISTING-11.1.

**LISTING-11.1**

The *Weight* Class Unit

```
unit WeightUnit;

interface
type
  Weight = object
      pounds : integer;
      ounces : integer;

      procedure SetWeight(lbs, oz : integer);
      function GetPounds:integer;
      function GetOunces:integer;
      function ConvertToMetric:real;
  end;

implementation
  procedure Weight.SetWeight(lbs, oz : Integer);
  begin
      {*** IF invalid parameters, exit operation ***}
      if (lbs < 0) OR (oz < 0) OR (oz > 15) then
          exit;
      {*** otherwise, assign values ***}
      pounds := lbs;
      ounces := oz;
  end;

  function Weight.GetPounds : integer;
  begin
      GetPounds := pounds;
  end;

  function Weight.GetOunces : integer;
  begin
      GetOunces := ounces;
  end;

  function Weight.ConvertToMetric : real;
  begin
      ConvertToMetric := (pounds*16+ounces)*0.0283495;
  end;

end.
```

**Activity 11.5**

Type in and compile the Pascal Unit given above.

There are 12 inches in a foot; 3 feet in a yard.

1 inch = 0.0254 metres

**Activity 11.6**

Complete your coding of the *Distance* class by adding the details for each method.
Save and compile your file as a Pascal Unit called *Distances.pas*.

## Using Objects

In our previous programs we created variables to help in the solution to our problems. Hence, if we needed to store someone's age we created an `integer` variable called *age*; if we needed to store an address, we created a `string` variable. And so, if we require to store the weight of a bunch of grapes we can create an object of the *Weight* class in which to store that weight.

In the next program we will create a *Weight* object, set it to some user-specified value and display that value in both imperial and metric values.

To make use of a class, a program needs to declare variables of that class. This is done using the normal variable declaration statement. The class name is used in the same way we would employ a user-defined type name or a basic type . The statement

```
var
    w1: Weight;
```

defines one *Weight* object, *w1*.

Rather than use the word variable, the terms **object** or **instance** are normally employed.

Conceptually, each object is an exact replica of the attributes and methods of the class. That is, each has its own copy of the attributes and methods of the class from which it is defined. The result of declaring the object *w1* is shown in FIG-11.3.

**FIG-11.3**

Creating a Weight Object

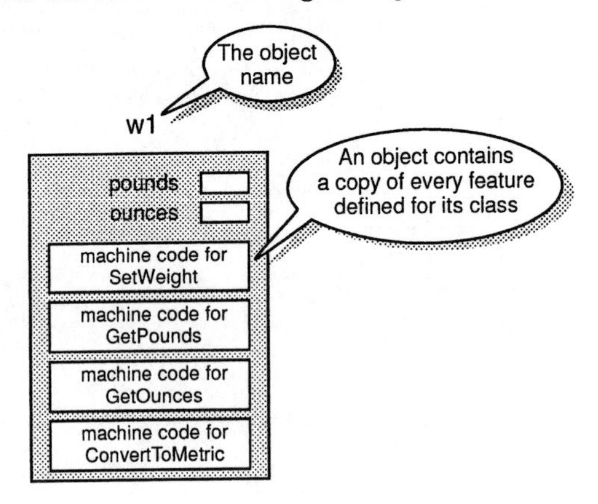


## Accessing Object Members

If *Weight* had been a normal record structure in which the fields *pounds* and *ounces* were declared, we could have accessed these fields in the variable *w1* with expressions such as:

`w1.pounds` and `w1.ounces`

And this is exactly how we access the features of an object. However, we are not restricted to accessing the data fields (attributes) within an object, but may also access and execute the methods of that object. Therefore, the statement

```
w1.SetWeight(10,3);
```

would cause the *SetWeight* procedure stored in the object *w1* to be executed and this would have the effect of setting the *pounds* attribute to 10 and the *ounces* attribute to 3 as shown in FIG-11.4.

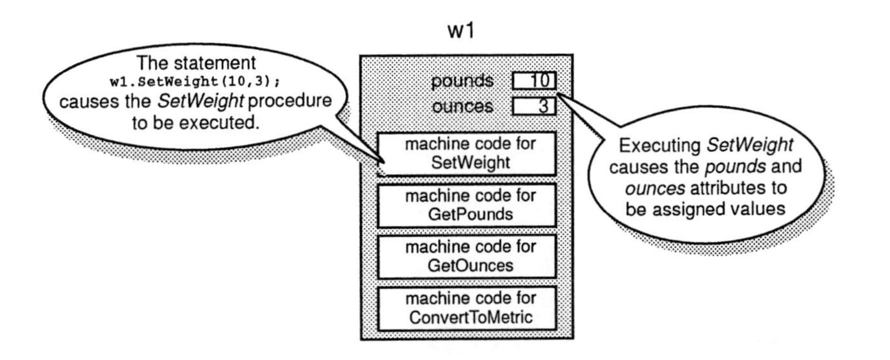
w1
The statement
w1.SetWeight(10,3);
causes the SetWeight procedure to be executed.
pounds 10
ounces 3
machine code for SetWeight
machine code for GetPounds
machine code for GetOunces
machine code for ConvertToMetric
Executing SetWeight causes the pounds and ounces attributes to be assigned values

> **Activity 11.7**
>
> What expression should we use to determine the value of the weight held in *w1* in kilogrammes?

We're now ready to attempt a complete program to demonstrate how to use a *Weight* object. The logic for this program (see LISTING-11.2) is:

```
Read in two integer values (lbs and oz)
Assign these values to the weight
Display the weight's value in pounds and ounces
Display the weight's value in kilogrammes
```

**LISTING-11.2**

Using a *Weight* Object

```
program UsingWeights;
uses WinCrt, Weights;
var
  lbs, oz : integer;
  w1 : Weight;                    {Create Weight object }
begin
  clrscr;
  write('Enter pounds : ');
  readln(lbs);
  write('Enter ounces : ');
  readln(oz);
  w1.SetWeight(lbs,oz);
  writeln('The weight entered was ',w1.GetPounds,' lbs ',
  ↳w1.GetOunces,' oz');
  writeln('This is ',w1.ConvertToMetric:0:2,' kilos');
end.
```

Note, we need to add a `uses Weights` statement in order to access the code for the *Weight* class.

> **Activity 11.8**
>
> Type in and test the program given in LISTING-11.2.

> **Activity 11.9**
>
> Create a program which uses a *Distance* object. The program should assign a value to the object and display the distance held in both imperial and metric form.

# Encapsulation

As you've experienced, there are two phases to using objects; first we design and code the class and then we create objects of that class.

Those two stages may be done separately with one person or company creating the class (the class designer) and another making use of objects of that class to produce applications (the application programmer).

The class designer would supply his software in the form of a compiled Unit

These two groups may never meet or have any contact with each other. All that is required of the class designer is that he produce sufficient documentation to allow the application programmer to manipulate the objects he wishes to create.

For example, if the class designer creates the *Weight* class, then he would have to produce documentation stating the name, parameters and purpose of each operation defined for the class; the application programmer would then be in a position to make use of *Weight* objects.

You may have noticed that when designing the *SetWeight* method, pre-condition checks have been made on the parameters. If the value to be assigned to *pounds* or *ounces* is invalid then no change is made, and the routine exits.

This stops the application programmer from placing invalid data in the *pounds* and *ounces* attributes of a *Weight* object should he accidentally type a line such as:

```
w1.setWeight(4,29);
```

However, there's a problem. What if the application programmer writes

```
w1.pounds = 4;
w1.ounces = 29;
```

Because he has assigned values directly to *pounds* and *ounces* rather than used *SetWeight*, no checks are carried out and the meaningless value of 29 is assigned to the *ounces* attribute (*pounds* is also assigned the value 4).

**Activity 11.10**

Load up the *UsingWeights* program and, when requested, enter 4 and 29 for the pounds and ounces respectively.

*The weight should display as 0 lbs 0 oz because* SetWeight *has exited without assigning any value.*

Replace the line

```
w1.setWeight(lbs, oz);
```

with

```
w1.pounds := lbs;
w1.ounces := oz;
```

Run the program again entering 4 and 29.

*This time the display reads 4 lbs 29 oz. The invalid value has been assigned.*

Obviously, it would be useful if there was some way to eliminate the possibility of such a mistake occurring. In fact, that's exactly what Pascal allows us to do.

The solution lies in the design of the *Weight* class. By changing the lines

```
pounds : integer;
ounces : integer;
```

to

```
private
    pounds : integer;
    ounces : integer;
```

we restrict access to the *pounds* and *ounces* attributes of any *Weight* object. Since we don't want to restrict access to the methods of the class, we also have to change the lines

```
procedure SetWeight(lbs, oz : integer);
function GetPounds:integer;
function GetOunces:integer;
function ConvertToMetric:real;
```

to

```
public
    procedure SetWeight(lbs, oz : integer);
    function GetPounds:integer;
    function GetOunces:integer;
    function ConvertToMetric:real;
```

This change has no effect on the other lines of code within the *Weight* class.

Pascal only treats a class member as `private` when the class is stored in a separate Unit from the main program.

If you keep everything in the same file there is no restriction on access.

**Activity 11.11**

Modify the code of the *Weight* class, as shown above, adding the keywords `private` and `public`.

Recompile the *Weight* class file.

Attempt to recompile the *UsingWeights* program, making sure it still contains the lines

```
w1.pounds := lbs;
w1.ounces := oz;
```

The line `w1.pounds := lbs;` *should be highlighted and the compilation error message* Field identifier expected *displayed in the status bar.*

With these changes the class designer has ensured that the application programmer can only access the data items within an object via the routines (such as *SetWeight*) designed for that purpose. And, since these routines will validate any value being passed as a parameter, there is no chance of an invalid value being stored in a class attribute.

**Activity 11.12**

Modify the code in your *Distance* class so that all attributes are private and all methods are public.

Test your application program containing a *Distance* object to ensure that it still functions correctly.

The inability to access the private members of a class is the first of many advantages of an object-oriented approach to programming.

There is a second, though more subtle, reason for not allowing the application programmer direct access to the attributes of a class. Let's assume that the *Weight* class designer has just had a flash of inspiration and has decided that the pounds and ounces of an imperial weight can be stored as a single real value in which the ounces are stored as a fraction of a pound. Hence, the weight 4 lbs 8 oz would be stored as 4.5. Using this approach the attributes of the *Weight* class can be rewritten as:

```
Weight = object
    private
        value : real;
    public
        procedure SetWeight(lbs, oz : integer);
        function GetPounds:integer;
        function GetOunces:integer;
        function ConvertToMetric:real;
end;
```

Although the names, parameters and purpose of each method remains the same, the code needed to implement them has changed. The new class's code is shown in LISTING-11.3.

**LISTING-11.3**

An Alternative Implementation of the *Weight* Class

```
Unit Weights2;

interface

type
  Weight = object
      private
          value : real;
      public
          procedure SetWeight(lbs, oz : integer);
          function GetPounds:integer;
          function GetOunces:integer;
          function ConvertToMetric:real;
  end;

implementation
  procedure Weight.SetWeight(lbs, oz : Integer);
  begin
      if (lbs < 0) OR (oz < 0) OR (oz > 15) then
          exit;
      value := lbs + oz/16;
  end;

  function Weight.GetPounds : integer;
  begin
      GetPounds := Trunc(value);
  end;

  function Weight.GetOunces : integer;
  begin
      GetOunces := Round((value-Trunc(value))*16);
  end;

  function Weight.ConvertToMetric : real;
  begin
      ConvertToMetric := value*16*0.0283495;
  end;

end.
```

Keen to distribute the new and improved version of the code, the class designer now sends his new implementation of the *Weight* class to the application programmer in a new version of the Pascal unit.

If the application programmer has been using lines such as

```
w1.pounds = 8;
w1.ounces = 4;
```

he is now in big trouble! The next time the application programmer tries to compile his program it will no longer be valid since the *pounds* and *ounces* fields no longer exist within the *Weight* class.

However, if the class designer prevents access to the attributes of an object except through the operations defined for that class, then such problems will not arise. The only constraint on the class designer is that the name, parameters, and purpose of each method must not be changed when new versions of a class are produced.

By following these rules, the application programmer will be unaware of the actual changes implemented between one version of an object class and the next.

This ability to conceal the details of a class implementation is known as **information hiding**. To achieve information hiding we need to restrict access to the data to the operations defined for that data. This linking of data and related operations is known as **encapsulation** (see FIG-11.5).

**FIG-11.5**

Encapsulation Concepts

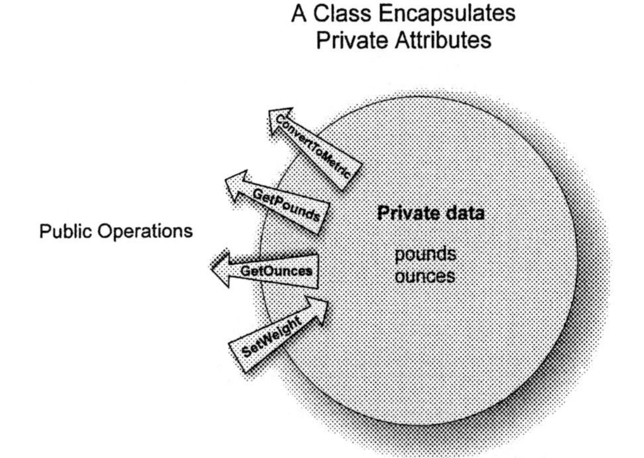


So, generally, it will be useful to stop the application programmer from accessing the attributes of a class directly; on the other hand we will want the application programmer to have access to the methods of the class. So we can say that in many cases the general structure for a class declaration is that shown in FIG-11.6.

**FIG-11.6**

Class Declaration Syntax

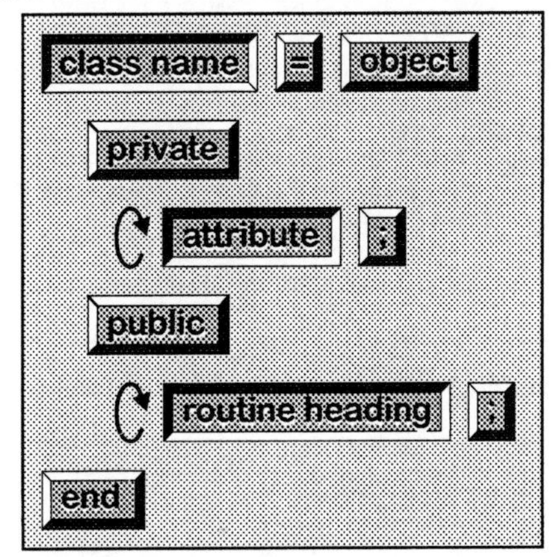

### Class Scope

The attributes and methods of a class belong to that class's **scope**. This means that the member functions can access any other component of the class, *private* or *public*, directly, without the need to specify them as parameters. Outside the class's scope, *public* members of the class can be accessed by objects of that class; *private* members cannot. For example, assuming the declaration

```
myclass = object
    private
        a, b, c : integer;
    public
        m, n : integer;
        function MyFunction : real;
                .
end
```

the code in *MyFunction* can reference any of the attributes, *a, b, c, m* or *n*.

But if an application program contains the definition

```
var
    x : myclass;
```

then the following expressions are valid

```
x.m
x.n
x.MyFunction
```

since they reference *public* components of the class, while the terms

```
x.a
x.b
x.c
```

are invalid since they attempt to access *private* parts of the class.

If a class operation contains a local variable which has the same name as a class attribute, that attribute is hidden by the local variable. So, creating local variables with the same name as data members should be avoided.

# Multiple Objects

Just as we might need several integer variables when writing a program, so it is likely that we will need more than a single object when creating applications.

For example, let's assume we need a program to read in two weights and determine which is the smaller. Our program could follow the logic:

```
Read in first weight
Read in second weight
IF first weight < second weight THEN
    Display first weight
ELSE
    Display second weight
ENDIF
```

The coding for this program is given in LISTING-11.4.

**LISTING-11.4**

Using Multiple Objects

```
program TwoWeights;
uses WinCrt, Weights;
var
  lbs, oz : integer;
  w1,w2 : Weight;
begin
  clrscr;
   {*** Read in first weight ***}
  write('Enter pounds : ');
  readln(lbs);
  write('Enter ounces : ');
  readln(oz);
  w1.SetWeight(lbs,oz);
  {*** Read in second weight ***}
  write('Enter pounds : ');
  readln(lbs);
  write('Enter ounces : ');
  readln(oz);
  w2.SetWeight(lbs,oz);
  {*** Display smaller weight ***}
  if w1.ConvertToMetric < w2.ConvertToMetric then
      writeln('Smaller weight is ',w1.getPounds,' lbs ',
      ↳w1.getOunces,' oz')
  else
      writeln('Smaller weight is ',w2.getPounds,' lbs ',
      ↳w2.getOunces,' oz');
end.
```

**Activity11.13**

Write a program, similar to the one above, which displays the longer of two distances.

# Designing a Class

The class designer has a difficult task on his hands. In creating a new class he has to attempt to predict what uses the application programmer is likely to require from the objects created. If the class designer doesn't build the correct features into the original class, then the application programmer may find it difficult or impossible to achieve the effects required.

For example, let's say the application programmer, having assigned values to two *Weight* objects (*w1* and *w2*), wishes to add *w2* to *w1*; how is this going to be achieved?

It is possible, but creates a rather complex piece of code.

We could try the line

```
w1.SetWeight(w1.GetPounds+w2.GetPounds,
↳w1.GetOunces+w2.GetOunces);
```

but this won't work if the expression

```
w1.getOunces+w2.GetOunces
```

gives a total of more than 15 ounces and hence supplies an invalid parameter to *setWeight()*.

A more foolproof approach would be:

```
carrypounds := (w1.getOunces+w2.getOunces) div 16;
w1.setWeight(w1.getPounds+w2.getPounds+carrypounds,
↳(w1.getOunces+w2.getOunces) mod 16);
```

But this seems too much like hard work for what should be such a simple operation. The limited operations of the *Weight* class are making the application programmer's job difficult.

As a starting point, the class designer will often create *set* (also known as **mutator methods**) and *get* (also called **accessor methods**) methods for each attribute in a class. We already have *GetPounds* and *GetOunces* in the *Weight* class.

Occasionally, a single operation will set more than one attribute if those attributes are closely linked. For example, the *Weight* class uses *SetWeight* to set both the *pounds* and *ounces* attributes.

However, if a *Customer* class contained both *name* and *address* as attributes, the class designer would create separate *set* methods for each of these attributes since they are not closely linked.

For classes, such as the *Weight* class, which are of a numeric nature, the class designer will often include methods to allow addition, subtraction, division and multiplication.

In addition, we need methods to allow comparisons between objects. For example, the program in LISTING-11.4 used the expression

```
w1.ConvertToMetric < w2.ConvertToMetric
```

to compare the weights *w1* and *w2*. If there had been an *IsLessThan* method included in the design of the *Weight* class, he could have replaced this with

```
w1.IsLessThan(w2)
```

# Summary

- **A class is the blueprint** for a structure containing data and functions designed to operate on that data.
- A class is described in terms of its **features.**
- The features of a class are its **attributes** and **operations**.
- **Using Unified Modelling Language**(UML) a class is shown in the form of a diagram.
- An **object** is an **instance** of a class.
- In Pascal classes are defined in a **object** statement.
- A class has both **private** and **public** members. In objects, **private** members can only be accessed through **public** operations; **public** members can be accessed freely.
- **Private** only operates correctly if the class definition is held in a **Pascal Unit**, separate from the code containing instances of the class.

- **Access to public members** takes the form

```
instance-name.public-member-name
```

- All members of a class have **class scope**. This means all members can be accessed freely within the code defining the methods of the class.

- **As a general rule**, classes should contain methods to *set* and *get* each of its attributes.

# MORE ON CLASS DESIGN AND OBJECTS

## Different Types of Class Methods

So far we've looked at very simple class operations. Below are some more complex examples.

### Using a Class Object as a Parameter

We commonly require to add one numeric value to another as in statements such as

```
count := count + 1;
```

and

```
total := total + nbr;
```

However, as we have already seen, adding one *Weight* object to another can be rather dfficult with the operations currently defined in the *Weight* class.To simplify the task of the application programmer the class designer needs to add a new function to the *Weight* class. This function needs to take a *Weight* object as a parameter. For example, we might create a new method, *Add*, which allows the value of another *Weight* object to be added to the object executing this new routine. That is to say, if the application programmer were to write

```
w1.Add(w2);
```

this would have the effect of adding the *pounds* and *ounces* in *w2* to those already held in the corresponding attributes of *w1*.

The *Add* method would have the heading:

```
procedure Add(w : Weight);
```

The *Weight* class would now be defined as:

```
type
    Weight = object
        private
            pounds : integer;
            ounces : integer;
        public
            procedure SetWeight(lbs, oz : integer);
            function GetPounds:integer;
            function GetOunces:integer;
            procedure Add(w : Weight);
            function ConvertToMetric : real;
    end;
```

With the new method being coded as

```
procedure Weight.Add(w : Weight);
var
    totaloz : integer;
begin
    totaloz := (pounds + w.pounds)*16 + ounces + w.ounces;
    pounds := totaloz div 16;
    ounces := totaloz mod 16;
end;
```

the application programmer can now use this new method in statements such as:

```
w1.Add(w2); {*** Add w2 to w1 ***}
```

**Activity 11.14**

Create an *Add* method for the *Distance* class. This operation should add one distance to another in a similar style to that given above for the *Weight* class.

Test the new method by creating two *Distance* objects *d1* and *d2*, assigning both values and then adding *d2* to *d1*.

The value of *d1* should then be displayed.

## The Assignment Operator ( := ) and Class Objects

Pascal automatically handles any use of the assignment operator involving two objects from the same class by copying the values held in the source object attributes to those in the destination object. For example, assuming execution of the statements

```
Weight w1,w2;

w1.SetWeight(10,2);
```

then the assignment

```
w2 := w1;
```

will result in the contents of *w1.pounds* and *w1.ounces* being copied to *w2.pounds* and *w2.ounces* respectively. This copying of each attribute from one object to another is known as **member-wise assignment.**

## Private Methods

Look at the coding of the *Weight* class and you'll see that many of its methods make use of the expression `pounds*16+ounces;` which calculates the total number of ounces in a weight. It may be useful to code this expression as a separate routine, *ToOunces*. Yet, *ToOunces* is not an operation of the class, rather it is a subsidiary function which comes in useful in coding the actual methods of the class. As such, we would not want the application programmer to have access to the routine.

To achieve this, we declare *ToOunces* within the `private` part of *Weight*. This prevents others accessing the routine, yet still allows it to be used in the definition of the other methods in the class.

```
type
    Weight = object
        private
            pounds : integer;
            ounces : integer;
            function ToOunces : integer;
        public
            procedure SetWeight(lbs, oz : integer);
            function GetPounds:integer;
            function GetOunces:integer;
            procedure Add(w : Weight);
            function ConvertToMetric : real;
    end;
```

Attempting to access *ToOunces* outside the class methods as in the code

```
var
    w : Weight;
    .
writeln(w.ToOunces);
```

would result in the compiler error message:

```
Field identifier expected
```

But we can now use the function in the definition of the other *Weight* methods. For example, *ConvertToMetric* could now be coded as:

```
function Weight.ConvertTometric:real;
begin
    ConvertTometric := ToOunces * 0.0283495;
end;
```

While *Add* would be coded as:

```
procedure Weight.Add(w : Weight);
var
    totaloz : integer;
begin
    totaloz := ToOunces + w.ToOunces;
    pounds  := totaloz div 16;
    ounces  := totaloz mod 16;
end;
```

**Activity 11.15**

Add a private function, *ToInches* to the *Distance* class and rewrite the *Add* method to make use of the *ToInches* function.

Test your program to ensure it still functions correctly.

## Comparison Methods

To allow two weights to be compared easily the class designer will have to add **comparison methods**. Such methods perform the same task as relational operators (<, <=, >, >=, =, <>) do on normal numeric variables. In the case of the *Weight* class the designer needs to add the following methods:

```
IsLessThan
IsLessThanOrEqualTo
IsGreaterThan
IsGreaterThanOrEqualTo
IsEqual
IsNotEqual
```

To give you an idea of how this is done, we can add the *IsLessThan* operation to the *Weight* class by inserting the following:

In the public section of the *Weight* class declaration:

```
function IsLessThan(w: Weight) : boolean;
```

Following the class declaration:

```
function Weight.IsLessThan(w : Weight) : boolean;
begin
    if ToOunces < w.ToOunces then
        IsLessThan := true
    else
        IsLessThan := false;
end;
```

The application programmer can then display the smaller of two weights with the statement:

```
if w1.IsLessThan(w2) then
    writeln('Smaller weight is ',w1.GetPounds,' lbs ',
    ↳w1.GetOunces,' oz')
else
    writeln('Smaller weight is ',w2.GetPounds,' lbs ',
    ↳w2.GetOunces,' oz');
```

**Activity 11.16**

Add an *IsGreaterThan* function to the *Distance* class.

Modify the program you created in Activity 11.13 to use this new method in determining the longer of the two distances.

## Returning a Class Object from a Method

One operation that the class designer might easily foresee as a requirement of the application programmer is division. For example, if the sum of several weights were to be calculated, we need to divide this figure by the number of weights involved to find their average weight. Such an operation would return a *Weight* object as its result.

The best approach to this would be to define a *Divide* function which started with the line:

```
function Divide (divisor : integer) : Weight;
```

Unfortunately, Pascal will not allow anything other than a normal variable type (`real`, `char`, etc.) to be returned by a function, so the operation must be written as a procedure. This is coded as:

```
procedure Weight.Divide(divisor : integer; var ans : Weight);
var
    ansinounces : integer;
begin
    if divisor <= 0 then
        halt;
    ansinounces := Round(ToOunces / divisor);
    ans.pounds := ansinounces div 16;
    ans.ounces := ansinounces mod 16;
end;
```

An application program which has declared *w1, w2* and *average* as *Weight* objects can calculate the average of the weights *w1* and *w2* using the following lines:

```
{*** Add weights ***}
w1.Add(w2);
{*** Calculate average ***}
w1.Divide(2,average);
{*** Display average ***}
writeln('Average of the two weights is ',average.GetPounds,
↳' lbs ',average.GetOunces,' oz');
```

**Activity 11.17**

Add a *Divide* operation to the *Distance* class.

Modify the program created in Activity 11.16 to display the average of the two distances.

## The Concept of Operation Overloading

The *Weight* class contains a method to set the values to be stored in the *pounds* and *ounces* attributes. This is the *SetWeight* procedure. But the *SetWeight* procedure takes two integers as arguments.What if we wanted to set the weight using a single, real number? For example, to store the weight 4 lbs 8 oz we would use the value 4.5.

It would be easy enough to add such a routine to the *Weight* class. Its code would be:

```
procedure Weight.SetWeightWithReal(v:real);
begin
    if v < 0 then
        exit;
    pounds := Trunc(v);
    ounces := Round((v - Trunc(v))*16);
end;
```

The application programmer could now use either routine to initialise a *Weight* object. For example, both of the following statements sets *w1* to 4 lbs 8 oz:

```
w1.SetWeight(4,8);
w1.SetWeightWithReal(4.5);
```

This may seem acceptable if you have never come across any other object-oriented language, but languages such as C++ and Java would allow both routines, *SetWeight* and *SetWeightWithReal* to be given exactly the same name, say *SetWeight.* The compiler then examines the parameters supplied to any function call to determine which version of the function is to be executed. Hence, in C++, the two statements above could be written as:

```
w1.setWeight(4,8);
w1.setWeight(4.5);
```

This idea of being able to give two or more routines within a class exactly the same name as long as the parameters of the routines differ in some way is known as **operation overloading**. Although not essential, its omission from Borland Pascal forces us to invent different names for routines that perform essentially the same task.

## Constructors

If we were to call a *Weight.* object's *GetPounds* before using its *SetWeight* method, a spurious value would be displayed on the screen. This is because the attribute, *pounds,* would contain an undefined value.

It would be more acceptable to display *0 lbs 0 oz* in such a situation. However, to do this we would need to ensure that *pounds* and *ounces*, rather than containing random values, were both set to zero.

To achieve the results we require, we have to add a new type of method to our class. Unlike other methods, a **constructor** is designed to be executed immediately after an object variable is created.

A constructor method is used to initialise class objects and perform some invisible housekeeping task which we'll hear more about later. In Borland Pascal a constructor is normally given the name *Init.* Although a constructor can have any number of parameters it cannot return a value.

To create a constructor, we begin by adding the constructor method to the class declaration:

```
type
    Weight = object
        private
            pounds : integer;
            ounces : integer;
            function ToOunces : integer;
        public
            constructor Init;
            procedure SetWeight(lbs, oz : integer);
            function GetPounds:integer;
            function GetOunces:integer;
            procedure Add(w : Weight);
            function ConvertToMetric : real;
            function IsLessThan(w : Weight) : boolean;
            procedure Divide(divisor : integer; var ans : Weight);
    end;
```

The definition of the constructor is then given:

```
constructor Weight.Init;
begin
    pounds := 0;
    ounces := 0;
end;
```

Now variables of this class can be assigned values as they are declared:

```
var
    w1, w2 : Weight;
begin
    w1.Init;
    w2.Init;
```

**Activity 11.18**

Write and test a constructor for the *Distance* class that sets all attributes of the class to zero.

The final version of the *Weight* class is given in LISTING-11.5.

**LISTING-11.5**

The Final Version of the *Weight* Class

```
Unit Weights;

interface
type
  Weight = object
      private
          pounds : integer;
          ounces : integer;
          function ToOunces : integer;
      public
          constructor Init;
          procedure SetWeight(lbs, oz : integer);
          function GetPounds:integer;
          function GetOunces:integer;
          function ConvertToMetric:real;
          procedure Add(w : Weight);
          function IsLessThan(w: Weight) : boolean;
          procedure Divide(divisor : integer; var ans:Weight);
  end;
```

**Continued on next page**

**LISTING-11.5**
(continued)

The Final Version of the *Weight* Class

```
implementation

  constructor Weight.Init;
  begin
      pounds := 0;
      ounces := 0;
  end;

  procedure Weight.SetWeight(lbs, oz : Integer);
  begin
      if (lbs < 0) OR (oz < 0) OR (oz > 15) then
          exit;
      pounds := lbs;
      ounces := oz;
  end;

  function Weight.GetPounds : integer;
  begin
      GetPounds := pounds;
  end;

  function Weight.GetOunces : integer;
  begin
      GetOunces := ounces;
  end;

  function Weight.ConvertToMetric : real;
  begin
      ConvertToMetric := (pounds*16+ounces)*0.0283495;
  end;

  procedure Weight.Add(w : Weight);
  var
      totalounces : integer;
  begin
      totalounces := ToOunces + w.ToOunces;
      pounds := totalounces div 16;
      ounces := totalounces mod 16;
  end;

  function Weight.ToOunces : integer;
  begin
      ToOunces := pounds * 16 + ounces;
  end;

  function Weight.IsLessThan(w : Weight) : boolean;
  begin
      if ToOunces < w.ToOunces then
          IsLessThan := true
      else
          IsLessThan := false;
  end;

  procedure Weight.Divide(divisor : integer; var ans : Weight);
  var
      ansinounces : integer;
  begin
      ansinounces := Round(ToOunces / divisor);
      ans.pounds := ansinounces div 16;
      ans.ounces := ansinounces mod 16;
  end;
end.
```

## Destructors

Just as we can call a constructor at the start of an object's life, we can write a **destructor** to be called just before the object's space is deallocated by the program.

Normally, destructors are only required if an object contains a pointer to dynamically allocated space. This space needs to be deallocated before the object itself is destroyed. Traditionally, destructors in Pascal are given the name ***Done***.

The program in LISTING-11.6 demonstrates the use of such a destructor. The class contains a set of 5 integer pointers. The constructor sets each of these to NIL, while the *SetValue* operation allocates space for a specified pointer and stores a value there. The destructor then disposes of any space allocated.

**LISTING-11.6**

Using Destructors

```
program UsingDestructors;
uses WinCrt;

type
  List = object
      private
          ptrlist : array[1..5] of ^integer;
      public
          constructor Init;
          procedure   SetValue(p, v : integer);
          function    GetValue(p :integer) : integer;
          destructor  Done;
  end;

constructor List.Init;
var
  c : integer;
begin
  {*** Set all pointers to NIL ***}
  for c := 1 to 5 do
      ptrlist[c] := NIL;
end;


procedure List.SetValue(p, v : integer);
begin
  {*** IF invalid position specified, exit ***}
  if (p < 1) or (p > 5) then
      exit;
  {*** IF position specified hasn't space, allocate it ***}
  if ptrlist[p] = NIL then
      New(ptrlist[p]);
  {*** Store the value ***}
  ptrlist[p]^ := v;
end;


function List.GetValue(p : integer) : integer;
begin
  {*** If position specified invalid or has no value, halt ***}
  if (p < 1) or (p > 5) or (ptrlist[p]=NIL) then
      halt;
  {*** Retrieve value ***}
  GetValue := ptrlist[p]^;
end;


destructor List.Done;
var
  c : integer;
begin
  {*** FOR each pointer DO ***}
  for c := 1 to 5 do
      {*** IF space has been allocated space, dipose of it ***}
      if ptrlist[c] <> NIL then
          Dispose(ptrlist[c]);
end;
```

**Continued on next page**

**LISTING-11.6**
(continued)

Using Destructors

```
var
  x : List;
begin
  x.Init;
  x.SetValue(1,89);
  writeln( value at position 1 is , x.GetValue(1));
  x.Done;
end      .
```

# Types of Objects

## Arrays of Objects

As well as individual objects, we can create arrays of objects. To set up an array of three *Weight* objects we use the declaration:

```
list: array[1..3] of Weight;
```

We can access the objects in this array with statements such as:

```
list[2].SetWeight(4,9);
```

As you can see, access to the array elements and the corresponding methods uses a combination of the array subscript syntax and object method access. For example, to display each *Weight* object we use:

```
for c := 1 to 3 do
    begin
        writeln('The weight ', list[c].GetPounds,' lbs ',
        ↳list[c].GetOunces,' oz is ',list[c].ConvertToMetric:0:2
        ↳,' kilos');
    end;
```

**Activity 11.19**

Create a program containing a 5 element array of *Distance* objects.

The program should calculate and display the average of these distances using the following logic:

```
Read in a value for each distance
Calculate the total of all 5 distances
Calculate the average as the total divided by 5
Display the average
```

## Dynamic Objects

The ability to create pointers to a value extends to classes, allowing statements such as

```
var
    wptr : ^Weight;
```

and this can be used either to reference some other variable of this type

```
wptr := @w1;
```

or to dynamically allocate object space:

```
New(wptr);
```

This will allocate space to a *Weight* class object, executing the class constructor to initialise the contents of the object.

The syntax of the `New` statement is extended in the case of object pointers to include the class constructor:

```
New(wptr, Init);
```

This not only creates space for the object with *wptr* referencing that space, but also executes the constructor's code immediately after the space is allocated.

The dynamically allocated object can then be accessed by dereferencing the pointer in a similar fashion to that used when dereferencing a pointer to a record:

```
wptr^.SetWeight(5,3);
writeln('The weight ',wptr^.GetPounds,' lbs ',wptr^.GetOunces,
↳' oz is ',wptr^.ConvertToMetric:0:2,' kilos');
```

Objects allocated in this way need to be deallocated using the normal `Dispose` command when no longer required:

```
Dispose(wptr);
```

Like `New`, an extended version of `Dispose` is available to allow a class destructor to be executed at the same time. So, if the *Weight* class had a destructor called *Done*, we could use the line

```
Dispose(wptr, Done);
```

to execute the destructor and dispose of the space allocated to *wptr*.

# Summary

- **Class Objects** can be used as **parameters** to an operation.
- **The assignment operator** (:=) when used with objects copies the attributes of the right-hand object to the corresponding attributes in the left-hand object.

  (e.g. `w1 := w2;` copies the *pounds* and *ounces* values from *w2* to *w1*.)
- Helper methods can be added as **private operations** in a class.
- **Comparison methods** will often need to be added to a class.
- **Objects may be returned from an operation**. In Pascal such operations must be written as procedures.
- Borland Pascal does not allow **operation overloading** where more than one operation within a class can be given the same name.
- A **constructor** is a method which is called when a class object is created.
- A **constructor** must have the same name as the class and may return no value.

- A **destructor** is a method which is called at the end of an object's lifetime.
- **Destructors** are normally used to clear up dynamically allocated space.

# DESIGNING CLASSES

## Introduction

At the beginning of this chapter we saw that one tool for helping with the design of an object-oriented system is the Unified Modelling Language (UML). The complete UML system and object-oriented design as a whole is outside the scope of this text. However, it will be useful to explore UML class diagrams in some more detail by showing how the *Weight* class would be represented in this system.

We've already seen that the basic diagram is a rectangle split into three areas. These areas contain:

- the class name
- the attributes of the class
- the operations of the class

In addition, the access modifier information can be added to the diagram: private items are started with a minus (-) sign; public features begin with a plus (+) sign.

The modified version of the *Weight* class is shown in FIG-11.7.

**FIG-11.7**

A UML Class Diagram for the Final Version of the *Weight*

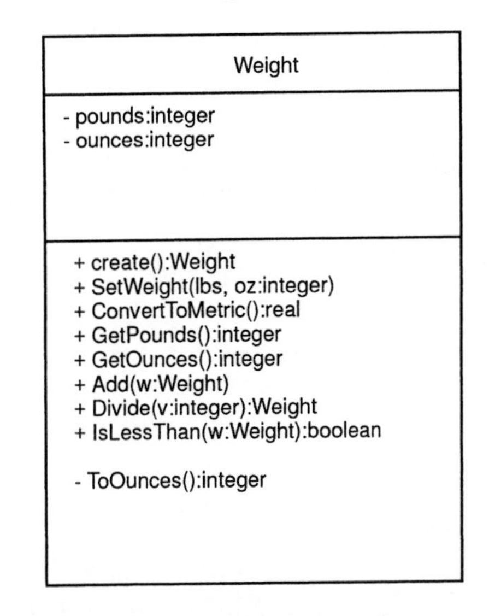


Notice that the constructor operation is named *create* and returns an object of the class being defined. This is a useful convention to follow with all classes. Of course, in the implementation, Pascal requires that the constructors are named *Init.*

Other documentation in the form of mini-specs will be required for each operation. In addition to the information given in previously discussed mini-specs, we'll need to add access details and which attributes are accessed by an operation. For example, the mini-spec for *SetWeight(lbs, oz : integer)* would be as shown overleaf:

```
Operation       :   SetWeight
Access          :   public
Parameters
    In          :   lbs : integer
                    oz  : integer
    Out:        :   None
    In/Out      :   None
Attributes Accessed
    read        :   None
    written     :   pounds
                    ounces
Pre-condition   :   lbs >= 0 AND oz >= 0 AND oz <= 15
Post-condition  :   pounds = lbs AND ounces = oz
Description     :   lbs copied to pounds and oz copied to ounces.
Outline Logic   :   Set pounds to lbs
                    Set ounces to oz
```

**Activity 11.20**

Create and test a class which meets the following specification:

*Clock* : Objects of this class are set to a specific time and made to increment by one second each time the *Tick* method is executed.

Attributes:

hours : integer
minutes : integer
seconds : integer

Operations:

**create() : Clock**
Creates a *Clock* object with the time set to midnight (0,0,0)

**SetTime(h,m,s:integer)**
Sets time to *h:m:s*. If the parameters are invalid, the time is unchanged.

**Tick()**
Adds one second to the current time.

**DisplayTime()**
Displays the values of the hours, minutes and seconds attributes using the format hh:mm:ss

**GetHours():integer**
Returns a copy of the hours attribute.

**GetMinutes():integer**
Returns a copy of the minutes attribute.

**GetSeconds():integer**
Returns a copy of the seconds attribute.

# INHERITANCE

## Relationships

### Introduction

We all have ancestors. From these ancestors we have inherited our features and basic abilities through our DNA. Although this DNA comes from both our parents, in asexual species the DNA is an exact copy of the parent. Nevertheless, even asexual species can adapt and modify inherited traits from generation to generation.

Inheriting what has gone before and adapting it to the current environment is not limited to the animal kingdom; for example, widescreen high-definition stereo television also has an ancestry which can be traced through radio; black-and-white TV; colour TV; stereo, colour TV; and 16:9 widescreen TV. At each step in the process the feature of its immediate predecessor were incorporated in the latest advance but these were then added to and modified where necessary to create the new product.

This approach of building on what has gone before, is one of the main goals of object-oriented programming. By adopting this technique it is hoped that classes can be reused and modified to create new classes with a minimum amount of development time and a reduction in errors.

### Class Relationships

If we were to create UML class diagrams for radio and black-and-white television we might come up with the diagrams shown in FIG-11.8.

**FIG-11.8**

*Radio* and *BWTV* Classes

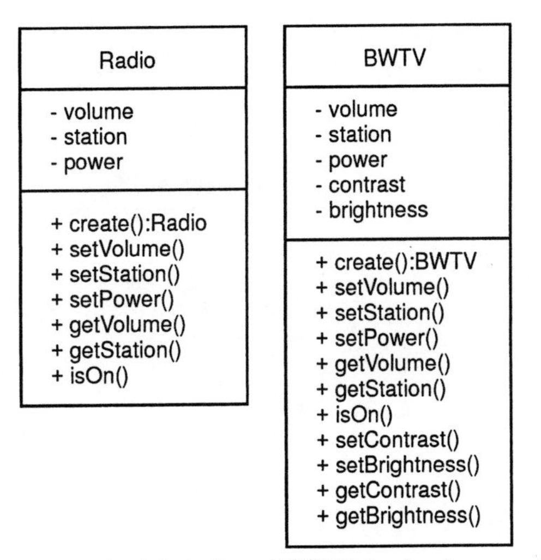


We can see that the television class (*BWTV*) is simply an extension of the *Radio* class with extra attributes and operations. That isn't surprising since, as we have already stated, television is simply a radio with pictures.

UML uses a diagram somewhat akin to a family tree, which illustrates this relationship (see FIG-11.9).

The diagram with the arrowed line shows that *BWTV* is a class which is descended from the *Radio* class. Notice also that only the features new to the *BWTV* class are included in its rectangle. This is because, in object-oriented design, any new class is automatically assumed to have inherited all its parent's features. The new class can then have additional features added and only these new features are shown in the diagram.

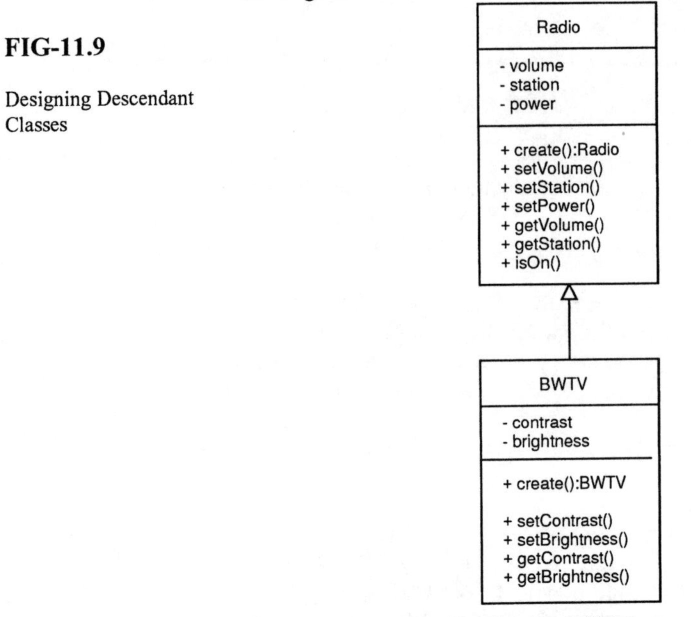


**FIG-11.9**

Designing Descendant Classes

If these two devices (*Radio* and *BWTV*) were to become part of a computer program (perhaps as part of a simulation game), then the traditional program approach would require each to be coded separately. Since both items have many features in common, the resulting code would contain a great deal of duplication.

> **Activity 11.21**
>
> From the diagram above, list the attributes of the *BWTV* class.

There are a few terms to note from FIG-11.9:

- The terms **base class, super class** or **parent class** are used to describe the class from which another class is derived. In the diagram above, *Radio* is the super class.

- The terms **derived class**, **sub-class** or **child class** are used to describe a descendant class.

There are no restrictions on the number of generations of derived classes that may be created or the number of child classes that can be derived from a single class.

> **Activity 11.22**
>
> Draw the UML diagram above.
>
> Add a new class, *ColourTV*, which is derived from *BWTV* class.
>
> The new class has the attributes:
> *volume, station, power, contrast, brightness,* and *colour intensity*
> It has the same operations as the *BWTV* class but adds *GetColourIntensity()* and *GetColourIntensity()* operations.

**Activity 11.23**

Add a fourth class, called *StereoRadio,* to your UML diagram.

This is a class derived from the *Radio* class but with an additional *balance* attribute and *SetBalance* and *GetBalance* operations.

# Implementing Derived Classes

In Activity 11.20 you created a *Clock* class. The code given in the solutions at the end of this chapter for that class is shown in LISTING-11.7.

**LISTING 11.7**

The *Clock* Class

```
Unit Clocks;

interface
type
  Clock = object
      private
          hours   : integer;
          minutes : integer;
          seconds : integer;

      public
          constructor Init;
          procedure SetTime(h,m,s : integer);
          procedure Tick;
          procedure DisplayTime;
          function GetHours : integer;
          function GetMinutes : integer;
          function GetSeconds : integer;
  end;

  implementation
  constructor Clock.Init;
  begin
      hours := 0;
      minutes := 0;
      seconds := 0;
  end;

  procedure Clock.SetTime(h,m,s:integer);
  begin
      if (h>23)OR(h<0)OR(m<0)OR(m>59)OR(s<0)OR(s>59) then
          exit;
      hours := h;
      minutes := m;
      seconds := s;
  end;

  procedure Clock.Tick;
  var
      totalsecs : longint;
  begin
      totalsecs := Trunc(hours*3600.0 + minutes*60 + seconds + 1);
      hours := (totalsecs div 3600) mod 24;
      minutes := (totalsecs mod 3600) div 60;
      seconds := totalsecs mod 60;
  end;

  procedure Clock.DisplayTime;
  begin
      writeln(hours,':',minutes,':',seconds);
  end;
```

**Continued on next page**

**LISTING 11.7**
(continued)

The *Clock* Class

```
   function Clock.GetHours : integer;
   begin
       GetHours := hours;
   end;

   function Clock.GetMinutes : integer;
   begin
       GetMinutes := minutes;
   end;

   function Clock.GetSeconds : integer;
   begin
       GetSeconds := seconds;
   end;

end.
```

We assume we now require a new class (*AlarmClock*) which displays an alarm message whenever a set time is reached. This class has the following additional features:

attributes

- ahours : integer
- aminutes : integer
- aseconds : integer

  These hold the time at which the alarm is to be activated.

operations

**SetAlarmTime(h,m,s:integer)**
  Sets the time at which the alarm is to be activated.

**IsAlarmTime():boolean**
  Returns *true* if the clock time and alarm time are exactly equal.

**GetAlarmHours() : integer**
  Returns the value of *ahours*.

**GetAlarmMinutes() : integer**
  Returns the value of *aminutes*.

**GetAlarmSeconds() : integer**
  Returns the value of *aseconds*.

We could create this new class by making it a descendant of the original *Clock* class. To do this, our program would begin with the statements:

```
uses Clocks;
    .
type
    AlarmClock = object(Clock)
```

This imports the existing *Clock* class and then defines *AlarmClock* as a descendant of *Clock* (Pascal names the base class in parentheses after the word `object` to achieve this).

As a subclass of *Clock, AlarmClock* inherits all the features of *Clock*. This means our new class only requires to specify the additional features. We need new attributes to record the time at which the alarm is to go off:

```
uses Clocks;

type
 AlarmClock = object(Clock)
    private
        ahours : integer;
```

```
        aminutes : integer;
        aseconds : integer;
```

We also need to add prototypes and code the new methods. That code is shown below:

```
procedure AlarmClock.SetAlarmTime(h,m,s : integer);
begin
    if (h<0)OR(h>23)OR(m<0)OR(m>59)OR(s<0)OR(s>59) then
        exit;
    ahours := h;
    aminutes := m;
    aseconds := s;
end;

function AlarmClock.IsAlarmTime: boolean;
begin
    if(hours = ahours )AND(minutes = aminutes)AND
    ↳(seconds = aseconds)then
        IsAlarmTime := true
    else
        IsAlarmTime := false;
end;

function AlarmClock.GetAlarmHours : integer;
begin
    GetAlarmHours := ahours;
end;

function AlarmClock.GetAlarmMinutes: integer;
begin
    GetAlarmMinutes := aminutes;
end;

function AlarmClock.GetAlarmSeconds : integer;
begin
    GetAlarmSeconds := aseconds;
end;
```

**Activity 11.24**

Create a Pascal Unit called *Alarms* containing the code for the *AlarmClock* class and attempt to compile it. Remember to add a `uses Clocks` clause.

If we try compiling this, we'll get the following error message

```
Unknown identifier
```

with the cursor flashing beside the *hours* term in the *IsAlarmTime* function.

The reason for this is that *hours, minutes* and *seconds* are declared as private within the parent *Clock* class. We've already seen that an attribute that is declared as private cannot be accessed by an application program which defines objects of that class. Now a further restriction has become apparent: private attributes inherited by a descendent class cannot be accessed from the methods added to that new class. To get round this we could rewrite *IsAlarmTime* using *GetHours, GetMinutes* and *GetSeconds:*

```
function AlarmClock.IsAlarmTime: boolean;
    begin
        if(GetHours = ahours )AND(GetMinutes = aminutes)AND
        ↳(GetSeconds = aseconds)then
            IsAlarmTime := true
        else
            IsAlarmTime := false;
    end;
```

**Activity 11.25**

Change the coding for the *IsAlarmTime* method and recompile the *AlarmClock* class.

## Overriding Methods

The program in LISTING-11.8 creates a simple application using an *AlarmClock* object and displays a message if the clock and alarm times are equal.

**LISTING-11.8**

Using an *AlarmClock* Object

```
program TestAlarm;
uses WinCrt, Alarms;

var
   ac : AlarmClock;
begin
   ac.Init;
   ac.SetTime(6,59,59);
   ac.SetAlarmTime(7,0,0);
   ac.Tick;
   if ac.IsAlarmTime then
       writeln('Time to get up');
end.
```

We can see that the *AlarmClock* object does not react to reaching the specified alarm time. Because of this, the above program contained the code:

```
ac.Tick;
if ac.isAlarmTime())
    writeln("Time to get up");
```

However, it might suit our purposes if this message was displayed by *Tick* itself when the appropriate time was reached.

To achieve this, the *AlarmClock* class needs a new version of the *Tick* method rather than the one it inherited from the *Clock* class. To create the replacement routine, we simply include the code for the new method within the *AlarmClock* class.

This is known as **overriding** the inherited method. To overwrite an inherited method the new version must have the same name and parameters as the original inherited method. For *Tick* the new method would be coded as:

```
procedure AlarmClock.Tick;
var
    totalsecs : longint;
begin
    totalsecs := Trunc(GetHours*3600.0 + GetMinutes*60 +
    ↳GetSeconds + 1);
    SetTime((totalsecs div 3600) mod 24,(totalsecs mod 3600)
    ↳div 60, totalsecs mod 60);
    if(GetHours = ahours )AND(GetMinutes = aminutes )AND
    ↳(GetSeconds = aseconds) then
        writeln('Time to get up');
end;
```

Notice that we're doing the same job as the original version of *Tick* (adding 1 second to the current time), but the code that does this is different because the methods of the *AlarmClock* class cannot access the private attributes of its parent class. In addition, the new version of *Tick* checks to see if the current time is equal to the alarm time and if so writes a message to the screen.

An alternative approach is to employ the following logic in *Tick:*

```
Execute the old version of Tick (adding 1 second to the time)
Check if the current and alarm times match
```

To run the inherited, but discarded, version of any routine we precede the normal call statement with the keyword `inherited`. Hence, the expression

```
inherited Tick;
```

executes the version of *Tick* defined in the *Clock* class.

This gives us the final code for the new version of *Tick* in the *AlarmClock* class:

```
procedure AlarmClock.Tick;
begin
    Inherited Tick;
    if(GetHours = ahours )AND(GetMinutes = aminutes )AND
    ↳(GetSeconds = aseconds) then
        writeln('Time to get up');
end;
```

**Activity 11.26**

Add the overridden version of *Tick* to *AlarmClock* and test the class.

## Inherited Constructors

Any new class derived from an existing class will also inherit the base class's constructor. Hence, we may use the following code for an *AlarmClock* object:

```
var
    ac : AlarmClock;
begin
    ac.Init;
```

which will set *hours, minutes* and *seconds* to zero.

Often the code a constructor contains will be insufficient for the new class. For example, in the case of the *AlarmClock* class the inherited constructor does not initialise the attributes *ahours, aminutes* and *aseconds.* The solution to this problem is simple - just override the constructor. The new constructor for the *AlarmClock* class needs to execute the *Clock* constructor and then add a few lines to initialise the new variables. The code for this is:

```
constructor AlarmClock.Init;
begin
    Clock.Init;
    ahours := 0;
    aminutes := 0;
    aseconds := 0;
end;
```

Notice that the call to the original constructor differs in syntax from the call to the old version of *Tick* in the earlier routine above. To call the base class's constructor we use the format:

```
BaseClass_name.constructor_name
```

Hence, in the example above we use:

```
Clock.Init;
```

**Activity 11.27**

Create a new Pascal unit called *Downs* containing a class, *CountdownClock*, which is a descendant of the *Clock* class, but differs from that class in that the *Tick* method reduces the time by one second.

Does the constructor need to be overridden?

Compile the file.

# Polymorphism

**Activity 11.28**

Create an application program containing both a *Clock* object and a *CountdownClock* object.

Set both objects to the time 12:00:00.

Execute the *Tick* methods of both objects and display the time of each.

From the results of Activity 11.28 we can see that each object executes its own version of *Tick.* So the *Clock* object moves on to 12:00:01 while the *CountdownClock* moves back to 11:59:59. This ability to execute the version of a routine appropriate to the type of object involved is an important one. The term **polymorphism** is used to describe this ability. As we will see below it is a very powerful feature.

## Polymorphism and Overridden Methods

Descendant classes have another unexpected feature; when we define a class reference variable, as in the statement

```
cl : ^Clock;
```

we can use that variable to reference an object of the stated class OR ANY DESCENDANT CLASS. In Borland Pascal we need to set up type declarations for each various class pointers:

```
program TestClocks;
uses WinCrt, Clocks, Alarms, Downs;

type
    ClockPtr = ^Clock;
    AlarmClockPtr = ^AlarmClock;
    CountdownClockPtr = ^CountdownClock;
```

then we can create our *Clock* pointer:

```
var
    ac : ^Clock;        {or ac : ClockPtr;}
```

Next, we allow the user to choose which type of clock is to be created:

```
clrscr;
writeln('What time of clock ?');
writeln('1 - Clock');
writeln('2 - Alarm clock');
writeln('3 - Countdown Clock');
readln(typeofclock);
case (typeofclock) of
    1:ac := new(ClockPtr,Init);
    2:ac := new(AlarmClockPtr, Init);
    3:ac := new(CountdownClockPtr,Init);
    else
        begin
            writeln('Invalid choice');
            exit;
        end;
end;
```

The object requested by the user is created using the `new` command. This command has the format:

```
new(ObjectPointerType, Class constructor name)
```

Finally, we execute methods of our object:

```
ac^.SetTime(6,59,59);
ac^.Tick;
ac^.DisplayTime;
```

Each type of clock has a different version of the method *Tick*. Polymorphism ensures that the version of *Tick* appropriate to the object created will be executed. Hence, if we create a *Clock* object, the time displayed should read 7:0:0 while a *CountdownClock* object will result in a display of 6:59:58. The complete example is given in LISTING-11.9.

**LISTING-11.9**

Using Object Pointers

```
program TestClocks;
uses WinCrt, Clocks, Alarms, Downs;
type
   ClockPtr = ^Clock;
   AlarmClockPtr = ^AlarmClock;
   CountdownClockPtr = ^CountdownClock;
var
   ac : ^Clock;
   typeofclock : integer;
begin
   {*** Let user choose clock type ***}
   clrscr;
   writeln('What time of clock ?');
   writeln('1 - Clock');
   writeln('2 - Alarm clock');
   writeln('3 - Countdown Clock');
   readln(typeofclock);
   {*** Create clock ***}
   case (typeofclock) of
       1:ac := new(ClockPtr,Init);
       2:ac := new(AlarmClockPtr, Init);
       3:ac := new(CountdownClockPtr,Init);
       else
           begin
               writeln('Invalid choice');
               exit;
           end;
   end;
   {*** Execute methods of the clock ***}
   ac^.SetTime(6,59,59);
   ac^.Tick;
   ac^.DisplayTime;
end.
```

**Activity 11.29**

Enter and compile the program given in LISTING-11.9.

On the first run create a *Clock* object. Is the time displayed 7:0:0?

On the second run create a *CountdownClock* object. Is the time displayed 6:59:58?

You'll see from Activity 11.29 that the *CountdownClock* object does not display the expected time. Why is that?

When we create a pointer to a class, Pascal decides on the version of *Tick* that is to be executed at compile time. Because the pointer *ac* is designed originally to reference a *Clock* object, Pascal assumes that it is the *Clock* version of *Tick* method that is to be executed. But at compile time the user has not yet chosen which type of object is to be created. If we want the program to work correctly we need to delay a decision on which version of *Tick* is to be executed until the program is running and the routine about to be executed. Then, if a *CountdownClock* object is chosen, the *Tick* method defined in that class can be run.

Deciding on the routine to be called at compile time is known as **early binding**.

This delay in deciding which version of a routine is to be executed until execution time is called **late binding** or **dynamic binding**.

## Virtual Methods

To achieve this effect, we need to tell the machine which methods should not have their addresses inserted at compile time. We do this by placing the term `virtual` at the end of the appropriate routine headings within the class declaration. Late binding of *Tick* requires the *Clock* declaration to be changed to:

```
procedure Tick; virtual;
```

All other classes in which the *Tick* method is overridden need to include the term `virtual` in the same way.

A second requirement of late binding is that the constructor of the object being created must be executed. If a class has no constructor then one must be created, even of this consists only of the terms `begin` and `end`.

**Activity 11.30**

Add the term virtual to the *Tick* methods of all three clock classes.

Re-run the program you produced in Activity 11.29.

On the first run, create a *Clock* object. The display should read 7:0:0.

On the second run, create a *CountdownClock* object. The display should read 6:59:58.

## Polymorphism within Methods

To demonstrate a final example of polymorphism at work we need to return to the *Clock* class and add a new operation to make the clock display the time as it counts through several seconds. The operation is called *RunTime.*

The code for the routine is

```
procedure Clock.RunTime(v : integer);
var
    c : integer;
begin
    for c := 1 to v do
    begin
        write(GetHours,':',GetMinutes,':',GetSeconds);
        Tick;
        Delay(1000);
        write(#8#8#8#8#8#8#8#8);
    end;
    write(GetHours,':',GetMinutes,':',GetSeconds);
end;
```

The clock ticks for *v* seconds. A `for` loop displays the current time; calls *Tick* and delays for about 1 second before continuing the iteration.

The line

```
write(#8#8#8#8#8#8#8#8);
```

causes the cursor to move back to its starting point so that the display updates over the same area of the screen.

The procedure *Delay* pauses the program for a given number of milliseconds. It is defined as a private method within the *Clock* class. The code for this routine is:

```
procedure Clock.Delay(milli : longint);
var
    x : real;
    c : longint;
begin
    for C := 1 to milli *100 do
        x := sin(c)*sqrt(c)/cos(c)/sin(c);
end;
```

*Delay* operates by the rather crude method of simply keeping the processor busy on some length calculations for about one millisecond. You may have to adjust the multiplication factor on your hardware.

**Activity 11.31**

Add the two routines to the *Clock* class and recompile the Pascal unit.

In the next Activity we'll see how the *RunTime* method works on a *Clock* object and then on a *CountdownClock* object.

**Activity 11.32**

Modify the program you created in Activity 11.29 to read as follows:

```
program TestRunTime;
uses WinCrt, Clocks, Alarms, Downs;
type
  ClockPtr = ^Clock;
  AlarmClockPtr = ^AlarmClock;
  CountdownClockPtr = ^CountdownClock;
```

**Continued on next page**

**Activity 11.32** (continued)

```
var
  ac : ^Clock;
  typeofclock : integer;
begin
  clrscr;
  writeln('What time of clock ?');
  writeln('1 - Clock');
  writeln('2 - Alarm clock');
  writeln('3 - Countdown Clock');
  readln(typeofclock);
  case (typeofclock) of
      1:ac := new(ClockPtr,Init);
      2:ac := new(AlarmClockPtr, Init);
      3:ac := new(CountdownClockPtr,Init);
      else
          begin
              writeln('Invalid choice');
              exit;
          end;
  end;
  ac^.SetTime(6,59,59);
  ac^.RunTime(10);
end.
```

Run the program twice.

On the first run create a *Clock* object. The time should count forwards.

On the second run create a *CountdownClock* object. Time should run backwards.

For the *CountdownClock* to function correctly the call in *RunTime* to *Tick* must be picking up the version appropriate to that class. Again, this is an example of polymorphism at work. As before, the term `virtual` is needed in the *Tick* definitions and the object constructor must be executed.

# A Shortcoming of Class Pointers

When a pointer is designed to reference one class as in

```
ac : ^Clock;
```

and is then made to reference an object of a descendant type:

```
new(AlarmClockPtr, Init)
```

a limitation is imposed on how that pointer may be used. Only methods named in the original class may be called. Hence, using the above example, the following expressions are acceptable:

```
ac^.SetTime(1,2,3)
ac^.GetHours
ac^.Tick
```

Attempting to access methods which are first named in the descendant class such as

```
ac^.SetAlarmTime(7,0,0);
ac^.IsAlarmTime
```

are invalid.

If you know a pointer contains the address of a descendant class, and you need to execute methods first mentioned in that class, then you need to cast the pointer to the new class's pointer type. For example, to execute *SetAlarmTime* we would use the expression:

```
(AlarmClockPtr)ac^.SetAlarmTime(7,0,0);
```

# Summary

- **Inheritance** allows a new class to be given the features of an existing class.
- The new class is known as the **derived class**.
- The existing class is known as the **base class**.
- The base class is the **parent** of the new class.
- The derived class is the **child** of the base class.
- **Derived classes can add new attributes and methods**.
- **Derived classes may override inherited methods**.
- **Constructors of derived classes can call their base class's constructor**.
- **Polymorphism** ensures that the version of a method appropriate to the object involved is executed.
- Polymorphism is activated in Pascal by including the term `virtual` in the method's declaration.
- **Virtual methods** have their address calculated at run-time. This is known as **late binding**.
- **Methods declared as virtual in the base class must be declared as virtual in all descendant classes**.
- If a class contains virtual methods **its constructor must be executed.**
- **A base class pointer can be used to reference a descendant class object.**
- **Only features mentioned in the base class can be accessed** when dereferencing the pointer.
- **To call features first defined in a descendant class** the object pointer must be cast to the appropriate pointer type.

# OTHER CLASS TYPES

## Aggregate Classes

### Introduction

An aggregate class is one in which some or all of its attributes are objects from other classes. For example, if a hospital system wished to record details of each new-born baby it might employ a *BabyClass* defined as:

```
type
    BabyClass = object
        private
            name : string;
            height : Distance;
            wght : Weight;
        public
            constructor Init;
            procedure SetName(n:string);
            procedure SetHeight(h:Distance);
            procedure SetWeight(w:Weight);
            function GetName:string;
            procedure GetHeight(var h:Distance);
            procedure GetWeight(var w:Weight);
    end;
```

*BabyClass* can be represented as a UML diagram in two ways. The first (see FIG-11.10) shows only the relationship between *BabyClass* and the *Distance* and *Weight* classes.

**FIG-11.10**

An Aggregate Class - Style 1

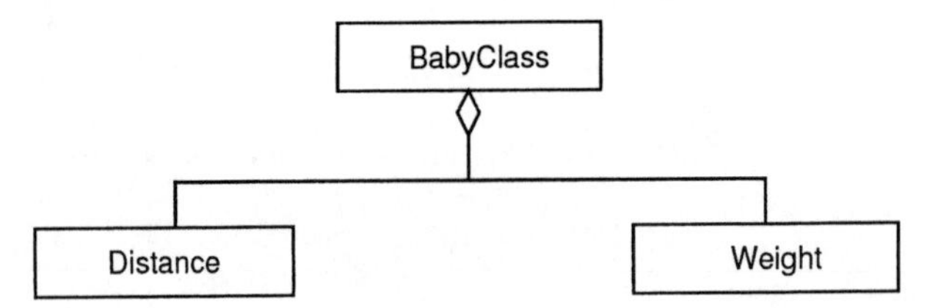


*Distance* and *Weight* components are shown to be "part of" *BabyClass.*

The second diagram (see FIG-11.11) shows more detail and names the features of the classes.

**FIG-11.11**

An Aggregate Class - Style 2

Early versions of the *Weight* and *Distance* classes are shown.

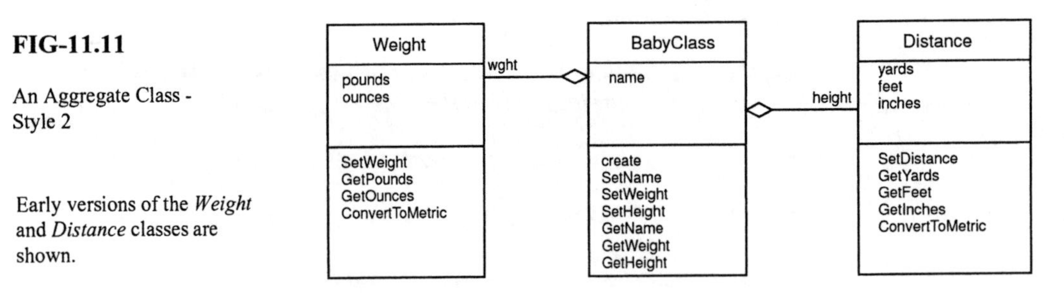


Since the attributes of *BabyClass* are private they cannot be accessed directly in any object of this class and hence access must be provided via new methods.

### Constructors in Aggregation

As a *BabyClass* object is created, so within it, *Weight* class and *Distance* class objects are also created. This means that the constructor for *BabyClass* needs to call each of the constructors of its constituent parts. This is done in the following manner:

```
constructor BabyClass.Init;
begin
    height.Init;
    wght.Init;
    name :='';
end;
```

### Creating Operations in an Aggregation

The remainder of the class's methods can then be defined. Most of these will make use of the methods defined for the objects which are attributes of the aggregate class. The new class has no special rights of access to its component objects and may only make use of public features of the class instances.

The code for the remaining methods is given in LISTING-11.10 below.

**LISTING-11.10**

The methods of *BabyClass*

```
procedure babyClass.SetName(n : string);
begin
    name := n;
end;

procedure BabyClass.SetHeight(h:Distance);
begin
    height.SetDistance(0,h.GetFeet,h.GetInches);
end;

procedure BabyClass.SetWeight(w:Weight);
begin
    wght.SetWeight(w.GetPounds, w.GetOunces);
end;

function BabyClass.GetName:string;
begin
    GetName := name;
end;

procedure BabyClass.GetHeight(var h:Distance);
begin
    h.SetDistance(0,height.GetFeet,height.GetInches);
end;

procedure BabyClass.GetWeight(var w : WEight);
begin
    w.SetWeight(wght.GetPounds, wght.GetOunces);
end;
```

**Activity 11.33**

Enter and compile *BabyClass*, saving it in a unit called *Baby*.

Create a program which exercises the methods of *BabyClass*.

## Container Classes

As well as creating objects capable of holding a single item, we can create classes which contain a collection of similar items. Such a class is known as a **container class.**

We've already met this idea in Chapter 8 when we created various data structures such as Lists, Stacks, Queues etc.

The operations required of a list are repeated below:

| | |
|---|---|
| **Create** | Creates an empty list. |
| **AddAt** | Adds a new value at a specified position in the list. |
| **DeleteFrom** | Deletes a value from a specified position in the list. |
| **Head** | Returns the first value in the list. |
| **Tail** | Removes the first item from the list |
| **Len** | Returns the number of entries in the list. |
| **IsEmpty** | Returns 1 if the list is empty, otherwise zero is returned. |
| **DisplayList** | Displays the complete sequence. |
| **DeleteList** | Removes all entries from an existing list. |
| **Give** | Returns the data held at a specified position within the list. |

We need to begin by declaring some auxiliary structures:

```
Data =
    record
        Ftext : string[21];
    end;

NodePointerType = ^Node;

Node =
    record
        value:Data;
        next:NodePointerType;
    end;
```

The class itself is then declared as:

```
List = object
    private
        start : NodePointerType;
        count : integer;
    public
        constructor Init;
        function  Len : integer;
        function  IsEmpty : boolean;
        function  AddAt(item : Data ; post : integer) : boolean;
        function  DeleteFrom(post:integer) : boolean;
        procedure Head(var front : Data);
        procedure Tail;
        procedure DisplayList;
        procedure DeleteList;
        function  IsAt(d:Data):integer;
        procedure Give(post:integer;var result:Data);
end;
```

The code for each class method closely reflects that produced in Chapter 8, but with the List variable missing from the routine's parameters (since the methods of the class have automatic access to the attributes of the class).

The code for the constructor and *AddAt* is given below:

```
constructor List.Init;
begin
    start := NIL;
    count := 0;
end;

function  List.AddAt(item : Data; post : integer) : boolean;
var
    current, previous, temp : NodePointerType;
```

```
    c : integer;
begin
    {*** IF invalid position THEN exit with zero ***}
    if(post < 1) or (post > Len + 1)then
        AddAt:=false;
    {*** Create space for new node ***}
    New (temp);
    {*** Place data in node ***}
    temp^.value := item;
    temp^.next := NIL;
    {*** IF placed at start update main pointer***}
    if post = 1 then
    begin
        current := start;
        start := temp;
        temp^.next := current;
    end
    else
    {*** ELSE find insert position ***}
    begin
        previous := NIL;
        current := start;
        for c := 2 to post do
        begin
            previous := current;
            current := current^.next;
        end;
        {** Link new node into chain **}
        previous^.next := temp;
        temp^.next := current;
    end;
    {*** Add 1 to count ***}
    Inc(count);
    AddAt:= true;
end;
```

**Activity 11.34**

Complete the coding for *List* class and add sufficient code to test your routines.

Convert the *List* class in a Pascal Unit named *ListClass*.

# Delegation

There are occasions when a new class needs less facilities than an existing one. For example, a stack is a type of list where values can only be added and removed from the head of the sequence. If we create a *Stack* class derived from a *List* class, it will inherit methods which are not appropriate to the new class. One way round this is to create an **aggregate** class containing only the original class which we wish to restrict. The operations of a stack are defined informally as:

| | |
|---|---|
| **Create** | Creates an empty stack. |
| **Push** | Adds a value to the top (front) of the stack. |
| **Top** | Returns the top element in the stack. |
| **Pop** | Removes the top element in the stack. |
| **IsEmpty** | Returns 1 if the stack is empty else zero. |
| **Len** | Returns the number of values in the stack. |
| **DisplayStack** | Displays the contents of the stack. |
| **EmptyStack** | Removes all entries from an existing stack. |

A program defining and using this class is given in LISTING-11.11 below.

**LISTING-11.11**

The *Stack* Class

```
program StackClass;
uses WinCrt,ListClass,Auxiliary;

type
  Stack = object
      private
          seq : List;
      public
          constructor Init;
          procedure Push(v : Data);
          procedure Top(var v : Data);
          procedure Pop;
          function IsEmpty : boolean;
          function Len : integer;
          procedure DisplayStack;
          procedure EmptyStack;
  end;

constructor Stack.Init;
begin
  seq.Init;
end;

procedure Stack.Push(v : Data);
begin
  seq.AddAt(v,1);
end;

procedure Stack.Top(var v : Data);
begin
  seq.Give(1,v);
end;

procedure Stack.Pop;
begin
  seq.DeleteFrom(1);
end;

function Stack.IsEmpty : boolean;
begin
  IsEmpty := seq.IsEmpty;
end;

function Stack.Len : integer;
begin
  Len := seq.Len;
end;

procedure Stack.DisplayStack;
begin
  seq.DisplayList;
end;

procedure Stack.EmptyStack;
begin
  seq.deleteList;
end;
{*************************************}
{*  End of Stack class definitions   *}
{*************************************}


procedure ExecuteOption(opt:integer; var s:Stack);
var
  value  : Data;
  post : integer;
  ch   : char;
begin
```

**Continued on next page**

**LISTING-11.11**
(continued)

The *Stack* Class

```
    case (opt) of
        1:  {Remove contents of stack}
            s.EmptyStack;
        2:  {Add item to stack}
            begin
                write('Enter value to be added : ');
                readln(value.Ftext);
                s.Push(value);
            end;
        3:  {Pop stack}
            if not s.IsEmpty then
                s.Pop;
            else
            begin
                writeln('The stack is empty');
                ch := readkey;
            end;
        4:  {Display top of stack}
            if not s.IsEmpty then
            begin
                s.Top(value);
                writeln('Top item in stack is : ',value.Ftext);
                ch := readkey;
            end
            else
            begin
                writeln('The stack is empty');
                ch := readkey;
            end;
        5:  {Number of items in stack }
            begin
                writeln('The stack contains ',s.Len,' values');
                ch := readkey;
            end;
        6:  {Check if empty}
            begin
                if s.IsEmpty then
                    writeln('The stack is empty')
                else
                    writeln('The stack is not empty');
                ch := readkey;
            end;
        7:  {Display contents}
            begin
                ClrScr;
                writeln('CONTENTS OF STACK');
                s.DisplayStack;
                ch := readkey;
            end;
        8:  {Terminate program}
            writeln('Program terminated');
    end
end;


const
    NL = #13#10;
var
    st : Stack;
    opt, noofopts : integer;
begin
    repeat
        ClrScr;
        noofopts := DisplayMenu('1 - Delete contents of stack'+NL+
                        '2 - Add value to stack'+NL+
                        '3 - Pop stack'+NL+
                        '4 - Display top of stack'+NL+
```

**Continued on next page**

**LISTING-11.11**
(continued)

The *Stack* Class

```
                        '5 - Display height of stack'+NL+
                        '6 - Check if stack empty'+NL+
                        '7 - Display stack'+NL+
                        '8 - QUIT'+NL);
        opt := GetOption(noofopts);
        ExecuteOption(opt, st);
    until opt = noofopts;
end.
```

**Activity 11.35**

Type in and test the program given in LISTING-11.11.

# Summary

## Aggregate Classes

- **An aggregate class** is one in which some or all of the attributes are themselves classes.
- **Default and zero-argument constructors of the attributes** of an aggregate class are executed automatically.
- **Other attribute constructors** must be called from within the aggregate class constructor.
- **Only public features of the attribute objects can be accessed within an aggregate class.**

## Container Classes

- **A container class is designed to hold several objects** of a given class or family of classes.

## Delegation

- **Delegation** allows access to the methods of an existing class to be restricted by enclosing the existing class in a new one.

# SOLUTIONS

## Activity 11.1

1. Characteristics
    - Length
    - Diameter
    - Colour of lead

   Operations
    - Write
    - Sharpen

2. Characteristics
    - Day
    - Month
    - Year

   Operations
    - SetDate
    - GetDate
    - Day of Week
    - Is Leap Year

## Activity11.2

1. class
2. object
3. class
4. object
5. class
6. object

## Activity 11.3

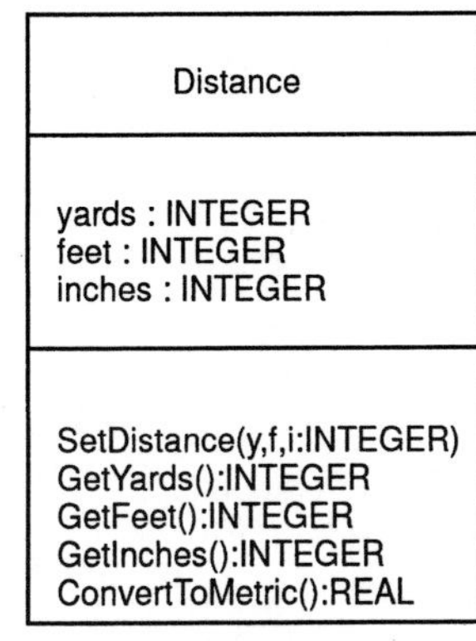


## Activity 11.4

```
type
    Distance = object
        yards : integer;
        feet : integer;
        inches : integer;

        procedure SetDistance(y,f,i:integer);
        function GetYards:integer;
        function GetFeet : integer;
        function GetInches : integer;
        function ConvertToMetric : real;
    end;
```

## Activiy 11.5

No solution required.

## Activity 11.6

```
Unit Distances;

interface

type
    Distance = object
        yards : integer;
        feet : integer;
        inches : integer;

        procedure SetDistance(y,f,i:integer);
        function GetYards:integer;
        function GetFeet : integer;
        function GetInches : integer;
        function ConvertToMetric : real;
    end;

implementation

    procedure Distance.SetDistance(y,f,i:integer);
    begin
        if (y < 0) OR (f < 0) OR (f > 2)
        ↳OR ( i< 0) OR (i > 11) then
            exit;
        yards := y;
        feet := f;
        inches := i;
    end;

    function Distance.GetYards : integer;
    begin
        GetYards := yards;
    end;

    function Distance.GetFeet : integer;
    begin
        GetFeet := feet;
    end;

    function Distance.GetInches : integer;
    begin
        GetInches := inches;
    end;

    function Distance.ConvertToMetric : real;
    begin
        ConvertToMetric := (yards*36+feet*12+inches)
        ↳*0.0254;
    end;

end.
```

## Activity 11.7

```
w1.ConvertToMetric
```

## Activity 11.8

No solution required.

## Activity 11.9

```
program WTest3;
uses WinCrt, Distances;
var
    y,f,i : integer;
    d1 : Distance;
begin
    clrscr;
    write('Enter yards : ');
    readln(y);
    write('Enter feet : ');
    readln(f);
    write('Enter inches : ');
    readln(i);
    d1.SetDistance(y,f,i);
    writeln('The distance entered was '
    ↳,d1.GetYards,' yds ',d1.GetFeet
    ↳,' ft ',d1.GetInches,' in');
    writeln('This is ',d1.ConvertToMetric:0:2
    ↳,' metres');
end.
```

## Activity 11.10

No solution required.

## Activity 11.11

No solution required.

## Activity 11.12

The interface part of the *Distances* unit should now read:

```
type
    Distance = object
        private
            yards : integer;
            feet : integer;
            inches : integer;

        public
            procedure SetDistance(y,f,i:integer);
            function GetYards:integer;
            function GetFeet : integer;
            function GetInches : integer;
            function ConvertToMetric : real;
    end;
```

The implementation section remains unchanged.

The application program should operate as before.

## Activity 11.13

```
program DTest;
uses WinCrt, Distances;
var
    y,f,i : integer;
    d1,d2 : Distance;
begin
    clrscr;
    {*** Read first distance ***}
    write('Enter yards : ');
    readln(y);
    write('Enter feet : ');
    readln(f);
    write('Enter inches : ');
    readln(i);
    d1.SetDistance(y,f,i);
    {*** Read second distance ***}
    write('Enter yards : ');
    readln(y);
    write('Enter feet : ');
    readln(f);
    write('Enter inches : ');
    readln(i);
    d2.SetDistance(y,f,i);
    {*** Display longer distance ***}
    if d1.ConvertToMetric > d2.ConvertToMetric
    ↳then
        writeln('Longer distance is ',d1.GetYards
        ↳,' yds ',d1.GetFeet,' ft ',d1.GetInches,
        ↳' in')
    else
        writeln('Longer distance is ',d2.GetYards
        ↳,' yds ',d2.GetFeet,' ft ',d2.GetInches,
        ↳' in')
end.
```

## Activity 11.14

The new code for the *Distance* class is:

```
Unit Distances;

interface

type
    Distance = object
        private
            yards : integer;
            feet : integer;
            inches : integer;
        public
            procedure SetDistance(y,f,i:integer);
            function GetYards:integer;
            function GetFeet : integer;
            function GetInches : integer;
            function ConvertToMetric : real;
            procedure Add(d : Distance);
    end;

implementation

    procedure Distance.SetDistance(y,f,i:integer);
    begin
        if (y < 0) OR (f < 0) OR (f > 2) OR
        ↳(i < 0) OR (i > 11) then
            exit;
        yards := y;
        feet := f;
        inches := i;
    end;

    function Distance.GetYards : integer;
    begin
        GetYards := yards;
    end;

    function Distance.GetFeet : integer;
    begin
        GetFeet := feet;
    end;

    function Distance.GetInches : integer;
    begin
        GetInches := inches;
    end;

    function Distance.ConvertToMetric : real;
    begin
        ConvertToMetric:=(yards*36+feet*12+inches)
        ↳*0.0254;
    end;

    procedure Distance.Add(d:Distance);
    var
        totalinches : integer;
    begin
        totalinches := (yards+d.yards)*36
        ↳+(feet+d.feet)*12 + inches + d.inches;
        yards := totalinches div 36;
        feet := totalinches mod 36 div 12;
        inches := totalinches mod 12;
    end;
end.
```

The application to add two distances is coded as:

```
program DTest3;
uses WinCrt, Distances;
var
    y,f,i : integer;
    d1,d2 : Distance;
begin
    clrscr;
    {*** Read first distance ***}
    write('Enter yards : ');
    readln(y);
    write('Enter feet : ');
    readln(f);
    write('Enter inches : ');
    readln(i);
    d1.SetDistance(y,f,i);
    {*** Read second distance ***}
    write('Enter yards : ');
    readln(y);
    write('Enter feet : ');
    readln(f);
    write('Enter inches : ');
    readln(i);
    d2.SetDistance(y,f,i);
    {*** Display longer distance ***}
    d1.Add(d2);
    writeln('Distance in d1 is ',d1.GetYards,
    ↳' yds ',d1.GetFeet,' ft ',d1.GetInches,' in')
end.
```

## Activity 11.15

The interface part of the *Distances* unit would now be :

```
type
    Distance = object
        private
            yards : integer;
```

```
            feet : integer;
            inches : integer;
            function ToInches : integer;

        public
            procedure SetDistance(y,f,i:integer);
            function GetYards:integer;
            function GetFeet : integer;
            function GetInches : integer;
            function ConvertToMetric : real;
            procedure Add(d : Distance);
    end;
```

The following code must be added to the implementation section:

```
function Distance.ToInches : integer;
begin
    ToInches := yards * 36 + feet * 12 + inches;
end;
```

The *Add* method should now be coded as:

```
procedure Distance.Add(d:Distance);
var
    totalinches : integer;
begin
    totalinches := ToInches + d.ToInches;
    yards := totalinches div 36;
    feet := totalinches mod 36 div 12;
    inches := totalinches mod 12;
end;
```

If you test the new code by re-running the application to add two distances, the result should be the same as before.

## Activity 11.16

The *Distance* class interface is now coded as:

```
type
    Distance = object
        private
            yards : integer;
            feet : integer;
            inches : integer;
            function ToInches : integer;

        public
            procedure SetDistance(y,f,i:integer);
            function GetYards:integer;
            function GetFeet : integer;
            function GetInches : integer;
            function ConvertToMetric : real;
            procedure Add(d : Distance);
            function IsGreaterThan(d : Distance)
            ↪: boolean;
    end;
```

The code for *IsGreaterThan* is:

```
function Distance.IsGreaterThan(d:Distance)
↪: boolean;
begin
    if ToInches > d.ToInches then
        IsGreaterThan := true
    else
        IsGreaterThan := false;
end;
```

The application code is:

```
program DTest4;
uses WinCrt, Distances;
var
    y,f,i : integer;
    d1,d2 : Distance;
begin
    clrscr;
    {*** Read first distance ***}
    write('Enter yards : ');
    readln(y);
    write('Enter feet : ');
    readln(f);
    write('Enter inches : ');
    readln(i);
    d1.SetDistance(y,f,i);
    {*** Read second distance ***}
    write('Enter yards : ');
    readln(y);
    write('Enter feet : ');
    readln(f);
    write('Enter inches : ');
    readln(i);
    d2.SetDistance(y,f,i);
    {*** Display longer distance ***}
    if d1.IsGreaterThan(d2) then
        writeln('The longer distance is '
        ↪,d1.GetYards,' yds ',d1.GetFeet
        ↪,' ft ',d1.GetInches,' in')
    else
        writeln('The longer distance is '
        ↪,d2.GetYards,' yds ',d2.GetFeet
        ↪,' ft ',d2.GetInches,' in');
end.
```

## Activity 11.17

The *Distance* class interface is now coded as:

```
type
    Distance = object
        private
            yards : integer;
            feet : integer;
            inches : integer;
            function ToInches : integer;

        public
            procedure SetDistance(y,f,i:integer);
            function GetYards:integer;
            function GetFeet : integer;
            function GetInches : integer;
            function ConvertToMetric : real;
            procedure Add(d : Distance);
            function IsGreaterThan(d : Distance)
            ↪: boolean;
            procedure Divide(divisor : integer;
            ↪var d : Distance);
    end;
```

The code for *Divide* is:

```
    procedure Distance.Divide(divisor : integer;
var d : Distance);
    var
        resultininches : integer;
    begin
      if divisor <= 0 then
        halt;
      resultininches := Round(ToInches/divisor);
      d.yards := resultininches div 36;
      d.feet := (resultininches mod 36) div 12;
      d.inches := resultininches mod 12;
    end;
```

The application code is:

```
program DTest5;
uses WinCrt, Distances;
var
    y,f,i : integer;
    d1,d2,average : Distance;
begin
    clrscr;
    {*** Read first distance ***}
    write('Enter yards : ');
    readln(y);
    write('Enter feet : ');
    readln(f);
    write('Enter inches : ');
    readln(i);
    d1.SetDistance(y,f,i);
    {*** Read second distance ***}
    write('Enter yards : ');
    readln(y);
    write('Enter feet : ');
    readln(f);
    write('Enter inches : ');
    readln(i);
    d2.SetDistance(y,f,i);
    {*** Display average distance ***}
    d1.Add(d2);
    d1.Divide(2,average);
    writeln('The average distance is '
    ↪,average.GetYards,' yds ',average.GetFeet
,' ft ',average.GetInches,' in');
end.
```

## Activity 11.18

The *Distance* class interface is now coded as:

```
type
    Distance = object
        private
            yards : integer;
            feet : integer;
            inches : integer;
            function ToInches : integer;

        public
            constructor Init;
            procedure SetDistance(y,f,i:integer);
            function GetYards:integer;
            function GetFeet : integer;
            function GetInches : integer;
            function ConvertToMetric : real;
            procedure Add(d : Distance);
            function IsGreaterThan(d : Distance)
            ↳: boolean;
            procedure Divide(divisor : integer;
            ↳var d : Distance);
    end;
```

The code for the constructor is:

```
    constructor Distance.Init;
    begin
        yards := 0;
        feet := 0;
        inches := 0;
    end;
```

## Activity 11.19

```
program DTest6;
uses WinCrt, Distances;
var
    y,f,i,c : integer;
    measures : array[1..5] of Distance;
    average,total : Distance;
begin
    clrscr;
    for c := 1 to 5 do
    begin
        {*** Read distance ***}
        write('Enter yards : ');
        readln(y);
        write('Enter feet : ');
        readln(f);
        write('Enter inches : ');
        readln(i);
        measures[c].SetDistance(y,f,i);
    end;
    {*** Calculate total ***}
    total.Init;
    for c := 1 to 5 do
        total.Add(measures[c]);
    {*** Display average distance ***}
    Total.Divide(5,average);
    writeln('The average distance is '
    ↳,average.GetYards,' yds ',average.GetFeet
    ↳,' ft ',average.GetInches,' in');
end.
```

## Activity 11.20

```
Unit Clocks;

interface
type
    Clock = object
        private
            hours   : integer;
            minutes : integer;
            seconds : integer;

        public
            constructor Init;
            procedure SetTime(h,m,s : integer);
            procedure Tick;virtual;
            procedure DisplayTime;
            function GetHours : integer;
            function GetMinutes : integer;
            function GetSeconds : integer;
    end;

    implementation
    constructor Clock.Init;
    begin
        hours := 0;
        minutes := 0;
        seconds := 0;
    end;

    procedure Clock.SetTime(h,m,s:integer);
    begin
        if (h>23)OR(h<0)OR(m<0)OR(m>59)OR(s<0)
        ↳OR(s>59) then
            exit;
        hours := h;
        minutes := m;
        seconds := s;
    end;

    procedure Clock.Tick;
    var
        totalsecs : longint;
    begin
        totalsecs := Trunc(hours*3600.0 +
        ↳minutes*60 + seconds + 1);
        hours := (totalsecs div 3600) mod 24;
        minutes := (totalsecs mod 3600) div 60;
        seconds := totalsecs mod 60;
    end;

    procedure Clock.DisplayTime;
    begin
        writeln(hours,':',minutes,':',seconds);
    end;

    function Clock.GetHours : integer;
    begin
        GetHours := hours;
    end;

    function Clock.GetMinutes : integer;
    begin
        GetMinutes := minutes;
    end;

    function Clock.GetSeconds : integer;
    begin
        GetSeconds := seconds;
    end;
end.
```

A test program:

```
program TestClock;
uses WinCrt, Clocks;

var
    cl: Clock;
    h,m,s : integer;
begin
    cl.Init;
    ClrScr;
    write('Enter hours :');
    readln(h);
    write('Enter minutes :');
    readln(m);
    write('Enter seconds :');
    readln(s);
    cl.SetTime(h,m,s);
    cl.DisplayTime;
    cl.Tick;
    writeln(cl.GetHours,':',cl.GetMinutes,':',
    ↳cl.GetSeconds);
end.
```

## Activity 11.21

The attributes of the *BWTV* class are:

```
volume
station
power
contrast
brightness
```

## Activity 11.22

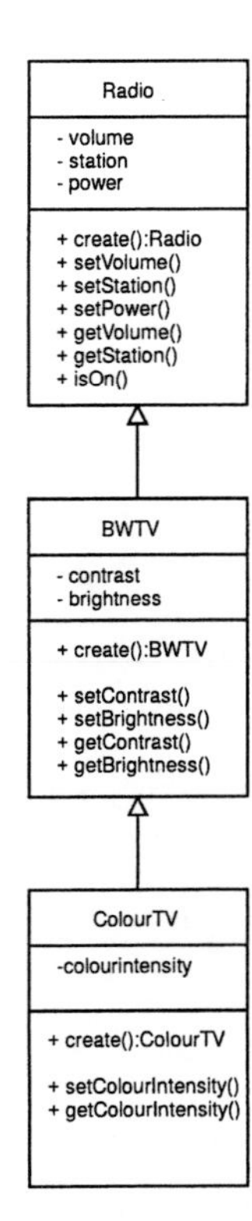


## Activity 11.23

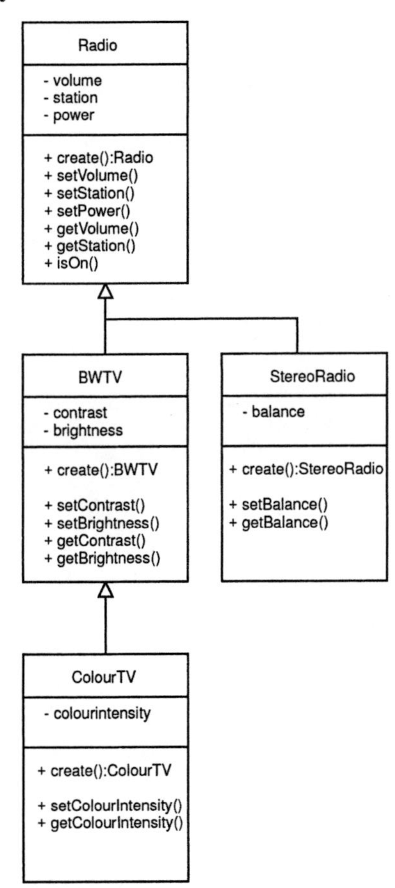


## Activity 11.24

```
Unit Alarms;

interface
uses Clocks;
type
    AlarmClock = object(Clock)
        private
            ahours : integer;
            aminutes : integer;
            aseconds : integer;

        public
        procedure SetAlarmTime(h,m,s : integer);
        function GetAlarmHours : integer;
        function GetAlarmMinutes : integer;
        function GetAlarmSeconds : integer;
        function IsAlarmTime : boolean;
        procedure Tick;
    end;

implementation

    procedure AlarmClock.SetAlarmTime
    ↳(h,m,s:integer);
    begin
        if(h>23)OR(h<0)OR(m<0)OR(m>59)OR(s<0)
        ↳OR(s>59)then
            exit;
        ahours := h;
        aminutes := m;
        aseconds := s;
    end;

    procedure AlarmClock.Tick;
    var
        totalsecs : longint;
    begin
        totalsecs := Trunc(GetHours*3600.0
        ↳+ GetMinutes*60 + GetSeconds + 1);
        SetTime((totalsecs div 3600) mod 24,
        ↳(totalsecs mod 3600) div 60,totalsecs
        ↳mod 60);
        if(GetHours = ahours )AND
        (GetMinutes = aminutes )AND
        (GetSeconds = aseconds) then
            writeln('Time to get up');
    end;

    function AlarmClock.GetAlarmHours:integer;
    begin
        GetAlarmHours := ahours;
    end;

    function AlarmClock.GetAlarmMinutes:integer;
    begin
        GetAlarmMinutes := aminutes;
    end;

    function AlarmClock.GetAlarmSeconds:integer;
    begin
        GetAlarmSeconds := aseconds;
    end;

    function AlarmClock.IsAlarmTime: boolean;
    begin
        if(hours = ahours )AND
        ↳(minutes = aminutes)AND
        ↳(seconds = aseconds)then
            IsAlarmTime := true
        else
            IsAlarmTime := false;
    end;
end.
```

## Activity 11.25

No solution required.

## Activity 11.26

No solution required.

## Activity 11.27

```
Unit Downs;

interface
uses Clocks;
type
    CountdownClock = object(Clock)
        public
            procedure Tick;
    end;

implementation

procedure CountdownClock.Tick;
    var
        totalsecs : longint;
    begin
        totalsecs := Trunc(GetHours*3600.0
        ↳+ GetMinutes*60 + GetSeconds - 1);
        SetTime((totalsecs div 3600) mod 24,
        ↳(totalsecs mod 3600) div 60,
        ↳totalsecs mod 60);
    end;
end.
```

The constructor does not need to be overridden since the inherited one already performs all operations required by the new class.

## Activity 11.28

```
program TwoClocks;
uses WinCrt, Clocks, Downs;

var
    cl : Clock;
    cd : CountdownClock;
begin
    cl.Init;
    cd.Init;
    cl.setTime(12,0,0);
    cd.setTime(12,0,0);
    cl.Tick;
    cd.Tick;
    cl.DisplayTime;
    cd.DisplayTime;
end.
```

## Activity 11.29

Both objects add 1 second to the time when *Tick* is executed.

## Activity 11.30

The *Clock* object adds 1 second to the time while the *CountdownClock* object correctly deducts 1 second.

## Activity 11.31

No solution required.

## Activity 11.32

No solution required.

## Activity 11.33

```
Unit Baby;

interface
uses Distances, Weights;

type
    BabyClass = object
        private
            name : string;
            height : Distance;
            wght : Weight;
        public
            constructor Init;
            procedure SetName(n:string);
            procedure SetHeight(h:Distance);
            procedure SetWeight(w:Weight);
            function GetName:string;
            procedure GetHeight(var h:Distance);
            procedure GetWeight(var w : Weight);
    end;

implementation
    constructor BabyClass.Init;
    begin
        name :='';
        height.Init;
        wght.Init;
    end;

    procedure babyClass.SetName(n :string);
    begin
        name := n;
    end;

    procedure BabyClass.SetHeight(h:Distance);
    begin
        height.SetDistance(0,h.GetFeet,h.GetInches);
    end;

    procedure BabyClass.SetWeight(w:Weight);
    begin
        wght.SetWeight(w.GetPounds, w.GetOunces);
    end;

    function BabyClass.GetName:string;
    begin
        GetName := name;
    end;

    procedure BabyClass.GetHeight(var h:Distance);
    begin
        h.SetDistance(0,height.GetFeet,
        ↳height.GetInches);
    end;

    procedure BabyClass.GetWeight(var w : WEight);
    begin
        w.SetWeight(wght.GetPounds, wght.GetOunces);
    end;

end.
```

A simple test program is given below.

```
program UBaby;
uses WinCrt, Babies, Weights, Distances;
var
    b : BabyClass;
    w1,w2 : Weight;
    d1,d2 : Distance;
begin
    ClrScr;
    b.Init;
    b.SetName('Avril Tait');
    w1.SetWeight(7,3);
    d1.SetDistance(0,1,0);
    b.SetHeight(d1);
    b.SetWeight(w1);
    b.GetHeight(d2);
    b.GetWeight(w2);
    writeln('Baby''s details:',#13,'Name :',
    ↳b.GetName,'   Height : ',d2.GetFeet,
    ↳' ft ',d2.GetInches,
    ' in    Weight : ',w2.GetPounds,' lbs ',
    ↳w2.GetOunces,' oz');
end.
```

## Activity 11.34

```
Unit ListClass;

interface
type
    Data =
        record
            Ftext:string[21];
        end;
    NodePointerType = ^Node;
    Node =
        record
            value:Data;
            next:NodePointerType;
        end;
```

```
    List = object
        private
            start : NodePointerType;
            count : integer;

        public
            constructor Init;
            function  Len : integer;
            function  IsEmpty : boolean;
            function  AddAt(item : Data ; post
            ↳: integer) : boolean;
            function  DeleteFrom(post:integer)
            ↳: boolean;
            procedure Head(var front : Data);
            procedure Tail;
            procedure DisplayList;
            procedure DeleteList;
            function  IsAt(d:Data):integer;
            procedure Give(post:integer;
            ↳var result:Data);
        end;

implementation


uses WinCrt;

constructor List.Init;
begin
    start := NIL;
    count := 0;
end;


function List.Len:integer;
begin
    Len := count;
end;


function List.IsEmpty : boolean;
begin
    IsEmpty := (count = 0);
end;


function  List.AddAt(item : Data; post :
integer) : boolean;
var
    current, previous, temp:NodePointerType;
    c:integer;
begin
    {*** IF invalid position THEN exit false ***}
    if(post<1)or(post > Len + 1)then
        AddAt:=false;
    {*** Create space for new node ***}
    new (temp);
    {*** Place data in node ***}
    temp^.value:=item;
    temp^.next:=NIL;
    {*** IF placed at start update main pointer***}
    if post=1 then
    begin
        current := start;
        start := temp;
        temp^.next:=current;
    end
    else
    {*** ELSE find insert position ***}
    begin
        previous := NIL;
        current := start;
        for c:=2 to post do
        begin
            previous := current;
            current := current^.next;
        end;
        {** Link new node into chain **}
        previous^.next := temp;
        temp^.next := current;
    end;
    {*** Add 1 to count ***}
    inc(count);
    AddAt:= true;
end;


function List.DeleteFrom(post:integer) : boolean;
var
    current, previous:NodePointerType;
    c:integer;
begin
    if(post < 1) or (post > Len)then
        DeleteFrom := false;
    {*** IF first node update main pointer***}
    if post = 1 then
    begin
        current := start;
        start := current^.next;
        Dispose(current);
    end
    else
    {*** ELSE find delete position ***}
    begin
        previous := NIL;
        current := start;
        for c:=2 to post do
        begin
            previous := current;
            current := current^.next;
        end;
        {** Remove node from chain **}
        previous^.next := current^.next;
        dispose (current);
    end;
    {*** Subtract 1 from count ***}
    dec(count);
    DeleteFrom := true;
end;

procedure List.Head(var front:Data);
begin
    if IsEmpty  then
    begin
    write('Invalid operation - Head');
        halt(1);
    end;
    front := start^.value;
end;


procedure List.Tail;
begin
    if IsEmpty then
    begin
        writeln('Invalid operation - Tail');
        halt(1);
    end;
    DeleteFrom(1);
end;


procedure List.DisplayList;
var
    current:NodePointerType;
    c:integer;
begin
    current:=start;
    for c:=1 to Len do
    begin
        writeln(current^.value.Ftext);
        current:=current^.next;
    end
end;

procedure List.DeleteList;
begin
    while not IsEmpty do
        DeleteFrom(1);
end;

function List.IsAt(d:Data):integer;
var
    nptr:NodePointerType;
    post :integer;
begin
    if Len=0 then
        IsAt:= 0;
    post := 1;
    nptr := start;
    while (nptr <> NIL) AND
    ↳(nptr^.value.Ftext<>d.Ftext) do
    begin
        nptr := nptr^.next;
        inc(post);
    end;
    if nptr <> NIL then
        IsAt:= post
    else
        IsAt:= 0;
end;

procedure List.Give(post:integer;
↳var result:Data);
var
    nptr:NodePointerType;
    c:integer;
begin
    if(post < 1)or( post > Len) then
    begin
        writeln('Invalid position - Give()');
        halt(1);
    end;
    nptr := start;
    for c := 1 to post - 1 do
```

```
        nptr := nptr^.next;
    result := nptr^.value;
end;
{***********************************************}
{*        End of List class definitions
*}
{***********************************************}


end.
```

## Activity 11.35

No solution required.

# APPENDIX A

# IBM Extended Character Set

IBM Extended Character Set

| | 00 | 01 | 02 | 03 | 04 | 05 | 06 | 07 | 08 | 09 | 0a | 0b | 0c | 0d | 0e | 0f |
|---|---|---|---|---|---|---|---|---|---|---|---|---|---|---|---|---|
| 00 | | ☺ | ☻ | ♥ | ♦ | ♣ | ♠ | • | ◘ | ○ | ◙ | ♂ | ♀ | ♪ | ♫ | ☼ |
| 10 | ► | ◄ | ↕ | ‼ | ¶ | § | ▬ | ↨ | ↑ | ↓ | → | ← | ∟ | ↔ | ▲ | ▼ |
| 20 | | ! | " | # | $ | % | & | ' | ( | ) | * | + | , | - | . | / |
| 30 | 0 | 1 | 2 | 3 | 4 | 5 | 6 | 7 | 8 | 9 | : | ; | < | = | > | ? |
| 40 | @ | A | B | C | D | E | F | G | H | I | J | K | L | M | N | O |
| 50 | P | Q | R | S | T | U | V | W | X | Y | Z | [ | \ | ] | ^ | _ |
| 60 | ` | a | b | c | d | e | f | g | h | i | j | k | l | m | n | o |
| 70 | p | q | r | s | t | u | v | w | x | y | z | { | ¦ | } | ~ | ⌂ |
| 80 | Ç | ü | é | â | ä | à | å | ç | ê | ë | è | ï | î | ì | Ä | Å |
| 90 | É | æ | Æ | ô | ö | ò | û | ù | ÿ | Ö | Ü | ¢ | £ | ¥ | ₧ | ƒ |
| a0 | á | í | ó | ú | ñ | Ñ | ª | º | ¿ | ⌐ | ¬ | ½ | ¼ | ¡ | « | » |
| b0 | ░ | ▒ | ▓ | │ | ┤ | ╡ | ╢ | ╖ | ╕ | ╣ | ║ | ╗ | ╝ | ╜ | ╛ | ┐ |
| c0 | └ | ┴ | ┬ | ├ | ─ | ┼ | ╞ | ╟ | ╚ | ╔ | ╩ | ╦ | ╠ | ═ | ╬ | ╧ |
| d0 | ╨ | ╤ | ╥ | ╙ | ╘ | ╒ | ╓ | ╫ | ╪ | ┘ | ┌ | █ | ▄ | ▌ | ▐ | ▀ |
| e0 | α | ß | Γ | π | Σ | σ | µ | τ | Φ | Θ | Ω | δ | ∞ | φ | ε | ∩ |
| f0 | ≡ | ± | ≥ | ≤ | ⌠ | ⌡ | ÷ | ≈ | ° | ∙ | · | √ | ⁿ | ² | ■ | |

# INDEX

**T**



**U**



**V**



**W**



**X**



**Z**